T0252236

VLSI Digital Signal Processing Systems

VLSI Digital Signal Processing Systems

Design and Implementation

KESHAB K. PARHI
University of Minnesota

A Wiley-Interscience Publication
JOHN WILEY & SONS, INC.

Library of Congress Cataloging-in-Publication Data:

Parhi, Keshab K., 1959–
    VLSI digital signal processing systems : design and implementation
/ Keshab K. Parhi.
      p. cm.
    "A Wiley-Interscience publication."
    Includes bibliographical references and index.
    ISBN 978-0-471-24186-7
    1. Integrated circuits—Very large scale integration.   I. Title.
TK7874.75.P37   1999
621.39'5 dc21   98-36462

To Jugu, Megha and Rahul

Contents

Preface

Digital signal processing (DSP) is used in numerous applications such as video compression, digital set-top box, cable modems, digital versatile disk, portable video systems/computers, digital audio, multimedia and wireless communications, digital radio, digital still and network cameras, speech processing, transmission systems, radar imaging, acoustic beamformers, global positioning systems, and biomedical signal processing. The field of DSP has always been driven by the advances in DSP applications and in scaled very-large-scale-integrated (VLSI) technologies. Therefore, at any given time, DSP applications impose several challenges on the implementations of the DSP systems. These implementations must satisfy the enforced sampling rate constraints of the real-time DSP applications and must require less space and power consumption.

This book addresses the methodologies needed to design custom or semi-custom VLSI circuits for these applications. Many of the techniques presented in the book are also applicable for faster implementations using off-the-shelf programmable digital signal processors. This book is intended to be used as a textbook for first-year graduate or senior courses on VLSI DSP architectures, or DSP structures for VLSI or High-Performance VLSI system design. This book is also an excellent reference for those involved in algorithm or architecture or circuit design for DSP applications.

This book brings together the distinct fields of computer architecture theory and DSP. DSP computation is different from general-purpose computation in the sense that the DSP programs are nonterminating programs. In DSP computation, the same program is executed repetitively on an infinite time series. The nonterminating nature can be exploited to design more efficient DSP systems by exploiting the dependency of tasks both within an iteration and among multiple iterations. Furthermore, long critical paths in DSP algorithms limit the performance of DSP systems. These algorithms need to be transformed for design of high-speed or low-area or low-power implementations. The emphasis of this book is on design of efficient architectures, algorithms, and circuits, which can be operated with either less area or power consumption or with higher speed or lower roundoff noise. The actual VLSI design of the circuits is not covered in this book.

DSP algorithms are used in various real-time applications with different sampling rate requirements that can vary from about 20 KHz in speech applications to over 500 MHz in radar and high-definition television applications. The computation requirement of a video compression system for high-definition TV (HDTV) can range from 10 to 100 gigaoperations per second. The dramatically different sample rate and computation requirements necessitate different architecture considerations for implementations of DSP algorithms. For example, in a speech application a time-multiplexed architecture may be preferred where many algorithm operations are mapped to the same hardware. However, the high-speed requirement in video applications can be met by one-to-one mapping of algorithm operations to processors. Thus it is important to study techniques to design not just a single architecture but a family of architectures out of which an appropriate architecture can be selected for a specified application.

The first part of the book (chapters 2 to 7) addresses several high-level architectural transformations that can be used to design families of architectures for a given algorithm. These transformations include pipelining, retiming, unfolding, folding, and systolic array design methodology. The second part of the book (chapters 8 to 12) deals with high-level algorithm transformations such as strength reduction, look-ahead and relaxed look-ahead. Strength reduction transformations are applied to reduce the number of multiplications in convolution, parallel finite impulse response (FIR) digital filters, discrete cosine transforms (DCTs), and parallel rank-order filters. Look-ahead and relaxed look-ahead transformations are applied to design pipelined direct-form and lattice recursive digital filters and adaptive digital filters, and parallel recursive digital filters. This part of the book exploits the interplay between algorithm design and integrated circuit implementations. The third part of the book (chapters 13 to 18) addresses architectures for VLSI addition, multiplication, and digital filters, and issues related to high-performance VLSI system design such as pipelining styles, low-power design, and architectures for programmable digital signal processors.

Chapter 1 of the book reviews various DSP algorithms and addresses their representation using block diagrams, signal flow graphs, and data-flow graphs. Chapter 2 addresses the iteration bound, which is a fundamental lower bound on the iteration period of any recursive signal processing algorithm. Two algorithms are described for determining this bound. The next 5 chapters address various transformations for improving performance of digital signal processing implementations. In Chapter 3, the basic concepts of pipelining and parallel processing are reviewed and the use of these techniques in design of high-speed or low-power applications is demonstrated. Chapter 4 addresses the retiming transformation, which is a generalization of the pipelining approach. Chapter 5 addresses unfolding, which can be used to design parallel architectures. Chapters 6 and 7 address folding techniques used to design time-multiplexed architectures where area reduction is important. While Chapter 6 addresses folding of arbitrary data-flow graphs, Chapter 7 addresses folding of regular data-flow graphs based on systolic design methodology.

Chapters 8 to 12 address design of algorithm structures for various DSP algorithms based on algorithm transformations such as strength reduction, look-ahead and relaxed look-ahead, and scaling and roundoff noise in digital filters. Chapter 8 addresses fast convolution based on Cook-Toom and Winograd convolution algorithms. In Chapter 9, algorithmic strength reduction is exploited to reduce the number of multiplication operations in parallel FIR filters, discrete cosine transforms, and parallel rank-order filters. Design of fast Fourier transform (FFT) structures is also based on strength reduction transformations but is not covered in this book since it is covered in many introductory DSP textbooks. While it is easy to achieve pipelining and parallel processing in nonrecursive computations, recursive and adaptive digital filters cannot be easily pipelined or processed in parallel due to the presence of feedback loops. In Chapter 10, the look-ahead technique is discussed and is used to pipeline first-order infinite impulse response (IIR) digital filters. For higher order filters, two types of look-ahead techniques, clustered and scattered look-ahead, are discussed. It is shown that the scattered look-ahead technique guarantees stability in pipelined IIR filters. The parallel implementations of IIR digital filters and how to combine pipelining and parallel processing in these digital filters are also addressed. Adaptive digital filters are pipelined based on relaxed look-ahead, which are based on certain approximations or relaxations of look-ahead. Chapter 11 addresses scaling and roundoff noise, which are important for VLSI implementations of DSP systems using fixed-point arithmetic. Roundoff noise computation techniques cannot be applied to many digital filters. These filters are preprocessed using slowdown, pipelining and/or retiming so that every roundoff noise node can be expressed as a state variable. The direct-form IIR digital filters cannot meet the filter requirements in certain applications. Lattice digital filters may be better suited for these applications due to their excellent roundoff noise property. Chapter 12 presents Schur polynomials, orthonormality of Schur polynomials, and use of these polynomials to design basic (two multiplier and one multiplier), normalized, and scaled-normalized lattice digital filters. Pipelined implementation of these lattice digital filters is also discussed.

Chapters 13 to 18 address VLSI implementations of arithmetic operations such as addition and multiplication and digital filters, high-performance VLSI system design issues such as pipelining styles and low-power design, and programmable digital signal processors. Design of adders and multipliers using various implementation styles, such as bit-parallel, bit-serial, and digit-serial, and various number systems such as two's complement, canonic signed digit, and carry-save are discussed in Chapter 13. This chapter also addresses distributed arithmetic. Chapter 14 addresses arithmetic architectures based on redundant or signed-digit implementations. The main advantage of redundant arithmetic lies in its carry-free property, which enables computation in both least significant bit and most significant bit first modes. Conversion from redundant to nonredundant and vice versa is also addressed. In these chapters, bit-serial multipliers are derived from bit-parallel designs by systolic design methodology. Residue arithmetic, which can be used for implementation of FIR digital filters and transforms, is not studied in this book. Chapter 15 presents strength reduction at numerical level to reduce the area and power consumption of two's complement and canonic signed digit number based digital filters. Chapter 16 discusses various pipelining styles, such as synchronous, wave, and asynchronous pipelining. Approaches to reduction of clock skew in synchronous systems and synthesis of interface circuits in asynchronous systems are also addressed. Chapter 17 on low-power design presents various approaches for reduction of power consumption at architectural and technology levels and for estimation of power consumption. Chapter 18 addresses various architectures used in programmable digital signal processors.

Seven appendixes in the book cover shortest path algorithms used for determining the iteration bound and for retiming, scheduling, and allocation techniques used for determining the folding sets for design of folded architectures; Euclid's GCD algorithm, which is used for Winograd's convolution; orthonormality of Schur polynomials used for design of lattice digital filters; fast bit-parallel addition and multiplication; scheduling techniques for bit-serial systems; and coefficient quantization in FIR filters.

The concepts in this book have been described in a technology-independent manner. The examples in this book are based on digital filters and transforms. Many real-time DSP systems make use of control flow constructs such as conditionals, interrupts, and jump. Design of control-dominated DSP systems is beyond the scope of this book. The exercises can be completed using any programming language such as MATLAB or C. Many application-driven problems have been included at the end of the chapters. For example, the problems at the end of the algorithmic strength reduction chapter address the use of fast filters in design of equalizers in communications systems, wavelets, two-dimensional FIR digital filters, and motion estimation. These problems introduce the reader to different applications where the concepts covered in the chapter can be applied.

This book is based on the material taught at the University of Minnesota in two current semester courses: EE 5329: VLSI Digital Signal Processing

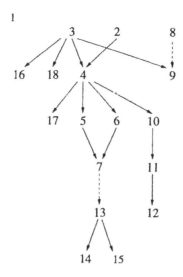

Fig. 0.1 Precedence constraints among different chapters.

Systems and EE 5549: Digital Signal Processing Structures for VLSI. EE 5329 (with a basic course on VLSI Design as prerequisite) covers chapters 2 through 7 and parts of chapters 13 through 18 (in that order). EE 5549 (with a basic course on digital signal processing as prerequisite) covers parts of chapters 2, 3, and 4, chapters 8 through 12, and some architectures for video compression based on journal and conference papers. These two semester courses were taught as three-quarter courses in the past. For a single semester course on VLSI Digital Signal Processing, chapters 2 through 7, parts of chapters 9, 10, 13 and 15, and an overview of topics in chapters 17 and 18 are recommended. However, the instructors can select the chapters that suit their needs.

The chapters need not be followed in the order they are presented. Many chapters can be taught independently. The precedence graph in Fig. 0.1 shows the dependencies among chapters. The dashed lines represent weak dependencies where a section of the current chapter is dependent on the preceding chapter.

The author has been fortunate to receive valuable help, support, and and suggestions from numerous colleagues, students, and friends. The author is grateful to Leilei Song for her constant and enthusiastic help during the writing of this book. He is also grateful to Jin-Gyun Chung, Tracy Denk, David Parker, Janardhan Satyanarayana, and Ching-Yi Wang for their help during the early part of the writing of this book. The author is thankful to Wayne Burleson, Francky Catthoor, Ed F. Deprettere, Graham Jullien, and Naresh R. Shanbhag for their thorough and constructive reviews of the first draft; their comments have resulted in reorganization of several chapters in the book. Ed F. Deprettere and Scott Douglas used the preliminary versions of the book at Delft University of Technology and at the University of Utah, respectively, and provided numerous suggestions.

The author appreciates the constant support and encouragement he has received from David G. Messerschmitt and Mos Kaveh. The author's research included in this book has been supported by the National Science Foundation, the Army Research Office, the Office of Naval Research, the Defense Advanced Research Projects Agency, Texas Instruments, Lucent Technologies, and NEC Corporation. The author is thankful to John Cozzens, Wanda Gass, Arup Gupta, Clifford Lau, Jose Munoz, Takao Nishitani, and Bill Sander for their encouragement.

Several chapters in the book are based on the joint research work of the author with his colleagues Jin-Gyun Chung, Tracy Denk, Kazuhito Ito, Lori Lucke, David G. Messerschmitt, Luis Montalvo, David Parker, Janardhan Satyanarayana, Naresh Shanbhag, H. R. Srinivas, and Ching-Yi Wang. The author also thanks many of his colleagues: Bryan Ackland, Jonathan Allen, Magdy Bayoumi, Don Boudlin, Robert W. Brodersen, Peter Cappello, Anantha Chandrakasan, Liang-Gee Chen, Gerhard Fettweis, Eby Friedman, Richard Hartley, Mehdi Hatamian, Sonia Heemstra, Yu Hen Hu, M. K. Ibrahim, Mary Irwin, Rajeev Jain, Leah Jamieson, Chein-Wei Jen, S.Y. Kung, Ichiro Kuroda, Edward Lee, K. J. R. Liu, Vijay Madisetti, John McCanny, Teresa Meng, Takao Nishitani, Tobias Noll, Robert Owens, Peter Pirsch, Miodrag Potkonjak, Jan Rabaey, Takayasu Sakurai, Edwin Sha, Bing Sheu, Michael Soderstrand, Mani Srivastava, Thanos Stouraitis, Earl Swartzlander, P. P. Vaidyanathan, Ingrid Verbauwhede, and Kung Yao. He has enjoyed numerous interactions with them. This book has been directly or indirectly influenced by these interactions. Thanks are also due to Carl Harris of Kluwer Academic Publishers for his permitting the author to reprint several parts of chapters 11 and 12 from an earlier monograph.

The author thanks Andrew Smith of John Wiley & Sons for his personal interest in this topic and for having invited the author to write this book. He also thanks Angioline Loredo, associate managing editor at Wiley, for her help in production of this book. It was truly a pleasure to work with them.

KESHAB K. PARHI

Minneapolis, MN

VLSI Digital Signal Processing Systems

1

Introduction to Digital Signal Processing Systems

1.1 INTRODUCTION

Digital signal processing (DSP) has many advantages over analog signal processing. Digital signals are more robust than analog signals with respect to temperature and process variations. The accuracy in digital representations can be controlled better by changing the wordlength of the signal. Furthermore, DSP techniques can cancel the noise and interference while amplifying the signal. In contrast, both signal and noise are amplified in analog signal processing. Digital signals can be stored and recovered, transmitted and received, processed and manipulated, all virtually without error. While analog signal processing is indispensable for systems that require extremely high frequencies such as the radio frequency transceiver in wireless communications, or extremely low area and low power such as micro machine sensors used to detect cracks and other stress-related material defects, many complex systems are realized digitally with high precision, high signal to noise ratio (SNR), repeatability, and flexibility.

DSP systems can be realized using programmable processors or custom designed hardware circuits fabricated using very-large-scale-integrated (VLSI) circuit technology. The goal of digital design is to maximize the performance while keeping the cost down. In the context of general digital design, performance is measured in terms of the amount of hardware circuitry and resources required (i.e., space or area); the speed of execution, which depends on both throughput and clock rate; and the amount of power dissipation or total energy required to perform a given task. For fixed-point DSP systems, the finite wordlength performance (i.e., quantization and roundoff noise) is the fourth measurement of performance, especially for digital filters, as a digital filter with large roundoff noise is of no use even if it has better performance in terms of area, speed, and power consumption.

Two important features that distinguish DSP from other general purpose computations are the *real-time throughput requirement* and the *data driven property*. The hardware should be designed to meet the tight throughput constraint of the *real-time processing* where new input samples need to be processed as they are received periodically from the signal source as opposed to first storing them in buffers and then processing them in batch mode. If the throughput of a system is less than the required sample rate, the new inputs need to be stalled (or buffered), which requires an infinite length buffer. However, once the sample rate is met by the hardware, there is no advantage in making the computation any faster. The second important attribute of signal processing systems is its *data-driven property*, implied by the fact that any subtasks or computations in a DSP system can be performed once all the input data are available. In this sense, these systems are synchronized by the flow of data, instead of the system clock. This enables the use of asynchronous circuits for DSP systems where no global clock is required.

This introductory chapter presents an overview of typical DSP algorithms, the current design challenges in multimedia signal processing, and the representations of DSP algorithms. Several typical DSP algorithms are reviewed in Section 1.2. Section 1.3 addresses the computation demands of a few multimedia DSP functions and the DSP system implementation opportunities presented by the scaled VLSI technologies. Section 1.4 addresses four different representations of DSP algorithm: block diagram, signal-flow graph, data-flow graph, and dependence graph representations. Section 1.5 presents an outline of various chapters in the book.

1.2 TYPICAL DSP ALGORITHMS

Some DSP algorithms and their typical applications are listed in Table 1.1 [1]. This section reviews several important DSP computations, including correlation, convolution, and digital filters; the stochastic-gradient and least-mean-square (LMS) adaptive filters; block matching algorithm for motion estimation (ME), discrete cosine transform (DCT) and vector quantization (VQ) for image processing and compression; Viterbi algorithm and dynamic programming; decimator and interpolator, and wavelets and filter banks for multirate signal processing.

Table 1.1 Examples of Common DSP Algorithms and Their Applications

DSP Algorithms	System Applications
Speech coding and decoding	Digital cellular phones, personal communication systems, digital cordless phones, multimedia computers, secure communications
Speech encryption and decryption	Digital cellular phones, personal communication systems, digital cordless phones, secure communications
Speech recognition	Advanced user interfaces, multimedia workstations, robotics and automotive applications, digital cellular phones, personal communication systems, digital cordless phones
Speech synthesis	Multimedia PCs, advanced user interfaces, robotics
Modem algorithms	Digital cellular phones, personal communication systems, digital cordless phones, digital audio broadcast, multimedia computers, wireless computing, navigation, data/facsimile modems, secure communications
Noise cancellation	Professional audio, advanced vehicular audio
Audio equalization	Consumer audio, professional audio, advanced vehicular audio
Image compression and decompression	Digital cameras, digital video, multimedia computers, consumer video
Beamforming	Navigation, radar/sonar, signals intelligence
Echo cancellation	Speakerphones, modems, telephone switches

1.2.1 Convolution

The convolution of 2 discrete sequences $h(n)$ and $x(n)$ is defined as

$$y(n) = x(n) * h(n) = \sum_{k=-\infty}^{\infty} x(k)h(n-k). \qquad (1.1)$$

The output at time instance n, $y(n)$, can be viewed as the inner product between $x(k)$ and $h(-k+n)$ (summed over $-\infty < k < \infty$).

Convolution is used to describe and analyze linear time-invariant (LTI) systems, which are completely characterized by their unit-sample (or impulse) response $h(n)$ [2]. The output sequence of an LTI system is computed as the convolution of the input sequence $x(n)$ and its unit-sample response $h(n)$. When the unit-sample response of a system contains a finite number of nonzero samples, i.e., $h(n)$ is of finite duration, the system is called *finite impulse response* (FIR); otherwise when $h(n)$ is of infinite duration, the system is called *infinite impulse response* (IIR). For example, the moving-average system with impulse response

$$h(n) = \frac{1}{M_1 + M_2 + 1} \sum_{-M_1}^{M_2} \delta(n - k)$$

is an FIR system; the accumulator with unit-sample response

$$h(n) = \sum_{k=-\infty}^{n} \delta(k),$$

is an IIR system. It is a step function, and equals 1 for $n \geq 0$ and 0 for $n < 0$.

A system is *causal* if the computation of $y(n_0)$ depends only on the past input samples $x(k)$, $k \leq n_0$. The unit-sample response of a causal LTI system satisfies $h(n) = 0$ for $n < 0$. Only causal digital filters are of interest since noncausal systems cannot be implemented in hardware or software.

1.2.2 Correlation

Correlation is a widely used computation in digital communications and other random signal processing systems. The correlation of 2 sequences $a(n)$ and $x(n)$ is defined as

$$y(n) = \sum_{k=-\infty}^{\infty} a(k)x(n + k). \tag{1.2}$$

The correlation operation in (1.2) can be described as a convolution as follows:

$$y(n) = \sum_{k=-\infty}^{\infty} a(-k)x(n - k)) = a(-n) * x(n). \tag{1.3}$$

If $a(n)$ and $x(n)$ have finite length N, i.e., these are nonzero for $n = 0, 1, \cdots, N - 1$, the digital correlation operation is given as follows:

$$y(n) = \sum_{k=0}^{N-1} a(k)x(n + k) \tag{1.4}$$

for $n = -N+1, -N+2, \cdots, -1, 0, 1, \cdots, N-2, N-1$. The digital correlation operation in (1.4) can also be written in matrix-vector multiplication form as

$$
\begin{bmatrix}
y(-3) \\
y(-2) \\
y(-1) \\
y(0) \\
y(1) \\
y(2) \\
y(3)
\end{bmatrix}
=
\begin{bmatrix}
0 & 0 & 0 & x(0) \\
0 & 0 & x(0) & x(1) \\
0 & x(0) & x(1) & x(2) \\
x(0) & x(1) & x(2) & x(3) \\
x(1) & x(2) & x(3) & 0 \\
x(2) & x(3) & 0 & 0 \\
x(3) & 0 & 0 & 0
\end{bmatrix}
\begin{bmatrix}
a(0) \\
a(1) \\
a(2) \\
a(3)
\end{bmatrix},
\tag{1.5}
$$

for $N = 4$.

1.2.3 Digital Filters

Digital filters are an important class of LTI systems designed to modify the frequency properties of the input signal $x(n)$ to meet certain specific design requirements. The properties of a causal digital filter can be completely characterized by its unit-sample response $h(n)$, or its frequency response $H(e^{j\omega})$ (or transfer function $H(z)$), or by difference equations. While unit-sample response and frequency response capture its time and frequency domain properties, difference equation representations explicitly show the computations required to implement the filter.

A linear, time-invariant, and causal filter is described by the difference equation

$$
y(n) = -\sum_{k=1}^{N} a_k y(n-k) + \sum_{k=0}^{M-1} b_k x(n-k).
\tag{1.6}
$$

If $a_k = 0$ for $1 \le k \le N$, (1.6) reduces to

$$
y(n) = \sum_{k=0}^{M-1} b_k x(n-k),
\tag{1.7}
$$

which is an M-tap finite impulse response (FIR) filter with unit-sample response $h(k) = b_k$ for $0 \le k \le M - 1$, and $h(k) = 0$ otherwise. This is a nonrecursive computation. If at least one $a_k \ne 0$ for $1 \le k \le N$, (1.6) represents a recursive computation where the computation of $y(n)$ requires the values of the past output samples, and is called a recursive filter. Its corresponding unit-sample response has infinite duration, hence, it is also referred to as an infinite impulse response (IIR) filter. The choice between an FIR filter and an IIR filter depends on the application requirements.

In designing frequency-selective digital filters, it is usually desirable to have approximately constant frequency-response magnitude and minimum phase distortion in the pass band [2]. A linear phase with integer slope corresponds to a simple delay in the time domain, and it reduces the phase distortion to a minimum in the frequency domain. Therefore, it is desirable to design digital filters with exactly or approximately linear phase. Linear phase FIR filters are particularly attractive as their unit-sample responses are symmetric and require only half the number of multiplications. For example, the unit-sample response of a M-tap linear phase FIR filter satisfies

$$h(n) = h(M - n).$$

Therefore, a 7-tap linear phase FIR filter with impulse response

$$h(0) = h(6) = b_0, \ h(1) = h(5) = b_1, \ h(2) = h(4) = b_2, \ h(3) = b_3$$

can be written as

$$
\begin{aligned}
y(n) = \ & b_0 x(n) + b_1 x(n-1) + b_2 x(n-2) + b_3 x(n-3) \\
& + b_0 x(n-6) + b_1 x(n-5) + b_2 x(n-4)
\end{aligned}
$$

$$(1.8)$$

and can be implemented as shown in Fig. 1.1(a) or in Fig. 1.1(b) using 4 multipliers, 6 adders, and 6 storage elements. Fig. 1.1(b) represents a data-broadcast structure since the input data is broadcast to all multipliers at the same time.

1.2.4 Adaptive Filters

Fixed-coefficient digital filters are ideal for frequency shaping in deterministic environments. Adaptive digital filters are used for applications such as echo cancellation, channel equalization, voiceband modems, digital mobile radio, system identification and control, acoustic beamforming, and speech and image processing [3]. Adaptive filters predict one random process $\{y(n)\}$ from observations of another random process $\{x(n)\}$ using linear models such as digital filters. Unlike the fixed-coefficient filters (such as FIR and IIR), the coefficients in adaptive digital filters are updated at each iteration in order to minimize the *difference* between the filter output and the desired signal. This updating process continues until the coefficients converge. Hence, adaptive digital filters usually consist of a general filter block and a coefficient update block. Various adaptation processes can be derived based on different difference minimization criteria. This subsection addresses the derivation of the LMS adaptive filters (with FIR filter block) and the stochastic-gradient adaptive lattice filters.

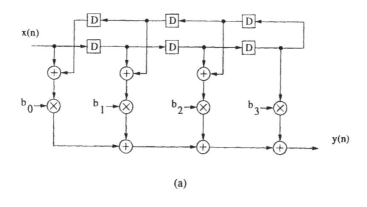

(a)

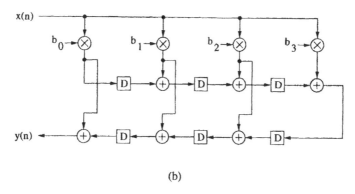

(b)

Fig. 1.1   Block diagrams of a 7-tap linear-phase FIR filter.

1.2.4.1   LMS Adaptive Filters   In the LMS adaptive algorithm, a weighted sum of all the observations

$$\hat{d}(n) \quad = \quad \mathbf{W}^T(n-1)\mathbf{U}(n) \tag{1.9}$$

is used as an estimate of the desired signal $d(n)$, where

$$\mathbf{W}^T(n) = [w_1(n), w_2(n), \cdots, w_N(n)]$$

is the weight vector and

$$\mathbf{U}^T(n) = [u(n), u(n-1), \cdots, u(n-N+1)]$$

contains the current and past input samples. The estimation error, denoted by $e(n)$, is the difference between the desired signal and the estimated signal, i.e.,

$$e(n) = d(n) - \hat{d}(n) = d(n) - \mathbf{W}^T(n-1)\mathbf{U}(n). \tag{1.10}$$

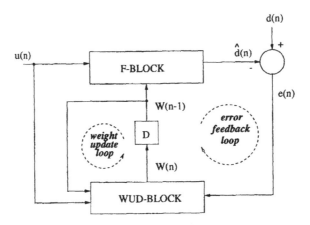

Fig. 1.2 System diagram of the LMS adaptive filter.

In the n-th iteration, the LMS algorithm selects $\mathbf{W}^T(n)$, which minimizes the square error $e^2(n)$. Therefore, the LMS adaptive filters consist of an FIR filter block (F-block) with coefficient vector $\mathbf{W}^T(n)$ and input sequence $u(n)$, and a weight (coefficient) update (WUD) block.

To derive the weight update algorithm, the derivative of $e^2(n)$ with respect to $\mathbf{W}^T(n-1)$ is calculated as follows (the time index n is dropped for simplicity):

$$\Delta_{\mathbf{W}^T}(e^2) = \frac{\partial e^2}{\partial \mathbf{W}^T} = -2d\mathbf{U} + 2\mathbf{W}^T\mathbf{U} \cdot \mathbf{U}$$
$$= -2(d - \mathbf{W}^T\mathbf{U})\mathbf{U} = -2e\mathbf{U}. \qquad (1.11)$$

The update of the weight vector is thus written as

$$\mathbf{W}(n) = \mathbf{W}(n-1) - \frac{1}{2}\mu\nabla_{\mathbf{W}^T}(e^2(n)). \qquad (1.12)$$

Finally, we obtain

$$\mathbf{W}(n) = \mathbf{W}(n-1) + \mu e(n)\mathbf{U}(n). \qquad (1.13)$$

The system level diagram of this LMS filter is shown in Fig.1.2, where in every iteration the error $e(n)$ (1.10) is computed by the filter block (F-block) and the weight vector (1.13) is updated by the WUD block. Fig. 1.3 shows the detailed LMS filter block diagram.

1.2.4.2 *Stochastic-Gradient Adaptive Lattice Filter*   The basic concepts and derivation of lattice filter structures are assumed, as these are covered in great detail in [4],[2] (see also Chapter 12).

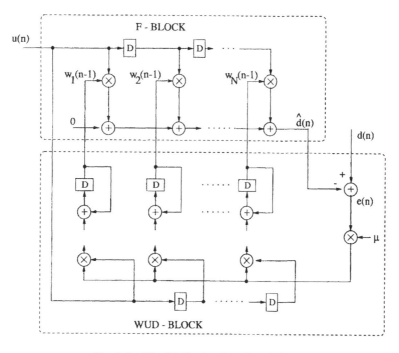

Fig. 1.3 The LMS adaptive digital filter.

Let n denote the time instance, and $m = 1, 2, \cdots, N$ denote the lattice stage number (N is the total number of stages or the order of the filter). Then the order update equations for the forward and backward prediction errors can be written as follows, respectively:

$$
\begin{aligned}
e_f(n|m) &= e_f(n|m-1) - k_m(n)e_b(n-1|m-1) \\
e_b(n|m) &= e_b(n-1|m-1) - k_m(n)e_f(n|m-1),
\end{aligned}
\tag{1.14}
$$

where k_m is the partial correlation coefficient (also called PARCOR or reflection coefficient) [5] (see Section 12.3.3). In Fig. 1.4, the shaded region represents a forward lattice stage and performs the computation in (1.14).

The stochastic-gradient adaptive algorithm adapts k_m to minimize

$$
J(n) = e_f^2(n|m) + e_b^2(n|m),
\tag{1.15}
$$

which represents the square sum of the forward and backward prediction errors. Expressing $J(n)$ in terms of $e_f(n|m-1)$, $e_b(n-1|m-1)$, and $k_m(n)$ and taking the derivative of $J(n)$ with respect to k_m, we have

$$
\begin{aligned}
\frac{\partial J(n)}{\partial k_m(n)} =& -2[e_f(n|m-1) - k_m(n)e_b(n-1|m-1)]e_b(n-1|m-1) \\
& -2[e_b(n-1|m-1) - k_m(n)e_f(n|m-1)]e_f(n|m-1).
\end{aligned}
$$

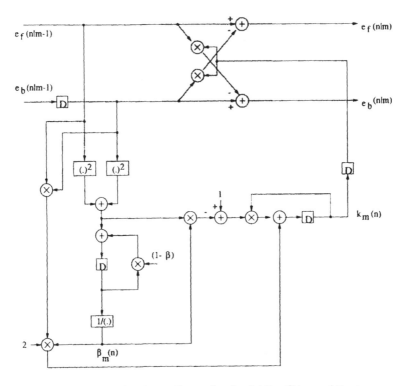

Fig. 1.4 The stochastic-gradient adaptive lattice filter architecture.

This derivative, calculated using the current estimate for $k_m(n)$, is weighted and subtracted from the current estimate to yield the new estimate $k_m(n)$. The update equation is written as

$$k_m(n+1) = k_m(n) - \frac{\beta_m(n)}{2} \frac{\partial J(n)}{\partial k_m} \tag{1.16}$$

$$= k_m(n)[1 - \beta_m(n)(e_f^2(n|m-1) + e_b^2(n-1|m-1))]$$
$$+ 2\beta_m(n)e_f(n|m-1)e_b(n-1|m-1),$$

where $\beta_m(n)$ is the adaptation constant. For the speed of adaptation to be relatively independent of the input signal levels, the step-size $\beta_m(n)$ needs to be normalized by an estimate of the sum of the $(m-1)$-th order prediction error variance. Hence, we can write

$$\beta_m(n) = \frac{1}{S(n|m-1)} \tag{1.17}$$

where $S(n|m-1)$ is estimated recursively as

$$S(n+1|m-1) = (1-\beta)S(n|m-1) \tag{1.18}$$
$$+e_f^2(n|m-1) + e_b^2(n-1|m-1),$$

where β is a constant which, in conjuction with the initial value of $S(0|m-1)$, controls the speed of adaptation.

The stochastic-gradient adaptive algorithm is completely described by the following equations:

$$k_m(n+1) = [1 - \beta_m(e_f^2(n|m-1) + e_b^2(n-1|m-1))]k_m(n)$$
$$+2\beta_m e_f(n|m-1)e_b(n-1|m-1) \tag{1.19}$$

$$S(n+1|m-1) = (1-\beta)S(n|m-1) \tag{1.20}$$
$$+e_f^2(n|m-1) + e_b^2(n-1|m-1)$$

$$\beta_m = \frac{1}{S(n|m-1)} \tag{1.21}$$

$$e_f(n|m) = e_f(n|m-1) - k_m(n)e_b(n-1|m-1) \tag{1.22}$$

$$e_b(n|m) = e_b(n-1|m-1) - k_m(n)e_f(n|m-1). \tag{1.23}$$

Equations (1.19)–(1.21) and (1.22)–(1.23) are referred to as the adaptation and order-update equations, respectively. This stochastic-gradient lattice filter block diagram is shown in Fig. 1.4, where the forward and backward prediction errors, e_f and e_b, are computed using forward lattice stages (in shaded region).

1.2.5 Motion Estimation

Motion estimation is used in interframe predictive coding and is the most computation-intensive part in video coding. In motion estimation, successive frames of a video sequence are analyzed to estimate the motion (or displacement) vectors of pixels or blocks of pixels. The motion vectors are transmitted instead of the corresponding blocks of the current frame. The best compression is obtained by motion-compensated prediction using blocks from previous coded frame. Block-matching algorithms (BMAs) are the most preferred schemes for motion estimation due to their relative simplicity. In BMAs, each frame is partitioned into N-by-N macro reference blocks and it is assumed that all the pixels in 1 block have the same motion. Each reference block in the current frame is compared with displaced candidate blocks in the previous frame and the offset between the best fitting candidate block and the reference block is defined as its motion vector. The search range in the previous frame

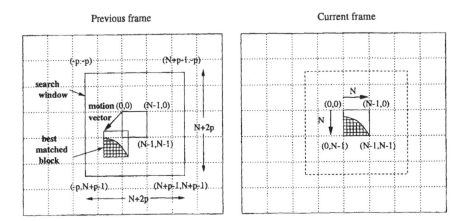

Fig. 1.5 Block-matching algorithm for motion estimation.

is called *search window* and is constrained to $+/-p$ pixels in both horizontal and vertical directions relative to the position of the reference block. Thus, the search window contains $(N + 2p)^2$ pixels. The block-matching algorithm is illustrated in Fig. 1.5.

Several search criteria can be used to define the best match, including cross-correlation function (CCF), mean-square error (MSE), and mean absolute difference (MAD). The MAD function is most widely used in practical implementations due to its simplicity and satisfactory performance. The displaced block difference $s(m, n)$ with displacement (m, n) using MAD is defined as

$$s(m,n) \;=\; \sum_{i=0}^{N-1}\sum_{j=0}^{N-1}|x(i,j) - y(i + m, j + n)|,$$
$$for \; -p \le m, \, n \le p, \tag{1.24}$$

where $x(i, j)$ and $y(i+m, j+n)$ correspond to the pixel values in the reference block in current frame and the candidate block in the search window in previous frame, respectively. Note that (1.24) requires $3N^2$ computations (one subtraction, one absolute value, and one accumulation are needed for each absolute difference computation). Several strategies can be used to determine the best matched block, out of which *full search* is the most straightforward method. It searches all the $(2p + 1)^2$ positions in the search window and computes the motion vector **v** as

$$u \;=\; min_{(m,n)}\{s(m,n)\}, \; for \; -p \le m, \, n \le p,$$
$$\mathbf{v} \;=\; (m,n)|_u.$$

Hence, for a $N_h \times N_v$ frame (N_h pixels per line, N_v lines per frame), the full-search BMA involves

$$\frac{N_h \times N_v}{N^2} \cdot (2p+1)^2 \cdot 3N^2 = 3(2p+1)^2 N_h N_v$$

computations per frame. Assume a frame rate of F frames/sec, the computation load of full-search BMA is $3(2p+1)^2 N_h N_v F$ operations/sec.

1.2.6 Discrete Cosine Transform

The discrete cosine transform (DCT) as a frequency transform was first introduced for pattern recognition in image processing and Wiener filtering [6]. It is currently extensively used as a transform coder for still and moving image and video compression. This section introduces the derivation of even symmetrical one-dimensional DCT (1D-DCT).

Consider a N-point sequence $x(n)$, i.e., $x(n) = 0$ for $n < 0$ and $n > N-1$. The N-point DCT and inverse DCT (IDCT) pair for this sequence is defined as:

$$X(k) = e(k) \sum_{n=0}^{N-1} x(n) \cos[\frac{(2n+1)k\pi}{2N}], \ k = 0, 1, \cdots, N-1 \qquad (1.25)$$

$$x(n) = \frac{2}{N} \sum_{k=0}^{N-1} e(k) X(k) \cos[\frac{(2n+1)k\pi}{2N}], \ n = 0, 1, \cdots, N-1, \qquad (1.26)$$

where

$$e(k) = \begin{cases} \frac{1}{\sqrt{2}}, & if \ k = 0, \\ 1, & otherwise. \end{cases} \qquad (1.27)$$

The N-point DCT and IDCT pair can be derived using a $2N$-point discrete Fourier transform (DFT) pair. Construct a $2N$-point sequence $y(n)$ using $x(n)$ and its mirror image as follows:

$$y(n) = x(n) + x(2N - n - 1) = \begin{cases} x(n), & 0 \le n \le N-1 \\ x(2N - n - 1), & N \le n \le 2N - 1. \end{cases} \qquad (1.28)$$

Hence $y(n)$ is symmetric with respect to the midpoint at $n = N - 1/2$. Fig. 1.6 shows an example for $N = 5$.

The $2N$-point DFT of $y(n)$ is given by

$$Y_D(k) = \sum_{n=0}^{2N-1} y(n) e^{-j\frac{2\pi}{2N}kn}$$

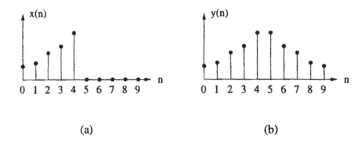

(a)   (b)

Fig. 1.6 Relation between N-point sequence $x(n)$ and $2N$-point sequence $y(n) = x(n) + x(2N - n - 1)$.

$$= \sum_{n=0}^{N-1} x(n)e^{-j\frac{2\pi}{2N}kn} + \sum_{n=N}^{2N-1} x(2N - n - 1)e^{-j\frac{2\pi}{2N}kn}, \quad (1.29)$$

for $0 \leq k \leq 2N - 1$. Substituting $n = 2N - n' - 1$ into the 2nd summation in (1.29), we obtain

$$\sum_{n=N}^{2N-1} x(2N - n - 1)e^{-j\frac{2\pi}{2N}kn} = \sum_{n'=N-1}^{0} x(n')e^{-j\frac{2\pi}{2N}k(2N-n'-1)}$$

$$= \sum_{n'=0}^{N-1} x(n')e^{j\frac{2\pi}{2N}kn'}e^{j\frac{2\pi}{2N}k}. \quad (1.30)$$

With (1.30), (1.29) can be rewritten as

$$Y_D(k) = \sum_{n=0}^{N-1} x(n)e^{-j\frac{2\pi}{2N}kn} + \sum_{n=0}^{N-1} x(n)e^{j\frac{2\pi}{2N}kn}e^{j\frac{2\pi}{2N}k}$$

$$= e^{j\frac{k\pi}{2N}}\left(\sum_{n=0}^{N-1} x(n)e^{-j\frac{(2n+1)k\pi}{2N}} + \sum_{n=0}^{N-1} x(n)e^{j\frac{(2n+1)k\pi}{2N}}\right)$$

$$= e^{j\frac{k\pi}{2N}} \sum_{n=0}^{N-1} 2x(n)\cos(\frac{(2n+1)k\pi}{2N}). \quad (1.31)$$

Define

$$\hat{X}(k) = \begin{cases} Y_D(k)e^{-j(\frac{k\pi}{2N})}, & 0 \leq k \leq N - 1 \\ 0, & otherwise. \end{cases} \quad (1.32)$$

Then the N-point DCT can be expressed as $X(k) = e(k)\hat{X}(k)/2$.

The inverse DCT is derived by relating $Y_D(k)$ to $X(k)$, computing $y(n)$ from $Y_D(k)$ using the inverse DFT, and reconstructing $x(n)$ from $y(n)$. Although $Y_D(k)$ is a $2N$-point sequence and $X(k)$ is a N-point sequence, the redundancy (symmetry) in $y(n)$ enables $Y_D(k)$ to be expressed using $X(k)$. For $0 \leq k \leq N - 1$, $Y_D(k) = e^{j\frac{k\pi}{2N}} \hat{X}(k)$; $Y_D(N) = 0$. For $N + 1 \leq k \leq 2N - 1$, $1 \leq 2N - k \leq N - 1$. Therefore,

$$Y_D(2N - k) = e^{j\frac{(2N-k)\pi}{2N}} \hat{X}(2N - k) = -e^{-j\frac{k\pi}{2N}} \hat{X}(2N - k). \qquad (1.33)$$

However, from (1.31),

$$
\begin{aligned}
Y_D(2N - k) &= e^{j\frac{(2N-k)\pi}{2N}} \sum_{n=0}^{N-1} 2x(n) \cos(\frac{(2n+1)(2N-k)\pi}{2N}) \\
&= -e^{j\frac{2N\pi}{2N}} e^{-j\frac{k\pi}{2N}} \sum_{n=0}^{N-1} 2x(n) \cos(\frac{(2n+1)k\pi}{2N}) \\
&= e^{-j\frac{2k\pi}{2N}} e^{j\frac{k\pi}{2N}} \sum_{n=0}^{N-1} 2x(n) \cos(\frac{(2n+1)k\pi}{2N}) \\
&= e^{-j\frac{2k\pi}{2N}} Y_D(k). \qquad (1.34)
\end{aligned}
$$

Hence,

$$
\begin{aligned}
Y_D(k) &= e^{j\frac{2k\pi}{2N}} Y_D(2N - k) \\
&= -e^{j\frac{2k\pi}{2N}} e^{-j\frac{k\pi}{2N}} \hat{X}(2N - k) \\
&= -e^{j\frac{k\pi}{2N}} \hat{X}(2N - k), \qquad (1.35)
\end{aligned}
$$

for $N + 1 \leq k \leq 2N - 1$. Therefore, we have

$$
Y_D(k) = \begin{cases}
e^{j\frac{k\pi}{2N}} \hat{X}(k), & 0 \leq k \leq N - 1 \\
0, & k = N \\
-e^{j\frac{k\pi}{2N}} \hat{X}(2N - k), & N + 1 \leq k \leq 2N - 1.
\end{cases} \qquad (1.36)
$$

Taking the inverse DFT of $Y_D(k)$, we have

$$
\begin{aligned}
y(n) &= \frac{1}{2N} \sum_{k=0}^{2N-1} Y_D(k) e^{j\frac{2\pi}{2N}kn} \\
&= \frac{1}{2N} \left(\sum_{k=0}^{N-1} \hat{X}(k) e^{j\frac{(2n+1)k\pi}{2N}} + \sum_{k=N+1}^{2N-1} (-e^{j\frac{k\pi}{2N}} \hat{X}(2N - k)) e^{j\frac{2\pi}{2N}kn} \right).
\end{aligned}
$$

$$(1.37)$$

After change of variable in the 2nd term and some algebraic manipulation, and using $1/e(0) = 2e(0)$ and $1/e(k) = e(k)$ for $k \neq 0$, (1.37) can be rewritten as

$$
\begin{aligned}
y(n) &= \frac{1}{2N}\left(\sum_{k=0}^{N-1} \hat{X}(k)e^{j\frac{(2n+1)k\pi}{2N}} + \sum_{k=1}^{N-1} \hat{X}(k)e^{-j\frac{(2n+1)k\pi}{2N}} \right) \\
&= \frac{1}{2N}\left(\hat{X}(0) + 2\sum_{k=1}^{N-1} \hat{X}(k)\cos\left(\frac{(2n+1)k\pi}{2N}\right) \right) \\
&= \frac{2}{N}\left(e(0)X(0) + \sum_{k=1}^{N-1} X(k)e(k)\cos\left(\frac{(2n+1)k\pi}{2N}\right) \right), \quad (1.38)
\end{aligned}
$$

for $0 \le n \le 2N-1$. The inverse DCT, obtained by retaining the 1st N points of $y(n)$, is given by

$$
x(n) = y(n) = \frac{2}{N}\sum_{k=0}^{N-1} e(k)X(k)\cos\left(\frac{(2n+1)k\pi}{2N}\right), \quad (1.39)
$$

for $0 \le n \le N-1$.

Express the N-point sequences $x(n)$ and $X(k)$ in vector form as

$$
\mathbf{x} = \begin{bmatrix} x(0) \\ x(1) \\ \cdots \\ x(N-1) \end{bmatrix}, \quad
\mathbf{X} = \begin{bmatrix} X(0) \\ X(1) \\ \cdots \\ X(N-1) \end{bmatrix}, \quad (1.40)
$$

and the DCT transform in (1.25) in matrix form as

$$
\mathbf{\Lambda} = \begin{bmatrix}
1/\sqrt{2} & 1/\sqrt{2} & \cdots & 1/\sqrt{2} \\
\cos(\frac{\pi}{2N}) & \cos(\frac{3\pi}{2N}) & \cdots & \cos(\frac{(2N-1)\pi}{2N}) \\
\cdots & \cdots & & \\
\cos(\frac{(N-1)\pi}{2N}) & \cos(\frac{3(N-1)\pi}{2N}) & \cdots & \cos(\frac{(2N-1)(N-1)\pi}{2N})
\end{bmatrix}. \quad (1.41)
$$

The DCT and IDCT coefficients can be computed using

$$
\mathbf{X} = \mathbf{\Lambda}\mathbf{x}, \quad \mathbf{x} = \tfrac{2}{N}\mathbf{\Lambda}^T\mathbf{X}. \quad (1.42)
$$

This leads to $\mathbf{\Lambda}\mathbf{\Lambda}^T = \frac{N}{2}\mathbf{I}_{N\times N}$, where $\mathbf{I}_{N\times N}$ is the identity matrix of dimension $N \times N$. Therefore, DCT is an orthogonal transform.

The N-point 1D-DCT in (1.25) requires N^2 multiplications and additions. For image compression, the image frame is divided into $N \times N$ blocks, and a $N \times N$ two-dimensional DCT (2D-DCT) is computed for each block. Direct computation of 2D-DCT of length N requires N^4 multiplications and additions. On the other hand, by utilizing the separability of 2D-DCT, it can be computed by performing N 1D-DCTs on the rows of the image block followed by N 1D-DCTs on the resulting columns [7]. With this simplification, $N \times N$

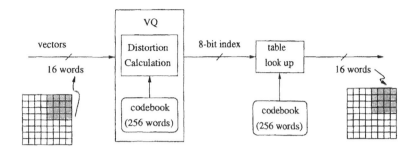

Fig. 1.7   Vector Quantization-based vector compression and decompression.

2D-DCT requires $2N^3$ multiply-add operations, or $4N^3$ arithmetic operations.

1.2.7   Vector Quantization

Vector quantization (VQ), which originated as a pattern matching scheme, is now commonly used for data compression in speech, image and video coding, and speech recognition. It is a lossy compression technique that exploits the spatial correlation that exists between neighboring signal samples. In VQ, a group of samples are quantized together rather than individually. A vector quantizer can operate directly on image blocks to achieve spatial information compression and quantization at the same time. In a VQ system, identical codebooks containing codeword vectors are available both in the transmitter and the receiver side. The vector quantizer transmits the index of the codeword rather than the codeword itself.

Fig. 1.7 illustrates the VQ encoding and decoding process. On the encoder side, the vector quantizer takes a group of input samples (pixels in the case of image compression in Fig. 1.7), compares this input vector to the codewords in the codebook and selects the codeword with minimum *distortion*. Assume that vectors are k-dimensional and the codebook size is N. If the wordlength of the vector elements is W and $N = 2^m$, then the m-bit address of the codebook is transmitted as opposed to kW-bit. This leads to a compression factor of m/kW. The decoder simply receives the m-bit index as the address of the codebook and retrieves the best codeword to reconstruct the input vector. In Fig. 1.7, each vector contains $k = 16$ pixels of wordlength $W = 8$. The codebook contains $N = 256$ codewords, hence $m = 8$. Therefore, the vector quantizer in Fig. 1.7 achieves a compression factor of $1/16$.

The encoding algorithm in vector quantizer can be viewed as an exhaustive search algorithm, where the computation of distortion is performed sequentially on every codeword vector in the codebook, keeping track of the minimum distortion so far, and continuing until every codeword vector has been tested.

Usually, the Euclidean distance between two vectors (also called square error)

$$d(\mathbf{x}, \mathbf{y}) = \|\mathbf{x} - \mathbf{y}\|^2 = \sum_{i=0}^{k-1} (x_i - y_i)^2 \tag{1.43}$$

is used as distortion measurement. In practical implementations, the distortion between the input vector $\mathbf{x}$ and the j-th codeword vector $\mathbf{c_j}$ ($0 \leq j \leq N - 1$) is computed based on their inner product, instead of direct squaring operations [8]. By expanding (1.43), we get

$$d(\mathbf{x}, \mathbf{c_j}) = \|\mathbf{x}\|^2 - 2(\mathbf{x} \cdot \mathbf{c_j} + e_j), \tag{1.44}$$

where

$$e_j = -\frac{1}{2}\|\mathbf{c_j}\|^2 = -\frac{1}{2}\sum_{i=0}^{k-1} c_{ji}^2, \tag{1.45}$$

and the inner product is given by

$$\mathbf{x} \cdot \mathbf{c_j} = \sum_{i=0}^{k-1} x_i c_{ji}. \tag{1.46}$$

Since e_j depends only on the codeword vector $\mathbf{c_j}$ and is a constant, it can be precomputed and treated as an additional component of the vector $\mathbf{c_j}$. Therefore, for a fixed input vector $\mathbf{x}$, minimizing the distortion in (1.44) among the N codeword vectors is equivalent to maximizing the quantity $\mathbf{x} \cdot \mathbf{c_j} + e_j$, where $0 \leq j \leq N - 1$. Therefore, the search process in VQ can be described as follows:

$$ind_n = (\min_{0 \leq j \leq N-i} d_j)^{-1} = (\max_{0 \leq j \leq N-1} \sum_{i=0}^{k-1} (x_i^n c_{ji} + e_j))^{-1}, \tag{1.47}$$

where the inverse means "output the index ind_n which achieves the minimum or maximum" and n represents the time instance. The search process can also be described equivalently in a matrix-vector multiplication formulation followed by comparisons as follows [9]:

$$\begin{aligned} \mathbf{D} &= [d_0\ d_1\ \cdots\ d_{N-1}]^T = \mathbf{Cx} + \mathbf{e} \\ ind_n &= (\mathbf{Max}\{d_i\})^{-1}, \end{aligned} \tag{1.48}$$

where $\mathbf{C} = \{c_{ji}\}$ is $N \times k$ matrix with the j-th codeword vector $\mathbf{c_j}^T$ as its j-th row, $\mathbf{x}$ is the input vector of dimension k, and $\mathbf{e} = [e_0\ e_1\ \cdots\ e_{N-1}]^T$.

The above searching algorithm is a bruteforce approach where the distortion between the input vector and every entry in the codebook is computed, and is called *full-search vector quantization*. Every full-search operation requires N distortion computations and each distortion computation involves k

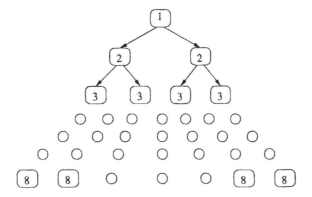

Fig. 1.8 Tree-structured vector quantization.

multiply-add operations. Hence, computing the index for one k-dimensional input vector requires Nk multiply-add operations and $N-1$ comparisons, without including memory access operations. This algorithm may be a bottleneck for high performance for large N. For these cases, a *tree-structured vector quantization* scheme can be used whose complexity is proportional to $\log_2 N$. The basic idea is to perform a sequence of binary search instead of an exhaustive search, as shown in Fig. 1.8. At each level of the tree, the input vector is compared with the 2 codeword vectors and 2 distortion computations are carried out. This process is repeated until the leaf of the tree is reached. For the example in Fig. 1.7, the tree search requires 16 distortion calculations, as compared to 256 in full search. The tree search VQ is a suboptimal quantizer that typically results in performance degradation. However, for carefully design codebook, the degradation can be minimized.

1.2.8   Viterbi Algorithm and Dynamic Programming

This section reviews the Viterbi algorithm, which is based on dynamic programming [10]. The Viterbi algorithm is widely used to detect sequential error-control codes such as convolutional codes, and to detect symbols in channels with memory. It is optimum in the maximum likelihood sense for finding the most likely noiseless sequence given a noise corrupted finite-state sequence. The finite-state signals are signals generated from finite-state transition diagram. For example, Fig. 1.9(a) is a state transition diagram with 4 states $S00$, $S01$, $S10$ and $S11$. There are two possible outgoing edges from each state assuming input of 0 and 1. The note on each edge denotes the current input bit and the corresponding output symbol. For example, the outgoing edge from state $S00$ with note 1/11 means that the current input is 1 and the output symbol is 11. This state transition diagram can be used to describe a convolutional encoding algorithm with code rate 1/2, memory length 2 and generator polynomials $g_1(z) = 1 + z^{-2}$ and $g_2(z) = 1 + z^{-1} + z^{-2}$.

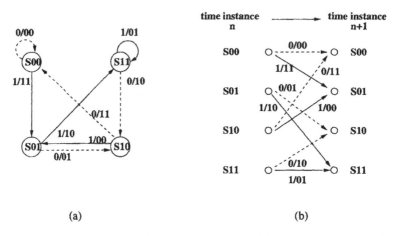

(a)   (b)

Fig. 1.9 Trellis description of a finite-state machine. (a) A 4-state machine. (b) The trellis description.

The state transition diagram in Fig. 1.9(a) can also be described using a time-indexed equivalent *trellis diagram* in Fig. 1.9(b), which describes all the state transitions from time instance n to $n + 1$. If a sequence of symbols, generated from a trellis, is corrupted by additive white Gaussian noise, the Viterbi algorithm can find the closest sequence of symbols in the given trellis, using either the Euclidean distance (optimal) or the Hamming distance (suboptimal) as distance measurement. The resulting sequence is called the *global most-likely sequence.*

For a received N-state sequence **v** containing L symbols

$$\mathbf{v} = \{v(0), v(1), \cdots, v(L-1)\},$$

where the first symbol $v(0)$ is received at time instance 0 and the last one $v(L-1)$ is received at time instance $L-1$, the Viterbi algorithm iteratively computes the *survivor path* entering each state at time instances $1, \cdots, L-1$. The survivor path for a given state at time instance n is the sequence of symbols closest in distance to the received sequence up to time n; a *path metric* $x_i(n)$ is assigned to each state denoting the distance between the survivor path for state i and the received sequence up to time n. From time instance n to $n+1$ (for $0 \le n \le L$), the Viterbi algorithm updates the survivor paths and the path metric values $x_j(n+1)$, for $1 \le j \le N$, from the survivor path metrics at time instance n and the branch metrics in the given trellis using *dynamic programming* (DP) [11] as follows:

$$x_j(n+1) = \min_i[x_i(n) + a_{ij}(n)], \quad i, j = 1, 2, \cdots, N, \qquad (1.49)$$

where $a_{ij}(n)$ is the branch metric for the transition from the i-th state at time instance n to the j-th state at time instance $n+1$ in the decoding trellis and is the difference in distance between the current received symbol $v(n)$ and the output symbol in the encoding trellis. Consider a sequence generated by the 4-state encoding trellis in Fig. 1.9(b). Assume that at time instance n, the path metrics for the 4 states are

$$x_1(n) - 2, \ x_2(n) = 0, \ x_3(n) = 1, \ x_4(n) = 2 \qquad (1.50)$$

and the received symbol is $v(n) = 11$. Using the Hamming distance, the branch metrics for all the transitions in the trellis can then be computed as

$$a_{11}(n) = weight(|11 - 00|) = 2, \quad a_{12} = weight(|11 - 11|) = 0,$$
$$a_{23}(n) = weight(|11 - 01|) = 1, \quad a_{24} = weight(|11 - 10|) = 1,$$
$$a_{31}(n) = weight(|11 - 11|) = 0, \quad a_{32} = weight(|11 - 00|) = 2,$$
$$a_{43}(n) = weight(|11 - 10|) = 1, \quad a_{44} = weight(|11 - 01|) = 1.$$

The survivor path and the path metric for each state from time n to $n+1$ can then be updated as shown in Fig. 1.10. There are 2 possible paths entering each state. The one with larger metric is discarded, and that with smaller metric is retained and added to the survivor path, as shown in darker lines in Fig. 1.10. This update process is carried out iteratively from $n = 1$ to $n = L$. The global most-likely sequence is the survivor path of the state with minimum path metric at time $n = L$, i.e., the survivor path of the state

$$i = ind^{-1}(\ min_j \ \{x_j(L)\} \ ), \qquad (1.51)$$

where ind^{-1} means "take the index of the corresponding state". Dynamic programming algorithms have the property that the optimum solution from an initial iteration to the iteration $n+m$ must consist of the optimum solution from initial iteration to iteration n, and from iteration n to iteration $n + m$. Hence, this iterative algorithm is optimum from this point of view.

Fig. 1.11 is an example run of Viterbi decoding algorithm. The input sequence 1 1 0 0 1 0 0 0 is encoded using the 4-state trellis in Fig. 1.9(b) and the transmitted symbol sequence is 11 10 10 11 11 01 11 00. The received sequence is corrupted by noise and deviates from the transmitted sequence by 3 symbols. Fig. 1.11 shows the decoding trellis from time instance 0 to 8, where the branches with an "x" are the discarded branches. The global most-likely sequence is the survivor path of the first state at time instance $n = L = 8$. It can be seen that the global most-likely sequence, drawn in darker lines in the decoding trellis, is exactly the same as the transmitted sequence.

The Viterbi algorithm includes computing of branch metrics $a_{ij}(n)$, updating the path metrics, selecting the final state, and tracing back its survivor path, out of which the path metric update requires addition, comparison, and selection (ACS) for every state at each time instance. The speed of the Viterbi decoder is limited by the recursive ACS operations.

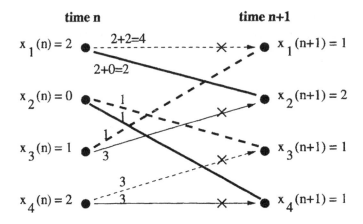

Fig. 1.10   Updated survivor paths for each state from time instance n to $n+1$.

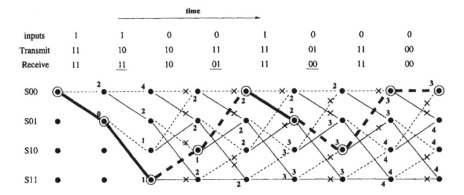

Fig. 1.11   An example of Viterbi decoding for a finite-state sequence generated by the state diagram in Fig. 1.9.

1.2.9   Decimator and Expander

The sampling rate in a DSP system can be changed internally by downsampling or upsampling operations. The resulting system is referred to as a multirate system. Applications of multirate signal processing include speech and image compression, digital audio systems, statistical and adaptive signal processing, etc. Decimators and expanders are the two basic building blocks in multirate systems.

A decimator processes an input $x(n)$ and produces an output sequence

$$y_D(n) = x(Mn), \qquad (1.52)$$

where M is a positive integer. The decimator is also referred to as compressor or downsampler. The notation of a decimator and its functionality are illus-

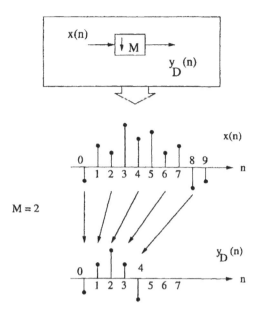

Fig. 1.12   The decimator and its functionality.

trated in Fig. 1.12. The decimator generates one output for every M input samples, and the output rate is thus M times slower than that of the input sequence.

Expansion is an upsampling process. It takes an input $x(n)$ and produces an output sequence

$$y_E(n) = \begin{cases} x(n/L), & if \ n \ is \ integer - multiple \ of \ L, \\ 0, & otherwise, \end{cases} \quad (1.53)$$

where L is an integer. The notation of an expander and its functionality are illustrated in Fig. 1.13. The expander is also referred to as interpolator or upsampler. An expander generates L output samples for every input sample by inserting $L - 1$ zeros. Hence, the sampling rate of the output sequence is L times faster than that of the input sequence.

Decimation and interpolation are nonlinear operations. Cascade of an M-fold decimator followed by an L-fold interpolator is generally not equivalent to the cascade of an L-fold interpolator followed by an M-fold decimator. Several identities are are used for analysis of multirate systems. The *noble identities* are used to transfer delay elements from the input of a decimator/expander to its output, as illustrated in Fig. 1.14. Note that n delay elements are equivalent to n/M delay elements after downsampling or nL delay elements after upsampling.

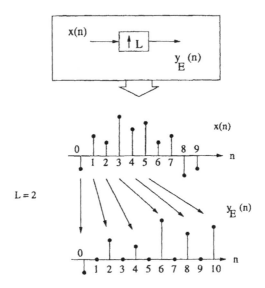

Fig. 1.13 The expander and its functionality.

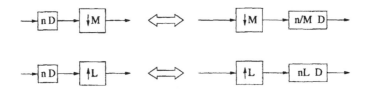

Fig. 1.14 The noble identities for multirate systems.

1.2.10   Wavelets and Filter Banks

Wavelet transform is used in speech and image compression [12],[13]. In wavelet analysis, signals are represented using a set of basis functions (wavelets) derived by shifting and scaling a single prototype function, referred to as "mother wavelet", in time. The wavelet transform can be viewed as a decomposition of a signal in the time-scale (frequency) plane.

One dimensional discrete wavelet transform (DWT) of $x(n)$ is defined as

$$y_i(n) = \sum_{k=-\infty}^{\infty} x(k)h_i(2^{i+1}n - k), \ for \ 0 \le i \le m - 2,$$

$$y_{m-1}(n) = \sum_{k=-\infty}^{\infty} x(k)h_{m-1}(2^{m-1}n - k), \ for \ i = m - 1, \quad (1.54)$$

where the shifted and scaled versions of the mother wavelet $h(n)$, $\{h_i(2^{i+1}n - k), \ for \ 0 \le i \le m - 1, -\infty < k < \infty\}$ are the basis functions, and $y_i(n)$ are

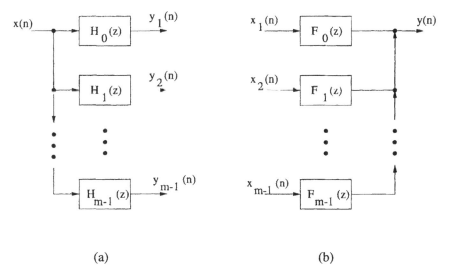

(a)   (b)

Fig. 1.15   (a) Analysis filter bank. (b) Synthesis filter bank.

the *wavelet coefficients*. The inverse transform is computed as follows:

$$x(n) = \sum_{i=0}^{m-2} \sum_{k=-\infty}^{\infty} y_i(k) f_i(n - 2^{i+1}k)$$

$$+ \sum_{k=-\infty}^{\infty} y_{m-1}(k) f_{m-1}(n - 2^{m-1}k), \quad (1.55)$$

where $\{f_i(n - 2^{i+1}k)\}$ are designed such that (1.55) perfectly reconstructs the original signal $x(n)$. Note that the computations in DWT and inverse DWT (IDWT) are similar to convolution operations. In fact, the DWT and IDWT can be calculated recursively as a series of convolutions and decimations and can be implemented using filter banks.

A digital *filter bank* is a collection of filters with a common input (referred to as the analysis filter bank) or a common output (referred to as the synthesis filter bank). Fig. 1.15 shows block diagrams of an analysis filter bank (part (a)) and a synthesis filter bank (part (b)). Filter banks are generally used for subband coding, where a single signal $x(n)$ is split into m subband signals in the analysis filter bank; in the synthesis filter bank, m input subband signals are combined to reconstruct the signal $y(n)$.

Consider the computation of the discrete wavelet transform for $m = 4$ using filter banks. The wavelet coefficients

$$y_0(n) = \sum_{k=-\infty}^{\infty} x(k) h_0(2n - k),$$

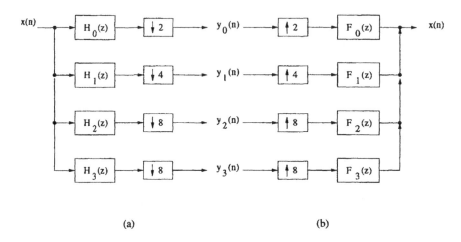

(a)   (b)

Fig. 1.16   Analysis (a) and synthesis (b) filter banks for DWT and IDWT.

$$y_1(n) = \sum_{k=-\infty}^{\infty} x(k)h_1(4n - k),$$

$$y_2(n) = \sum_{k=-\infty}^{\infty} x(k)h_2(8n - k),$$

$$y_3(n) = \sum_{k=-\infty}^{\infty} x(k)h_3(8n - k) \tag{1.56}$$

can be computed using the analysis filter bank with decimators in Fig. 1.16(a). The signal $x(n)$ can then be reconstructed through inverse wavelet transform using interpolators and synthesis filter bank, as shown in Fig. 1.16(b).

In practice, the discrete wavelet transform periodically processes M input samples every time and generates M output samples at various frequency bands, where $M = 2^m$ and m is the number of bands or levels of the wavelet. It is often implemented using a *tree-structured* filter bank, where the M wavelet coefficients are computed through $\log_2 M$ octave levels and each octave performs one low-pass and one high-pass filtering operations. At each octave level j, an input sequence $s_{j-1}(n)$ is fed into low-pass and high-pass filters $g(n)$ and $h(n)$, respectively. The output from the high-pass filter $h(n)$ represents the detail information in the original signal at the given level j, which is denoted by $w_j(n)$, and the output from the low-pass filter $g(n)$ represents the remaining (coarse) information in the original signal, which is denoted as $s_j(n)$. The computation in octave j can be expressed as follows:

$$s_j(n) = \sum_k s_{j-1}(k)g(2n - k) = \sum_k g(k)s_{j-1}(2n - k)$$

$$w_j(n) \;=\; \sum_k s_{j-1}(k)h(2n-k) = \sum_k h(k)s_{j-1}(2n-k), \qquad (1.57)$$

where n is the sample index and j is the octave index. Initially, $s_0(n) = x(n)$. Fig. 1.17 shows the block diagram of a 3-octave tree-structured DWT. It is worth pointing out that since each filtered output is decimated by a factor of 2, only signals that are not thrown away need to be computed. For example, consider an $m = \log_2 M$-level wavelet with an input sequence containing M samples (assume M is power of 2). The total number of samples generated at the output of the 1st octave is M ($M/2$ outputs from high-pass filter and $M/2$ from low-pass filter); the total number of samples generated at 2nd octave is $M/2$; the 3rd octave is $M/4$, etc. Hence in this m-level wavelet, the total number of samples that needs to be computed for every M inputs equals

$$M + M/2 + M/4 + \cdots + 2 = 2(M - 1). \qquad (1.58)$$

For this periodic wavelet computation with M input samples, the number of samples computed every sample period is $2(M-1)/M$ or $2(1 - 1/M)$ [14].

The two analysis filter banks in Fig. 1.16(a) and Fig. 1.17(a) carry out the same functions. Using noble identities, the transfer function of the analysis filters in Fig. 1.17(a) can be expressed in terms of $h(n)$ and $g(n)$ as follows:

$$
\begin{aligned}
H_0(z) &= H(z), \; H_1(z) = G(z)H(z^2), \\
H_2(z) &= G(z)G(z^2)H(z^4), \; H_3(z) = G(z)G(z^2)G(z^4), \qquad (1.59)
\end{aligned}
$$

where $H_0(z)$ is a high-pass filter, $H_1(z)$ and $H_2(z)$ are bandpass filters, and $H_3(z)$ is a low-pass filter. The width of the passband of these filters decreases from $H_0(z)$ to $H_3(z)$, and hence wavelet transform can also be viewed as nonuniform subband coding.

1.3   DSP APPLICATION DEMANDS AND SCALED CMOS TECHNOLOGIES

The field of VLSI DSP continues to be driven by the increasing demand of DSP applications, particularly in multimedia and wireless communications, and by advances in scaled CMOS technologies. This section presents the computation requirements needed in digital video processing applications and in scaled CMOS VLSI technologies. It is shown that video processing systems require computation rates in the range of $10-100$ GOPs/sec (gigaoperations per second) and, therefore, design of these systems is quite challenging!

A color digital image consists of picture elements (pixels), which are represented using three primary color elements, red (R), green (G) and blue (B). The RGB representation is converted to YUV representation based on human

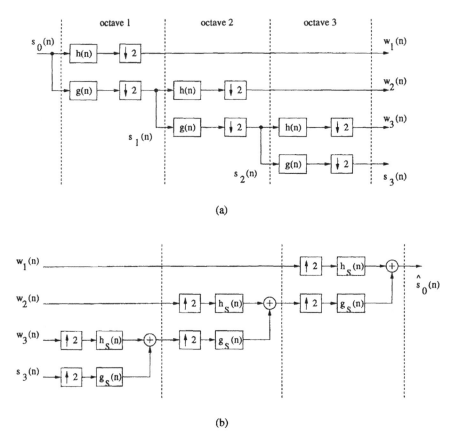

Fig. 1.17 Block diagrams of tree-structured analysis (a) and synthesis filter banks (b) DWT.

visual systems, where Y stands for the luminance information and U and V are the color differences between Y and blue, Y and red, respectively, and are called chrominances. A full-sampling of YUV is represented as $4:4:4$ sampling and the resulting pixel is represented using 24 bits, 8 bits for each variable. With $4:4:4$ sampling, a CIF (common intermediate format) frame with a frame size of 288×352 pixels and a frame rate of 30 frame/sec requires storage of size 2.433 megabits (Mb) and the video source data rate is 72.99 Mb/sec for a single frame. For high-definition TV (HDTV) video with a frame size of 1920×1250 pixels and a frame rate of 50 frame/sec, one frame requires storage size of 57.6 Mb and the video source data rate of 2.88 gigabits per sec (Gb/sec). With a sequence of video containing hundreds and thousands of frames, storage and transmission in real-time is impossible with today's technology. In reality, video pixels are downsampled and video frames are compressed before these are stored or transmitted.

Human eyes have fewer receptors with less spatial resolution for color than

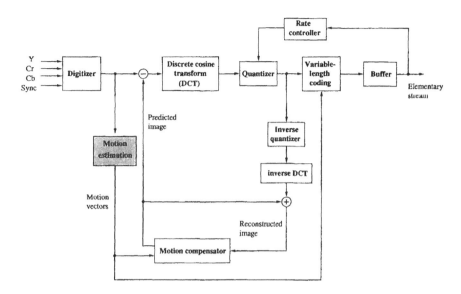

Fig. 1.18   Block diagram of MPEG-2 encoder.

those for luminance. Hence the chrominance can be downsampled to reduce the source data rate and frame storage size. Typically, a $4 : 2 : 2$ or $4 : 2 : 0$ sampling is used. In $4 : 2 : 2$, the luminance Y is sampled for every pixel, while the chrominances U and V are sampled every other pixel horizontally resulting in 33% savings. In $4 : 2 : 0$, U and V are downsampled by half both horizontally and vertically, resulting in 50% savings.

Besides downsampling, video compression is the key for reduction in bandwidth requirement of source data streams. Generally speaking, video sequences contain significant amount of spatial and temporal redundancy within a single frame and between consecutive frames. MPEG, a video communication standard developed by the Moving Picture Experts Group, reduces the bit-rate by exploiting both the spatial and temporal redundancies through intra- and interframe coding techniques. The ultimate goal of MPEG standard is to optimize image or video quality for a specified bit rate subject to "objective" or "subjective" optimization criteria [15]. Fig. 1.18 shows the block diagram of the MPEG-2 encoding process, where a temporal motion-compensated prediction is followed by transform coding of the remaining spatial information and entropy coding of the transmitted sequences are used to achieve high data compression rate [16].

Using motion-compensated video compression technique, digital video sequences can be stored and transmitted in real time. However, these sophisticated compression techniques involve substantial amount of computations at high speed. For example, the complexity of a full-search block-matching algorithm is proportional to $3(2p+1)^2 N_h N_v F$ operations/sec, where $N_h \times N_v$ is the frame size, $+/- p$ is the search area and F is the frame rate in frames/sec.

For a CIF frame with a frame size of 288×352 pixels, a frame rate of 30 frames/sec and a search range of $+/-$ 7 pixels, the full-search BMA requires about 2 GOPs/sec. The required number of operations gets even larger for higher resolution pictures with higher frame rates and larger search range. For HDTV video with a frame size of 1920×1250 pixels, a frame rate of 50 frames/sec and a search range of $+16/-15$ pixels, the full-search BMA demands a computation rate of about 368.64 GOPs/sec. The DCT in video communications is also very demanding. The $N \times N$ 2D-DCT requires $2N^3$ multiply-add operations, or $4N^3$ arithmetic operations. For a CIF frame with image blocks of size 8×8, the computation requirement for 2D-DCT is 97.32 MOPs/sec (megaoperations per second). For HDTV video with image blocks of size 8×8, the computation requirement for 2D-DCT is 3.84 GOPs/sec. These high processing requirements can only be met using parallel processing techniques with carefully designed hardware and software. Design and implementation of video compression and multimedia signal processing systems is a major challenge.

Complexity of digital signal processing has not only been driven by theoretical advances, but also by the rapid advances in the scaled CMOS VLSI technologies. The dramatic increase in the integration levels in recent years has led to an increase in the number of possible DSP applications that can be integrated onto single chips. In previous years the focus of the increased integration levels was to design dedicated (or application-specific) architectures for high-performance DSP applications. This trend still continues today as more complex DSP and image/video processing algorithms are implemented on single chips. For example, current submicron technology allows a single chip to be designed that can perform real-time MPEG-2 motion estimation (which requires approximately $10-30$ GOPs/sec). An example is a chip from NEC [17] that contains 3.7M transistors and has a peak performance of 12 GOPs/sec. Lately a second trend has been gaining more momentum where DSP systems are implemented using programmable DSPs and microprocessors specialized for media processing. This trend is primarily driven by the demand for decreased time-to-market and more portability/mobility.

The design of complex multimedia systems has become possible due to the advances in scaled VLSI technologies. It is predicted that the CMOS technology will scale down to 0.07μm-devices with corresponding improvements in density, speed, and cost as shown in Table 1.2 [18]. Note that the number of transistors on single chips is expected to increase from the current $6M$ to $90M$ by year 2010. The main challenge to maintaining the pace of scaling is the availability of a large-field lithographic technology. If this is not available, manufacturing at high yields and low costs might be difficult. Optical lithography might have to be used for technologies below 0.25μm. For technologies below 0.18μm, even more dramatic changes in lithographic systems is required. The limits of practical device feasibility begin to be seriously challenged at dimensions of 0.05μm due to contact resistance and statistically significant dopant distribution fluctuations.

Table 1.2 Characteristics of Scaled CMOS Technologies

Year of first DRAM shipment	1998	2001	2004	2010
Minimum feature size (μm)	0.25	0.18	0.13	0.07
Memory				
Bits/chip (DRAM/Flash)	256M	1G	4G	64G
Cost/bit@volume (millicents)	0.007	0.003	0.001	0.0002
Logic (high-volume: microprocessor)				
Logic transistors/cm^2 (packed)	7M	13M	25M	90M
Bits/cm^2 (cache SRAM)	6M	20M	50M	300M
Cost/transistor@volume (millicents)	0.5	0.2	0.1	0.02
Logic (low-volume ASIC)				
Transistors/cm^2 (auto layout)	4M	7M	12M	40M
Non-recurring engineering cost/transistor (millicents)	0.1	0.05	0.03	0.01

It is also interesting to observe the evolution of applications as shown in Fig. 1.19 [19]. This figure shows that the applications like desktop video that were primarily implemented using application-specific integrated circuits (ASICs) are now being executed by programmable DSPs (PDSPs). Therefore, there is a general shift in the nature of applications from ASIC to PDSP to microprocessors to field-programmable gate arrays (FPGAs). Another way to look at it is that as technology improves the "best" implementation of a given function will move from ASIC to DSP to microprocessor to FPGA with time.

1.4 REPRESENTATIONS OF DSP ALGORITHMS

DSP algorithms are described by *nonterminating programs* which execute the same code repetitively. For example, a 3-tap FIR digital filter described by the non-terminating program

$$y(n) = ax(n) + bx(n-1) + cx(n-2) \ for \ n = 1 \ to \ n = \infty. \qquad (1.60)$$

Execution of all the computations in the algorithm once is referred to as an *iteration*. The *iteration period* is the time required for execution of one iteration of the algorithm. The *iteration rate* is the reciprocal of the iteration period. During each iteration, the 3-tap FIR filter in (1.60) processes one input signal, completes 3 multiplication and 2 addition operations (in serial or in parallel), and generates 1 output sample. DSP systems are also characterized by the *sampling rate* (also referred to as *throughput*) in terms of number of samples processed per second. The *critical path* of a combinational logic circuit

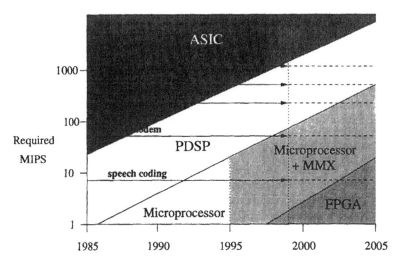

Fig. 1.19 Evolution of applications.

is defined as the longest path between inputs and outputs, where the length of a path is proportional to its computation time. DSP systems generally are implemented using sequential circuits, where the critical path is defined as the longest path between any two storage elements (or delay elements). The critical path computation time determines the minimum feasible *clock period* of a DSP system. The *latency* is defined as the difference between the time an output is generated and the time at which its corresponding input was received by the system. For systems containing combinational logic only, latency is usually represented in terms of absolute time units, or the number of gate delays; for sequential systems, latency is usually represented in terms of number of clock cycles. Generally, the clock rate of a DSP system is not the same as its sampling rate.

DSP algorithms are described using mathematical formulations at a higher level where it is more important to specify the functionality of the system than the order and structure of the internal operations. For architectural design, these mathematical formulations need to be converted to behavioral description languages or graphical representations.

The behavioral description languages include applicative languages, prescriptive languages, and descriptive languages. The *applicative languages* represent a set of equations that are satisfied by the variables in the algorithm, rather than a sequence of actions (assignments to be carried out, i.e., the order of the assignment statements is not important). Applicative languages are popular for the description of DSP systems. For example, the Silage language [20] used in the Cathedral synthesis tool [21] is applicative. The *prescriptive languages* explicitly specify the order of the assignment statements. Some examples of these types of languages include high-level programming languages such as Pascal, C, or Fortran. More recently, many applications are being defined using *descriptive languages* that represent the structure of a DSP system. Examples of these are the hardware description languages such as Verilog or VHDL [22],[23].

Graphical representations are efficient for investigating and analyzing data flow properties of DSP algorithms and for exploiting the inherent parallelism among different subtasks. More importantly, graphical representations can be used to map DSP algorithms to hardware implementations. Hence, these representations can bridge the gap between algorithmic descriptions and structural implementations. The absolute measures of the performance metrics of DSP systems, area, speed, power, and roundoff noise cannot be obtained without the knowledge of the supporting technology in which the system is implemented. However, the graphical representations exhibit all the parallelism and data-driven properties of the system, and provide insight into space and time tradeoffs. With graphical representations, the architectural design space can be explored and an appropriate architecture can be selected in a technology-independent manner.

This section addresses four types of graphical representations of DSP algorithms; these include block diagram, signal-flow graph (SFG), data-flow graph (DFG) and dependence graph (DG) representations, all of which are described by directed graphs. These representations describe the algorithms at various levels of abstraction. In general, the DG exhibits the inherent parallelism and data-flow constraints in an algorithm to the maximum extend and has the least structural bias; the parallelism in a DG can be exploited in various ways by mapping it to SFG or DFG. In practice, DG is used for systolic array design. SFG and DFG are used for analyzing structural properties and to explore architectural alternatives using high-level transformations [24].

1.4.1 Block Diagrams

Block diagrams are most frequently used to graphically represent DSP systems. All the DSP algorithms in Section 1.2 are illustrated using block diagrams. A block diagram consists of functional blocks connected with directed edges, which represent the data flow from its input block to its output block. These edges may or may not contain delay elements. Block diagrams can be constructed for all systems with different levels of abstraction.

For example, the 3-tap FIR filter

$$y(n) = b_0 x(n) + b_1 x(n-1) + b_2 x(n-2) \tag{1.61}$$

can be described using the block diagram in Fig. 1.20, which consists of two types of functional blocks, $\boxed{\text{adder}}$ and $\boxed{\text{multiplier}}$. The unit-delay elements can also be treated as functional blocks as they are implemented using registers in reality. The unit-delay element is denoted as $\boxed{z^{-1}}$ (or $\boxed{D}$) in Fig. 1.20.

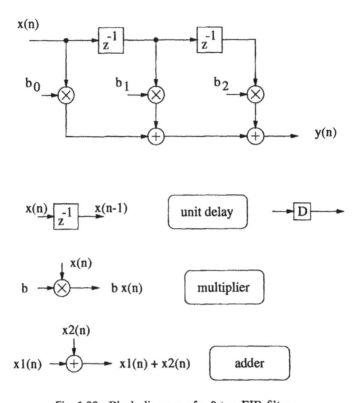

Fig. 1.20 Block diagram of a 3-tap FIR filter.

A system can be represented using various block diagrams, each of which represents a different implementation of the same functionality. For example, the 3-tap FIR filter in (1.61) can also be represented using the block diagram in Fig. 1.21, which is referred to as a *data-broadcast* structure.

A block diagram is a concrete model that captures the exact functionality of a system. Each signal and functional unit are expressed explicitly in the diagram. Various block diagrams can be derived for the same system with different arrangements leading to different distinct realizations.

1.4.2 Signal-Flow Graph

A signal-flow graph (SFG) is a collection of nodes and directed edges [25]. The nodes represent computations or tasks. A directed edge (j, k) denotes a branch originating from node j and terminating at node k. With input signal at node j and output signal at node k, the edge (j, k) denotes a linear transformation from the signal at node j to the signal at node k. SFGs have been used for the analysis, representation, and evaluation of linear digital networks, especially digital filter structures. In digital networks, the edges are usually restricted to

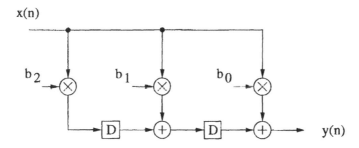

Fig. 1.21   Block diagram of a 3-tap data-broadcast FIR filter.

constant gain multipliers (the output of the edge is a constant multiple of the input signal), or delay elements (the output of the edge is a delayed version of the input signal). Adders and multipliers can be described by a node with multiple incoming edges and one outgoing edge. There are 2 special types of nodes in an SFG, source nodes and sink nodes. A *source node* is a node with no entering edges, and is used to represent the injection of external inputs into a graph. A *sink node* is a node with only entering edges, and is used to extract outputs from a graph. The SFG of the direct-form 3-tap FIR filter (corresponding to the block diagram in Fig. 1.20) is shown in Fig. 1.22(a), where an edge with no explicit indication of operation indicates an edge with unit-gain (identity transformation). Note that the source and sink nodes in this SFG are connected to the rest of the graph through unit-gain edges in order to clearly show the input and output of the system.

Linear SFGs can be transformed into different forms without changing the system functions. *Flow graph reversal* or *transposition* is one of these transformations and is applicable to single-input–single-output systems to obtain equivalent transposed structures. Transposition of an SFG is carried out by reversing the directions of all the edges, exchanging the input and output nodes while keeping the edge gain or edge delay unchanged. The resulting SFG maintains the same system functionality. Fig. 1.22(b) shows the derivation of the transpose FIR filter SFG (corresponding to the data-broadcast block diagram in Fig. 1.21) from the direct-form SFG. The reader can verify that the data-broadcast symmetric FIR filter in Fig. 1.1(b) can be derived from Fig. 1.1(a) by transposition. Transpose operations are also applicable to multiple-input multiple-output (MIMO) systems described by symmetric transformation matrices (see Chapter 9).

SFGs provide an abstract flowgraph representation of linear networks and have been extensively used in digital filter structure design and analysis of finite wordlength effects. In general, SFGs are only applicable to linear networks; they cannot be used to describe multirate DSP systems.

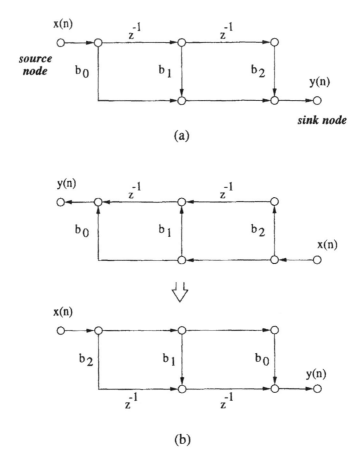

Fig. 1.22 An SFG of a 3-tap FIR filter. (a) Direct-form FIR filter SFG; (b) transposed FIR filter SFG.

1.4.3 Data-Flow Graph

In data-flow graph (DFG) representations, the nodes represent computations (or functions or subtasks) and the directed edges represent data paths (communications between nodes) and each edge has a nonnegative number of delays associated with it. For example, Fig. 1.23(b) is a data-flow graph of the computation $y(n) = ay(n-1) + x(n)$, where node A represents addition and node B represents multiplication, the edge from A to B (denoted as $A \rightarrow B$) contains one delay and the edge from B to A ($B \rightarrow A$) contains no delay. Associated with each node is its execution time in terms of normalized time units (u.t.; units of time). For example, the execution time of node A is 2 u.t. and the execution time of node B is 4 u.t., as shown in Fig. 1.23(b). The iteration period of this DFG equals 6 u.t.

The data-flow graph captures the *data-driven* property of DSP algorithms

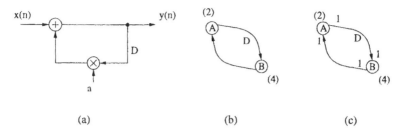

Fig. 1.23 (a) Block diagram description of the computation $y(n) = ay(n-1) + x(n)$.
(b) Conventional DFG representation. (c) Synchronous DFG representation.

where any node can fire (perform its computation) whenever all the input data are available. This implies that a node with no input edges can fire at any time; thus many nodes can be fired simultaneously, leading to concurrency. Conversely, a node with multiple input edges can only fire after all its precedent nodes have fired. The latter case imposes the precedence constraints on a DFG, where each edge describes a precedence constraint between two nodes. This precedence constraint is an *intra-iteration precedence constraint* if the edge has zero delays or an *inter-iteration precedence constraint* if the edge has one or more delays. Together, the intra-iteration and inter-iteration precedence constraints specify the order in which the nodes in the DFG can be executed. For example, the edge from node A to node B in Fig. 1.23(b) enforces the inter-iteration precedence constraint, which states that the execution of the k-th iteration of A must be completed before the $(k+1)$-th iteration of B. The edge from B to A enforces the intra-iteration precedence constraint, which states that the k-th iteration of B must be executed before the k-th iteration of A.

DFGs, as well as block diagrams, can be used to describe both linear single-rate and nonlinear multirate DSP systems. The block diagram description is closer to actual hardware architectures where the signal processing functions are represented using functional units (blocks). The DFG, on the other hand, describes the data flow among subtasks (or elementary computations modeled as nodes) in a signal processing algorithm. Various DFGs derived for one algorithm can be obtained from each other through high-level transformations [24]. Fig. 1.24 shows the DFGs for the 3-tap FIR filter in (1.61). Fig. 1.24(a) is obtained from the direct-form block diagram in Fig. 1.20 and Fig. 1.24(b) is obtained from the transpose form block diagram in Fig. 1.21. DFGs are generally used for high-level synthesis to derive concurrent implementations of DSP applications onto parallel hardware, where subtask scheduling and resource allocation are of major concerns (a *schedule* determines when and in which hardware units nodes can be executed).

The nodes in a DFG can be as simple as elementary indivisible operations such as addition or basic logic operations. Such DFGs are said to be *atomic*. If the granularity is at the level of signal processing subtasks such as filtering,

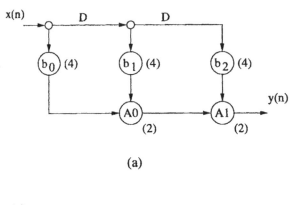

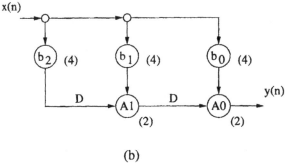

Fig. 1.24 (a) DFG of a direct-form 3-tap FIR filter. (b) DFG for transposed 3-tap FIR filter.

the DFG is a *coarse-grain* data-flow graph.

A *synchronous* data-flow graph (SDFG) is a special case of data-flow graph (either atomic or coarse-grain) where the number of data samples produced or consumed by each node in each execution is specified *a priori* [26]. For example, Fig. 1.23(c) is a synchronous data-flow graph for the computation $y(n) = ay(n-1) + x(n)$, which explicitly specifies that one execution of both nodes A and B consumes one data sample and produces one output. This describes a single-rate system. The SDFG can describe multirate systems in a simple way. For example, Fig. 1.25(a) shows an SDFG representation of a multirate system, where nodes A, B, and C are operated at different frequencies f_A, f_B, and f_C, respectively. Note that A processes f_A input samples per time unit and produces $3f_A$ output samples per time unit. Node B consumes 5 input samples during each execution, hence consumes $5f_B$ input samples per time unit. Using the equality $3f_A = 5f_B$, we have $f_B = 3f_A/5$. Similarly, the operating rate of node C can be computed as $f_C = 2f_B/3 = 2f_A/5$. For a specified input sampling rate, the operating frequencies for nodes A, B, and C can be computed. However, as described in Section 2.5, single-rate DFGs (SRDFGs) can also be used to represent multirate systems by

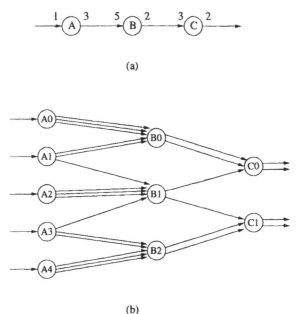

(a)

(b)

Fig. 1.25 Multirate DFG (in (a)) can be converted into single-rate DFG (in (b)), which can then be represented using linear SFG.

first unfolding (unrolling) the multirate systems to single rate. An equivalent single-rate DFG for the multirate DFG (MRDFG) in Fig. 1.25(a) is shown in Fig. 1.25(b). However, this single-rate DFG contains 10 nodes and 30 edges, as compared with 3 nodes and 4 edges in the SDFG representation.

1.4.4 Dependence Graph

A dependence graph (DG) is a directed graph that shows the dependence of the computations in an algorithm. The nodes in a DG represent computations (designated as nodes) and the edges represent precedence constraints among nodes. In a DG, a new node is created whenever a new computation is called for in the algorithm (program) and no node in a DG is ever reused on a single computation basis [27]. DG representation is similar to DFG representation as it explicitly exhibits the dependence of nodes on other nodes in the graph. The difference is that the nodes in DFG only cover the computations in one iteration of the corresponding algorithm and they are executed repetitively from iteration to iteration, whereas DG contains computations for all iterations in an algorithm. DFGs contain delay elements that store and pass data from current iteration to subsequent iterations while DG does not contain delay elements. The 3-tap FIR filter in (1.61) is described using a 2D-DG in Fig. 1.26.

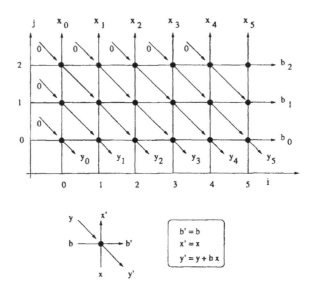

Fig. 1.26 Data dependence graph for a 3-tap FIR filter $y(n) = b_0 x(n) + b_1 x(n-1) + b_2 x(n-2)$.

Dependence graphs are used for systolic array design, where various implementations (DFGs or block diagrams) can be derived from a single DG by exploiting the parallelism presented in DG in different ways (see Chapter 7).

1.5 BOOK OUTLINE

The chapters in this book present various approaches to improve the performance characteristics of DSP systems in terms of area, speed, power, and roundoff noise. Chapter 1 reviews various DSP algorithms, presents the computation requirements of current DSP systems, and describes various representations of DSP algorithms using block diagrams, signal flow graphs, and data-flow graphs. The remaining chapters can be grouped into three parts.

The first part of the book (chapters 2 to 7) addresses several high-level architectural transformations that can be used to design families of architectures for a given algorithm. These transformations include pipelining, retiming, unfolding, folding, and systolic array design methodology. The second part of the book (chapters 8 to 12) deals with high-level algorithm transformations such as strength reduction, look-ahead and relaxed look-ahead. Strength reduction transformations are applied to reduce the number of multiplications in convolution, parallel finite impulse response (FIR) digital filters, discrete cosine transforms (DCTs), and parallel rank-order filters. Look-ahead and relaxed look-ahead transformations are applied to design pipelined direct-form and lattice recursive digital filters and adaptive digital filters, and parallel recursive digital filters. This part of the book exploits the interplay between algorithm design and integrated circuit implementations. The third part of the book (chapters 13 to 18) addresses architectures for VLSI addition, multiplication, and digital filters, and issues related to high-performance VLSI system design such as pipelining styles, low-power design, and architectures for programmable digital signal processors.

Seven appendixes in the book cover shortest path algorithms that are used for determining the iteration bound and for retiming, scheduling and allocation techniques used for determining the folding sets for design of folded architectures; Euclid's greatest common divisor (GCD) algorithm, which is used for Winograd's convolution; orthonormality of Schur polynomials, which are used for design of lattice digital filters; fast bit-parallel addition and multiplication; scheduling for bit-serial systems; and coefficient quantization in FIR filters.

The techniques used in this book can be used for high-speed, low-area and low-power implementations of DSP systems for various applications such as multimedia [28], wired and wireless communications.

REFERENCES

1. P. Lapsley, J. Bier, A. Shoham, and E. A. Lee, *DSP Processor Fundamentals: Architectures and Features.* Elsevier, 1993.

2. A. V. Oppenheim and R. W. Schafer, *Discrete-Time Signal Processing.* Prentice Hall, 1989.

3. S. Haykin, *Adaptive Filter Theory.* Prentice Hall, 1991.

4. J. G. Chung and K. K. Parhi, *Pipelined Lattice and Wave Digital Recursive Filters.* Kluwer, 1996.

5. M. L. Honig and D. G. Messerschmitt, *Adaptive Filters: Structures, Algorithms and Applications.* Kluwer, 1984.

6. N. Ahmed, T. Natarajan, and K. R. Rao, "Discrete cosine transform," *IEEE Trans. on Computers*, pp. 90−93, Jan. 1974.

7. P. Pirsch, N. Demassieux, and W. Cehrke, "VLSI architectures for video compression − a survey," *Proc. IEEE*, no. 2, pp. 220−245, Feb. 1995.

8. G. A. Davidson, P. R. Cappello, and A. Gersho, "Systolic architectures for vector quantization," *IEEE Trans. on Acoustics, Speech, and Signal Processing*, vol. 36, pp. 1651−1664, Oct. 1988.

9. S. Y. Kung, *VLSI Array Processors.* Prentice Hall, 1988.

10. G. D. Forney, "The Viterbi algorithm," *Proc. IEEE*, pp. 268−278, March 1973.

11. R. Bellman and S. Dreyfus, *Applied Dynamic Programming.* Princeton University Press, 1962.

12. P. P. Vaidyanathan, *Multirate Digital Signal Processing*. Prentice Hall, 1993.

13. R. E. Crochiere and L. R. Rabiner, *Multirate Digital Signal Processing*. Prentice Hall, 1983.

14. O. Rioul and M. Vetterli, "Wavelets and signal processing," *IEEE Signal Processing Magazine*, pp. 14–38, Oct. 1991.

15. T. Sikora, "MPEG digital video-coding standards," *IEEE Signal Processing Magazine*, pp. 82–100, Sept. 1997.

16. B. Bhatt, D. Birks, and D. Hermreck, "Digital television: making it work," *IEEE Spectrum*, pp. 19–28, Oct. 1997.

17. M. Mizuno et al., "A 1.5W single-chip MPEG2 MP@ML encoder with low-power motion estimation and clocking," in *Proc. of IEEE International Solid State Circuits Conference (ISSCC97)*, pp. 256–257, Feb. 1997.

18. W. F. Brinkman, "The transistor: 50 glorious years and where we are going," in *Proc. of IEEE International Solid State Circuits Conference (ISSCC)*, pp. 22–26, Feb. 1997.

19. B. Ackland, "Programmable multimedia signal processors," in *Circuits and Systems in the Information Age* (Y.-F. Huang and C.-H. Wei, eds.), pp. 23–30, IEEE Press, 1997.

20. P. Hilfinger, "A high-level language and silicon compiler for digital signal processing," in *Proc. of IEEE Custom Integrated Circuits Conference*, pp. 213–216, 1985.

21. H. De Man, J. Rabaey, P. Six, and L. J. Claesen, "Cathedral-II: a silicon compiler for digital signal processing," *IEEE Design and Test*, vol. 3, no. 6, pp. 13–25, Dec. 1986.

22. A. Stoll and P. Duzy, "High-level synthesis from VHDL with exact timing constraints," in *Proc. of 29th ACM/IEEE Design Automation Conference*, June 1992.

23. S. Amellal and B. Kaminska, "Functional synthesis of digital systems with tass," *IEEE Trans. on Computer-Aided Design*, vol. 13, no. 5, pp. 537–552, May 1994.

24. K. K. Parhi, "Algorithm transformation techniques for concurrent processors," *Proc. IEEE*, pp. 1879–1895, Dec. 1989.

25. R. E. Crochiere and A. V. Oppenheim, "Analysis of linear digital networks," *Proc. IEEE*, no. 4, pp. 581–595, Apr. 1975.

26. E. A. Lee and D. G. Messerschmitt, "Synchronous data flow," *Proc. IEEE, special issue on hardware and software for digital signal processing*, pp. 1235–1245, Sept. 1987.

27. J. Allen, "Computer architecture for digital signal processing," *Proc. IEEE*, no. 5, pp. 852–873, May 1985.

28. K. K. Parhi and T. Nishitani, eds., *Digital Signal Processing for Multimedia Systems*. Marcel Dekker, 1999.

2

Iteration Bound

2.1 INTRODUCTION

Many DSP algorithms such as recursive and adaptive digital filters contain feedback loops, which impose an inherent fundamental lower bound on the achievable iteration or sample period. This bound is referred to as the iteration period bound, or simply the iteration bound. The iteration bound is a characteristic of the representation of an algorithm in the form of a data-flow graph (DFG); different representations of the same algorithm may lead to different iteration bounds. It is not possible to achieve an iteration period less than the iteration bound even when infinite processors are available. This chapter defines the iteration bound and presents two techniques to compute the iteration bound; these include the longest path matrix (LPM) and the minimum cycle mean (MCM) methods. The iteration bound of multirate DFGs is also addressed.

2.2 DATA-FLOW GRAPH REPRESENTATIONS

DSP programs are considered to be nonterminating programs that run from time index $n = 0$ to time $n = \infty$. For example, a DSP program that computes $y(n) = ay(n - 1) + x(n)$ represents the following program:

```
for n = 0 to ∞
    y(n) = ay(n - 1) + x(n)
```

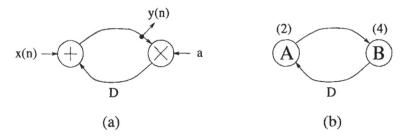

Fig. 2.1 (a) A graphical representation of $y(n) = ay(n-1) + x(n)$. (b) A DFG for this program. The numbers in parentheses are the execution times for the nodes.

The input to this DSP program is the sequence $x(n)$ for $n = 0, 1, 2, \ldots$, and the initial condition $y(-1)$. The output is the sequence $y(n)$ for $n = 0, 1, 2, \ldots$.

A DSP program is often represented using a DFG, which is a directed graph (i.e., each edge has a distinct direction) that describes the program (see also Section 1.4.3). For example, the program $y(n) = ay(n-1) + x(n)$ is graphically represented in Fig. 2.1(a). A simplified version of this program is shown in Fig. 2.1(b). The structure in Fig. 2.1(b) is a DFG, which consists of a set of nodes and edges. The nodes represent tasks or computations (the node A represents addition and the node B represents multiplication), and each node has an execution time associated with it. The edges represent communication between the nodes, and each edge has a nonnegative number of delays associated with it. In our example, the edge $A \rightarrow B$ has zero delays and the edge $B \rightarrow A$ has one delay. An *iteration* of a node is the execution of the node exactly once, and an iteration of the DFG is the execution of each node in the DFG exactly once.

Each edge in a DFG describes a precedence constraint between two nodes. This precedence constraint is an *intra-iteration precedence constraint* if the edge has zero delays or an *inter-iteration precedence constraint* if the edge has one or more delays. Together, the intra-iteration and inter-iteration precedence constraints specify the order in which the nodes in the DFG can be executed. The edge from A to B in Fig. 2.1(b) enforces the intra-iteration precedence constraint, which states that the k-th iteration of A must be executed before the k-th iteration of B. The edge from B to A enforces the inter-iteration precedence constraint, which states that the k-th iteration of B must be executed before the $(k+1)$-th iteration of A. Let X_k denote the k-th iteration of the node X. When it is important to distinguish between intra-iteration and inter-iteration precedence constraints, an intra-iteration precedence constraint is denoted using a single arrow such as $A_k \rightarrow B_k$, and an inter-iteration precedence constraint is denoted using a double arrow such as $B_k \Rightarrow A_{k+1}$. Otherwise, all precedence constraints are denoted using single arrows.

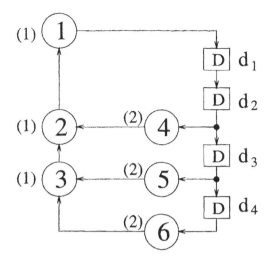

Fig. 2.2   A DFG with three loops that have loop bounds of 4/2 u.t., 5/3 u.t., and 5/4 u.t. The iteration bound for this DFG is $T_\infty = 2$ u.t.

The *critical path* of a DFG is defined to be the path with the longest computation time among all paths that contain zero delays. The critical path in the DFG in Fig. 2.1(b) is the path $A \rightarrow B$, which requires 6 u.t. The DFG in Fig. 2.2 contains several paths with no delays. The maximum computation time among these paths is 5 u.t. (the two paths $6 \rightarrow 3 \rightarrow 2 \rightarrow 1$ and $5 \rightarrow 3 \rightarrow 2 \rightarrow 1$ are both critical paths), so the critical path computation requires 5 u.t. The critical path is the longest path for combinational rippling in the DFG, so the computation time of the critical path is the minimum computation time for one iteration of the DFG.

A DFG can be classified as nonrecursive or recursive. A nonrecursive DFG contains no loops, while a recursive DFG contains at least one loop. For example, an FIR filter is nonrecursive, while the DFG in Fig. 2.1(b) is recursive because it contains the loop $A \rightarrow B \rightarrow A$. A recursive DFG has a fundamental limit on how fast the underlying DSP program can be implemented in hardware. This limit, called the *iteration bound*, T_∞ [1],[2], holds regardless of the computing power available for the implementation of the DSP program.

2.3   LOOP BOUND AND ITERATION BOUND

A *loop* is a directed path that begins and ends at the same node, such as the path $A \rightarrow B \rightarrow A$ in Fig. 2.1(b). The terms "loop" and "cycle" are used interchangeably to describe a directed cycle in a directed graph. The amount of time required to execute a loop can be determined from the precedence relations described by the edges of the DFG. For the DFG in Fig. 2.1(b), the

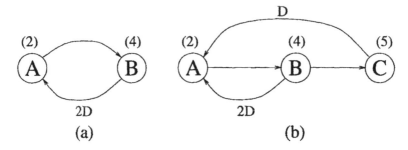

Fig. 2.3 (a) A DFG with one loop that has a loop bound of $6/2 = 3$ u.t. The iteration bound for this DFG is 3 u.t. (b) A DFG with iteration bound $T_\infty = \max\{6/2, 11/1\} = 11$ u.t.

edges describe the precedence constraints

$$A_0 \to B_0 \Rightarrow A_1 \to B_1 \Rightarrow A_2 \to B_2 \Rightarrow A_3 \to \cdots$$

where single arrows ($\to$) represent intra-iteration precedence constraints and double arrows ($\Rightarrow$) represent inter-iteration precedence constraints. According to these precedence constraints, iteration k of the loop consists of the sequential execution of A_k and B_k. Given that the execution times of nodes A and B are 2 and 4 u.t., respectively, one iteration of the loop requires 6 u.t. This is the *loop bound*, which represents the lower bound on the loop computation time. Formally, the loop bound of the l-th loop is defined as t_l/w_l, where t_l is the loop computation time and w_l is the number of delays in the loop. We can verify that the loop bound for the loop in Fig. 2.1(b) is $6/1 = 6$ u.t.

The loop in Fig. 2.3(a) has two delays, requires 6 u.t. to compute, and has a loop bound of $6/2 = 3$ u.t. To see how one iteration of this loop can be executed in 3 u.t., we need to examine the precedence constraints

$$A_0 \to B_0 \Rightarrow A_2 \to B_2 \Rightarrow A_4 \to B_4 \Rightarrow A_6 \to \cdots$$
$$A_1 \to B_1 \Rightarrow A_3 \to B_3 \Rightarrow A_5 \to B_5 \Rightarrow A_7 \to \cdots$$

This shows two independent sets of precedence constraints, one set for the even iterations and one set for the odd iterations. In this case, two iterations can be computed in 6 u.t., resulting in a loop bound of $6/2 = 3$.

The DFG in Fig. 2.3(b) contains two loops, namely, the loops $l_1 = A \to B \to A$ and $l_2 = A \to B \to C \to A$. The loop bounds for l_1 and l_2 are $6/2 = 3$ u.t. and $11/1 = 11$ u.t., respectively. The *critical loop* is the loop with the maximum loop bound, so the loop l_2 is the critical loop in this example. The loop bound of the critical loop is the *iteration bound* of the DSP program, which is the lower bound on the iteration or sample period of the DSP program regardless of the amount of computing resources available.

Formally, the iteration bound is defined as

$$T_\infty = \max_{l \in L} \left\{ \frac{t_l}{w_l} \right\}, \tag{2.1}$$

where L is the set of loops in the DFG, t_l is the computation time of the loop l, and w_l is the number of delays in the loop l. For the DFG in Fig. 2.3(b) we have

$$T_\infty = \max \left\{ \frac{6}{2}, \frac{11}{1} \right\} = 11 \text{ u.t.}$$

A straightforward technique for finding the iteration bound of a DFG is to locate all loops and directly compute T_∞ using (2.1); however, the number of loops in a DFG can be exponential with respect to the number of nodes, so this technique can require long execution times. Three techniques have been developed for computing T_∞ in polynomial time, namely the longest path matrix algorithm [3], the minimum cycle mean algorithm [4], and the negative cycle detection algorithm [5]. The first two techniques are described in Section 2.4.

2.4   ALGORITHMS FOR COMPUTING ITERATION BOUND

The two iteration-bound algorithms described in this section are demonstrated using the DFG in Fig. 2.2. This DFG has three loops: loop $l_1 = 1 \to 4 \to 2 \to 1$ with loop bound 4/2 u.t., loop $l_2 = 1 \to 5 \to 3 \to 2 \to 1$ with loop bound 5/3 u.t., and loop $l_3 = 1 \to 6 \to 3 \to 2 \to 1$ with loop bound 5/4 u.t. Therefore, the iteration bound of this DFG is

$$T_\infty = \max \left\{ \frac{4}{2}, \frac{5}{3}, \frac{5}{4} \right\} = 2 \text{ u.t.}$$

2.4.1   Longest Path Matrix Algorithm

In the longest path matrix (LPM) algorithm [3], a series of matrices is constructed, and the iteration bound is found by examining the diagonal elements of the matrices. Let d be the number of delays in the DFG. These matrices, $\mathbf{L}^{(m)}$, $m = 1, 2, \ldots, d$, are constructed such that the value of the element $l_{i,j}^{(m)}$ is the longest computation time of all paths from delay element d_i to delay element d_j that pass through exactly $m - 1$ delays (not including d_i and d_j). If no such path exists, then $l_{i,j}^{(m)} = -1$. Note that longest path between any two nodes can be computed using any path algorithm in Appendix A. For example, to determine $l_{3,1}^{(1)}$ for the DFG in Fig. 2.2, all paths from the delay element d_3 to the delay element d_1 that pass through exactly zero delay elements must be considered. There is one such path, namely, the path

$d_3 \to n_5 \to n_3 \to n_2 \to n_1 \to d_1$. This path has computation time 5, so $l_{3,1}^{(1)} = 5$. To determine $l_{4,3}^{(1)}$, we note that there are no paths from the delay element d_4 to the delay element d_3 that pass through zero delay elements, so $l_{4,3}^{(1)} = -1$. After determining the rest of the elements of $\mathbf{L}^{(1)}$, we find

$$\mathbf{L}^{(1)} = \begin{bmatrix} -1 & 0 & -1 & -1 \\ 4 & -1 & 0 & -1 \\ 5 & -1 & -1 & 0 \\ 5 & -1 & -1 & -1 \end{bmatrix}.$$

The higher order matrices, $\mathbf{L}^{(m)}$, $m = 2, 3, \ldots, d$, do not need to be determined directly from the DFG. Rather, they can be recursively computed according to the rule

$$l_{i,j}^{(m+1)} = \max_{k \in K}(-1, l_{i,k}^{(1)} + l_{k,j}^{(m)}),$$

where K is the set of integers k in the interval $[1, d]$ such that neither $l_{i,k}^{(1)} = -1$ nor $l_{k,j}^{(m)} = -1$ holds. For example, to compute $l_{2,1}^{(2)}$, the first step is to find the set K from the possible set $\{1, 2, 3, 4\}$. The value 3 is in K because $l_{2,3}^{(1)} = 0$ and $l_{3,1}^{(1)} = 5$, and the values $k = 1, 2, 4$ are not in K because at least one of $l_{2,k}^{(1)}$ or $l_{k,1}^{(1)}$ is equal to -1 for each of these. Using $K = \{3\}$, the value of $l_{2,1}^{(2)}$ can be computed as

$$\begin{aligned} l_{2,1}^{(2)} &= \max_{k \in \{3\}}(-1, l_{2,k}^{(1)} + l_{k,1}^{(1)}) \\ &= \max(-1, 0 + 5) = 5. \end{aligned}$$

Computing the remaining values of $l_{i,j}^{(2)}$ results in

$$\mathbf{L}^{(2)} = \begin{bmatrix} 4 & -1 & 0 & -1 \\ 5 & 4 & -1 & 0 \\ 5 & 5 & -1 & -1 \\ -1 & 5 & -1 & -1 \end{bmatrix}.$$

While $\mathbf{L}^{(2)}$ is computed using only $\mathbf{L}^{(1)}$, the matrix $\mathbf{L}^{(3)}$ is computed using both $\mathbf{L}^{(1)}$ and $\mathbf{L}^{(2)}$. To compute $l_{3,3}^{(3)}$, $K = \{1\}$ because $l_{3,1}^{(1)} = 5$ and $l_{1,3}^{(2)} = 0$, and for the values of $k = 2, 3, 4$, at least one of $l_{3,k}^{(1)}$ or $l_{k,3}^{(3)}$ is equal to -1. The value of $l_{3,3}^{(3)}$ is

$$\begin{aligned} l_{3,3}^{(3)} &= \max_{k \in \{1\}}(-1, l_{3,k}^{(1)} + l_{k,3}^{(2)}) \\ &= \max(-1, 5 + 0) = 5. \end{aligned}$$

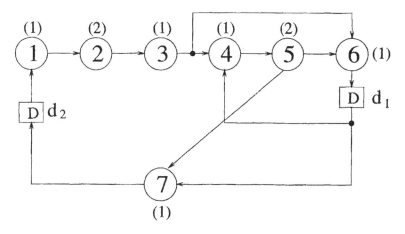

Fig. 2.4   A filter with iteration bound $T_\infty = 8$.

Computing the rest of $\mathbf{L}^{(3)}$ and $\mathbf{L}^{(4)}$ results in

$$
\mathbf{L}^{(3)} = \begin{bmatrix} 5 & 4 & -1 & 0 \\ 8 & 5 & 4 & -1 \\ 9 & 5 & 5 & -1 \\ 9 & -1 & 5 & -1 \end{bmatrix}
$$

and

$$
\mathbf{L}^{(4)} = \begin{bmatrix} 8 & 5 & 4 & -1 \\ 9 & 8 & 5 & 4 \\ 10 & 9 & 5 & 5 \\ 10 & 9 & -1 & 5 \end{bmatrix}.
$$

Once the matrices $\mathbf{L}^{(m)}$ have been computed, the iteration bound can be determined as

$$
T_\infty = \max_{i,m\in\{1,2,\ldots d\}} \left\{ \frac{l_{i,i}^{(m)}}{m} \right\},
$$

which for this example is

$$
T_\infty = \max\left\{ \frac{4}{2}, \frac{4}{2}, \frac{5}{3}, \frac{5}{3}, \frac{5}{3}, \frac{8}{4}, \frac{8}{4}, \frac{5}{4}, \frac{5}{4} \right\} = 2.
$$

As another example, consider the DFG in Fig. 2.4. The matrices $\mathbf{L}^{(m)}$, $m = 1, 2$, are

$$
\mathbf{L}^{(1)} = \begin{bmatrix} 4 & 4 \\ 8 & 8 \end{bmatrix}
$$

and

$$\mathbf{L}^{(2)} = \left[\begin{array}{cc} 12 & 12 \\ 16 & 16 \end{array} \right],$$

and the iteration bound is

$$T_\infty = \max\left\{\frac{4}{1}, \frac{8}{1}, \frac{12}{2}, \frac{16}{2}\right\} = 8.$$

The LPM algorithm works because the value $l_{i,i}^{(m)}$ represents the longest computation time of all loops that have m delays and contain the delay element d_i. By taking the maximum of $l_{i,i}^{(m)}/m$ for all possible values of i and m, we find the maximum loop bound of all loops in the DFG, which is the iteration bound.

The time complexity of computing $\mathbf{L}^{(k+1)}$ from $\mathbf{L}^{(1)}$ and $\mathbf{L}^{(k)}$ is $\mathcal{O}(d^3)$ since there are d^2 elements in $\mathbf{L}^{(k+1)}$ and each computation has time complexity $\mathcal{O}(d)$. Therefore, computing $\mathbf{L}^{(d)}$ from $\mathbf{L}^{(1)}$ has time complexity $\mathcal{O}(d^4)$. Although we determined $\mathbf{L}^{(1)}$ by inspection, an algorithm with time complexity $\mathcal{O}(de)$ is given in [3] for finding $\mathbf{L}^{(1)}$, where d and e are the number of delays and edges in the DFG, respectively. Hence, the time complexity of the LPM algorithm of computing the iteration bound is $\mathcal{O}(d^4 + de)$. For the interested reader, improvements have been suggested in [3] to improve this complexity to $\mathcal{O}(d^3 \log d + de)$. Note that $\mathbf{L}^{(d)}$ can be computed in $\mathcal{O}(d^3 \log d)$ complexity by computing $\mathbf{L}^{(2)}$ from $\mathbf{L}^{(1)}$, $\mathbf{L}^{(4)}$ from $\mathbf{L}^{(2)}$, $\mathbf{L}^{(8)}$ from $\mathbf{L}^{(4)}$, etc.

2.4.2 The Minimum Cycle Mean Algorithm

The minimum cycle mean (MCM) algorithm [4] reduces the problem of determining the iteration bound to the problem of finding the MCM of a graph. The technique in [6] is then used to efficiently compute the MCM. Recall that the terms "cycle" and "loop" can be used interchangeably.

The algorithm described in this section uses the concepts of a cycle mean, the maximum cycle mean, and the MCM. The cycle mean $m(c)$ of a cycle c is the average length of the edges in c, which can be found by simply taking the sum of the edge lengths and dividing by the number of edges in the cycle. The MCM λ_{min} is simply the minimum value of all of the cycle means, i.e.,

$$\lambda_{min} = \min_c m(c).$$

Similarly, the maximum cycle mean λ_{max} is

$$\lambda_{max} = \max_c m(c).$$

The cycle means of a new graph G_d are used to compute the iteration bound, where G_d can be found from the DFG for which we are computing

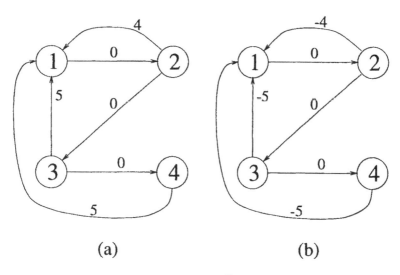

Fig. 2.5   The graphs (a) G_d and (b) $\bar{G}_d$ for the DFG in Fig. 2.2.

the iteration bound (call this DFG G). If d is the number of delay elements in G, then the graph G_d has d nodes where each node corresponds to one of the delays in G. The weight $w(i, j)$ of the edge from the node i to the node j in G_d is the longest path length among all paths in G from the delay d_i to the delay d_j that do not pass through any delays. If no zero-delay path exists from the delay d_i to the delay d_j, then the edge $i \to j$ does not exist in G_d. The graph G_d for the DFG in Fig. 2.2 is shown in Fig. 2.5(a). Note that constructing G_d is essentially the same as constructing the matrix $\mathbf{L}^{(1)}$ in the LPM algorithm described in Section 2.4.1.

The sum of the edge weights in a cycle c in G_d is the maximum computation time of all cycles in G that contain the delays represented by the nodes in the cycle c. This is because the edge weights in G_d are the maximum computation times between the delays in G. For example there are two cycles that contain the delays D_α and D_β in the graph G in Fig. 2.6(a), and these cycles have computation times of 6 u.t. and 4 u.t. The corresponding graph G_d in Fig. 2.6(b) has one cycle that passes through the nodes corresponding to D_α and D_β. The sum of the edge weights in this cycle is 6, which is the maximum computation time of the two cycles in G in Fig. 2.6(a). In G_d, the number of edges in a cycle equals the number of nodes in the cycle, and this equals the number of delays in the cycle in G. Therefore, the cycle mean of a cycle c in G_d is

$$\frac{\text{max computation time of all cycles in } G \text{ that contain the delays in } c}{\text{the number of delays in these cycles in } G}.$$

This is the maximum cycle bound of the cycles in G that contain the delays

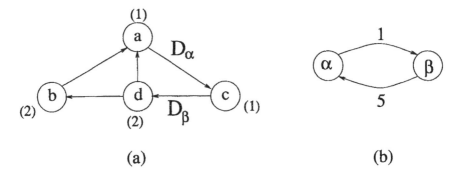

Fig. 2.6 (a) A graph G with two cycles that contain the delays D_α and D_β. (b) The corresponding graph G_d.

in the cycle c. The maximum cycle mean of G_d is the maximum cycle bound of all cycles in G, which is the iteration bound of G.

To compute the maximum cycle mean of G_d, the graph $\bar{G}_d$ is constructed from G_d by simply multiplying the weights of the edges by -1, i.e., $\bar{G}_d$ has the same topology as G_d and the weights $\bar{w}(i,j)$ of the edge $i \rightarrow j$ in $\bar{G}_d$ are given by $\bar{w}(i,j) = -w(i,j)$, where $w(i,j)$ is the weight of the edge $i \rightarrow j$ in G_d. The graph $\bar{G}_d$ for the DFG in Fig. 2.2 is given in Fig. 2.5(b). The maximum cycle mean of G_d is simply the MCM of $\bar{G}_d$ multiplied by -1. So the iteration bound of G can be found by finding the MCM of $\bar{G}_d$ and multiplying it by -1.

The MCM of $\bar{G}_d$ is found by first constructing the series of $d+1$ vectors, $\mathbf{f}^{(m)}$, $m = 0, 1, \ldots, d$, which are each of dimension $d \times 1$. An arbitrary reference node is chosen in $\bar{G}_d$ (call this node s). The initial vector $\mathbf{f}^{(0)}$ is formed by setting $f^{(0)}(s) = 0$ and setting the remaining entries of $\mathbf{f}^{(0)}$ to ∞. If node 1 is chosen as the reference node for the graph $\bar{G}_d$ in Fig. 2.5(b), then

$$\mathbf{f}^{(0)} = \begin{bmatrix} 0 \\ \infty \\ \infty \\ \infty \end{bmatrix}.$$

The remaining vectors, $\mathbf{f}^{(m)}$, $m = 1, 2, \ldots, d$, are recursively computed according to

$$f^{(m)}(j) = \min_{i \in I}(f^{(m-1)}(i) + \bar{w}(i,j)) \tag{2.2}$$

where $\bar{w}(i,j)$ is the weight of the edge $i \rightarrow j$ in $\bar{G}_d$ and I is the set of nodes in $\bar{G}_d$ such that there exists an edge from node i to node j ($i \rightarrow j$). This series

Table 2.1   Values of $\frac{f^{(4)}(i)-f^{(m)}(i)}{4-m}$ for $1 \le i \le 4$ and $0 \le m \le 3$

	$m = 0$	$m = 1$	$m = 2$	$m = 3$	$\max_{0 \le m \le 3}\left\{\frac{f^{(4)}(i)-f^{(m)}(i)}{4-m}\right\}$
$i = 1$	-2	$-\infty$	-2	-3	-2
$i = 2$	$-\infty$	$-5/3$	$-\infty$	-1	-1
$i = 3$	$-\infty$	$-\infty$	-2	$-\infty$	-2
$i = 4$	$\infty - \infty$	$\infty - \infty$	$\infty - \infty$	∞	∞

of vectors found from $\bar{G}_d$ in Fig. 2.5(b) is

$$\mathbf{f}^{(1)} = \begin{bmatrix} \infty \\ 0 \\ \infty \\ \infty \end{bmatrix} \quad \mathbf{f}^{(2)} = \begin{bmatrix} -4 \\ \infty \\ 0 \\ \infty \end{bmatrix} \quad \mathbf{f}^{(3)} = \begin{bmatrix} -5 \\ -4 \\ \infty \\ 0 \end{bmatrix} \quad \mathbf{f}^{(4)} = \begin{bmatrix} -8 \\ -5 \\ -4 \\ \infty \end{bmatrix}.$$

For example, $f^{(4)}(1)$ is computed as

$$\begin{aligned} f^{(4)}(1) &= \min(f^{(3)}(2) - w(2,1), f^{(3)}(3) - w(3,1), f^{(3)}(4) - w(4,1)) \\ &= \min(-4 - 4, \infty - 5, 0 - 5) = -8. \end{aligned}$$

From the vectors $\mathbf{f}^{(m)}$, $m = 0, 1, \ldots, d$, the iteration bound can be computed as

$$T_\infty = -min_{i \in \{1,2,\ldots,d\}}\left(\max_{m \in \{0,1,\ldots,d-1\}}\left(\frac{f^{(d)}(i) - f^{(m)}(i)}{d - m}\right)\right).$$

In our example, $d = 4$. Table 2.1 shows the values of

$$\frac{f^{(4)}(i) - f^{(m)}(i)}{4 - m}$$

for $1 \le i \le 4$ and $0 \le m \le 3$. In some cases we may encounter $f^{(d)}(i) - f^{(m)}(i) = \infty - \infty$. In this case, $\infty - \infty$ should be treated as zero. For example, $f^{(4)}(4) - f^{(1)}(4) = \infty - \infty$, so the value $(\infty - \infty)/3 = 0/3 = 0$ is given for $i = 4$ and $m = 1$ in Table 2.1.

Using the right column of Table 2.1, we can determine

$$T_\infty = -\min\{-2, -1, -2, \infty\} = 2,$$

as desired.

As another example, consider the DFG in Fig. 2.4. The graphs G_d and $\bar{G}_d$

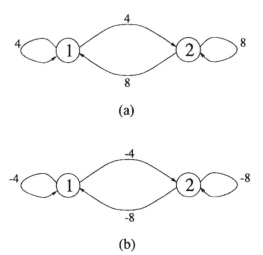

(a)

(b)

Fig. 2.7 The graphs (a) G_d and (b) $\bar{G}_d$ for the DFG in Fig. 2.4.

Table 2.2 Values of $\frac{f^{(2)}(i)-f^{(m)}(i)}{2-m}$ for $1 \le i \le 2$ and $0 \le m \le 1$

	$m = 0$	$m = 1$	$\max_{0 \le m \le 1}\left\{\dfrac{f^{(2)}(i)-f^{(m)}(i)}{2-m}\right\}$
$i = 1$	$-12/2$	$-8/1$	-6
$i = 2$	$-\infty$	$-8/1$	-8

are shown in Fig. 2.7. The set of vectors $\mathbf{f}^{(m)}$, $m = 0, 1, 2$, is

$$\mathbf{f}^{(0)} = \begin{bmatrix} 0 \\ \infty \end{bmatrix} \quad \mathbf{f}^{(1)} = \begin{bmatrix} -4 \\ -4 \end{bmatrix} \quad \mathbf{f}^{(2)} = \begin{bmatrix} -12 \\ -12 \end{bmatrix}.$$

Table 2.2 shows the values of

$$\frac{f^{(2)}(i) - f^{(m)}(i)}{2 - m}$$

for $1 \le i \le 2$ and $0 \le m \le 1$.

Using the right column of Table 2.2, we can determine

$$T_\infty = -\min\{-8, -6\} = 8.$$

The time complexity of constructing G_d and $\bar{G}_d$ from the original DFG is $\mathcal{O}(de)$. Note that this is the same as the complexity of computing $\mathbf{L}^{(1)}$ in the LPM algorithm because these are equivalent problems. The MCM of G_d is

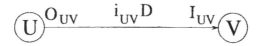

Fig. 2.8   An edge $U \to V$ in an multirate DFG.

computed in $\mathcal{O}(de_d)$ time, where e_d is the number of edges in G_d. The total time complexity for computing the iteration bound using the MCM algorithm is $\mathcal{O}(de + de_d)$.

2.5   ITERATION BOUND OF MULTIRATE DATA-FLOW GRAPHS

Up to this point, we have only considered single-rate DFGs (SRDFGs), i.e., DFGs where each node is executed exactly once per iteration. Another class of DFGs, called multirate DFGs (MRDFGs) [7], allows each node to be executed more than once per iteration, and 2 nodes are not required to execute the same number of times in an iteration (see Section 1.4.3). A 2-step process can be used to compute the iteration bound of a multirate DFG. This 2-step process is

1. Construct a SRDFG that is equivalent to the MRDFG.

2. Compute the iteration bound of the equivalent SRDFG using the LPM algorithm, or the MCM algorithm.

The iteration bound of the MRDFG is the same as the iteration bound of the equivalent SRDFG. In this section, MRDFGs are defined and an algorithm is presented for constructing an equivalent SRDFG from an MRDFG (Step 1) so that 1 of the 2 algorithms described in this chapter can be used to compute the iteration bound of the equivalent SRDFG (step 2).

An edge from the node U to the node V in an MRDFG is shown in Fig. 2.8. The value O_{UV} is the number of samples produced on the edge by an invocation of the node U, and the value I_{UV} is the number of samples consumed from the edge by an invocation of the node V. The value i_{UV} is the number of delays on the edge.

If the nodes U and V are invoked k_U times and k_V times, respectively, in an iteration, then the number of samples produced on the edge from the node U to the node V in 1 iteration is $O_{UV}k_U$, and then number of samples consumed from the edge by the node V in 1 iteration is $I_{UV}k_V$. To avoid a buildup or deficiency of samples on the edge, the number of samples produced in 1 iteration must equal the number of samples consumed in one iteration. This relationship can be described mathematically as

$$O_{UV}k_U = I_{UV}k_V. \tag{2.3}$$

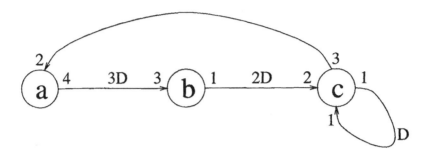

Fig. 2.9 An multirate DFG.

1.   For each node U in the MRDFG
2.   For $k = 0$ to $k_U - 1$
3.   Draw a node U^k in the SRDFG with the same computation
              time as U in the MRDFG.
4.   For each edge $U \xrightarrow{i_{UV}} V$ in the MRDFG
5.   For $j = 0$ to $O_{UV} k_U - 1$
6.   Draw an edge $U^{j/O_{UV}} \to V^{((j+i_{UV})/I_{UV})\%k_V}$ in the SRDFG
              with $(j + i_{UV})/(I_{UV} k_V)$ delays

Fig. 2.10 Algorithm for constructing an equivalent SRDFG from an MRDFG.

To determine how many times each node must be executed in an iteration, the
set of equations found by writing (2.3) for each edge in the MRDFG must be
solved so the number of invocations of the nodes are coprime. For example,
the set of equations for the MRDFG in Fig. 2.9 is

$$
\begin{aligned}
4k_a &= 3k_b \\
k_b &= 2k_c \\
k_c &= k_c \\
3k_c &= 2k_a,
\end{aligned}
$$

which has a solution $k_a = 3$, $k_b = 4$, $k_c = 2$. Once the numbers of invocations
of the nodes has been determined, an equivalent SRDFG can be constructed
for the MRDFG.

To simplify notation, let a/b denote the integer part of division, and let $a\%b$
denote the remainder. For example, $10/3 = 3$ and $10\%3 = 1$. Mathematically,
we can write $a/b = \lfloor \frac{a}{b} \rfloor$ and $a\%b = a - \lfloor \frac{a}{b} \rfloor b$, where $\lfloor x \rfloor$ is the floor of x, which
is the largest integer less than or equal to x. An algorithm for constructing
an equivalent SRDFG from an MRDFG is given in Fig. 2.10.

For the DFG in Fig. 2.9, the algorithm in Fig. 2.10 can be used to construct
the DFG in Fig. 2.11. The iteration bound of the SRDFG in Fig. 2.11 is the

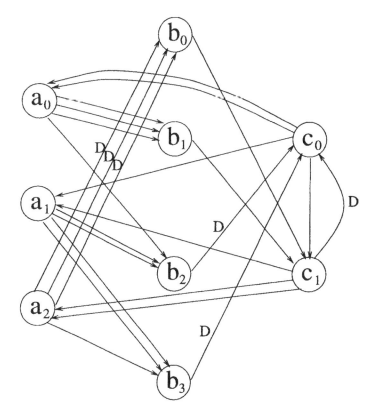

Fig. 2.11   An equivalent SRDFG for the MRDFG in Fig. 2.9.

same as the iteration bound of the MRDFG in Fig. 2.9.

Various techniques have been suggested to reduce the number of nodes and edges in an equivalent SRDFG without affecting the iteration bound of the graph. These reductions can be used to reduce the complexity of determining the iteration bound of the equivalent SRDFG, which directly leads to reduced complexity for determining the iteration bound of the MRDFG. The interested reader can find algorithms for reducing the complexity of the equivalent SRDFG in [4].

2.6   CONCLUSIONS

DSP programs have the property that they are executed from $n = 0$ to $n = \infty$. These programs are often represented using DFGs, which can be recursive or nonrecursive. When the DFG is recursive, the iteration bound is the fundamental limit on the minimum sample period of a hardware implementation of the DSP program. Two algorithms for computing the iteration bound were

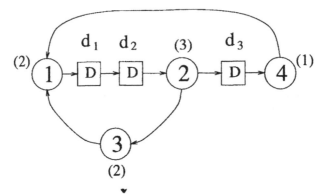

Fig. 2.12 The DFG used in Problem 1.

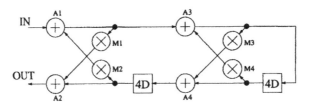

Fig. 2.13 A 4-level pipelined all-pass 8th-order IIR digital filter.

discussed. The LPM algorithm finds the iteration bound with time complexity $\mathcal{O}(d^4 + de)$, and the MCM algorithm finds the iteration bound with time complexity $\mathcal{O}(de + de_d)$. The MCM algorithm is usually faster than the LPM algorithm because $e_d \leq d^2$ holds for most cases.

The iteration bound of a multirate DFG can be determined by first constructing an equivalent single-rate DFG and then computing the iteration bound of the single-rate DFG using 1 of the 2 algorithms described in this chapter. The algorithm in Fig. 2.10 can be used to construct an equivalent single-rate DFG from the multirate DFG.

2.7 PROBLEMS

1. For the DFG shown in Fig. 2.12, the computation times of the nodes are shown in parentheses. Compute the iteration bound of this DFG using

   (a) the LPM algorithm, and

   (b) the MCM algorithm.

2. Repeat Problem 1 for the DFG shown in Fig. 2.13 assuming that addition and multiplication require 1 u.t. and 2 u.t., respectively.

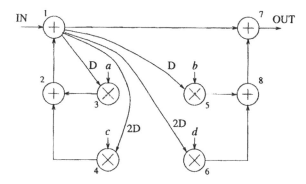

Fig. 2.14 The biquad filter.

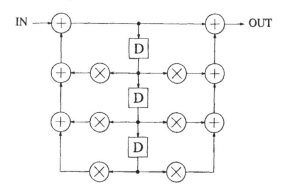

Fig. 2.15 Direct-form 3rd-order IIR filter.

3. Repeat Problem 1 for the DFG shown in Fig. 2.14 assuming that addition and multiplication require 1 u.t. and 2 u.t., respectively.

4. Repeat Problem 1 for the DFG shown in Fig. 2.15 assuming that addition and multiplication require 1 and 2 u.t., respectively.

5. Repeat Problem 1 for the DFG shown in Fig. 2.16 assuming that addition and multiplication require 1 and 2 u.t., respectively.

6. Repeat Problem 1 for the DFG shown in Fig. 2.17 assuming that addition and multiplication require 1 and 2 u.t., respectively.

7. Repeat Problem 1 for the DFG shown in Fig. 2.18 assuming that addition and multiplication require 1 and 2 u.t., respectively.

8. Repeat Problem 1 for the DFG in Fig. 2.11 assuming that the execution time of each node is 1 u.t.

9. Determine the iteration bound of the MRDFG in Fig. 2.19. Assume the execution time of each node to be 1 u.t. The following steps should be used:

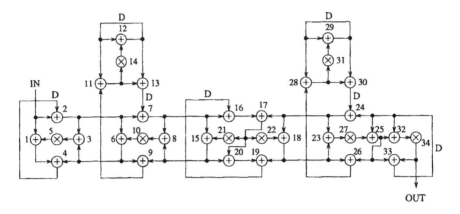

Fig. 2.16   Fifth-order wave digital elliptic filter.

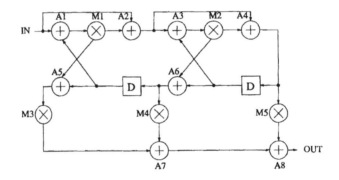

Fig. 2.17   The lattice filter used in Problem 6.

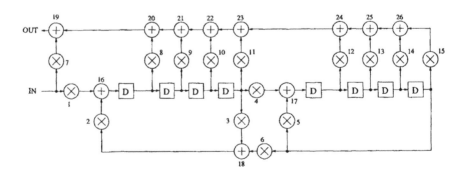

Fig. 2.18   The normalized lattice filter used in Problem 7.

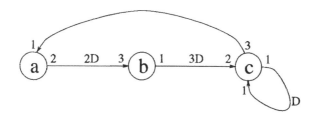

Fig. 2.19 The DFG used in Problem 9.

(a) construct the equivalent SRDFG, and

(b) use any algorithm in this chapter to determine the iteration bound of the equivalent SRDFG.

REFERENCES

1. M. Renfors and Y. Neuvo, "The maximum sampling rate of digital filters under hardware speed constraints," *IEEE Trans. on Circuits and Systems*, vol. CAS-28, no. 3, pp. 196–202, March 1981.

2. K. K. Parhi and D. G. Messerschmitt, "Static rate-optimal scheduling of iterative data-flow programs via optimum unfolding," *IEEE Trans. on Computers*, vol. 40, no. 2, pp. 178–195, Feb. 1991.

3. S. H. Gerez, S. M. Heemstra de Groot, and O. E. Herrmann, "A polynomial-time algorithm for the computation of the iteration-period bound in recursive data-flow graphs," *IEEE Trans. on Circuits and Systems—I: Fundamental Theory and Applications*, vol. 39, no. 1, pp. 49–52, Jan. 1992.

4. K. Ito and K. K. Parhi, "Determining the minimum iteration period of an algorithm," *Journal of VLSI Signal Processing*, vol. 11, pp. 229–244, 1995.

5. D. Y. Chao and D. T. Wang, "Iteration bounds of single-rate data flow graphs for concurrent processing," *IEEE Trans. on Circuits and Systems—I: Fundamental Theory and Applications*, vol. 40, no. 9, pp. 629–634, Sept. 1993.

6. R. M. Karp, "A characterization of the minimum cycle mean in a digraph," *Discrete Mathematics*, vol. 23, pp. 309–311, 1978.

7. E. A. Lee and D. G. Messerschmitt, "Static scheduling of synchronous data flow programs for digital signal processing," *IEEE Trans. on Computers*, vol. C-36, no. 1, pp. 24–35, Jan. 1987.

8. D. A. Schwartz and T. P. Barnwell, III, "Cyclo-static solutions: optimal multiprocessor realizations of recursive algorithms," in *Proc. of IEEE VLSI Signal Processing Workshop*, 1986.

3

Pipelining and Parallel Processing

3.1 INTRODUCTION

Pipelining transformation leads to a reduction in the critical path, which can be exploited to either increase the clock speed or sample speed or to reduce power consumption at same speed. In parallel processing, multiple outputs are computed in parallel in a clock period. Therefore, the effective sampling speed is increased by the level of parallelism. Similar to the pipelining, parallel processing can also be used for reduction of power consumption.

Consider the three-tap finite impulse response (FIR) digital filter

$$y(n) = ax(n) + bx(n-1) + cx(n-2). \tag{3.1}$$

The block diagram implementation of this filter is shown in Fig. 3.1. The

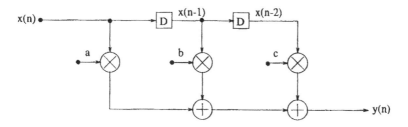

Fig. 3.1 A 3-tap FIR filter.

critical path or the minimum time required for processing a new sample is limited by 1 multiply and 2 add times, i.e., if T_M is the time taken for multiplication and T_A is time needed for addition operation then the "sample period" (T_{sample}) is given by,

$$T_{sample} \geq T_M + 2T_A. \qquad (3.2)$$

Therefore, the sampling frequency (f_{sample}) (also referred to as the throughput or the iteration rate) is given by

$$f_{sample} \leq \frac{1}{T_M + 2T_A}. \qquad (3.3)$$

Note that the *direct-form structure* shown in Fig. 3.1 can only be used when (3.2) is satisfied. But if some real-time application demands a faster input rate (sample rate), then this structure cannot be used! In that case, the *effective critical path* can be reduced by using either pipelining or parallel processing.

Pipelining reduces the *effective critical path* by introducing pipelining latches along the datapath. Pipelining has been used in the context of architecture design [1] –[4], and compiler synthesis [5] –[10], etc. Parallel processing increases the sampling rate by replicating hardware so that several inputs can be processed in parallel and several outputs can be produced at the same time [11] –[13]. Consider the simple structure in Fig. 3.2(a), where the computation time of the critical path is $2T_A$. Fig. 3.2(b) shows the 2-level pipelined structure, where 1 latch is placed between the 2 adders and hence the critical path is reduced by half. Its 2-level parallel processing structure is shown in Fig. 3.2(c), where the same hardware is duplicated so that 2 inputs can be processed at the same time and 2 outputs are produced simultaneously. Therefore, the sample rate is increased by two.

This chapter is organized as follows. Sections 3.2 and 3.3, respectively, present pipelining and parallel processing approaches in the context of non-recursive computations such as FIR digital filters. Section 3.4 presents use of pipelining and parallel processing for reduction of power consumption at same sample speed using lower supply voltage.

3.2 PIPELINING OF FIR DIGITAL FILTERS

Consider the pipelined implementation of the 3-tap FIR filter of (3.1) obtained by introducing 2 additional latches as shown in Fig. 3.3.

The critical path is now reduced from $T_M + 2T_A$ to $T_M + T_A$. In this arrangement while the left adder initiates the computation of the current iteration the right adder is completing the computation of the previous iteration result. The schedule of events for this *pipelined* system is shown in Table 3.1. In this system, at any time, 2 consecutive outputs are computed in an interleaved manner.

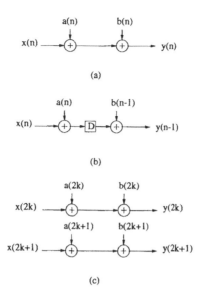

(a)

(b)

(c)

Fig. 3.2 (a) A datapath. (b) The 2-level pipelined structure of (a). (c) The 2-level parallel processing structure of (a).

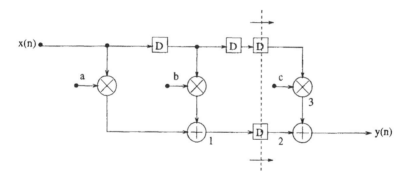

Fig. 3.3 Pipelined FIR filter. The dashed vertical line represents a feed-forward cutset.

Table 3.1   Schedule of Events in the Pipelined FIR Filter in Fig. 3.3

Clock	Input	Node 1	Node 2	Node 3	Output
0	$x(0)$	$ax(0) + bx(-1)$	—	—	—
1	$x(1)$	$ax(1) + bx(0)$	$ax(0) + bx(-1)$	$cx(-2)$	$y(0)$
2	$x(2)$	$ax(2) + bx(1)$	$ax(1) + bx(0)$	$cx(-1)$	$y(1)$
3	$x(3)$	$ax(3) + bx(2)$	$ax(2) + bx(1)$	$cx(0)$	$y(2)$

One must note that in an M-level pipelined system, the number of delay elements in any path from input to output is $(M - 1)$ greater than that in the same path in the original sequential circuit. While pipelining reduces the critical path, it leads to a penalty in terms of an increase in *latency*. Latency essentially is the difference in the availability of the first output data in the pipelined system and the sequential system. For example if latency is 1 clock cycle then the k-th output is available in $(k + 1)$-th clock cycle in a 1-stage pipelined system. The two main drawbacks of the pipelining are increase in the number of latches and in system latency.

The following points may be noted:

1. The speed of an architecture (or the clock period) is limited by the longest path between any 2 latches or between an input and a latch or between a latch and an output or between the input and the output.

2. This longest path or the "critical path" can be reduced by suitably placing the pipelining latches in the architecture.

3. The pipelining latches can only be placed across any *feed-forward cutset* of the graph.

In order to explain item 3, we need to introduce 2 definitions.

- **Cutset** A cutset is a set of edges of a graph such that if these edges are removed from the graph, the graph becomes disjoint.

- **Feed-forward Cutset** A cutset is called a feed-forward cutset if the data move in the forward direction on all the edges of the cutset. For example, the cutset used to pipeline the FIR filter in Fig. 3.3 is a feed-forward cutset.

We can arbitrarily place latches on a feed-forward cutset of any FIR filter structure without affecting the functionality of the algorithm.

Example 3.2.1 *In the signal-flow graph (SFG) shown in Fig. 3.4(a), the computation time for each node is assumed to be 1 u.t.*

(a) Calculate the critical path computation time.

(b) The critical path has been reduced to 2 u.t. by inserting 3 extra delay elements as shown in Fig. 3.4(b). Is this a valid pipelining? If not, obtain an appropriate pipelined circuit with critical path of 2 u.t.

Solution

(a) The critical path (the longest path between any two latches) is $A_3 \rightarrow A_5 \rightarrow A_4 \rightarrow A_6$ and its computation time is 4 u.t.

(b) This is not a valid pipelining. Let the dashed line in Fig. 3.4(b) denote 1 feed-forward cutset. We can see that only 3 latches are placed across the

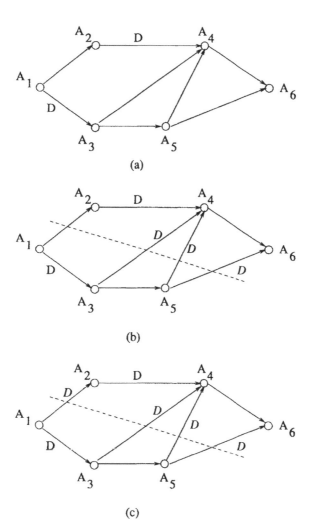

(a)

(b)

(c)

Fig. 3.4   Signal-flow graph for Example 3.2.1.

cutset. Although the critical path has been reduced to one-half of the original system, the functionality has been changed! To obtain an appropriate pipelining circuit, pipelining latches should be inserted on all the edges in the feed-forward cutset. Fig. 3.4(c) shows a valid pipelined circuit that has critical path of 2 u.t.

Comments: Adding delay elements at the feed-forward cutset in Fig. 3.4(c) leads to a 2-stage pipeline. In the 2-level pipelined system, the number of delay elements in any path from the input to the output is increased by 1. ■

3.2.1 Data-Broadcast Structures

The critical path of the original 3-tap FIR filter can be reduced without introducing any pipelining latches by transposing the structure. The *transposition theorem* states that

"Reversing the direction of all the edges in a given SFG and interchanging the input and output ports preserves the functionality of the system."

A 3-tap FIR filter is represented in SFG form in Fig. 3.5.

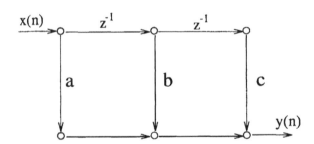

Fig. 3.5 Signal-flow graph representation of the FIR filter.

The SFG of the transposed filter is shown in Fig. 3.6 and its equivalent block diagram is shown in Fig. 3.7.

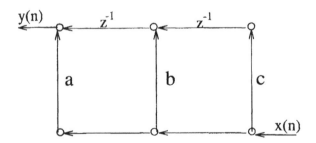

Fig. 3.6 Transposed SFG representation of the FIR filter.

This leads to the *data-broadcast structure* where data are not stored but are broadcast to all the multipliers simultaneously. Notice that now we have a critical path of $T_M + T_A$, the same as in Fig. 3.3.

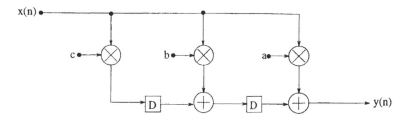

Fig. 3.7 Data-broadcast structure of the FIR filter.

3.2.2 Fine-Grain Pipelining

Let $T_M = 10$ units and $T_A = 2$ units, and the desired clock period be $(T_M + T_A)/2$, i.e., 6 units. In this case the multiplier is broken into 2 smaller units with processing times of 6 units and 4 units, respectively. Now by placing the latches on the horizontal cutset across the multiplier, the desired clock speed can be achieved. This is referred to as *fine-grain pipelining*. A fine-grain pipelined version of the 3-tap data-broadcast FIR filter is shown in Fig. 3.8.

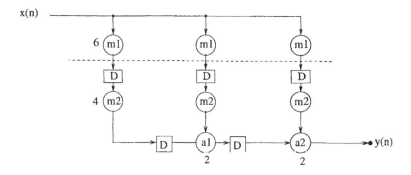

Fig. 3.8 Fine-grain pipelining of the FIR filter.

3.3 PARALLEL PROCESSING

It is of interest to note that parallel processing and pipelining techniques are duals of each other, and if a computation can be pipelined, it can also be processed in parallel. Both techniques exploit concurrency available in the computation in different ways. While independent sets of computations are computed in an interleaved manner in a pipelined system, they are computed using duplicate hardware in parallel processing mode.

3.3.1 Designing a Parallel FIR System

Consider the 3-tap FIR filter described by (3.1). This system is a single-input single-output (SISO) system and is described by

$$y(n) = ax(n) + bx(n-1) + cx(n-2). \tag{3.4}$$

To obtain a parallel processing structure, the SISO system must be converted into a MIMO (multiple-input multiple-output) system. For example, the following set of equations describe a parallel system with 3 inputs per clock cycle (i.e., level of parallel processing $L = 3$).

$$
\begin{aligned}
y(3k) &= ax(3k) + bx(3k-1) + cx(3k-2) & (3.5)\\
y(3k+1) &= ax(3k+1) + bx(3k) + cx(3k-1)\\
y(3k+2) &= ax(3k+2) + bx(3k+1) + cx(3k).
\end{aligned}
$$

Here k denotes the clock cycle. As can be seen, at the k-th clock cycle the 3 inputs $x(3k)$, $x(3k+1)$ and $x(3k+2)$ are processed and 3 samples are generated at the output. Parallel processing systems are also referred to as *block processing* systems and the number of inputs processed in a clock cycle is referred to as the *block size*. Because of the MIMO structure, placing a latch at any line produces an effective delay of L clock cycles at the sample rate. Each delay element is referred to as a *block delay* (also referred to as *L*-slow). For example, delaying the signal $x(3k)$ by 1 clock cycle would result in $x(3k-3)$ instead of $x(3k-1)$, which has been input in another input line. The block architecture for a 3-parallel FIR filter is shown in Fig. 3.9 and its details are shown in Fig. 3.10.

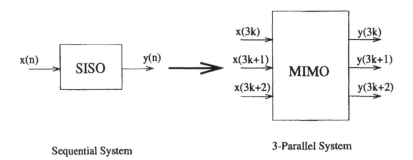

Sequential System   3-Parallel System

Fig. 3.9 A block processing example.

Note that the critical path of the block or parallel processing system has remained unchanged and the clock period (T_{clk}) must satisfy:

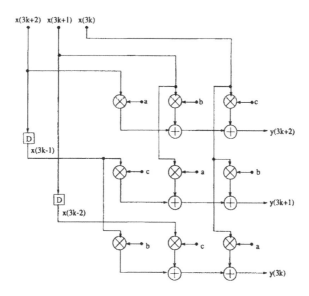

Fig. 3.10   Parallel processing architecture for a 3-tap FIR filter with block size 3.

$$T_{clk} \geq T_M + 2T_A. \qquad (3.6)$$

But since 3 samples are processed in 1 clock cycle instead of 3, the iteration period is given by

$$T_{iter} = T_{sample} = \frac{1}{L}T_{clk} \geq \frac{1}{3}(T_M + 2T_A). \qquad (3.7)$$

It is important to understand that in a parallel system $T_{clk} \neq T_{sample}$ whereas in a pipelined system $T_{clk} = T_{sample}$. Fig. 3.11 shows a complete parallel processing system including serial-to-parallel and parallel-to-serial converters, shown in detail in Fig. 3.12 and Fig. 3.13, respectively.

Now the question arises why use parallel processing when we can use pipelining equally well. Why do we want to duplicate so many copies of the hardware? The answer lies in the fact that there is a fundamental limit to pipelining imposed by the input/output (I/O) bottlenecks.

Consider the chip set shown in Fig. 3.14. If, for example, output-pad delay plus input-pad delay and the wire delay between the two chips is 8 nsec then T_{clk} has to be greater than or equal to 8 nsec. If the critical path computation time is less than 8 nsec, then the I/O bound dominates and this system is *communication bounded*. This essentially means that pipelining can be used only to the extent such that the critical path computation time is limited by the communication or I/O bound, and once this has been reached, pipelining can no longer increase the speed. At this point, pipelining can be combined with parallel processing to further increase the speed of the architecture. As

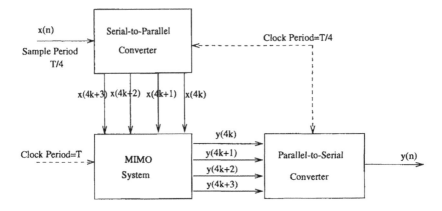

Fig. 3.11 Complete parallel processing system with block size 4.

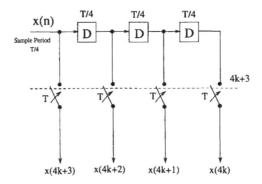

Fig. 3.12 A serial-to-parallel converter.

an example, consider the parallel filter in Fig. 3.10. Assume the computation time for 1 multiplication (T_M) to be 10 u.t. and the computation time for 1 adder (T_A) to be 2 u.t. Fine grain pipelining can be applied to the parallel filter to further reduce the critical path. In this case, the multiplier is broken up into two smaller units, $m1$ and $m2$, with computation time 7 u.t. and 3 u.t., respectively, and pipelining latches are placed on the horizontal cutsets across the multipliers as shown in Fig. 3.15. Although these horizontal cutsets may appear to be invalid, they are, however, valid since cutting the edges of these cutsets will lead to disjoint components. Therefore, by combining parallel processing and pipelining, the sample period has been reduced to

$$T_{iter} = T_{sample} = \frac{1}{LM}T_{clk} = \frac{1}{6}(T_M + 2T_A). \tag{3.8}$$

Parallel processing is also used for reduction of power consumption while using slow clocks. This reduces the power consumption due to the clock lines as compared with a pipelined system, which needs to be operated using a

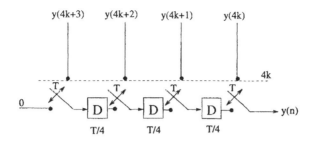

y(4k+3)   y(4k+2)   y(4k+1)   y(4k)

4k

0

T/4   T/4   T/4

y(n)

Fig. 3.13   A parallel-to-serial converter.

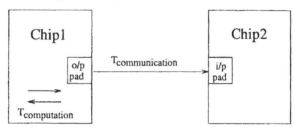

Chip1

o/p
pad

$T_{communication}$

Chip2

i/p
pad

$T_{computation}$

Fig. 3.14   A chip set.

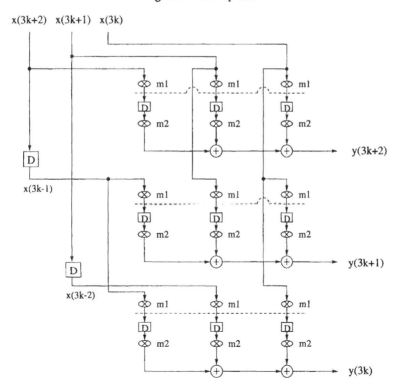

x(3k+2)   x(3k+1)   x(3k)

m1   m1   m1

D   D   D

m2   m2   m2

y(3k+2)

x(3k-1)

m1   m1   m1

D   D   D

m2   m2   m2

y(3k+1)

x(3k-2)

m1   m1   m1

D   D   D

m2   m2   m2

y(3k)

Fig. 3.15   Combined fine-grain pipelining and parallel processing for 3-tap FIR filter.

faster clock for equivalent throughput or sample speed. Furthermore, use of fine-grain pipelining such as bit-level pipelining may not be desirable, since the hardware overhead and the latency increase due to latches may be significant.

3.4 PIPELINING AND PARALLEL PROCESSING FOR LOW POWER

There are two main advantages of using pipelining and parallel processing:

- Higher speed

- Lower power

It has already been shown that pipelining and parallel processing can increase the sample speed. Now consider use of these techniques for lowering the power consumption where sample speed does not need to be increased [14].

Before moving on, two formulas are reviewed: one for computing the propagation delay of CMOS circuits and the other for computing the power consumption. The propagation delay T_{pd} is associated with charging and discharging of the various gate and stray capacitances in the critical path. For CMOS circuits, the propagation delay can be written as:

$$T_{pd} = \frac{C_{charge}V_0}{k(V_0 - V_t)^2},$$ (3.9)

where C_{charge} denotes the capacitance to be charged/discharged in a single clock cycle, i.e., the capacitance along the critical path, V_0 is the supply voltage and V_t is the threshold voltage. Parameter k is a function of technology parameters μ, $\frac{W}{L}$, and C_{ox}. The power consumption of a CMOS circuit can be estimated using the following equation,

$$P = C_{total}V_0^2 f,$$ (3.10)

where C_{total} denotes the total capacitance of the circuit, V_0 is the supply voltage, and f is the clock frequency of the circuit. Note that (3.9) and (3.10) are based on simple approximations and are appropriate only for a 1st-order analysis.

3.4.1 Pipelining for Low Power

As mentioned earlier, pipelining can be used to reduce the power consumption of a FIR filter. Let

$$P_{seq} = C_{total}V_0^2 f$$ (3.11)

represent the power consumed in the original filter. It should be noted that $f = \frac{1}{T_{seq}}$, where T_{seq} is the clock period of the original sequential filter. Now consider an M-level pipelined system, where the critical path is reduced to $\frac{1}{M}$ of its original length and the capacitance to be charged/discharged in a single clock cycle is reduced to $\frac{C_{charge}}{M}$. Notice that the total capacitance does not change. If the same clock speed is maintained, i.e., the clock frequency f is maintained, only a fraction of the original capacitance, $\frac{C_{charge}}{M}$, is being charged/discharged in the same amount of time that was previously needed to charge/discharge the capacitance, C_{charge} (see Fig. 3.16). This implies, then, that the supply voltage can be reduced to βV_0, where β is a positive constant less than 1. Hence, the power consumption of the pipelined filter will be

$$P_{pip} = C_{total}\beta^2 V_0^2 f = \beta^2 P_{seq}. \tag{3.12}$$

Therefore, the power consumption of the pipelined system has been reduced by a factor of β^2 as compared with the original system.

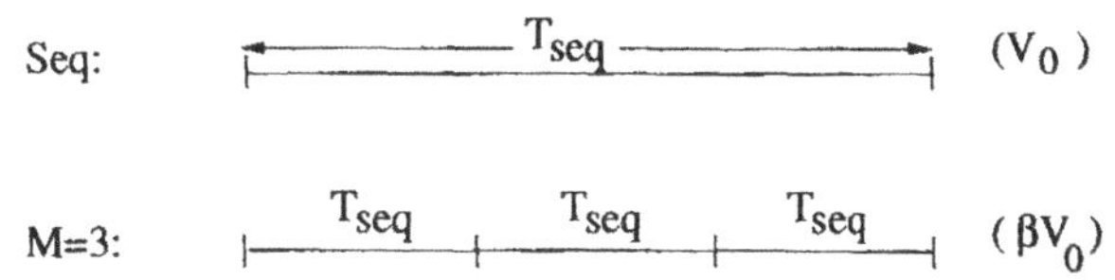

Seq: |———————— T_{seq} ————————| (V_0)

M=3: |—— T_{seq} ——|—— T_{seq} ——|—— T_{seq} ——| (βV_0)

Fig. 3.16   Critical path lengths for original and 3-level pipelined systems.

The power consumption reduction factor, β, can be determined by examining the relationship between the propagation delay of the original filter and the pipelined filter. The propagation delay of the original filter is given by

$$T_{seq} = \frac{C_{charge} V_0}{k(V_0 - V_t)^2}. \tag{3.13}$$

The propagation delay of the pipelined filter is given by

$$T_{pip} = \frac{\frac{C_{charge}}{M}\beta V_0}{k(\beta V_0 - V_t)^2}. \tag{3.14}$$

It should be noted that the clock period, T_{clk}, is usually set equal to the maximum propagation delay, T_{pd}, in a circuit. Since the same clock speed is maintained for both filters, from (3.13) and (3.14), the following quadratic equation can be obtained to solve for β,

$$M(\beta V_0 - V_t)^2 = \beta(V_0 - V_t)^2. \tag{3.15}$$

Once β is obtained, the reduced power consumption of the pipelined filter can be computed using (3.12).

Example 3.4.1 *Consider the 3-tap FIR filter shown in Fig. 3.7 and its fine-grain pipelined version shown in Fig. 3.8. Assume that the multiplication operation takes 10 u.t. and the addition operation takes 2 u.t. For power* *estimation purposes, assume that the capacitance of the multiplier is 5 times that of an adder. In the fine-grain pipelined filter, the multiplier is broken into 2 parts, m1 and m2, with computation time of 6 u.t. and 4 u.t. respectively, with capacitance 3 times and 2 times that of an adder, respectively. Assume the device threshold voltage to be 0.6 V. Also assume the nonpipelined filter to be operated at the supply voltage 5.0 V.*

(a) What is the supply voltage of the pipelined filter if the clock period remains unchanged?

(b) What is the power consumption of the pipelined filter as a percentage of the original filter?

Solution

(a) Let C_M be the capacitance of 1 multiplier and C_A be the capacitance of 1 adder. For the original filter, the charging capacitance along the critical path is

$$C_{charge} = C_M + C_A = 6C_A. \tag{3.16}$$

For the pipelined filter, the charging capacitance along the critical path is

$$C_{charge} = C_{m1} = C_{m2} + C_A = 3C_A, \tag{3.17}$$

where C_{m1} and C_{m2} are capacitances for parts m1 and m2 of 1 multiplier respectively. Notice the pipelining level $M = 2$ and the charging capacitance of the pipelined filter is one-half of that of the original filter. Assume the pipelined filter is operated at supply voltage βV_0. Substitute $M = 2$, $V_0 = 5.0$, $V_t = 0.6$ into (3.15):

$$50\beta^2 - 31.36\beta + 0.72 = 0. \tag{3.18}$$

Solve (3.18) to get

$$\beta = 0.6033, \ or \ \beta = 0.0239 \tag{3.19}$$

Note that $\beta = 0.0239$ is infeasible since the supply voltage for this case (0.1195 V) is less than the threshold voltage and the device is off all the time. Therefore, the supply voltage of the pipelined filter should be

$$V_{pip} = \beta V_0 = 3.0165 \ V. \tag{3.20}$$

(b) Since the total capacitance of the pipelined filter is the same as the original filter and the 2 filters are operated at the same clock period, from (3.12),

$$Ratio = \beta^2 = 36.4\%. \ \blacksquare \tag{3.21}$$

3.4.2 Parallel Processing for Low Power

Parallel processing, like pipelining, can reduce the power consumption of a system by allowing the supply voltage to be reduced. In an L-parallel system, the charging capacitance does not usually change while the total capacitance is increased by L times. In order to maintain the same sample rate, the clock period of the L-parallel circuit must be increased to LT_{seq}, where T_{seq} is the propagation delay of the sequential circuit given by (3.13). This means that C_{charge} is charged in time LT_{seq} rather than in time T_{seq}. In other words, there is more time to charge the same capacitance (see Fig. 3.17). This means that the supply voltage can be reduced to βV_0.

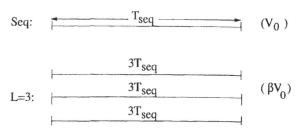

Fig. 3.17 Critical path lengths for sequential and 3-parallel systems.

The propagation delay considerations can again be used to compute the supply voltage of the L-parallel system. The propagation delay of the original system is given by (3.13), while the propagation delay of the L-parallel system is given by

$$LT_{seq} = \frac{C_{charge}\beta V_0}{k(\beta V_0 - V_t)^2}.\qquad(3.22)$$

From (3.13) and (3.22), the following quadratic equation can be obtained to compute β:

$$L(\beta V_0 - V_t)^2 = \beta(V_0 - V_t)^2.\qquad(3.23)$$

Once β is computed, the power consumption of the L-parallel system can be calculated as

$$\begin{aligned}P_{par} &= (LC_{charge})(\beta V_0)^2\frac{f}{L}\qquad(3.24)\\ &= \beta^2 C_{charge}V_0^2 f\\ &= \beta^2 P_{seq},\end{aligned}$$

where P_{seq} is power consumption of the sequential system given by (3.11). Therefore, as in the pipelined system, the power consumption of the L-parallel system has been reduced by a factor of β^2 as compared with the original sequential system.

Example 3.4.2 *Consider a 4-tap FIR filter shown in Fig. 3.18(a) and its 2-parallel version in 3.18(b). The parallel filter has exactly 2 copies of the original filter. The dashed lines in Fig. 3.18 denote the critical path. Assume that the multiplication operation takes 8 u.t. and addition operation takes 1 u.t. For power calculation purposes, assume that the capacitance of the multiplier is 8 times that of an adder. The two architectures are operated at*

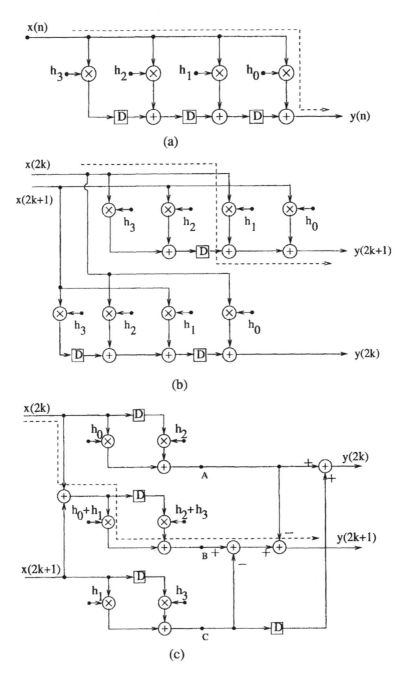

Fig. 3.18 (a) A 4-tap FIR filter. (b) A 2-parallel filter. (c) An area-efficient 2-parallel filter.

the sample period 9 u.t. Assume the device threshold voltage to be 0.45 V. Also assume the sequential filter to be operated at an initial supply voltage of 3.3 V.

(a) What is the supply voltage of the 2-parallel filter?

(b) What is the power consumption of the 2-parallel filter as a percentage of the original filter?

Solution

(a) Let C_M be the capacitance of 1 multiplier and C_A be the capacitance of 1 adder. For the sequential filter, the charging capacitance along the critical path is

$$C_{charge} = C_M + C_A = 9C_A. \tag{3.25}$$

For the 2-parallel filter, the charging capacitance along the critical path is

$$C_{charge} = C_M + 2C_A = 10C_A. \tag{3.26}$$

Assume the parallel filter is operated at the supply voltage βV_0. Notice that the charging capacitances for the sequential filter and the 2-parallel filter are not equal. We cannot use (3.23) directly. From (3.13), the propagation delays of the 2 filters are given by

$$T_{seq} = \frac{9C_A V_0}{k(V_0 - V_t)^2}, \tag{3.27}$$

$$T_{par} = \frac{10C_A \beta V_0}{k(\beta V_0 - V_t)^2}.$$

The critical path for sequential filter is 1 multiply and 1 add, i.e., 9 u.t., which implies that the sample period $T_{sample} = T_{seq}$. Combining the fact $T_{par} = 2T_{sample} = 2T_{seq}$ with (3.27), we have

$$5\beta(V_0 - V_t)^2 = 9(\beta V_0 - V_t)^2. \tag{3.28}$$

Substitute $V_0 = 3.3$ V, $V_t = 0.45$ V into (3.28) to get

$$98.01\beta^2 - 67.3425\beta + 1.8225 = 0. \tag{3.29}$$

Solving (3.29), we obtain

$$\beta = 0.6589, \text{ or } \beta = 0.0282. \tag{3.30}$$

The only feasible supply voltage for the 2-parallel filter is $\beta V_0 = 2.17437$ V. (The other root $\beta = 0.0282$ is discarded since $\beta V_0 = 0.09306$ V is less than the threshold voltage.)

(b) From (3.24),

$$\text{Ratio} = \beta^2 = 43.41\%. \blacksquare \tag{3.31}$$

Example 3.4.3 *Consider the 4-tap FIR filter in Fig. 3.18(a) and its 2-parallel version in Fig. 3.18(c). The 2-parallel filter in Fig. 3.18(c) is more efficient than the parallel filter in Fig. 3.18(b) in the sense that it requires 6 multipliers as opposed to 8 required by the parallel filter in Fig. 3.18(b). Use the same assumptions as in example 3.4.2. Our objective is to compare the power consumption of the sequential filter and its 2-parallel version for a sample period of 9 u.t. The 2-parallel filter can be operated at a lower supply voltage such that it achieves an effective sample period of 9 u.t. but this supply voltage must be greater than or equal to 0.9 V.*

(a) Tracing the computation paths, verify that the 2-parallel structure correctly computes the outputs $y(2k)$ and $y(2k+1)$.

(b) Calculate the supply voltage at which the 2-parallel filter should be operated.

(c) Using the result of (b), calculate the power consumption of the 2-parallel filter as a percentage of the sequential filter.

Solution

(a) The system equation for the given 4-tap FIR filter is as follows:

$$y(n) = h_0 x(n) + h_1 x(n-1) + h_2 x(n-2) + h_3 x(n-3). \tag{3.32}$$

Defining the outputs at node A, B, and C as y_A, y_B, and y_C, respectively, we have

$$
\begin{aligned}
y_A &= h_0 x(2k) + h_2 x(2k-2), & (3.33)\\
y_B &= (h_0 + h_1)(x(2k) + x(2k+1)) + (h_2 + h_3)(x(2k-2) + x(2k-1)),\\
y_C &= h_1 x(2k+1) + h_3 x(2k-1).
\end{aligned}
$$

Then

$$
\begin{aligned}
y(2k) &= y_A + [y_C \ after \ 1 \ block \ delay] & (3.34)\\
&= h_0 x(2k) + h_1 x(2k-1) + h_2 x(2k-2) + h_3 x(2k-3),\\
y(2k+1) &= y_B - y_A - y_C\\
&= h_0 x(2k+1) + h_1 x(2k) + h_2 x(2k-1) + h_3 x(2k-2).
\end{aligned}
$$

It is easy to verify that the proceeding equations satisfy the system equation (3.32).

(b). Let C_M denote the capacitance of 1 multiplier and C_A denote the capacitance of 1 adder. For the sequential filter, the charging capacitance along the critical path is given by (3.25). For its 2-parallel version, the charging capacitance along the critical path is

$$C_{charge} = C_M + 4C_A = 12C_A. \tag{3.35}$$

From Example 3.4.2, we already know that $T_{sample} = T_{seq} = 9$ u.t. In order to *operate the 2-parallel filter at the sample period of 9 u.t., $T_{par} = 2T_{sample} = 2T_{seq}$ must be satisfied. This leads to*

$$\frac{2 \cdot 9 C_A V_0}{k(V_0 - V_t)^2} = \frac{12 C_A \beta V_0}{k(\beta V_0 - V_t)^2}. \tag{3.36}$$

Substituting $V_0 = 3.3$ V, $V_t = 0.45$ V into (3.36), we get

$$32.67\beta^2 - 25.155\beta + 0.6075 = 0. \tag{3.37}$$

Solving (3.37), we get

$$\beta = 0.745, \ or \ \beta = 0.025. \tag{3.38}$$

The 2-parallel filter should be operated at the supply voltage $\beta V_0 = 2.4585$ V. (The other root is not valid because $\beta V_0 = 0.0825$ V is less than the threshold voltage).

(c) Let $C_{total}^{(seq)}$ be the total capacitance for the 4-tap FIR filter. Let $C_{total}^{(par)}$ be the total capacitance for the 2-parallel filter. From (3.10), the power consumption for 4-tap FIR filter and that for 2-parallel filter are as follows:

$$P_{seq} = C_{total}^{(seq)} V_0^2 f_{seq}, \ P_{par} = C_{total}^{(par)} V_{par}^2 f_{par}, \tag{3.39}$$

where $C_{total}^{(seq)} = 4C_M + 3C_A = 35C_A$, $C_{total}^{(par)} = 6C_M + 7C_A = 55C_A$. From part (b), we know that $f_{par} = \frac{1}{2} f_{seq} = \frac{1}{2} f_s$, where f_s is the sample frequency. Therefore, we have

$$P_{seq} = 35 C_A \cdot V_0^2 \cdot f_s, \tag{3.40}$$

$$P_{par} = 55 C_A \cdot \beta^2 V_0^2 \cdot \frac{1}{2} f_s.$$

Therefore,

$$Ratio = \frac{P_{par}}{P_{seq}} = \frac{0.5 \cdot 55\beta^2}{35} = 43.6\%. \ \blacksquare \tag{3.41}$$

Note that the structures in Fig. 3.18(b) and Fig. 3.18(c) consume similar power but the structure in Fig. 3.18(c) consumes much less area.

3.4.3 Combining Pipelining and Parallel Processing

The techniques of pipelining and parallel processing can be combined for lower power consumption. The principles remain the same, i.e., pipelining reduces the capacitance to be charged/discharged in 1 clock period and parallel processing increases the clock period for charging/discharging the original capacitance (see Fig. 3.19). The propagation delay of the parallel-pipelined filter is

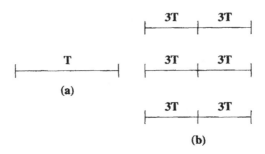

Fig. 3.19   (a) Charging/discharging of entire capacitance in clock period T. (b) Charging/discharging of capacitance in clock period 3T using a 3-parallel filter and 2 stages of pipelining.

obtained as follows

$$LT_{pd} = \frac{(C_{charge}/M)\beta V_o}{k(\beta V_0 - V_t)^2} = \frac{LC_{charge}V_0}{k(V_0 - V_t)^2}. \tag{3.42}$$

Using this equation, the following quadratic equation is obtained

$$ML(\beta V_0 - V_t)^2 = \beta(V_0 - V_t)^2 \tag{3.43}$$

which can be used to solve for β. As an example, consider the case when $L = M = 2$, $V_0 = 5$ V and $V_t = 0.6$ V. Using (3.43), β is found to be approximately 0.4, which means that the power consumption can be reduced by a factor of 0.16. It should be noted that the supply voltage cannot be lowered indefinitely by applying more and more levels of pipelining and parallelism. There is a lower bound on the supply voltage that is dictated by the process parameters and noise margins.

3.5   CONCLUSIONS

This chapter has addressed the methodologies of pipelining and parallel processing in the context of nonrecursive digital filters. Both approaches can be used to increase the sampling frequency of a filter. In pipelining, pipelining latches are placed across the feed-forward cutsets in the SFG and the computation time of the critical path is reduced. As a result, the clock frequency can be increased and hence the sampling rate is increased. In parallel processing, the hardware for the original serial system is duplicated and the resulting system is an MIMO parallel system. In this case, the clock frequency stays the same, and the sampling frequency is increased. Use of pipelining and parallel processing for low-power design has been illustrated. The basic idea is to trade the increased sampling speed for reduction of power consumption using lower supply voltage. Parallel FIR filters can be implemented using less than linear increase in hardware with respect to the level of parallelism using fast algorithms (see Chapter 9). Pipelining and parallel processing of recursive digital filters using look-ahead techniques are addressed in Chapter 10.

3.6 PROBLEMS

1. Consider the DFG shown in Fig. 3.20. Assume the time required for each operation is T.

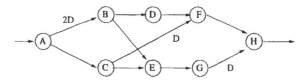

Fig. 3.20 Data-flow graph for Problem 1.

(a) What is the maximum achievable sample rate in this system?

(b) Place pipelining registers at appropriate feed-forward cutsets such that the sample rate of this system can be approximately equal to $1/T$. Clearly identify the feed-forward cutsets and count the total number of pipelining registers required.

2. Consider the IIR digital filter block diagram shown in Fig. 3.21. Assume that the multiplication operation takes 2 u.t. and the addition operation takes 1 u.t.

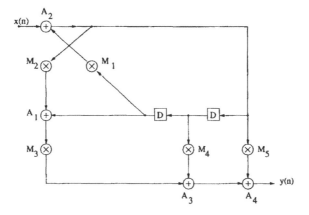

Fig. 3.21 Digital IIR filter for Problem 2.

(a) Calculate the critical path of the IIR filter.

(b) Pipeline the IIR filter by placing latches at appropriate feed-forward cutsets to reduce the critical path to 3 u.t.

3. Consider the nonrecursive signal processing structure shown in Fig. 3.22. Find an equivalent data-broadcast implementation of this algorithm to

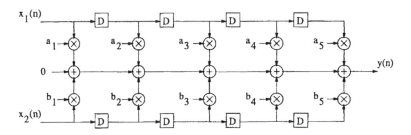

Fig. 3.22 Data-flow graph for Problem 3.

improve the speed of the system. Do not use any additional latches. Calculate the throughput or sample speed of the broadcast architecture. (Hint: Transpose operation is not applicable to the 2-input 1-output system in Fig. 3.22.)

4. Consider the 2D FIR digital filter of size 3×3

$$y(n_1, n_2) = \sum_{i=0}^{2} \sum_{j=0}^{2} a_{ij} x(n_1 - i, n_2 - j)$$

shown in Fig. 3.23.

Obtain an equivalent data-broadcast FIR filter structure.

5. Consider a direct-form implementation of the FIR filter

$$y(n) = ax(n) + bx(n - 2) + cx(n - 3). \tag{3.44}$$

Assume that the time required for 1 multiply-add operation is T.

(a) Pipeline this filter such that the clock period is approximately T.

(b) Draw a block filter architecture for a block size of three. Pipeline this block filter such that the clock period is about T. What is the system sample rate?

(c) Pipeline the block filter in part (b) such that the clock period is about $T/2$. Show the appropriate cutsets and label the outputs clearly. What is the system sample rate now?

6. Repeat Problem 5 using the broadcast filter architecture. In each case, how many latches can you save?

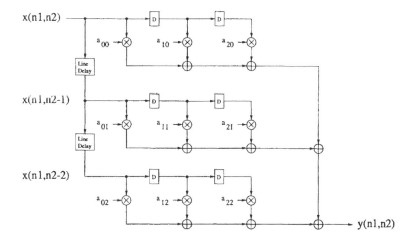

x(n1,n2)

x(n1,n2-1)

x(n1,n2-2)

y(n1,n2)

Fig. 3.23   Two-dimensional FIR filter for Problem 4.

7. Consider the 6th-order FIR filter

$$y(n) = ax(n) + bx(n-4) + cx(n-6). \qquad (3.45)$$

(a) Draw a topology for this filter such that the clock period is limited by 1 multiply-add time. Do this without adding any new latches.

(b) Draw a block architecture for the structure in (a) for block size of 3. Rearrange this block structure such that the clock period of this block structure is one-fourth of a multiply-add time. Assume that the multiply computation time is three times the add computation time.

8. Consider the recursive filter

$$x(n) = ax(n-2) + u(n). \qquad (3.46)$$

(a) Pipeline this multiply-add operator by 2 stages, by first breaking up the multiply-add operation into 2 components and by redistributing the delay elements in the loop.

(b) Interleave the computation in (3.46) with (3.47)

$$y(n) = by(n-2) + v(n). \qquad (3.47)$$

using the same hardware. Now pipeline the multiply-add operation by 4 stages. Show all the circuits needed for this implementation.

9. It is necessary to reduce the power consumption of a system by at least 5 times using pipelining. For the threshold voltage of 0.4 V and initial

supply voltage of 5 V, at what level should the system be pipelined? What is the supply voltage of the pipelined system?

10. Two implementations of an 8-tap FIR filter are shown in Fig. 3.24. Assume the critical path (or the propagation delay) of a multiplier to

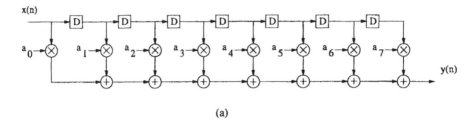

(a)

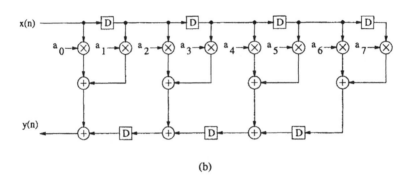

(b)

Fig. 3.24 Two implementations of an 8-tap FIR filter in Problem 10.

be twice that of an adder, i.e., $T_m = 2T_a$. Therefore, the charging capacitance of a multiplier is twice that of an adder. Further assume that the total capacitance of a multiplier is 10 times that of an adder, i.e., $C_m = 10C_a$. The critical path of the direct-form structure in Fig. 3.24(a) is $T_m + 7T_a = 9T_a$. The structure in Fig. 3.24(b) can be operated with a lower supply voltage to meet the clock period or sampling period constraint of $9T_a$. Thus, the structure in Fig. 3.24(b) can be used to reduce the power consumption. Assume that the structure in Fig. 3.24(a) is operated with a supply voltage of 4 V. Assume the technology threshold voltage to be 0.5 V. The supply voltage must be greater than 1.2 V to achieve the acceptable noise margin.

What is the minimum supply voltage at which the structure shown in Fig. 3.24(b) can be operated to achieve the desired sampling period of $9T_a$? Calculate the percentage of reduction in power consumption for the structure in Fig. 3.24(b) as compared with that in Fig. 3.24(a). Neglect the propagation delay and capacitance of delay elements in calculation of critical path or power consumption.

11. Consider a datapath with a total capacitance of C_{total}. This datapath is pipelined by M levels. Let C_{latch} represent the total capacitance of the latches used for 1 pipelining stage. The pipelined system is operated with lower supply voltage to reduce the power consumption. Assume both systems are operated at same speed and assume the propagation delay of the latch to be negligible. Let $C_{total} = 10C_{latch}$, $V_{dd} = 4$ V and $V_t = 0.6$ V. Calculate the power consumption of the pipelined system as a percentage of that of the sequential system for different values of M. What is the optimal M for least power consumption?

12. Calculate the power reduction of a computation if it is pipelined by 4 stages and processed using a block structure with block size 4, but is operated with the same sample rate as the original system. Assume that the original system was operated at a supply voltage of 5 V, and assume the threshold voltage V_t of the CMOS process to be 0.4 V. Calculate the power consumption of the parallel-pipelined system as compared with the original system. What is the operating supply voltage of the parallel-pipelined system?

13. Consider an FIR digital filter operated with a clock or sample period T. This problem can be solved without knowing the order of the filter. The filter circuit is operated with a supply voltage of 5 V using a technology with threshold voltage of 0.4 V. The consumer demand imposes the constraint that the sample speed of the filter be increased by 4 times, i.e., the new system should achieve a sample period of $T/4$. In addition, the power should also be reduced, possibly at the expense of increasing the area. To reduce the power consumption, a lower supply voltage can be used. Assume the availability of a variable voltage supply that can generate voltages from 1.0 to 5 V. The supply voltage cannot be less than 1.0 V.

The simultaneous speed increase and power reduction can be achieved by using block processing using block size that is a multiple of 4. For example, we can use a parallel FIR filter with block size 8 and operate this system with clock period $2T$ to achieve a sample period $T/4$. Similarly, we can use parallel filters with block size $4p$ and operate the filter with clock period pT to achieve sample period $T/4$ where p is any positive integer. These filters can then be operated with lower supply voltage to reduce power consumption.

   (a) What value of p or block size should be chosen to obtain a circuit with the least power consumption? Calculate the supply voltage and power consumption for this p.

   (b) If the goal is not to reduce the power, but to reduce the area-power product, what value of p or block size should be chosen? Calculate the supply voltage, power consumption, and area-power product for this p. For area calculation, assume that the cost of adders is negligible compared to the cost of multipliers.

14. Pipeline the circuit shown in Fig. 3.18(c) by placing latches at appropriate feed-forward locations such that the critical path is reduced by a factor of 2 to 6 u.t. Consider the capacitance of a circuit element to be proportional to its path length. Calculate the power consumption of the circuit as a percentage of the original sequential circuit in Fig. 3.18(a). (Use the same parameters as in Examples 3.4.2 and 3.4.3).

15. Consider power consumption reduction of a circuit at same speed by use of pipelining and parallel processing. Let V_0 be the original supply voltage of the sequential system. Let β represent the supply voltage reduction factor of an L-parallel M-level pipelined system, i.e., this system is operated with supply voltage βV_0. Let β_1 be the supply voltage reduction factor for an M-level pipelined system operated at the same speed, i.e., this system is operated with supply voltage $\beta_1 V_0$. Let β_2 be the supply voltage reduction factor of an L-parallel system operating at the same speed as sequential circuit operated with supply voltage $\beta_1 V_0$. Show that $\beta = \beta_1 \beta_2$.

REFERENCES

1. J. Hennessy and D. Patterson, *Computer Architecture A Quantitative Approach, 2nd ed.*. Morgan Kaufmann Publishers, 1996.

2. K. Hwang and F. A. Briggs, *Computer Architecture and Parallel Processing.* McGraw-Hill, 1984.

3. P. M. Kogge, *The Architecture of Pipelined Computers.* McGraw-Hill, 1981.

4. H. T. Kung, "Why systolic architectures?" *IEEE Computers Magazine*, vol. 15, pp. 37–45, Jan. 1982.

5. U. Banerjee et al., "Time and parallel processor bounds for fortran like loops," *IEEE Trans. on Computers*, vol. 28, pp. 660–670, 1979.

6. N. Jouppi and D. Wall, "Available instruction level parallelism for superscalar and super-pipelined machines," in *Proc. of 3rd International Conference on Architectural Support for Programming Languages and Operating Systems*, (Boston), pp. 272–282, May 1989.

7. M. Lam, "Software pipelining: an effective scheduling technique for VLIW machines," in *Proc. of the ACM SIGPLAN Conference on Programming Language Design and Implementation*, (Atlanta), pp. 318–328, June 1988.

8. D. A. Padua and M. J. Wolfe, "Advanced compiler organizations for supercomputers," *Communications of the ACM*, vol. 29, pp. 1184–1201, 1986.

9. B. R. Rau et al., "Efficient code generation for horizontal architectures: compiler techniques and architectural support," in *Proc. of 9th International Symposium on Computer Architecture*, 1982.

10. M. E. Wolf and M. S. Lam, "A loop transformation theory and an algorithm to maximize parallelism," *IEEE Trans. on Parallel and Distributed Systems*, vol. 2, pp. 452–471, 1991.

11. K. K. Parhi and D. G. Messerschmitt, "Pipeline interleaving and parallelism in recursive digital filters—part I: pipelining using scattered look-ahead and decomposition," *IEEE Trans. on Acoustics, Speech, and Signal Processing*, vol. 37, no. 7, pp. 1099–1117, July 1989.

12. K. K. Parhi and D. G. Messerschmitt, "Pipeline interleaving and parallelism in recursive digital filters—part II: pipelined incremental block filtering," *IEEE Trans. on Acoustics, Speech, and Signal Processing*, vol. 37, no. 7, pp. 1118–1135, July 1989.

13. C. W. Wu and P. R. Cappello, "Application-specific CAD of VLSI second-order sections," *IEEE Trans. on Acoustics, Speech, and Signal Processing*, vol. 36, pp. 813–825, 1988.

14. A. P. Chandrakasan, S. Sheng, and R. W. Brodersen, "Low-power CMOS digital design," *IEEE Journal of Solid-State Circuits*, vol. 27, no. 4, pp. 473–483, April 1992.

4

Retiming

4.1 INTRODUCTION

Retiming [1] is a transformation technique used to change the locations of delay elements in a circuit without affecting the input/output characteristics of the circuit. For example, consider the IIR filter in Fig. 4.1(a). This filter is described by

$$
\begin{aligned}
w(n) &= ay(n-1) + by(n-2) \\
y(n) &= w(n-1) + x(n) \\
&= ay(n-2) + by(n-3) + x(n).
\end{aligned}
$$

The filter in Fig. 4.1(b) is described by

$$
\begin{aligned}
w_1(n) &= ay(n-1) \\
w_2(n) &= by(n-2) \\
y(n) &= w_1(n-1) + w_2(n-1) + x(n) \\
&= ay(n-2) + by(n-3) + x(n).
\end{aligned}
$$

Although the filters in Fig. 4.1(a) and Fig. 4.1(b) have delays at different locations, these filters have the same input/output characteristics. These 2 filters can be derived from one another using retiming.

Retiming has many applications in synchronous circuit design. These applications include reducing the clock period of the circuit, reducing the number of registers in the circuit, reducing the power consumption of the circuit, and

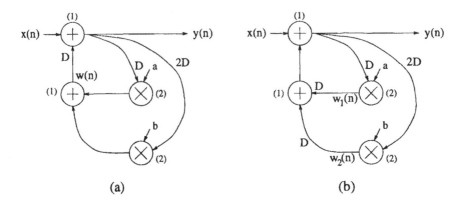

Fig. 4.1 Two versions of an IIR filter. The computation times of the nodes are shown in parentheses.

logic synthesis. The topics of retiming to reduce the clock period and to reduce the number of registers are discussed in detail in this chapter. Retiming for logic synthesis is beyond the scope of this book.

Retiming can be used to increase the clock rate of a circuit by reducing the computation time of the critical path. Recall that the critical path is defined to be the path with the longest computation time among all paths that contain zero delays, and the computation time of the critical path is the lower bound on the clock period of the circuit. The critical path of the filter in Fig. 4.1(a) passes through 1 multiplier and 1 adder and has a computation time of 3 u.t., so this filter cannot be clocked with a clock period of less than 3 u.t. The retimed filter in Fig. 4.1(b) has a critical path that passes through 2 adders and has a computation time of 2 u.t., so this filter can be clocked with a clock period of 2 u.t. By retiming the filter in Fig. 4.1(a) to obtain the filter in Fig. 4.1(b), the clock period has been reduced from 3 u.t. to 2 u.t., or by 33%. A polynomial-time algorithm for retiming for clock period minimization is described in Section 4.4.2.

Retiming can be used to decrease the number of registers in a circuit. The filter in Fig. 4.1(a) uses 4 registers while the filter in Fig. 4.1(b) uses 5 registers. Since retiming can affect the clock period *and* the number of registers, it is sometimes desirable to take both of these parameters into account. A polynomial time algorithm for retiming to minimize the number of registers for a given clock period is described in Section 4.4.3.

Retiming can be used to reduce the power consumption of a circuit by reducing switching, which can lead to dynamic power dissipation in static CMOS circuits [2]. Placing registers at the inputs of nodes with large capacitances can reduce the switching activities at these nodes, which can lead to low-power solutions (see Section 17.5.4).

In Section 4.2, a mathematical description of retiming is addressed and

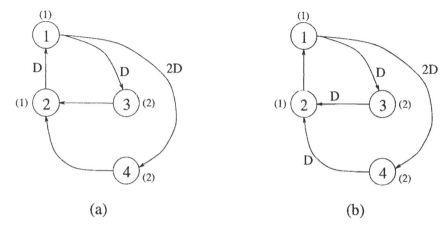

Fig. 4.2 (a) A DFG. (b) The retimed DFG obtained using $r(1) = 0$, $r(2) = 1$, $r(3) = 0$, and $r(4) = 0$.

some properties of retiming are discussed. Techniques for solving systems of inequalities are described in Section 4.3. These techniques are used in Section 4.4, where algorithms for retiming a circuit to achieve various objectives, such as clock period minimization, are described.

4.2 DEFINITIONS AND PROPERTIES

4.2.1 Quantitative Description of Retiming

Retiming maps a circuit G to a retimed circuit G_r. In the context of retiming, the terms circuit and graph and DFG are often used interchangeably, as they are in this chapter. A retiming solution is characterized by a value $r(V)$ for each node V in the graph. Let $w(e)$ denote the weight of the edge e in the original graph G, and let $w_r(e)$ denote the weight of the edge e in the retimed graph G_r. The weight of the edge $U \xrightarrow{e} V$ in the retimed graph is computed from the weight of the edge in the original graph using

$$w_r(e) = w(e) + r(V) - r(U). \tag{4.1}$$

To demonstrate some formal retiming concepts, the filter in Fig. 4.1(a) is redrawn in Fig. 4.2(a), and the retimed filter in Fig. 4.1(b) is redrawn in Fig. 4.2(b). The retiming values $r(1) = 0$, $r(2) = 1$, $r(3) = 0$, and $r(4) = 0$ can be used to obtain the retimed DFG in Fig. 4.2(b) from the DFG in Fig. 4.2(a). For example, the edge $3 \xrightarrow{e} 2$ in the retimed DFG contains

$$w_r(3 \xrightarrow{e} 2) \quad = \quad w(3 \xrightarrow{e} 2) + r(2) - r(3)$$

$$= 0 + 1 - 0 = 1$$

delay, and the edge $2 \overset{e}{\rightarrow} 1$ contains

$$
\begin{aligned}
w_r(2 \overset{e}{\rightarrow} 1) &= w(2 \overset{e}{\rightarrow} 1) + r(1) - r(2) \\
&= 1 + 0 - 1 = 0
\end{aligned}
$$

delays.

A retiming solution is feasible if $w_r(e) \geq 0$ holds for all edges. While the solution that maps Fig. 4.2(a) to Fig. 4.2(b) is feasible because all of the edges in Fig. 4.2(b) have nonnegative weights, the solution $r(1) = 0$, $r(2) = -1$, $r(3) = 0$, and $r(4) = 0$ is infeasible because, for example, the edge $3 \overset{e}{\rightarrow} 2$ in the retimed system contains

$$
\begin{aligned}
w_r(3 \overset{e}{\rightarrow} 2) &= w(3 \overset{e}{\rightarrow} 2) + r(2) - r(3) \\
&= 0 + (-1) - 0 = -1
\end{aligned}
$$

delays.

4.2.2 Properties of Retiming

Several properties of retiming can be derived from the retiming equation (4.1). Before considering these, the concepts of paths and cycles are reviewed. A path is a sequence of edges and nodes $V_0 \overset{e_0}{\rightarrow} V_1 \overset{e_1}{\rightarrow} \cdots \overset{e_{k-2}}{\rightarrow} V_{k-1} \overset{e_{k-1}}{\rightarrow} V_k$. The weight of the path p is $w(p) = \sum_{i=0}^{k-1} w(e_i)$ and the computation time of the path is $t(p) = \sum_{i=0}^{k} t(V_i)$. A cycle is a closed path $V_0 \overset{e_0}{\rightarrow} V_1 \overset{e_1}{\rightarrow} \cdots \overset{e_{k-2}}{\rightarrow} V_{k-1} \overset{e_{k-1}}{\rightarrow} V_0$. The weight of the cycle c is $w(c) = \sum_{i=0}^{k-1} w(e_i)$ and the delay of the cycle is $t(c) = \sum_{i=0}^{k-1} t(V_i)$.

Property 4.2.1 *The weight of the retimed path* $p = V_0 \overset{e_0}{\rightarrow} V_1 \overset{e_1}{\rightarrow} \cdots \overset{e_{k-1}}{\rightarrow} V_k$ *is given by* $w_r(p) = w(p) + r(V_k) - r(V_0)$.

The retimed path weight is

$$
\begin{aligned}
w_r(p) &= \sum_{i=0}^{k-1} w_r(e_i) \\
&= \sum_{i=0}^{k-1} (w(e_i) + r(V_{i+1}) - r(V_i)) \\
&= \sum_{i=0}^{k-1} w(e_i) + \left(\sum_{i=0}^{k-1} r(V_{i+1}) - \sum_{i=0}^{k-1} r(V_i) \right) \\
&= w(p) + r(V_k) - r(V_0).
\end{aligned}
$$

For example, the path $2 \to 1 \to 3$ in Fig. 4.2(a) has 2 delays, and this path in the retimed DFG in Fig. 4.2(b) has $2 + r(3) - r(2) = 2 + 0 - 1 = 1$ delay.

Property 4.2.2 *Retiming does not change the number of delays in a cycle.*

This is a special case of Property 4.2.1 where $V_k = V_0$. The weight of the retimed cycle c is $w_r(c) = w(c) + r(V_0) - r(V_0) = w(c)$. In Fig. 4.2, the cycle $1 \to 3 \to 2 \to 1$ contains 2 delays in the unretimed and retimed DFGs, and the cycle $1 \to 4 \to 2 \to 1$ contains 3 delays in the unretimed and retimed DFGs.

Property 4.2.3 *Retiming does not alter the iteration bound in a DFG.*

Property 4.2.4 *Adding the constant value j to the retiming value of each node does not change the mapping from G to G_r.*

After replacing $r(V)$ with $r(V) + j$ for each node, the weight of the retimed edge $U \xrightarrow{e} V$ in G_r is

$$w_r(e) = w(e) + (r(V) + j) - (r(U) + j) = w(e) + r(V) - r(U),$$

which is the same for any value of j (including $j = 0$). Recall that the retiming values $r(1) = 0, r(2) = 1, r(3) = 0$, and $r(4) = 0$ were used to obtain the retimed DFG in Fig. 4.2(b) from the unretimed DFG in Fig. 4.2(a). By adding, for example, the constant -38 to these retiming values, the retiming values $r(1) = -38, r(2) = -37, r(3) = -38$, and $r(4) = -38$ can be used to obtain the retimed DFG in Fig. 4.2(b) from the DFG in Fig. 4.2(a).

4.3 SOLVING SYSTEMS OF INEQUALITIES

Given a set of M inequalities in N variables, where each inequality has the form $r_i - r_j \le k$ for integer values of k, one of the shortest path algorithms in Appendix A can be used to determine if a solution exists and to find a solution if one does indeed exist. This is done using the following procedure.

1. Draw a constraint graph.

    (a) Draw the node i for each of the N variables $r_i, i = 1, 2, \ldots, N$.

    (b) Draw the node $N + 1$.

    (c) For each inequality $r_i - r_j \le k$, draw the edge $j \to i$ from node j to node i with length k.

    (d) For each node $i, i = 1, 2, \ldots, n$, draw the edge $N + 1 \to i$ from the node $N + 1$ to the node i with length 0.

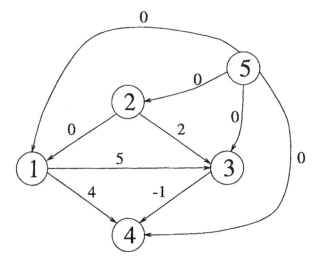

Fig. 4.3   The constraint graph for Example 4.3.1.

2. Solve using a shortest path algorithm.

    (a) The system of inequalities has a solution if and only if the constraint graph contains no negative cycles.

    (b) If a solution exists, one solution is where r_i is the minimum-length path from the node $N + 1$ to the node i.

Example 4.3.1 *In this example we demonstrate how shortest path algorithms can be used to solve a system of $M = 5$ inequalities*

$$
\begin{aligned}
r_1 - r_2 &\le 0 \\
r_3 - r_1 &\le 5 \\
r_4 - r_1 &\le 4 \\
r_4 - r_3 &\le -1 \\
r_3 - r_2 &\le 2.
\end{aligned}
$$

in $N = 4$ variables. The 1st step is to draw the constraint graph, which is shown in Fig. 4.3.

    Using the Bellman-Ford algorithm (described in Section A.2 of Appendix A), where the origin U is the node 5, we find that there are no negative cycles, so the solution can be found by examining $r^{(4)}(V)$. From $r^{(4)}(1) = 0$, $r^{(4)}(2) = 0$, $r^{(4)}(3) = 0$, $r^{(4)}(4) = -1$, and $r^{(4)}(5) = 0$, a solution to the system of inequalities is determined to be $r_1 = 0$, $r_2 = 0$, $r_3 = 0$, and $r_4 = -1$.

Using the Floyd-Warshall algorithm (described in Section A.3 of Appendix A), we find that there are no cycles, so the solution can be found by examining

$$
\mathbf{R}^{(6)} = \begin{bmatrix} \infty & \infty & 5 & 4 & \infty \\ 0 & \infty & 2 & 1 & \infty \\ \infty & \infty & \infty & -1 & \infty \\ \infty & \infty & \infty & \infty & \infty \\ 0 & 0 & 0 & -1 & \infty \end{bmatrix},
$$

where the element U, V in the matrix $\mathbf{R}^{(6)}$ is $r^{(6)}(U, V)$. The bottom row of $\mathbf{R}^{(6)}$ gives $r^{(6)}(5, V)$ for $V = 1, 2, 3, 4, 5$. The solution to the system of inequalities, given by $r^{(6)}(5, V)$ for $V = 1, 2, 3, 4$, is $r_1 = 0$, $r_2 = 0$, $r_3 = 0$, and $r_4 = -1$. ∎

When solving systems of inequalities, there may be multiple inequalities with identical left-hand sides, which can lead to parallel edges in Step 1(c). For example, the 2 inequalities $r(1) - r(2) \le 9$ and $r(1) - r(2) \le 7$ would lead to 2 edges from node 2 to node 1 with weights 9 and 7. When this happens, the most restrictive of these inequalities should be selected to avoid drawing parallel edges in Step 1(c). For example, the 2 inequalities $r(1) - r(2) \le 9$ and $r(1) - r(2) \le 7$ can be represented by simply using $r(1) - r(2) \le 7$ because this is the most restrictive of the two, and Step 1(c) results in only 1 edge from node 2 to node 1 with weight 7.

4.4   RETIMING TECHNIQUES

This section considers some techniques used for retiming. First, two special cases of retiming, namely, *cutset retiming* and *pipelining*, are considered. Two algorithms are then considered for retiming to minimize the clock period and retiming to minimize the number of registers that are required to implement the circuit.

4.4.1   Cutset Retiming and Pipelining

Cutset retiming is a useful technique that is a special case of retiming. A *cutset* is a set of edges that can be removed from the graph to create 2 disconnected subgraphs. Cutset retiming only affects the weights of the edges in the cutset. If the 2 disconnected subgraphs are labeled G_1 and G_2, then cutset retiming consists of adding k delays to each edge from G_1 to G_2 and removing k delays from each edge from G_2 to G_1. For example, a cutset is shown with a dashed line in Fig. 4.4(a). The 3 edges in the cutset are $2 \to 1$, $3 \to 2$, and $1 \to 4$. The 2 subgraphs G_1 and G_2 found by removing the 3 edges in the cutset are shown in Fig. 4.4(b). For $k = 1$, the result of cutset retiming is shown in Fig. 4.4(c). The edges from G_1 to G_2 are $3 \to 2$ and $1 \to 4$, and one delay

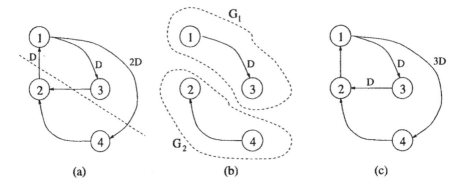

Fig. 4.4 (a) The unretimed DFG with a cutset shown as a dashed line. (b) The 2 graphs G_1 and G_2 formed by removing the edges in the cutset. (c) The retimed graph found using cutset retiming with $k = 1$.

is added to each of these edges. The edge from G_2 to G_1 is $2 \to 1$, and one delay is subtracted from this edge.

Cutset retiming is a special case of retiming where each node in the subgraph G_1 has the retiming value j and each node in the subgraph G_2 has the retiming value $j + k$. The value of j is unimportant due to Property 4.2.4. For the example in Fig. 4.4, using the values $j = 0$ and $k = 1$ results in $r(1) = 0$, $r(2) = 1$, $r(3) = 0$, and $r(4) = 1$, and this maps the DFG in Fig. 4.4(a) to the DFG in Fig. 4.4(c). Any value of j results in the same retimed graph.

For feasibility of the retimed graph, $w_r(e) \geq 0$ must hold for all edges e in G_r. Let $e_{1,2}$ represent an edge from G_1 to G_2, and let $e_{2,1}$ represent an edge from G_2 to G_1. Since cutset retiming adds k delays to each edge from G_1 to G_2, $w_r(e_{1,2}) \geq 0 \Rightarrow w(e_{1,2}) + k \geq 0$ must hold. Similarly, since k delays are subtracted from each edge $e_{2,1}$ from G_2 to G_1, $w_r(e_{2,1}) \geq 0 \Rightarrow w(e_{2,1}) - k \geq 0$ must hold. Combining these 2 inequalities and considering all of the edges in the cutset result in

$$ - \min_{G_1 \overset{e}{\to} G_2} \{w(e)\} \leq k \leq \min_{G_2 \overset{e}{\to} G_1} \{w(e)\} $$

as the condition on k for cutset retiming to give a feasible solution. In Fig. 4.4, $\min_{G_1 \overset{e}{\to} G_2} \{w(e)\} = \min\{0, 2\} = 0$ and $\min_{G_2 \overset{e}{\to} G_1} \{w(e)\} = 1$, so $0 \leq k \leq 1$ must hold. Since $k = 0$ does nothing, $k = 1$ is the only value of k that results in a feasible retimed graph, and this graph is shown in Fig. 4.4(c).

It is interesting to see what happens when the cutset is chosen so the subgraph G_2 is a single node and the subgraph G_1 is the rest of the graph minus the edges going into and out of the chosen node. An example of such a cutset is shown in Fig. 4.5(a), and the 2 subgraphs G_1 and G_2 are shown in Fig. 4.5(b). The graph G_2 consists of the node 2, and the graph G_1 consists of the rest of the graph except the 3 edges that go into and out of the node 2.

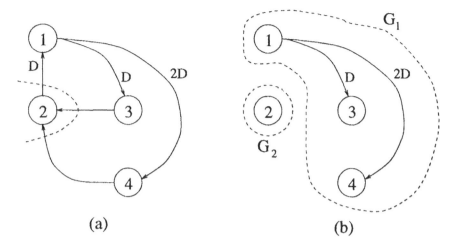

Fig. 4.5 (a) The unretimed DFG with a cutset shown as a dashed line. (b) The 2 graphs G_1 and G_2 formed by removing the edges in the cutset. The retimed graph is shown in Fig. 4.2(c).

The result of cutset retiming in this case is found by adding 1 delay to each edge incident into the node 2 and subtracting 1 delay from each edge outgoing from the node 2 as shown in Fig. 4.2(c). Therefore, this special case of cutset retiming consists of choosing a node as a cutset and subtracting one delay from each edge outgoing from the node and adding one delay to each edge incident into the node.

Pipelining is a special case of cutset retiming where there are no edges in the cutset from the subgraph G_2 to the subgraph G_1, i.e., pipelining applies to graphs without loops. These cutsets are referred to as feed-forward cutsets. The feed-forward cutset shown in Fig. 4.6(a) divides the graph into the 2 subgraphs shown in Fig. 4.6(b). All 3 of the edges in the cutset go from G_1 to G_2, and performing cutset retiming with $k = 2$ results in 2 additional delays on each edge in the cutset, resulting in the retimed (or pipelined, in this case) graph in Fig. 4.6(c). This demonstrates that pipelining can be viewed as a special case of retiming.

Cutset retiming is often used in combination with *slow-down*. The procedure is to first replace each delay in the DFG with N delays to create an *N-slow* version of the DFG and then to perform cutset retiming on the N-slow DFG. Note that in an N-slow system, $N - 1$ null operations (or 0 samples) must be interleaved after each useful signal sample to preserve the functionality of the algorithm. For example, consider the 100-stage lattice filter in Fig. 4.7(a), which has a critical path of 101 adders and 2 multipliers. Assuming that addition and multiplication take 1 and 2 u.t., respectively, the minimum sample period is $(101)(1) + (2)(2) = 105$ u.t. The 2-slow version of this circuit is shown in Fig. 4.7(b), and cutset retiming can be used to obtain

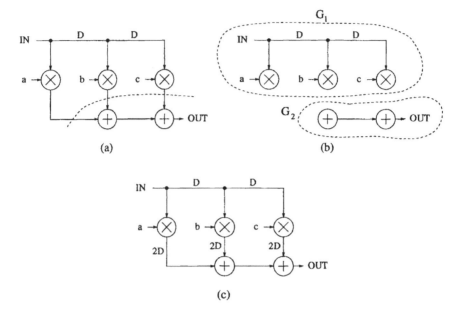

Fig. 4.6 (a) The unretimed DFG with a cutset shown as a dashed line. (b) The 2 graphs G_1 and G_2 formed by removing the edges in the cutset. (c) The graph obtained by cutset retiming with $k = 2$.

the circuit in Fig. 4.7(c). The critical path of the retimed circuit has 2 adders and 2 multipliers and has computation time $(2)(1) + (2)(2) = 6$ u.t. Since this circuit is 2-slow, the minimum sample period is $(2)(6) = 12$ u.t. In this example, slow-down and cutset retiming reduce the sample period from 105 u.t. to 12 u.t.

To summarize, cutset retiming is a special case of retiming, and pipelining is a special case of cutset retiming. Cutset retiming and pipelining are graphical techniques that can be used to perform complex retiming operations in a simple manner.

4.4.2   Retiming for Clock Period Minimization

This section presents a retiming algorithm for minimizing the clock period of a synchronous circuit. For a circuit G, the minimum feasible clock period is the computation time of the critical path, which is the path with the longest computation time among all paths with no delays. Mathematically, the minimum feasible clock period, $\Phi(G)$, is defined as

$$\Phi(G) = \max\{t(p) : w(p) = 0\}.$$

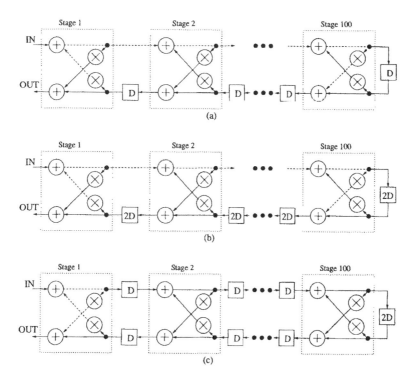

Fig. 4.7 In each of the 3 filters in this figure, the critical path is shown with dotted lines, and addition and multiplication are assumed to take 1 and 2 u.t., respectively. (a) A 100-stage lattice filter with minimum sample period of 105 u.t. (b) The 2-slow version of the circuit. (c) A retimed version of the 2-slow circuit with critical path of 6 u.t. and minimum sample period of 12 u.t.

The algorithm presented in this section finds a retiming solution r_0 such that $\Phi(G_{r_0}) \leq \Phi(G_r)$ for any other retiming solution r.

The 2 quantities $W(U, V)$ and $D(U, V)$ are used in this algorithm. The quantity $W(U, V)$ is the minimum number of registers on any path from node U to node V, and $D(U, V)$ is the maximum computation time among all paths from U to V with weight $W(U, V)$. Formally,

$$W(U, V) = \min\{w(p) : U \overset{p}{\leadsto} V\}$$
$$D(U, V) = \max\{t(p) : U \overset{p}{\leadsto} V \text{ and } w(p) = W(U, V)\}.$$

The following algorithm can be used to compute $W(U, V)$ and $D(U, V)$.

1. Let $M = t_{max}n$, where t_{max} is the maximum computation time of the nodes in G and n is the number of nodes in G.

2. Form a new graph G' which is the same as G except the edge weights are replaced by $w'(e) = Mw(e) - t(U)$ for all edges $U \overset{e}{\to} V$.

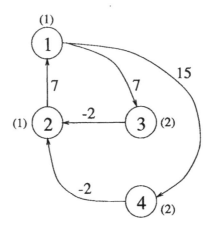

Fig. 4.8 The graph G' used to compute $W(U,V)$ and $D(U,V)$ for the DFG in Fig. 4.2(a).

3. Solve the all-pairs shortest path problem on G'. Let S'_{UV} be the shortest path from U to V.

4. If $U \neq V$, then $W(U,V) = \left\lceil \frac{S'_{UV}}{M} \right\rceil$ and $D(U,V) = MW(U,V) - S'_{UV} + t(V)$. If $U = V$, then $W(U,V) = 0$ and $D(U,V) = t(U)$.

The value of $\lceil x \rceil$ is the ceiling of x, which is the smallest integer greater than or equal to x.

To demonstrate this algorithm, the values of $W(U,V)$ and $D(U,V)$ are computed for the DFG in Fig. 4.2(a). In the first step, $t_{max} = 2$ and $n = 4$, so $M = 8$. The new graph G' (found in the second step) is shown in Fig. 4.8. The solution to the all-pairs shortest path problem for G' can be found using the Floyd-Warshall algorithm, which is described in Section A.3 of Appendix A. This solution (found in the third step), and the values of $W(U,V)$ and $D(U,V)$ (found in the final step) are given in Table 4.1.

The values of $W(U,V)$ and $D(U,V)$ are used to determine if there is a retiming solution that can achieve a desired clock period. Given a desired clock period c, there is a feasible retiming solution r such that $\Phi(G_r) \leq c$ if the following constraints hold

1. (feasibility constraint) $r(U) - r(V) \leq w(e)$ for every edge $U \xrightarrow{e} V$ of G, and

2. (critical path constraint) $r(U) - r(V) \leq W(U,V) - 1$ for all vertices U, V in G such that $D(U,V) > c$.

The feasibility constraint forces the number of delays on each edge in the retimed graph to be nonnegative, and the critical path constraint enforces

Table 4.1   Values of S'_{UV}, $W(U,V)$, and $D(U,V)$ for the DFG in Fig. 4.2(a)

S'_{UV}	1	2	3	4	$W(U,V)$	1	2	3	4
1	12	5	7	15	1	0	1	1	2
2	7	12	14	22	2	1	0	2	3
3	5	-2	12	20	3	1	0	0	3
4	5	-2	12	20	4	1	0	2	0

$D(U,V)$	1	2	3	4
1	1	4	3	3
2	2	1	4	4
3	4	3	2	6
4	4	3	6	2

$\Phi(G) \leq c$. If $D(U,V) > c$, then $W(U,V) + r(V) - r(U) \geq 1$ must hold for the critical path to have computation time less than or equal to c. This leads to the critical path constraint. For the DFG in Fig. 4.2(a), if c is chosen to be 3, the inequalities $r(U) - r(V) \leq w(e)$ for every edge $U \xrightarrow{e} V$ are

$$
\begin{aligned}
r(1) - r(3) &\leq 1 \\
r(1) - r(4) &\leq 2 \\
r(2) - r(1) &\leq 1 \\
r(3) - r(2) &\leq 0 \\
r(4) - r(2) &\leq 0,
\end{aligned}
\tag{4.2}
$$

and the inequalities $r(U) - r(V) \leq W(U,V) - 1$ for all vertices U, V in G such that $D(U,V) > 3$, found using Table 4.1, are

$$
\begin{aligned}
r(1) - r(2) &\leq 0 \\
r(2) - r(3) &\leq 1 \\
r(2) - r(4) &\leq 2 \\
r(3) - r(1) &\leq 0 \\
r(3) - r(4) &\leq 2 \\
r(4) - r(1) &\leq 0 \\
r(4) - r(3) &\leq 1.
\end{aligned}
\tag{4.3}
$$

If there is a solution to the 12 inequalities in (4.2) and (4.3), then the solution is a feasible retiming solution such that the circuit can be clocked with period $c = 3$. Checking for a solution can be performed by constructing a constraint graph and solving a single-source shortest path problem, as described in Section 4.3. The constraint graph for the 12 inequalities in (4.2) and (4.3) is shown in

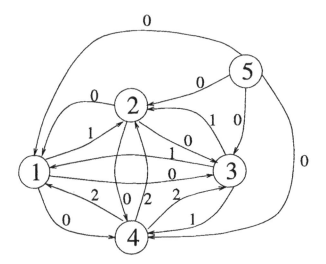

Fig. 4.9 The constraint graph for the inequalities in (4.2) and (4.3).

Fig. 4.9. Using either the Bellman-Ford algorithm or the Floyd-Warshall algorithm, it can be determined that the constraint graph in Fig. 4.9 contains no negative cycles, so the retiming solution for $c = 3$ is the solution to the single-source shortest path problem with the origin at the node 5, which is $r(1) = r(2) = r(3) = r(4) = 0$. This is intuitive since the DFG in Fig. 4.2(a) already has $\Phi(G) = 3$ so no retiming needs to be performed to achieve a clock period of 3 u.t.

The fact that the 12 inequalities in (4.2) and (4.3) have a solution indicates that the minimum clock period for the circuit in Fig. 4.2(a) is less than or equal to 3. It has been shown that the minimum clock period for the DFG is $D(U, V)$ for some pair U, V [1]. To find the minimum feasible clock period, we can attempt to solve the retiming equations for c equal to each unique value of $D(U, V)$ and find the minimum value of c with a solution. From the $D(U, V)$ values in Table 4.1, the unique values of $D(U, V)$ are 1, 2, 3, 4, and 6. A clock period of $c = 1$ is not feasible because the nodes 3 and 4 have computation time greater than 1 u.t. A clock period of $c = 3$ is feasible because the constraint graph in Fig. 4.9 has a solution, so in order to determine the minimum feasible clock period for the DFG in Fig. 4.2(a), only the value of $c = 2$ must be checked.

For $c = 2$, the inequalities $r(U) - r(V) \leq w(e)$ for every edge $U \xrightarrow{e} V$ are given in (4.2) (these inequalities are a function of the DFG and not c) and the inequalities $r(U) - r(V) \leq W(U, V) - 1$ for all vertices U, V in G such that $D(U, V) > 2$ are

$$r(1) - r(2) \leq 0$$
$$r(1) - r(3) \leq 0$$

$$r(1) - r(4) \leq 1$$
$$r(2) - r(3) \leq 1$$
$$r(2) - r(4) \leq 2$$
$$r(3) - r(1) \leq 0$$
$$r(3) - r(2) \leq -1$$
$$r(3) - r(4) \leq 2$$
$$r(4) - r(1) \leq 0$$
$$r(4) - r(2) \leq -1$$
$$r(4) - r(3) \leq 1. \tag{4.4}$$

The equations for a feasible retiming solution with clock period $c = 2$ are given in (4.2) and (4.4). Combining the equations in (4.2) and (4.4) that have identical left-hand sides results in the set of equations

$$r(1) - r(3) \leq 0$$
$$r(1) - r(4) \leq 1$$
$$r(2) - r(1) \leq 1$$
$$r(3) - r(2) \leq -1$$
$$r(4) - r(2) \leq -1$$
$$r(1) - r(2) \leq 0$$
$$r(2) - r(3) \leq 1$$
$$r(2) - r(4) \leq 2$$
$$r(3) - r(1) \leq 0$$
$$r(3) - r(4) \leq 2$$
$$r(4) - r(1) \leq 0$$
$$r(4) - r(3) \leq 1. \tag{4.5}$$

The constraint graph for the 12 inequalities in (4.5) is shown in Fig. 4.10. Using the Bellman-Ford algorithm or Floyd-Warshall algorithm, it can be determined that this graph contains no negative cycles, so the retiming solution for $c = 2$ is the solution to the single-source shortest path problem with the origin at the node 5, which is $r(1) = -1$, $r(2) = 0$, $r(3) = -1$, and $r(4) = -1$. This solution, which has clock period $\Phi(G_r) = 2$, is the retimed version of Fig. 4.2(a) and is shown in Fig. 4.2(b).

The general approach to finding a retiming solution with the minimum clock period is to 1st compute $W(U, V)$ and $D(U, V)$ and then sort the values of $D(U, V)$ and perform a *binary search* on these values to find the retiming solution with the minimum clock period. Computation of $W(U, V)$ and $D(U, V)$ can be done in $\mathcal{O}(n^3)$ time using the Floyd-Warshall algorithm. The maximum number of distinct values of $D(U, V)$ is n^2 (if all values of $D(U, V)$ are

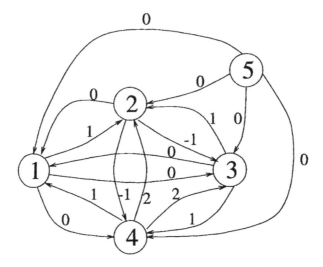

Fig. 4.10   The constraint graph for the inequalities in (4.5).

distinct), so the binary search takes $\mathcal{O}(\log n)$ steps. Checking if one of these values is greater than or equal to the minimum clock period takes $\mathcal{O}(n^3)$ time using either the Floyd-Warshall algorithm or the Bellman-Ford algorithm. Therefore, the time complexity required to find a retimed circuit with the minimum clock period is $\mathcal{O}(n^3 \log n)$. Note that if the iteration bound is known, then only those values in $D(U, V)$ that are greater than or equal to the iteration bound should be considered.

4.4.3   Retiming for Register Minimization

This section presents an algorithm for finding a retiming solution that uses the minimum number of registers while satisfying the clock period constraint.

If a node has several output edges carrying the same signal, the number of registers required to implement these edges is the maximum number of registers on any one of the edges. This is demonstrated in Fig. 4.11, where the naive implementation in Fig. 4.11(a) uses $1 + 3 + 7 = 11$ registers while the clever implementation in Fig. 4.11(b) uses $\max(1, 3, 7) = 7$ registers. Using this concept, the number of registers required to implement the output edges of the node V in the retimed graph is

$$R_V = \max_{V \xrightarrow{e} ?}\{w_r(e)\},$$

and the total register cost in the retimed circuit is $COST = \sum R_V$.

The formulation of retiming to minimize the number of registers under the constraint that the clock period is not greater than c is: Minimize $COST =$

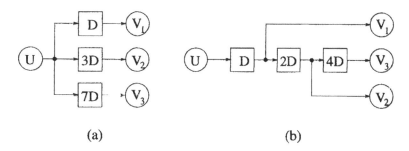

Fig. 4.11 (a) Fanout implementation using $1 + 3 + 7 = 11$ registers. (b) Fanout implementation using $\max(1, 3, 7) = 7$ registers.

$\sum R_V$ subject to

1. (fanout constraint) $R_V \geq w_r(e)$ for all V and all edges $V \xrightarrow{e} ?$.

2. (feasibility constraint) $r(U) - r(V) \leq w(e)$ for every edge $U \xrightarrow{e} V$.

3. (clock period constraint) $r(U) - r(V) \leq W(U, V) - 1$ for all vertices U, V such that $D(U, V) > c$.

The fanout constraint simply makes sure that $R_V = \max_{V \xrightarrow{e} ?}\{w_r(e)\}$. An algorithm for computing $W(U, V)$ and $D(U, V)$ is presented in Section 4.4.2, along with descriptions of the feasibility constraint and clock period constraint.

While this formulation of retiming indeed minimizes the number of registers under a clock period constraint, it is not in a form that can be solved using linear programming (LP) techniques because some solutions may not be integers. To get the formulation in such a form, a "gadget" is used to represent nodes with multiple output edges [1]. This gadget is shown in Fig. 4.12. Fig. 4.12(a) shows a fanout node with k output edges. The gadget in Fig. 4.12(b) is used to model the fanout node. Each of the k edges e_i, $1 \leq i \leq k$, has an associated weight $w(e_i)$ which is known from the DFG. The node $\hat{U}$ is a dummy node with zero computation time $(t(\hat{U}) = 0)$, and the edges $\hat{e}_i$, $1 \leq i \leq k$, are dummy edges introduced so the retiming for register minimization problem can be modeled as a linear programming problem. The weight of the edge $\hat{e}_i$ is defined to be $w(\hat{e}_i) = w_{max} - w(e_i)$, where $w_{max} = \max_{1 \leq i \leq k} w(e_i)$. In addition to its weight, each edge in this model also has a breadth β associated with it. This breadth of an edge is simply a number used so that the gadget in Fig. 4.12(b) properly models the memory required by the edges e_i, $1 \leq i \leq k$, in the retimed DFG (the details of this are explained a bit later). The breadth of each of the edges e_i and $\hat{e}_i$ for $1 \leq i \leq k$ is $\beta = 1/k$, as shown in Fig. 4.12(b).

Using the fanout model in Fig. 4.12, the retiming formulation is: Minimize $COST = \sum_e \beta(e)w_r(e)$ subject to

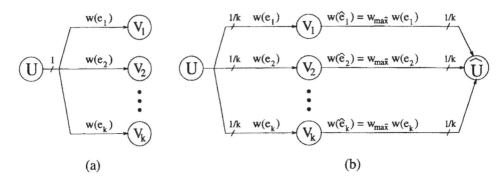

Fig. 4.12 (a) A node U with k output edges. (b) A gadget used to model the node U.

1. (feasibility constraint) $r(U) - r(V) \leq w(e)$ for every edge $U \overset{e}{\rightarrow} V$.

2. (clock period constraint) $r(U) - r(V) \leq W(U,V) - 1$ for all vertices U, V such that $D(U,V) > c$.

The expression for $COST$ can be rewritten as

$$
\begin{aligned}
COST &= \sum_e \beta(e) w_r(e) \\
&= \sum_e \beta(e)(w(e) + r(V) - r(U)) \\
&= \sum_e \beta(e) w(e) + \sum_e \beta(e)(r(V) - r(U)) \\
&= K + \sum_e \beta(e)(r(V) - r(U)) \\
&= K + \sum_V r(V) \left(\sum_{? \overset{e}{\rightarrow} V} \beta(e) - \sum_{V \overset{e}{\rightarrow} ?} \beta(e) \right).
\end{aligned}
$$

Since K is a constant, the formulation can be written as Minimize $COST' = \sum_V r(V) \left(\sum_{? \overset{e}{\rightarrow} V} \beta(e) - \sum_{V \overset{e}{\rightarrow} ?} \beta(e) \right)$ subject to

1. (feasibility constraint) $r(U) - r(V) \leq w(e)$ for every edge $U \overset{e}{\rightarrow} V$.

2. (clock period constraint) $r(U) - r(V) \leq W(U,V) - 1$ for all vertices U, V such that $D(U,V) > c$.

To demonstrate this, the DFG in Fig. 4.2(a) is retimed so the number of registers is minimized while maintaining a clock period of $\Phi(G_r) \leq 2$. The 1st step is to redraw this DFG as shown in Fig. 4.13(a) using the fanout model for node 1 because this node has more than one output edge. The 2nd step

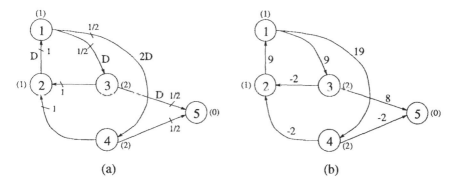

Fig. 4.13 (a) The DFG in Fig. 4.2(a) redrawn using the fanout gadget in Fig. 4.12. (b) The graph G' used to compute $W(U,V)$ and $D(U,V)$.

Table 4.2 Values of S'_{UV}, $W(U,V)$, and $D(U,V)$ for the DFG in Fig. 4.13(a)

S'_{UV}	1	2	3	4	5
1	16	7	9	19	17
2	9	16	18	28	26
3	7	-2	16	26	8
4	7	-2	16	26	-2
5	-	-	-	-	-

$W(U,V)$	1	2	3	4	5
1	0	1	1	2	2
2	1	0	2	3	3
3	1	0	0	3	1
4	1	0	2	0	0
5	-	-	-	-	0

$D(U,V)$	1	2	3	4	5
1	1	4	3	3	3
2	2	1	4	4	4
3	4	3	2	6	2
4	4	3	6	2	2
5	-	-	-	-	0

is to compute $W(U,V)$ and $D(U,V)$ for the DFG in Fig. 4.13(a). Using the procedure described in Section 4.4.2, $M = 10$, G' is shown in Fig. 4.13(b), and the values of S'_{UV}, $W(U,V)$, and $D(U,V)$ are shown in Table 4.2.

The LP formulation of the problem is: Minimize

$$\begin{aligned} COST' &= r(1)(1-1) + r(2)(2-1) + r(3)(1/2 - 3/2) + r(4)(1/2 - 3/2) \\ &\quad + r(5)(1-0) \\ &= r(2) - r(3) - r(4) + r(5) \end{aligned}$$

subject to the feasibility constraints

$$\begin{aligned} r(1) - r(3) &\leq 1 \\ r(1) - r(4) &\leq 2 \end{aligned}$$

$$r(2) - r(1) \leq 1$$
$$r(3) - r(2) \leq 0$$
$$r(3) - r(5) \leq 1$$
$$r(4) - r(2) \leq 0$$
$$r(4) - r(5) \leq 0$$

and the clock period constraints

$$r(1) - r(2) \leq 0$$
$$r(1) - r(3) \leq 0$$
$$r(1) - r(4) \leq 1$$
$$r(1) - r(5) \leq 1$$
$$r(2) - r(3) \leq 1$$
$$r(2) - r(4) \leq 2$$
$$r(2) - r(5) \leq 2$$
$$r(3) - r(1) \leq 0$$
$$r(3) - r(2) \leq -1$$
$$r(3) - r(4) \leq 2$$
$$r(4) - r(1) \leq 0$$
$$r(4) - r(2) \leq -1$$
$$r(4) - r(3) \leq 1.$$

This linear programming problem is in the form of a minimum-cost flow problem, for which algorithms exist (e.g., see [3]); however, these algorithms can be quite involved. To solve this problem, a linear programming software package such as GAMS [4] can be used. Using GAMS, the solution to this problem is $r(1) = 1$, $r(2) = 2$, $r(3) = 1$, $r(4) = 0$, and $r(5) = 0$, and the retimed graph, which uses proper register sharing between the 2 output edges of the node 1, is shown in Fig. 4.14.

It remains to show that the fanout gadget in Fig. 4.12(b) properly models the amount of memory used by a node with multiple output edges. The goal is for the sum of the weights (scaled by the breadths β) of all of the edges e_i and $\hat{e}_i$ in the fanout gadget to equal the maximum of the weights on the edges e_i in the gadget. In other words, the goal is to show that

$$\sum_{i=1}^{k} (w_r(e_i)\beta(e_i) + w_r(\hat{e}_i)\beta(\hat{e}_i)) = w_{r,max},$$

where $w_{r,max} = \max_{1 \leq i \leq k} w_r(e_i)$. This is shown using the following 3 steps.

Step 1: Assume that $w_r(e_j) = w_{r,max}$. Show that $w_r(e_j) = w_{max} + r(\hat{U}) - r(U)$.

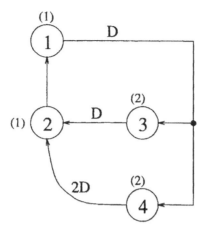

Fig. 4.14 The result of retiming the DFG in Fig. 4.2(a) to minimize the number of registers while maintaining a clock period of 2 u.t.

Step 2: Show that

$$\sum_{i=1}^{k} (w_r(e_i)\beta(e_i) + w_r(\hat{e}_i)\beta(\hat{e}_i)) = w_{max} + r(\hat{U}) - r(U).$$

Step 3: Combining steps 1 and 2 results in

$$\sum_{i=1}^{k} (w_r(e_i)\beta(e_i) + w_r(\hat{e}_i)\beta(\hat{e}_i)) = w_{max} + r(\hat{U}) - r(U) = w_r(e_j) = w_{r,max}.$$

While step 3 is trivial (assuming that steps 1 and 2 can be shown), steps 1 and 2 are not trivial. These 2 steps are described in detail.

Details of Step 1: Assume that $w_r(e_j) = w_{r,max}$. The weight of each path $p_i = U \xrightarrow{e_i} V_i \xrightarrow{\hat{e}_i} \hat{U}$ in the original DFG is

$$
\begin{aligned}
w(p_i) &= w(e_i) + (w_{max} - w(e_i)) \\
&= w_{max}.
\end{aligned}
$$

The weight of each path p_i in the retimed DFG is

$$
\begin{aligned}
w_r(p_i) &= w_r(e_i) + w_r(\hat{e}_i) \\
&= (w(e_i) + r(V_i) - r(U)) + \left(w_{max} - w(e_i) + r(\hat{U}) - r(V_i)\right) \\
&= w_{max} + r(\hat{U}) - r(U).
\end{aligned}
$$

Solving to minimize $COST$ causes $r(\hat{U})$ to be as small as possible while still forcing $w_r(\hat{e}_i) \geq 0$ for $1 \leq i \leq k$. Therefore, $w_r(\hat{e}_i) = 0$ for at least 1 edge $\hat{e}_i$. Since the value of $w_r(p_i) = w_r(e_i) + w_r(\hat{e}_i) = w_{max} + r(\hat{U}) - r(U)$ is the same for $1 \leq i \leq k$, the edge e_j with $w_r(e_j) = w_{r,max}$ is in the path p_j which has $w_r(\hat{e}_j) = 0$. Thus, $w_r(e_j) = w_r(p_j) = w_{max} + r(\hat{U}) - r(U)$. ∎

Details of Step 2: The cost of the edges in the fanout model is

$$
\begin{aligned}
COST &= \sum_{i=1}^{k} (w_r(e_i)\beta(e_i) + w_r(\hat{e}_i)\beta(\hat{e}_i)) \\
&= \frac{1}{k} \left(\sum_{i=1}^{k} (w_r(e_i) + w_r(\hat{e}_i)) \right) \\
&= \frac{1}{k}(k)\left(w_{max} + r(\hat{U}) - r(U) \right). \blacksquare
\end{aligned}
$$

4.5 CONCLUSIONS

Synchronous systems can be retimed to reduce critical path or clock period, number of storage or delay elements, or power consumption. Shortest path algorithms can be used to obtain a retiming solution if one exists. All possible retiming solutions can also be obtained by *exhaustive retiming* using approaches in [5],[6]. Retiming can also be used as a preprocessing step for folding and for computation of roundoff noise as discussed in Chapters 6 and 11, respectively. Use of retiming for reduction of power consumption is covered in Section 17.5.4. Retiming of multirate DFGs is addressed in the context of multirate folding in Section 6.5. Retiming of 2D DFGs has been addressed in [7],[8].

4.6 PROBLEMS

1. Consider the wave digital filter shown in Fig. 4.15. Assume that each multiply operation requires 20 nsec and each add operation requires 8 nsec.

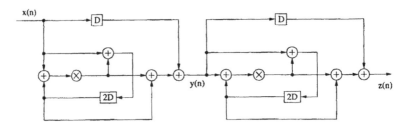

Fig. 4.15 The wave digital filter structure in Problem 1.

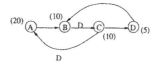

Fig. 4.16 Data-flow graph for Problem 2.

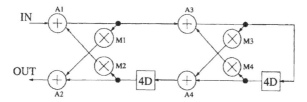

Fig. 4.17 A 4-level pipelined all-pass 8th-order IIR digital filter.

(a) Calculate the iteration period bound of this filter by inspection.

(b) What is the critical path?

(c) Manually pipeline and/or retime this filter to achieve a critical path equal to the iteration period bound.

2. Consider the DFG shown in Fig. 4.16, where the number at each node denotes its execution time.

   (a) What is the maximum sample rate of this DFG?

   (b) What is the fundamental limit on the sample period for the system described by this DFG?

   (c) Manually retime this DFG to minimize the clock period.

3. Consider the 4-level pipelined all-pass 8th-order IIR digital filter DFG in Fig. 4.17. Assume that addition and multiplication require 1 and 2 u.t., respectively.

   (a) By inspection, calculate the iteration bound.

   (b) Compute the critical path time of the circuit.

   (c) Pipeline and/or retime this system to achieve a critical path of 2 u.t. Do this by inspection (manually).

4. Consider the 6th-order orthogonal filter structure shown in Fig. 4.18. All operations in this structure are CORDIC (coordinate rotation digital computer) rotation operations, which are orthonormal. Assume that each CORDIC rotation operation requires T nsec.

   What is the iteration bound of this filter? What is the critical path of this filter? Manually pipeline and/or retime the filter structure to

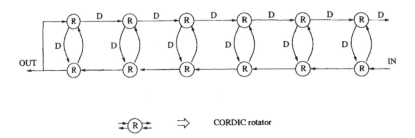

Fig. 4.18 A 6th-order orthogonal filter for Problem 4.

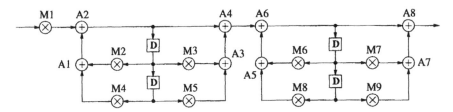

Fig. 4.19 The DFG for the 4th-order IIR filter in Problem 5.

achieve a critical path of computation $2T$ nsec. Show all the cutset locations used for retiming explicitly.

5. The DFG shown in Fig. 4.19 describes a 4th-order IIR digital filter implemented as cascade of 2 2nd-order sections. Assume each multiply requires 2 u.t. and add requires 1 u.t.

   (a) What is the critical path of this DFG? What is the iteration bound of this DFG?

   (b) Manually retime and pipeline the DFG to minimize the clock period. What is the minimum achievable clock period obtained with pipelining and retiming?

6. For the biquad filter in Fig. 4.20, assume that addition and multiplication require 1 and 2 u.t., respectively. There are 120 unique retiming solutions that retime this filter to have a clock period of 4 u.t. Find 10 of these solutions by inspection.

7. For the DFG in Fig. 4.20, find the retimed DFG for $r(1) = 0$, $r(2) = 0$, $r(3) = -1$, $r(4) = -2$, $r(5) = -1$, $r(6) = 0$, $r(7) = 0$, and $r(8) = 0$.

8. Draw a constraint graph and use it to determine if the following system of inequalities has a solution, and find a solution if one exists using

   (a) the Bellman-Ford algorithm, and

   (b) the Floyd-Warshall algorithm.

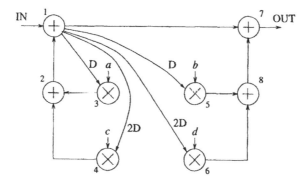

Fig. 4.20 The biquad filter. The numbers next to the nodes are node labels used in Problem 7, not execution times.

$$r_1 - r_2 \leq 1$$
$$r_3 - r_1 \leq 3$$
$$r_4 - r_1 \leq 2$$
$$r_4 - r_3 \leq -1$$
$$r_3 - r_2 \leq 1$$
$$r_5 - r_1 \leq 2$$
$$r_3 - r_5 \leq -1$$
$$r_4 - r_5 \leq -2.$$

9. Draw a constraint graph and use it to determine if the following system of inequalities has a solution, and find a solution if one exists using

   (a) the Bellman-Ford algorithm, and
   (b) the Floyd-Warshall algorithm.

$$r_1 - r_2 \leq 1$$
$$r_3 - r_1 \leq 3$$
$$r_4 - r_1 \leq 2$$
$$r_4 - r_3 \leq -1$$
$$r_3 - r_2 \leq 1$$
$$r_5 - r_1 \leq 2$$
$$r_3 - r_5 \leq -6$$
$$r_4 - r_5 \leq -2.$$

10. Retime/pipeline the IIR digital filter shown in Fig. 3.21 (see Problem 2 of Chapter 3) to reduce the critical path to 2 time units.

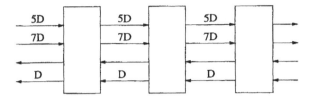

Fig. 4.21   The recursive DFG used in Problem 11(a).

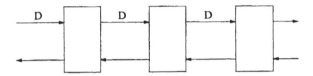

Fig. 4.22   The recursive DFG used in Problem 11(b).

11. This problem addresses interblock pipelining of recursive DFGs.

   (a) Retime the system shown in Fig. 4.21 to achieve interblock pipelin-
       ing, i.e., each interblock communicating edge should have at least
       one delay element.

   (b) To obtain interblock pipelining for the system shown in Fig. 4.22,
       use an appropriate slow-down approach and then use retiming.
       What is the hardware utilization efficiency of this system?

12. Consider the N-stage normalized lattice filter in Fig. 4.23. Let $N = 25$,
    i.e., the filter has 25 modules, and assume that addition and multiplica-
    tion take 1 and 2 u.t., respectively.

   (a) Compute the critical path and the minimum clock period for this
       filter.

   (b) Using a 2-slow transformation, retime the filter so that it is pipelined
       at the module level, i.e., each wire between modules has at least one
       delay. What is the clock period and sample period of the retimed
       filter?

13. The objective of this problem is to write a program to retime a DFG
    for clock period minimization. Assume that addition and multiplication
    require 1 and 2 u.t., respectively. Formulate the constraints for retiming
    and use your program to determine the minimum clock period for the
    direct-form 3rd-order IIR filter in Fig. 4.24.

14. Repeat Problem 13 for the DFG in Fig. 4.25, which represents a 5th-
    order wave digital elliptic filter.

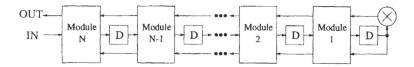

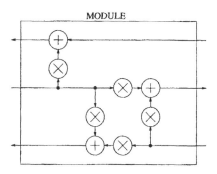

Fig. 4.23   The *N*-stage normalized lattice filter.

15. Repeat Problem 13 for the DFG in Fig. 2.17, which represents a 1-multiplier basic lattice IIR digital filter.

16. Systematically retime the DFG used in Problem 13 to minimize the number of registers while achieving a clock period of 4 u.t. Assume that addition and multiplication require 1 and 2 u.t., respectively.

17. Systematically retime the DFG used in Problem 3 to minimize the number of registers while achieving a clock period of 2 u.t. Assume that addition and multiplication require 1 and 2 u.t., respectively.

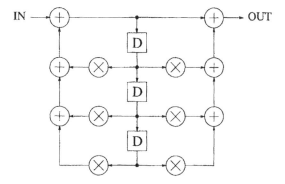

Fig. 4.24   Direct-form 3rd-order IIR filter.

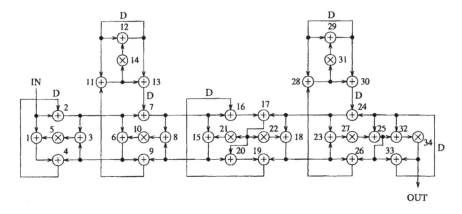

Fig. 4.25   A 5th-order wave digital elliptic filter.

REFERENCES

1. C. Leiserson, F. Rose, and J. Saxe, "Optimizing synchronous circuitry by re-timing," in *Third Caltech Conference on VLSI*, pp. 87–116, 1983.

2. J. Monteiro, S. Devadas, and A. Ghosh, "Retiming sequential circuits for low power," in *Proc. of IEEE International Conference on Computer Aided Design*, pp. 398–402, 1993.

3. E. L. Lawler, *Combinatorial Optimization: Networks and Matriods*. Holt, Rinehard and Winston, 1976.

4. A. Brooke, D. Kendrick, and A. Meeraus, *GAMS: A User's Guide, Release 2.25*. The Scientific Press, 1992.

5. S. Simon, E. Bernard, M. Sauer, and J. Nossek, "A new retiming algorithm for circuit design," in *Proc. of IEEE International Symposium on Circuits and Systems (ISCAS)*, (London, England), May 1994.

6. T. C. Denk and K. K. Parhi, "Exhaustive scheduling and retiming of digital signal processing systems," *IEEE Trans. on Circuits and Systems–II: Analog and Digital Signal Processing*, vol. 45, no. 7, pp. 821-838, July 1998.

7. T. C. Denk and K. K. Parhi, "Two-dimensional retiming", *IEEE Trans. on VLSI Systems*, vol. 7, 1999.

8. N. Passos and E. H.-M. Sha, "Full parallelism in uniform nested loops using multi-dimensional retiming," in *Proc. of International Conference on Parallel Processing*, 1994.

5
Unfolding

5.1 INTRODUCTION

Unfolding is a transformation technique that can be applied to a DSP program
to create a new program describing more than one iteration of the original
program. More specifically, unfolding a DSP program by the *unfolding factor*
J creates a new program that describes J consecutive iterations of the original
program. Unfolding is also referred to as loop unrolling and has been used in
compiler theory [1].

For example, consider the DSP program

$$y(n) = ay(n-9) + x(n) \tag{5.1}$$

for $n = 0$ to ∞, which is shown in Fig. 5.1(a). Replacing the index n with $2k$
results in $y(2k) = ay(2k-9) + x(2k)$ for $k = 0$ to ∞. Similarly, replacing the
index n with $2k + 1$ results in $y(2k+1) = ay(2k-8) + x(2k+1)$ for $k = 0$
to ∞. Together, the 2 equations

$$
\begin{aligned}
y(2k) &= ay(2k-9) + x(2k) \\
y(2k+1) &= ay(2k-8) + x(2k+1)
\end{aligned}
\tag{5.2}
$$

describe the same program as (5.1). The program in (5.2) describes 2 consecutive iterations of the program in (5.1). For example, for $k = 7$, the equations
in (5.2) are $y(14) = ay(5) + x(14)$ and $y(15) = ay(6) + x(15)$. These equations are the same as those described in (5.1) for the 2 consecutive iterations
$n = 14$ and $n = 15$. The program in (5.2) describes a 2-*unfolded* version of

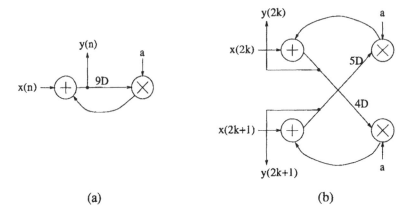

(a)   (b)

Fig. 5.1   (a) The original DSP program describing $y(n) = ay(n-9) + x(n)$ for $n = 0$ to ∞. (b) The 2-unfolded DSP program describing $y(2k) = ay(2k-9) + x(2k)$ and $y(2k+1) = ay(2k-8) + x(2k+1)$ for $k = 0$ to ∞.

the program in (5.1).

In unfolded systems, each delay is *J-slow*. This means that if the input to a delay element is the signal $x(kJ + m)$, the output of the delay element is $x((k-1)J + m) = x(kJ + m - J)$. The 2-unfolded program corresponding to the equations in (5.2) is shown in Fig. 5.1(b). Using the concept of *J*-slow delays, Fig. 5.1(b) describes the computations $y(2k) = ay(2(k-5)+1)+x(2k)$ and $y(2k+1) = ay(2(k-4)+0) + x(2k+1)$, as desired.

The 2-unfolded program shown in Fig. 5.1(b) was created by substituting $n = 2k$ and $n = 2k + 1$ into (5.1). While this technique results in a correct 2-unfolded program, it can often be tedious to write the equations for the original and *J*-unfolded programs and then draw the corresponding unfolded data-flow graph (DFG), especially for larger values of *J*. In this chapter, we describe a graph-based technique for directly unfolding the DFG to create the DFG of the *J*-unfolded program without explicitly writing the equations describing the original or unfolded program [2].

Unfolding has applications in designing high-speed and low-power VLSI architectures [3] –[5]. One application is to unfold the program to reveal hidden concurrencies so that the program can be scheduled to a smaller iteration period, thus increasing the throughput of the implementation. Another application is to design parallel architectures at the word level and bit level. At the word level, these architectures can be used to design word-parallel architectures from word-serial architectures to increase the throughput or decrease the power consumption of the implementation (see Chapter 3). At the bit-level, unfolding can be used to design bit-parallel and digit-serial architectures from bit-serial architectures to achieve the same objectives as word-level unfolding [6],[7].

In Section 5.2, the graph-based algorithm is presented for unfolding a DFG without writing the equations for J consecutive iterations of the program. Some properties of unfolding are discussed in Section 5.3, the relationship between critical path and order of unfolding and retiming is explored in Section 5.4, and applications of unfolding are discussed in Section 5.5. In this chapter, we always assume that the node cannot be split into two subnodes with smaller computation times.

5.2   AN ALGORITHM FOR UNFOLDING

In this section, an algorithm for unfolding a DFG by an unfolding factor J is described. Before this algorithm is presented, some notations are introduced and some basic properties of unfolded DFGs are described.

The operation $\lfloor x \rfloor$ is the floor of x, which is the largest integer less than or equal to x. For example, $\lfloor \frac{11}{4} \rfloor = 2$ and $\lfloor \frac{25}{3} \rfloor = 8$. The operation $a\%b$ is the remainder after dividing a by b, where a and b are integers. For example, $11\%4 = 3$ and $25\%3 = 1$.

For each node U in the original DFG, there are J nodes with the same function as U in the J-unfolded DFG. For example, for the adder in Fig. 5.1(a), there are 2 adders in the 2-unfolded DFG in Fig. 5.1(b). Similarly, there are 2 multipliers in Fig. 5.1(b) corresponding to the multiplier in Fig. 5.1(a).

For each edge in the original DFG, there are J edges in the J-unfolded DFG. This can be observed in Fig. 5.1, where the edge from the adder to the multiplier in the original DFG results in 2 edges from an adder to a multiplier in the unfolded DFG.

Keeping in mind that the DFG of the J-unfolded program contains J times as many nodes and edges as the DFG of the original DFG, the following unfolding algorithm can be used to construct a J-unfolded DFG.

Unfolding Algorithm

1. For each node U in the original DFG, draw the J nodes U_0, U_1, ..., U_{J-1}.

2. For each edge $U \to V$ with w delays in the original DFG, draw the J edges $U_i \to V_{(i+w)\%J}$ with $\lfloor \frac{i+w}{J} \rfloor$ delays for $i = 0, 1, \ldots, J - 1$.

A proof of correctness for this unfolding algorithm is given at the end of this section.

To demonstrate the unfolding algorithm, a DFG is constructed for the DSP program in Fig. 5.1(a), and this DFG is unfolded with unfolding factor 2 to obtain the DSP program in Fig. 5.1(b). A DFG representing the DSP program in Fig. 5.1(a) is shown in Fig. 5.2(a). In this DFG, the nodes A and B represent input and output, respectively, and the nodes C and D represent addition and multiplication by a, respectively. To unfold this DFG by unfolding factor 2,

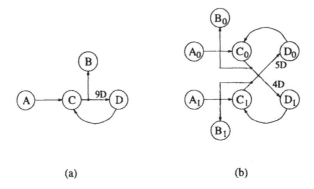

(a)   (b)

Fig. 5.2 (a) A DFG corresponding to the DSP program in Fig. 5.1(a). (b) The 2-unfolded DFG corresponding to the 2-unfolded DSP program in Fig. 5.1(b).

the 8 nodes A_i, B_i, C_i, and D_i, for $i = 0, 1$, are first drawn according to the 1st step of the unfolding algorithm. After these nodes have been drawn, the 2nd step of the unfolding algorithm needs to be performed. For an edge $U \rightarrow V$ with no delays, this step reduces to drawing the J edges $U_i \rightarrow V_i$ with no delays for $i = 0, 1, \ldots, J - 1$. For example, the edge $D \rightarrow C$ with no delays in Fig. 5.2(a) results in the two edges $D_0 \rightarrow C_0$ and $D_1 \rightarrow C_1$ with no delays in the 2-unfolded DFG in Fig. 5.2(b). For the edge $C \rightarrow D$ with $w = 9$ delays in Fig. 5.2(a), we draw the edges $C_0 \rightarrow D_{(9+0)\%2}$ with $\lfloor \frac{9+0}{2} \rfloor$ delays and $C_1 \rightarrow D_{(9+1)\%2}$ with $\lfloor \frac{9+1}{2} \rfloor$ delays, which correspond to the edges $C_0 \rightarrow D_1$ with 4 delays and $C_1 \rightarrow D_0$ with 5 delays, respectively, in Fig. 5.2(b).

Referring to Fig. 5.2, the nodes C_0 and C_1 in the 2-unfolded DFG represent addition because the node C in the original DFG represents addition (recall that the DFG in Fig. 5.2(a) represents the DSP program in Fig. 5.1(a)). Similarly, the nodes D_0 and D_1 in the 2-unfolded DFG represent multiplication by the constant a, because the node D in the original DFG represents multiplication by a. The node A in the original DFG represents the input $x(n)$. The k-th iteration of the node A_i in the unfolded DFG executes the $(Jk + i)$-th iteration of the node A in the original DFG for $i = 0, 1, \ldots, J - 1$ and $k = 0$ to ∞, so the node A_0 corresponds to the input samples $x(2k + 0)$ and the node A_1 corresponds to the input samples $x(2k + 1)$. Similarly, the node B_0 corresponds to the output samples $y(2k + 0)$ and the node B_1 corresponds to the output samples $y(2k + 1)$. Hence, the 2-unfolded DFG in Fig. 5.2(b) corresponds to the 2-unfolded DSP program in Fig. 5.1(b).

Two more examples of unfolding are shown in Figs. 5.3 and 5.4. The DFG in Fig. 5.3(a) is unfolded using unfolding factor 4 to get the DFG in Fig. 5.3(b), and the DFG in Fig. 5.4(a) is unfolded using unfolding factor 3 to get the DFG in Fig. 5.4(b).

Note that unfolding of an edge with w delays in the original DFG produces $J - w$ edges with no delays and w edges with 1 delay in J-unfolded DFG when

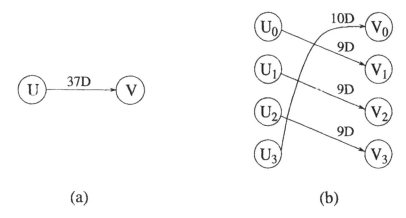

Fig. 5.3   (a) The original DFG. (b) The 4-unfolded DFG.

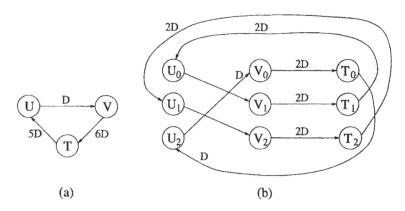

Fig. 5.4   (a) The original DFG. (b) The 3-unfolded DFG.

$w < J$.

An important property of unfolding is that *unfolding preserves precedence constraints* of a DSP program. The e edges in the original DFG explicitly show the precedence constraints for 1 iteration of the original program, and the Je edges in the J-unfolded DFG explicitly show the precedence constraints for J iterations of the program. To show that the unfolding algorithm described in this section indeed creates an unfolded DFG with the same precedence constraints as the original DFG, we need to show that the edge $U_i \rightarrow V_{(i+w)\%J}$ with $\lfloor \frac{i+w}{J} \rfloor$ delays in the unfolded DFG corresponds to the edge $U \rightarrow V$ with w delays in the original DFG.

The unfolding transformation is based on the fact that the k-th iteration of the node U_i in the J-unfolded DFG executes the $(Jk + i)$-th iteration of the node U in the original DFG. Due to the $\lfloor \frac{i+w}{J} \rfloor$ delays on the edge $U_i \rightarrow V_{(i+w)\%J}$, the output of the k-th iteration of the node U_i is consumed by the $\left(k + \lfloor \frac{i+w}{J} \rfloor\right)$-th iteration of the node $V_{(i+w)\%J}$ in the unfolded DFG. The k-th iteration of U_i corresponds to the $(Jk + i)$-th iteration of the node U, and the $\left(k + \lfloor \frac{i+w}{J} \rfloor\right)$-th iteration of $V_{(i+w)\%J}$ corresponds to the $\left(J\left(k + \lfloor \frac{i+w}{J} \rfloor\right)\right) + (i + w)\%J$-th iteration of the node V. Therefore, in the original DFG, the output of the $(Jk + i)$-th iteration of the node U is consumed by the $\left(J\left(k + \lfloor \frac{i+w}{J} \rfloor\right)\right) + (i + w)\%J$-th iteration of the node V, so the number of delays on the edge $U \rightarrow V$ is

$$J\left(k + \left\lfloor \frac{i + w}{J} \right\rfloor\right) + (i + w)\%J - (Jk + i),$$

which can be simplified as

$$\left(J\left\lfloor \frac{i + w}{J} \right\rfloor + (i + w)\%J\right) - i.$$

The value

$$J\left\lfloor \frac{i + w}{J} \right\rfloor + (i + w)\%J$$

is simply $i + w$, so the number of delays on the edge $U \rightarrow V$ is $(i + w) - i = w$, as desired.

5.3 PROPERTIES OF UNFOLDING

Some basic properties of unfolding are discussed in this section. These properties are useful when applications of unfolding are considered in Section 5.5.

Property 5.3.1 *Unfolding preserves the number of delays in a DFG.*

This property is based on the fact that the sum of the delays on the J unfolded edges $U_i \rightarrow V_{(i+w)\%J}$, $i = 0, 1, \ldots, J - 1$, is same as the number of delays on the edge $U \rightarrow V$ in the original DFG. Mathematically, this can be stated as

$$\left\lfloor \frac{w}{J} \right\rfloor + \left\lfloor \frac{w + 1}{J} \right\rfloor + \cdots + \left\lfloor \frac{w + J - 1}{J} \right\rfloor = w. \tag{5.3}$$

The proof of this is left as an exercise (see Problem 3). This property can be observed in Figs. 5.2, 5.3, and 5.4.

It is interesting to observe what happens when a loop is unfolded. Let l be a loop with w_l delays in the original DFG, and let A be a node in l. The loop l can be denoted as the path $A \xrightarrow{l} A$ with w_l delays. If the loop l is traversed p times $(p \geq 1)$, this results in the path $A \xrightarrow{l} A \xrightarrow{l} \cdots \xrightarrow{l} A$ with pw_l delays. The corresponding unfolded path starting at the the node A_i, $0 \leq i \leq J - 1$, in the J-unfolded DFG is $A_i \rightarrow A_{(i+pw_l)\%J}$, and this path forms a loop in the unfolded DFG if $i = (i + pw_l)\%J$. We would like to find the minimum value

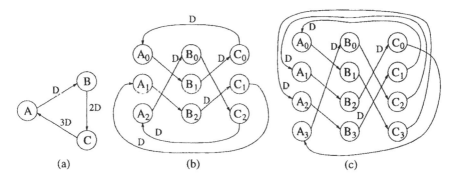

Fig. 5.5 (a) The original DFG containing a single loop. (b) The 3-unfolded DFG containing 3 loops. (c) The 4-unfolded DFG containing 2 loops.

of p (i.e., the minimum number of times that the loop l is traversed) such that the path $A_i \to A_{(i+pw_l)\%J}$ is a loop in the unfolded DFG.

For example, the DFG in Fig. 5.5(a) contains a single loop $l = A \to B \to C \to A$ with $w_l = 6$ delays. The 3-unfolded and 4-unfolded DFGs are shown in Figs. 5.5(b) and 5.5(c), respectively. For $J = 3$, the equation $i = (i + pw_l)\%J$ becomes $i = (i + 6p)\%3$, which holds for $i = 0, 1, 2$ for $p = 1$. Therefore, unfolding $p = 1$ instance of the loop results in a loop in the 3-unfolded DFG. Starting at A_0, unfolding the loop l results in the loop $A_0 \to B_1 \to C_0 \to A_0$. Starting at A_1, unfolding the loop l results in the loop $A_1 \to B_2 \to C_1 \to A_1$. Starting at A_2, unfolding the loop l results in the loop $A_2 \to B_0 \to C_2 \to A_2$. The 3-unfolded DFG consists of these 3 loops. For $J = 4$, the equation $i = (i + pw_l)\%J$ becomes $i = (i + 6p)\%4$, which does not hold for $p = 1$ but holds for $i = 0, 1, 2, 3$ for $p = 2$. Therefore, unfolding $p = 2$ instances of the loop results in a loop in the 4-unfolded DFG. Starting at A_0, unfolding the loop $l' = A \to B \to C \to A \to B \to C \to A$ results in the loop $A_0 \to B_1 \to C_3 \to A_2 \to B_3 \to C_1 \to A_0$. Starting at A_1, unfolding the loop l' results in the loop $A_1 \to B_2 \to C_0 \to A_3 \to B_0 \to C_2 \to A_1$. The 4-unfolded DFG consists of these 2 loops.

When a loop is unfolded, the number of resulting unfolded loops can be determined without going through the process of unfolding. This number can be determined by finding the minimum value of p such that the path $A_i \to A_{(i+pw_l)\%J}$ forms a loop, i.e., finding the minimum value of p such that $i = (i + pw_l)\%J$. The following 2 lemmas are used to show this. The first lemma is stated without proof.

Lemma 5.3.1 $i = (i + pw_l)\%J \Leftrightarrow pw_l = qJ$ for an integer q.

Lemma 5.3.2 *The smallest positive integer p that satisfies $pw_l = qJ$ is* $J/\gcd(w_l, J)$.

Proof of Lemma 5.3.2: The expression $pw_l = qJ$ can be written as $\left(\frac{a}{w_l}\right)w_l$ $= \left(\frac{a}{J}\right)J$. The values $p = \frac{a}{w_l}$ and $q = \frac{a}{J}$ must be integers, and a is to be as small as possible because $p = \frac{a}{w_l}$ is to be as small as possible, so $a = \text{lcm}\{w_l, J\}$. Using the fact that $\text{lcm}\{w_l, J\}\gcd\{w_l, J\} = w_l J$, the minimum value of p is $p = \frac{\text{lcm}\{w_l, J\}}{w_l} = \frac{J}{\gcd\{w_l, J\}}$. $\square$

From Lemma 5.3.1, the path $A_i \rightarrow A_{(i+nw_l)\%J}$ is a loop if and only if $pw_l = qJ$ holds. The minimum value of p that satisfies this is equal to the number of times the loop l is traversed to form an unfolded loop, and Lemma 5.3.2 states that this number is $J/\gcd(w_l, J)$, where $\gcd(a, b)$ represents the greatest common divisor of a and b. Therefore, an unfolded loop contains $J/\gcd(w_l, J)$ copies of each node in l. The unfolded DFG contains a total of J copies of each node, so there must be $J/(J/\gcd(w_l, J)) = \gcd(w_l, J)$ unfolded loops that result from unfolding l. The unfolded DFG contains w_l delays (from Property 5.3.1), and each of the $\gcd(w_l, J)$ unfolded loops contains $w_l/\gcd(w_l, J)$ delays. This is summarized in the following property.

Property 5.3.2 *J-unfolding of a loop l with w_l delays in the original DFG leads to $\gcd(w_l, J)$ loops in the unfolded DFG, and each of these $\gcd(w_l, J)$ loops contains $w_l/\gcd(w_l, J)$ delays and $J/\gcd(w_l, J)$ copies of each node that appears in l.*

The following property describes how the iteration bound is affected by unfolding.

Property 5.3.3 *Unfolding a DFG with iteration bound T_∞ results in a J-unfolded DFG with iteration bound JT_∞.*

Intuitively, since the J-unfolded DFG represents J iterations of the original DFG, the iteration bound of the J-unfolded DFG should be J times the iteration bound of the original DFG. Mathematically, the iteration bound of the original DFG is $T_\infty = \max_l \left\{\frac{t_l}{w_l}\right\}$, and Property 5.3.2 can be used to show that the iteration bound of the unfolded DFG is

$$T'_\infty = \max_l \left\{\frac{(J/\gcd(w_l, J))t_l}{w_l/\gcd(w_l, J)}\right\} = J\max_l \left\{\frac{t_l}{w_l}\right\} = JT_\infty.$$

As an example, assume that addition and multiplication in Fig. 5.1 require 3 and 6 u.t., respectively. The iteration bound of the original DFG in Fig. 5.1(a) is $9/9 = 1$ u.t., and the iteration bound of the 2-unfolded DFG in Fig. 5.1(b) is $18/9 = 2$ u.t.

5.4 CRITICAL PATH, UNFOLDING, AND RETIMING

This section relates the critical path of the original DFG, G, to that of the J-unfolded DFG, G_J. The relationship between the critical path of the J-unfolded version of a retimed DFG, $(G_r)_J$, and the retimed version of the J-unfolded DFG, $(G_J)_r$, is also explored [8]–[10].

Property 5.4.1 *Consider a path with w delays in the original DFG. J-unfolding of this path leads to $(J - w)$ paths with no delays and w paths with 1 delay each, when $w < J$.*

Corollary 5.4.1 *Any path in the original DFG containing J or more delays leads to J paths with 1 or more delays in each path. Therefore, a path in the original DFG with J or more delays cannot create a critical path in the J-unfolded DFG.*

Using Property 5.4.1, we can retime the original DFG such that the J-unfolded version of the retimed DFG will meet a specified critical path computation time, c. The critical path of the unfolded DFG can be c if there exists a path in the original DFG with computation time c and less than J delay elements. This leads to the critical path constraint for retiming for critical path reduction in the unfolded version of the retimed DFG. If $D(U, V) \geq c$, then $W_r(U, V) = W(U, V) + r(V) - r(U) \geq J$, or $r(U) - r(V) \leq W(U, V) - J$. The usual feasibility constraint, $w(e) + r(V) - r(U) \leq 0$, should be used with this critical path constraint.

Lemma 5.4.1 *Any feasible clock cycle period that can be obtained by retiming the J-unfolded DFG, G_J, can be achieved by retiming the original DFG, G, directly and then unfolding it by unfolding factor J.*

Proof: Let r' be a legal retiming for the unfolded DFG, G_J, which leads to critical path c. Let r be a retiming for G defined as

$$r(U) = \sum_{i=0}^{J-1} r'(U_i).$$

We prove that r is a feasible retiming on the original DFG such that the J-unfolded version of the DFG, G_r, will have a critical path c. First consider the proof of feasibility of the retiming r. Consider an edge $U \to V$ with w delays in G. Since r' is a legal retiming on the unfolded DFG,

$$r'(U_i) - r'(V_{(i+w)\%J}) \leq \left\lfloor \frac{i + w}{J} \right\rfloor.$$

Summing the above inequalities for $i = 0$ to $J - 1$, we obtain $r(U) - r(V) \leq w$, which proves that r is a feasible retiming. Now consider the proof that the critical path in the J-unfolded DFG is c. Since r' satisfies the critical path constraint for the unfolded DFG, i.e.,

$$r'(U_i) - r'(V_{(i+w)\%J}) \leq \left\lfloor \frac{i+w}{J} \right\rfloor - 1$$

if $D(U_i \rightarrow V_{(i+w)\%J}) > c$, summing this for all i ranging from 0 to $J - 1$ results in

$$r(U) - r(V) \leq W(U, V) - J,$$

which is the desired inequality. □

5.5   APPLICATIONS OF UNFOLDING

5.5.1   Sample Period Reduction

The iteration bound, T_∞, is the lower bound on the iteration period of a recursive DSP program. An implementation of the DSP program can never achieve an iteration period less than the iteration bound, even if infinite processors are available. A thorough description of the iteration bound is found in Chapter 2. In some cases, the DSP program cannot be implemented with the iteration period equal to the iteration bound without the use of unfolding. This section considers 2 such cases where unfolding allows the DSP program to be implemented with an iteration period equal to the iteration bound.

The 1st case where the iteration period cannot be made equal to the iteration bound is when there is a node in the DFG that has computation time greater than T_∞ (we assume here that the node cannot be split into 2 subnodes with smaller computation times). In this case, even retiming cannot be used to reduce the computation time of the critical path of the DFG to T_∞. For example, the DFG in Fig. 5.6(a) has iteration bound $T_\infty = 3$, but the nodes S and T each require computation times of 4 u.t., so the minimum sample period after retiming is 4 u.t. This DFG can be unfolded with unfolding factor 2 to get the DFG in Fig. 5.6(b). This unfolded DFG has iteration bound $T_\infty = 6$, and its critical path is 6 u.t. The unfolded DFG performs 2 iterations of the original DSP program in 6 u.t., so the sample period of the unfolded DFG is $6/2 = 3$ u.t., which is the same as the iteration bound of the original DFG. To summarize, the original DFG in Fig. 5.6(a) cannot achieve a sample period equal to the iteration bound because a node computation time is larger than the iteration bound, but the unfolded DFG in Fig. 5.6(b) can have a sample period equal to the iteration bound of the original DFG. In general, if the computation time of node U, t_U, is greater than the iteration bound, T_∞, then $\lceil t_U/T_\infty \rceil$-unfolding should be used, where $\lceil x \rceil$ is the ceiling of x, which is the smallest integer greater than or equal to x. In the above example, $t_U = 4$ and $T_\infty = 3$, so $\lceil 4/3 \rceil$-unfolding (i.e., 2-unfolding) was used.

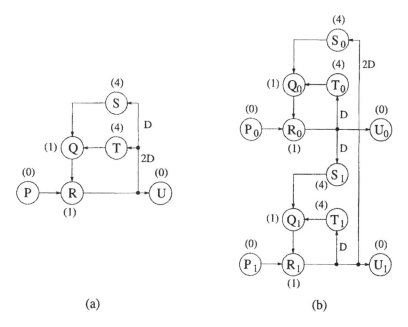

(a)   (b)

Fig. 5.6 (a) The original DFG with iteration bound $T_\infty = 3$ and minimum sample period of 4. (b) The 2-unfolded DFG with iteration bound $T_\infty = 6$ and minimum sample period of $6/2 = 3$.

The second case where the iteration period cannot be made equal to the iteration bound is when the iteration bound is not an integer. A simple example of this is shown in Fig. 5.7(a), where the DFG has iteration bound $T_\infty = 4/3$; however, even retiming cannot be used to achieve a critical path of less than 2 u.t. This DFG can be unfolded with unfolding factor 3 to get the DFG in Fig. 5.7(b). This unfolded DFG has iteration bound $T_\infty = 4$, and its critical path is 4 u.t. The unfolded DFG performs 3 iterations of the original DSP program in 4 u.t., so the sample period of the unfolded DFG is $4/3$ u.t., which is the same as the iteration bound of the original DFG. To summarize, the original DFG in Fig. 5.7(a) cannot achieve a sample period equal to the iteration bound because the iteration bound is not an integer, but the unfolded DFG in Fig. 5.7(b) can have a sample period equal to the iteration bound of the original DFG. In general, if a critical loop bound is of the form t_l/w_l where t_l and w_l are mutually coprime, then w_l-unfolding should be used. For example, if $t_l = 60$ and $w_l = 45$, then t_l/w_l should be written as $t_l/w_l = 4/3$, and 3-unfolding should be used.

Situations may also occur where the longest node computation time is larger than the iteration bound, T_∞, *and* T_∞ is not an integer. In this case, the minimum unfolding factor that allows the iteration period to equal the iteration bound is the minimum value of J such that JT_∞ is an integer and

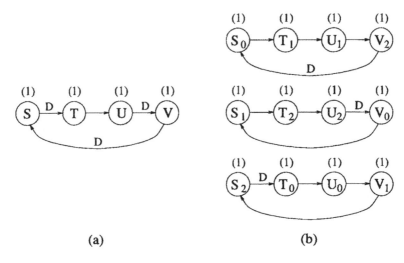

(a)   (b)

Fig. 5.7 (a) The original DFG with iteration bound $T_\infty = 4/3$ and minimum sample period of 2. (b) The 3-unfolded DFG with iteration bound $T_\infty = 4$ and minimum sample period of 4/3.

is greater than or equal to the longest node computation time. For example, if $T_\infty = 4/3$ and the longest node computation time is 6, then the minimum unfolding factor that allows the iteration period to equal the iteration bound is $J = 6$ because this is the minimum value of J such that $J(4/3)$ is an integer and $J(4/3) \geq 6$.

Any DFG with 1 delay in each loop is referred to as a *perfect-rate* DFG. A perfect-rate DFG can always be scheduled such that the iteration period is equal to the iteration bound of the DFG. If a DFG is not perfect rate, it can always be unfolded so the unfolded DFG is perfect rate. To see how this can be done, recall that Property 5.3.2 states that J-unfolding a loop l with w_l delays forms $\gcd(w_l, J)$ loops in the unfolded DFG, and each of these $\gcd(w_l, J)$ loops contains $w_l/\gcd(w_l, J)$ delays. Therefore, if $\gcd(w_l, J) = w_l$ (i.e., if J is a multiple of w_l), the unfolded loops contain 1 delay each, and the unfolded DFG is perfect rate. For $\gcd(w_l, J) = w_l$ to hold for all loops l in the original DFG, J must be a multiple of w_l for each loop l. Choosing J to be equal to the least common multiple of the number of loop delays guarantees that J is a multiple of w_l for each loop l, which guarantees that the unfolded DFG is perfect rate. For example, the least common multiple (lcm) of the number of loop delays in Fig. 5.6(a) is $\mathrm{lcm}\{2,3\} = 6$. Therefore, unfolding this DFG using unfolding factor 6 guarantees an unfolded DFG with sample period equal to the iteration period. However, we just showed that the unfolding factor 2 can be used to make the sample period equal to the iteration period, so the lcm of the number of loop delays is not necessarily the minimum unfolding factor that can be used to guarantee that the sample period of the unfolded DFG is equal to the iteration period (in fact, it is the

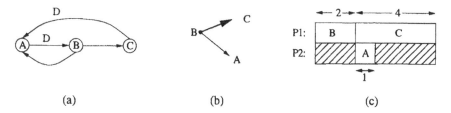

(a)   (b)   (c)

Fig. 5.8 (a) A DFG where execution times of the nodes A, B and C are assumed to be 1, 2 and 4 u.t., respectively, (b) corresponding acyclic precedence graph, and (c) periodic non-overlapped schedule with period 6 u.t.

upper bound on the unfolding factor). Note that the lcm is independent of the node computation times. The topics of determining the minimum unfolding factor and combining unfolding and retiming are beyond the scope of this book.

Unfolding can be exploited to reduce the iteration period in programmable DSPs. Periodic schedules can be constructed from the acyclic precedence graphs that are obtained by deleting all edges with delay elements from the DFG (see Appendix B). If the period of a periodic schedule for a J-unfolded DFG is T, then the average iteration period is T/J. Schedules can be *overlapped* or *nonoverlapped*. In a nonoverlapped schedule, the period of the schedule is the same as the critical path of the acyclic precedence graph. In an overlapped schedule, the period of the schedule is smaller than the critical path of the acyclic precedence graph [2]. As an example, consider the DFG in Fig. 5.8(a) whose acyclic precedence graph and periodic schedule are shown in Fig. 5.8(b) and Fig. 5.8(c), respectively. The schedule in this case is nonoverlapped. For this DFG, the iteration bound is 3.5 u.t. and the period of the nonoverlapped periodic schedule is 6 u.t. Note that the path marked by bold lines in the acyclic precedence graph represents the critical path. A corresponding 2-unfolded DFG, its acyclic precedence graph and periodic schedule are shown in Fig. 5.9. The period of the overlapped periodic schedule is 7 u.t.; therefore, the average iteration period is 3.5 u.t., which is the same as the iteration bound. The reader can verify that retiming the DFG in Fig. 5.8(a) by removing the delay element from the input edge of node B and adding a delay element to each outgoing edge of node B can reduce the critical path from 6 u.t. to 4 u.t. Furthermore, 2-unfolding of this retimed DFG will lead to a *nonoverlapped* schedule with average iteration period, which is the same as the iteration bound. In general, constructing overlapped schedules is significantly more complex than nonoverlapped schedules.

5.5.2   Parallel Processing

A direct application of the general unfolding transformation is to design parallel processing architectures from serial processing architectures. At the word

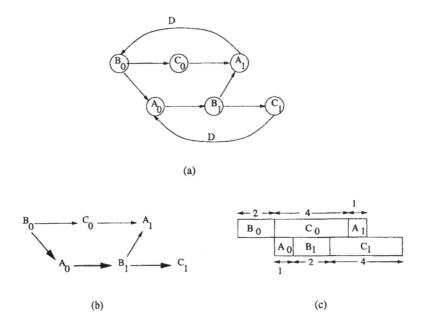

Fig. 5.9 (a) A 2-unfolded DFG, (b) its acyclic precedence graph, and (c) an overlapped periodic schedule with period 7 u.t.

level, this means that word-parallel architectures can be designed from word-serial architectures. At the bit level, it means that bit-parallel and digit-serial architectures can be designed from bit-serial architectures. The following sections describe how to design parallel processing architectures using unfolding.

5.5.2.1 Word-Level Parallel Processing   The unfolding transformation can be used to design a word-parallel architecture from a word-serial architecture. This has already been demonstrated in Fig. 5.1. The original architecture in Fig. 5.1(a) processes 1 input sample per clock cycle to compute 1 output sample, and the 2-unfolded architecture in Fig. 5.1(b) processes 2 input samples per clock cycle to compute two output samples. In general, unfolding a word-serial architecture by J creates a word-parallel architecture that processes J words per clock cycle. Note that parallel processing architectures as described in Chapter 3 can be designed using the unfolding technique.

As another example, consider the DSP program $y(n) = ax(n) + bx(n - 4) + cx(n - 6)$, which is shown in Fig. 5.10(a). To create an architecture that can process more than 1 word per clock cycle, the first step is to draw a corresponding DFG as shown in Fig. 5.10(b). The next step is to unfold the DFG. The 3-unfolded DFG is shown in Fig. 5.10(c), and the corresponding DSP program is shown in Fig. 5.10(d). The DSP program in Fig. 5.10(d) is a 3-parallel version of the DSP program in Fig. 5.10(a).

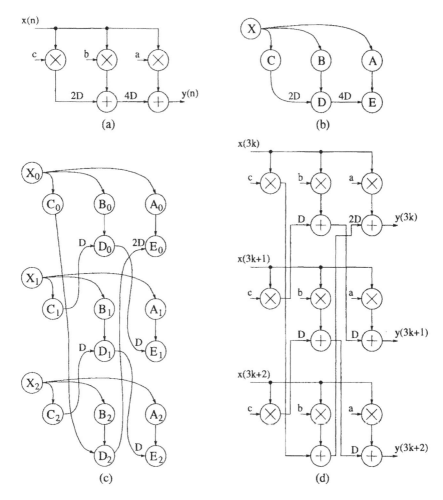

Fig. 5.10 (a) The original DSP program. (b) The DFG for the original DSP program. (c) The 3-unfolded DFG. (d) The 3-parallel DSP program.

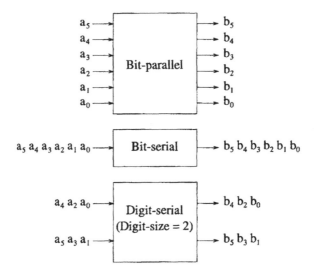

Fig. 5.11 A demonstration of bit-parallel, bit-serial, and digit-serial processing styles for wordlength $W = 6$.

5.5.2.2 Bit-Level Parallel Processing The goal of this section is to show how bit-parallel and digit-serial architectures can be derived from bit-serial architectures using the unfolding transformation. A description of the bit-serial, bit-parallel, and digit-serial processing styles is given below. Assume that W is the wordlength of the data.

- *Bit-serial processing:* One bit is processed per clock cycle and a complete word is processed in W clock cycles.

- *Bit-parallel processing:* One word of W bits is processed every clock cycle.

- *Digit-serial processing:* N bits are processed per clock cycle and a word is processed in W/N clock cycles. The parameter N is referred to as the *digit size*.

Fig. 5.11 shows the difference between these 3 processing styles for wordlength $W = 6$. For digit-serial architectures, N or digit-size number of bits are processed per clock cycle. We begin with the assumption that N is a divisor of W. This restriction is lifted later in this section.

Fig. 5.12 shows a bit-serial adder architecture for wordlength $W = 4$. This adder adds the two 4-bit numbers $a_3a_2a_1a_0$ and $b_3b_2b_1b_0$ to get the 4-bit sum $s_3s_2s_1s_0$, where bit 0 is the least significant bit and bit 3 is the most significant bit. To obtain a digit-serial or bit-parallel adder architecture, the bit-serial adder must be unfolded. The bit-serial adder is typical of most bit-serial architectures in that it contains an edge with a switch (which corresponds

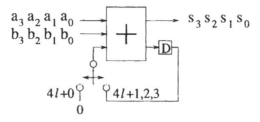

$$a_3\, a_2\, a_1\, a_0 \qquad s_3\, s_2\, s_1\, s_0$$
$$b_3\, b_2\, b_1\, b_0$$

$$4l+0 \qquad 4l+1,2,3$$
$$0$$

Fig. 5.12 Bit-serial addition $s = a + b$ for wordlength $W = 4$.

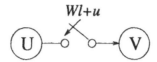

$$Wl+u$$

$$U \qquad V$$

Fig. 5.13 A switch.

to a multiplexer in hardware). Therefore, the process of unfolding edges with switches is first described and then applied to design digit-serial and bit-parallel architectures from bit-serial architectures.

Consider the edge $U \to V$ in Fig. 5.13. To unfold this edge with unfolding factor J, two basic assumptions are made:

- The wordlength W is a multiple of the unfolding factor J, i.e., $W = W'J$.

- All edges into and out of the switch have no delays.

With these two assumptions in mind, the edge in Fig. 5.13 can be unfolded using the following 2 steps:

1. Write the switching instance as

$$Wl + u = J\left(W'l + \left\lfloor \frac{u}{J} \right\rfloor\right) + (u\%J).$$

2. Draw an edge with no delays in the unfolded graph from the node $U_{u\%J}$ to the node $V_{u\%J}$, which is switched at time instance $\left(W'l + \left\lfloor \frac{u}{J} \right\rfloor\right)$.

The proof of this is left as an exercise (see Problem 18). For example, consider unfolding the switch in Fig. 5.13 for unfolding factor $J = 3$ assuming $W = 12$ and $u = 7$. This satisfies the two assumptions because $W = W'J \Rightarrow 12 = (4)(3)$ and the edge has no delays. The switching instance can be written as

$$12l + 7 = 3\left(4l + \left\lfloor \frac{7}{3} \right\rfloor\right) + (7\%3) = 3(4l + 2) + 1.$$

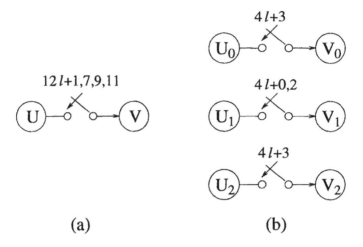

(a)   (b)

Fig. 5.14   (a) The original DFG. (b) The 3-unfolded DFG.

In the unfolded DFG, the unfolded edge is from the node U_1 to the node V_1 and is switched at $4l + 2$.

If the switch has multiple instances, then each switching instance is treated separately. The switch in Fig. 5.14(a) closes at the 4 switching instances $12l + 1$, $12l + 7$, $12l + 9$, and $12l + 11$. To unfold the DFG by $J = 3$, these switching instances are written as

$$
\begin{aligned}
12l + 1 &= 3(4l + 0) + 1 \\
12l + 7 &= 3(4l + 2) + 1 \\
12l + 9 &= 3(4l + 3) + 0 \\
12l + 11 &= 3(4l + 3) + 2.
\end{aligned}
$$

The unfolded DFG is shown in Fig. 5.14(b).

If an edge contains a switch and a positive number of delays, a dummy node can be used to reduce this problem to the case where the edge contains zero delays. The DFG in Fig. 5.15(a) contains an edge $A \to C$ that has a switch and 2 delays. Before unfolding, this DFG can be redrawn using the dummy node D as in Fig. 5.15(b). To unfold by $J = 3$, the 6 switching instances in this DFG can be written as

$$
\begin{aligned}
6l + 0 &= 3(2l + 0) + 0 \\
6l + 1 &= 3(2l + 0) + 1 \\
6l + 2 &= 3(2l + 0) + 2 \\
6l + 3 &= 3(2l + 1) + 0 \\
6l + 4 &= 3(2l + 1) + 1 \\
6l + 5 &= 3(2l + 1) + 2.
\end{aligned}
$$

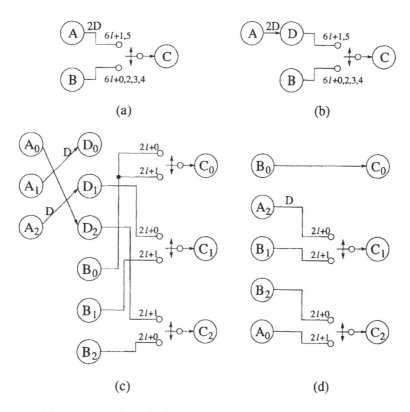

Fig. 5.15 (a) The original DFG. (b) The original DFG with a dummy node D. (c) The unfolded DFG. (d) The unfolded DFG with the dummy nodes and dead nodes removed.

The unfolded DFG is shown in Fig. 5.15(c). The dummy nodes D_i, $i = 0, 1, 2$, and the "dead" node A_1 can be eliminated as shown in the simplified unfolded DFG in Fig. 5.15(d). It may be noted that the number of delays is not preserved by unfolding of circuits containing switches.

Using these techniques for unfolding switches, bit-parallel and digit-serial architectures can be systematically designed from bit-serial architectures. This is demonstrated using the bit-serial adder in Fig. 5.12. A DFG corresponding to this adder is shown in Fig. 5.16. The 4-unfolded and 2-unfolded versions of this DFG are shown in Fig. 5.17, and the architectures corresponding to these unfolded DFGs are shown in Fig. 5.18. The 4-unfolded architecture in Fig. 5.18(a) is simply a bit-parallel ripple-carry adder. The 2-unfolded architecture in Fig. 5.18(b) is a digit-serial adder with digit size equal to 2.

If the wordlength W is not a multiple of the unfolding factor J, the DFG can still be unfolded by determining $L = \text{lcm}\{W, J\}$ and replacing the switching instance $Wl + u$ with the L/W switching instances $Ll + u + wW$ for $w = 0$ to $L/W - 1$. The switch periodicity has now been changed from W to L

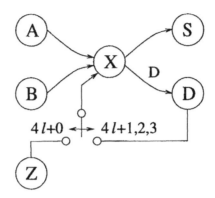

Fig. 5.16 The DFG corresponding to the bit-serial adder in Fig. 5.12.

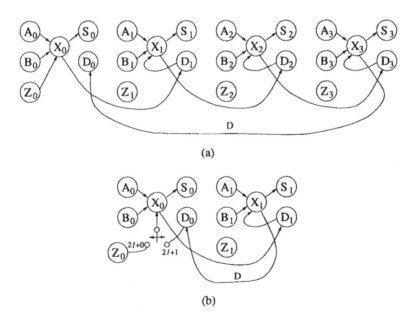

Fig. 5.17 The DFGs that result from unfolding the DFG in Fig. 5.16 using unfolding factors (a) $J = 4$, and (b) $J = 2$.

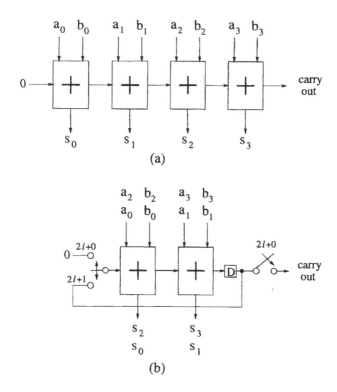

Fig. 5.18 (a) The bit-parallel adder designed by unfolding the bit-serial adder in Fig. 5.12 using $J = 4$. (b) The digit-serial adder designed by unfolding the bit-serial adder in Fig. 5.12 using $J = 2$.

and each switching instance has been expanded by a factor L/W. Since the switch periodicity is a multiple of the unfolding factor, unfolding can be performed as previously described. This is demonstrated by unfolding the DFG in Fig. 5.16 using unfolding factor $J = 3$. This DFG is redrawn in Fig. 5.19(a) such that all switching instances have the form $12l + m$ because $L = \text{lcm}\{4, 3\} = 12$. Note that the switching instance $4l$ is equivalent to $12l$, $12l + 4$, and $12l + 8$. Similarly, the switching instance $4l + 1$ is expanded as $12l + 1$, $12l + 5$, and $12l + 9$; $4l + 2$ is expanded as $12l + 2$, $12l + 6$, and $12l + 10$; $4l + 3$ is expanded as $12l + 3$, $12l + 7$, and $12l + 11$. The 3-unfolded DFG is shown in Fig. 5.19(b). This results in the digit-serial adder with digit size of 3 shown in Fig. 5.19(c). Since the wordlength is 4, this adder processes 3 words every 4 clock cycles. Note that this is an example of a digit-serial architecture where the wordlength is not a multiple of the digit size. The use of a digit size that is not a divisor of the wordlength requires more complex control circuitry, but this circuit processes a word in an average of 4/3 clock cycles. If the digit size is restricted to be a divisor of the wordlength, then in this example the wordlength needs to be extended to 6 bits (using 2 sign extension bits) and a word can be processed in 2 clock cycles.

5.6 CONCLUSIONS

It has been shown that the unfolding transformation can unravel hidden concurrency in digital signal processing systems described by DFGs. Therefore, unfolding can be used to reduce the iteration period in DSP algorithms. Unfolding can be applied to generate word-parallel architectures that can be used for high-speed or low-power applications. In the context of programmable DSPs, unfolding can be used to reduce the number of clock cycles needed to compute an output sample.

5.7 PROBLEMS

1. Unfold the DFG in Fig. 5.20 using unfolding factors 3 and 4.

2. Unfold the DFGs in Fig. 5.21 using unfolding factors 2 and 5.

3. Prove the relationship in (5.3) used to show that unfolding preserves the number of delays.

4. This problem attempts to show that a complex loop, which is a combination of 2 simple or fundamental loops, cannot introduce a new iteration bound. To show this, consider two loops with loop computation times T_1 and T_2, respectively, and with number of delay elements N_1 and N_2, respectively. Let $T_1/N_1 > T_2/N_2$ hold. Show that

$$\frac{T_1 + T_2}{N_1 + N_2} < \frac{T_1}{N_1}. \tag{5.4}$$

5. Our objective in this problem is to prove that the critical path of a J-unfolded DFG is a monotonically nondecreasing function with respect to J [11]. To show this, prove that the critical path of a J-unfolded DFG is greater than or equal to the critical path of the $(J-1)$-unfolded DFG.

6. Prove that the following iterative algorithm computes the minimum unfolding factor for a nonrecursive DFG such that the iteration period of T is achievable. It is assumed that pipelining and/or retiming are not used to reduce the critical path.

Repeat until $T_{crit} \le JT$
{
$\qquad J = \lceil \frac{T_{crit}}{T} \rceil$

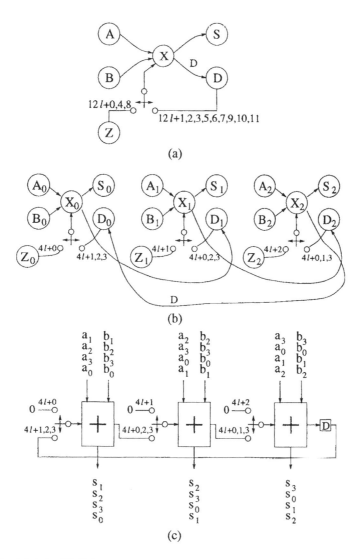

Fig. 5.19 (a) The DFG in Fig. 5.16 redrawn so it is compatible with the unfolding factor $J = 3$. (b) The 3-unfolded DFG. (c) The digit-serial adder with digit size of 3.

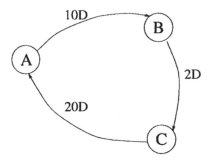

Fig. 5.20 The DFG for Problem 1.

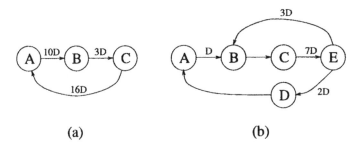

(a)   (b)

Fig. 5.21 The DFGs for Problem 2.

$$T_{crit} = \text{critical path of } J\text{-unfolded DFG.}$$
}

(Hint: Use the result of Problem 5.)

7. Consider the DFG in Fig. 5.22. Find the minimum unfolding factor required to obtain an equivalent DFG that can achieve a required iteration period of 8 u.t. Do not perform pipelining and/or retiming on this DFG. Find the minimum J such that the critical path of the J-unfolded DFG should be less than or equal to $8J$. The minimum unfolding factor can be computed using the algorithm given in Problem 6.

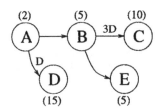

Fig. 5.22 The DFG for Problem 7. The numbers in parentheses are computation times of the nodes.

8. In this problem, we wish to show that changing the ordering of retiming and unfolding is immaterial when we wish to minimize the critical path of the unfolded DFG. Perform (a) and (b) for the DFG in Fig. 5.23:

   (a) Unfold the DFG with unfolding factor $J = 2$, and then retime the unfolded DFG to minimize the clock period.

   (b) Let the retiming function determined in part (a) of this problem be denoted r'. Let the retiming function r be $r(A) = r'(A_0) + r'(A_1)$; $r(B) = r'(B_0) + r'(B_1)$; $r(C) = r'(C_0) + r'(C_1)$; $r(D) = r'(D_0) + r'(D_1)$. Show that retiming the DFG in Fig. 5.23 using r results in a DFG that, when unfolded, achieves the same critical path as the result of part (a) of this problem. Do this by showing that if $D(U, V) \geq c$, then $W(U, V) + r(V) - r(U) \geq J$ holds for all pairs of nodes U, V in the retimed version of the original DFG.

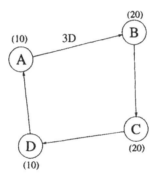

Fig. 5.23   The DFG for Problem 8.

9. Retime the DFG in Fig. 5.24 such that the 4-unfolded version of the retimed DFG will achieve a critical path of 14 u.t. Assume that addition and multiplication require 2 and 4 u.t., respectively.

10. Retime the DFG in Fig. 5.25 such that the 3-unfolded version of the retimed DFG will achieve a critical path of 4 u.t. Assume that addition and multiplication require 1 and 2 u.t., respectively.

11. For the 8-th order 4-stage pipelined lattice all-pole lattice filter shown in Fig. 5.24, assume that addition and multiplication require 2 and 4 u.t., respectively.

   (a) Use retiming to minimize the critical path of the DFG.

   (b) Determine the minimum unfolding factor J such that the J-unfolded DFG can be retimed so that the critical path of this unfolded and retimed DFG is JT_∞, where T_∞ is the iteration bound of the original DFG in Fig. 5.24.

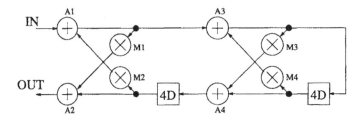

Fig. 5.24 A 4-level pipelined all-pass 8th-order IIR digital filter.

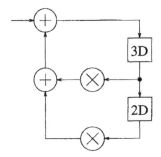

Fig. 5.25 The DFG used in Problem 13.

12. Repeat Problem 11 assuming that addition and multiplication require 1 and 2 u.t., respectively.

13. For the DFG in Fig. 5.25, find the minimum unfolding factor J such that the J-unfolded DFG can be retimed so that the critical path of this unfolded and retimed DFG is JT_∞. Assume that addition and multiplication require 1 and 2 u.t., respectively.

14. Draw the DFGs for the direct-form and data-broadcast forms of the FIR filter $y(n) = ax(n) + bx(n-2) + cx(n-5)$ and unfold these two DFGs using unfolding factor $J = 3$.

15. Repeat Problem 14 using $J = 4$.

16. Consider the DFG in Fig. 5.26. The numbers in parentheses are the computation times of the nodes.

   (a) What is the iteration bound of this DFG? What is the actual iteration period?

   (b) Retime this DFG to minimize the iteration period. What is the actual iteration period of the retimed DFG?

   (c) Unfold both the original DFG and the retimed DFG by a factor of 2. What are their actual iteration periods?

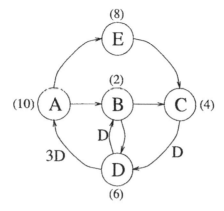

Fig. 5.26 The DFG for Problem 16.

(d) Determine the minimum unfolding factor J such that the J-unfolded DFG (unfold from the original DFG) can be retimed so that the critical path of this unfolded and retimed DFG is JT_∞, where T_∞ is the iteration bound of the original DFG in Fig. 5.26. Unfold the DFG by this minimum unfolding factor and retime the unfolded DFG so that its critical path is JT_∞.

17. This problem addresses loop unfolding (unrolling) in software in order to maximize the hardware utilization efficiency for a fixed hardware structure, and a given algorithm (program). It exploits unfolding for parallel computation for a programmable DSP (PDSP) with three MAC (multiply-accumulate) units. Our objective is to use unfolding to maximize the hardware utilization in parallel FIR filtering applications with the PDSP architecture in Fig. 5.27. This PDSP has a data bottleneck, i.e., we can fetch only one input operand in each clock cycle from the random access memory (RAM) representing the inputs. Assume that only the input data need to be fetched through this data bus, which creates the bottleneck, while filter coefficients are stored in other local memory unit(s) and can be accessed by each MAC unit freely during the clock cycle. Draw a schedule for a 7-tap FIR filter computation with appropriate unfolding factor so that hardware utilization efficiency is maximized.

18. Prove that the technique described in Section 5.5.2 for unfolding switches when the wordlength W is a multiple of the unfolding factor J is correct.

19. Unfold the circuit in Fig. 5.28 by unfolding factors 2, 3, and 4.

20. Obtain a 2-parallel structure of the computation in Fig. 5.29 using unfolding transformation.

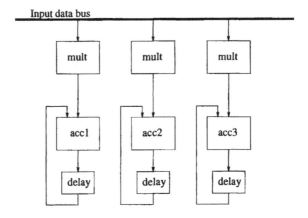

Fig. 5.27   The PDSP architecture.

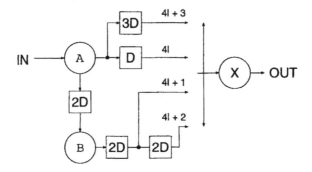

Fig. 5.28   The DFG for Problem 19.

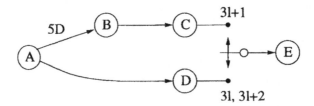

Fig. 5.29   The DFG for Problem 20.

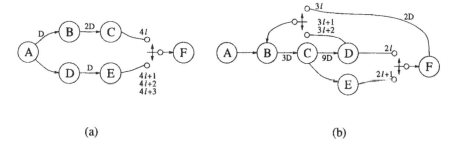

(a)   (b)

Fig. 5.30 The DFGs for Problem 21.

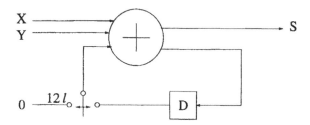

Fig. 5.31 The DFG for Problem 22.

21. Perform the following unfolding operations.

  (a) Unfold the DFG in Fig. 5.30(a) by unfolding factors 2 and 5.

  (b) Unfold the DFG in Fig. 5.30(b) by unfolding factor 4.

22. Unfold the bit-serial adder with wordlength = 12 in Fig. 5.31 by factors 4 and 5 to obtain the corresponding digit-serial adders.

23. The bit-serial system shown in Fig. 5.32 implements $y(n) = \frac{9}{8}y(n-1) + x(n)$ for a wordlength of 5 bits. Unfold this system by a factor of 2 to obtain a digit-serial architecture with digit size 2.

REFERENCES

1. A. Aho, R. Sethi, and J. D. Ullman, *Compilers: Principles, Techniques and Tools*. Addison-Wesley, 1986.

2. K. K. Parhi and D. G. Messerschmitt, "Static rate-optimal scheduling of iterative data-flow programs via optimum unfolding," *IEEE Trans. on Computers*, vol. 40, no. 2, pp. 178–195, Feb. 1991.

3. K. K. Parhi and D. G. Messerschmitt, "Pipeline interleaving and parallelism in recursive digital filters−part I: pipelining using scattered look-ahead and decom-

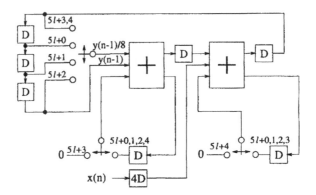

Fig. 5.32 The DFG for Problem 23.

position," *IEEE Trans. on Acoustics, Speech, and Signal Processing*, vol. 37, no. 7, pp. 1099–1117, July 1989.

4. K. K. Parhi and D. G. Messerschmitt, "Pipeline interleaving and parallelism in recursive digital filters—part II: pipelined incremental block filtering," *IEEE Trans. on Acoustics, Speech, and Signal Processing*, vol. 37, no. 7, pp. 1118–1135, July 1989.

5. A. P. Chandrakasan, A. Sheng, and R. W. Brodersen, "Low-power CMOS digital design," *IEEE Journal of Solid-State Circuits*, vol. 27, no. 4, pp. 473–484, April 1992.

6. K. K. Parhi, "A systematic approach for design of digit-serial signal processing architectures," *IEEE Trans. on Circuits and Systems*, vol. 38, no. 4, pp. 358–375, April 1991.

7. R. I. Hartley and K. K. Parhi, *Digit-Serial Computation.* Kluwer, 1995.

8. L.-F. Chao and E. Sha, "Retiming and unfolding data-flow graphs," in *Proc. of 1992 International Conference on Parallel Processing, part II*, (St. Charles, IL), pp. 33–40, Aug. 1992.

9. L.-G. Jeng and L.-G. Chen, "Rate-optimal DSP synthesis by pipeline and minimum unfolding," *IEEE Trans. on VLSI Systems*, vol. 2, no. 1, pp. 81–88, March 1994.

10. D.-J. Wang and Y.-H. Hu, "Fully static multiprocessor array realizability criteria for real-time recurrent DSP applications," *IEEE Trans. on Signal Processing*, vol. 42, no. 5, pp. 1288–1292, May 1994.

11. L. E. Lucke and K. K. Parhi, "Data-flow transformations for critical path time reduction in high-level DSP synthesis," *IEEE Trans. on Computer-Aided Design of Integrated Circuits and Systems*, vol. 12, no. 7, pp. 1063–1068, July 1993.

6

Folding

6.1 INTRODUCTION

In synthesizing DSP architectures, it is important to minimize the silicon area of the integrated circuits, which is achieved by reducing the number of functional units (such as adders and multipliers), registers, multiplexers, and interconnection wires. The folding transformation is used to systematically determine the control circuits in DSP architectures where multiple algorithm operations (such as addition operations) are time-multiplexed to a single functional unit (such as a pipelined adder) [1],[2]. By executing multiple algorithm operations on a single functional unit, the number of functional units in the implementation is reduced, resulting in an integrated circuit with low silicon area. Although folding technique can be used for synthesis of DSP architectures that can be operated using single or multiple clocks, this chapter only addresses synthesis of circuits operated by a single clock.

Fig. 6.1 shows an example of how 2 addition operations can be time-multiplexed on a single pipelined hardware adder. The DSP program in Fig. 6.1(a) computes $y(n) = a(n) + b(n) + c(n)$. In Fig. 6.1(b), the 2 addition operations shown in Fig. 6.1(a) are time-multiplexed on a single pipelined adder. The time-multiplexed hardware in Fig. 6.1(b) operates as follows. In cycle 0, the samples $a(0)$ and $b(0)$ are switched into the adder, and the sum $(a(0) + b(0))$ is stored in the delay element until cycle 1, when $(a(0) + b(0))$ is switched into the adder along with $c(0)$. The sum $(a(0) + b(0) + c(0))$ is stored in the delay until cycle 2, when the sum $(a(0) + b(0) + c(0))$ is output and the intermediate result $(a(1) + b(1))$ is computed by the adder. This process continues as shown in Table 6.1. One output sample is produced every 2 clock cycles, and one

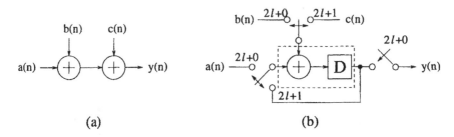

Fig. 6.1 (a) A simple DSP program with 2 addition operations. (b) A folded architecture where the 2 addition operations are folded to a single hardware adder with 1
stage of pipelining.

Table 6.1   Operation of the First Six Cycles of the Folded Hardware in Fig. 6.1(b)

Cycle	Adder Input (left)	Adder Input (top)	System Output
0	$a(0)$	$b(0)$	—
1	$a(0) + b(0)$	$c(0)$	—
2	$a(1)$	$b(1)$	$a(0) + b(0) + c(0)$
3	$a(1) + b(1)$	$c(1)$	—
4	$a(2)$	$b(2)$	$a(1) + b(1) + c(1)$
5	$a(2) + b(2)$	$c(2)$	—

sample of each input signal is consumed every 2 clock cycles (e.g., $a(i)$ is used
in cycle $2i$). As a result, an input sample must remain valid for 2 clock cycles
before changing. In general, the data on the input of the folded realization is
assumed to be valid for N cycles before changing, where N is the number of
algorithm operations executed on a single functional unit in hardware.

The architecture in Fig. 6.1(b) is simple enough to be designed using ad hoc
techniques; however, general DSP programs are more complex than the program in Fig. 6.1(a). In such cases, the systematic folding techniques described
in this chapter can be used to design the time-multiplexed architectures.

Folding provides a means for trading area for time in a DSP architecture.
One way to implement the DSP program in Fig. 6.1(a) is to use two adders
in hardware with a pipelining delay between the two adders. This implementation requires two hardware adders and computes one iteration of the
program in the time required to perform addition, T_{add}. On the other hand,
the folded implementation in Fig. 6.1(b) uses one hardware adder and computes one iteration of the program in $2T_{add}$ time. In general, folding can be
used to reduce the number of hardware functional units by a factor of N at
the expense of increasing the computation time by a factor of N. The two
extremes of this are when a fully parallel implementation is used (i.e., each

algorithm operation is assigned its own functional unit in hardware) and when a single processor is used (i.e., the entire program is implemented on a single functional unit).

While the folding transformation reduces the number of functional units in the architecture, it may also lead to an architecture that uses a large number of registers. To avoid architectures using excessive amounts of registers, techniques can be used to compute the minimum number of registers required to implement a folded DSP architecture and to allocate data to these registers [3]. These techniques are described in detail in this chapter. Using register minimization along with the folding transformation not only reduces the number of functional units but also keeps the area consumed by memory in the folded architecture to a minimum.

This chapter begins with mathematical descriptions of folding and retiming for folding in Section 6.2. General techniques for designing DSP architectures that use the minimum possible number of registers are discussed in Section 6.3, and these techniques are applied to folded architectures in Section 6.4. Section 6.5 describes the folding transformation that can be used to systematically synthesize architectures for multirate DSP programs [4].

6.2 FOLDING TRANSFORMATION

The folding transformation provides a systematic technique for designing control circuits for hardware where several algorithm operations are time-multiplexed on a single functional unit. The derivation of the folding equation, which is the basis for this technique, is included in this section along with the derivation of the retiming for the folding equation used to retime a DFG prior to folding.

Consider the edge e connecting the nodes U and V with $w(e)$ delays, as shown in Fig. 6.2(a). Let the executions of the l-th iteration of the nodes U and V be scheduled at the time units $Nl + u$ and $Nl + v$, respectively, where u and v are the *folding orders* of the nodes U and V that satisfy $0 \le u, v \le N-1$. The folding order of a node is the time partition to which the node is scheduled to execute in hardware. The functional units that execute the nodes U and V are denoted as H_U and H_V, respectively. Note that N is the number of operations folded to a single functional unit and is also referred to as the *folding factor*. If H_U is pipelined by P_U stages, then the result of the l-th iteration of the node U is available at the time unit $Nl + u + P_U$. Since the edge $U \xrightarrow{e} V$ has $w(e)$ delays, the result of the l-th iteration of the node U is used by the $(l + w(e))$-th iteration of the node V, which is executed at $N(l + w(e)) + v$. Therefore, the result must be stored for

$$D_F(U \xrightarrow{e} V) = [N(l + w(e)) + v] - [Nl + P_U + u] = Nw(e) - P_U + v - u \quad (6.1)$$

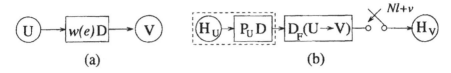

(a)   (b)

Fig. 6.2 (a) An edge $U \xrightarrow{e} V$ with $w(e)$ delays. (b) The corresponding folded data path. The data begin at the functional unit H_U which has P_U pipelining stages, pass through $D_F(U \xrightarrow{e} V)$ delays, and are switched into the functional unit H_V at the time instances $Nl + v$.

time units, which is independent of the iteration number l. The edge $U \xrightarrow{e} V$ is implemented as a path from H_U to H_V in the architecture with $D_F(U \xrightarrow{e} V)$ delays, and data on this path are input to H_V at $Nl + v$, as illustrated in Fig. 6.2(b).

A folding set is an ordered set of operations executed by the same functional unit. Each folding set contains N entries, some of which may be null operations. The operation in the j-th position within the folding set (where j goes from 0 to $N - 1$) is executed by the functional unit during the time partition j. For example, consider the folding set $S_1 = \{A_1, \emptyset, A_2\}$ for $N = 3$. The operation A_1 belongs to the folding set S_1 with folding order 0 (this is also denoted as $(S_1|0)$), and the operation A_2 belongs to the folding set S_1 with folding order 2 (this is also denoted as $(S_1|2)$). Due to the null operation in position 1 within S_1, the functional unit that executes operations A_1 and A_2 will not be utilized at time instances $3l + 1$.

The use of systematic folding techniques is demonstrated by folding the retimed biquad filter in Fig. 6.3. Assume that addition and multiplication require 1 and 2 u.t., respectively, and 1-stage pipelined adders and 2-stage pipelined multipliers are available (i.e., $P_A = 1$ and $P_M = 2$). The functional units can be clocked with period 1 u.t. This filter is folded with folding factor $N = 4$ using the folding sets shown in the figure. The folding factor $N = 4$ means that the iteration period of the folded hardware is 4 u.t., i.e., each node of the biquad filter is executed exactly once every 4 u.t. in the folded architecture. It also means that a functional unit in the folded hardware executes 4 operations (nodes) of the DSP program. To see this, the folding sets in Fig. 6.3 can be written as $S_1 = \{4, 2, 3, 1\}$ and $S_2 = \{5, 8, 6, 7\}$. The folding set S_1 contains only addition operations, and the nodes in this folding set are executed by the same hardware adder. Similarly, the folding set S_2 contains only multiplication operations, and the nodes in this folding set are executed by the same hardware multiplier. For example, node 3 is executed in the folded architecture at time instances $4l + 2$ on the adder that implements the operations in the folding set S_1. The folded architecture is shown in Fig. 6.4. This is obtained from the data-flow graph (DFG) in Fig. 6.3 by writing the folding equation in (6.1) for each of the 11 edges in the DFG.

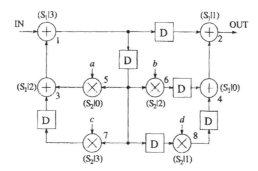

Fig. 6.3   The retimed biquad filter with valid folding sets assigned.

These 11 equations are

$$
\begin{aligned}
D_F(1 \to 2) &= 4(1) - 1 + 1 - 3 = 1 \\
D_F(1 \to 5) &= 4(1) - 1 + 0 - 3 = 0 \\
D_F(1 \to 6) &= 4(1) - 1 + 2 - 3 = 2 \\
D_F(1 \to 7) &= 4(1) - 1 + 3 - 3 = 3 \\
D_F(1 \to 8) &= 4(2) - 1 + 1 - 3 = 5 \\
D_F(3 \to 1) &= 4(0) - 1 + 3 - 2 = 0 \\
D_F(4 \to 2) &= 4(0) - 1 + 1 - 0 = 0 \\
D_F(5 \to 3) &= 4(0) - 2 + 2 - 0 = 0 \\
D_F(6 \to 4) &= 4(1) - 2 + 0 - 2 = 0 \\
D_F(7 \to 3) &= 4(1) - 2 + 2 - 3 = 1 \\
D_F(8 \to 4) &= 4(1) - 2 + 0 - 1 = 1.
\end{aligned}
\tag{6.2}
$$

For example, $D_F(1 \to 8) = 5$ means that there is an edge from the adder to the multiplier in the folded DFG with 5 delays. Since this edge ends at the node 8, which has folding order 1 in Fig. 6.3, the folded edge is switched at the input of the multiplier in the folded DFG at $4l + 1$. This folded edge can be seen in Fig. 6.4.

For a folded system to be realizable, $D_F(U \xrightarrow{e} V) \geq 0$ must hold for all of the edges in the DFG. Once valid folding sets have been assigned, retiming can be used to either satisfy this property or determine that the folding sets are not feasible. Recall that the edge $U \xrightarrow{e} V$ in Fig. 6.2(a) is folded using (6.1). Using retiming, the number of delays on the edge $U \xrightarrow{e} V$ is changed from $w(e)$ to

$$
w_r(e) = w(e) + r(V) - r(U),
\tag{6.3}
$$

where $w_r(e)$ is the number of delays on the edge $U \xrightarrow{e} V$ in the retimed DFG, and $r(X)$ denotes the retiming value of the node X (see Chapter 4). Let $D'_F(U \xrightarrow{e} V)$ denote the number of folded delays obtained by folding the edge $U \xrightarrow{e} V$ in the *retimed* DFG. To ensure that the corresponding edge in the folded hardware has a nonnegative number of delays, the constraint

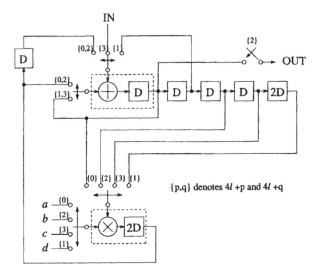

Fig. 6.4   The folded biquad filter using the folding sets given in Fig. 6.3.

$D'_F(U \xrightarrow{e} V) \geq 0$ must hold, which implies

$$Nw_r(e) - P_U + v - u \geq 0. \tag{6.4}$$

This constraint ensures that the folding set is valid after retiming. Combining (6.3) and (6.4) results in

$$N(w(e) + r(V) - r(U)) - P_U + v - u \geq 0.$$

Substituting $D_F(U \to V)$ for $Nw(e) - P_U + v - u$ and solving for $r(U) - r(V)$ results in

$$r(U) - r(V) \leq \frac{D_F(U \xrightarrow{e} V)}{N}.$$

Since the retiming values of the nodes are restricted to be integers, this can be rewritten as

$$r(U) - r(V) \leq \left\lfloor \frac{D_F(U \xrightarrow{e} V)}{N} \right\rfloor, \tag{6.5}$$

where $\lfloor x \rfloor$ is the floor of x, which is the largest integer less than or equal to x.

Once the set of constraints for the DFG is found using (6.5) (there is one such constraint for each edge in the DFG), the technique described in Section 4.3 can be used to determine if a solution exists and to find a solution if one indeed exists. As an example, consider the biquad DFG in Fig. 6.5. Assume that 1-stage pipelined adders and 2-stage pipelined multipliers (i.e., $P_A = 1$ and $P_M = 2$) are available. The folding equations (see (6.1)) and the

Table 6.2 Folding Equations and Retiming for Folding Constraints for the DFG in Fig. 6.5(a)

Edge	Folding Equation	Retiming for Folding Constraint
$1 \to 2$	$D_F(1 \to 2) = -3$	$r(1) - r(2) \leq -1$
$1 \to 5$	$D_F(1 \to 5) = 0$	$r(1) - r(5) \leq 0$
$1 \to 6$	$D_F(1 \to 6) = 2$	$r(1) - r(6) \leq 0$
$1 \to 7$	$D_F(1 \to 7) = 7$	$r(1) - r(7) \leq 1$
$1 \to 8$	$D_F(1 \to 8) = 5$	$r(1) - r(8) \leq 1$
$3 \to 1$	$D_F(3 \to 1) = 0$	$r(3) - r(1) \leq 0$
$4 \to 2$	$D_F(4 \to 2) = 0$	$r(4) - r(2) \leq 0$
$5 \to 3$	$D_F(5 \to 3) = 0$	$r(5) - r(3) \leq 0$
$6 \to 4$	$D_F(6 \to 4) = -4$	$r(6) - r(4) \leq -1$
$7 \to 3$	$D_F(7 \to 3) = -3$	$r(7) - r(3) \leq -1$
$8 \to 4$	$D_F(8 \to 4) = -3$	$r(8) - r(4) \leq -1$

retiming for folding constraints (see (6.5)) for the DFG in Fig. 6.5(a) are given in Table 6.2. According to the technique in Section 4.3 for solving systems of inequalities, the 1st step is to draw a constraint graph. The constraint graph for the inequalities in the right column of Table 6.2 is shown in Fig. 6.6. If this constraint graph contains a negative cycle, then there is no solution to the retiming for folding constraints. If no negative cycle exists, one solution is $r(i)$, which is the shortest path from the node 9 to the node i. A shortest path algorithm, such as the Bellman-Ford algorithm (see Section A.2 of Appendix A) or the Floyd-Warshall algorithm (see Section A.3 of Appendix A) can be used to determine if a negative cycle exists and find a solution if no negative cycle exists. Using either of these algorithms, we find that the set of constraints has a solution, and one solution is $r(1) = -1, r(2) = 0, r(3) = -1,$ $r(4) = 0, r(5) = -1, r(6) = -1, r(7) = -2,$ and $r(8) = -1$. The retimed DFG is shown in Fig. 6.3, the folding equations for the retimed DFG are given in (6.2), and the folded DFG is shown in Fig. 6.4.

The retiming for folding can also be carried out by inspection for simple DFGs such as the biquad filter. From Table 6.2, the edges with negative $D_F(U \to V)$ are the edges $1 \to 2, 6 \to 4, 8 \to 4,$ and $7 \to 3$. Note that adding (subtracting) w delays on the edge $U \to V$ increases (decreases) the $D_F(U \to V)$ by Nw. Thus, the $D_F(1 \to 2), D_F(6 \to 4), D_F(8 \to 4),$ and $D_F(7 \to 3)$ can be made nonnegative by increasing the number of delays by 1 on each of these edges. This can be achieved by performing cutset retiming for the cutsets marked $c1$ and $c2$ in Fig. 6.5. The reader can verify that the retimed DFG obtained in this manner is identical to the DFG in Fig. 6.3.

Note that unfolding the folded circuit in Fig. 6.4 with unfolding factor 4 leads to the DFG in Fig. 6.3, which is the retimed version of the DFG in

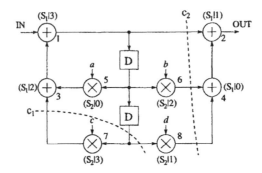

Fig. 6.5 (a) The original DFG resulting in some negative folded edge delays. The retimed DFG resulting in all nonnegative folded edge delays is shown in Fig. 6.3.

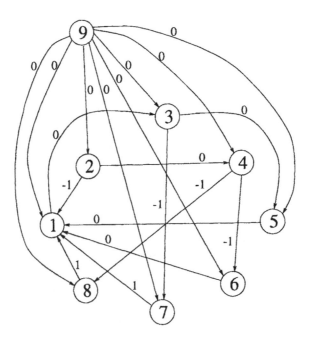

Fig. 6.6 The constraint graph for the set of inequalities in the right-hand column of Table 6.2. Node 9 is the host node.

Fig. 6.5. In general, the original DFG and the N-unfolded version of the folded DFG (synthesized with folding factor N) are retimed and/or pipelined versions of each other. Furthermore, an arbitrary DFG can be unfolded by factor N and the unfolded DFG can be folded with many possible folding sets to generate a family of architectures. An appropriate folding set can be used to obtain the original DFG.

In hardware synthesis, folding can be used for *connection binding* of the functional units. The folding sets are typically obtained from a scheduling and allocation algorithm (see Appendix B).

6.3   REGISTER MINIMIZATION TECHNIQUES

The focus of this section is on minimizing the number of registers used in a DSP architecture so that the silicon area due to the registers remains small. Techniques are presented for computing the minimum number of registers and for allocating the data to these registers. Section 6.4 discusses how these techniques can be used to design folded architectures that use the minimum possible number of registers.

6.3.1   Lifetime Analysis

Lifetime analysis is a procedure used to compute the minimum number of registers required to implement a DSP algorithm in hardware. A data sample (also called a *variable*) is *live* from the time it is produced through the time it is consumed. After the variable is consumed, it is *dead*. A variable occupies one register during each time unit that it is live. In *lifetime analysis*, the number of live variables at each time unit is computed, and the maximum number of live variables at any time unit is determined [5]. This is the minimum number of registers required to implement the DSP program.

For example, consider a DSP program that produces the 3 variables a, b, and c. Let the variable a be live during time units $n \in \{1, 2, 3, 4\}$, let the variable b be live during time units $n \in \{2, 3, 4, 5, 6, 7\}$, and let the variable c be live during time units $n \in \{5, 6, 7\}$. Assuming that the lifetimes of variables from the previous and subsequent iterations of the program do not overlap with the lifetimes of a, b, or c, the number of live variables during the time units $1, 2, 3, 4, 5, 6, 7$ is $1, 2, 2, 2, 2, 2, 2$, respectively. The minimum number of registers required to implement this DSP program is the maximum number of live variables at any time unit, which is $\max\{1, 2, 2, 2, 2, 2, 2\} = 2$. In this section, graphical techniques for lifetime analysis are described.

A *linear lifetime chart* is used to graphically represent the lifetime of each variable in a linear (as opposed to circular) fashion. The linear lifetime chart for our example is shown in Fig. 6.7(a). The horizontal lines represent clock cycles (or time units), and the vertical lines represent the lifetimes of the

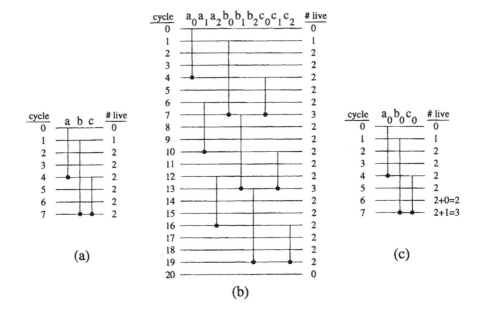

Fig. 6.7 (a) A linear lifetime chart. (b) The linear lifetime chart explicitly showing 3 iterations of the DSP program assuming the period is $N = 6$. (c) The linear lifetime chart implicitly taking into account the periodicity of the DSP program assuming the period is $N = 6$.

variables. Note that this lifetime chart uses the convention that a variable *is not* live during the clock cycle in which it is produced, and the variable *is* live during the clock cycle in which it is consumed. For example, the variable a is produced during cycle 0 and consumed during cycle 4, and this variable is live during the cycles $1, 2, 3, 4$. At the right of the lifetime chart, the number of live variables during each cycle is shown. The maximum number of live variables at any time step is 2, so the minimum number of registers that can be used to implement the underlying DSP program is 2.

In general, DSP programs are periodic. The lifetimes of a, b, and c from one iteration of the underlying DSP program may overlap with the lifetimes of these same variables from other iterations. For example, let the iteration period be $N = 6$, and let a_i, b_i, and c_i denote the variables a, b, and c resulting from iteration i of the DSP program. The lifetime chart for three consecutive iterations of the DSP program is shown in Fig. 6.7(b). Notice that the lifetime of a_1 overlaps with the lifetimes of b_0 and c_0, and as a result the DSP program requires 3 registers when the periodic nature of the DSP program is taken into account. Recall that only 2 registers were required in Fig. 6.7(a) where the periodic nature of the DSP program was not taken into account. This periodic nature of DSP programs must always be taken into account during lifetime analysis. Fortunately, this periodic nature can be taken into account without

Table 6.3   Lifetimes for 3×3 Matrix Transpose Operation

Sample	T_{input}	T_{zlout}	T_{diff}	T_{output}	Life Period $(T_{input} \rightarrow T_{output})$
a	0	0	0	4	$0 \rightarrow 4$
b	1	3	2	7	$1 \rightarrow 7$
c	2	6	4	10	$2 \rightarrow 10$
d	3	1	-2	5	$3 \rightarrow 5$
e	4	4	0	8	$4 \rightarrow 8$
f	5	7	2	11	$5 \rightarrow 11$
g	6	2	-4	6	$6 \rightarrow 6$
h	7	5	-2	9	$7 \rightarrow 9$
i	8	8	0	12	$8 \rightarrow 12$

explicitly drawing the lifetimes of several iterations. This is done by drawing the lifetimes of the variables for the 0-th iteration and letting the number of live variables at the time partitions $n \geq N$ be the sum of the number of live variables due to the 0-th iteration at cycles $n - kN$ for all integers $k \geq 0$. This is shown in Fig. 6.7(c) where the number of live variables in cycle 7 is the sum of the number of live variables due to the 0-th iteration at cycles 7 and 1, which is $2 + 1 = 3$.

In general, lifetime analysis begins with the construction of a lifetime table, such as the one in Table 6.3. This table represents the transpose operation of a 3×3 matrix, i.e., the matrix

$$\begin{bmatrix} a & b & c \\ d & e & f \\ g & h & i \end{bmatrix}$$

is reordered from row-by-row to column-by-column ordering. Each variable in Table 6.3 has an input time, T_{input}, and a zero-latency output time, T_{zlout}, which is the output time of the variable ignoring the latency of the system. Each variable in the zero-latency system is live for $T_{diff} = T_{zlout} - T_{input}$ clock cycles; however, this violates causality if any of the life periods are negative. For example, the variable d is input at $T_{input} = 3$ and output at $T_{zlout} = 1$ and is live for $1 - 3 = -2$ time units, which is not possible. To force the system to be causal, a latency is added to the system. The latency, T_{lat}, is the magnitude of the most negative value of T_{diff}, and $T_{lat} = -(-4) = 4$ in Table 6.3. The actual output time of the variables is $T_{output} = T_{zlout} + T_{lat}$, and the life period of the variables is $(T_{input} \rightarrow T_{output})$. Using these life periods, the lifetime chart can be drawn. The lifetime chart for Table 6.3 is shown in Fig. 6.8. Note that the period of this DSP program is $N = 9$.

Another way to represent the periodic behavior of DSP programs using a

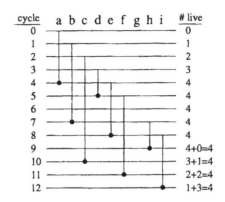

Fig. 6.8 The linear lifetime chart for the 3×3 matrix transposer with period $N = 9$. The life periods of the variables are given in Table 6.3.

lifetime chart is to use a *circular lifetime chart*. In a circular lifetime chart of periodicity N, the point marked i (where i is an integer satisfying $0 < i < N - 1$) represents the time partition i and all time instances $\{(Nl + i)\}$, where l is any nonnegative integer. For example, for $N = 8$, the time partition $i = 3$ represents the time instances $\{3, 11, 19, \ldots\}$. The circular lifetime chart corresponding to the linear lifetime chart in Fig. 6.8 is shown in Fig. 6.9. The numbers in parentheses represent the number of live variables at each time partition. Note that a variable produced during the time unit j and consumed during the time unit k is shown to be alive from the time unit $j + 1$ to the time unit k because we use the convention that a variable does not need to be stored during the time unit in which it is produced.

6.3.2 Data Allocation Using Forward-Backward Register Allocation

Once the minimum number of registers required to implement the DSP program has been determined, the data need to be allocated to these registers. *Forward-backward register allocation* is an allocation scheme that can be used to allocate data to the minimum number of registers [6]. In this section, forward-backward register allocation is described and used to generate architectures that use the minimum number of registers required to implement a DSP program. Other allocation schemes can also be used [7],[8].

Register allocation can be performed using an allocation table. The allocation scheme dictates how the variables are assigned to registers in the allocation table. The allocation table that uses the forward-backward scheme to allocate the data for the 3×3 matrix transposer is shown in Fig. 6.10(b). The steps used to perform forward-backward register allocation are as follows.

Step 1: Determine the minimum number of registers using lifetime anal-

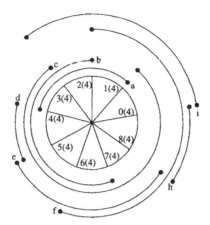

Fig. 6.9 The circular lifetime chart for the 3×3 matrix transposer. The corresponding linear lifetime chart is in Fig. 6.8, and the life periods of the variables are given in Table 6.3.

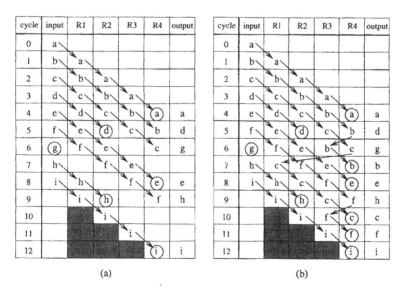

Fig. 6.10 (a) The allocation table for the 3 × 3 matrix transposer after steps 1 through 4 of forward-backward register allocation have been performed. (b) The allocation table after the allocation has been completed.

ysis.

Step 2: Input each variable at the time step corresponding to the beginning of its lifetime. If multiple variables are input in a given cycle, these are allocated to multiple registers such that the variable with the longest lifetime is allocated to the initial register and the other variables are allocated to consecutive registers in decreasing order of lifetime.

Step 3: Each variable is allocated in a forward manner until it is dead or it reaches the last register. In forward allocation, if the register i holds the variable in the current cycle, then the register $i + 1$ holds the same variable in the next cycle. If the register $i + 1$ is not available, then the variable is allocated to the first available forward register.

Step 4: Since the allocation is periodic, the allocation of the current iteration also repeats itself in subsequent iterations. Thus, if R_j is occupied with a variable in cycle l, then R_j would occupy the corresponding variable in cycle $l + N$, where N denotes the periodicity of the allocation. Therefore, we "hash" the position for R_j at time unit $l + N$ for each j and l.

Step 5: For variables that reach the last register and are not yet dead, the remaining life period is calculated, and these variables are allocated to a register in a backward manner on a first-come first-served basis. If multiple registers are available for backward allocation, first try to choose a register such that backward allocation has already been performed from the last register to this register. In the case where more than one register qualifies for backward allocation, choose the register with the minimum number of forward registers among all candidate registers that have a sufficient number of forward registers to complete the allocation of the variable. After a variable has been allocated backward, allocate it forward until it is dead or it again reaches the last register.

Step 6: Repeat steps 4 and 5 as required until the allocation is complete.

■

Fig. 6.10 shows the forward-backward register allocation table for the 3×3 matrix transposer whose lifetime table is given in Table 6.3. Step 1 has been performed in Section 6.3.1, where it has been determined that the 3×3 matrix transposer requires 4 registers (see Figs. 6.8 and 6.9). Steps 2, 3, and 4 are shown in Fig. 6.10(a). In step 2, each variable is input at the cycle corresponding to the beginning of its lifetime. Note that no cycle has more than one input variable in this example. In step 3, the variables are all allocated in a forward manner. In step 4, the hashing is performed to avoid conflicts when backward allocation is performed. For example, the register R_2 is hashed in cycle 11 because this register is occupied by the variable a in the cycle $11 - 9 = 2$. Step 5 is shown in Fig. 6.10(b). In this step, the variables are allocated backward. For example, the variable b is allocated backward to R_3 because this is the only register available for backward allocation. After each of the variables b, c, and f have been allocated backward and then allocated forward until they are dead, the allocation is complete.

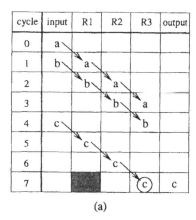
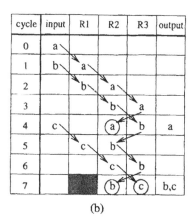

(a)   (b)

Fig. 6.11 (a) The allocation table for the data represented in Fig. 6.7(c) after steps 1 through 4 of forward-backward register allocation have been performed. (b) The allocation table after the allocation has been completed.

As another example of forward-backward register allocation, the allocation table for the data represented in Fig. 6.7(c) is shown in Fig. 6.11. Fig. 6.11(a) shows the allocation table after steps 1 through 4 of forward-backward register allocation have been performed, and Fig. 6.11(b) shows the table after the allocation has been completed.

From the allocation table, an architecture for the memory unit can be synthesized. The architecture for the 3×3 matrix transposer is shown in Fig. 6.12. This architecture is completely specified by the allocation table in Fig. 6.10(b). For example, the backward allocation for the variable b during cycle 5 from R_4 to R_3 in Fig. 6.10(b) is implemented using a feedback path in Fig. 6.12 from the output of R_4 to the input of R_3, which is switched at time $9l + 5$. Similarly, the feedback path for c is implemented using a feedback path from the output of R_4 to the input of R_1, which is switched at time $9l + 6$. The switching instance in the architecture for the feedback of the variable f is $9l + 0$ because this feedback occurs in Fig. 6.10(b) during cycle 9, and all switching instances must be of the form $9l + m$ for $0 \leq m \leq 8$.

As another example, the architecture corresponding to the allocation table in Fig. 6.11(b) is shown in Fig. 6.13.

6.4   REGISTER MINIMIZATION IN FOLDED ARCHITECTURES

The register minimization techniques described in Section 6.3 can be used to synthesize control circuits in folded architectures that use the minimum possible number of registers. The basic procedure is as follows:

1. Perform retiming for folding (see Section 6.2).

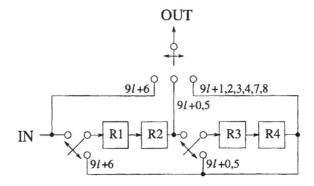

Fig. 6.12 The architecture corresponding to the allocation table in Fig. 6.10(b) for the 3 × 3 matrix transposer.

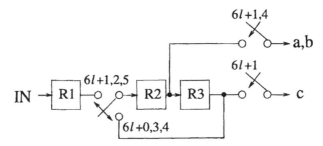

Fig. 6.13 The architecture corresponding to the allocation table in Fig. 6.11(b).

2. Write the folding equations (see Section 6.2).

3. Use the folding equations to construct a lifetime table.

4. Draw the lifetime chart and determine the required number of registers (see Section 6.3.1).

5. Perform forward-backward register allocation (see Section 6.3.2).

6. Draw the folded architecture that uses the minimum number of registers.

This procedure is demonstrated in this section with 2 examples.

6.4.1 Biquad Filter Example

In this example, a minimum-register architecture is constructed for the DFG in Fig. 6.5. The DFG after retiming for folding is shown in Fig. 6.3, and the folding equations for this DFG are given in (6.2). The folded architecture without any register minimization is shown in Fig. 6.4. This architecture uses 6 registers (the 3 pipelining registers that are internal to the adder and multiplier are not counted).

Table 6.4   Lifetimes for the Retimed Biquad Filter Shown in Fig. 6.3

node	$T_{input} \rightarrow T_{output}$
1	$4 \rightarrow 9$
2	–
3	$3 \rightarrow 3$
4	$1 \rightarrow 1$
5	$2 \rightarrow 2$
6	$4 \rightarrow 4$
7	$5 \rightarrow 6$
8	$3 \rightarrow 4$

Since retiming for folding has already been performed and the folding equations are written in (6.2), the next step is to construct the lifetime table shown in Table 6.4. In the lifetime table, there is one entry for each node in the DFG that specifies the lifetime ($T_{input} \rightarrow T_{output}$) for the node. The time T_{input} for the node U is $u + P_U$, where u is the folding order of U and P_U is the number of pipelining stages in the functional unit that executes U. This value of T_{input} is the time unit in which the node produces data in hardware for the 0-th iteration of the DSP program. For example, T_{input} for the node 1 is $3 + 1 = 4$. The time T_{output} for the node U is $u + P_U + \max_V\{D_F(U \rightarrow V)\}$, where $\max_V\{D_F(U \rightarrow V)\}$ represents the longest folded path delay among all edges that begin at the node U. This value of T_{output} is the latest time that the result of the 0-th iteration of the node is used. For example, T_{output} for the node 1 is $3 + 1 + \max\{1, 0, 2, 3, 5\} = 3 + 1 + 5 = 9$. Note that in this lifetime table it is not necessary to add a latency to the output times because the retiming for folding step guarantees the causality of the system.

The linear lifetime chart for the lifetime table in Table 6.4 is in Fig. 6.14. Note that $N = 4$ is the period of operation. From this lifetime chart, it can be seen that the folded architecture requires 2 registers. The next step is to perform forward-backward register allocation. The allocation table is shown in Fig. 6.15. The variable n_i in this table denotes the output of the node i. This table only shows the 3 variables n_1, n_7, and n_8 because these are the only variables with lifetimes that have nonzero duration. Also, the table shows that the variable n_1 is output in cycle 9. Note that this variable is also output in cycles 4, 5, 6, and 8. For the sake of clarity, the table only shows the latest output time of each variable.

From the allocation table in Fig. 6.15 and the folding equations in (6.2), the final architecture in Fig. 6.16 can be synthesized. For example, the edge $(1 \rightarrow 2)$ has $D_F(1 \rightarrow 2) = 1$ delay in the folded architecture. This edge starts at the node 1, and after 1 delay the variable n_1 is located in the register R_1 in Fig. 6.15, so there exists an edge from R_1 to the adder in the folded

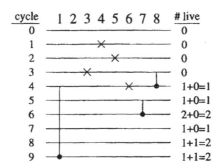

Fig. 6.14   The lifetime chart corresponding to the lifetime table in Table 6.4.

cycle	input	R1	R2	output
0				
1				
2				
3	n_8			
4	n_1	(n_8)		n_8
5	n_7	n_1		
6		(n_7)	n_1	n_7
7			n_1	
8			n_1	
9			(n_1)	n_1

Fig. 6.15   The allocation table for the folded biquad filter.

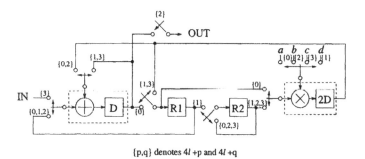

{p,q} denotes 4*l* +p and 4*l* +q

Fig. 6.16 A folded biquad filter architecture implementing the DFG in Fig. 6.3 using the minimum number of registers, which is 2.

architecture, and this edge is switched into the adder at the time instances $4l + 1$ because the node 2 has folding order 1. As another example, the edge $(1 \rightarrow 7)$ has $D_F(1 \rightarrow 7) = 3$ delays, and the variable n_1 is in R_2 in after 2 delays, so there is an edge from R_2 to the multiplier in the folded architecture. This edge is switched into the multiplier at the time instances $4l + 3$ because node 7 has folding order 3. Note that in this example, the number of registers in the folded architecture has been reduced from 6 (see Fig. 6.4) to 2 (see Fig. 6.16).

6.4.2   IIR Filter Example

In this example, the IIR filter in Fig. 6.17(a) that computes $y(n) = ay(n-3) + by(n-5) + x(n)$ is folded. All 6 steps outlined at the beginning of Section 6.4 are performed to find the folded architecture that uses the minimum number of registers. In the 1st step, retiming for folding is performed. The folding equations and retiming for folding inequalities are given in Table 6.5. Using the technique in Section 4.3 to solve the retiming for folding inequalities results in the retiming solution $r(1) = 0$, $r(2) = 0$, $r(3) = -2$, and $r(4) = -1$. The retimed DFG is shown in Fig. 6.17(b).

Table 6.5 Folding Equations and Retiming for Folding Equations for the DFG in Fig. 6.17(a)

Edge	Folding Equation	Retiming for Folding Equation
$1 \rightarrow 2$	$D_F(1 \rightarrow 2) = 0$	$r(1) - r(2) \leq 0$
$2 \rightarrow 3$	$D_F(2 \rightarrow 3) = 9$	$r(2) - r(3) \leq 4$
$2 \rightarrow 4$	$D_F(2 \rightarrow 4) = 4$	$r(2) - r(4) \leq 2$
$3 \rightarrow 1$	$D_F(3 \rightarrow 1) = -3$	$r(3) - r(1) \leq -2$
$4 \rightarrow 1$	$D_F(4 \rightarrow 1) = -2$	$r(4) - r(1) \leq -1$

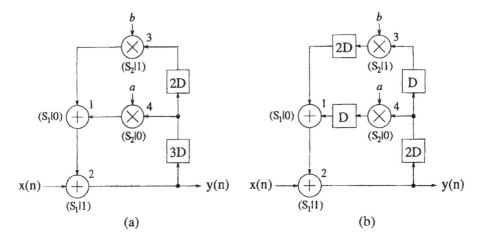

Fig. 6.17   (a) The IIR filter that computes $y(n) = ay(n-3) + by(n-5) + x(n)$. (b) A retimed version of the filter with nonnegative folded edge delays.

Table 6.6   Lifetimes for the Equations in (6.6)

Node	$T_{input} \rightarrow T_{output}$
1	$1 \rightarrow 1$
2	$2 \rightarrow 7$
3	$3 \rightarrow 4$
4	$2 \rightarrow 2$

The folding equations for the retimed DFG in Fig. 6.17(b) are

$$
\begin{aligned}
D_F(1 \rightarrow 2) &= 2(0) - 1 + 1 - 0 = 0 \\
D_F(2 \rightarrow 3) &= 2(3) - 1 + 1 - 1 = 5 \\
D_F(2 \rightarrow 4) &= 2(2) - 1 + 0 - 1 = 2 \\
D_F(3 \rightarrow 1) &= 2(2) - 2 + 0 - 1 = 1 \\
D_F(4 \rightarrow 1) &= 2(1) - 2 + 0 - 0 = 0.
\end{aligned}
\tag{6.6}
$$

The lifetime table for these equations is shown in Table 6.6, the lifetime chart is given in Fig. 6.18, and the allocation table is shown in Fig. 6.19(a). From the allocation table and the folding equations in (6.6), the architecture in Fig. 6.19(b) can be synthesized. This architecture requires 3 registers (not including the pipelining registers) as opposed to 6 registers needed in a straightforward implementation without register minimization.

cycle	1 2 3 4	# live
0	———————	0
1	—✕———————	0
2	——————✕—	0+0=0
3	———————┼—	1+0=1
4	————————●—	2+0=2
5	———————┼—	1+1=2
6	———————┼—	1+2=3
7	———————●—	1+2=3

Fig. 6.18 The lifetime chart corresponding to the lifetimes in Table 6.6.

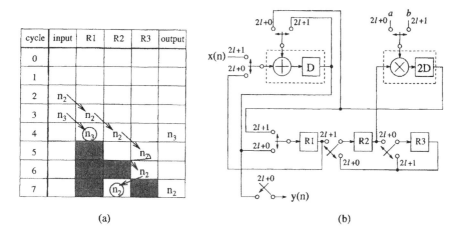

(a)   (b)

Fig. 6.19 (a) The allocation table for the IIR filter example. (b) The minimum-register architecture for the IIR filter example.

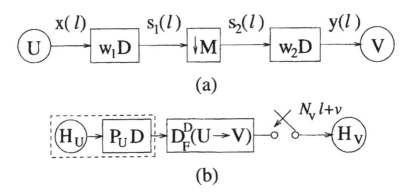

Fig. 6.20 (a) Decimation by M. (b) Expansion by M.

Fig. 6.21 (a) An arc $U \to V$ containing a decimator. (b) The corresponding folded arc.

6.5 FOLDING OF MULTIRATE SYSTEMS

Multirate DSP algorithm descriptions contain decimators and/or expanders (see Section 1.2.9). Fig. 6.20 shows a decimator and an expander. The decimator obeys the input-output relationship $y_D(n) = x(Mn)$, and the expander obeys the input-output relationship

$$y_E(n) = \begin{cases} x(\frac{n}{M}) & \text{if } n \text{ is a multiple of } M \\ 0 & \text{otherwise.} \end{cases}$$

The decimator throws away $(M - 1)$ out of M samples and the expander inserts $(M - 1)$ zero-samples between 2 nonzero samples. The decimator and the expander both have the effect of changing the sample rate.

The folding equation for an edge that contains no decimators or expanders is given in (6.1). Folding equations can also be derived for an edge that contains a decimator or an expander [9]. In this section we derive the equation for edges that contain a decimator; the case where an edge contains an expander is left as an exercise (see Problem 22).

Consider the edge $U \to V$ in Fig. 6.21(a), where the output of the node U passes through w_1 delays, decimation by M, and w_2 delays before reaching the node V. Let the l-th iteration of the node U be executed at time unit $N_U l + u$ and the l-th iteration of V execute at $N_V l + v$, where the folding orders u and v satisfy $u \in [0, N_U)$ and $v \in [0, N_V)$. The signals labeled in

Fig. 6.21(a) are related by

$$
\begin{aligned}
s_1(l) &= x(l - w_1) \\
s_2(l) &= s_1(Ml) = x(Ml - w_1) \\
y(l) &= s_2(l - w_2) = x(M(l - w_2) - w_1),
\end{aligned}
$$

which implies that the sample $y(l)$, which is consumed during the l-th iteration of V, is produced during the $(Ml - (Mw_2 + w_1))$-th iteration of U. The sample $y(l)$ is consumed by H_V in time unit $N_V l + v$ and is computed by H_U in time unit $N_U(Ml - (Mw_2 + w_1)) + u$. If H_U is pipelined by P_U stages, then $y(l)$ is available at time unit $N_U(Ml - (Mw_2 + w_1)) + u + P_U$. Therefore, $y(l)$ must be stored for

$$
\begin{aligned}
D_F^D(U \to V) &= [N_V l + v] - [N_U(Ml - (Mw_2 + w_1)) + u + P_U] \\
&= (N_V - MN_U)l + N_U(Mw_2 + w_1) - P_U + v - u
\end{aligned}
$$

time units. As in the single-rate case, this expression should be independent of the iteration number, l. This can be achieved by forcing $N_V = MN_U$, which implies that the node U executes M times for each execution of the node V. This appeals to our intuition because the output of the node U is decimated by M before reaching the node V. With $N_V = MN_U$, the folding equation becomes

$$
D_F^D(U \to V) = N_U(Mw_2 + w_1) - P_U + v - u, \tag{6.7}
$$

which is independent of the iteration number, l.

Since the node V is scheduled to execute on hardware operator H_V at time units $N_V l + v$, the data on the edge $U \to V$ are input to H_V at time units $N_V l + v$ as illustrated in Fig. 6.21(b). For the case of $M = 1$, i.e., where the decimator does not affect the data stream, w_1 and w_2 can be combined as $w = w_1 + w_2$, and $N_U = N_V = N$, where N is the iteration period of the nodes U and V. Substituting these expressions into (6.7) gives the single-rate folding equation, (6.1), as expected.

As an example of folding edges that contain decimators, consider the DFG in Fig. 6.22(a). The folding factors or the iteration periods of the nodes are $N_U = 2$ and $N_{V_0} = N_{V_1} = N_{V_2} = N_{V_3} = 6$. The folding orders are $u = 1$, $v_0 = 1$, $v_1 = 2$, $v_2 = 4$, and $v_3 = 5$. Node U is assigned to a processor that is pipelined by one stage, i.e., $P_U = 1$. The folding equations are

$$
\begin{aligned}
D_F^D(U \overset{e_0}{\to} V_0) &= 2(3(1) + 2) - 1 + 1 - 1 = 9 \\
D_F^D(U \overset{e_1}{\to} V_1) &= 2(3(0) + 1) - 1 + 2 - 1 = 2 \\
D_F^D(U \overset{e_2}{\to} V_2) &= 2(3(0) + 3) - 1 + 4 - 1 = 8 \\
D_F^D(U \overset{e_3}{\to} V_3) &= 2(3(2) + 0) - 1 + 5 - 1 = 15.
\end{aligned}
$$

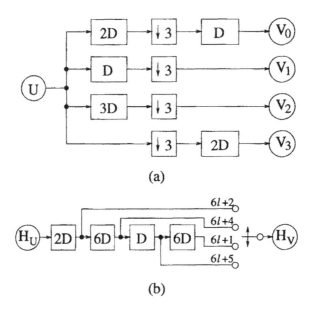

Fig. 6.22 (a) A DFG with edges containing decimators. (b) The folded architecture.

$$\xrightarrow{\quad} \boxed{\downarrow M} \xrightarrow{\;z^{-w}\;} \quad \equiv \quad \xrightarrow{\;z^{-Mw}\;} \boxed{\downarrow M} \xrightarrow{\quad}$$

(a)

$$\xrightarrow{\;z^{-w}\;} \boxed{\uparrow M} \xrightarrow{\quad} \quad \equiv \quad \xrightarrow{\quad} \boxed{\uparrow M} \xrightarrow{\;z^{-Mw}\;}$$

(b)

Fig. 6.23 Redistribution of delays in a multirate system using the noble identities.

If the four nodes V_i, $i = 1, 2, 3, 4$, are all executed by the same functional unit, H_V, then the folded architecture is shown in Fig. 6.22(b). Note that the number of registers can be reduced using lifetime analysis.

For (6.7) to be useful, $D_F^D(U \to V) \geq 0$ must hold given a feasible schedule. Retiming for folding can be used for multirate DFGs (MRDFGs) in a manner similar to that used in single-rate DFGs (SRDFGs). Before deriving the retiming for folding constraints for edges containing decimators, some multirate fundamentals are reviewed.

The noble identities are useful for theory and implementation of multirate DSP [4]. Special cases of these identities are shown in Fig. 6.23. These relationships are used to derive conditions for retiming an MRDFG for folding.

The DFG can be retimed to satisfy the condition $D_F^D(U \to V) \geq 0$. Let w_1' and w_2' be the number of delays on arc $U \to V$ after retiming. Using (6.7), the number of delays on the folded arc after retiming is

$$D_F'^D(U \to V) = N_U(Mw_2' + w_1') - P_U + v - u.$$

The values of w_1' and w_2' are related to w_1 and w_2 by

$$w_1' = w_1 + Mr(D_{uv}) - r(U)$$

and

$$w_2' = w_2 + r(V) - r(D_{uv}),$$

where $r(u)$ and $r(v)$ are the retiming values of nodes U and V, respectively, i.e., the number of times one delay is removed from each of the output arcs of the node and one delay is added to each of the input arcs of the node. According to the noble identity in Fig. 6.23(a), the retiming value of the decimator, $r(D_{uv})$, is the number of times one delay is removed from its output and M delays are added to its input. Substituting the expressions for w_1' and w_2', we find

$$\begin{aligned} D_F'^D(U \to V) &= N_U[M(w_2 + r(V) - r(D_{uv})) + w_1 \\ &\quad + Mr(D_{uv}) - r(U)] - P_U + v - u \\ &= D_F^D(U \to V) + N_U(Mr(V) - r(U)), \end{aligned}$$

which is independent of $r(D_{uv})$. We can retime the DFG for folding by forcing $D_F'^D(U \to V) \geq 0$, which results in

$$r(U) - Mr(V) \leq \frac{D_F^D(U \to V)}{N_U}.$$

Since M, $r(U)$, and $r(V)$ are all restricted to be integers, this can be written as

$$r(U) - Mr(V) \leq \left\lfloor \frac{D_F^D(U \to V)}{N_U} \right\rfloor. \tag{6.8}$$

Caution must be exercised when retiming a MRDFG due to its periodically time-varying nature. For example, consider the MRDFG in Fig. 6.24(a). If we retime this DFG by assigning the adder a retiming value of -1 and assigning the multiplier a retiming value of 0, we get the DFG in Fig. 6.24(b). The problem is that these 2 circuits have completely different functionality. In the single-rate case, retiming an input node simply results in a delay at the output signal, where this example shows that retiming an input node of an MRDFG can completely change the functionality of the circuit.

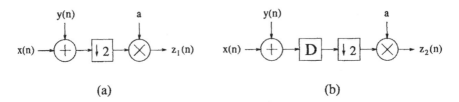

Fig. 6.24 (a) An MRDFG that computes $z_1(n) = a(x(2n) + y(2n))$. (b) Retimed version that computes $z_2(n) = a(x(2n-1) + y(2n-1))$.

6.6 CONCLUSIONS

Folding is a systematic transformation technique for design of time-multiplexed architectures and is a generalization of the techniques in [10],[11]. Although folded circuits require less silicon area, these can be operated at higher speed by exploiting fine-grain pipelining of the functional units. This results in no net loss in the sample rate of the system for small folding factors. Folding sets can be designed by any scheduling and allocation techniques (see Appendix B). Lifetime analysis, a technique used in compiler theory, can be used to reduce the number of storage units in folded circuits. This chapter has concentrated on storage unit reduction for scalars or one-dimensional variables. Register minimization for systems involving vectors or multidimensional signals is beyond the scope of this book (see [12],[13]). Extension of folding to one-dimensional multirate systems has been addressed. For folding of multi-dimensional single-rate and multirate systems, the reader is referred to [14].

6.7 PROBLEMS

1. Consider the 6-tap FIR filter

$$y(n) = \sum_{i=0}^{5} h_i x(n-i)$$

implemented using data-broadcast form shown in Fig. 6.25. This filter is implemented using folding factor 2 with folding set

$$S_0 = \{MA5, MA4\}, \quad S_1 = \{MA3, MA2\}, \quad S_2 = \{MA1, MA0\}.$$

(a) Design the folded architecture.

(b) Construct a schedule corresponding to the folded architecture and verify that the folded architecture generates the desired filter output samples.

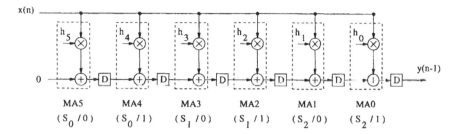

Fig. 6.25   A 6-tap data-broadcast FIR filter for Problem 1.

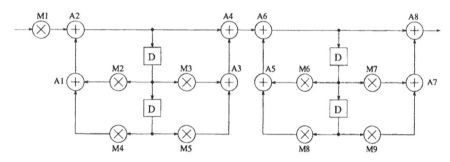

Fig. 6.26   The DFG to be folded in Problem 2.

2. Perform retiming for folding on the DFG in Fig. 6.26 so that the folding sets shown below result in nonnegative edge delays in the folded architecture. Assume that the folding factor $N = 5$, and assume that each multiplier is pipelined by 2 stages and each adder is pipelined by 1 stage. Each operator is clocked with clock period of one u.t. The multiplication operation requires 2 u.t. and the addition operation requires 1 u.t. Note that ϕ represents a null operation.

$$S_{M1} = \{M_2, M_1, M_3, M_6, M_7\}$$
$$S_{M2} = \{M_4, \phi, M_5, M_8, M_9\}$$
$$S_{A1} = \{A_4, \phi, A_1, A_2, A_3\}$$
$$S_{A2} = \{A_5, A_6, A_7, A_8, \phi\}$$

3. Fold the retimed DFG obtained in Problem 2 using the folding sets given in Problem 2.

4. Using the same assumptions as used in Problem 2, fold the DFG in Fig. 6.27 assuming the following folding sets for the iteration period $N = 4$.

$$S_M = \{M_4, M_1, M_3, M_2\}$$
$$S_A = \{A_1, A_3, A_4, A_2\}$$

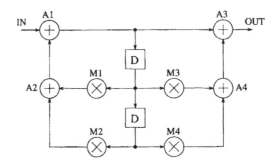

Fig. 6.27 The DFG to be folded in Problems 4, 5, and 6.

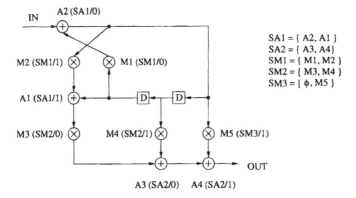

Fig. 6.28 The lattice filter used in Problem 7.

(a) Perform retiming for folding so that the folding sets result in non-negative edge delays in the folded architecture.

(b) Fold the retimed DFG.

5. Repeat Problem 4 using the folding sets

$$S_M = \{M_2, M_1, M_3, M_4\}$$
$$S_A = \{A_1, A_4, A_3, A_2\}.$$

6. Repeat Problem 4 using the folding sets

$$S_M = \{M_4, M_1, M_2, M_3\}$$
$$S_A = \{A_1, A_4, A_3, A_2\}.$$

7. The goal of this problem is to fold the lattice filter shown in Fig. 6.28 using the folding set description shown in the figure. Assume the multiply operations to be mapped to multiply hardware operators pipelined by 2 stages and assume the add operations to be mapped to 1-stage

Table 6.7 Specifications for the Converter Discussed in Problem 8

Variable Name	Input Time Units	Zero-Latency Output Time Units
x_0	0	0
x_1	0	6
x_2	2	0
x_3	2	6
x_4	4	0
x_5	4	6
x_6	6	3
x_7	6	9
x_8	8	3
x_9	8	9
x_{10}	10	3
x_{11}	10	9

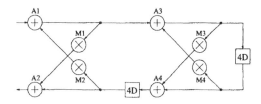

Fig. 6.29 The DFG to be folded in problems 9-13.

pipelined adders. The hardware architecture needs to be clocked with a clock period of 1 u.t.

(a) Systematically perform retiming for folding so that all folded edge delays are nonnegative.

(b) Fold the retimed DFG.

8. Table 6.7 shows the name of the variables, the input time units, and the ideal zero-latency output time units for a data-format converter. Our problem is to design an architecture that will satisfy these constraints. Obtain the latency (T_{lat}), the minimum number of registers, the allocation table, and the associated synthesized architecture using the forward-backward allocation scheme.

9. Using the same assumptions as used in Problem 2, fold the DFG in Fig. 6.29 assuming the following folding sets for the iteration period $N = 2$.

$$S_{M1} = \{M_2, M_1\}$$

$$S_{M2} = \{M_3, M_4\}$$
$$S_{A1} = \{A_1, A_2\}$$
$$S_{A2} = \{A_4, A_3\}$$

(a) Perform retiming for folding so that the folding sets result in non-negative edge delays in the folded architecture.

(b) Fold the retimed DFG.

(c) Minimize the number of registers and redesign the folded architecture.

10. Repeat Problem 9 for iteration period $N = 2$ using the folding sets

$$S_{M1} = \{M_2, M_1\}$$
$$S_{M2} = \{M_4, M_3\}$$
$$S_{A1} = \{A_1, A_2\}$$
$$S_{A2} = \{A_3, A_4\}.$$

11. Repeat Problem 9 for iteration period $N = 2$ using the folding sets

$$S_{M1} = \{M_3, M_1\}$$
$$S_{M2} = \{M_2, M_4\}$$
$$S_{A1} = \{A_1, A_3\}$$
$$S_{A2} = \{A_4, A_2\}.$$

12. Repeat Problem 9 for iteration period $N = 4$ using the folding sets

$$S_M = \{M_3, M_1, M_2, M_4\}$$
$$S_A = \{A_1, A_3, A_4, A_2\}.$$

13. Repeat Problem 9 for iteration period $N = 4$ using the folding sets

$$S_M = \{M_4, M_1, M_2, M_3\}$$
$$S_A = \{A_1, A_4, A_3, A_2\}.$$

14. This problem addresses the implementation of a 6-tap FIR filter shown in Fig. 6.30 using a ring architecture containing 2 processing elements (PEs) where each PE contains a multiply-adder, using folding technique. Due to the cyclic property of the ring architecture, the hardware is not fully utilized.

Full hardware utilization of the folded architecture can be achieved by implementing a 2-unfolded 6-tap filter. First, the 6-tap FIR filter is unfolded by a factor of 2, as shown in Fig. 6.31. The two independent

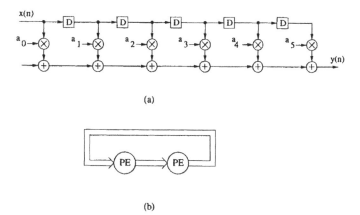

(a)

(b)

Fig. 6.30 The 6-tap FIR filter (in (a)) to be implemented using the ring structure (in (b)) in Problem 14.

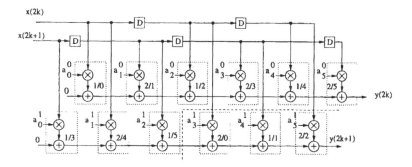

Fig. 6.31 The 2-unfolded 6-tap FIR filter in Problem 14.

computations can then be scheduled in an interleaved manner. The 2 folding sets for the 2-unfolded filter with folding factor 6 are as follows:

$$S1 = \{a_0^0, a_4^1, a_2^0, a_0^1, a_4^0, a_2^1\},$$
$$S2 = \{a_3^1, a_1^0, a_5^1, a_3^0, a_1^1, a_5^0\},$$

where the coefficients with the superscripts i are used to compute $y(2k+i)$, for $i = 0, 1$. The folding sets are also shown in Fig. 6.31. For folding, the multiplication and its associated addition operation are considered as a single operation.

(a) Verify that retiming for folding leads to pipelining of the DFG where the delay elements are placed at the feed-forward cutset shown in Fig. 6.31.

(b) Design the folded architecture for the 6-tap FIR filter.

(c) To minimize the number of registers required, replace the parallel delay lines for $x(2k)$ and $x(2k+1)$ by a single delay line with input $x(n)$. Assume that $x(n)$ is sampled at time unit $3n$. Show that the minimum number of registers required for the folded circuit is 7.

(d) Synthesize the folded architecture using the minimum number of registers based on forward-backward allocation.

15. Dynamic programming (DP) has been used to solve problems in communications and controls, artificial intelligence, and operations research, etc. (see Section 1.2.8). The DP problems have the property that the optimum solution from an initial iteration to the iteration $i+j$ must consist of the optimum solution from initial iteration to iteration i, and from iteration i to iteration $i+j$. In signal processing, DP is frequently used in Viterbi decoders in communication systems, and in hidden Markov models based speech recognition systems [15]. Consider the N-state DP problem given by

$$x_i(n+1) = \max_j[x_j(n) + a_{ji}(n)], \quad i, j = 1, 2, \cdots, N, \qquad (6.9)$$

where $x_i(n)$ is the value for state i in n-th iteration, and variables $\{a_{ji}\}$ are referred to as the trellis or path coefficients. The fundamental operation in (6.9) is add-compare-select (ACS). An N-state DP problem requires N^2 ACS operations in order to update the N state values. The DFG for $N = 4$ is shown in Fig. 6.32, which corresponds to a ring systolic structure. The coefficient a_{ji} is stored in node A_{ji}, and the DFG is wrapped around with edge $\bigcirc i$ on the right connected to the edge on the left with the same number.

(a) Write down the computations performed by all ACS units in the DFG in Fig. 6.32 during n-th iteration, and verify that this DFG updates $x_1(n+1)$, $x_2(n+1)$, $x_3(n+1)$, and $x_4(n+1)$ along the first, second, third, and fourth column, respectively.

(b) Fold the DFG using a folding factor 4, pipelining level of 1 and the following folding sets:

$$\begin{aligned} S_1 &= \{A_{41}, A_{31}, A_{21}, A_{11}\} \\ S_2 &= \{A_{12}, A_{42}, A_{32}, A_{22}\} \\ S_3 &= \{A_{23}, A_{13}, A_{43}, A_{33}\} \\ S_4 &= \{A_{34}, A_{24}, A_{14}, A_{44}\}. \end{aligned}$$

(Hint: You should get a ring systolic structure.)

(c) Fold the DFG using a folding factor 8, pipelining level of 2, and the following folding sets:

$$S_1 = \{A_{41}, A_{23}, A_{31}, A_{13}, A_{21}, A_{43}, A_{11}, A_{33}\}$$

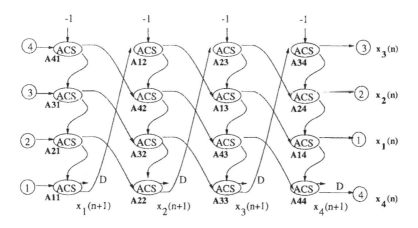

Fig. 6.32   The DFG for the DP in Problem 15.

$$S_2 \; = \; \{A_{12}, A_{34}, A_{42}, A_{24}, A_{32}, A_{14}, A_{22}, A_{44}\}.$$

(d) Fold all the nodes in the DFG onto one processing element using folding factor 16, pipelining level of 4 and the following folding set:

$$S_1 \; = \; \{A_{41}, A_{12}, A_{23}, A_{34}, A_{31}, A_{42}, A_{13}, A_{24},$$
$$A_{21}, A_{32}, A_{43}, A_{14}, A_{11}, A_{22}, A_{33}, A_{44}\}.$$

16. For the lattice filter in Fig. 6.33, let the folding factor be $N = 8$ and the folding sets be

$$S_A \; = \; \{A_1, A_4, A_7, A_2, A_3, A_5, A_8, A_6\}$$
$$S_M \; = \; \{M_4, M_1, M_5, \phi, \phi, M_2, M_3, \phi\}.$$

Assume that addition and multiplication require 1 and 2 units of time, respectively.

(a) Perform retiming for folding so that all folded edges contain non-negative delays.

(b) Synthesize the folded architecture for this system.

(c) Using lifetime analysis, minimize the number of delay elements used in the architecture. Allocate the variables to the minimum number of delay elements using forward-backward allocation. Redraw the folded synthesized architecture.

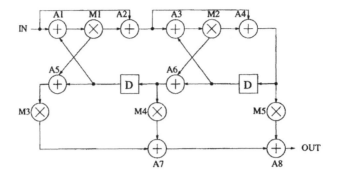

Fig. 6.33 The lattice filter used in Problem 16.

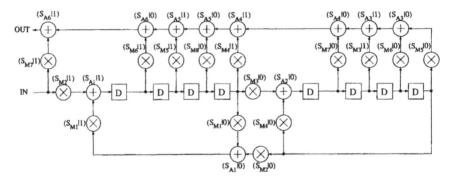

Fig. 6.34 The normalized lattice filter used in Problem 17.

17. Fold the lattice filter shown in Fig. 6.34 using folding factor $N = 2$. Perform retiming for folding if necessary.

18. Design the folded architecture for the pipelined/retimed biquad filter shown in Fig. 6.35 using folding factor 4 for the folding sets

$$S_{M_1} = \{M1, M2, M3, M4\}$$
$$S_{A_1} = \{A3, A4, A1, A2\}.$$

Unfold the folded DFG by unfolding factor 4 and verify that this unfolded DFG is identical to the pipelined/retimed biquad DFG in Fig. 6.35.

19. Consider the folded lattice filter in Problem 7. From the folded edge delays obtained in Problem 7, determine the minimum number of registers required to store the output of each functional unit (a functional unit is an adder or multiplier) using lifetime analysis. Then synthesize a storage unit for each functional unit using forward-backward register allocation. Draw the complete folded architecture using these minimum-register storage units. Compare the number of registers in the architecture with

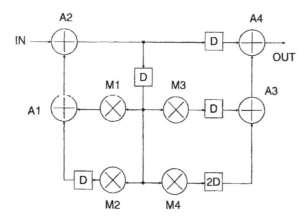

Fig. 6.35   The biquad filter used in Problem 18.

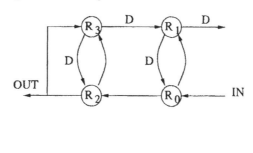

CORDIC rotator

Fig. 6.36   The DFG for Problem 21.

the number of registers obtained in your solution to Problem 7.

20. Let w_l and t_l be the number of delays and the computation time of the loop l. Assume that a node with computation time t is executed on a processor pipelined by t stages.

   (a) Show that

   $$\sum_l D_F(U \to V) = Nw_l - t_l$$

   must hold, where N is the folding factor.

   (b) Use the result in part (a) to show that the folding factor N cannot be less than the iteration bound T_∞.

21. Consider the portion of a retimed 4th-order orthogonal filter structure shown in Fig. 6.36, where all computations are CORDIC rotation operations. This structure is to be implemented using 1 hardware CORDIC

rotator, which can be achieved using folding technique. Let the folding factor be N. Register minimization is not required in this problem.

Assume that each CORDIC rotation operation requires T nsec when operated using a supply voltage of 3.3 V. The folded architecture should be designed such that a sampling period of $4T$ can be achieved, while the power consumption is minimized by use of a lower supply voltage along with possible pipelining of functional units. Assume that the threshold voltage of the technology is 0.5 V and the technology requires use of a minimum supply voltage of 2 V to maintain high noise immunity.

(a) First consider the possibility of using a fine-grain pipelined CORDIC rotator. Assume that the pipelining level of the CORDIC rotator is equal to P. Systematically prove that:

   i. P cannot be greater than 2 if the folding factor N is equal to 4. (Hint: use the constraints imposed by the loops in the algorithm, see Problem 20(a).)

   ii. There are no feasible folding sets for $P = 2$ and $N = 4$.

(b) Design the folded architecture using a 1-state pipelined CORDIC rotator and the folding set $S = \{R_0, R_1, R_2, R_3\}$.

(c) In this part, a 2-level pipelined CORDIC rotator is to be used. Design the folded architecture using a folding factor of 5 and the folding set $S = \{R_0, R_3, \phi, R_1, R_2\}$. Note that the 2-level pipelined CORDIC rotator has a critical path of $0.5T$; however, a clock period of $0.8T$ is enough to meet the sampling period requirement of $4T$. Hence this architecture can be operated at lower supply voltage such that its power consumption can be reduced.

(d) Assume that latches, multiplexers and buses do not consume any power. Compare the power consumption of the designs in part (b) and part (c), to a 1st order approximation. Ignore any capacitive loading effects due to fanout and the effect of glitching. For this, assume the design in part (b) is operated with supply voltage of 3.3 V. (Hint: calculate the appropriate supply voltage for the design in part (c) first.)

(e) Can the power consumption be further reduced by using deeper-pipelined CORDIC rotator ($P \geq 2$) and a larger folding factor $N \geq 5$? Explain your answer with 1 or 2 examples.

22. Consider the edge $U \rightarrow V$ in Fig. 6.37(a), where the output of node U passes through w_1 delays, expansion by L, and w_2 delays before reaching node V. Let the l-th iteration of node U be executed at time unit $N_U l + u$ and the l-th iteration of V be executed at $N_V l + v$, where the folding orders satisfy $u \in [0, N_U)$ and $v \in [0, N_V)$.

(a) Write an expression for $x(l)$ in terms of the signal y.

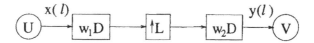

Fig. 6.37 (a) An arc $U \to V$ containing an expander. (b) The corresponding folded arc.

Table 6.8 Schedule for the 3-level Orthonormal DWT Example with Period 8

	0	1	2	3	4	5	6	7
Processor M_1	M_{10}	M_{11}	M_{10}	M_{12}	M_{10}	M_{11}	M_{10}	X
Processor M_2	M_{20}	M_{21}	M_{20}	M_{22}	M_{20}	M_{21}	M_{20}	X
Processor M_3	M_{30}	X	M_{30}	M_{31}	M_{30}	M_{32}	M_{30}	M_{31}
Processor M_4	M_{40}	X	M_{40}	M_{41}	M_{40}	M_{42}	M_{40}	M_{41}
Processor M_5	M_{52}	M_{50}	M_{51}	M_{50}	X	M_{50}	M_{51}	M_{50}
Processor M_6	M_{62}	M_{60}	M_{61}	M_{60}	X	M_{60}	M_{61}	M_{60}
Processor A_1	A_{10}	A_{11}	A_{10}	X	A_{10}	A_{11}	A_{10}	A_{12}
Processor A_2	A_{20}	A_{21}	A_{20}	X	A_{20}	A_{21}	A_{20}	A_{22}
Processor A_3	A_{31}	A_{30}	A_{32}	A_{30}	A_{31}	A_{30}	X	A_{30}
Processor A_4	A_{41}	A_{40}	A_{42}	A_{40}	A_{41}	A_{40}	X	A_{40}

(b) At what time instance is the result of the l-th iteration of U produced by the functional unit H_U that is pipelined by P_U stages? At what time instance is this sample consumed by the functional unit H_V?

(c) Using the results of part (b), derive the folding equation for the edge in Fig. 6.37(a). What is the relationship between N_U and N_V that forces this expression to be independent of the iteration number, l?

(d) Derive the retiming inequality for folding for this edge.

23. In this problem, multirate folding is used to design an architecture for the discrete wavelet transform (see Section 1.2.10). Fold the 3-level orthogonal discrete wavelet transform analysis filter bank that uses 3rd-order wavelet filters, as shown in Fig. 6.38. This DFG has already been retimed so all folded edges have nonnegative number of delays. What is the hardware utilization of the folded architecture? The schedule for the architecture is given in Table 6.8. An X in the schedule represents a null operation.

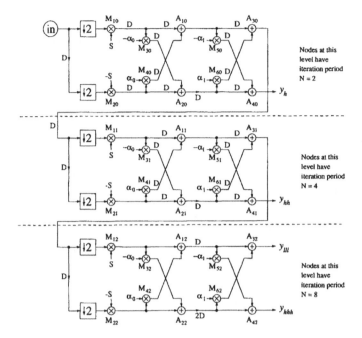

Fig. 6.38   Three-level orthogonal discrete wavelet transform analysis filter bank using 3rd-order wavelet filters.

REFERENCES

1. K. K. Parhi, C.-Y. Wang, and A. P. Brown, "Synthesis of control circuits in folded pipelined DSP architectures," *IEEE Journal of Solid-State Circuits*, vol. 27, no. 1, pp. 29–43, Jan. 1992.

2. K. K. Parhi, "High-level algorithm and architecture transformations for DSP synthesis," *Journal of VLSI Signal Processing*, vol. 9, no. 1, pp. 121–143, Jan. 1995.

3. K. K. Parhi, "Calculation of minimum number of registers in arbitrary life time chart," *IEEE Trans. on Circuits and Systems– II*, vol. 41, no. 6, pp. 434–436, June 1994.

4. P. P. Vaidyanathan, *Multirate Systems and Filter Banks*. Prentice Hall, 1993.

5. A. Aho, R. Sethi, and J. D. Ullman, *Compilers: Principles, Techniques and Tools*. Addison-Wesley, 1986.

6. K. K. Parhi, "Systematic synthesis of DSP data format converters using life time analysis and forward-backward register allocation," *IEEE Trans. on Circuits and Systems - II*, vol. 39, no. 7, pp. 423–440, July 1992.

7. A. Tucker, "Coloring a family of circular arcs," *SIAM Journal of Applied Mathematics*, vol. 29, no. 3, pp. 493–502, Nov. 1975.

8. L. Stok and J. A. G. Jess, "Foreground memory management in data path synthesis," *International Journal of Circuit Theory and Applications*, vol. 20,

no. 3, pp. 235-255, 1992.

9. T. C. Denk and K. K. Parhi, "Synthesis of folded pipelined architectures for multirate DSP algorithms," *IEEE Trans. on VLSI Systems*, vol. 6, no. 4, Dec. 1998.

10. E. F. Girczyc, "Loop winding—a data flow approach to functional pipelining," in *Proc. of IEEE Symposium on Circuits and Systems*, pp. 382–385, May 1987.

11. G. Goossens, J. Rabaey, J. Vandewalle, and H. De Man, "An efficient microcode compiler for application specific DSP processors," *IEEE Trans. on Computer Aided Design of Integrated Circuits and Systems*, pp. 925–937, 1990.

12. F. Franssen, F. Balasa, M. van Swaaij, F. Catthoor, and H. De Man, "Modeling multi-dimensional data and control flow," *IEEE Trans. on VLSI Systems*, vol. 1, pp. 319–327, Sept. 1993.

13. F. Balasa, F. Catthoor, and H. De Man, "Dataflow-driven memory allocation for multi-dimensional signal processing systems," in *Proc. of IEEE International Conference on Computer-Aided Design*, (Santa Clara, CA), pp. 31–34, Nov. 1994.

14. V. Sundararajan and K. K. Parhi, "Synthesis of folded, pipelined architectures for multi-dimensional multirate systems", in *Proc. of IEEE International Conference on Acoustics, Speech, and Signal Processing*, (Seattle, WA), pp. 3089–3092, May 1998.

15. K. K. Parhi, "Pipelining in dynamic programming architectures," *IEEE Trans. on Signal Processing*, pp. 1442–1450, 1991.

7

Systolic Architecture Design

7.1 INTRODUCTION

Systolic architectures (also referred to as systolic arrays) represent a network of processing elements (PEs) that *rhythmically* compute and pass data through the system. These PEs regularly *pump* data in and out such that a regular flow of data is maintained [1],[2]. As a result, systolic systems feature modularity and regularity, which are important properties for VLSI design. The systolic array may be used as a coprocessor in combination with a host computer where the data samples received from the host computer pass through the PEs and the final result is returned to the host computer (see Fig. 7.1). This operation is analogous to the flow of blood through the heart, thus the name "systolic".

Typically, all the PEs in a systolic array are uniform and fully pipelined, i.e., all communicating edges among the PEs contain delay elements, and the whole system usually contains only local interconnections [3]. However, some relaxations have been introduced to increase the utility of systolic arrays. These relaxations include use of not only local but also neighbor (near, but not nearest) interconnections, use of data broadcast operations, and use of different PEs in the system, especially at the boundaries. With these relaxations, a family of modular, regular, and efficient data-driven array architectures can be designed for DSP applications.

This chapter presents the systolic architecture design methodology where many systolic architectures can be designed for any given regular iterative algorithm using linear mapping or projection techniques. The linear systolic mapping methodology is introduced in section 7.2 and is used to derive systolic arrays for FIR filters in section 7.3. Section 7.4 describes how the scheduling vector is selected. Section 7.5 derives several systolic arrays for matrix-matrix multiplication problem. Section 7.6 extends the mapping technique to accommodate regular iterative algorithms that lead to dependence graphs with delays.

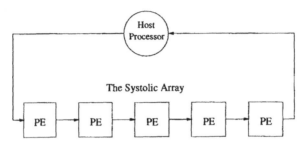

Fig. 7.1 Basic principle of a systolic system.

7.2 SYSTOLIC ARRAY DESIGN METHODOLOGY

Systolic architectures are designed by using linear mapping techniques on *regular* dependence graphs [3] −[7]. The edges in dependence graphs represent precedence constraints. A dependence graph (DG) is said to be regular if the presence of an edge in a certain direction at any node in the DG represents presence of an edge in the same direction at all nodes in the DG.

Example 7.2.1 *As an example, consider the DG for a 3-tap FIR filter*

$$y(n) = \omega_0 x(n) + \omega_1 x(n-1) + \omega_2 x(n-2) \tag{7.1}$$

shown in Fig. 7.2. This DG has 3 fundamental edges: input moving upward represented by an edge in $[0\ 1]^T$ direction, coefficient moving toward the right represented by an edge in $[1\ 0]^T$ direction, and the result moving in $[1\ -1]^T$ direction. Since all nodes in the DG contain the same three edges, this DG is regular. ■

The DG corresponds to a *space representation* where no time instance is assigned to any computation. Typically this corresponds to a $t = 0$ plane. The mapping technique transforms a space representation to a *space-time representation* where each node is mapped to a certain processing element and is scheduled to a certain time instance.

The systolic design methodology maps an N-dimensional DG to a lower dimensional systolic architecture. In this chapter, only one-level mapping is considered where a N-dimensional DG is mapped to an $(N − 1)$-dimensional systolic array.

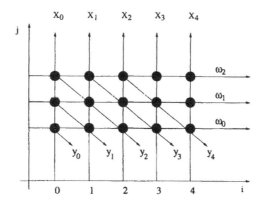

Fig. 7.2 Space representation for FIR filtering.

The basic vectors involved in the systolic array design are now defined.

- Projection vector (also called iteration vector), $\mathbf{d} = \begin{pmatrix} d_1 \\ d_2 \end{pmatrix}$

  Two nodes that are displaced by $\mathbf{d}$ or multiples of $\mathbf{d}$ are executed by the same processor.

- The processor space vector, $\mathbf{p}^T = \begin{pmatrix} p_1 & p_2 \end{pmatrix}$

  Any node with index $I^T = (i, j)$ would be executed by processor

$$\mathbf{p}^T I = \begin{pmatrix} p_1 & p_2 \end{pmatrix} \begin{pmatrix} i \\ j \end{pmatrix}.$$

- Scheduling vector, $\mathbf{s}^T = \begin{pmatrix} s_1 & s_2 \end{pmatrix}$

  Any node with index I would be executed at time, $\mathbf{s}^T I$.

- Hardware Utilization Efficiency, $HUE = 1/|\mathbf{s}^T \mathbf{d}|$.

  This is because two tasks executed by the same processor are spaced $|\mathbf{s}^T \mathbf{d}|$ time units apart.

Many systolic architectures can be designed for a given problem by selecting different projection, processor space and scheduling vectors. These vectors must satisfy the feasibility constraints derived below.

- Processor space vector and the projection vector must be orthogonal to each other. If points A and B differ by the projection vector, i.e., $I_A - I_B$ is same as $\mathbf{d}$, then they must be executed by the same processor. In other words, $\mathbf{p}^T I_A = \mathbf{p}^T I_B$. This leads to

$$\mathbf{p}^T (I_A - I_B) = 0 \Rightarrow \mathbf{p}^T \mathbf{d} = 0. \tag{7.2}$$

- If A and B are mapped to the same processor, then they cannot be executed at the same time, i.e.,

$$\mathbf{s}^T I_A \neq \mathbf{s}^T I_B, \ i.e., \ \mathbf{s}^T \mathbf{d} \neq 0. \tag{7.3}$$

- Edge mapping: If an edge $\mathbf{e}$ exists in the space representation or DG, then an edge $\mathbf{p}^T \mathbf{e}$ is introduced in the systolic array with $\mathbf{s}^T \mathbf{e}$ delays.

The space representation or DG can be transformed to a space-time representation or geometric representation by interpreting one of the spatial dimensions as temporal dimension [8]. For a two-dimensional (2D) DG, the general transformation is described by $i' = t = 0$, $j' = \mathbf{p}^T I$ and $t' = \mathbf{s}^T I$, or equivalently,

$$\begin{pmatrix} i' \\ j' \\ t' \end{pmatrix} = T \begin{pmatrix} i \\ j \\ t \end{pmatrix} = \begin{pmatrix} 0 & 0 & 1 \\ \mathbf{p}^T & & 0 \\ \mathbf{s}^T & & 0 \end{pmatrix} \begin{pmatrix} i \\ j \\ t \end{pmatrix}. \tag{7.4}$$

In the space-time representation, the j' axis represents the processor axis (recall that the 2D-DG is mapped to a one-dimensional (1D) systolic array) and t' represents the scheduling time instance.

7.3   FIR SYSTOLIC ARRAYS

This section derives a family of systolic arrays for FIR digital filters using the linear mapping technique.

7.3.1   Design B_1 (Broadcast Inputs, Move Results, Weights Stay)

The systolic design B_1 is derived by selecting the projection vector, processor vector, and scheduling vector as follows:

$$\mathbf{d} = \begin{pmatrix} 1 \\ 0 \end{pmatrix}, \quad \mathbf{p}^T = (\ 0 \quad 1\ ), \quad \mathbf{s}^T = (\ 1 \quad 0\ ). \tag{7.5}$$

Using these definitions, we can show that:

- Any node with index $I^T = (i, j)$ is mapped to processor

$$\mathbf{p}^T I = (\ 0 \quad 1\ ) \begin{pmatrix} i \\ j \end{pmatrix} = j.$$

Therefore, all nodes on a horizontal line are mapped to the same processor.

- Any node with index $I^T = (i, j)$ is executed at time

$$s^T I = (1 \quad 0) \begin{pmatrix} i \\ j \end{pmatrix} = i.$$

- Since

$$s^T d = (1 \quad 0) \begin{pmatrix} 1 \\ 0 \end{pmatrix} = 1,$$

  then

$$HUE = \frac{1}{|s^T d|} = 1. \tag{7.6}$$

- Edge mapping: The 3 fundamental edges corresponding to weight, input, and result can be mapped to corresponding edges in the systolic array according to Table 7.1.

Table 7.1   Edge Mapping Table for Design B_1

e^T	$p^T e$	$s^T e$
wt(1 0)	0	1
i/p(0 1)	1	0
result(1 − 1)	−1	1

The block diagram of B_1 systolic array design is then constructed as shown in Fig. 7.3. The low-level implementation of this architecture is shown in

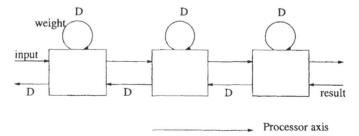

Fig. 7.3   Block diagram of the B_1 design.

Fig. 7.4.

The space-time representation of the B_1 design is shown in Fig. 7.5 from which we can see that the incoming x value is available at all the processors at the same time. Specifically, the input data is "broadcast" to the processors.

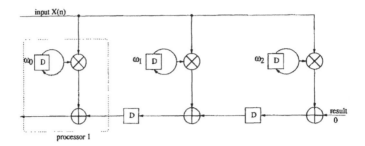

Fig. 7.4 Low-level implementation of the B_1 design.

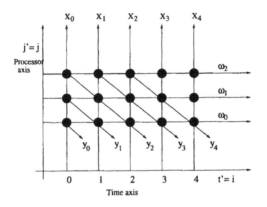

Fig. 7.5 Space-time representation of the B_1 design.

Similarly, the weights, w_i, appear at the processors at the same spatial coordinates. Thus, w_i values "stay". And the outputs, y_i, appear at the processors at different space and time. Hence, the outputs "move".

7.3.2   Design B_2 (Broadcast Inputs, Move Weights, Results Stay)

The projection vector, processor vector, and scheduling vector used to design B_2 are chosen as:

$$\mathbf{d} = \begin{pmatrix} 1 \\ -1 \end{pmatrix}, \quad \mathbf{p}^T = (\ 1 \ \ 1\ ), \quad \mathbf{s}^T = (\ 1 \ \ 0\ ). \tag{7.7}$$

It can be shown that these vectors satisfy the foregoing constraints and

$$\mathbf{s}^T\mathbf{d} = (\ 1 \ \ 0\ )\begin{pmatrix} 1 \\ -1 \end{pmatrix} = 1.$$

Therefore, $HUE = 1$. The edge mapping of design B_2 is shown in Table 7.2.

In the case of design B_2, we observe that the weights move instead of the

Table 7.2 Edge Mapping for Design B_2

e	$\mathbf{p}^T\mathbf{e}$	$\mathbf{s}^T\mathbf{e}$
wt(1, 0)	1	1
i/p(0, 1)	1	0
result(1, −1)	0	1

results as in B_1. But, the inputs are broadcast in both cases. The systolic array for this design is shown in Fig. 7.6 and the low-level representation is shown in Fig. 7.7.

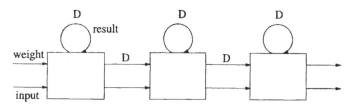

Fig. 7.6 Block diagram of the B_2 design.

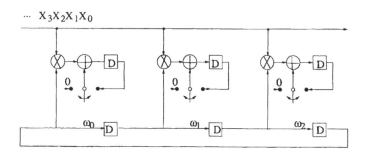

Fig. 7.7 Low-level implementation of the B_2 design.

Applying the space-time transformation, we have

$$j' \;=\; \mathbf{p}^T \begin{pmatrix} i \\ j \end{pmatrix} = i + j \qquad\qquad (7.8)$$

$$t' \;=\; \mathbf{s}^T \begin{pmatrix} i \\ j \end{pmatrix} = i.$$

Therefore, the space-time representation of B_2 is shown in Fig. 7.8. From the figure, it is clear that the input data, x_i, appear to the processors at the same time. Thus, the input data are broadcast. The weights, w_i, appear to the processors at different space and time. Hence, the weights "move". The

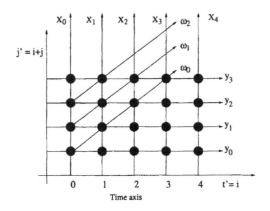

Fig. 7.8 Space-time representation of the B_2 design.

output, y_i, stays in the same processor.

7.3.3   Design F (Fan-In Results, Move Inputs, Weight Stay)

The projection vector, processor vector, and scheduling vector for Design F are chosen as:

$$\mathbf{d} = \begin{pmatrix} 1 \\ 0 \end{pmatrix}, \quad \mathbf{p}^T = (\ 0 \quad 1 \ ), \quad \mathbf{s}^T = (\ 1 \quad 1 \ ). \tag{7.9}$$

In this case, the hardware utilization efficiency HUE is equal to 1. Again, using these vectors, the edges are mapped as shown in Table 7.3. From Table

Table 7.3   Edge Mapping for Design F

$\mathbf{e}^T$	$\mathbf{p}^T \mathbf{e}$	$\mathbf{s}^T \mathbf{e}$
wt(1, 0)	0	1
i/p(0, 1)	1	1
result(1, −1)	-1	0

7.3, it is clear that the weights, w_i, are fixed in space, and the input vector, x_i, moves from left to right with 1 delay element. The output, y_i, moves from right to left with no delay elements. The systolic array and its low-level implementation are shown in Figs. 7.9 and 7.10, respectively. The output in this architecture is "fanned in".

This can also be verified using the geometric (space-time) transformation

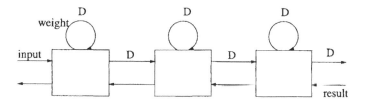

Fig. 7.9 Block diagram of the F design.

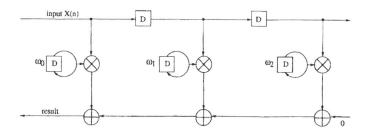

Fig. 7.10 Low-level implementation of the F design.

as follows:

$$j' = \mathbf{p}^T \begin{pmatrix} i \\ j \end{pmatrix} = j, \quad t' = \mathbf{s}^T \begin{pmatrix} i \\ j \end{pmatrix} = i + j.$$

Therefore, the space-time representation of F design is shown in Fig. 7.11. From the geometric representation, we notice that the weights stay, the inputs move, and the outputs are fanned in.

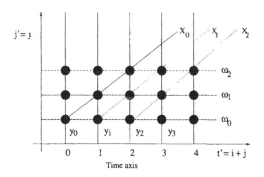

Fig. 7.11 Space-time representation of the F design.

7.3.4 Design R_1 (Results Stay, Inputs and Weights Move in Opposite Directions)

The projection vector, processor vector, and scheduling vector for design R_1 are chosen as:

$$\mathbf{d} = \begin{pmatrix} 1 \\ -1 \end{pmatrix}, \quad \mathbf{p}^T = (1 \quad 1), \quad \mathbf{s}^T = (1 \quad -1), \quad (7.10)$$

and

$$\mathbf{s}^T \mathbf{d} = (1 \quad -1) \begin{pmatrix} 1 \\ -1 \end{pmatrix} = 2.$$

Therefore, the hardware utilization efficiency is given by 1/2. The edge mapping of design R_1 is summarized in Table 7.4, the systolic array architecture and the lower-level implementation of design R_1 are shown in Figs. 7.12 and 7.13, respectively. Note that the input direction has been reversed to guarantee $\mathbf{s}^T \mathbf{e} \geq 0$ for all edges. This is permissible only when there are no precedence constraints for the computations along the edge. Similar to design B_2, the results are accumulated in the same processor. However, 3 outputs are completed in 6 clock cycles. Thus, the average rate of output is 1 per 2 clock cycles.

Table 7.4 Edge Mapping for Design R_1

$\mathbf{e}^T$	$\mathbf{p}^T\mathbf{e}$	$\mathbf{s}^T\mathbf{e}$
wt(1, 0)	1	1
i/p(0, −1)	−1	1
result(1, −1)	0	2

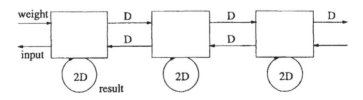

Fig. 7.12 Block diagram of the R_1 design.

Following the same analysis, 5 other systolic array designs can be derived. The projection vectors, processor vectors, and scheduling vectors used to derive these designs are summarized in the following sections but details are omitted.

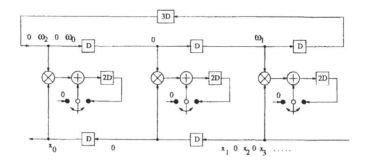

Fig. 7.13 Low-level implementation of the R_1 design.

7.3.5 Design R_2 and Dual R_2 (Results Stay, Inputs and Weights Move in the Same Direction but at Different Speeds)

The projection vector and processor vector of designs R_2 and dual R_2 are the same:

$$\mathbf{d} = \begin{pmatrix} 1 \\ -1 \end{pmatrix}, \quad \mathbf{p}^T = \begin{pmatrix} 1 & 1 \end{pmatrix}. \tag{7.11}$$

The scheduling vectors of design R_2 and dual R_2 are different and are given by :

$$R_2 : \ \mathbf{s}^T = \begin{pmatrix} 2 & 1 \end{pmatrix}; \quad Dual \ R_2 : \ \mathbf{s}^T = \begin{pmatrix} 1 & 2 \end{pmatrix}. \tag{7.12}$$

The 2 designs have the same hardware utilization efficiency $HUE = 1$. Their edge mappings are summarized in Table 7.5. Note that the result edge in design dual R_2 has been reversed to guarantee $\mathbf{s}^T \mathbf{e} \geq 0$.

Table 7.5 Edge Mapping for Designs R_2 and Dual R_2

R_2			Dual R_2		
$\mathbf{e}^T$	$\mathbf{p}^T \mathbf{e}$	$\mathbf{s}^T \mathbf{e}$	$\mathbf{e}^T$	$\mathbf{p}^T \mathbf{e}$	$\mathbf{s}^T \mathbf{e}$
wt$(1, \ 0)$	1	2	wt$(1, \ 0)$	1	1
i/p$(0, \ 1)$	1	1	i/p$(0, \ 1)$	1	2
result$(1, \ -1)$	0	1	result$(-1, \ 1)$	0	1

7.3.6 Design W_1 (Weights Stay, Inputs and Results Move in Opposite Directions)

The projection vector, processor vector, and scheduling vector are

$$d = \begin{pmatrix} 1 \\ 0 \end{pmatrix}, \quad p^T = (\ 0 \quad 1\ ), \quad s^T = (\ 2 \quad 1\ ), \tag{7.13}$$

and the hardware utilization efficiency is $HUE = 1/2$. The edge mapping table is summarized in Table 7.6.

Table 7.6   Edge Mapping for Design W_1

e^T	$p^T e$	$s^T e$
wt(1, 0)	0	2
i/p(0, 1)	1	1
result(1, −1)	−1	1

7.3.7 Design W_2 and Dual W_2 (Weights Stay, Inputs and Results Move in Same Direction but at Different Speeds)

The projection vector and processor vector for design W_2 and dual W_2 are the same; their scheduling vectors are different, as follows:

$$d = \begin{pmatrix} 1 \\ 0 \end{pmatrix}, p^T = (\ 0 \quad 1\ )$$
$$W_2: \ s^T = (\ 1 \quad 2\ ); Dual\ W_2: \ s^T = (\ 1 \quad -1\ ). \tag{7.14}$$

The hardware utilization efficiency of both designs are equal to 1. Their edge mapping are summarized in Table 7.7. Note that both the input edge and the result edge for design dual W_2 are reversed to guarantee $s^T e \geq 0$.

Table 7.7   Edge Mapping for Designs W_2 and Dual W_2

W_2			Dual W_2		
e^T	$p^T e$	$s^T e$	e^T	$p^T e$	$s^T e$
wt(1, 0)	0	1	wt(1, 0)	0	1
i/p(0, 1)	1	2	i/p(0, −1)	−1	1
result(−1, 1)	1	1	result(1, −1)	−1	2

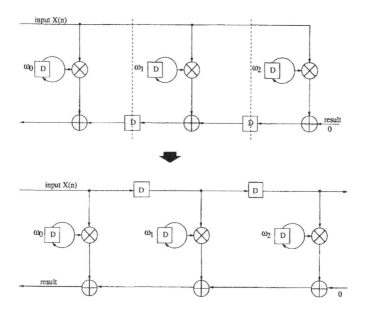

Fig. 7.14   Derivation of design F from design B_1 using cutset retiming.

7.3.8   Relating Systolic Designs Using Transformations

The FIR systolic architectures obtained using the same projection vector and processor space vector, but different scheduling vectors, can be derived from each other using transformations, such as edge reversal, associativity, slow-down, retiming, and pipelining. *Edge reversal* transformation denotes reversing the direction of an edge in the DG when there is no precedence constraints along that directed edge. *Associativity* can be used to change the order of additions when accumulating several elements, i.e., $(a+b)+c = a+(b+c)$. The readers may refer to chapters 4 and 3 for the definitions of other transformations.

It can be observed that the design F can be obtained by applying cutset retiming to the design B_1, as shown in Fig. 7.14; the design W_1 can be obtained from the design F by first slowing down by a factor of 2, then applying cutset retiming, etc. Derivations of these systolic arrays from each other are left as exercises as the end of this chapter.

7.4   SELECTION OF SCHEDULING VECTOR

For any specified projection vector, processor space vector and scheduling vector, the systolic array can be designed using linear mapping technique. In this section, the method of selecting feasible scheduling vectors using scheduling inequalities is discussed. Based on the selected scheduling vector s^T, the projection vector $\mathbf{d}$ and the processor space vector $\mathbf{p}^T$ can be selected according to equations (7.3) and (7.2). Hence the desired systolic array can be obtained.

7.4.1   Selection of s^T Based on Scheduling Inequalities

Consider the dependence relation $X \rightarrow Y$,

$$X : I_x = \begin{pmatrix} i_x \\ j_x \end{pmatrix} \longrightarrow Y : I_y = \begin{pmatrix} i_y \\ j_y \end{pmatrix}, \tag{7.15}$$

where I_x and I_y are the indices of node X and node Y, respectively. The scheduling inequality for this dependence is defined as

$$S_y \geq S_x + T_x, \tag{7.16}$$

where T_x is the time to compute node X and S_x, S_y are the scheduling times for nodes X, Y, respectively. The scheduling equations can be classified into 2 types:

1. Linear scheduling, where

$$\begin{aligned} S_x &= s^T I_x = \begin{pmatrix} s_1 & s_2 \end{pmatrix} \begin{pmatrix} i_x \\ j_x \end{pmatrix} \\ S_y &= s^T I_y = \begin{pmatrix} s_1 & s_2 \end{pmatrix} \begin{pmatrix} i_y \\ j_y \end{pmatrix}. \end{aligned} \tag{7.17}$$

2. Affine scheduling, where

$$\begin{aligned} S_x &= s^T I_x + \gamma_x = \begin{pmatrix} s_1 & s_2 \end{pmatrix} \begin{pmatrix} i_x \\ j_x \end{pmatrix} + \gamma_x \\ S_y &= s^T I_y + \gamma_y = \begin{pmatrix} s_1 & s_2 \end{pmatrix} \begin{pmatrix} i_y \\ j_y \end{pmatrix} + \gamma_y. \end{aligned} \tag{7.18}$$

Using the foregoing definition, we can rewrite the scheduling equation for affine scheduling as

$$s^T I_y + \gamma_y \geq s^T I_x + \gamma_x + T_x. \tag{7.19}$$

Note that the scheduling equation for linear scheduling can be obtained by setting γ_x and γ_y equal to zero. Define the edge from node X to node Y as $e_{x-y} = I_y - I_x$. Then the scheduling inequality for an edge is described as follows:

$$s^T e_{x-y} + \gamma_y - \gamma_x \geq T_x. \tag{7.20}$$

Therefore, one scheduling inequality can be obtained for each fundamental edge in the dependence graph and the scheduling vector $\mathbf{s}^T$ can be obtained by solving these inequalities. Hence the selection of scheduling vector consists of 2 steps.

1. Capture all the fundamental edges. The reduced dependence graph (RDG) is used to capture the fundamental edges and the regular iterative algorithm (RIA) description of the corresponding problem is used to construct RDGs. Both are discussed in detail in the following subsections.

2. Construct the scheduling inequalities according to (7.20) and solve them for feasible $\mathbf{s}^T$.

7.4.2   RIA Description

In this section, the regular iterative algorithm (RIA) is introduced and the method for constructing RDGs using RIA is illustrated.

The RIA has two standard forms, which are defined as follows:

- The RIA is in *standard input RIA* form if the index of the inputs are the same for all equations.

- The RIA is in *standard output RIA* form if all output indices, i.e., indices on the left side, are the same.

Using the same FIR filtering example, the RIA description is written as

$$
\begin{aligned}
W(i+1,j) &= W(i,j) \\
X(i,j+1) &= X(i,j) \\
Y(i+1,j-1) &= Y(i,j) + W(i+1,j-1)X(i+1,j-1). \quad (7.21)
\end{aligned}
$$

It is obvious that the FIR filtering problem cannot be expressed in standard input RIA form. It, however, can be described using the standard output RIA description, as shown in (7.22).

$$
\begin{aligned}
W(i,j) &= W(i-1,j) \\
X(i,j) &= X(i,j-1) \\
Y(i,j) &= Y(i-1,j+1) + W(i,j)X(i,j). \quad (7.22)
\end{aligned}
$$

From these equations, the RDG in Fig. 7.15 can be obtained.

7.4.3   Scheduling Vector and Systolic Array Design Using RDG

This section considers the construction of scheduling inequalities using RDG, the selection of scheduling vector using scheduling inequalities, and the sys-

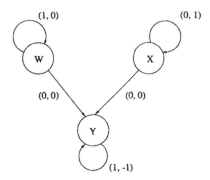

Fig. 7.15 Reduced dependence graph of the FIR filtering example.

tolic mapping using the scheduling vector. The FIR filter example is used to illustrate this approach. This formulation, due to its generality, can accommodate different computation times for various operations.

Example 7.4.1 *Assume that the time to perform multiplication, addition, and communication are as follows:*

$$T_{mult} = 5, \quad T_{add} = 2, \quad T_{com} = 1.$$

Recall the scheduling inequality for an edge in a DG is given by:

$$\mathbf{s}^T \mathbf{e} + \gamma_y - \gamma_x \geq T_x$$

where

$$\mathbf{s} = \begin{pmatrix} s_1 \\ s_2 \end{pmatrix}.$$

There are 5 edges in the RDG shown in Fig. 7.15. The scheduling inequality for each of these edges is as follows:

$$W \rightarrow Y: \quad \mathbf{e} = \begin{pmatrix} 0 \\ 0 \end{pmatrix}, \quad \gamma_y - \gamma_w \geq 0$$

$$X \rightarrow X: \quad \mathbf{e} = \begin{pmatrix} 0 \\ 1 \end{pmatrix}, \quad s_2 + \gamma_x - \gamma_x \geq 1$$

$$W \rightarrow W: \quad \mathbf{e} = \begin{pmatrix} 1 \\ 0 \end{pmatrix}, \quad s_1 + \gamma_w - \gamma_w \geq 1$$

$$X \rightarrow Y: \quad \mathbf{e} = \begin{pmatrix} 0 \\ 0 \end{pmatrix}, \quad \gamma_y - \gamma_x \geq 0$$

$$Y \rightarrow Y: \quad \mathbf{e} = \begin{pmatrix} 1 \\ -1 \end{pmatrix}, \quad s_1 - s_2 + \gamma_y - \gamma_y \geq 5 + 2 + 1.$$

For linear scheduling, $\gamma_x = \gamma_y = \gamma_w = 0$. Simplifying these equations, we have

$$s_1 \geq 1, \quad s_2 \geq 1, \quad s_1 - s_2 \geq 8.$$

Therefore, one of the solutions is

$$s_2 = 1, s_1 = 8 + 1 = 9 \Rightarrow s^T = (9, 1). \tag{7.23}$$

Now, select $\mathbf{d} = (1, -1)$ such that $\mathbf{s}^T\mathbf{d} \neq 0$ and select $\mathbf{p}^T$ such that $\mathbf{p}^T\mathbf{d} = 0$. Choose $\mathbf{p}^T = (1, 1)$. Since

$$\mathbf{s}^T\mathbf{d} = \begin{pmatrix} 9 & 1 \end{pmatrix} \begin{pmatrix} 1 \\ -1 \end{pmatrix} = 8,$$

therefore $HUE = 1/8$. Now, the edges can be mapped using Table 7.8. The

Table 7.8   Edge Mapping for Example 7.4.1

e^T	$p^T e$	$s^T e$
wt(1, 0)	1	9
i/p(0, 1)	1	1
result(1, −1)	0	8

systolic array architecture is shown in Fig. 7.16. ■

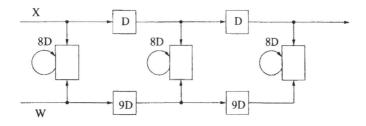

Fig. 7.16   Systolic array architecture of the Example 7.4.1.

7.5   MATRIX-MATRIX MULTIPLICATION AND 2D SYSTOLIC ARRAY DESIGN

In this section, systolic arrays are designed for matrix-matrix multiplication [4]. The DG for this problem corresponds to a three-dimensional (3D) space representation. Linear projection is used to design 2D systolic arrays for matrix-matrix multiplication.

Given 2 matrices A and B, we can denote their product as $C = AB$, where A, B, and C are $n \times n$ matrices. For $n = 2$, we have

$$\begin{pmatrix} c_{11} & c_{12} \\ c_{21} & c_{22} \end{pmatrix} = \begin{pmatrix} a_{11} & a_{12} \\ a_{21} & a_{22} \end{pmatrix} \begin{pmatrix} b_{11} & b_{12} \\ b_{21} & b_{22} \end{pmatrix}$$

$$\begin{aligned} c_{11} &= a_{11}b_{11} + a_{12}b_{21} \\ c_{12} &= a_{11}b_{12} + a_{12}b_{22} \\ c_{21} &= a_{21}b_{11} + a_{22}b_{21} \\ c_{22} &= a_{21}b_{12} + a_{22}b_{22}. \end{aligned}$$

These equations can be represented in a space representation as shown in Fig. 7.17.

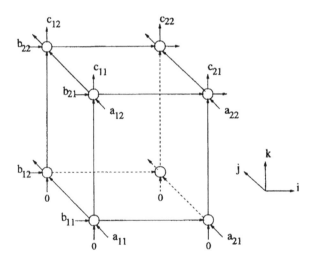

Fig. 7.17 Systolic array architecture of the matrix product computation.

From the space diagram, we can write the iteration in standard output RIA form as follows:

$$\begin{aligned} a(i, j, k) &= a(i, j - 1, k) \\ b(i, j, k) &= b(i - 1, j, k) \\ c(i, j, k) &= c(i, j, k - 1) + a(i, j, k)b(i, j, k). \end{aligned}$$

The corresponding RDG is shown in Fig. 7.18. Now, applying the scheduling inequality for each edge in the RDG $s^T e + \gamma_y - \gamma_x \geq T_x$ and assuming

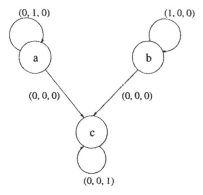

Fig. 7.18 Reduce dependence graph of the matrix product computation.

$T_{mult-add} = 1$ and $T_{com} = 0$, we have,

$$a \rightarrow a: \quad \mathbf{e} = \begin{pmatrix} 0 \\ 1 \\ 0 \end{pmatrix}, \quad s_2 \geq 0$$

$$b \rightarrow b: \quad \mathbf{e} = \begin{pmatrix} 1 \\ 0 \\ 0 \end{pmatrix}, \quad s_1 \geq 0$$

$$c \rightarrow c: \quad \mathbf{e} = \begin{pmatrix} 0 \\ 0 \\ 1 \end{pmatrix}, \quad s_3 \geq 1$$

$$a \rightarrow c: \quad \mathbf{e} = \begin{pmatrix} 0 \\ 0 \\ 0 \end{pmatrix}, \quad \gamma_c - \gamma_a \geq 0$$

$$b \rightarrow c: \quad \mathbf{e} = \begin{pmatrix} 0 \\ 0 \\ 0 \end{pmatrix}, \quad \gamma_c - \gamma_b \geq 0.$$

For linear scheduling, $\gamma_a = \gamma_b = \gamma_c = 0$. Consider the following possible solutions:

- Solution 1:

$$\mathbf{s}^T = (1,1,1), \quad \mathbf{d} = \begin{pmatrix} 0 \\ 0 \\ 1 \end{pmatrix}, \quad \mathbf{P}^T = \begin{pmatrix} 1 & 0 & 0 \\ 0 & 1 & 0 \end{pmatrix}.$$

$$\mathbf{P}^T\mathbf{d} \;=\; \begin{pmatrix} 1 & 0 & 0 \\ 0 & 1 & 0 \end{pmatrix}\begin{pmatrix} 0 \\ 0 \\ 1 \end{pmatrix} = \begin{pmatrix} 0 \\ 0 \end{pmatrix}$$

$$\mathbf{s}^T\mathbf{d} \;=\; \begin{pmatrix} 1 & 1 & 1 \end{pmatrix}\begin{pmatrix} 0 \\ 0 \\ 1 \end{pmatrix} = 1.$$

Therefore, *HUE* is 1. The edge mapping of the DG is summarized in Table 7.9. The corresponding 2D systolic array architecture of this design is shown in Fig. 7.19.

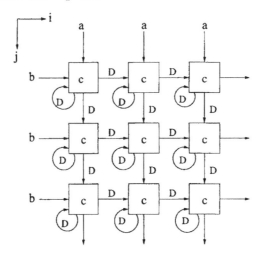

Fig. 7.19 Two-dimensional systolic array by S. Y. Kung [3].

- Solution 2: Consider the projection vector, scheduling vector, and processor space vector shown below:

$$\mathbf{s}^T = (1,1,1), \quad \mathbf{d} = \begin{pmatrix} 1 \\ 1 \\ -1 \end{pmatrix}, \quad \mathbf{P}^T = \begin{pmatrix} 1 & 0 & 1 \\ 0 & 1 & 1 \end{pmatrix}.$$

For this design,

$$\mathbf{P}^T\mathbf{d} \;=\; \begin{pmatrix} 1 & 0 & 1 \\ 0 & 1 & 1 \end{pmatrix}\begin{pmatrix} 1 \\ 1 \\ -1 \end{pmatrix} = \begin{pmatrix} 0 \\ 0 \end{pmatrix}$$

$$\mathbf{s}^T\mathbf{d} \;=\; \begin{pmatrix} 1 & 1 & 1 \end{pmatrix}\begin{pmatrix} 1 \\ 1 \\ -1 \end{pmatrix} = 1.$$

Therefore, *HUE* = 1. The edge mapping of the DG is summarized in

Table 7.9. The corresponding two dimensional systolic array design is shown in Fig. 7.20.

Table 7.9   Edge Mapping for Solutions 1 and 2 of Matrix-Matrix Multiplication

	Sol. 1		Sol. 2	
$\mathbf{e}^T$	$\mathbf{P}^T\mathbf{e}$	$\mathbf{s}^T\mathbf{e}$	$\mathbf{P}^T\mathbf{e}$	$\mathbf{s}^T\mathbf{e}$
a(0, 1, 0)	(0, 1)	1	(0, 1)	1
b(1, 0, 0)	(1, 0)	1	(1, 0)	1
C(0, 0, 1)	(0, 0)	1	(1, 1)	1

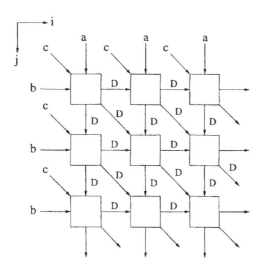

Fig. 7.20   Two-dimensional systolic array by Weiser-Davis [4].

The following are some other solutions:

- Solution 3:

$$\mathbf{s}^T = (1,1,1), \quad \mathbf{d} = \begin{pmatrix} 1 \\ 0 \\ 1 \end{pmatrix}, \quad \mathbf{P}^T = \begin{pmatrix} 1 & 0 & -1 \\ 0 & 1 & 0 \end{pmatrix}$$

This solution leads to the *Schreiher-Rao* 2D systolic array.

- Solution 4:

$$\mathbf{s}^T = (1,1,1), \quad \mathbf{d} = \begin{pmatrix} 1 \\ 1 \\ 1 \end{pmatrix}, \quad \mathbf{P}^T = \begin{pmatrix} 1 & 0 & -1 \\ 0 & 1 & -1 \end{pmatrix}$$

This solution leads to the *Kung-Leiserson* systolic array.

- Solution 5:

$$\mathbf{s}^T = (1, 2, 1), \quad \mathbf{d} = \begin{pmatrix} 0 \\ 1 \\ -1 \end{pmatrix}, \quad \mathbf{P}^T = \begin{pmatrix} 0 & 1 & 1 \\ 1 & 0 & 0 \end{pmatrix}$$

- Solution 6:

$$\mathbf{s}^T = (1, 1, 1), \quad \mathbf{d} = \begin{pmatrix} 2 \\ 1 \\ 1 \end{pmatrix}, \quad \mathbf{P}^T = \begin{pmatrix} 1 & -1 & -1 \\ 0 & 1 & -1 \end{pmatrix}$$

- Solution 7:

$$\mathbf{s}^T = (1, 2, 1), \quad \mathbf{d} = \begin{pmatrix} -1 \\ -1 \\ 2 \end{pmatrix}, \quad \mathbf{P}^T = \begin{pmatrix} 1 & 1 & 1 \\ 1 & -1 & 0 \end{pmatrix}.$$

7.6 SYSTOLIC DESIGN FOR SPACE REPRESENTATIONS CONTAINING DELAYS

Systolic mapping methodology can be modified to accommodate delay elements in the space representation [9]. The precedence constraints in such space representations represent inter-iteration and intra-iteration precedence constraints. This methodology can also be used to for multilevel systolic mapping (for example, for design of 1D systolic arrays for matrix-matrix multiplication).

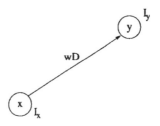

Fig. 7.21 Dependence graph containing delays.

Consider the DG shown in Fig. 7.21, where I_x, I_y are the indices of nodes x and y, respectively, and w is the number of delay elements from node x to node y. Strictly speaking, the DG containing delay elements should be referred to as data-flow graphs. Nevertheless, we refer to them as DGs here. Before we derive the scheduling constraint for each edge in the DG with delays, we need to define the following parameters:

- N' : number of nodes mapped to a processor.

- $\mathbf{s}^T \mathbf{d}$: If a processor computes the node x at $\mathbf{s}^T I$, then it computes the node displaced from x by $\mathbf{d}$ at $\mathbf{s}^T(I + d)$.

Now, assume that the iteration l of node x is executed at T_l. Then, the $(l + 1)$-th iteration of node x is executed at $T_l + N'|\mathbf{s}^T \mathbf{d}|$. Therefore, the iteration period is equal to $N'|\mathbf{s}^T \mathbf{d}|$. The iteration l of node x is scheduled at time instance $S^T I_x + lN'|\mathbf{s}^T \mathbf{d}|$, and the $(l + w)$-th iteration of node y is scheduled at time instance $\mathbf{s}^T I_y + (l+w)N'|\mathbf{s}^T \mathbf{d}|$. This leads to the scheduling inequality:

$$\mathbf{s}^T I_y + (l + w)N'|\mathbf{s}^T \mathbf{d}| \geq \mathbf{s}^T I_x + lN'|\mathbf{s}^T \mathbf{d}| + T_x.$$

After simplification, this leads to:

$$\mathbf{s}^T \mathbf{e} + wN'|\mathbf{s}^T \mathbf{d}| \geq T_x. \tag{7.24}$$

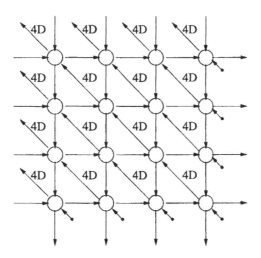

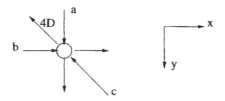

Fig. 7.22 Single cell of a DG.

Example 7.6.1 *Consider a single cell in the DG of Fig. 7.22. Assuming $T_x = 1$ and applying the scheduling inequality to the three fundamental edges,* *we have*

$$\mathbf{e_a} = \begin{pmatrix} 0 \\ 1 \end{pmatrix}, \quad (s_1 \quad s_2) \begin{pmatrix} 0 \\ 1 \end{pmatrix} + 0 \cdot N' \left| S^T \mathbf{d} \right| \geq 1 \Rightarrow s_2 \geq 1$$

$$\mathbf{e_b} = \begin{pmatrix} 1 \\ 0 \end{pmatrix}, \qquad\qquad s_1 \geq 1$$

$$\mathbf{e_c} = \begin{pmatrix} -1 \\ -1 \end{pmatrix}, \qquad -s_1 - s_2 + 4N'(s_1 d_1 + s_2 d_2) \geq 1.$$

Assume

$$\mathbf{d} = \begin{pmatrix} 0 \\ 1 \end{pmatrix}.$$

Therefore, all tasks on a column are mapped to the same processor. Let us further assume that there are 4 nodes on each column in the DG, i.e., $N' = 4$. Substituting these values into the proceeding inequalities, we have

$$-s_1 - s_2 + 16(s_2) \quad \geq \quad 1$$
$$15 s_2 - s_1 \quad \geq \quad 1.$$

Choose $s_1 = s_2 = 1$, i.e., $\mathbf{s}^T = (1\ 1)$. Then $HUE = 1$. Select $\mathbf{p}^T = (1\ 0)$. Then, the edge mapping of the fundamental edges can be computed as Table 7.10. The block diagram of this systolic array is shown in Fig. 7.23. ■

Table 7.10 Edge Mapping for Systolic Array Design in Example 7.6.1

$\mathbf{e}^T$	$\mathbf{p}^T\mathbf{e}$	$\mathbf{s}^T\mathbf{e} + wN' \left| \mathbf{s}^T\mathbf{e} \right|$
a(0, 1)	0	1
b(1, 0)	1	1
c(−1, −1)	−1	14

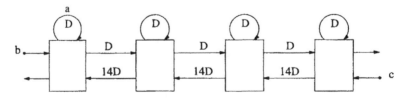

Fig. 7.23 Reduced DG of the FIR filtering example.

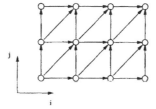

Fig. 7.24   Figure for Problem 1.

7.7   CONCLUSIONS

This chapter has addressed the systolic architecture design methodology where many systolic architectures can be designed for any given regular iterative algorithm using linear mapping or projection techniques. The methodology is illustrated using FIR filters and matrix-matrix multiplications as examples. For theory of multilevel systolic mapping, the readers are referred to [10].

7.8   PROBLEMS

1. For the DG shown in Fig. 7.24,

    (a) Which of the following sets of scheduling and projection are permissible?

        i. $\mathbf{s} = [1\ 0]^T$, $\mathbf{d} = [1\ 0]^T$
        ii. $\mathbf{s} = [1\ 2]^T$, $\mathbf{d} = [2\ -1]^T$
        iii. $\mathbf{s} = [1\ 1]^T$, $\mathbf{d} = [1\ 0]^T$
        iv. $\mathbf{s} = [1\ -2]^T$, $\mathbf{d} = [1\ 0]^T$

    (b) Derive the projected systolic array for each permissible set.

2. Draw the space-time mapping of design R_1.

3. Using one or more transformations such as edge reversal, associativity, slow-down, retiming, and pipelining, derive design R_1 from B_2.

4. For the two designs R_2 and dual R_2, draw the architecture block diagrams and their space-time mappings.

5. Using one or more transformations such as edge reversal, associativity, slow-down, retiming, and pipelining, show all steps needed to obtain dual R_2 from R_2.

6. Draw the space-time representation and the systolic architecture of the design W1 with $\mathbf{d} = \begin{bmatrix} 1 \\ 0 \end{bmatrix}$, $\mathbf{p}^T = [\ 0\ \ 1\ ]$, and $\mathbf{s}^T = [\ 2\ \ 1\ ]$.

7. Derive design W_1 from design F using transformations such as edge reversal, associativity, slow-down, retiming, and pipelining.

8. For the two designs W_2 and dual W_2, draw the architecture block diagrams and their space-time mappings. Why are these two architectures dual of each other?

9. Consider the DG of a 5-tap convolution filter shown in Fig. 7.25. Assume

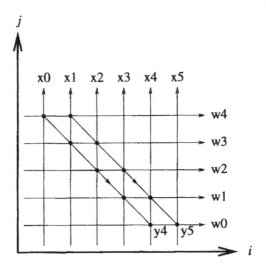

Fig. 7.25   Figure for Problem 9.

that the inputs and the coefficients can be broadcast (with no time delay) to all processors simultaneously or can be delayed for fully systolic design. Further assume that the multiply-add processor requires 4 time units, i.e., each processor contains a 4-stage pipelined multiply-adder.

(a) Write down all the inequalities that the elements of the scheduling vector $s^T = \begin{bmatrix} s_1 & s_2 \end{bmatrix}$ must satisfy. Choose a scheduling vector to maximize the hardware utilization efficiency.

(b) Draw systolic architectures for the iteration vector $d^T = \begin{bmatrix} 1 & 0 \end{bmatrix}$. Use the scheduling vector obtained in part (a). What is the hardware utilization efficiency of this array?

(c) Repeat part (b) for $d^T = \begin{bmatrix} 1 & -1 \end{bmatrix}$.

10. This problem considers design of fully pipelined (i.e., all interconnection edges must contain at least 1 delay element) systolic architectures for the DG shown in Fig. 7.26.

(a) Design fully pipelined systolic architectures using the projection vector $d^T = [0\ 1]$. Specify the processor displacement and scheduling vectors. The scheduling vectors must be chosen such that the

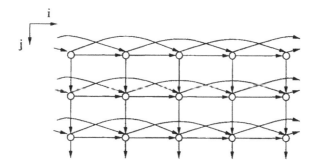

Fig. 7.26 Dependence graph for Problem 10.

hardware utilization efficiency is maximized. Explicitly show the appropriate number of PEs used in the systolic design.

(b) Repeat part (a) for the projection vector $\mathbf{d}^T = [1\ 1]$.

11. Vector Quantization (VQ) is commonly used for data compression in speech, image and video coding, and speech recognition. An overview of VQ can be found in subsection 1.2.7 in Chapter 1. This problem considers the design of systolic architectures for the searching process in VQ, which is described as follows:

$$ind_n = (\min_{0 \le j \le N-1} d_j)^{-1} = (\max_{0 \le j \le N-1} \sum_{i=0}^{k-1} (x_i^n y_{ji} + e_j))^{-1}, \qquad (7.25)$$

where the inverse means "output the index ind_n that achieves the minimum" and n represents the time instance. The search process can also be described equivalently in a matrix-vector multiplication formulation followed by comparisons as follows [3]:

$$\mathbf{D} = [d_0\ d_1\ \cdots\ d_{N-1}]^T = \mathbf{Y}\mathbf{x} + \mathbf{e} \qquad (7.26)$$
$$ind_n = (\mathbf{Max}\{d_i\})^{-1},$$

where $\mathbf{Y} = \{y_{ji}\}$ is $N \times k$ matrix with the j-th codevector $\mathbf{y_j}^T$ as its j-th row, $\mathbf{x}$ is the input vector and $\mathbf{e} = [e_0\ e_1\ \cdots\ e_{N-1}]^T$ (see Section 1.2.7). The DG for the computation in (7.26), and the definitions of the 2 basic processing elements, multiply-accumulate (MAC) and compare/select, are shown in Fig. 7.27. The input vector $\mathbf{x}$ is propagated along the i direction, and the elements in the codevectors y_{ji} are preloaded to the (j, i) nodes in the DG. The initial values $\{e_j\}$ are input from the top row to the j-th column. In this problem, assume $k = 4$ and $N = 16$.

(a) Using the DG and edge information, derive the systolic architecture for the computation in (7.26) using projection vector $\mathbf{d} = [1\ 0]^T$, scheduling vector $\mathbf{s} = [1\ 1]^T$, and processor space vector $\mathbf{p} = [0\ 1]^T$.

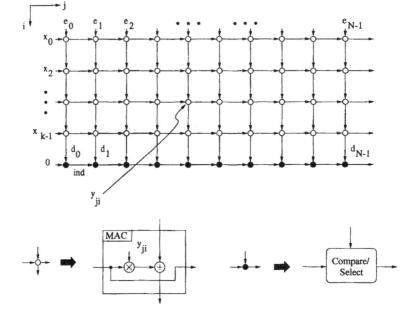

Fig. 7.27 The DG and the processing elements for vector quantization in Problem 11.

Assume each processing element has local storage. In this case, the local memory (storage elements of codevectors) should be organized as a recirculating queue (shift register or read only memory (ROM) with modulo addressing mode). Draw the memory structure and explicitly show the initial content at each location.

(b) Derive another systolic architecture for the computation in (7.26) using projection vector $\mathbf{d} = [0\ 1]^T$, $\mathbf{s} = [1\ 1]^T$, and $\mathbf{p} = [1\ 0]^T$. Note that this architecture requires switches. Show the content of each local memory location.

12. This problem addresses systolic architecture design for matrix-vector multiplication, with emphasis on Toeplitz-matrix vector multiplication and its application in digital correlator design. In this problem, we assume that each processing element can only access its local memory, and the elements in matrix $\mathbf{A}$ are constant.

(a) Consider the following matrix-vector multiplication:

$$\begin{bmatrix} y_0 \\ y_1 \\ y_2 \\ y_3 \end{bmatrix} = \begin{bmatrix} a_{00} & a_{01} & a_{02} & a_{03} \\ a_{10} & a_{11} & a_{12} & a_{13} \\ a_{20} & a_{21} & a_{22} & a_{23} \\ a_{30} & a_{31} & a_{32} & a_{33} \end{bmatrix} \cdot \begin{bmatrix} x_0 \\ x_1 \\ x_2 \\ x_3 \end{bmatrix} . \tag{7.27}$$

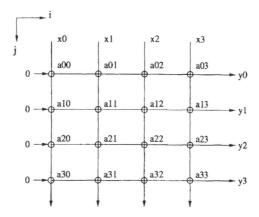

Fig. 7.28 The DG for matrix-vector multiplication in Problem 12(a, b).

Its data dependency graph is shown in Fig. 7.28, where the element a_{ij} of the coefficient matrix $\mathbf{A}$ is stored at position (i, j). Draw the space-time representation and the systolic architecture for the matrix-vector multiplication using

$$\mathbf{d}^T = [1\ 0], \quad \mathbf{p}^T = [0\ 1], \quad \mathbf{s}^T = [1\ 1]. \tag{7.28}$$

Assume that storage is localized to each processing element. Explicitly show the contents of local memory.

(b) The digital correlation operation is given as follows:

$$y_n = \sum_{k=0}^{N-1} x_k a_{n+k}, \tag{7.29}$$

for $n = 0, 1, 2, \cdots, N-1$. It can also be written in terms of matrix-vector multiplication, where the matrix is Toeplitz, i.e., all the elements along the diagonal direction are the same. For example, a 4-level digital correlator can be written as:

$$\begin{bmatrix} y_0 \\ y_1 \\ y_2 \\ y_3 \end{bmatrix} = \begin{bmatrix} a_3 & a_2 & a_1 & a_0 \\ a_4 & a_3 & a_2 & a_1 \\ a_5 & a_4 & a_3 & a_2 \\ a_6 & a_5 & a_4 & a_3 \end{bmatrix} \cdot \begin{bmatrix} x_3 \\ x_2 \\ x_1 \\ x_0 \end{bmatrix}. \tag{7.30}$$

Note that there are only 7 distinct elements in the $\mathbf{A}$ matrix. Replace this Toeplitz $\mathbf{A}$ matrix into the DG in Fig. 7.28 and map the digital correlator algorithm into systolic array using

   i. $\mathbf{d}^T = [1\ 1], \mathbf{p}^T = [1\ -1], \mathbf{s}^T = [1\ 0].$
   ii. $\mathbf{d}^T = [1\ 1], \mathbf{p}^T = [1\ -1], \mathbf{s}^T = [0\ 1].$

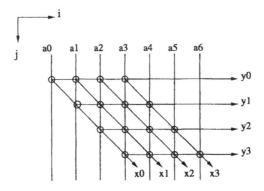

Fig. 7.29 The DG for Problem 12(c).

iii. $\mathbf{d}^T = [1\ 1], \mathbf{p}^T = [1\ -1], \mathbf{s}^T = [1\ 1]$.

Draw the space-time representation and the systolic architecture for each design. Compare the hardware complexity (in terms of the number of local storage elements, processing elements, delay elements, etc.) and throughput of these three designs and the design from part (a) for digital correlator. (Hint: Fixed-coefficient multipliers can be used for the designs in part (b), while variable-coefficient multipliers must be used for the designs in part (a) designed without considering the special feature of Toeplitz matrix.)

(c) In this part, we want to show that an algorithm can be represented by several DGs, which can lead to the same systolic architectures by use of different projection vectors. The digital correlation operation can also be described in a way similar to the FIR filtering operation using the DG shown in Fig. 7.29. Find the projection vector $\mathbf{d}$, the processor space vector $\mathbf{p}$ and the scheduling vector $\mathbf{s}$ based on this DG for the systolic designs obtained in part (a) and (b) for the digital correlator.

(d) If the global memory, i.e., memory common to processing elements, is used, what are the advantages and disadvantages of the designs in part (b) compared with the designs in part (a) for the digital correlator?

13. Draw high-level architectures for matrix-matrix multiplication for the following iteration vectors (the row vectors represent the transpose of the iteration vectors). Do not draw complete architectures. Just show direction of data flow among processors. For each array, choose the scheduling vector to obtain the best iteration period. What is the hardware utilization efficiency of each of these architectures?

(a) $\begin{bmatrix} 2 & 1 & 0 \end{bmatrix}$

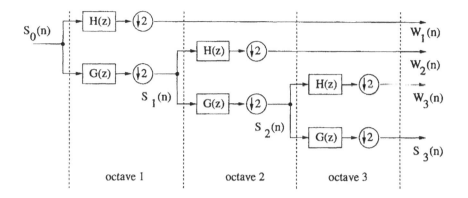

Fig. 7.30 Block diagram of DWT.

(b) $\begin{bmatrix} 2 & -1 & 0 \end{bmatrix}$

(c) $\begin{bmatrix} 2 & -1 & 1 \end{bmatrix}$

14. The discrete wavelet transform (DWT) is a discrete-time, discrete-scale decomposition of finite energy sequences used to represent frequency content as it evolves in time (see Section 1.2.10). The DWT may be calculated recursively as a series of convolutions and decimations. At each octave level j, an input sequence $S_{j-1}(n)$ is fed into a low-pass and a high-pass filter with coefficients $G(n)$ and $H(n)$, respectively. The computation in octave j can be expressed as follows:

$$S_j(n) = \sum_k g_k S_{j-1}(2n - k)$$

$$W_j(n) = \sum_k h_k S_{j-1}(2n - k), \tag{7.31}$$

where n is the sample index and j is the octave index. Fig. 7.30 shows the block diagram of a 3-octave DWT. Usually, the DWT is characterized by a nonuniform data dependence structure owing to the decimation operations. In [11], some nonlinear transformations are introduced to first regularize the DWT algorithm and then transform the regularized 3D algorithm to a 2D index space (DG).

Consider a 3-octave DWT for which the DGs for the computations in the first, second, and third octave are illustrated in Figs. 7.31, 7.32, and 7.33, respectively. Alternatively, they can be combined into 1 DG as shown in Fig. 7.34, with the n index along x-axis and the k index along the y-axis, where n and k are as in (7.31). Note that the S outputs of octave $j - 1$ are fed as inputs to octave j.

(a) Write the equations $S_j(n) = \sum_{k=0}^{3} g_k S_{j-1}(2n - k)$ for $j = 1, 2, 3$ and $n = 2, 3$. Locate these computations in the DG of Fig. 7.34.

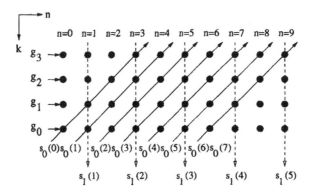

Fig. 7.31   The DG for computations in octave 1.

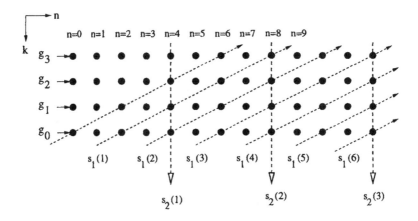

Fig. 7.32   The DG for computations in octave 2.

(b) The edge vector for the outputs of octave j (j=1,2,3) is $\mathbf{e} = [0 \ 1]^T$. The edge vector for the inputs of octave 1 is $\mathbf{e} = [1 \ -1]^T$. Determine $\mathbf{e}$ for

   i. the octave 2 inputs;

   ii. the octave 3 inputs;

   iii. the weight g_i.

(c) The edge vector $\mathbf{e} = [1 \ 0]^T$ describes the transition where the outputs of octave 1 are fed as inputs to octave 2. Similarly, $\mathbf{e} = [2 \ 0]^T$ describes the transition where the outputs of octave 2 are fed as inputs to octave 3. Using this information and the edge vectors obtained in part (b), find the systolic architecture for the DWT using

$$\mathbf{p} = [0 \ 1]^T, \ \mathbf{s} = [1 \ 1]^T, \ \mathbf{d} = [1 \ 0]^T. \quad (7.32)$$

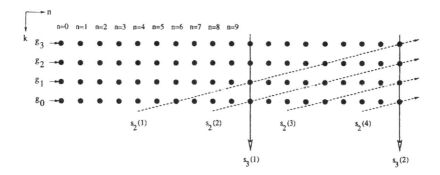

Fig. 7.33 The DG for computations in octave 3.

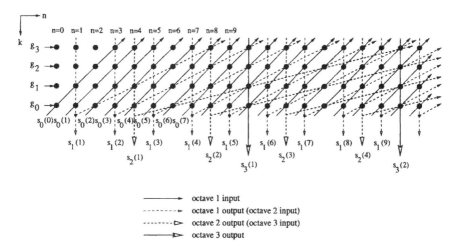

Fig. 7.34 The DG for computations in octaves 1, 2 and 3.

15. Consider the space representation shown in Fig. 7.35 for the computation of the filtering operation

$$y(n) = ax(n) + bx(n-2) + cx(n-4) + dx(n-6). \qquad (7.33)$$

(a) Formulate an equivalent RIA description of this algorithm. Show the reduced DG and write down the scheduling inequalities if the multiply-add operation requires 2 time units. Assume that the input and weight coefficients can be propagated in a broadcast manner.

(b) Select the projection vector $\mathbf{d}^T = [1\ 0]$. Select a processor space vector $\mathbf{p}$. Obtain the solution to the scheduling inequalities so that the designed systolic architecture requires fewest number of delays.

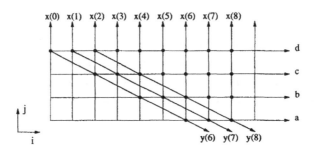

Fig. 7.35 DG for Problem 15.

Draw the systolic architecture.

(c) What is the hardware utilization efficiency of the architecture in part (b)? If that architecture does not achieve 100% hardware utilization efficiency, obtain another systolic architecture that achieves 100% hardware efficiency. (Hint: Try to see if reversing certain directions in the space representation helps.)

16. In this problem we wish to design systolic arrays for a DG in which some edges may contain delays. Consider the DG shown in Fig. 7.36.

   (a) Write down all equations that the scheduling vector elements $s^T = \begin{bmatrix} s_1 & s_2 \end{bmatrix}$ must satisfy.

   (b) For the iteration vector $d^T = \begin{bmatrix} 0 & 1 \end{bmatrix}$, obtain the values of s_1 and s_2 to maximize the hardware utilization efficiency. For this scheduling vector, obtain the systolic array. What is the hardware utilization efficiency of this array?

17. Repeat Example 7.6.1 for $d^T = \begin{bmatrix} 1 & 1 \end{bmatrix}$.

18. Consider the motion estimation computation

$$s(m,n) = \sum_{i=0}^{N-1} \sum_{j=0}^{N-1} |x(i,j) - y(i+m, j+n)|, \quad 0 \le m, n \le 2p$$

$$v = (m,n)|u, \quad u = min_{(m,n)} s(m,n) \quad (7.34)$$

using the 2D and 1D systolic architectures shown in Fig. 7.37 and Fig. 7.38 for $N = 3$ and $p = 2$ [12]. In these architectures, the "dots" represent delay elements.

   (a) Verify the operation of these systolic architectures.

   (b) How many clock cycles are needed for calculation of one motion vector in each systolic array?

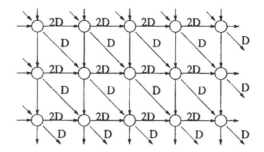

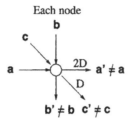

Each node

Fig. 7.36 Figure for Problem 16.

19. Consider the motion estimation computation

$$s(m, n) = \sum_{i=0}^{N-1} \sum_{j=0}^{N-1} |x(i, j) - y(i + m, j + n)|, \ 0 \leq m, n \leq 2p$$

$$v = (m, n)|u, \ u = min_{(m,n)} s(m, n) \quad (7.35)$$

using the 2D and 1D systolic architectures shown in Fig. 7.39 and Fig. 7.40 for $N = 3$ and $p = 2$ [12]. In these architectures, the "dots" represent delay elements.

(a) Verify the operation of these systolic architectures.

(b) How many clock cycles are needed for calculation of one motion vector in each systolic array?

REFERENCES

1. H. T. Kung and C. E. Leiserson, "Systolic arrays (for VLSI)," in *Sparse Matrix Symposium, SIAM*, pp. 256–282, 1978.

2. H. T. Kung, "Why systolic architectures?" *IEEE Computers Magazine*, vol. 15, pp. 37–45, Jan. 1982.

3. S. Y. Kung, *VLSI Array Processors*. Prentice Hall, 1988.

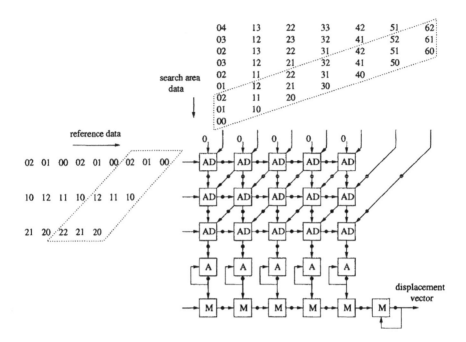

Fig. 7.37 Two-dimensional systolic array for motion estimation in Problem 18. The processing element AD computes the absolute difference; A computes addition; and M compares $s(m, n)$ and selects the displacement vector. The indexes are data $x(i, j)$ and $y(i + m, j + n)$.

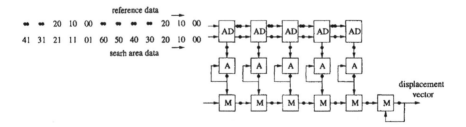

Fig. 7.38 One-dimensional systolic array for motion estimation in Problem 18.

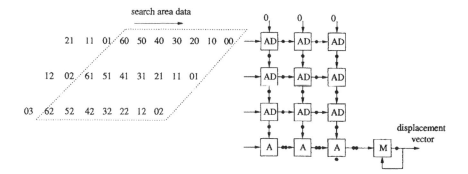

Fig. 7.39 Two-dimensional systolic array for motion estimation in Problem 19.

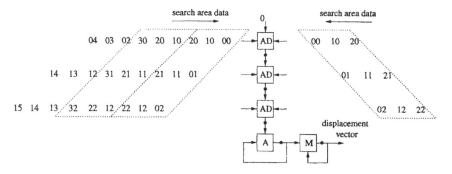

Fig. 7.40 One-dimensional systolic array for motion estimation in Problem 19.

4. H. V. Jagadish, S. K. Rao, and T. Kailath, "Array architecture for iterative algorithms," *Proc. IEEE*, vol. 75, no. 9, pp. 1304–1321, Sept. 1987.

5. P. Quinton, "Automatic synthesis of systolic arrays from uniform recurrent equations," in *Proc. of 11th Annual Symposium on Computer Architecture*, pp. 208–214, June 1984.

6. D. I. Moldovan and J. A. B. Fortes, "Partioning and mapping of algorithms into fixed size systolic arrays," *IEEE Trans. on Computers*, pp. 1–12, Jan. 1986.

7. G. Li and B. W. Wah, "The design of optimal systolic arrays," *IEEE Trans. on Computers*, pp. 67–77, Jan. 1985.

8. P. R. Cappello and K. Steiglitz, "Unifying VLSI array design with linear transformation of space time," *Advances Comput. Res.*, vol. 2, pp. 23–65, 1984.

9. K. K. Parhi, C.-Y. Wang, and A. P. Brown, "Synthesis of control circuits in folded pipelined DSP architectures," *IEEE Journal of Solid-State Circuits*, vol. 27, no. 1, pp. 29–43, Jan. 1992.

10. Y. T. Hwang and Y. H. Hu, "MSSM—a design aid for multi-stage systolic mapping," *Journal of VLSI Signal Processing*, vol. 4, pp. 125–145, 1992.

11. J. Fridman and E. S. Manolakos, "Discrete wavelet transform: data dependence analysis and synthesis of distributed memory and control array architectures," *IEEE Trans. on Signal Processing*, vol. 45, pp. 1291–1308, May 1997.

12. T. Komarek and P. Pirsch, "Array architectures for block matching algorithms," *IEEE Trans. on Circuits and Systems*, no. 10, pp. 1301–1308, Oct. 1989.

8

Fast Convolution

8.1 INTRODUCTION

This chapter addresses implementation of convolution algorithms using fewer
multiplication operations. These algorithms, referred to as *fast convolution*
algorithms, belong to the class of *algorithmic strength reduction*, where the
number of strong operations, such as multiplication operations, is reduced
possibly at the expense of an increase in the number of weaker operations,
such as addition operations. These implementations are best suited for implementation using either programmable or dedicated hardware.

The importance of the fast algorithms in reducing the arithmetic complexity becomes obvious from the following complex multiplication example.
Assume $(a+jb)(c+jd) = e+jf$, where $(a+jb)$ is a signal sample and $(c+jd)$
is a coefficient. This can be expressed using the matrix form

$$\begin{bmatrix} e \\ f \end{bmatrix} = \begin{bmatrix} c & -d \\ d & c \end{bmatrix} \begin{bmatrix} a \\ b \end{bmatrix}.$$

This direct implementation requires 4 multiplications and 2 additions. However, using the identities

$$\begin{aligned} ac - bd &= a(c - d) + d(a - b) \\ ad + bc &= b(c + d) + d(a - b), \end{aligned} \tag{8.1}$$

the coefficient matrix can be decomposed as the product of a 2×3, a 3×3

and a 3×2 matrix:

$$\begin{bmatrix} 1 & 0 & 1 \\ 0 & 1 & 1 \end{bmatrix} \begin{bmatrix} c-d & 0 & 0 \\ 0 & c+d & 0 \\ 0 & 0 & d \end{bmatrix} \begin{bmatrix} 1 & 0 \\ 0 & 1 \\ 1 & -1 \end{bmatrix} \begin{bmatrix} a \\ b \end{bmatrix}. \qquad (8.2)$$

The $\begin{bmatrix} 1 & 0 \\ 0 & 1 \\ 1 & -1 \end{bmatrix}$ is the precomputation matrix, which requires 1 addition.

Note that $\begin{bmatrix} 1 & 0 \\ 0 & 1 \\ 1 & -1 \end{bmatrix} \begin{bmatrix} a \\ b \end{bmatrix} = \begin{bmatrix} a \\ b \\ a-b \end{bmatrix}$. The $\begin{bmatrix} 1 & 0 & 1 \\ 0 & 1 & 1 \end{bmatrix}$ is the postcomputation matrix and requires 2 additions. Also notice that the number of multiplications is the number of entries of the 3×3 diagonal matrix. Therefore, the arithmetic complexity has been reduced to 3 multiplications and 3 additions. One multiplication has been traded off for one addition, which leads to worthwhile savings in hardware. The parameters $c-d$ and $c+d$ are assumed to be precomputed.

This chapter presents two well-known approaches to the design of fast short-length convolution algorithms [1],[2]. The Cook-Toom algorithm based on Lagrange Interpolation is discussed in Section 8.2 [3]. The Winograd algorithm, based on the Chinese remainder theorem (CRT), is discussed in Section 8.3 [4]. The use of these short convolution algorithms to derive computationally efficient implementations for convolution of long-length sequences is illustrated in Section 8.4. The circular convolution and its relationship with linear convolution is discussed in Section 8.5. Design of fast convolution algorithms by inspection is addressed in Section 8.6.

8.2 COOK-TOOM ALGORITHM

The Cook-Toom algorithm is a linear convolution algorithm for polynomial multiplication. It is based on the *Lagrange interpolation theorem*. The Lagrange interpolation theorem states that,

"Let $\beta_0,..., \beta_n$ be a set of $n+1$ distinct points, and let $f(\beta_i)$, for $i = 0, 1, \cdots, n$ be given. There is *exactly* one polynomial $f(p)$ of degree n or less that has value $f(\beta_i)$ when evaluated at β_i for $i = 0, 1, \cdots, n$. It is given by

$$f(p) = \sum_{i=0}^{n} f(\beta_i) \frac{\prod_{j \neq i}(p - \beta_j)}{\prod_{j \neq i}(\beta_i - \beta_j)}." \qquad (8.3)$$

Consider an N-point sequence $h = \{h_0, h_1, \cdots, h_{N-1}\}$ and an L-point sequence $x = \{x_0, x_1, \cdots, x_{L-1}\}$. The linear convolution of h and x can be expressed in terms of polynomial multiplication as follows:

$$s(p) = h(p)x(p), \tag{8.4}$$

where $h(p) = h_{N-1}p^{N-1} + \cdots + h_1 p + h_0$, $x(p) = x_{L-1}p^{L-1} + \cdots + x_1 p + x_0$ and $s(p) = s_{L+N-2}p^{L+N-2} + \cdots + s_1 p + s_0$. The output polynomial $s(p)$ has degree $L + N - 2$ and has $L + N - 1$ different coefficients. Therefore, it can be uniquely determined by its values at $L + N - 1$ different points. Let $\beta_0, \beta_1, \cdots, \beta_{L+N-2}$ be $L + N - 1$ different real numbers. If $s(\beta_i)$, for $i = 0, 1, \cdots, L + N - 2$ are known, $s(p)$ can be computed using the Lagrange interpolation theorem as

$$s(p) = \sum_{i=0}^{L+N-2} s(\beta_i) \frac{\prod_{j \neq i}(p - \beta_j)}{\prod_{j \neq i}(\beta_i - \beta_j)}. \tag{8.5}$$

It can be proved that (8.5) is the unique solution for $s(p)$ given the values of $s(\beta_i)$, for $i = 0, 1, \cdots, L + N - 2$.

The steps using the Cook-Toom algorithm to compute linear convolution in (8.4) are summarized in the following algorithm.

Algorithm 8.2.1 Cook-Toom Algorithm

1. *Choose $L + N - 1$ different real numbers $\beta_0, \beta_1, \cdots, \beta_{L+N-2}$.*

2. *Compute $h(\beta_i)$ and $x(\beta_i)$, for $i = 0, 1, \cdots, L + N - 2$.*

3. *Compute $s(\beta_i) = h(\beta_i)x(\beta_i)$, for $i = 0, 1, \cdots, L + N - 2$.*

4. *Compute $s(p)$ using (8.5).*

Notice that the goal of the fast-convolution algorithm is to reduce the multiplication complexity. If $\beta_i, i = 0, 1, \cdots, L + N - 2$, are chosen properly, the computation in step 2 for evaluating $h(\beta_i)$ and $x(\beta_i)$ will involve some additions and multiplications by small constants (such as positive and negative powers of 2). We will ignore these multiplication operations when β_i's are small numbers. (However, one must keep in mind that as the size of the problem increases, these additions and multiplications may contribute to increased hardware complexity, which should not be ignored.) The multiplications are used in step 3, for computing $s(\beta_i) = h(\beta_i)x(\beta_i)$, $i = 0, 1, \cdots, L + N - 2$. These are the only $L + N - 1$ general multiplications needed. Therefore, the number of multiplications have been reduced from $O(LN)$ to $L + N - 1$ at the expense of an increase in the number of additions. Since an adder has much smaller area and computation time than a multiplier, the Cook-Toom algorithm can lead to large savings in hardware complexity and hence can be used to generate computationally efficient implementations.

Example 8.2.1 *Construct a* 2×2 *convolution algorithm using Cook-Toom algorithm with* $\beta = 0, \pm 1$.

Solution

Write 2×2 *convolution in polynomial multiplication form as*

$$s(p) = h(p)x(p), \qquad (8.6)$$

where $h(p) = h_0 + h_1 p$, $x(p) = x_0 + x_1 p$, *and* $s(p) = s_0 + s_1 p + s_2 p^2$. *A direct implementation can be expressed in matrix form as follows:*

$$\begin{bmatrix} s_0 \\ s_1 \\ s_2 \end{bmatrix} = \begin{bmatrix} h_0 & 0 \\ h_1 & h_0 \\ 0 & h_1 \end{bmatrix} \begin{bmatrix} x_0 \\ x_1 \end{bmatrix}, \qquad (8.7)$$

which requires 4 multiplications and 1 addition. Next the Cook-Toom algorithm is used to construct an efficient convolution algorithm with reduced number of multiplications. First, $h(\beta_i)$ *and* $x(\beta_i)$ *are calculated for* $i = 0, 1, 2$ *to obtain*

$$\begin{aligned} \beta_0 &= 0, & h(\beta_0) &= h_0, & x(\beta_0) &= x_0 \\ \beta_1 &= 1, & h(\beta_1) &= h_0 + h_1, & x(\beta_1) &= x_0 + x_1 \\ \beta_2 &= -1, & h(\beta_2) &= h_0 - h_1, & x(\beta_2) &= x_0 - x_1. \end{aligned} \qquad (8.8)$$

Then, $s(\beta_0)$, $s(\beta_1)$, *and* $s(\beta_2)$ *are calculated as*

$$\begin{aligned} s(\beta_0) &= h(\beta_0)x(\beta_0) \\ s(\beta_1) &= h(\beta_1)x(\beta_1) \\ s(\beta_2) &= h(\beta_2)x(\beta_2) \end{aligned} \qquad (8.9)$$

using 3 multiplications. From the Lagrange interpolation formula (8.5), we get

$$\begin{aligned} s(p) &= s(\beta_0)\frac{(p - \beta_1)(p - \beta_2)}{(\beta_0 - \beta_1)(\beta_0 - \beta_2)} + s(\beta_1)\frac{(p - \beta_0)(p - \beta_2)}{(\beta_1 - \beta_0)(\beta_1 - \beta_2)} \\ &\quad + s(\beta_2)\frac{(p - \beta_0)(p - \beta_1)}{(\beta_2 - \beta_0)(\beta_2 - \beta_1)} \\ &= s(\beta_0)(-p^2 + 1) + s(\beta_1)\frac{p^2 + p}{2} + s(\beta_2)\frac{p^2 - p}{2} \\ &= s(\beta_0) + p\left(\frac{s(\beta_1)}{2} - \frac{s(\beta_2)}{2}\right) + p^2\left(-s(\beta_0) + \frac{s(\beta_1)}{2} + \frac{s(\beta_2)}{2}\right) \\ &= s_0 + ps_1 + p^2 s_2. \end{aligned} \qquad (8.10)$$

The preceding computation leads to the matrix form:

$$
\begin{bmatrix} s_0 \\ s_1 \\ s_2 \end{bmatrix} = \begin{bmatrix} 1 & 0 & 0 \\ 0 & 1 & -1 \\ -1 & 1 & 1 \end{bmatrix} \begin{bmatrix} s(\beta_0) \\ \frac{s(\beta_1)}{2} \\ \frac{s(\beta_2)}{2} \end{bmatrix} \tag{8.11}
$$

$$
= \begin{bmatrix} 1 & 0 & 0 \\ 0 & 1 & -1 \\ -1 & 1 & 1 \end{bmatrix} \begin{bmatrix} h(\beta_0) & 0 & 0 \\ 0 & \frac{h(\beta_1)}{2} & 0 \\ 0 & 0 & \frac{h(\beta_2)}{2} \end{bmatrix} \begin{bmatrix} x(\beta_0) \\ x(\beta_1) \\ x(\beta_2) \end{bmatrix}
$$

$$
= \begin{bmatrix} 1 & 0 & 0 \\ 0 & 1 & -1 \\ -1 & 1 & 1 \end{bmatrix} \begin{bmatrix} h_0 & 0 & 0 \\ 0 & \frac{h_0+h_1}{2} & 0 \\ 0 & 0 & \frac{h_0-h_1}{2} \end{bmatrix} \begin{bmatrix} 1 & 0 \\ 1 & 1 \\ 1 & -1 \end{bmatrix} \begin{bmatrix} x_0 \\ x_1 \end{bmatrix}.
$$

The computation is carried out as follows:

1. $H_0 = h_0$, $H_1 = \frac{h_0+h_1}{2}$, $H_2 = \frac{h_0-h_1}{2}$. *(precomputed)*

2. $X_0 = x_0$, $X_1 = x_0 + x_1$, $X_2 = x_0 - x_1$.

3. $S_0 = H_0 X_0$, $S_1 = H_1 X_1$, $S_2 = H_2 X_2$.

4. $s_0 = S_0$, $s_1 = S_1 - S_2$, $s_2 = -S_0 + S_1 + S_2$.

This algorithm requires 3 multiplications and 5 additions. Therefore, the number of multiplications has been reduced by 1 at the expense of 4 extra addition operations. ∎

Example 8.2.2 *Consider a 2 × 3 linear convolution*

$$
s(p) = h(p)x(p), \tag{8.12}
$$

where $h(p) = h_0 + h_1 p$, $x(p) = x_0 + x_1 p + x_2 p^2$. Use the Cook-Toom algorithm to construct an efficient implementation for the given linear convolution.

Solution

The degree of $s(p)$ is 3. Let $s(p) = s_0 + s_1 p + s_2 p^2 + s_3 p^3$. Let $\beta_0 = 0$, $\beta_1 = 1$, $\beta_2 = -1$, $\beta_3 = 2$. Then

$$
\begin{aligned}
\beta_0 &= 0, & h(\beta_0) &= h_0, & x(\beta_0) &= x_0 \\
\beta_1 &= 1, & h(\beta_1) &= h_0 + h_1, & x(\beta_1) &= x_0 + x_1 + x_2 \\
\beta_2 &= -1, & h(\beta_2) &= h_0 - h_1, & x(\beta_1) &= x_0 - x_1 + x_2 \\
\beta_3 &= 2, & h(\beta_2) &= h_0 + 2h_1, & x(\beta_1) &= x_0 + 2x_1 + 4x_2
\end{aligned} \tag{8.13}
$$

and

$$
\begin{aligned}
s(\beta_0) &= h(\beta_0)x(\beta_0) \\
s(\beta_1) &= h(\beta_1)x(\beta_1)
\end{aligned}
$$

$$s(\beta_2) = h(\beta_2)x(\beta_2)$$
$$s(\beta_3) = h(\beta_3)x(\beta_3), \tag{8.14}$$

which requires 4 multiplications. From Lagrange interpolation formula (8.5), we get

$$
\begin{aligned}
s(p) &= s(\beta_0)\frac{(p-\beta_1)(p-\beta_2)(p-\beta_3)}{(\beta_0-\beta_1)(\beta_0-\beta_2)(\beta_0-\beta_3)} \\
&\quad + s(\beta_1)\frac{(p-\beta_0)(p-\beta_2)(p-\beta_3)}{(\beta_1-\beta_0)(\beta_1-\beta_2)(\beta_1-\beta_3)} \\
&\quad + s(\beta_2)\frac{(p-\beta_0)(p-\beta_1)(p-\beta_3)}{(\beta_2-\beta_0)(\beta_2-\beta_1)(\beta_2-\beta_3)} \\
&\quad + s(\beta_3)\frac{(p-\beta_0)(p-\beta_1)(p-\beta_2)}{(\beta_3-\beta_0)(\beta_3-\beta_1)(\beta_3-\beta_2)} \\
&= \frac{s(\beta_0)}{2}(p^3 - 2p^2 - p + 2) + \frac{s(\beta_1)}{-2}(p^3 - p^2 - 2p) \\
&\quad + \frac{s(\beta_2)}{-6}(p^3 - 3p^2 + 2p) + \frac{s(\beta_3)}{6}(p^3 - p) \\
&= s(\beta_0) \\
&\quad + p\left(-\frac{s(\beta_0)}{2} + s(\beta_1) - \frac{s(\beta_2)}{3} - \frac{s(\beta_3)}{6}\right) \\
&\quad + p^2\left(-s(\beta_0) + \frac{s(\beta_1)}{2} + \frac{s(\beta_2)}{2}\right) \\
&\quad + p^3\left(\frac{s(\beta_0)}{2} - \frac{s(\beta_1)}{2} - \frac{s(\beta_2)}{6} + \frac{s(\beta_3)}{6}\right). \tag{8.15}
\end{aligned}
$$

Finally, the convolution operation is expressed in matrix-vector form as

$$
\begin{bmatrix} s_0 \\ s_1 \\ s_2 \\ s_3 \end{bmatrix}
=
\begin{bmatrix}
2 & 0 & 0 & 0 \\
-1 & 2 & -2 & -1 \\
-2 & 1 & 3 & 0 \\
1 & -1 & -1 & 1
\end{bmatrix}
\begin{bmatrix} \frac{s(\beta_0)}{2} \\ \frac{s(\beta_1)}{2} \\ \frac{s(\beta_2)}{6} \\ \frac{s(\beta_3)}{6} \end{bmatrix}
$$

$$
=
\begin{bmatrix}
2 & 0 & 0 & 0 \\
-1 & 2 & -2 & -1 \\
-2 & 1 & 3 & 0 \\
1 & -1 & -1 & 1
\end{bmatrix}
\begin{bmatrix}
\frac{h_0}{2} & 0 & 0 & 0 \\
0 & \frac{h_0+h_1}{2} & 0 & 0 \\
0 & 0 & \frac{h_0-h_1}{6} & 0 \\
0 & 0 & 0 & \frac{h_0+2h_1}{6}
\end{bmatrix}
$$

$$
\begin{bmatrix}
1 & 0 & 0 \\
1 & 1 & 1 \\
1 & -1 & 1 \\
1 & 2 & 4
\end{bmatrix}
\begin{bmatrix} x_0 \\ x_1 \\ x_2 \end{bmatrix}. \tag{8.16}
$$

The computation is carried out as follows:

1. $H_0 = \frac{h_0}{2}$, $H_1 = \frac{h_0+h_1}{2}$, $H_2 = \frac{h_0-h_1}{6}$, $H_3 = \frac{h_0+2h_1}{6}$ (precomputed).

2. $X_0 = x_0$, $X_1 = (x_0+x_2)+x_1$, $X_2 = (x_0+x_2)-x_1$, $X_3 = x_0+2x_1+4x_2$.

3. $S_0 = H_0X_0$, $S_1 = H_1X_1$, $S_2 = H_2X_2$, $S_3 = H_3X_3$.

4. $s_0 = 2S_0$, $s_1 = -(S_0+S_3)+2(S_1-S_2)$, $s_2 = -2S_0+S_1+3S_2$, $s_3 = (S_0+S_3)-(S_1+S_2)$.

This algorithm requires 4 multiplications and 12 additions, compared with 6 multiplications and 2 additions required for direct implementation. ■

Comments

- Notice that some additions in the preaddition matrix can be shared, i.e., $x_0 + x_2$ in Example 8.2.2 as illustrated by the underlines in (8.16). When we count the number of additions, we only count one instead of two. The same thing can be done for the postaddition matrix, i.e., $S_0 + S_3$ can be shared.

- If we consider this convolution as passing three data samples through a 2-tap FIR filter, take h_0, h_1 as the filter coefficients and take x_0, x_1, x_2 as the data sequence. Then the terms H_0, H_1, H_2, H_3 need not be recomputed each time the filter is used. They can be precomputed once off-line and stored. Therefore we ignore these computations when we count the number of operations.

- As can be seen from Examples 8.2.1 and 8.2.2, the Cook-Toom algorithm can be understood as a matrix decomposition. In general, a convolution can be expressed in matrix-vector form as

$$
\begin{bmatrix} s_0 \\ s_1 \\ s_2 \\ s_3 \end{bmatrix} = \begin{bmatrix} h_0 & 0 & 0 \\ h_1 & h_0 & 0 \\ 0 & h_1 & h_0 \\ 0 & 0 & h_1 \end{bmatrix} \begin{bmatrix} x_0 \\ x_1 \\ x_2 \end{bmatrix}, \tag{8.17}
$$

or

$$ \mathbf{s} = \mathbf{T}\mathbf{x}. \tag{8.18} $$

Generally, equations (8.18) can be expressed as

$$ \mathbf{s} = \mathbf{CHDx}, \tag{8.19} $$

where $\mathbf{C}$ is a postaddition matrix, $\mathbf{D}$ is a preaddition matrix and $\mathbf{H}$ is a diagonal matrix with $H_i, i = 0, 1, \cdots, L + N - 2$ on the main diagonal. From (8.18) and (8.19), we have $\mathbf{T} = \mathbf{CHD}$. This implies that the Cook-Toom algorithm provides a way to factorize the convolution matrix $\mathbf{T}$ into multiplication of one postaddition matrix, one diagonal matrix and one preaddition matrix, such that the total number of general multiplications is determined solely by the non-zero elements on the main diagonal of the diagonal matrix $\mathbf{H}$.

- Although the number of multiplications has been reduced by one-third, the number of additions has increased.

At this point, the Cook-Toom algorithm is modified in order to further reduce the number of addition operations. Define

$$s'(p) = s(p) - s_{L+N-2}p^{L+N-2}. \tag{8.20}$$

Notice that the degree of $s(p)$ is $L+N-2$ and s_{L+N-2} is its highest order coefficient. Therefore the degree of $s'(p)$ is $L+N-3$. The modified Cook-Toom algorithm is summarized as follows.

Algorithm 8.2.2 Modified Cook-Toom Algorithm

1. *Choose $L+N-2$ different real numbers $\beta_0, \beta_1, \cdots, \beta_{L+N-3}$.*

2. *Compute $h(\beta_i)$ and $x(\beta_i)$, for $i = 0, 1, \cdots, L+N-3$.*

3. *Compute $s(\beta_i) = h(\beta_i)x(\beta_i)$, for $i = 0, 1, \cdots, L+N-3$.*

4. *Compute $s'(\beta_i) = s(\beta_i) - s_{L+N-2}\beta_i^{L+N-2}$, for $i = 0, 1, \cdots, L+N-3$.*

5. *Compute $s'(p)$ using (8.5).*

6. *Compute $s(p) = s'(p) + s_{L+N-2}p^{L+N-2}$.*

Example 8.2.3 *Derive a 2×2 convolution algorithm using the modified Cook-Toom algorithm with $\beta_0 = 0$ and $\beta_1 = -1$ and compare the result with that in Example 8.2.1.*

Solution

Consider the Lagrange interpolation for

$$s'(p) = s(p) - h_1 x_1 p^2 \tag{8.21}$$

at $\beta_0 = 0$ and $\beta_1 = -1$. First, find $s'(\beta_i) = h(\beta_i)x(\beta_i) - h_1 x_1 \beta_i^2$.

$$\begin{aligned} \beta_0 = 0, \quad & h(\beta_0) = h_0, \quad & x(\beta_0) = x_0 \\ \beta_1 = -1, \quad & h(\beta_1) = h_0 - h_1, \quad & x(\beta_1) = x_0 - x_1 \end{aligned} \tag{8.22}$$

and

$$\begin{aligned} s'(\beta_0) = & \ h(\beta_0)x(\beta_0) - h_1 x_1 \beta_0^2 = h_0 x_0 \\ s'(\beta_1) = & \ h(\beta_1)x(\beta_1) - h_1 x_1 \beta_1^2 = (h_0 - h_1)(x_0 - x_1) - h_1 x_1, \end{aligned} \tag{8.23}$$

which requires 2 multiplications not counting the $h_1 x_1$ multiplication. Applying the Lagrange interpolation formula (8.5) to $s'(p)$, we get

$$
\begin{aligned}
s'(p) &= s'(\beta_0)\frac{(p-\beta_1)}{(\beta_0-\beta_1)} + s'(\beta_1)\frac{(p-\beta_0)}{(\beta_1-\beta_0)} \\
&= s'(\beta_0) + p(s'(\beta_0) - s'(\beta_1)).
\end{aligned}
\tag{8.24}
$$

Therefore,

$$
\begin{aligned}
s(p) &= s'(p) + h_1 x_1 p^2 \\
&= s_0 + s_1 p + s_2 p^2 = s_0 + s_1 p.
\end{aligned}
\tag{8.25}
$$

Finally, we have

$$
\begin{bmatrix} s_0 \\ s_1 \\ s_2 \end{bmatrix} =
\begin{bmatrix} 1 & 0 & 0 \\ 1 & -1 & 0 \\ 0 & 0 & 1 \end{bmatrix}
\begin{bmatrix} s'(\beta_0) \\ s'(\beta_1) \\ h_1 x_1 \end{bmatrix}.
\tag{8.26}
$$

Notice that

$$
\begin{bmatrix} s'(\beta_0) \\ s'(\beta_1) \\ h_1 x_1 \end{bmatrix} =
\begin{bmatrix} 1 & 0 & 0 \\ 0 & 1 & -1 \\ 0 & 0 & 1 \end{bmatrix}
\begin{bmatrix} s(\beta_0) \\ s(\beta_1) \\ h_1 x_1 \end{bmatrix}.
\tag{8.27}
$$

Therefore,

$$
\begin{aligned}
\begin{bmatrix} s_0 \\ s_1 \\ s_2 \end{bmatrix} &=
\begin{bmatrix} 1 & 0 & 0 \\ 1 & -1 & 0 \\ 0 & 0 & 1 \end{bmatrix}
\begin{bmatrix} 1 & 0 & 0 \\ 0 & 1 & -1 \\ 0 & 0 & 1 \end{bmatrix}
\begin{bmatrix} s(\beta_0) \\ s(\beta_1) \\ h_1 x_1 \end{bmatrix} \\
&= \begin{bmatrix} 1 & 0 & 0 \\ 1 & -1 & 1 \\ 0 & 0 & 1 \end{bmatrix}
\begin{bmatrix} h_0 & 0 & 0 \\ 0 & h_0 - h_1 & 0 \\ 0 & 0 & h_1 \end{bmatrix}
\begin{bmatrix} 1 & 0 \\ 1 & -1 \\ 0 & 1 \end{bmatrix}
\begin{bmatrix} x_0 \\ x_1 \end{bmatrix}.
\end{aligned}
\tag{8.28}
$$

The computation is carried out as folows:

1. $H_0 = h_0$, $H_1 = h_0 - h_1$, $H_2 = h_1$. *(precomputed)*

2. $X_0 = x_0$, $X_1 = x_0 - x_1$, $X_2 = x_1$.

3. $S_0 = H_0 X_0$, $S_1 = H_1 X_1$, $S_2 = H_2 X_2$.

4. $s_0 = S_0$, $s_1 = S_0 - S_1 + S_2$, $s_2 = S_2$.

The total number of operations are 3 multiplications and 3 additions. Compared with the convolution algorithm in Example 8.2.1, the number of addition operations has been reduced by two while the number of multiplication operations remains the same. ■

Example 8.2.4 *Derive a 2×3 convolution algorithm using the modified Cook-Toom algorithm with $\beta = 0, \pm 1$ and compare the complexity of this algorithm with that in Example 8.2.2.*

Solution

Since the degree of $s'(p)$ is $L + N - 3 = 2$, three different real values for β_i's, i.e., $\beta_0 = 0$, $\beta_1 = 1$, $\beta_2 = -1$, are sufficient. Then

$$
\begin{aligned}
\beta_0 &= 0, & h(\beta_0) &= h_0, & x(\beta_0) &= x_0 \\
\beta_1 &= 1, & h(\beta_1) &= h_0 + h_1, & x(\beta_1) &= x_0 + x_1 + x_2 \\
\beta_2 &= -1, & h(\beta_2) &= h_0 - h_1, & x(\beta_1) &= x_0 - x_1 + x_2
\end{aligned} \tag{8.29}
$$

and

$$
\begin{aligned}
s'(\beta_0) &= h(\beta_0)x(\beta_0) - h_1 x_2 \beta_0^3 \\
s'(\beta_1) &= h(\beta_1)x(\beta_1) - h_1 x_2 \beta_1^3 \\
s'(\beta_2) &= h(\beta_2)x(\beta_2) - h_1 x_2 \beta_2^3,
\end{aligned} \tag{8.30}
$$

which requires 3 multiplications not including the $h_1 x_2$ multiplication. Applying the Lagrange interpolation formula (8.5) to $s'(p)$, we get

$$
\begin{aligned}
s'(p) &= s'(\beta_0)\frac{(p - \beta_1)(p - \beta_2)}{(\beta_0 - \beta_1)(\beta_0 - \beta_2)} + s'(\beta_1)\frac{(p - \beta_0)(p - \beta_2)}{(\beta_1 - \beta_0)(\beta_1 - \beta_2)} \\
&\quad + s'(\beta_2)\frac{(p - \beta_0)(p - \beta_1)}{(\beta_2 - \beta_0)(\beta_2 - \beta_1)} \\
&= s'(\beta_0) + p\left(\frac{s'(\beta_1)}{2} - \frac{s'(\beta_2)}{2}\right) + p^2\left(-s'(\beta_0) + \frac{s'(\beta_1)}{2} + \frac{s'(\beta_2)}{2}\right).
\end{aligned} \tag{8.31}
$$

Therefore,

$$
\begin{aligned}
s(p) &= s'(p) + h_1 x_2 p^3 \\
&= s_0 + s_1 p + s_2 p^2 + s_3 p^3.
\end{aligned} \tag{8.32}
$$

Finally, we have

$$
\begin{bmatrix} s_0 \\ s_1 \\ s_2 \\ s_3 \end{bmatrix} =
\begin{bmatrix} 1 & 0 & 0 & 0 \\ 0 & 1 & -1 & 0 \\ -1 & 1 & 1 & 0 \\ 0 & 0 & 0 & 1 \end{bmatrix}
\begin{bmatrix} s'(\beta_0) \\ \frac{s'(\beta_1)}{2} \\ \frac{s'(\beta_2)}{2} \\ h_1 x_2 \end{bmatrix}
$$

$$
=
\begin{bmatrix} 1 & 0 & 0 & 0 \\ 0 & 1 & -1 & 0 \\ -1 & 1 & 1 & 0 \\ 0 & 0 & 0 & 1 \end{bmatrix}
\begin{bmatrix} 1 & 0 & 0 & 0 \\ 0 & 1 & 0 & -\frac{1}{2} \\ 0 & 0 & 1 & \frac{1}{2} \\ 0 & 0 & 0 & 1 \end{bmatrix}
$$

$$\begin{bmatrix} h_0 & 0 & 0 & 0 \\ 0 & \frac{h_0+h_1}{2} & 0 & 0 \\ 0 & 0 & \frac{h_0-h_1}{2} & 0 \\ 0 & 0 & 0 & h_1 \end{bmatrix} \begin{bmatrix} x_0 \\ x_0 + x_1 + x_2 \\ x_0 - x_1 + x_2 \\ x_2 \end{bmatrix}$$

$$= \begin{bmatrix} 1 & 0 & 0 & 0 \\ 0 & 1 & -1 & -1 \\ -1 & 1 & 1 & 0 \\ 0 & 0 & 0 & 1 \end{bmatrix} \begin{bmatrix} h_0 & 0 & 0 & 0 \\ 0 & \frac{h_0+h_1}{2} & 0 & 0 \\ 0 & 0 & \frac{h_0-h_1}{2} & 0 \\ 0 & 0 & 0 & h_1 \end{bmatrix}$$

$$\begin{bmatrix} 1 & 0 & 0 \\ 1 & 1 & 1 \\ 1 & -1 & 1 \\ 0 & 0 & 1 \end{bmatrix} \begin{bmatrix} x_0 \\ x_1 \\ x_2 \end{bmatrix} . \tag{8.33}$$

The computation is carried out as follows:

1. $H_0 = h_0$, $H_1 = \frac{h_0+h_1}{2}$, $H_2 = \frac{h_0-h_1}{2}$, $H_3 = h_1$ *(precomputed)*.

2. $X_0 = x_0$, $X_1 = (x_0 + x_2) + x_1$, $X_2 = (x_0 + x_2) - x_1$, $X_3 = x_2$.

3. $S_0 = H_0 X_0$, $S_1 = H_1 X_1$, $S_2 = H_2 X_2$, $S_3 = H_3 X_3$.

4. $s_0 = S_0$, $s_1 = S_1 - S_2 - S_3$, $s_2 = -S_0 + S_1 + S_2$, $s_3 = S_3$.

This computation requires 4 multiplications and 7 additions, compared with 4 multiplications and 12 additions in Example 8.2.2. ■

The Cook-Toom algorithm is efficient as measured by the number of multiplications. However, as mentioned earlier, it is not efficient when the size of the problem increases, because for a large system, when the number of samples in the output sequence is large, β may take values other than $0, \pm 1, \pm 2, \pm 4$, etc. This may not result in simple preaddition and postaddition matrices. For larger problems, the Winograd algorithm described in the next section is more efficient.

8.3   WINOGRAD ALGORITHM

The Winograd short convolution algorithm is based on the CRT over an integer ring, which can be stated as:

"It is possible to uniquely determine a nonnegative integer given only its remainders with respect to the given moduli, provided that the moduli are relatively prime and the integer is known to be smaller than the product of the moduli."

In a polynomial ring over any field, there again exists a CRT. Both the CRT over an integer ring and the CRT over a polynomial ring are summarized below.

Theorem 8.3.1 CRT for Integers

Given $c_i = R_{m_i}[c]$, for $i = 0, 1, \cdots, k$, where m_i are moduli and are relatively prime, then

$$c = \sum_{i=0}^{k} c_i N_i M_i \; mod \; M, \tag{8.34}$$

where $M = \prod_{i=0}^{k} m_i$, $M_i = M/m_i$ and N_i is the solution of

$$N_i M_i + n_i m_i = GCD(M_i, m_i) = 1, \tag{8.35}$$

provided that $0 \le c < M$. The notation $R_{m_i}[c]$ represents the remainder when c is divided by m_i.

Theorem 8.3.2 CRT for Polynomials

Given $c^{(i)}(p) = R_{m^{(i)}(p)}[c(p)]$, for $i = 0, 1, \cdots, k$, where $m^{(i)}(p)$ are relatively prime, then

$$c(p) = \sum_{i=0}^{k} c^{(i)}(p) N^{(i)}(p) M^{(i)}(p) \; mod \; M(p), \tag{8.36}$$

where $M(p) = \prod_{i=0}^{k} m^{(i)}(p)$, $M^{(i)}(p) = \frac{M(p)}{m^{(i)}(p)}$ and $N^{(i)}(p)$ is the solution of

$$N^{(i)}(p) M^{(i)}(p) + n^{(i)}(p) m^{(i)}(p) = GCD(M^{(i)}(p), m^{(i)}(p)) = 1, \tag{8.37}$$

provided that the degree of $c(p)$ is less than the degree of $M(p)$.

To solve (8.35) and (8.37) for N_i and $N^{(i)}(p)$, one needs to use the Euclidean greatest common divisor (GCD) algorithm for integer and polynomial rings, respectively. The Euclidean GCD algorithms are described in detail in Appendix C.

Consider an example for using the CRT for integers. Choose moduli $m_0 = 3$, $m_1 = 4$, $m_2 = 5$. Then $M = m_0 m_1 m_2 = 60$, and $M_i = \frac{M}{m_i}$. Then

$$\begin{aligned}
m_0 &= 3, & M_0 &= 20, & (-1)20 + 7(3) &= 1 \\
m_1 &= 4, & M_1 &= 15, & (-1)15 + (4)4 &= 1 \\
m_2 &= 5, & M_2 &= 12, & (-2)12 + (5)5 &= 1, \tag{8.38}
\end{aligned}$$

where N_i and n_i are obtained using the Euclidean GCD algorithm. Given the integer c satisfying $0 \le c < M$, let $c_i = R_{m_i}[c]$. The CRT states that for any $0 \le c < M$, there is a one-to-one map between the M values that c takes on and the M values that the vector of residues (c_0, c_1, c_2) can take on. (Notice that $0 \le c_0 < m_0$, $0 \le c_1 < m_1$, $0 \le c_2 < m_2$.) The integer c can be calculated as

$$c = \sum_{i=0}^{k} c_i N_i M_i \bmod M$$
$$= (-20c_0 - 15c_1 - 24c_2) \bmod 60. \qquad (8.39)$$

Example 8.3.1 For $c = 17$, $c_0 = R_3(17) = 2$, $c_1 = R_4(17) = 1$, $c_2 = R_5(17) = 2$

$$c = (-20 * 2 - 15 * 1 - 24 * 2) \bmod 60$$
$$= -103 \bmod 60$$
$$= 17. \blacksquare \qquad (8.40)$$

The remainder of a polynomial with regard to modulus $p^i + f(p)$, where $deg\ f(p) \le i - 1$, can be evaluated by substituting p^i by $-f(p)$ in the polynomial.

Example 8.3.2 (a). $R_{x+2}[5x^2 + 3x + 5] = 5(-2)^2 + 3(-2) + 5 = 19$.
  (b). $R_{x^2+2}[5x^2 + 3x + 5] = 5(-2) + 3x + 5 = 3x - 5$.
  (c). $R_{x^2+x+2}[5x^2 + 3x + 5] = 5(-x - 2) + 3x + 5 = -2x - 5$. $\blacksquare$

Now consider the CRT over a polynomial ring. Consider the computation of

$$s(p) = h(p)x(p) \bmod m(p), \qquad (8.41)$$

where $m(p) = m^{(0)}(p)m^{(1)}(p) \cdots m^{(k)}(p)$ and $m^{(i)}(p)$ are pairwise relatively prime. Suppose $M^{(i)}(p) = m(p)/m^{(i)}(p)$ and $N^{(i)}(p)$ can be found by (8.37). Let $s^{(i)}(p) = R_{m_{(i)}(p)}[s(p)]$, for $i = 0, 1, \cdots, k$. As long as $deg\ s(p) < deg\ m(p)$, the polynomial $s(p)$ can be uniquely determined by

$$s(p) = \sum_{i=0}^{k} s^{(i)}(p)N^{(i)}(p)M^{(i)}(p) \bmod m(p). \qquad (8.42)$$

Notice that when $deg\ h(p)x(p) < deg\ m(p)$,

$$s(p) = h(p)x(p) \bmod m(p) = h(p)x(p). \qquad (8.43)$$

Equation (8.41) is a trivial restatement of the linear convolution. Efficient implementation for linear convolution can be constructed using the CRT by choosing and factoring the polynomial $m(p)$ appropriately. This leads to the Winograd fast convolution algorithm. The structure of a Winograd convolution algorithm is summarized as follows.

Algorithm 8.3.1 Winograd Algorithm

1. *Choose a polynomial $m(p)$ with degree higher than the degree of $h(p)x(p)$ and factor it into $k+1$ relatively prime polynomials with real coefficients, i.e., $m(p) = m^{(0)}(p)m^{(1)}(p)\cdots m^{(k)}(p)$.*

2. *Let $M^{(i)}(p) = \frac{m(p)}{m^{(i)}(p)}$ and use the Euclidean GCD algorithm to solve (8.37) for $N^{(i)}(p)$.*

3. *Compute*

$$
\begin{aligned}
h^{(i)}(p) &= h(p) \bmod m^{(i)}(p), \\
x^{(i)}(p) &= x(p) \bmod m^{(i)}(p),
\end{aligned}
\qquad (8.44)
$$

for $i = 0, 1, \cdots, k$.

4. *Compute*

$$
s^{(i)}(p) = h^{(i)}(p)x^{(i)}(p) \bmod m^{(i)}(p), \qquad (8.45)
$$

for $i = 0, 1, \cdots, k$.

5. *Compute $s(p)$ using (8.42).*

Note that only the short convolutions represented by polynomial products $h^{(i)}(p)x^{(i)}(p)$ in step 4 require multiplications.

Example 8.3.3 *Consider a 2×3 linear convolution as in Example 8.2.2. Construct an efficient realization using Winograd algorithm with $m(p) = p(p-1)(p^2 + 1)$.*

Solution

Let

$$
\begin{aligned}
m^{(0)}(p) &= p \\
m^{(1)}(p) &= p - 1 \\
m^{(2)}(p) &= p^2 + 1
\end{aligned}
\qquad (8.46)
$$

and $M^{(i)}(p) = \frac{m(p)}{m^{(i)}(p)}$, $i = 0, 1, 2$. Use the relationship

$$
N^{(i)}(p)M^{(i)}(p) + n^{(i)}(p)m^{(i)}(p) = 1 \qquad (8.47)
$$

to construct the following table:

i	$m^{(i)}(p)$	$M^{(i)}(p)$	$n^{(i)}(p)$	$N^{(i)}(p)$
0	p	$p^3 - p^2 + p - 1$	$p^2 - p + 1$	-1
1	$p - 1$	$p^3 + p$	$-\frac{1}{2}(p^2 + p + 2)$	$\frac{1}{2}$
2	$p^2 + 1$	$p^2 - p$	$-\frac{1}{2}(p - 2)$	$\frac{1}{2}(p - 1)$

Compute residues

$$h^{(0)}(p) = h_0, \qquad x^{(0)}(p) = x_0$$
$$h^{(1)}(p) = h_0 + h_1, \qquad x^{(1)}(p) = x_0 + x_1 + x_2$$
$$h^{(2)}(p) = h_0 + h_1 p, \qquad x^{(2)}(p) = (x_0 - x_2) + x_1 p \qquad (8.48)$$

and

$$
\begin{aligned}
s^{(0)}(p) &= h_0 x_0 = s_0^{(0)} \\
s^{(1)}(p) &= (h_0 + h_1)(x_0 + x_1 + x_2) = s_0(1) \\
s^{(2)}(p) &= (h_0 + h_1 p)((x_0 - x_2) + x_1 p) \bmod (p^2 + 1) \\
&= h_0(x_0 - x_2) - h_1 x_1 + (h_0 x_1 + h_1(x_0 - x_2))p \\
&= s_0^{(2)} + s_1^{(2)} p. \qquad (8.49)
\end{aligned}
$$

Notice that it takes 1 multiplication to compute $s^{(0)}(p)$, 1 to compute $s^{(1)}(p)$. The computation of $s^{(2)}(p)$ requires 4 multiplications. However, it can be further reduced to 3 multiplications as shown below.

$$
\begin{bmatrix} s_0^{(2)} \\ s_1^{(2)} \end{bmatrix} = \begin{bmatrix} 1 & 0 & -1 \\ 1 & -1 & 0 \end{bmatrix} \begin{bmatrix} h_0 & 0 & 0 \\ 0 & h_1 - h_0 & 0 \\ 0 & 0 & h_0 + h_1 \end{bmatrix} \begin{bmatrix} x_0 + x_1 - x_2 \\ x_0 - x_2 \\ x_1 \end{bmatrix}.
$$

Then

$$
\begin{aligned}
s(p) &= \sum_{i=0}^{2} s^{(i)}(p) N^{(i)}(p) M^{(i)}(p) \bmod m(p) \\
&= [-s^{(0)}(p)(p^3 - p^2 + p - 1) + \frac{s^{(1)}(p)}{2}(p^3 + p) \\
&\quad + \frac{s^{(2)}(p)}{2}(p^3 - 2p^2 + p)] \bmod (p^4 - p^3 + p^2 - p). \qquad (8.50)
\end{aligned}
$$

Substitute $s^{(0)}(p)$, $s^{(1)}(p)$, and $s^{(2)}(p)$ into (8.50) and write the coefficients of $s(p)$ in tabular form as

p^0	p^1	p^2	p^3
$s_0^{(0)}$	$-s_0^{(0)}$	$s_0^{(0)}$	$-s_0^{(0)}$
0	$\dfrac{s_0^{(1)}}{2}$	0	$\dfrac{s_0^{(1)}}{2}$
0	$\dfrac{s_0^{(2)}}{2}$	$-s_0^{(2)}$	$\dfrac{s_0^{(2)}}{2}$
0	$\dfrac{s_1^{(2)}}{2}$	0	$-\dfrac{s_1^{(2)}}{2}$

Therefore, we have

$$
\begin{bmatrix} s_0 \\ s_1 \\ s_2 \\ s_3 \end{bmatrix} = \begin{bmatrix} 1 & 0 & 0 & 0 \\ -1 & 1 & 1 & 1 \\ 1 & 0 & -2 & 0 \\ -1 & 1 & 1 & -1 \end{bmatrix} \begin{bmatrix} s_0^{(0)} \\ \frac{1}{2}s_0^{(1)} \\ \frac{1}{2}s_0^{(2)} \\ \frac{1}{2}s_1^{(2)} \end{bmatrix}. \tag{8.51}
$$

Notice that

$$
\begin{bmatrix} s_0^{(0)} \\ \frac{1}{2}s_0^{(1)} \\ \frac{1}{2}s_0^{(2)} \\ \frac{1}{2}s_1^{(2)} \end{bmatrix} = \begin{bmatrix} 1 & 0 & 0 & 0 & 0 \\ 0 & 1 & 0 & 0 & 0 \\ 0 & 0 & 1 & 0 & -1 \\ 0 & 0 & 1 & 1 & 0 \end{bmatrix} \tag{8.52}
$$

$$
\begin{bmatrix} h_0 & 0 & 0 & 0 & 0 \\ 0 & \frac{h_0+h_1}{2} & 0 & 0 & 0 \\ 0 & 0 & \frac{h_0}{2} & 0 & 0 \\ 0 & 0 & 0 & \frac{h_1-h_0}{2} & 0 \\ 0 & 0 & 0 & 0 & \frac{h_0+h_1}{2} \end{bmatrix} \begin{bmatrix} x_0 \\ x_0 + x_1 + x_2 \\ x_0 + x_1 - x_2 \\ x_0 - x_2 \\ x_1 \end{bmatrix}.
$$

So finally we have

$$
\begin{bmatrix} s_0 \\ s_1 \\ s_2 \\ s_3 \end{bmatrix} = \begin{bmatrix} 1 & 0 & 0 & 0 & 0 \\ -1 & 1 & 2 & 1 & -1 \\ 1 & 0 & -2 & 0 & 2 \\ -1 & 1 & 0 & -1 & -1 \end{bmatrix} \tag{8.53}
$$

$$
\begin{bmatrix} h_0 & 0 & 0 & 0 & 0 \\ 0 & \frac{h_0+h_1}{2} & 0 & 0 & 0 \\ 0 & 0 & \frac{h_0}{2} & 0 & 0 \\ 0 & 0 & 0 & \frac{h_1-h_0}{2} & 0 \\ 0 & 0 & 0 & 0 & \frac{h_0+h_1}{2} \end{bmatrix} \begin{bmatrix} 1 & 0 & 0 \\ 1 & 1 & 1 \\ 1 & 1 & -1 \\ 1 & 0 & -1 \\ 0 & 1 & 0 \end{bmatrix} \begin{bmatrix} x_0 \\ x_1 \\ x_2 \end{bmatrix}.
$$

This completes the construction of the Winograd convolution algorithm. This algorithm requires 5 multiplications and 11 additions compared with 6 multiplications and 2 additions for direct implementation. ∎

The number of multiplications in the Winograd algorithm is highly dependent on the degree of each $m^{(i)}(p)$. Therefore, the degree of $m(p)$ should be as small as possible. According to the CRT, the extreme case will be when $deg\ m(p) = deg\ s(p) + 1$. However, a more efficient form of Winograd algorithm can be obtained by choosing $m(p)$ with a degree equal to that of $s(p)$ and applying the CRT to $s'(p) = s(p) - h_{N-1}x_{L-1}m(p)$. Notice that $s'(p)\ mod\ m(p) = s(p)\ mod\ m(p)$. The modified Winograd convolution algorithm is addressed next.

Algorithm 8.3.2 Modified Winograd Algorithm

1. *Choose a polynomial $m(p)$ with degree equal to that of $s(p)$ and factor it into $k + 1$ relatively prime polynomials, i.e.,*

$$m(p) = m^{(0)}(p)m^{(1)}(p) \cdots m^{(k)}(p). \tag{8.54}$$

2. *Let $M^{(i)}(p) = \frac{m(p)}{m^{(i)}(p)}$ and solve (8.37) for $N^{(i)}(p)$ using the Euclidean GCD algorithm.*

3. *Compute*

$$\begin{aligned} h^{(i)}(p) &= h(p) \bmod m^{(i)}(p), \\ x^{(i)}(p) &= x(p) \bmod m^{(i)}(p), \end{aligned} \tag{8.55}$$

for $i = 0, 1, \cdots, k$.

4. *Compute*

$$s'^{(i)}(p) = h^{(i)}(p)x^{(i)}(p) \bmod m^{(i)}(p), \tag{8.56}$$

for $i = 0, 1, \cdots, k$.

5. *Compute $s'(p)$ using (8.42).*

6. *Compute $s(p) = s'(p) + h_{N-1}x_{L-1}m(p)$.*

Example 8.3.4 *Construct a 2×3 convolution algorithm using modified Winograd algorithm with $m(p) = p(p-1)(p+1)$.*
Solution
Let

$$\begin{aligned} m^{(0)}(p) &= p \\ m^{(1)}(p) &= p - 1 \\ m^{(2)}(p) &= p + 1 \end{aligned} \tag{8.57}$$

and $M_{(i)}(p) = \frac{m(p)}{m^{(i)}(p)}$, $i = 0, 1, 2$. Use the relationship in (8.47) to construct the following table:

i	$m^{(i)}(p)$	$M^{(i)}(p)$	$n^{(i)}(p)$	$N^{(i)}(p)$
0	p	$p^2 - 1$	p	-1
1	$p - 1$	$p^2 + p$	$-\frac{1}{2}(p+2)$	$\frac{1}{2}$
2	$p + 1$	$p^2 - p$	$-\frac{1}{2}(p-2)$	$\frac{1}{2}$

Compute residues

$$h^{(0)}(p) = h_0, \qquad x^{(0)}(p) = x_0$$

$$h^{(1)}(p) = h_0 + h_1, \quad x^{(1)}(p) = x_0 + x_1 + x_2$$
$$h^{(2)}(p) = h_0 - h_1, \quad x^{(2)}(p) = x_0 - x_1 + x_2 \tag{8.58}$$

and

$$
\begin{aligned}
s'^{(0)}(p) &= h_0 x_0 \\
s'^{(1)}(p) &= (h_0 + h_1)(x_0 + x_1 + x_2) \\
s'^{(2)}(p) &= (h_0 - h_1)(x_0 - x_1 + x_2).
\end{aligned} \tag{8.59}
$$

Since the degree of $m^{(i)}(p)$ is equal to 1, $s'^{(i)}(p)$ is a polynomial of degree 0, i.e., a constant number. Therefore, we have

$$
\begin{aligned}
s(p) &= s'(p) + h_1 x_2 m(p) \\
&= s'^{(0)}(-p^2 + 1) + \frac{s'^{(1)}}{2}(p^2 + p) + \frac{s'^{(2)}}{2}(p^2 - p) + h_1 x_2(p^3 - p) \\
&= s'^{(0)} + p\left(\frac{s'^{(1)}}{2} - \frac{s'^{(2)}}{2} - h_1 x_2\right) \\
&\quad + p^2\left(-s'^{(0)} + \frac{s'^{(1)}}{2} + \frac{s'^{(2)}}{2}\right) + p^3(h_1 x_2).
\end{aligned} \tag{8.60}
$$

This algorithm can be written in matrix form as

$$
\begin{bmatrix} s_0 \\ s_1 \\ s_2 \\ s_3 \end{bmatrix}
=
\begin{bmatrix}
1 & 0 & 0 & 0 \\
0 & 1 & -1 & -1 \\
-1 & 1 & 1 & 0 \\
0 & 0 & 0 & 1
\end{bmatrix}
\begin{bmatrix}
s'^{(0)} \\
\frac{s'^{(1)}}{2} \\
\frac{s'^{(2)}}{2} \\
h_1 x_2
\end{bmatrix}
$$

$$
=
\begin{bmatrix}
1 & 0 & 0 & 0 \\
0 & 1 & -1 & -1 \\
-1 & 1 & 1 & 0 \\
0 & 0 & 0 & 1
\end{bmatrix}
\begin{bmatrix}
h_0 & 0 & 0 & 0 \\
0 & \frac{h_0 + h_1}{2} & 0 & 0 \\
0 & 0 & \frac{h_0 - h_1}{2} & 0 \\
0 & 0 & 0 & h_1
\end{bmatrix}
$$

$$
\begin{bmatrix}
1 & 0 & 0 \\
1 & 1 & 1 \\
1 & -1 & 1 \\
0 & 0 & 1
\end{bmatrix}
\begin{bmatrix} x_0 \\ x_1 \\ x_2 \end{bmatrix}. \tag{8.61}
$$

This algorithm requires 4 multiplications and 7 additions. ■

8.4   ITERATED CONVOLUTION

The *iterated convolution algorithm* makes use of efficient short-length convolution algorithms iteratively to build long convolutions [3]. While these algorithms do not achieve minimal multiplication complexity, they achieve a good balance between multiplication and addition complexity.

Example 8.4.1 *Construct a 4×4 linear convolution algorithm using 2×2 short convolution.*

Solution

Let $h(p) = h_0 + h_1 p + h_2 p^2 + h_3 p^3$, $x(p) = x_0 + x_1 p + x_2 p^2 + x_3 p^3$, and $s(p) = h(p)x(p)$. First we need to decompose the 4×4 convolution into a 2×2 convolution. Define $h_0'(p) = h_0 + h_1 p$, $h_1'(p) = h_2 + h_3 p$, $x_0'(p) = x_0 + x_1 p$, $x_1'(p) = x_2 + x_3 p$, and $q = p^2$. Then we have

$$h(p) = h_0'(p) + h_1'(p)p^2, \quad i.e., \quad h(p) = h(p, q) = h_0'(p) + h_1'(p)q$$
$$x(p) = x_0'(p) + x_1'(p)p^2, \quad i.e., \quad x(p) = x(p, q) = x_0'(p) + x_1'(p)q \quad (8.62)$$

and

$$
\begin{aligned}
s(p) &= h(p)x(p) = h(p, q)x(p, q) \\
&= (h_0'(p) + h_1'(p)q)(x_0'(p) + x_1'(p)q) \\
&= s(p, q) = s_0'(p) + s_1'(p)q + s_2'(p)q^2. \quad (8.63)
\end{aligned}
$$

Therefore, the 4×4 convolution is decomposed into two levels of nested 2×2 convolutions. Let us start from the top-level 2×2 convolution, which is expressed in terms of variable q. Using the 2×2 convolution algorithm derived from the previous section, we have

$$
\begin{bmatrix} s_0'(p) \\ s_1'(p) \\ s_2'(p) \end{bmatrix}
=
\begin{bmatrix} 1 & 0 & 0 \\ 1 & -1 & 1 \\ 0 & 0 & 1 \end{bmatrix}
\begin{bmatrix} h_0'(p) & 0 & 0 \\ 0 & h_0'(p) - h_1'(p) & 0 \\ 0 & 0 & h_1'(p) \end{bmatrix}
$$
$$
\begin{bmatrix} 1 & 0 \\ 1 & -1 \\ 0 & 1 \end{bmatrix}
\begin{bmatrix} x_0'(p) \\ x_1'(p) \end{bmatrix}, \quad (8.64)
$$

which uses 3 polynomial multiplications, 1 degree-1 polynomial addition and 2 degree-2 polynomial additions. The 3 polynomial multiplications which are used to compute $s_0'(p)$, $s_1'(p)$, and $s_2'(p)$ are again 2×2 convolutions, each of which requires 3 multiplications and 3 additions. Note that 2 additions are required due to the overlap terms between $s_0'(p)$ and $s_1'(p)$, $s_1'(p)$ and $s_2'(p)$. Therefore, the total number of operations used in this 4×4 iterated convolution algorithm is 9 multiplications and 19 additions. ■

The procedure for the iterated convolution algorithm is summarized as follows.

Algorithm 8.4.1 Iterated Convolution Algorithm

1. *Decompose the long convolution into several levels of short convolutions.*

2. *Construct fast convolution algorithms for short convolutions.*

3. *Use the short convolution algorithms to iteratively (hierarchically) implement the long convolution.*

The order of short convolutions in the decomposition affects the complexity of the derived long convolution structure.

8.5 CYCLIC CONVOLUTION

Cyclic convolution is also known as circular convolution. Let $h = \{h_0, h_1, \cdots, h_{n-1}\}$ be the filter coefficients and $x = \{x_0, x_1, \cdots, x_{n-1}\}$ be the data sequence. The cyclic convolution can be expressed as

$$s(p) = h \bigcirc_n x = h(p)x(p) \ mod \ (p^n - 1) \qquad (8.65)$$

and the output samples are given by

$$s_i = \sum_{k=0}^{n-1} h_{((i-k))} x_k, \ i = 0, 1, \cdots, n-1, \qquad (8.66)$$

where $((i-k))$ denotes $(i-k) \ mod \ n$. The cyclic convolution can be computed as a linear convolution reduced by modulo $p^n - 1$. (Notice that there are $2n-1$ different output samples for this linear convolution). Alternatively, the cyclic convolution can be computed using CRT with $m(p) = p^n - 1$, which is much simpler.

Example 8.5.1 *Construct a 4×4 cyclic convolution algorithm using CRT with $m(p) = p^4 - 1 = (p-1)(p+1)(p^2+1)$.*

Solution

Let $h(p) = h_0 + h_1 p + h_2 p^2 + h_3 p^3$ and $x(p) = x_0 + x_1 p + x_2 p^2 + x_3 p^3$. Let $m^{(0)}(p) = p - 1$, $m^{(1)}(p) = p + 1$, $m^{(2)}(p) = p^2 + 1$. Let $M^{(i)}(p) = \frac{m(p)}{m^{(i)}(p)}$. Use the relationship (8.37) to construct the following table:

i	$m^{(i)}(p)$	$M^{(i)}(p)$	$n^{(i)}(p)$	$N^{(i)}(p)$
0	$p - 1$	$p^3 + p^2 + p + 1$	$-\frac{p^2+2p+3}{4}$	$\frac{1}{4}$
1	$p + 1$	$p^3 - p^2 + p - 1$	$\frac{p^2-2p+3}{4}$	$-\frac{1}{4}$
2	$p^2 + 1$	$p^2 - 1$	$\frac{1}{2}$	$-\frac{1}{2}$

Compute residues

$$h^{(0)}(p) = h_0 + h_1 + h_2 + h_3 = h_0^{(0)},$$
$$h^{(1)}(p) = h_0 - h_1 + h_2 - h_3 = h_0^{(1)},$$

$$h^{(2)}(p) = (h_0 - h_2) + (h_1 - h_3)p = h_0^{(2)} + h_1^{(2)}p,$$
$$x^{(0)}(p) = x_0 + x_1 + x_2 + x_3 = x_0^{(0)}$$
$$x^{(1)}(p) = x_0 - x_1 + x_2 - x_3 = x_0^{(1)}$$
$$x^{(2)}(p) = (x_0 - x_2) + (x_1 - x_3)p = x_0^{(2)} + x_1^{(2)}p \qquad (8.67)$$

and

$$
\begin{aligned}
s^{(0)}(p) &= h^{(0)}(p)x^{(0)}(p) = h_0^{(0)}x_0^{(0)} = s_0^{(0)} \\
s^{(1)}(p) &= h^{(1)}(p)x^{(1)}(p) = h_0^{(1)}x_0^{(1)} = s_0^{(1)} \\
s^{(2)}(p) &= s_0^{(2)} + s_1^{(2)}p = h^{(2)}(p)x^{(2)}(p) \bmod (p^2 + 1) \\
&= (h_0^{(2)}x_0^{(2)} - h_1^{(2)}x_1^{(2)}) + (h_0^{(2)}x_1^{(2)} + h_1^{(2)}x_0^{(2)})p. \qquad (8.68)
\end{aligned}
$$

Notice that it takes 1 multiplication to compute $s_0^{(0)}$ and 1 to compute $s_0^{(1)}$. The computation of $s_0^{(2)}$ and $s_1^{(2)}$ requires 4 multiplications. However, using the identities

$$
\begin{aligned}
s_0^{(2)} &= h_0^{(2)}x_0^{(2)} - h_1^{(2)}x_1^{(2)} \\
&= h_0^{(2)}(x_0^{(2)} + x_1^{(2)}) - (h_0^{(2)} + h_1^{(2)})x_1^{(2)} \\
s_1^{(2)} &= h_0^{(2)}x_1^{(2)} + h_1^{(2)}x_0^{(2)} \\
&= h_0^{(2)}(x_0^{(2)} + x_1^{(2)}) + (h_1^{(2)} - h_0^{(2)})x_0^{(2)}, \qquad (8.69)
\end{aligned}
$$

or

$$
\begin{bmatrix} s_0^{(2)} \\ s_1^{(2)} \end{bmatrix} =
\begin{bmatrix} 1 & 0 & -1 \\ 1 & 1 & 0 \end{bmatrix}
\begin{bmatrix} h_0^{(2)} & 0 & 0 \\ 0 & h_1^{(2)} - h_0^{(2)} & 0 \\ 0 & 0 & h_0^{(2)} + h_1^{(2)} \end{bmatrix}
$$
$$
\begin{bmatrix} x_0^{(2)} + x_1^{(2)} \\ x_0^{(2)} \\ x_1^{(2)} \end{bmatrix}, \qquad (8.70)
$$

the number of multiplications is reduced to 3. Then

$$
\begin{aligned}
s(p) &= \sum_{i=0}^{2} s^{(i)}(p)N^{(i)}(p)M^{(i)}(p) \bmod m(p) \qquad (8.71) \\
&= s_0^{(0)}\frac{p^3 + p^2 + p + 1}{4} + s_0^{(1)}\frac{p^3 - p^2 + p - 1}{-4} \\
&\quad + s_0^{(2)}\frac{p^2 - 1}{-2} + s_1^{(2)}p\frac{p^2 - 1}{-2}
\end{aligned}
$$

$$= \frac{s_0^{(0)}}{4} + \frac{s_0^{(1)}}{4} + \frac{s_0^{(2)}}{2} + p\left(\frac{s_0^{(0)}}{4} - \frac{s_0^{(1)}}{4} + \frac{s_1^{(2)}}{2}\right)$$

$$+ p^2\left(\frac{s_0^{(0)}}{4} + \frac{s_0^{(1)}}{4} - \frac{s_0^{(2)}}{2}\right) + p^3\left(\frac{s_0^{(0)}}{4} - \frac{s_0^{(1)}}{4} - \frac{s_1^{(2)}}{2}\right).$$

We have

$$
\begin{bmatrix} s_0 \\ s_1 \\ s_2 \\ s_3 \end{bmatrix} =
\begin{bmatrix} 1 & 1 & 1 & 0 \\ 1 & -1 & 0 & 1 \\ 1 & 1 & -1 & 0 \\ 1 & -1 & 0 & -1 \end{bmatrix}
\begin{bmatrix} \frac{s_0^{(0)}}{4} \\ \frac{s_0^{(1)}}{4} \\ \frac{s_0^{(2)}}{2} \\ \frac{s_1^{(2)}}{2} \end{bmatrix}.
\tag{8.72}
$$

Notice that

$$
\begin{bmatrix} \frac{s_0^{(0)}}{4} \\ \frac{s_0^{(1)}}{4} \\ \frac{s_0^{(2)}}{2} \\ \frac{s_1^{(2)}}{2} \end{bmatrix} =
\begin{bmatrix} 1 & 0 & 0 & 0 & 0 \\ 0 & 1 & 0 & 0 & 0 \\ 0 & 0 & 1 & 0 & -1 \\ 0 & 0 & 1 & 1 & 0 \end{bmatrix}
\tag{8.73}
$$

$$
\begin{bmatrix} \frac{h_0^{(0)}}{4} & 0 & 0 & 0 & 0 \\ 0 & \frac{h_0^{(1)}}{4} & 0 & 0 & 0 \\ 0 & 0 & \frac{h_0^{(2)}}{2} & 0 & 0 \\ 0 & 0 & 0 & \frac{h_1^{(2)}-h_0^{(2)}}{2} & 0 \\ 0 & 0 & 0 & 0 & \frac{h_0^{(2)}+h_1^{(2)}}{2} \end{bmatrix}
\begin{bmatrix} x_0^{(0)} \\ x_0^{(1)} \\ x_0^{(2)}+x_1^{(2)} \\ x_0^{(2)} \\ x_1^{(2)} \end{bmatrix}.
$$

Therefore, we have

$$
\begin{bmatrix} s_0 \\ s_1 \\ s_2 \\ s_3 \end{bmatrix} =
\begin{bmatrix} 1 & 1 & 1 & 0 & -1 \\ 1 & -1 & 1 & 1 & 0 \\ 1 & 1 & -1 & 0 & 1 \\ 1 & -1 & -1 & -1 & 0 \end{bmatrix}
$$

$$
\begin{bmatrix} \frac{h_0+h_1+h_2+h_3}{4} & 0 & 0 & 0 & 0 \\ 0 & \frac{h_0-h_1+h_2-h_3}{4} & 0 & 0 & 0 \\ 0 & 0 & \frac{h_0-h_2}{2} & 0 & 0 \\ 0 & 0 & 0 & \frac{-h_0+h_1+h_2-h_3}{2} & 0 \\ 0 & 0 & 0 & 0 & \frac{h_0+h_1-h_2-h_3}{2} \end{bmatrix}
$$

$$
\begin{bmatrix} 1 & 1 & 1 & 1 \\ 1 & -1 & 1 & -1 \\ 1 & 1 & -1 & -1 \\ 1 & 0 & -1 & 0 \\ 0 & 1 & 0 & -1 \end{bmatrix}
\begin{bmatrix} x_0 \\ x_1 \\ x_2 \\ x_3 \end{bmatrix}.
\tag{8.74}
$$

This algorithm requires 5 multiplications and 15 additions, while the direct implementation

$$
\begin{bmatrix} s_0 \\ s_1 \\ s_2 \\ s_3 \end{bmatrix} = \begin{bmatrix} h_0 & h_3 & h_2 & h_1 \\ h_1 & h_0 & h_3 & h_2 \\ h_2 & h_1 & h_0 & h_3 \\ h_3 & h_2 & h_1 & h_0 \end{bmatrix} \begin{bmatrix} x_0 \\ x_1 \\ x_2 \\ x_3 \end{bmatrix}
\tag{8.75}
$$

requires 16 multiplications and 12 additions. (Notice that the cyclic convolution matrix is a circulant matrix). ∎

An efficient cyclic convolution algorithm can often be easily extended to construct efficient linear convolution.

Example 8.5.2 *Construct a 3×3 linear convolution using 4×4 cyclic convolution algorithm in Example 8.5.1.*

Solution

Let the 3-point coefficient sequence be $h = \{h_0, h_1, h_2\}$ and the 3-point data sequence be $x = \{x_0, x_1, x_2\}$. First extend them to 4-point sequences as

$$
h = \{h_0, h_1, h_2, 0\}, \quad x = \{x_0, x_1, x_2, 0\}.
\tag{8.76}
$$

Then the 3×3 linear convolution of h and x is

$$
\begin{bmatrix} h_0 x_0 \\ h_1 x_0 + h_0 x_1 \\ h_2 x_0 + h_1 x_1 + h_0 x_2 \\ h_2 x_1 + h_1 x_2 \\ h_2 x_2 \end{bmatrix},
\tag{8.77}
$$

and the 4×4 cyclic convolution of h and x, $h \bigcirc_4 x$, is

$$
\begin{bmatrix} h_0 x_0 + h_2 x_2 \\ h_1 x_0 + h_0 x_1 \\ h_2 x_0 + h_1 x_1 + h_0 x_2 \\ h_2 x_1 + h_1 x_2 \end{bmatrix}.
\tag{8.78}
$$

Therefore, we have $s(p) = h(p)x(p) = h \bigcirc_4 x + h_2 x_2 (p^4 - 1)$. Using the result of Example 8.5.1 for $h \bigcirc_4 x$, the following convolution algorithm for 3×3 linear convolution is obtained:

$$
\begin{bmatrix} s_0 \\ s_1 \\ s_2 \\ s_3 \\ s_4 \end{bmatrix} = \begin{bmatrix} 1 & 1 & 1 & 0 & -1 & -1 \\ 1 & -1 & 1 & 1 & 0 & 0 \\ 1 & 1 & -1 & 0 & 1 & 0 \\ 1 & -1 & -1 & -1 & 0 & 0 \\ 0 & 0 & 0 & 0 & 0 & 1 \end{bmatrix}
$$

$$
\begin{bmatrix}
\frac{h_0+h_1+h_2}{4} & 0 & 0 & 0 & 0 & 0 \\
0 & \frac{h_0-h_1+h_2}{4} & 0 & 0 & 0 & 0 \\
0 & 0 & \frac{h_0-h_2}{2} & 0 & 0 & 0 \\
0 & 0 & 0 & \frac{-h_0+h_1+h_2}{2} & 0 & 0 \\
0 & 0 & 0 & 0 & \frac{h_0+h_1-h_2}{2} & 0 \\
0 & 0 & 0 & 0 & 0 & h_2
\end{bmatrix}
$$

$$
\begin{bmatrix}
1 & 1 & 1 \\
1 & -1 & 1 \\
1 & 1 & -1 \\
1 & 0 & -1 \\
0 & 1 & 0 \\
0 & 0 & 1
\end{bmatrix}
\begin{bmatrix}
x_0 \\
x_1 \\
x_2
\end{bmatrix}, \tag{8.79}
$$

which requires 6 multiplications and 16 additions. ∎

Comments   The same 3×3 linear convolution algorithm can be constructed using the modified Winograd algorithm with $m(p) = p^4 - 1 = (p-1)(p+1)(p^2+1)$. However, since we already have derived the 4×4 cyclic convolution algorithm in Example 8.5.1, the design process is much more simplified by using the existing cyclic convolution algorithm instead of using the modified Winograd algorithm.

In general, an efficient linear convolution algorithm can be used to obtain an efficient cyclic convolution algorithm. Conversely, an efficient cyclic convolution algorithm can be used to derive an efficient linear convolution algorithm.

8.6   DESIGN OF FAST CONVOLUTION ALGORITHM BY INSPECTION

All efficient convolution algorithms cannot be generated by the Cook-Toom or the Winograd algorithms. Sometimes, a clever factorization by inspection may generate a better algorithm.

Example 8.6.1 *Construct a 3×3 fast convolution algorithm by inspection.*
   Solution
   The 3×3 linear convolution can be written as

$$
\begin{bmatrix}
s_0 \\
s_1 \\
s_2 \\
s_3 \\
s_4
\end{bmatrix}
=
\begin{bmatrix}
h_0 x_0 \\
h_1 x_0 + h_0 x_1 \\
h_2 x_0 + h_1 x_1 + h_0 x_2 \\
h_2 x_1 + h_1 x_2 \\
h_2 x_2
\end{bmatrix}, \tag{8.80}
$$

which requires a multiplication and 4 additions. Using the following identities

$$
\begin{aligned}
s_1 &= h_1 x_0 + h_0 x_1 = (h_0 + h_1)(x_0 + x_1) - h_0 x_0 - h_1 x_1 \\
s_2 &= h_2 x_0 + h_1 x_1 + h_0 x_2 = (h_0 + h_2)(x_0 + x_2) - h_0 x_0 + h_1 x_1 - h_2 x_2 \\
s_3 &= h_2 x_1 + h_1 x_2 = (h_1 + h_2)(x_1 + x_2) - h_1 x_1 - h_2 x_2,
\end{aligned}
\tag{8.81}
$$

the 3×3 linear convolution can be written as

$$
\begin{bmatrix} s_0 \\ s_1 \\ s_2 \\ s_3 \\ s_4 \end{bmatrix}
=
\begin{bmatrix}
1 & 0 & 0 & 0 & 0 & 0 \\
-1 & -1 & 0 & 1 & 0 & 0 \\
-1 & 1 & -1 & 0 & 1 & 0 \\
0 & -1 & -1 & 0 & 0 & 1 \\
0 & 0 & 1 & 0 & 0 & 0
\end{bmatrix}
$$
$$
\begin{bmatrix}
h_0 & 0 & 0 & 0 & 0 & 0 \\
0 & h_1 & 0 & 0 & 0 & 0 \\
0 & 0 & h_2 & 0 & 0 & 0 \\
0 & 0 & 0 & h_0 + h_1 & 0 & 0 \\
0 & 0 & 0 & 0 & h_0 + h_2 & 0 \\
0 & 0 & 0 & 0 & 0 & h_1 + h_2
\end{bmatrix}
\begin{bmatrix}
1 & 0 & 0 \\
0 & 1 & 0 \\
0 & 0 & 1 \\
1 & 1 & 0 \\
1 & 0 & 1 \\
0 & 1 & 1
\end{bmatrix}
\begin{bmatrix} x_0 \\ x_1 \\ x_2 \end{bmatrix},
\tag{8.82}
$$

which requires 6 multiplications and 10 additions. This efficient algorithm cannot be obtained by the Cook-Toom or the Winograd algorithms. ■

8.7   CONCLUSIONS

This chapter has introduced various short-length fast convolution algorithms, including the Cook-Toom algorithm, the modified Cook-Toom algorithm, the Winograd algorithm, and the modified Winograd algorithm. Based on the fast short-length convolution algorithms, long convolution algorithms can be derived using iterated convolution method. The relationship between the cyclic convolution and the linear convolution and how they can be derived from each other has also been addressed. Fast convolution algorithms form the basis for design of fast parallel FIR filters (see Section 9.2.2.3).

8.8   PROBLEMS

1. Compute the product of 3 complex numbers

$$
x + jy = (a + jb)(c + jd)(e + jf)
\tag{8.83}
$$

using the fewest number of multiplication operations.

2. Calculate $f_1 = ax + by$ and $f_2 = bx + ay$ using 2 multiplications.

3. Calculate f_1 and f_2 given by

$$f_1 = (a_1 + ja_2)(x_1 + jx_2) + (b_1 + jb_2)(y_1 + jy_2)$$
$$f_2 = (b_1 + jb_2)(x_1 + jx_2) + (a_1 + ja_2)(y_1 + jy_2)$$

using 6 real multiplication operations.

4. Construct a 2×2 convolution algorithm using the Cook-Toom algorithm with $\beta = 0, 1, 2$.

5. Construct a 3×3 convolution algorithm using the Cook-Toom algorithm with β_i's as 0,1,-1, 2, -2.

6. Construct a 3×3 convolution algorithm using the modified Cook-Toom algorithm with β_i's as 0, 1, -1, 2.

7. Construct a 3×3 convolution algorithm using the modified Cook-Toom algorithm with β_i's as 0, 1, 2, -2.

8. Use the Cook-Toom algorithm to construct a convolution algorithm for filtering a sequence of 3 data inputs with a 4-tap FIR filter, i.e., 4×3 linear convolution.

9. Use the Cook-Toom algorithm to construct a 3×4 convolution algorithm.

10. Use the modified Cook-Toom algorithm to construct a convolution algorithm for 4×3 linear convolution.

11. Construct a 2×2 convolution algorithm using the Winograd algorithm with $m(p) = p(p-1)(p+1)$.

12. Construct a 2×2 convolution algorithm using the modified Winograd algorithm with $m(p) = p(p-1)$.

13. Design a Winograd convolution for 4-point by 3-point linear convolution using $m(p) = p^2(p+1)(p-1)(p^2+1)$.

14. Design a 4-point by 3-point linear convolution using the modified Winograd algorithm using $m(p) = p(p+1)(p-1)(p^2+1)$.

15. Construct a 3-point circular convolution algorithm using $m(p) = p^3 - 1 = (p-1)(p^2+p+1)$.

16. Evaluate the linear convolution $h = \{h_0, h_1\} * x = \{x_0, x_1, x_2, x_3\}$ by the modified Winograd method using $m(p) = p(p+1)(p^2+1)$.

17. Using the result of Problem 15, compute a 2×3 point linear convolution. Calculate the number of multiplication and addition operations required. Compare the result with the linear convolution algorithms

derived using Cook-Toom and Winograd algorithms. (Hint: note that
$h * x = h \bigcirc_3 x + h_1 x_2 (p^3 - 1)$.)

18. Use the iterated convolution algorithm to evaluate a 6×4 convolution
using efficient short-convolution algorithms for the 2×2 and 3×2 cases.
Note that the order in which the short convolution algorithms are used
is important. Calculate the multiplication and addition operations for
all possible orders and determine the best one. (Hint: For 3×2
convolution, use $h(p) = h'_0(p^3) + p h'_1(p^3) + p^2 h'_2(p^3)$, where $h'(q) =
h_i + h_{i+3} q$ and $q = p^3$.)

19. A 3×3 fast convolution requiring 6 multiplication and 10 addition operations was presented in Example 8.6.1. By inspection, obtain an-
other algorithm for 3×3 convolution using the terms $h_0 x_0$, $h_1 x_1$, $h_2 x_2$,
$(h_0 + h_1)(x_0 + x_1)$, $(h_1 + h_2)(x_1 + x_2)$, and $(h_0 + h_1 + h_2)(x_0 + x_1 + x_2)$.
Show that this convolution requires 6 multiplication and 9 addition operations.

REFERENCES

1. R. E. Blahut, *Fast Algorithms for Digital Signal Processing*. Addison-Wesley,
1985.

2. R. Tolimieri, M. An, and C. Lu, *Algorithms for Discrete Fourier Transform and
Convolution*. Springer-Verlag, 1989.

3. R. C. Agarwal and J. W. Cooley, "New algorithms for digital convolution," *IEEE
Trans. on Acoustics, Speech, and Signal Processing*, vol. ASAP-25, pp. 392–410,
1977.

4. S. Winograd, "On computing the discrete Fourier transform," *Math. Comp.*,
vol. 32, pp. 175–199, 1978.

9

Algorithmic Strength Reduction in Filters and Transforms

9.1 INTRODUCTION

This chapter presents applications of algorithmic strength reduction in parallel FIR filters, discrete cosine transforms (DCTs) and parallel rank-order filter. Strength reduction leads to a reduction in hardware complexity by exploiting substructure sharing. This transformation can lead to reduction in silicon area or power consumption in a VLSI implementation or iteration period in a programmable DSP implementation.

The FIR filter is one of the fundamental processing elements in any digital signal processing (DSP) system. FIR filters are used in DSP applications ranging from video and image processing to wireless communications. In some applications, such as video processing, the FIR filter circuit must be able to operate at high frequencies, while in other applications, such as cellular telephony, the FIR filter circuit must be a low-power circuit, capable of operating at moderate frequencies. Parallel, or block processing can be applied to digital FIR filters to either increase the effective throughput of the original filter or reduce the power consumption of the original filter. Traditionally, the application of parallel processing to an FIR filter involves the replication of the hardware units that exist in the original filter. If the area required by the original circuit is A, then the L-parallel circuit requires an area of $L \times A$. In other words, the circuit area increases linearly with the block size. In many design situations, the hardware overhead incurred by parallel processing cannot be tolerated due to limitations in design area. Therefore, it is advantageous to realize parallel FIR filtering structures that consume less area than traditional parallel FIR filtering structures. In Section 9.2, algorithmic strength reduction is exploited to design parallel FIR filter implementations that require a less-than-linear increase in the circuit area. Fast filtering algorithms for smaller block sizes are developed and combined to design parallel FIR filters for larger block sizes.

The DCT is widely used in DSP. It has become a major tool for image coding and has been successfully applied for coding of high resolution images. Due to its increasing importance, numerous attempts have been made to accelerate the DCT computation in order to facilitate real-time, high-throughput implementations. In Section 9.3, fast DCT architectures are designed using algorithm-architecture transformation and the decimation-in-frequency approach.

Rank-order filters belong to the class of nonlinear filters and are useful in cancelling non-Gaussian noise such as impulse noise and flicker noise. Design of parallel programmable rank-order filters is considered in Section 9.4. Substructure sharing is exploited to design these architectures using the fewest number of compare-swap (**C&S**) units.

9.2   PARALLEL FIR FILTERS

This section considers the implementation of parallel FIR filters using algorithmic strength reduction transformation.

9.2.1   Formulation of Parallel FIR Filtering Using Polyphase Decomposition

This section addresses the formulation of parallel FIR filters using polyphase decomposition, a technique used in multirate signal processing [1].

An N-tap FIR filter can be expressed in time domain as

$$y(n) = h(n) * x(n) = \sum_{i=0}^{N-1} h(i)x(n-i), \ n = 0, 1, 2, \cdots, \infty, \qquad (9.1)$$

where $\{x(n)\}$ is an infinite length input sequence and the sequence $\{h(n)\}$ contains FIR filter coefficients of length N, or in z-domain as

$$Y(z) = H(z)X(z) = \sum_{n=0}^{N-1} h(n)z^{-n} \sum_{n=0}^{\infty} x(n)z^{-n}. \qquad (9.2)$$

The input sequence $\{x(0), x(1), x(2), x(3), \cdots\}$ can be decomposed into even-numbered part and odd-number part as follows:

$$X(z) \quad = \quad x(0) + x(1)z^{-1} + x(2)z^{-2} + x(3)z^{-3} + \cdots$$

$$
\begin{aligned}
&= x(0) + x(2)z^{-2} + x(4)z^{-4} + \cdots \\
&\quad + z^{-1}[x(1) + x(3)z^{-2} + x(5)z^{-4} + \cdots] \\
&= X_0(z^2) + z^{-1}X_1(z^2),
\end{aligned}
\tag{9.3}
$$

where $X_0(z^2)$ and $X_1(z^2)$ are the z-transforms of $x(2k)$ and $x(2k+1)$ (for $0 \le k < \infty$), respectively. In (9.3), $X(z)$ is decomposed into two polyphases. Similarly, the length-N filter coefficients $H(Z)$ can be decomposed as

$$
H(Z) = H_0(z^2) + z^{-1}H_1(z^2),
\tag{9.4}
$$

where $H_0(z^2)$ and $H_1(z^2)$ are of length $N/2$ and are referred to as even subfilter and odd subfilter, respectively. For example, the even and odd subfilters of the 6-tap FIR filter $H(z) = h(0) + h(1)z^{-1} + h(2)z^{-2} + h(3)z^{-3} + h(4)z^{-4} + h(5)z^{-5}$ are $H_0(z) = h(0) + h(2)z^{-1} + h(4)z^{-2}$ and $H_1(z) = h(1) + h(3)z^{-1} + h(5)z^{-2}$. The even-numbered output sequence $y(2k)$ and the odd-numbered output sequence $y(2k+1)$ (for $0 \le k < \infty$) can be computed as

$$
\begin{aligned}
Y(z) &= Y_0(z^2) + z^{-1}Y_1(z^2) \\
&= (X_0(z^2) + z^{-1}X_1(z^2))(H_0(z^2) + z^{-1}H_1(z^2)) \\
&= X_0(z^2)H_0(z^2) + z^{-1}(X_0(z^2)H_1(z^2) \\
&\quad + X_1(z^2)H_0(z^2)) + z^{-2}X_1(z^2)H_1(z^2),
\end{aligned}
\tag{9.5}
$$

i.e.,

$$
\begin{aligned}
Y_0(z^2) &= X_0(z^2)H_0(z^2) + z^{-2}X_1(z^2)H_1(z^2) \\
Y_1(z^2) &= X_0(z^2)H_1(z^2) + X_1(z^2)H_0(z^2),
\end{aligned}
\tag{9.6}
$$

where $Y_0(z^2)$ and $Y_1(z^2)$ correspond to $y(2k)$ and $y(2k+1)$ in time domain, respectively. The filtering operation in (9.6) processes two inputs $x(2k)$ and $x(2k+1)$ and generates two outputs $y(2k)$ and $y(2k+1)$ every iteration, and is referred to as a 2-parallel FIR filter. This 2-parallel FIR filter can be rewritten in matrix form as

$$
\begin{bmatrix} Y_0 \\ Y_1 \end{bmatrix} = \begin{bmatrix} H_0 & z^{-2}H_1 \\ H_1 & H_0 \end{bmatrix} \begin{bmatrix} X_0 \\ X_1 \end{bmatrix}.
\tag{9.7}
$$

Fig. 9.1 shows the resulting 2-parallel FIR filtering structure, which requires $2N$ multiplications and $2(N-1)$ additions.

For 3-phase polyphase decomposition, the input sequence $X(z)$ and the filter coefficients $H(z)$ can be decomposed as follows:

$$
X(z) = X_0(z^3) + z^{-1}X_1(z^3) + z^{-2}X_2(z^3)
\tag{9.8}
$$

$$
H(z) = H_0(z^3) + z^{-1}H_1(z^3) + z^{-2}H_2(z^3),
\tag{9.9}
$$

where $X_0(z^3)$, $X_1(z^3)$, and $X_2(z^3)$ correspond to $x(3k)$, $x(3k+1)$ and $x(3k+$

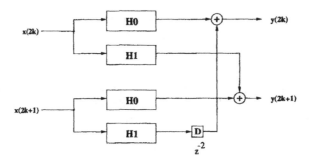

Fig. 9.1   Traditional 2-parallel FIR filter implementation.

2) in time domain, respectively; and $H_0(z)$, $H_1(z)$ and $H_2(z)$ are the three subfilters of $H(z)$. The output can be computed as

$$
\begin{aligned}
Y(z) &= Y_0(z^3) + z^{-1}Y_1(z^3) + z^{-2}Y_2(z^3) \qquad\qquad\qquad (9.10)\\
&= (X_0 + z^{-1}X_1 + z^{-2}X_2)(H_0 + z^{-1}H_1 + z^{-2}H_2)\\
&= X_0H_0 + z^{-1}(X_0H_1 + X_1H_0) + z^{-2}(X_0H_2 + X_1H_1 + X_2H_0)\\
&\quad + z^{-3}(X_1H_2 + X_2H_1) + z^{-4}X_2H_2\\
&= X_0H_0 + z^{-3}(X_1H_2 + X_2H_1) + z^{-1}(X_0H_1 + X_1H_0 + z^{-3}X_2H_2)\\
&\quad + z^{-2}(X_0H_2 + X_1H_1 + X_2H_0).
\end{aligned}
$$

Hence,

$$
\begin{aligned}
Y_0(z^3) &= X_0(z^3)H_0(z^3) + z^{-3}X_1(z^3)H_2(z^3) + z^{-3}X_2(z^3)H_1(z^3),\\
Y_1(z^3) &= X_0(z^3)H_1(z^3) + X_1(z^3)H_0(z^3) + z^{-3}X_2(z^3)H_2(z^3),\\
Y_2(z^3) &= X_0(z^3)H_2(z^3) + X_1(z^3)H_1(z^3) + X_2(z^3)H_0(z^3), \qquad (9.11)
\end{aligned}
$$

where $Y_0(z^3)$, $Y_1(z^3)$, and $Y_2(z^3)$ correspond to $y(3k)$, $y(3k + 1)$, and $y(3k + 2)$, respectively. This 3-parallel FIR filter processes 3 input samples $x(3k)$, $x(3k+1)$, and $x(3k+2)$ and generates 3 output samples $y(3k)$, $y(3k+1)$, and $y(3k + 2)$ in one iteration and can be rewritten in matrix form as

$$
\begin{bmatrix} Y_0 \\ Y_1 \\ Y_2 \end{bmatrix} =
\begin{bmatrix}
H_0 & z^{-3}H_2 & z^{-3}H_1(z^3) \\
H_1 & H_0 & z^{-3}H_2(z^3) \\
H_2(z^3) & H_1(z^3) & H_0(z^3)
\end{bmatrix}
\begin{bmatrix} X_0 \\ X_1 \\ X_2 \end{bmatrix}. \qquad (9.12)
$$

Fig. 9.2 shows the resulting 3-parallel FIR filtering structure, which requires $3N$ multiplications and $3(N - 1)$ additions.

Generally, the polyphase decomposition can be used to derive L-parallel FIR filters by decomposing $X(z)$, $H(z)$, and $Y(z)$ into L subsequences as

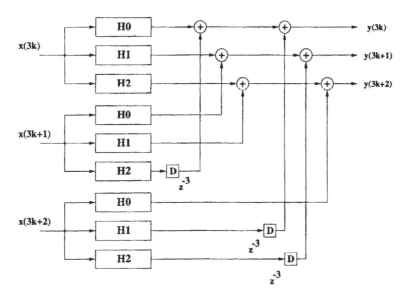

Fig. 9.2 Traditional 3-parallel FIR filter implementation.

follows:

$$X_i(z) = \sum_{k=0}^{\infty} z^{-k} x(Lk+i), \; i = 0, 1, \cdots, L-1$$

$$H_j(z) = \sum_{k=0}^{N/L-1} z^{-k} h(Lk+j), \; j = 0, 1, \cdots, L-1$$

$$Y_l(z) = \sum_{k=0}^{\infty} z^{-k} y(Lk+l), \; l = 0, 1, \cdots, L-1. \quad (9.13)$$

The L output subsequences $y(Lk+i)$ $(0 \le i \le L-1, \; 0 \le k < \infty)$ can be computed using a combination of L subfilters from the L input subsequences $x(Lk+i)$ $(0 \le i \le L-1, \; 0 \le k < \infty)$ as

$$\sum_{l=0}^{L-1} Y_l(z^L) z^{-l} = \sum_{i=0}^{L-1} X_i(z^L) z^{-i} \sum_{j=0}^{L-1} H_j(z^L) z^{-j}, \quad (9.14)$$

or more explicitly,

$$Y_k = z^{-L} \sum_{i=k+1}^{L-1} H_i X_{L+k-i} + \sum_{i=0}^{k} H_i X_{k-i}, \; 0 \le k \le L-2,$$

$$Y_{L-1} = \sum_{i=0}^{L-1} H_i X_{L-1-i}. \tag{9.15}$$

This can also be written in matrix form as

$$\mathbf{Y} = \mathbf{HX} \tag{9.16}$$

$$
\begin{bmatrix} Y_0 \\ Y_1 \\ \vdots \\ Y_{L-1} \end{bmatrix}
=
\begin{bmatrix}
H_0 & z^{-L}H_{L-1} & \cdots & z^{-L}H_1 \\
H_1 & H_0 & \ddots & z^{-L}H_2 \\
\vdots & \vdots & \ddots & \vdots \\
H_{L-1} & H_{L-2} & \cdots & H_0
\end{bmatrix}
\begin{bmatrix} X_0 \\ X_1 \\ \vdots \\ X_{L-1} \end{bmatrix}.
\tag{9.17}
$$

It should be noted that $\mathbf{H}$ is a *pseudocirculant* matrix [1]. This L-parallel FIR filter requires L^2 subfiltering operations, each of which is of length N/L and requires N/L multiply-add operations. Hence, the L-parallel FIR filter requires $L^2 \cdot N/L$ or LN multiply-add operations, which is linear in the block-size L. Although the polyphase formulation does not reduce the parallel filter complexity, it can be exploited to derive fast parallel FIR filters.

9.2.2   Fast FIR Algorithms

Since the work of Winograd [2], it is known that 2 polynomials of degree $L-1$ can be multiplied using only $(2L-1)$ product terms [3]. This reduction in the number of multiplications comes at the expense of increasing the number of additions required for implementation. Since the product terms in the polynomial formulation of the FIR filter are equivalent to filtering operations in the block formulation, this implies that the parallel FIR filter can be realized using approximately $(2L-1)$ FIR filters of length-N/L.

A relatively new class of algorithms, termed fast FIR algorithms (FFAs) [4],[5], rely upon this approach to produce reduced complexity parallel filtering structures [6]. Using this approach, the L-parallel filter can be implemented using approximately $(2L-1)$ filtering operations of length (N/L). The resulting parallel filtering structure would require $(2N - N/L)$ multiplications. As an example, if we let $N = 4$ and let $L = 2$, the traditional 2-parallel approach would require 8 multiplications while the 2-parallel fast filtering approach would require only 6 multiplications. For large values of N, the FFAs can reduce the number of multiplications significantly.

This section addresses the derivation of hardware-efficient parallel FIR filters using the fast FIR algorithms.

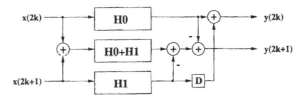

Fig. 9.3 Reduced-complexity 2-parallel FIR filter implementation.

9.2.2.1 Two-Parallel and Three-Parallel Low-Complexity FIR Filters

Two-Parallel Fast FIR Filter   The 2-parallel FIR filter in (9.6) requires $2N$ multiplication and addition operations. Note that (9.6) can be rewritten as

$$
\begin{aligned}
Y_0 &= H_0 X_0 + z^{-2} H_1 X_1 \\
Y_1 &= (H_0 + H_1)(X_0 + X_1) - H_0 X_0 - H_1 X_1.
\end{aligned}
\tag{9.18}
$$

This 2-parallel fast FIR filter contains 5 subfilters; however, the 2 terms $H_0 X_0$ and $H_1 X_1$ are common and can be shared for the computation of Y_0 and Y_1. This low-complexity 2-parallel filter structure is shown in Fig. 9.3, which computes a block of 2 outputs using 3 distinct subfilters of length $N/2$ and 4 pre/postprocessing addition operations. It requires $3N/2 = 1.5N$ multiplications and $3(N/2 - 1) + 4 = 1.5N + 1$ additions, as opposed to $2N$ multiplications and $2(N - 1)$ additions in the traditional parallel filter derived directly from polyphase decomposition. For example, when $N = 8$ and $H = \{h_0, h_1, h_2, \cdots, h_6, h_7\}$, the 3 subfilters are

$$
\begin{aligned}
H_0 &= \{h_0, h_2, h_4, h_6\} \\
H_1 &= \{h_1, h_3, h_5, h_7\} \\
H_0 + H_1 &= \{h_0 + h_1, h_2 + h_3, h_4 + h_5, h_6 + h_7\},
\end{aligned}
\tag{9.19}
$$

and $H_0 + H_1$ can be precomputed. This low-complexity 2-parallel filter requires 12 multiplications and 13 additions, as opposed to 16 multiplications and 14 addition operations required for the traditional parallel filter.

The 2-parallel filter in (9.18) can also be written in matrix form as

$$
\mathbf{Y_2 = Q_2 H_2 P_2 X_2}
$$

$$
\begin{bmatrix} Y_0 \\ Y_1 \end{bmatrix} = \begin{bmatrix} 1 & 0 & z^{-2} \\ -1 & 1 & -1 \end{bmatrix} diag \begin{bmatrix} H_0 \\ H_0 + H_1 \\ H_1 \end{bmatrix} \begin{bmatrix} 1 & 0 \\ 1 & 1 \\ 0 & 1 \end{bmatrix} \begin{bmatrix} X_0 \\ X_1 \end{bmatrix}.
\tag{9.20}
$$

Note that the notation

$$diag \begin{bmatrix} a_1 \\ a_2 \\ \vdots \\ a_N \end{bmatrix}$$

represents an $N \times N$ diagonal matrix with diagonal elements $a_1, a_2, ..., a_N$. In the matrix representation, Q_2 is a postprocessing matrix and P_2 is a pre-processing matrix. P_2 determines the manner in which the inputs should be combined, while Q_2 determines the manner in which the filter outputs should be combined to correctly produce the parallel outputs. It should be noted that the application of an FFA diagonalizes the pseudocirculant matrix of (9.7). The entries on the diagonal of $\mathbf{H_2}$ are the subfilters required in this parallel FIR filter.

Many different equivalent parallel FIR filter structures can be obtained. For example, the 2-parallel filter can be implemented using subfilters H_0, $H_0 - H_1$, and H_1 (see Problem 1). Furthermore, all parallel filters can be transposed to obtain other equivalent structures (see Section 9.2.2.2). While the performance of these filters may be similar in a programmable DSP implementation, their performance in a hardware VLSI implementation may be significantly different. For example, in a narrow-band low-pass filter, the subfilter $H_0 + H_1$ may require more nonzero bits than $H_0 - H_1$ [7]. Similarly, the subfilter $H_0 + H_1$ may require less nonzero bits in a narrow-band high-pass filter. Thus, appropriate filter structures can be selected to reduce area and power consumption for a specified frequency spectrum. It may be noted that the sum or difference coefficients can also be used for reducing the strength of a sequential filter (see Problem 20). In addition, different structures also lead to different roundoff noise properties. An appropriate filter structure may also be selected to reduce roundoff noise.

Three-Parallel Fast FIR Filter   A fast 3-parallel FIR algorithm can be derived by recursively applying a 2-parallel fast FIR algorithm.

$$\begin{aligned} Y &= Y_0 + z^{-1}Y_1 + z^{-2}Y_2 \\ &= (X_0 + z^{-1}X_1 + z^{-2}X_2)(H_0 + z^{-1}H_1 + z^{-2}H_2) \\ &= (X_0 + z^{-1}V)(H_0 + z^{-1}W), \end{aligned} \qquad (9.21)$$

where $V = X_1 + z^{-1}X_2$ and $W = H_1 + z^{-1}H_2$. Using the fast FIR algorithm in (9.18), Y can be computed as

$$\begin{aligned} Y &= H_0X_0 + z^{-2}VW + z^{-1}((H_0 + W)(X_0 + V) - H_0X_0 - VW) \\ &= [H_0X_0 + z^{-2}VW] \\ &\quad + z^{-1}[(H_0 + H_1 + z^{-1}H_2)(X_0 + X_1 + z^{-1}X_2) - H_0X_0 - VW] \end{aligned} \qquad (9.22)$$

where $VW = (X_1 + z^{-1}X_2)(H_1 + z^{-1}H_2)$ can be computed as

$$VW = \begin{aligned}[t] &[H_1X_1 + z^{-2}H_2X_2] \\ &+ z^{-1}[(H_1 + H_2)(X_1 + X_2) - H_1X_1 - H_2X_2]. \end{aligned} \tag{9.23}$$

Substituting (9.23) into (9.22), we have

$$\begin{aligned}
Y =\; & [H_0X_0 + z^{-2}([H_1X_1 + z^{-2}H_2X_2] \\
& + z^{-1}[(H_1 + H_2)(X_1 + X_2) - H_1X_1 - H_2X_2])] \\
& + z^{-1}[((H_0 + H_1) + z^{-1}H_2)((X_0 + X_1) + z^{-1}X_2) - H_0X_0 \\
& - ([H_1X_1 + z^{-2}H_2X_2] + z^{-1}[(H_1 + H_2)(X_1 + X_2) - H_1X_1 - H_2X_2])] \\
=\; & H_0X_0 \\
& + z^{-1}[(H_0 + H_1)(X_0 + X_1) - H_0X_0 - H_1X_1] \\
& + z^{-2}[H_1X_1 + (H_0 + H_1)X_2 + H_2(X_0 + X_1) \\
& - (H_1 + H_2)(X_1 + X_2) + H_1X_1 + H_2X_2] \\
& + z^{-3}[(H_1 + H_2)(X_1 + X_2) - H_1X_1 - H_2X_2 + H_2X_2 - H_2X_2] \\
& + z^{-4}[H_2X_2] \\
=\; & H_0X_0 - z^{-3}H_2X_2 + z^{-3}[(H_1 + H_2)(X_1 + X_2) - H_1X_1] \\
& + z^{-1}([(H_0 + H_1)(X_0 + X_1) - H_1X_1] - [H_0X_0 - z^{-3}H_2X_2]) \\
& + z^{-2}([(H_0 + H_1 + H_2)(X_0 + X_1 + X_2)] - [(H_0 + H_1)(X_0 + X_1) \\
& - H_1X_1] - [(H_1 + H_2)(X_1 + X_2) - H_1X_1]).
\end{aligned} \tag{9.24}$$

The resulting 3-parallel FFA filter is given by

$$\begin{aligned}
Y_0 =\; & H_0X_0 - z^{-3}H_2X_2 + z^{-3}[(H_1 + H_2)(X_1 + X_2) - H_1X_1] \\
Y_1 =\; & [(H_0 + H_1)(X_0 + X_1) - H_1X_1] - [H_0X_0 - z^{-3}H_2X_2] \\
Y_2 =\; & [(H_0 + H_1 + H_2)(X_0 + X_1 + X_2)] \\
& - [(H_0 + H_1)(X_0 + X_1) - H_1X_1] \\
& - [(H_1 + H_2)(X_1 + X_2) - H_1X_1],
\end{aligned} \tag{9.25}$$

and can be expressed in matrix form as

$$\mathbf{Y_3 = Q_3 H_3 P_3 X_3}$$

$$\mathbf{Y_3} = \begin{bmatrix} Y_0 \\ Y_1 \\ Y_2 \end{bmatrix}, \mathbf{Q_3} = \begin{bmatrix} 1 & 0 & z^{-3} & 0 \\ -1 & 1 & 0 & 0 \\ 0 & -1 & -1 & 1 \end{bmatrix} \begin{bmatrix} 1 & 0 & -z^{-3} & 0 & 0 & 0 \\ 0 & -1 & 0 & 1 & 0 & 0 \\ 0 & -1 & 0 & 0 & 1 & 0 \\ 0 & 0 & 0 & 0 & 0 & 1 \end{bmatrix},$$

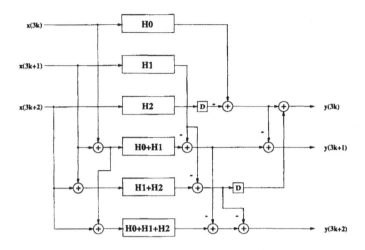

Fig. 9.4 Reduced-complexity 3-parallel FIR filter implementation.

$$\mathbf{H_3} = diag \begin{bmatrix} H_0 \\ H_1 \\ H_2 \\ H_0 + H_1 \\ H_1 + H_2 \\ H_0 + H_1 + H_2 \end{bmatrix}, \mathbf{P_3} = \begin{bmatrix} 1 & 0 & 0 \\ 0 & 1 & 0 \\ 0 & 0 & 1 \\ 1 & 1 & 0 \\ 0 & 1 & 1 \\ 1 & 1 & 1 \end{bmatrix}, \mathbf{X_3} = \begin{bmatrix} X_0 \\ X_1 \\ X_2 \end{bmatrix}. \quad (9.26)$$

The P_3 and Q_3 matrices are the pre- and postprocessing matrices, respectively, while the H_3 matrix is the diagonalized subfilter matrix. Hence, the 3-parallel FIR filter is constructed using 6 subfilters of length $N/3$, including H_0X_0, H_1X_1, H_2X_2, $(H_0 + H_1)(X_0 + X_1)$, $(H_1 + H_2)(X_1 + X_2)$ and $(H_0 + H_1 + H_2)(X_0 + X_1 + X_2)$, and 3 preprocessing and 7 postprocessing additions, as shown in Fig. 9.4. The overall computation requirement includes $2N$ multiplications and $2N + 4$ additions. Comparing the cost of the traditional and reduced-complexity 3-parallel structures, it is clear that the reduced-complexity filtering structure provides a savings of approximately 33% over the traditional structure.

9.2.2.2 Parallel Filters by Transposition

Any parallel FIR filter structure can be used to derive another parallel equivalent structure by transpose operation (or transposition). Generally the transposed architecture has the same hardware complexity, but different finite wordlength performance. This section addresses derivation of parallel FIR filters using transposition.

Consider the parallel filtering operation in matrix form $\mathbf{Y} = \mathbf{HX}$, as shown in (9.16), where $\mathbf{H}$ is an $L \times L$ matrix. An equivalent realization of this parallel filtering algorithm can be generated by taking the transpose of the $\mathbf{H}$ matrix and flipping the vectors $\mathbf{X}$ and $\mathbf{Y}$:

$$\mathbf{Y}_F = \mathbf{H}^T \mathbf{X}_F,$$

where $\mathbf{X}_F$ and $\mathbf{Y}_F$ are as follows:

$$\mathbf{X}_F = \begin{bmatrix} X_{L-1} & X_{L-2} & \cdots & X_0 \end{bmatrix}^T$$
$$\mathbf{Y}_F = \begin{bmatrix} Y_{L-1} & Y_{L-2} & \cdots & Y_0 \end{bmatrix}^T. \qquad (9.27)$$

For example, the 2-parallel FIR filter in (9.7) can be reformulated by using $\mathbf{H}^T$ and the flipped input and output vectors as

$$\begin{bmatrix} Y_1 \\ Y_0 \end{bmatrix} = \begin{bmatrix} H_0 & H_1 \\ z^{-2}H_1 & H_0 \end{bmatrix} \begin{bmatrix} X_1 \\ X_0 \end{bmatrix}. \qquad (9.28)$$

Transposition of the 2-parallel fast filter in (9.20)

$$\mathbf{Y_2} = \mathbf{Q_2 H_2 P_2 X_2}$$

leads to another equivalent structure

$$\mathbf{Y_{2_F}} = (\mathbf{Q_2 H_2 P_2})^T \mathbf{X_{2_F}}$$
$$= \mathbf{P_2}^T \mathbf{H_2}^T \mathbf{Q_2}^T \mathbf{X_{2_F}}$$

$$\begin{bmatrix} Y_1 \\ Y_0 \end{bmatrix} = \begin{bmatrix} 1 & 1 & 0 \\ 0 & 1 & 1 \end{bmatrix} diag \begin{bmatrix} H_0 \\ H_0 + H_1 \\ H_1 \end{bmatrix} \begin{bmatrix} 1 & -1 \\ 0 & 1 \\ z^{-2} & -1 \end{bmatrix} \begin{bmatrix} X_1 \\ X_0 \end{bmatrix}. \qquad (9.29)$$

Notice that the computational complexity of the filtering algorithm remains the same. Fig. 9.5(c) shows the reduced-complexity 2-parallel FIR filter architecture of (9.29), which is obtained by transposition.

The transposed architecture can also be obtained by transposing the signal-flow graph of the original parallel filter, as shown in Fig. 9.5(a) and (b). Generally, both matrix transposition and signal-flow graph transposition are applicable to any FFA to generate equivalent parallel filtering structures.

9.2.2.3 Parallel Filtering Algorithms from Linear Convolutions
Any $L \times L$ convolution algorithm can also be used to derive an L-parallel fast filter structure. For example, the transpose of the matrix in a 2×2 linear convolution algorithm

$$\begin{bmatrix} s_2 \\ s_1 \\ s_0 \end{bmatrix} = \begin{bmatrix} h_1 & 0 \\ h_0 & h_1 \\ 0 & h_0 \end{bmatrix} \begin{bmatrix} x_1 \\ x_0 \end{bmatrix} \qquad (9.30)$$

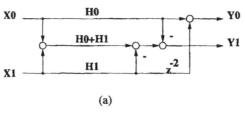

(a)

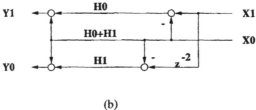

(b)

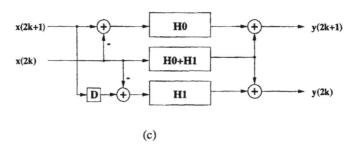

(c)

Fig. 9.5 (a) Signal-flow graph of the 2-parallel FIR filter in Fig. 9.3. (b) Transposed signal-flow graph. (c) Block diagram of the transposed reduced-complexity 2-parallel FIR filter implementation.

can be used to obtain the 2-parallel filter

$$
\begin{bmatrix} Y_0 \\ Y_1 \end{bmatrix} = \begin{bmatrix} H_1 & H_0 & 0 \\ 0 & H_1 & H_0 \end{bmatrix} \begin{bmatrix} z^{-2}X_1 \\ X_0 \\ X_1 \end{bmatrix}. \tag{9.31}
$$

Generally, the L-parallel filter

$$
\mathbf{Y} = \mathbf{HX}
$$

is first expressed as

$$\begin{bmatrix} Y_0 & Y_1 & \vdots & Y_{L-1} \end{bmatrix}^T \tag{9.32}$$

$$= \begin{bmatrix} H_{L-1} & H_{L-2} & \cdots & H_1 & H_0 & 0 & \cdots & 0 \\ 0 & H_{L-1} & \cdots & H_2 & H_1 & H_0 & \cdots & 0 \\ 0 & 0 & \cdots & H_3 & H_2 & H_1 & \cdots & 0 \\ \vdots & \vdots & \vdots & \ddots & \vdots & \vdots & \vdots & \vdots \\ 0 & \cdots & \cdots & 0 & H_{L-1} & H_{L-2} & \cdots & H_0 \end{bmatrix} \begin{bmatrix} z^{-L}X_1 \\ z^{-L}X_2 \\ \cdots \\ z^{-L}X_{L-1} \\ X_0 \\ X_1 \\ \cdots \\ X_{L-1} \end{bmatrix}.$$

Notice that this form of the standard parallel filtering algorithm is similar to the transpose form of a linear convolution [8]. Using this idea, reduced-complexity parallel filtering algorithms can be generated. The basic idea is to start with an optimal linear convolution and take its transposition to generate the parallel filtering algorithm. To generate a 2-parallel filter using 2×2 fast convolution, consider the following optimal 2×2 linear convolution:

$$s = \mathbf{CHAx}$$

$$\begin{bmatrix} s_2 \\ s_1 \\ s_0 \end{bmatrix} = \begin{bmatrix} 1 & 0 & 0 \\ -1 & 1 & -1 \\ 0 & 0 & 1 \end{bmatrix} diag \begin{bmatrix} h_1 \\ h_0 + h_1 \\ h_0 \end{bmatrix} \begin{bmatrix} 1 & 0 \\ 1 & 1 \\ 0 & 1 \end{bmatrix} \begin{bmatrix} x_1 \\ x_0 \end{bmatrix}. \tag{9.33}$$

Note that flipping the samples in the sequences $\{s\}$, $\{h\}$, and $\{x\}$ preserves the convolution formulation, i.e., the same $\mathbf{C}$ and $\mathbf{A}$ matrices can be used with the flipped sequences. Taking the transpose of this algorithm and by proper substitutions for s_i, h_i and x_i, we have:

$$\mathbf{Y} = (\mathbf{CHA})^T \mathbf{X} = \mathbf{QHPX}$$

$$\begin{bmatrix} Y_0 \\ Y_1 \end{bmatrix} = \begin{bmatrix} 1 & 1 & 0 \\ 0 & 1 & 1 \end{bmatrix} diag \begin{bmatrix} H_1 \\ H_1 + H_0 \\ H_0 \end{bmatrix} \begin{bmatrix} 1 & -1 & 0 \\ 0 & 1 & 0 \\ 0 & -1 & 1 \end{bmatrix} \begin{bmatrix} z^{-2}X_1 \\ X_0 \\ X_1 \end{bmatrix}. \tag{9.34}$$

The resulting 2-parallel architecture is shown in Fig. 9.5(c). It should not be a surprise that this method leads to the same architecture that was obtained using the direct transposition of the 2-parallel FFA since the original 2-parallel FFA is based upon the optimal linear convolution (9.33). The previous technique used a direct transposition of the FFA, while this technique uses a transposition of the linear convolution. This method can be applied to any FFA to generate an equivalent parallel filtering realization.

9.2.2.4   Fast Parallel FIR Algorithms for Large Block Sizes   Parallel FIR filters with long block sizes can be designed by cascading smaller length fast parallel filters. For example, an m-parallel FFA can be cascaded with an n-parallel FFA to produce an $(m \times n)$-parallel filtering structure. The set of FIR filters that result from the application of the m-parallel FFA are further decomposed, one at a time, by the application of the n-parallel FFA. The resulting set of filters will be of length $N/(m \times n)$. When cascading the FFAs, it is important to keep track of both the number of multiplications and the number of additions required for the filtering structure. The number of required multiplications for an L-parallel filter with $L = L_1 L_2 ... L_r$ is given by:

$$M = \frac{N}{\prod_{i=1}^{r} L_i} \prod_{i=1}^{r} M_i \tag{9.35}$$

where r is the number of FFAs used, L_i is the block size of the FFA at step-i, M_i is the number of filters that result from the application of the i-th FFA and N is the length of the filter. The number of required adders can be calculated as follows:

$$A = A_1 \prod_{i=2}^{r} L_i + \sum_{i=2}^{r} \left[A_i \left(\prod_{j=i+1}^{r} L_j \right) \left(\prod_{k=1}^{i-1} M_k \right) \right] + \left[\prod_{i=1}^{r} M_i \right] \left[\frac{N}{\prod_{i=1}^{r} L_i} - 1 \right]$$

$$\tag{9.36}$$

where A_i is the number of pre/postprocessing adders required by the i-th FFA. Consider the case of cascading two 2-parallel FFAs. The resulting 4-parallel filtering structure would require a total of $9N/4$ multiplications and $20 + 9(N/4 - 1)$ additions for implementation. The reduced-complexity 4-parallel filtering structure represents a hardware (area) savings of nearly 44% when compared to the $4N$ multiplications required in the traditional 4-parallel FIR filtering structure.

Example 9.2.1 *Calculating the Hardware Complexity*
In this example, the number of multiplications and additions required to implement a 24-tap filter with a block size of $L = 6$ is calculated. The calculation is performed for both the $L_1 = 2$, $L_2 = 3$ and the $L_1 = 3$, $L_2 = 2$ forms.

$$\underline{L_1 = 2, \ L_2 = 3}$$

$$M_1 = 3, \ A_1 = 4$$
$$M_2 = 6, \ A_2 = 10$$

$$M = \tfrac{24}{(2 \times 3)} \times (3 \times 6) = 72$$
$$A = (4 \times 3) + (10 \times 3) + (3 \times 6) \left[\tfrac{24}{2 \times 3} - 1 \right] = 96$$

$$\underline{L_1 = 3, \; L_2 = 2}$$

$$M_1 = 6, \; A_1 = 10$$
$$M_2 = 3, \; A_2 = 4$$

$$M = \tfrac{24}{(3 \times 2)} \times (6 \times 3) = 72$$
$$A = (10 \times 2) + (4 \times 6) + (6 \times 3)\left[\tfrac{24}{3 \times 2} - 1\right] = 98. \quad \blacksquare$$

In order to understand how the FFAs are cascaded, it is useful to consider (9.15) once again. Consider the design of a parallel FIR filter with a block size of 4. From (9.15), we have

$$\begin{aligned} Y = \; & Y_0 + z^{-1}Y_1 + z^{-2}Y_2 + z^{-3}Y_3 \\ = \; & (X_0 + z^{-1}X_1 + z^{-2}X_2 + z^{-3}X_3)(H_0 \\ & + z^{-1}H_1 + z^{-2}H_2 + z^{-3}H_3). \end{aligned} \tag{9.37}$$

The reduced-complexity 4-parallel FIR filtering structure is obtained by first applying the 2-parallel FFA to (9.37) and then applying the FFA a second time to each of the filtering operations that result from the first application of the FFA. From (9.37), we have

$$Y = (X_0' + z^{-1}X_1')(H_0' + z^{-1}H_1')$$

where

$$\begin{aligned} X_0' &= X_0 + z^{-2}X_2, \quad X_1' = X_1 + z^{-2}X_3 \\ H_0' &= H_0 + z^{-2}H_2, \quad H_1' = H_1 + z^{-2}H_3. \end{aligned} \tag{9.38}$$

Application 1

$$Y = X_0'H_0' + z^{-1}[(X_0' + X_1')(H_0' + H_1') - X_0'H_0' - X_1'H_1'] + z^{-2}X_1'H_1'. \tag{9.39}$$

The 2-parallel FFA is then applied a second time to each of the filtering operations $X_0'H_0'$, $X_1'H_1'$ and $(X_0' + X_1')(H_0' + H_1')$ of (9.39).

Application 2, Filtering Operation $X_0'H_0'$

$$\begin{aligned} X_0'H_0' = \; & (X_0 + z^{-2}X_2)(H_0 + z^{-2}H_2) \\ = \; & X_0H_0 + z^{-2}[(X_0 + X_2)(H_0 + H_2) \\ & - X_0H_0 - X_2H_2] + z^{-4}X_2H_2. \end{aligned} \tag{9.40}$$

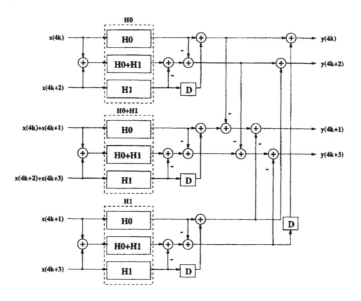

Fig. 9.6 Reduced-complexity 4-parallel FIR filter.

Application 2, Filtering Operation $X_1' H_1'$

$$
\begin{aligned}
X_1' H_1' = & \ (X_1 + z^{-2} X_3)(H_1 + z^{-2} H_3) \\
= & \ X_1 H_1 + z^{-2}[(X_1 + X_3)(H_1 + H_3) \\
& -X_1 H_1 - X_3 H_3] + z^{-4} X_3 H_3.
\end{aligned} \tag{9.41}
$$

Application 2, Filtering Operation $(X_0' + X_1')(H_0' + H_1')$

$$
\begin{aligned}
& (X_0' + X_1')(H_0' + H_1') \\
& = [(X_0 + X_1) + z^{-2}(X_2 + X_3)][(H_0 + H_1) + z^{-2}(H_2 + H_3)] \\
& = (X_0 + X_1)(H_0 + H_1) \\
& \quad + z^{-2}[(X_0 + X_1 + X_2 + X_3)(H_0 + H_1 + H_2 + H_3) \\
& \quad - (X_0 + X_1)(H_0 + H_1) - (X_2 + X_3)(H_2 + H_3)] \\
& \quad + z^{-4}(X_2 + X_3)(H_2 + H_3).
\end{aligned} \tag{9.42}
$$

The second application of the 2-parallel FFA leads to the 4-parallel filtering structure shown in Fig. 9.6, which requires 9 length $N/4$ filtering operations. In matrix form, the reduced-complexity 4-parallel FIR filter is represented as follows:

$$
\mathbf{Y_{4p}} = \mathbf{B_4}(\mathbf{I_{3x3}} \otimes \mathbf{Q_4})\mathbf{H_4}(\mathbf{P_2} \otimes \mathbf{P_2})\mathbf{X_{4p}}
$$

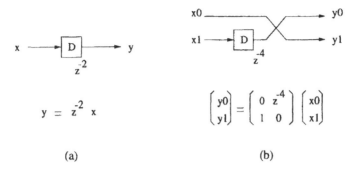

Fig. 9.7 Unfolding of a delay element, (a) Representation of z^{-2} in a 2-parallel design, (b) 2-unfolded representation to obtain the 4-parallel design where a delay element corresponds to z^{-4}.

where

$$\mathbf{Y_{4p}} = \begin{bmatrix} Y_0 \\ Y_2 \\ Y_1 \\ Y_3 \end{bmatrix}, \quad \mathbf{B_4} = \begin{bmatrix} 1 & 0 & 0 & 0 & 0 & z^{-4} \\ 0 & 1 & 0 & 0 & 1 & 0 \\ -1 & 0 & 1 & 0 & -1 & 0 \\ 0 & -1 & 0 & 1 & 0 & -1 \end{bmatrix},$$

$$\mathbf{Q_4} = \begin{bmatrix} 1 & 0 & z^{-4} \\ -1 & 1 & -1 \end{bmatrix}, \quad \mathbf{H_4} = diag \begin{bmatrix} H_0 \\ H_0 + H_2 \\ H_2 \\ H_0 + H_1 \\ H_0 + H_1 + H_2 + H_3 \\ H_2 + H_3 \\ H_1 \\ H_1 + H_3 \\ H_3 \end{bmatrix},$$

$$\mathbf{P_2} = \begin{bmatrix} 1 & 0 \\ 1 & 1 \\ 0 & 1 \end{bmatrix}, \quad \mathbf{X_{4p}} = \begin{bmatrix} X_0 \\ X_2 \\ X_1 \\ X_3 \end{bmatrix}. \tag{9.43}$$

Note that $\mathbf{X_{4p}}$ and $\mathbf{Y_{4p}}$ are permuted versions of $\mathbf{X_4}$ and $\mathbf{Y_4}$, respectively. Note that $\mathbf{B_4}$ can be obtained from $\mathbf{Q_2}$ by replacing 1 by $\mathbf{I_{2 \times 2}}$, 0 by $\mathbf{0_{2 \times 2}}$ and by appropriate unfolding of the delay operator z^{-2} of the 2-parallel design as shown in Fig. 9.7. (For details of unfolding, see Chapter 5). The $\otimes$ operator is the tensor or Kronecker product operator [9]. The tensor product is extremely useful in signal processing applications because it allows large matrices to be represented using smaller matrices. The tensor product is defined as follows:

Definition 9.2.1 Tensor Product
Let $\mathbf{A}$ and $\mathbf{B}$ be 2 arbitrary matrices of dimension k by l and m by n, respec-

tively.

$$\mathbf{A} = \begin{bmatrix} a_{0,0} & a_{0,1} & \cdots & a_{0,l-1} \\ a_{1,0} & a_{1,1} & \cdots & a_{1,l-1} \\ \cdot & \cdot & \cdots & \cdot \\ a_{k-1,0} & a_{k-1,1} & \cdots & a_{k-1,l-1} \end{bmatrix},$$

$$\mathbf{B} = \begin{bmatrix} b_{0,0} & b_{0,1} & \cdots & b_{0,n-1} \\ b_{1,0} & b_{1,1} & \cdots & b_{1,n-1} \\ \cdot & \cdot & \cdots & \cdot \\ b_{m-1,0} & b_{m-1,1} & \cdots & b_{m-1,n-1} \end{bmatrix}.$$

The tensor product of $\mathbf{A}$ *and* $\mathbf{B}$, $\mathbf{C} = \mathbf{A} \otimes \mathbf{B}$, *is defined to be the km by ln matrix given by*

$$\mathbf{C} = \begin{bmatrix} a_{0,0}\mathbf{B} & a_{0,1}\mathbf{B} & \cdots & a_{0,l-1}\mathbf{B} \\ a_{1,0}\mathbf{B} & a_{1,1}\mathbf{B} & \cdots & a_{1,l-1}\mathbf{B} \\ \cdot & \cdot & \cdots & \cdot \\ a_{k-1,0}\mathbf{B} & a_{k-1,1}\mathbf{B} & \cdots & a_{k-1,l-1}\mathbf{B} \end{bmatrix}.$$

Using the tensor product, we can represent the reduced-complexity 4-parallel FIR filter in a relatively compact form. It should be noted that the Q_4 matrix is essentially identical to the Q_2 matrix of the 2-parallel FFA with the only difference being the power of the delay operator in the matrices. The 4-parallel structure shown in Fig. 9.6 can be thought of as 3 separate 2-parallel FFAs each producing 2 outputs, which are combined by $\mathbf{B_4}$ to produce the 4 filter outputs. As stated earlier, this structure uses approximately 44% less hardware than the traditional 4-parallel FIR filter.

In the remainder of this section, we present 2 more parallel filtering structures: the 6-parallel FIR filter and the 8-parallel FIR filter. The 6-parallel FIR filter is generated by cascading a 2-parallel FFA with a 3-parallel FFA. The process is essentially identical to the process that was used to generate the 4-parallel filtering structure. Beginning with (9.15), the 2-parallel FFA is applied resulting in 3 filtering operations. The 3-parallel FFA is then applied to each of these filters producing the 18 filtering operations that are required in the 6-parallel filtering structure. Note that when 2-parallel and 3-parallel FFAs are cascaded, the 2-parallel FFA is always applied first as this will lead to the lowest implementational cost (see (9.35) and (9.36)). The resulting 6-parallel filtering structure requires $18N/6$, or $3N$, multiplications and $42 + 18(N/6 - 1) = 3N + 24$ additions. This reduced-complexity 6-parallel filtering structure provides an area savings of approximately 50% compared to the traditional 6-parallel filtering structure. In matrix form, the reduced-complexity 6-parallel FIR filter is represented as follows:

$$\mathbf{Y_{6p}} = \mathbf{B_6}(\mathbf{I_{3x3}} \otimes \mathbf{Q_6})\mathbf{H_6}(\mathbf{P_2} \otimes \mathbf{P_3})\mathbf{X_{6p}}$$

where

$$
\mathbf{Y_{6p}} = \begin{bmatrix} Y_0 \\ Y_2 \\ Y_4 \\ Y_1 \\ Y_3 \\ Y_5 \end{bmatrix}, \quad
\mathbf{B_6} = \begin{bmatrix} 1 & 0 & 0 & 0 & 0 & 0 & 0 & 0 & z^{-6} \\ 0 & 1 & 0 & 0 & 0 & 0 & 1 & 0 & 0 \\ 0 & 0 & 1 & 0 & 0 & 0 & 0 & 1 & 0 \\ -1 & 0 & 0 & 1 & 0 & 0 & -1 & 0 & 0 \\ 0 & -1 & 0 & 0 & 1 & 0 & 0 & -1 & 0 \\ 0 & 0 & -1 & 0 & 0 & 1 & 0 & 0 & -1 \end{bmatrix},
$$

$$
\mathbf{Q_6} = \begin{bmatrix} 1 & 0 & z^{-6} & 0 \\ -1 & 1 & 0 & 0 \\ 0 & -1 & -1 & 1 \end{bmatrix} \begin{bmatrix} 1 & 0 & -z^{-6} & 0 & 0 & 0 \\ 0 & -1 & 0 & 1 & 0 & 0 \\ 0 & -1 & 0 & 0 & 1 & 0 \\ 0 & 0 & 0 & 0 & 0 & 1 \end{bmatrix},
$$

$$
\mathbf{H_6} = diag \begin{bmatrix} H_0 \\ H_2 \\ H_4 \\ \vdots \\ H_1 + H_3 \\ H_3 + H_5 \\ H_1 + H_3 + H_5 \end{bmatrix}, \quad
\mathbf{P_2} = \begin{bmatrix} 1 & 0 \\ 1 & 1 \\ 0 & 1 \end{bmatrix},
$$

$$
\mathbf{P_3} = \begin{bmatrix} 1 & 0 & 0 \\ 0 & 1 & 0 \\ 0 & 0 & 1 \\ 1 & 1 & 0 \\ 0 & 1 & 1 \\ 1 & 1 & 1 \end{bmatrix}, \quad
\mathbf{X_{6p}} = \begin{bmatrix} X_0 \\ X_2 \\ X_4 \\ X_1 \\ X_3 \\ X_5 \end{bmatrix}. \tag{9.44}
$$

Notice that $\mathbf{X_{6p}}$ and $\mathbf{Y_{6p}}$ are permuted versions of $\mathbf{X_6}$ and $\mathbf{Y_6}$, respectively, and $\mathbf{Q_6}$ is the same as the $\mathbf{Q_3}$ matrix with the delay operators changed from z^{-3} to z^{-6}. The matrix $\mathbf{B_6}$ is obtained from $\mathbf{Q_2}$ by replacing 1 by $\mathbf{I_{3\times3}}$, 0 by $\mathbf{0_{3\times3}}$, and z^{-2} by its 3-unfolded version. The reduced-complexity 6-parallel FIR filter structure is shown in Fig. 9.8.

The 8-parallel FIR filtering structure is generated by cascading three 2-parallel FFAs. This results in a filtering structure that performs 27 filtering operations. The 8-parallel FIR filtering structure requires $27N/8$ multiplications and $76 + 27(N/8 - 1) = 27N/8 + 49$ additions. This filtering structure provides an area savings of approximately 58% when compared to the traditional 8-parallel FIR filter. In matrix form, the reduced-complexity 8-parallel FIR filter is represented as follows:

$$
\mathbf{Y_{8p}} = \mathbf{B_8}(\mathbf{I_{3\times3}} \otimes \mathbf{Q_{8_2}})[\mathbf{I_{3\times3}} \otimes (\mathbf{I_{3\times3}} \otimes \mathbf{Q_{8_1}})]\mathbf{H_8}[\mathbf{P_2} \otimes (\mathbf{P_2} \otimes \mathbf{P_2})]\mathbf{X_{8p}}
$$

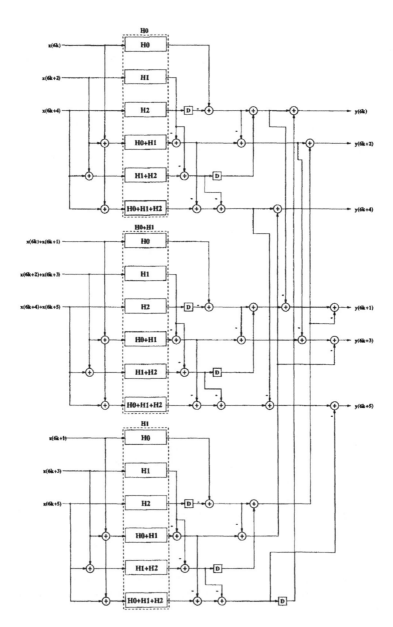

Fig. 9.8 Reduced-complexity 6-parallel FIR filter. The subfilters in this architecture are the subfilters of H_0, $H_0 + H_1$, and H_1, which are obtained from the original filter.

where

$$
\mathbf{Y}_{8p} = \begin{bmatrix} Y_0 \\ Y_4 \\ Y_2 \\ Y_6 \\ Y_1 \\ Y_5 \\ Y_3 \\ Y_7 \end{bmatrix}, \quad
\mathbf{Q}_{8_2} = \begin{bmatrix} 1 & 0 & 0 & 0 & 0 & z^{-8} \\ 0 & 1 & 0 & 0 & 1 & 0 \\ -1 & 0 & 1 & 0 & -1 & 0 \\ 0 & -1 & 0 & 1 & 0 & -1 \end{bmatrix}, \quad
\mathbf{X}_{8p} = \begin{bmatrix} X_0 \\ X_4 \\ X_2 \\ X_6 \\ X_1 \\ X_5 \\ X_3 \\ X_7 \end{bmatrix},
$$

$$
\mathbf{B}_8 = \begin{bmatrix}
1 & 0 & 0 & 0 & 0 & 0 & 0 & 0 & 0 & 0 & 0 & z^{-8} \\
0 & 1 & 0 & 0 & 0 & 0 & 0 & 0 & 0 & 0 & 1 & 0 \\
0 & 0 & 1 & 0 & 0 & 0 & 0 & 0 & 1 & 0 & 0 & 0 \\
0 & 0 & 0 & 1 & 0 & 0 & 0 & 0 & 0 & 1 & 0 & 0 \\
-1 & 0 & 0 & 0 & 1 & 0 & 0 & 0 & -1 & 0 & 0 & 0 \\
0 & -1 & 0 & 0 & 0 & 1 & 0 & 0 & 0 & -1 & 0 & 0 \\
0 & 0 & -1 & 0 & 0 & 0 & 1 & 0 & 0 & 0 & -1 & 0 \\
0 & 0 & 0 & -1 & 0 & 0 & 0 & 1 & 0 & 0 & 0 & -1
\end{bmatrix},
$$

$$
\mathbf{Q}_{8_1} = \begin{bmatrix} 1 & 0 & z^{-8} \\ -1 & 1 & -1 \end{bmatrix}, \quad
\mathbf{P}_2 = \begin{bmatrix} 1 & 0 \\ 1 & 1 \\ 0 & 1 \end{bmatrix}, \quad
\mathbf{H}_8 = diag \begin{bmatrix} H_0 \\ H_0 + H_4 \\ \vdots \\ H_3 + H_7 \\ H_7 \end{bmatrix}.
$$

$$(9.45)$$

The reduced-complexity 8-parallel FIR filter structure is shown in Fig. 9.9. The Q_{8_1}, Q_{8_2} matrices are essentially identical to the Q_2, Q_4 matrices, respectively, that are used in the matrix representations of the 2-parallel and 4-parallel FIR filters. They only differ with respect to the power of the delay operators in both matrices.

9.2.2.5 Applications of Fast Parallel FIR Filters   Fast parallel FIR filters can be applied in many applications to reduce the number of multiplication operations. These can be used to design efficient wavelet transforms [10] (see Problems 16 and 17) and subband coders, adaptive equalizers [11] (see Problems 18 and 19), two-dimensional parallel FIR filters (see Problem 23) and motion estimation in video compression [12] (see Problem 24).

9.3 DISCRETE COSINE TRANSFORM AND INVERSE DCT

The discrete cosine transform (DCT) is a frequency transform used in still and moving video compression [13] (see Section 1.2.6). This section addresses fast implementations of DCT based on algorithm-architecture transformations

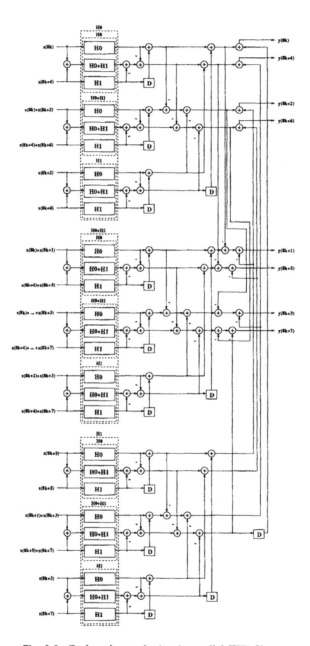

Fig. 9.9 Reduced-complexity 8-parallel FIR filter.

and the decimation-in-frequency approach.

Denote the DCT of the data sequence $x(n)$, $n = 0, 1, \cdots, N - 1$, by $X(k)$, $k = 0, 1, \cdots, N - 1$. The DCT and inverse DCT (IDCT) algorithms are described by the following equations:

DCT:

$$X(k) = e(k) \sum_{n=0}^{N-1} x(n) \cos[\frac{(2n+1)\pi k}{2N}], \quad k = 0, 1, \cdots, N - 1 \qquad (9.46)$$

and

IDCT:

$$x(n) = \frac{2}{N} \sum_{k=0}^{N-1} e(k) X(k) \cos[\frac{(2n+1)\pi k}{2N}], \quad n = 0, 1, \cdots, N - 1, \qquad (9.47)$$

where

$$e(k) = \begin{cases} \frac{1}{\sqrt{2}}, & if \ k = 0, \\ 1, & otherwise. \end{cases} \qquad (9.48)$$

Notice that the DCT is an *orthogonal* transform, i.e., the transformation matrix for IDCT is a scaled version of the transpose of that for the DCT and vice versa. Therefore, the DCT architecture can be obtained by "transposing" the IDCT, i.e., reversing the direction of the arrows in the flow graph of IDCT, and the IDCT can be obtained by "transposing" the DCT.

It is easy to verify that a direct implementation of DCT or IDCT requires $N(N - 1)$ multiplication operations, i.e., $O(N^2)$, which is very hardware expensive. Therefore, an algorithm that can minimize the number of calculations required is a problem of particular interest for DCT.

9.3.1   Algorithm-Architecture Transformation

The *algorithm-architecture transformations* can be used to derive efficient DCT implementations where the number of multiplications can be reduced dramatically [14]. The algorithm-architecture mapping technique works in a hierarchical way to adapt an architecture to a given algorithm or change the algorithm's description in a systematic way. An 8-point DCT architecture is derived in Example 9.3.1 using this technique, where the number of multiplications is reduced from 56 to 13.

Example 9.3.1 *Consider the 8-point DCT*

$$X(k) = e(k) \sum_{n=0}^{7} x(n) \cos[\frac{(2n+1)\pi k}{16}], \quad k = 0, 1, \cdots, 7 \qquad (9.49)$$

where

$$e(k) = \begin{cases} \frac{1}{\sqrt{2}}, & if \ k = 0, \\ 1, & otherwise. \end{cases} \tag{9.50}$$

It can be written in matrix form as follows:

$$\begin{bmatrix} X(0) \\ X(1) \\ X(2) \\ X(3) \\ X(4) \\ X(5) \\ X(6) \\ X(7) \end{bmatrix} = \begin{bmatrix} c_4 & c_4 & c_4 & c_4 & c_4 & c_4 & c_4 & c_4 \\ c_1 & c_3 & c_5 & c_7 & c_9 & c_{11} & c_{13} & c_{15} \\ c_2 & c_6 & c_{10} & c_{14} & c_{18} & c_{22} & c_{26} & c_{30} \\ c_3 & c_9 & c_{15} & c_{21} & c_{27} & c_1 & c_7 & c_{13} \\ c_4 & c_{12} & c_{20} & c_{28} & c_4 & c_{12} & c_{20} & c_{28} \\ c_5 & c_{15} & c_{25} & c_3 & c_{13} & c_{23} & c_1 & c_{11} \\ c_6 & c_{18} & c_{30} & c_{10} & c_{22} & c_2 & c_{14} & c_{26} \\ c_7 & c_{21} & c_3 & c_{17} & c_{31} & c_{13} & c_{27} & c_9 \end{bmatrix} \begin{bmatrix} x(0) \\ x(1) \\ x(2) \\ x(3) \\ x(4) \\ x(5) \\ x(6) \\ x(7) \end{bmatrix}, \tag{9.51}$$

where $c_i = \cos \frac{i\pi}{16}$. *The algorithm-architecture mapping for the 8-point DCT can be carried out in three steps. In the first step, the DCT algorithm is modified in a systematic way that is simpler to implement. Using trigonometric properties, we have*

$$\begin{bmatrix} X(0) \\ X(1) \\ X(2) \\ X(3) \\ X(4) \\ X(5) \\ X(6) \\ X(7) \end{bmatrix} = \begin{bmatrix} c_4 & c_4 & c_4 & c_4 & c_4 & c_4 & c_4 & c_4 \\ c_1 & c_3 & c_5 & c_7 & -c_7 & -c_5 & -c_3 & -c_1 \\ c_2 & c_6 & -c_6 & -c_2 & -c_2 & -c_6 & c_6 & c_2 \\ c_3 & -c_7 & -c_1 & -c_5 & c_5 & c_1 & c_7 & -c_3 \\ c_4 & -c_4 & -c_4 & c_4 & c_4 & -c_4 & -c_4 & c_4 \\ c_5 & -c_1 & c_7 & c_3 & -c_3 & -c_7 & c_1 & -c_5 \\ c_6 & -c_2 & c_2 & -c_6 & -c_6 & c_2 & -c_2 & c_6 \\ c_7 & -c_5 & c_3 & -c_1 & c_1 & -c_3 & c_5 & -c_7 \end{bmatrix} \begin{bmatrix} x(0) \\ x(1) \\ x(2) \\ x(3) \\ x(4) \\ x(5) \\ x(6) \\ x(7) \end{bmatrix} \tag{9.52}$$

Then the 8-point DCT can be rewritten as

$$\begin{aligned} X(1) &= M_0 c_1 + M_1 c_7 + M_2 c_3 + M_3 c_5 \\ X(7) &= M_0 c_7 - M_1 c_1 - M_2 c_5 + M_3 c_3 \\ X(3) &= M_0 c_3 - M_1 c_5 - M_2 c_7 - M_3 c_1 \\ X(5) &= M_0 c_5 + M_1 c_3 - M_2 c_1 + M_3 c_7 \\ X(2) &= M_{10} c_2 + M_{11} c_6 \\ X(6) &= M_{10} c_6 - M_{11} c_2 \\ X(4) &= M_{100} c_4 \\ X(0) &= P_{100} c_4, \end{aligned} \tag{9.53}$$

where

$$\begin{array}{ll} M_0 = x_0 - x_7 & P_0 = x_0 + x_7 \\ M_1 = x_3 - x_4 & P_1 = x_3 + x_4 \\ M_2 = x_1 - x_6 & P_2 = x_1 + x_6 \end{array}$$

$$M_3 = x_2 - x_5 \qquad P_3 = x_2 + x_5$$
$$M_{10} = P_0 - P_1 \qquad P_{10} = P_0 + P_1$$
$$M_{11} = P_2 - P_3 \qquad P_{11} = P_2 + P_3$$
$$M_{100} = p_{10} - P_{11} \qquad P_{100} = P_{10} + P_{11}. \tag{9.54}$$

Fig. 9.10 shows the DCT architecture according to (9.53) and (9.54) with 22 multiplications. In the 2nd step, the DCT structure in Fig. 9.10 is grouped

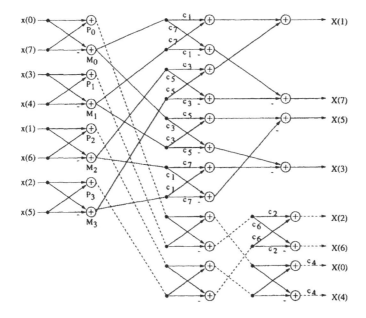

Fig. 9.10 First step 8-point DCT structure in Example 9.3.1.

into different functional units represented by blocks and then the whole DCT structure is transformed into a block diagram. Two major blocks are defined as shown in Fig. 9.11. The transformed block diagram for an 8-point DCT is shown in Fig. 9.12. In the 3rd step, reduced complexity implementations of various blocks are exploited. The block $\boxed{XC\pm}$ *can be realized using 3 multiplications and 3 additions instead of using 4 multiplications and 2 additions, as shown in Fig. 9.13(a). Furthermore, define the block* $\boxed{XC\pm}$ *with* $a = \sin\theta$ *and* $b = \cos\theta$ *and reversed outputs as a rotator block* $\boxed{rot\ \theta}$ *that computes*

$$\begin{bmatrix} x' \\ y' \end{bmatrix} = \begin{bmatrix} \cos\theta & -\sin\theta \\ \sin\theta & \cos\theta \end{bmatrix} \begin{bmatrix} x \\ y \end{bmatrix}, \tag{9.55}$$

as shown in Fig. 9.13(b). Notice that the angles of cascaded rotators can be simply added, as shown in the transformation block in Fig. 9.13(c). Fig. 9.13(d) is based on the fact that a rotator with $\theta = \pi/4$ *is just the block* $\boxed{X\pm}$ *whose*

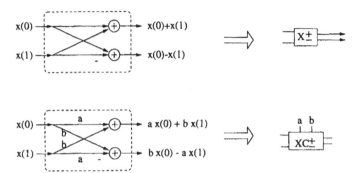

Fig. 9.11 Block definitions in Example 9.3.1.

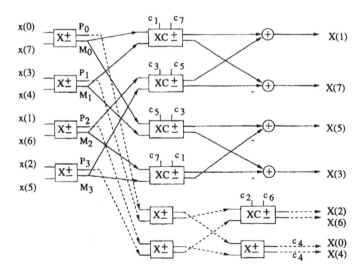

Fig. 9.12 Second step 8-point DCT structure in Example 9.3.1.

outputs are both reversed and multiplied by $\cos(\pi/4)$. *Applying all the trans-*

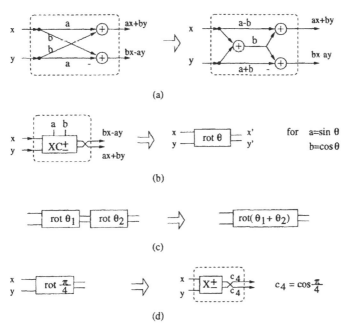

Fig. 9.13 Graph transformations used in Example 9.3.1.

formations in Fig. 9.13 to the DCT block diagram in Fig. 9.12, we obtain the final structure in Fig. 9.14 where only 13 multiplications are required. ∎

The number of multipliers can be further reduced to 11 if the scaled DCT, $X(k)/c_4$, is computed instead of $X(k)$ (see Problem 29).

9.3.2 Decimation-in-Frequency Fast DCT for 2^m-Point DCT

Fast 2^m-point DCT/IDCT structures can be derived by the decimation-in-frequency approach [15],[16], which is commonly used to derive the discrete-Fourier transform (DFT). This algorithm reduces the number of multiplications to about $(N/2)\log_2 N$ by power-of-2 decomposition.

First the fast IDCT computation is considered. For simplicity, the $2/N$ scaling factor in (9.47) is ignored in this derivation. Define

$$\hat{X}(k) = e(k)X(k) \tag{9.56}$$

and decompose $x(n)$ into even and odd indexes of k as follows:

$$x(n) = \sum_{k=0}^{N-1} \hat{X}(k) \cos \frac{(2n+1)\pi k}{2N} \tag{9.57}$$

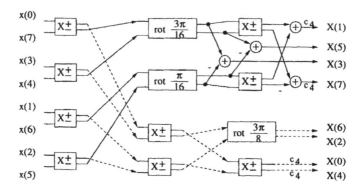

Fig. 9.14   Final 8-point DCT structure in Example 9.3.1.

$$= \sum_{k=0}^{N/2-1} \hat{X}(2k) \cos \frac{(2n+1)\pi(2k)}{2N}$$

$$+ \sum_{k=0}^{N/2-1} \hat{X}(2k+1) \cos \frac{(2n+1)\pi(2k+1)}{2N}$$

$$= \sum_{k=0}^{N/2-1} \hat{X}(2k) \cos \frac{(2n+1)\pi k}{2(N/2)}$$

$$+ \frac{1}{2\cos \frac{(2n+1)\pi}{2N}} \sum_{k=0}^{N/2-1} 2\hat{X}(2k+1) \cos \frac{(2n+1)\pi(2k+1)}{2N} \cos \frac{(2n+1)\pi}{2N}.$$

Notice that

$$2\cos \frac{(2n+1)\pi(2k+1)}{2N} \cos \frac{(2n+1)\pi}{2N} = \cos \frac{(2n+1)\pi(k+1)}{N} + \cos \frac{(2n+1)\pi k}{N}.$$
$$\tag{9.58}$$

Therefore,

$$\sum_{k=0}^{N/2-1} 2\hat{X}(2k+1) \cos \frac{(2n+1)\pi(2k+1)}{2N} \cos \frac{(2n+1)\pi}{2N} \tag{9.59}$$

$$= \sum_{k=0}^{N/2-1} \hat{X}(2k+1) \cos \frac{(2n+1)\pi(k+1)}{N} + \sum_{k=0}^{N/2-1} \hat{X}(2k+1) \cos \frac{(2n+1)\pi k}{N}$$

$$= \sum_{k=0}^{N/2-2} \hat{X}(2k+1) \cos \frac{(2n+1)\pi(k+1)}{N} + \sum_{k=0}^{N/2-1} \hat{X}(2k+1) \cos \frac{(2n+1)\pi k}{N},$$

since $\cos \frac{(2n+1)\pi(N/2-1+1)}{N} = 0$. Substitute $k' = k + 1$ into the 1st term of

(9.60) and it becomes

$$\sum_{k=0}^{N/2-2} \hat{X}(2k+1) \cos \frac{(2n+1)\pi(k+1)}{N} \tag{9.60}$$

$$= \sum_{k'=1}^{N/2-1} \hat{X}(2k'-1) \cos \frac{(2n+1)\pi k'}{N}$$

$$= \sum_{k'=0}^{N/2-1} \hat{X}(2k'-1) \cos \frac{(2n+1)\pi k'}{N},$$

with $\hat{X}(-1) = 0$. Then the IDCT (9.58) can be written as

$$x(n) = \sum_{k=0}^{N/2-1} \hat{X}(2k) \cos \frac{(2n+1)\pi k}{2(N/2)} \tag{9.61}$$

$$+ \frac{1}{2\cos\frac{(2n+1)\pi}{2N}} \sum_{k=0}^{N/2-1} [\hat{X}(2k+1) + \hat{X}(2k-1)] \cos \frac{(2n+1)\pi k}{2(N/2)}.$$

Define

$$G(k) = \hat{X}(2k),$$
$$H(k) = \hat{X}(2k+1) + \hat{X}(2k-1), \quad for\ k = 0, 1, \cdots, N/2 - 1 \tag{9.62}$$

and

$$g(n) = \sum_{k=0}^{N/2-1} \hat{X}(2k) \cos \frac{(2n+1)\pi k}{2(N/2)},$$

$$h(n) = \sum_{k=0}^{N/2-1} [\hat{X}(2k+1) + \hat{X}(2k-1)] \cos \frac{(2n+1)\pi k}{2(N/2)},$$

$$for\ n = 0, 1, \cdots, N/2 - 1. \tag{9.63}$$

Clearly, $G(k)$ and $H(k)$ are the DCT of $g(n)$ and $h(n)$, respectively. And we have

$$x(n) = g(n) + \frac{1}{2\cos\frac{(2n+1)\pi}{2N}} h(n), \tag{9.64}$$

$$x(N-1-n) = g(n) - \frac{1}{2\cos\frac{(2n+1)\pi}{2N}} h(n), \tag{9.65}$$

$$for\ n = 0, 1, \cdots, N/2 - 1$$

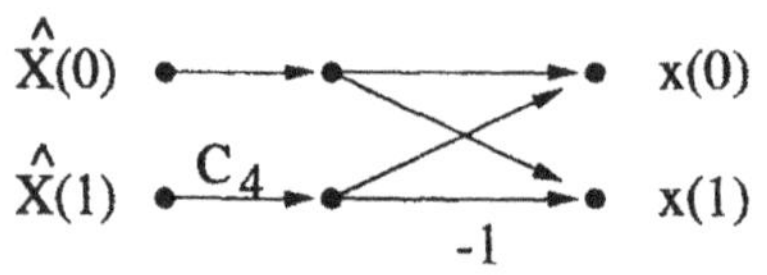

Fig. 9.15 Two-point IDCT butterfly architecture.

since

$$\cos \frac{(2(N-1-n)+1)\pi k}{N} = \cos \frac{(2n+1)\pi k}{N},$$

$$\cos \frac{(2(N-1-n)+1)\pi}{2N} = -\cos \frac{(2n+1)\pi}{2N}. \qquad (9.66)$$

Therefore, the N-point IDCT in (9.47) has been expressed in terms of two $N/2$-point IDCTs in (9.63). By repeating this process, the IDCT can be decomposed further until it can be expressed in terms of 2-point IDCTs.

The DCT algorithm can also be decomposed similarly. Alternatively, it can be obtained by transposing the IDCT, as mentioned in a previous subsection.

Example 9.3.2 *Construct the 2-point IDCT butterfly architecture. The 2-point IDCT can be computed as*

$$x(0) = \hat{X}(0) + \hat{X}(1) \cos \frac{\pi}{4}$$

$$x(1) = \hat{X}(0) - \hat{X}(1) \cos \frac{\pi}{4}. \qquad (9.67)$$

This 2-point IDCT butterfly architecture is shown in Fig. 9.15.

Example 9.3.3 *Construct the 8-point fast DCT architecture using 2-point IDCT butterfly architecture. With $N=8$, (9.62)–(9.66) are rewritten as:*

$$G(k) = \hat{X}(2k), \qquad (9.68)$$

$$H(k) = \hat{X}(2k+1) + \hat{X}(2k-1), \quad k = 0, 1, 2, 3 \qquad (9.69)$$

and

$$g(n) = \sum_{k=0}^{3} G(k) \cos \frac{(2n+1)\pi k}{2(N/2)}, \qquad (9.70)$$

$$h(n) = \sum_{k=0}^{3} H(k) \cos \frac{(2n+1)\pi k}{2(N/2)}, \qquad (9.71)$$

$$x(n) = g(n) + \frac{1}{2 \cos \frac{(2n+1)\pi}{16}} h(n), \qquad (9.72)$$

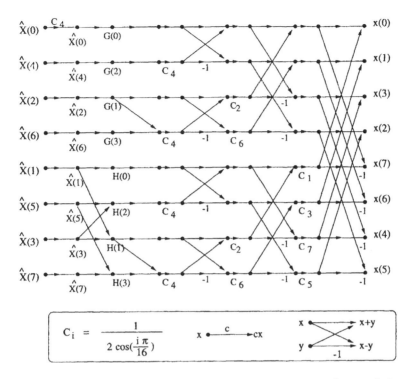

Fig. 9.16 Eight-point fast IDCT flowgraph. The scaling factor $2/N = 1/4$ has not been included in this structure.

$$x(7 - n) = g(n) - \frac{1}{2\cos\frac{(2n+1)\pi}{16}}h(n), \quad n = 0, 1, 2, 3. \qquad (9.73)$$

The 8-point fast IDCT is shown in Fig. 9.16, where only 13 multiplication operations are needed. This structure can be transposed to get the fast 8-point DCT architecture shown in Fig. 9.17. (Notice for N=8, the $C_4 = \frac{1}{2\cos(4\pi/16)} = \cos\frac{\pi}{4}$ in both figures.) ■

9.4 PARALLEL ARCHITECTURES FOR RANK-ORDER FILTERS

Rank-order filters are widely used in image processing for applications such as smoothing, noise reduction, edge detection, etc. They are nonlinear filters that sort the input sequence and choose an output based on its rank. The input output relationship of a rank-order filter is given by (9.74):

$$y_r(n) = r^{th} rank \quad [x(n - N), x(n - N + 1), \cdots,$$
$$x(n), \cdots, x(n + N - 1), x(n + N)], \qquad (9.74)$$

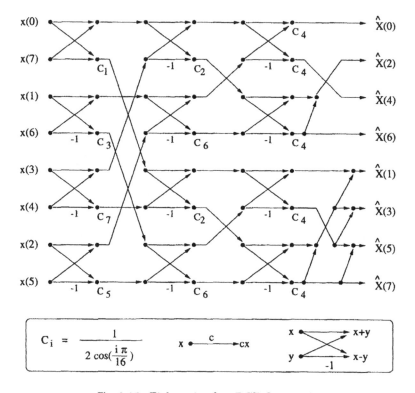

Fig. 9.17 Eight-point fast DCT flowgraph.

where $r = 1, 2, ...2N + 1$. The window size of the filter is $W = 2N + 1$. A corresponding system diagram for $W = 5$ case is shown in Fig. 9.18. This section is mostly concerned with programmable rank-order filters where outputs for all values of r are available. The set of all outputs $\{y_r(n)\}$ for all values of r is denoted simply as $y(n)$.

This section addresses the parallel architectures of the rank-order filters designed based on the Batcher's *odd-even merge-sort* algorithm [17] and algorithmic strength reduction. By sharing some of the merge units in different parallel blocks, the hardware complexity of the parallel rank-order filters can be reduced.

9.4.1 Odd-Even Merge-Sort Architecture

The rank-order filters sort the inputs with respect to their magnitudes based on merge-sort operations. This subsection introduces the odd-even merge-sort algorithm that can be used to efficiently realize the merge-sort operations.

The odd-even merge-sort algorithm processes 2 presorted sequences and merges them into 1 sorted sequence. There are 2 merging units, *odd-merge*

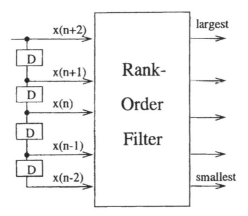

Fig. 9.18 A rank-order filter with window size $W=5$.

and *even-merge*. All inputs with odd subscripts are input to the odd-merge. All inputs with even subscripts are input to the even-merge. The outputs of each merge unit are again compared with each other except the first output of odd-merge, which is the largest element, and the last output of the even-merge, which is the smallest element. The ith output of the odd merge unit is compared with the $(i-1)^{th}$ output of the even merge unit to obtain the sorted outputs. Large merge-sort units can be built using small merge-sort units. The smallest merge-sort unit is a 1×1 merge-sort unit, which is usually denoted as **C&S** and referred to as a *compare-and-swap* unit. The derivation of hardware complexity and latency of the merge-sort architecture is left as an exercise to the reader (see Problem 35).

Example 9.4.1 *Fig. 9.19 shows a 4×4 merge-sort circuit. It consists of an*

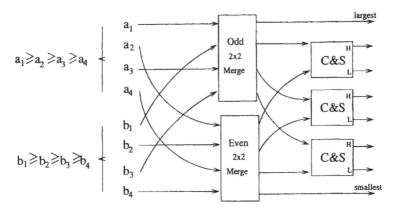

Fig. 9.19 A 4×4 merge-sort circuit.

*odd and an even 2×2 merge units and some **C&S** units for sorting purposes.*

*The 2×2 merge can be built using 3 **C&S** units as shown in Fig. 9.20. Notice that the 2 input sequences are assumed to be presorted, i.e., $a_1 \geq a_2$*

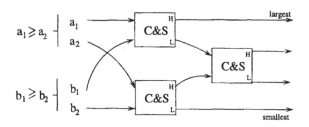

Fig. 9.20   A 2×2 merge unit.

*and $b_1 \geq b_2$. (Otherwise, 2 extra **C&S** units are required to sort them in order, which means that for a complete 4-element sorter, a total of 5 **C&S** units are required.) Therefore, the 4×4 merge-sort circuit shown in Fig. 9.19 requires 9 **C&S** units.* ■

Example 9.4.2 *Consider the design of a 4×2 merge unit shown in Fig. 9.21. This structure can be easily derived from that of the 4×4 merge unit by simply*

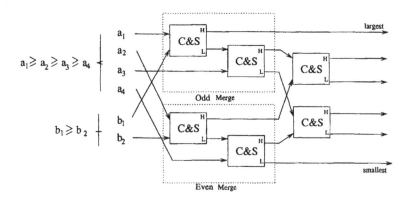

Fig. 9.21   A 4×2 merge unit.

*treating the last 2 data elements as dummy and throwing away any **C&S** unit that has at least one of these dummy elements as inputs. It is not hard to verify that a 4×2 merge unit requires 6 **C&S** units.* ■

Note that a merger merges 2 input vectors into 1 output vector with elements in ascending (or descending) order. Hence, an $m \times n$ merger has the same hardware complexity as an $n \times m$ merger.

9.4.2 Rank-Order Filter Architectures

This subsection considers design of rank-order filters based on Batcher's odd-even merge-sort algorithm.

Example 9.4.3 *Fig. 9.22 shows an architecture of the rank-order filter with window size $W = 5$. Notice that the inputs to the filter are tapped off a delay line to form a window for the sorter. The total number of* **C&S** *units is 9 as*

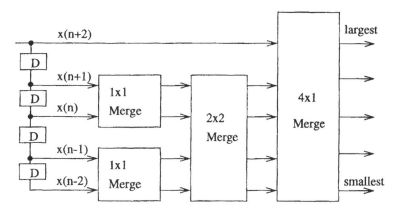

Fig. 9.22 $W = 5$, rank-order filter.

the 4×1 merge requires 4 **C&S** *units (see Fig. 9.23).* ∎

Example 9.4.4 *Consider a rank-order filter with window size $W = 7$. Its structure is shown in Fig. 9.24. A 4×3 merge unit is required, which consists of 8* **C&S** *units as shown in Fig. 9.25. As can be seen, a total of 16* **C&S** *units are required.* ∎

9.4.3 Parallel Rank-Order Filters

Efficient parallel rank-order filters can be designed by taking advantage of shared comparisons within the block structure such that the hardware complexity of the resulting parallel filter is reduced substantially [18]. This subsection illustrates these substructure sharing techniques for design of low-complexity parallel rank-order filters using examples. Systematic design methodologies can be found in [18].

Example 9.4.5 *Consider a parallel rank-order filter with window size 5 and 2 levels of parallel processing (i.e., $L = 2$). The function of parallel rank-order filter can be described by the following equations:*

$$y_r(2k) = r^{th} rank[x(2k - 2), x(2k - 1), x(2k), x(2k + 1), x(2k + 2)],$$

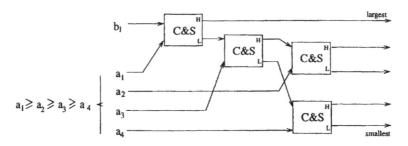

Fig. 9.23   A 4 × 1 merge unit.

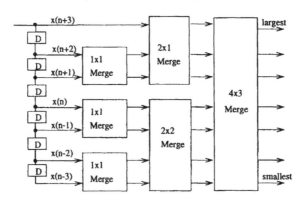

Fig. 9.24 $W = 7$, Rank-order filter.

$$y_r(2k+1) = r^{th}rank[x(2k-1), x(2k), x(2k+1), x(2k+2), x(2k+3)].$$
$$(9.75)$$

*A straightforward implementation can be designed by repeating the same hardware twice, as shown in Fig. 9.26, where $9 \times 2 = 18$ **C&S** units are required. However, this is not an efficient architecture since there are many redundant comparisons in this structure. To eliminate redundant computations, drop $2k$ from the indexes in (9.75) and rewrite them as in Fig. 9.27. As can be seen from Fig. 9.27, two identical hardware pieces are used to sort the -1, 0, 1, and 2 elements in the block structure. This redundancy can be exploited to achieve the efficient architecture shown in Fig. 9.28. Now only 13 **C&S** units are required as opposed to 18 in the implementation in Fig. 9.26.* ∎

Example 9.4.6 *Consider a parallel rank-order filter with window size $W = 5$ and block-size $L = 3$. The sorting operation in the 3-parallel system can be described by the diagram in Fig. 9.29 (the indexes $3k$ have been dropped). Partition the input sequences into groups as shown in Fig. 9.29. Those comparisons in the same group can be carried out by one **C&S** unit. The corresponding parallel filter architecture is shown in Fig. 9.30. In this case, 21 **C&S** units are required as opposed to 27 **C&S** units required for standard im-*

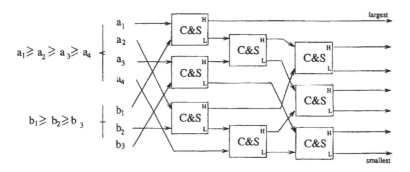

Fig. 9.25 A 4×3 merge unit.

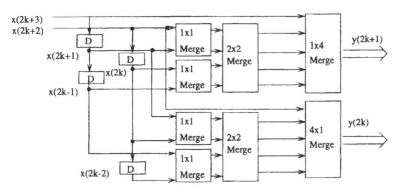

Fig. 9.26 $W = 5$, rank-order filter architecture with 2 levels of parallel processing.

plementation. The most efficient parallel architecture is obtained by grouping 2 samples at a time. The reader may verify that in this example considering sorting of $y(3k), y(3k + 1)$, and $y(3k + 2)$ as a group would also require 21 C&S units (see Problem 38). ■

As can be seen from Examples 9.4.5 and 9.4.6, the basic idea for designing efficient parallel rank-order filters involves finding pairs of inputs common to multiple outputs, then finding pairs of pairs of inputs, etc. The goal is to make use of as much substructure sharing as possible. Example 9.4.7 shows a more involved searching process for designing parallel rank-order filters.

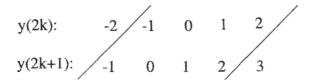

Fig. 9.27 $W = 5, L = 2$ rank-order filter indices.

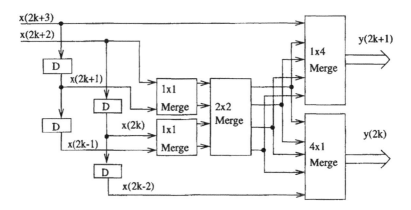

Fig. 9.28 $W = 5, L = 2$ rank-order filter architecture with substructure sharing.

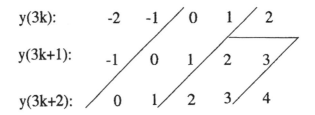

Fig. 9.29 $W = 5, L = 3$ rank-order filter indices.

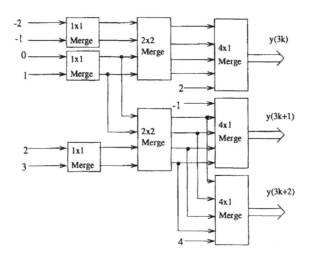

Fig. 9.30 $W = 5, L = 3$ rank-order filter architecture with substructure sharing.

Example 9.4.7 *Consider the design of a 4-parallel rank-order filter with window size=7. Fig. 9.31 shows the search process. The common elements are grouped and the sorting process is repeated by replacing multiple elements as groups in a hierarchical manner. This sorting approach is used to design the parallel architecture in Fig. 9.32, which requires 43 C&S units as opposed to 64 needed for direct implementation.* ■

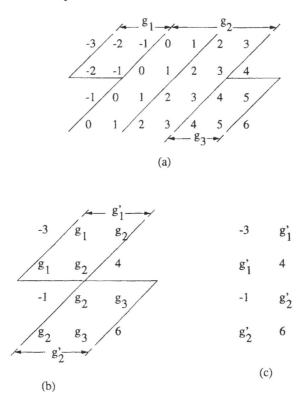

(a)

(b)

(c)

Fig. 9.31 Searching process for shared comparisons for rank-order filter with $W = 7$ and $L = 4$.

9.4.4 Running Order Merge-Sorter — Time-Mapping Technique

Batcher's odd/even merge-sorter has been used in rank-order filtering so far. One may notice from (9.74) that the inputs in the sample window are consecutive time samples and only one output leaves the window and one input enters the window as the input window slides in time. Therefore by taking advantage of the time relationship between the inputs, the total number of merge units can be further reduced. This is exploited by the *running order merge-sorter*, where those units whose inputs are separated by the same number of time steps are mapped onto a single merge unit by using extra memory

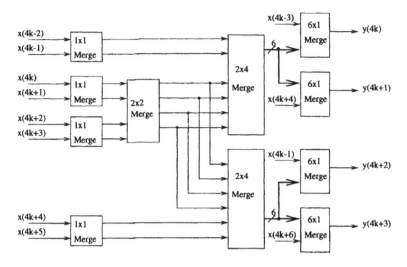

Fig. 9.32 $W = 7, L = 4$ rank-order filter architecture with substructure sharing.

units for each level of merging [19]. However, the latency of this sorter is equal to the window size W since each merging level generates a serial sorted output stream. A *time-mapping technique* can be used to generate all the sorted outputs in parallel, as illustrated in the following example.

Example 9.4.8 *Consider a rank-order filter with window size $W = 8$ shown in Fig. 9.33. This direct implementation using Batcher's odd/even merge-sorter algorithm requires four 1×1 mergers, two 2×2 mergers and one 4×4 merger, i.e., 19 C&S units. The time mapped rank-order filter structure is shown in Fig. 9.34. As can be seen, three 1×1 merger and one 2×2 merger, i.e., 6 C&S units have been saved using time mapping technique.* ■

The time-mapping technique is most efficient when the window size is a power-of-2. For other window sizes, savings in hardware can be achieved by adapting both the Batcher's merge-sorter and the merge-sorter with time mapping carefully.

9.4.5 Low Power Rank-Order Filter

Power consumption reduction using parallel processing is achieved by reducing the supply voltage while maintaining the same sample rate as the sequential system. However, there is a fundamental limit imposed on the supply voltage, or the power reduction factor β, i.e., the supply voltage βV_0 cannot be lower than the threshold voltage V_t of the CMOS device. Usually for reliable operation the supply voltage is maintained at twice the threshold voltage. For trivial block processing, the same amount of hardware is duplicated L

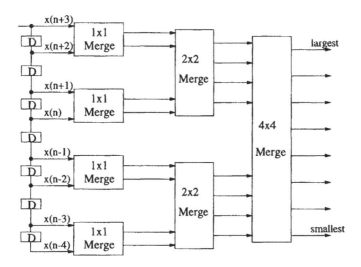

Fig. 9.33 Block structure for $W=8$ rank-order filter.

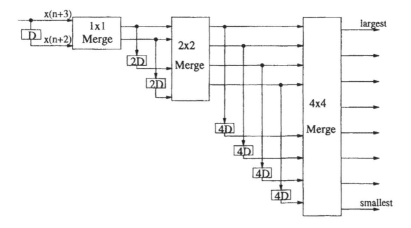

Fig. 9.34 Block structure for time mapped $W=8$ rank-order filter.

times. In other words, the area of the parallel system is increased linearly with respect to the block size L. Therefore, the power consumption of the parallel system is $P_{par} = \beta^2 P_{seq}$, where P_{seq} denotes the power consumption of the original sequential system. This imposes a lower bound on power reduction. However, for parallel rank-order filters, by using the substructure sharing to reduce the number of **C&S** units, the area (or total capacitance) of the parallel filter grows less than linearly with the block size L, i.e.,

$$C_{total}^{par} = \alpha L C_{total}^{seq}, \tag{9.76}$$

where $\alpha < 1$. Therefore, the power consumption of the parallel rank-order filter can be written as

$$P_{par} = \alpha \beta^2 P_{seq}. \tag{9.77}$$

Hence it is possible to continue to reduce the power consumption beyond the supply voltage limit by increasing block size L.

Example 9.4.9 *Consider the odd-even merge based rank-order filter with window size $W = 5$ shown in Fig. 9.22. The total number of **C&S** units is 9. Assume the filter to be pipelined at the **C&S** unit level and total capacitance for one **C&S** unit to be C_0. Then the power consumption for the sequential filter is*

$$P_{seq} = 9 C_0 V_0^2 f_{seq}. \tag{9.78}$$

Now consider the parallel filters without minimizing the redundancies. The total power consumption will be:

$$P_{par} = \frac{9 L C_0 \beta^2 V_0^2 f_{seq}}{L} = \beta^2 P_{seq}. \tag{9.79}$$

Note that since we are not minimizing the redundancies, the total capacitance is $9 L C_0$. Once the supply voltage or β reaches its lower limit, the power consumption cannot be reduced any more.

*Consider the parallel rank-order filter with substructure sharing. It turns out that for L levels of block processing, the total number of **C&S** units is*

$$N_{cs} = 6L + 1, \quad \text{when } L \text{ even}$$
$$N_{cs} = 6L + 3, \quad \text{when } L \text{ odd} \tag{9.80}$$

(see Problem 40). In this case the power consumption is (for even L),

$$P_{parallel} = (6 + \frac{1}{L}) C_0 \beta^2 V^2 f_{seq}. \tag{9.81}$$

Notice that even if the lower limit of β has been reached, there still can be a reduction in power consumption as L increases. The lower limit on the power consumption is obtained when $L \to \infty$. ∎

9.5   CONCLUSIONS

Algorithmic strength reduction transformation approaches have been presented. These transformations exploit substructure sharing and reduce the number of stronger operations, possibly at the expense of increasing the number of weaker operations. Strength reduction has been applied to design fast parallel FIR filters, DCTs, and parallel rank-order filters. These architectures can reduce the area and power consumption in a VLSI implementation or reduce the iteration period in a programmable DSP implementation. Strength reduction can also be applied at numerical level to reduce the implementation complexity (see Chapter 15).

9.6   PROBLEMS

1. Express the 2-parallel filter algorithm:

$$Y_0 = X_0 H_0 + z^{-2} X_1 H_1$$
$$Y_1 = X_0 H_0 + X_1 H_1 - (X_0 - X_1)(H_0 - H_1).$$

   in terms of a postprocessing matrix, a diagonal matrix, and a preprocessing matrix. Obtain another 2-parallel structure using the transpose of this formulation.

2. Consider a 6-tap FIR filter with unit-sample response

$$h(n) = \{a, 0, b, b, c, c\} \tag{9.82}$$

   and

$$H(z) = a + bz^{-2} + bz^{-3} + cz^{-4} + cz^{-5}. \tag{9.83}$$

   The sequential filter has 3 distinct coefficients and can be implemented using 3 multiplication operations as shown in Fig. 9.35. The 2-parallel filter will not require more than 6 multiplication operations. Design the structure of a 2-parallel implementation of this filter. Show the coefficients of all multipliers in your structure.

3. Design a 3-parallel filter structure using the transpose of the 3-parallel filter algorithm presented in Section 9.2.2.1.

4. Using the following 3-parallel linear convolution:

$$
\begin{bmatrix} s_4 \\ s_3 \\ s_2 \\ s_1 \\ s_0 \end{bmatrix} =
\begin{bmatrix} 2 & 0 & 0 & 0 & 0 \\ -1 & 2 & -2 & -1 & 2 \\ -2 & 1 & 3 & 0 & -1 \\ 1 & -1 & -1 & 1 & -2 \\ 0 & 0 & 0 & 0 & 1 \end{bmatrix}
diag
\begin{bmatrix} h_2/2 \\ (h_2 + h_1 + h_0)/2 \\ (h_2 - h_1 + h_0)/6 \\ (h_2 + 2h_1 + 4h_0)/6 \\ h_0 \end{bmatrix}
$$

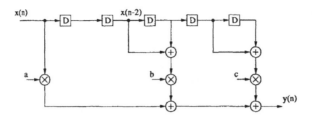

Fig. 9.35 Figure for Problem 2.

$$
\begin{bmatrix}
1 & 0 & 0 \\
1 & 1 & 1 \\
1 & -1 & 1 \\
1 & 2 & 4 \\
0 & 0 & 1
\end{bmatrix}
\begin{bmatrix}
x_2 \\
x_1 \\
x_0
\end{bmatrix}
$$

obtain a 3-parallel filter that requires 5 subfiltering operations.

5. Use the following fast 2×2 convolution

$$
\begin{aligned}
h_0 x_0 &= h_0 x_0 \\
h_0 x_1 + h_1 x_0 &= \tfrac{h_0 + h_1}{2}(x_0 + x_1) - \tfrac{h_0 - h_1}{2}(x_0 - x_1) \\
h_1 x_1 &= -h_0 x_0 + \tfrac{h_0 + h_1}{2}(x_0 + x_1) + \tfrac{h_0 - h_1}{2}(x_0 - x_1)
\end{aligned}
$$

and the transposition operation to design a 2-parallel FIR filter.

6. Transpose the 2-parallel filter structure obtained in Problem 5 to obtain another 2-parallel filter.

7. Derive (9.35) and (9.36).

8. Prove that a block filter of block size 2^n can be designed based on 2-parallel fast filter algorithms using $(1.5)^n N$ multiplications and $(1.5)^n N^n + 3^{n+1} - 2^{n+2}$ additions, where N corresponds to the length of the filter.

9. Consider the 2-parallel filtering algorithm:

$$
\begin{aligned}
Y_0 &= X_0 H_0 + z^{-2} X_1 H_1 \\
Y_1 &= X_0 H_0 + X_1 H_1 - (X_0 - X_1)(H_0 - H_1).
\end{aligned}
$$

Design a 4-parallel filter based upon this algorithm.

10. A 36-tap FIR filter is to be implemented using a block size of 12. A 12-parallel FIR filter can be generated by using 2-parallel fast algorithms twice and a 3-parallel fast algorithm once. Find the total number of additions and multiplications required for the implementation if the following orderings of the fast algorithms are used:

    (a) $2 \times 2 \times 3$;

(b) $3 \times 2 \times 2$;

(c) $2 \times 3 \times 2$.

For each case, determine the number of adders that are used for the filter sections and the number of adders that are used for pre/postprocessing.

11. Consider a 12-parallel implementation of a 60-tap FIR filter using a programmable DSP (PDSP). The PDSP can implement one add, one multiply, or one multiply-add in a single clock cycle. The 12-parallel filter is organized as $2 \times 2 \times 3$. How many clock cycles are needed to implement this 12-parallel filter using the PDSP? Do not include the clock cycles needed for load and store instructions.

12. Determine the fast algorithm ordering that will lead to the best block structure for a 72-tap FIR filter for block sizes 12 and 36 such that the sum of the number of addition and multiplication operations is minimized.

13. Calculate the number of additions and multiplications required to implement a FIR filter using the following block sizes and fast algorithm ordering (assume the filter is of length N):

    (a) block size: 9, ordering: 3×3;

    (b) block size: 36, ordering: $2 \times 2 \times 3 \times 3$;

    (c) block size: 10, ordering: 2×5;

    (d) block size: 27, ordering: $3 \times 3 \times 3$.

14. Parallel processing can be exploited to reduce the power consumption of FIR filters at same sampling speed. Assume that a 20-tap ($N = 20$) fast parallel FIR filter is implemented with a block size of 4 to reduce the power consumption of the filter. Assume the use of broadcast FIR filter structures. Calculate the power reduction factor. Assume $V_o = 5\ V$ and $V_t = .4\ V$.

15. This problem considers the implementation of a 100-tap FIR filter using a programmable DSP. The programmable DSP can implement an add, a multiply, or a multiply-add operation in a single clock cycle. Let the clock period of the programmable DSP be T nsec. This filter can be implemented in a straightforward manner to meet the sampling period constraint of $100T$ nsec as imposed by the real-time application. However, a low-power implementation can be obtained by using fast parallel filter algorithms to reduce the number of clock cycles and by increasing the clock period proportionately by operating the programmable DSP with a lower supply voltage.

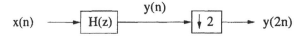

y(n)

$x(n) \longrightarrow \boxed{H(z)} \longrightarrow \boxed{\downarrow 2} \longrightarrow y(2n)$

Fig. 9.36 Figure for Problem 16.

(a) This filter is implemented using the 4-parallel filter structure shown in Fig. 9.6. How many clock cycles are needed to compute one output sample using the 4-parallel filter structure? Calculate the percentage of power reduction of this implementation by operating the programmable DSP with reduced supply voltage. Your implementation should still achieve a sample period of $100T$ nsec. Assume that the programmable DSP was initially operated with a supply voltage of 5 V and assume the technology threshold voltage to be 0.5 V.

(b) Repeat (a) using the 8-parallel structure shown in Fig. 9.9.

16. Consider the implementation of the discrete-time system in Fig. 9.36, where $H(z)$ is an N-tap FIR filter. This system requires N multiplications and $(N-1)$ add operations per input sample period. However, since the odd outputs are not retained by the decimator, these outputs need not be computed. Then the computation requirement can be reduced to $\frac{N}{2}$ multiplications and $\frac{N-1}{2}$ add operations per input sample period. This computation requirement can be reduced further by use of parallel filter structures.

   (a) By using polyphase representation, derive a structure for the implementation of this system that only computes the even output samples and requires $\frac{N}{2}$ multiplications and $\frac{N-1}{2}$ add operations per input sample period.

   (b) Using 2-parallel filter structures, reduce the structure in (a) to a fast structure that requires less number of multiplication operations. Show that this structure requires $\frac{3N}{8}$ multiplications and $\frac{3N}{8}+1$ add operations per input sample period.

17. Consider the implementation of one level of a wavelet filter shown in Fig. 9.37. Let $H(z)$ and $G(z)$ be N-tap FIR filters. A straightforward implementation that computes only even outputs $v(2n)$ and $w(2n)$ requires N multiplications and $(N-1)$ addition operations per input sample period.

   (a) Implement this filter using the 2-parallel fast FIR algorithm in (9.18) and show that the resulting fast structure requires $\frac{3N}{4}$ multiplications and $(\frac{3N}{4}+1.5)$ additions per input sample.

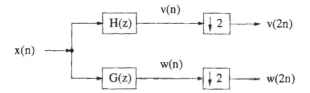

Fig. 9.37   One level of wavelet filter for Problem 17.

(b) Show that using the transpose form of the 2-parallel filter in (a)

$$
\begin{aligned}
Y_0 &= (X_1 z^{-2} - X_0)H_1 + (H_0 + H_1)X_0 \\
Y_1 &= (X_1 - X_0)H_0 + (H_0 + H_1)X_0
\end{aligned}
\tag{9.84}
$$

can reduce the number of additions per input sample period to $\left(\frac{3N}{4} + 1\right)$.

18. A cross-coupled equalizer used in a complex two-dimensional (2D) adaptive filtering application is described by

$$y(n) = \mathbf{w}^H(n-1)\mathbf{x}(n)$$

where

$$
\begin{aligned}
\mathbf{x}(n) &= \mathbf{x}_r(n) + j\mathbf{x}_i(n), \\
\mathbf{w}^H(n) &= \mathbf{w}_r^T(n) - j\mathbf{w}_i^T(n), \\
\mathbf{w}_i^T(n) &= (w_{i1}(n), w_{i2}(n), \cdots, w_{iN}(n))
\end{aligned}
$$

and $\mathbf{w}^H(n)$ represents the Hermitian or transpose-conjugate of $\mathbf{w}(n)$. The N-length vectors $\mathbf{w}_r(n)$, $\mathbf{x}_r(n)$ and $\mathbf{x}_i(n)$ are defined similar to $\mathbf{w}_i(n)$. The weights in this equalizer are updated by the least-mean-square (LMS) algorithm using

$$\mathbf{w}(n) = \mathbf{w}(n-1) + \mu e^*(n)x(n),$$

where $e^*(n)$ represents the conjugate of $e(n)$.

(a) The real and imaginary parts of the filter output

$$
\begin{aligned}
y_r(n) &= \mathbf{w}_r^T(n-1)\mathbf{x}_r(n) + \mathbf{w}_i^T(n-1)\mathbf{x}_i(n) \\
y_i(n) &= \mathbf{w}_r^T(n-1)\mathbf{x}_i(n) - \mathbf{w}_i^T(n-1)\mathbf{x}_r(n)
\end{aligned}
$$

can be computed using 4 filters. Using fast FIR algorithm, obtain another implementation using the 3 filters $\mathbf{w}_r^T(n-1) + \mathbf{w}_i^T(n-1)$, $\mathbf{w}_r^T(n-1) - \mathbf{w}_i^T(n-1)$, and $\mathbf{w}_i^T(n-1)$.

(b) Derive the weight update equations for $\mathbf{w}_r(n)$ and $\mathbf{w}_i(n)$. The computation in (a) is best implemented by updating $\mathbf{w}_r(n) + \mathbf{w}_i(n)$

and $\mathbf{w}_r(n) - \mathbf{w}_i(n)$, rather than updating $\mathbf{w}_r(n)$ and $\mathbf{w}_i(n)$. After $\mathbf{w}_r(n) \pm \mathbf{w}_i(n)$ are updated, $\mathbf{w}_i(n)$ can be calculated by taking the half of the difference of these updated coefficients. Express update equations for $\mathbf{w}_r(n) + \mathbf{w}_i(n)$ and $\mathbf{w}_r(n) - \mathbf{w}_i(n)$ using 4 filters. Based on fast FIR algorithms, update these using 3 filters.

19. Consider the implementation of an adaptive equalizer in a 3-dimensional (3D) signaling environment with fewer number of multiplication operations based on fast filtering techniques. Let the 3D filtering operation of the signal $\mathbf{X}$ and coefficient $\mathbf{W}$ be defined as

$$
\begin{aligned}
\mathbf{W}^T\mathbf{X} &= (\mathbf{i}\mathbf{w}_i^T + \mathbf{j}\mathbf{w}_j^T + \mathbf{k}\mathbf{w}_k^T)(\mathbf{i}\mathbf{x}_i + \mathbf{j}\mathbf{x}_j + \mathbf{k}\mathbf{x}_k) \\
&= \mathbf{i}(\mathbf{w}_i^T\mathbf{x}_i + \mathbf{w}_k^T\mathbf{x}_j - \mathbf{w}_j^T\mathbf{x}_k) + \mathbf{j}(\mathbf{w}_j^T\mathbf{x}_j + \mathbf{w}_i^T\mathbf{x}_k - \mathbf{w}_k^T\mathbf{x}_i) \\
&\quad + \mathbf{k}(\mathbf{w}_k^T\mathbf{x}_k + \mathbf{w}_j^T\mathbf{x}_i - \mathbf{w}_i^T\mathbf{x}_j)
\end{aligned}
$$

where $\mathbf{w}_r$ and $\mathbf{x}_r$ represent column vectors of size N. This equalizer requires 9 filters and 6 vector additions. Implement this filter using 4 filters and 6 vector additions. (Hint: Use the filters $\mathbf{w}_i + \mathbf{w}_j + \mathbf{w}_k$, $\mathbf{w}_i + \mathbf{w}_j$, $\mathbf{w}_i + \mathbf{w}_k$ and $\mathbf{w}_j + \mathbf{w}_k$.)

20. The hardware complexity in an FIR filter can be reduced by using a set of transformed coefficients with less dynamic range [20],[21]. Consider an N-tap FIR filter given by

$$
y(n) = \sum_{i=0}^{N-1} h_i x(n-i). \tag{9.85}
$$

(a) For a narrow-band low-pass filter, the coefficients vary slowly. As a result, the dynamic range of the difference of the consecutive coefficients is much less than that of the original coefficients. In other words, $(h_{i+1} - h_i)$ coefficients require less nonzero bits than $\{h_i\}$. A transfer function with difference coefficients can be obtained by multiplying $(1 - z^{-1})$ to the numerator and the denominator of the original transfer function. Therefore,

$$
\begin{aligned}
H(z) &= \frac{(\sum_{i=0}^{N-1} h_i z^{-i})(1 - z^{-1})}{1 - z^{-1}} \\
&= \frac{h_0 + \sum_{i=0}^{N-2}(h_{i+1} - h_i)z^{-(i+1)} - h_{N-1}z^{-N}}{1 - z^{-1}}
\end{aligned}
$$

can be implemented as a cascade of an FIR filter with coefficients h_0, h_{N-1} and $(N-1)$ difference coefficients, and an IIR filter with transfer function $1/(1 - z^{-1})$. Draw a block diagram of this filter for $N = 6$.

(b) For narrow-band high-pass filters, the dynamic range of the sum of the consecutive coefficients is much less than that of the original

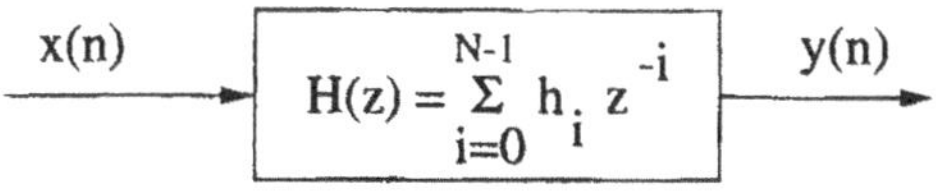

$$x(n) \longrightarrow \boxed{H(z) = \sum_{i=0}^{N-1} h_i \, z^{-i}} \longrightarrow y(n)$$

Fig. 9.38 Figure for Problem 21.

coefficients. Following the approach similar to part (a), obtain an equivalent transfer function of the FIR filter based on the sum of the consecutive coefficients $\{h_{i+1} + h_i\}$. Implement the N-tap FIR narrow-band high-pass filter using the sum coefficients. Draw a block diagram of this filter for $N = 6$.

21. The input to the narrow-band low-pass FIR digital filter in Fig. 9.38, $x(n)$, is known to be slowly varying. In this problem, we explore several alternate structures for low-power implementation.

   (a) Since $x(n)$ is slowly varying, $x(n) - x(n-1)$ has a smaller dynamic range and can be represented using a smaller wordlength. Thus the area of the multipliers is reduced. Obtain an equivalent filter structure that exploits this observation.

   (b) In this part, assume that the slowly varying signal is filtered by a narrow-band low-pass filter, obtain an equivalent filter structure that can be implemented using less area and lower power consumption by exploiting wordlength reduction.

   (c) Obtain an equivalent structure if the signal $x(n)$ is rapidly varying and is filtered by a narrow-band high-pass filter.

22. Consider the design of a low-power vector quantizer (VQ) (see Section 1.2.7) by appropriate algorithm selection. The goal is to select an algorithm with fewer operations. Consider the full-search, tree-search, and differential tree-search VQ algorithms listed below. The tree-search VQ algorithms lead to slightly degraded but acceptable performance. Calculate the number of multiplications and add/subtract operations for each of the VQ algorithm. Assume the vector dimension to be 16 and the codebook size to be 256.

   (a) Full-search vector quantizer that computes

   $$\sum_{i=0}^{15} (x_i - c_{ji})^2, \; j = 0 \; to \; 255 \tag{9.86}$$

   (b) Tree-search vector quantizer (see Fig. 1.8) that computes

   $$\sum_{i=0}^{15} (x_i - c_{ji})^2, \; j = 2 \times 8 \tag{9.87}$$

where 2 distances are computed at each of the 8 levels of the tree

(c) Differential tree-search vector quantizer that computes

$$
\begin{aligned}
& \sum_{i=0}^{15}(x_i - c_{ji})^2 - \sum_{i=0}^{15}(x_i - c_{ki})^2 \\
= \;& \sum_{i=0}^{15} 2x_i(c_{ki} - c_{ji}) + \sum_{i=0}^{15}(c_{ji}^2 - c_{ki}^2)
\end{aligned}
\tag{9.88}
$$

for each level of the tree. The vectors c_j and c_k represent the codewords associated with the two leaf words at each level of the tree. Assume that $\sum_{i=0}^{15} c_{ji}^2$ is precomputed.

23. Consider the implementation of a 2D FIR filter

$$
z(m, n) = \sum_{i=0}^{N-1}\sum_{j=0}^{N-1} x(i, j)y(i + m, j + n), \quad 0 \le m, n \le M - 1 \tag{9.89}
$$

using fast parallel filter techniques. A straightforward implementation of $z(m, n)$ requires N^2 multiplications per output sample. The multiplication complexity per output sample can be reduced from N^2 to $9N^2/16$ by using fast parallel filtering techniques [12].

(a) Show that the computation in (9.89) can be transformed to

$$
\begin{bmatrix}
z(2m, 2n) \\
z(2m + 1, 2n) \\
z(2m, 2n + 1) \\
z(2m + 1, 2n + 1)
\end{bmatrix}
= \begin{bmatrix} \mathbf{Y}_{00} & \mathbf{Y}_{10} & \mathbf{Y}_{01} & \mathbf{Y}_{11} \end{bmatrix} \cdot
\begin{bmatrix}
\mathbf{X}_{00} \\
\mathbf{X}_{10} \\
\mathbf{X}_{01} \\
\mathbf{X}_{11}
\end{bmatrix}
$$

where

$$
\mathbf{Y}_{00} = \begin{bmatrix}
\mathbf{Y}(2m, 2n) \\
\mathbf{Y}(2m + 1, 2n) \\
\mathbf{Y}(2m, 2n + 1) \\
\mathbf{Y}(2m + 1, 2n + 1)
\end{bmatrix}, \quad
\mathbf{Y}_{10} = \begin{bmatrix}
\mathbf{Y}(2m + 1, 2n) \\
\mathbf{Y}(2m + 2, 2n) \\
\mathbf{Y}(2m + 1, 2n + 1) \\
\mathbf{Y}(2m + 2, 2n + 1)
\end{bmatrix},
$$

$$
\mathbf{Y}_{01} = \begin{bmatrix}
\mathbf{Y}(2m, 2n + 1) \\
\mathbf{Y}(2m + 1, 2n + 1) \\
\mathbf{Y}(2m, 2n + 2) \\
\mathbf{Y}(2m + 1, 2n + 2)
\end{bmatrix}, \quad
\mathbf{Y}_{11} = \begin{bmatrix}
\mathbf{Y}(2m + 1, 2n + 1) \\
\mathbf{Y}(2m + 2, 2n + 1) \\
\mathbf{Y}(2m + 1, 2n + 2) \\
\mathbf{Y}(2m + 2, 2n + 2)
\end{bmatrix},
$$

$$
\begin{aligned}
\mathbf{X}_{ij} &= \begin{bmatrix} \mathbf{x}_{i,j} & \mathbf{x}_{i,j+2} & \cdots & \mathbf{x}_{i,j+N-2} \end{bmatrix}^T \\
\mathbf{Y}(i, j) &= \begin{bmatrix} \mathbf{y}(i, j) & \mathbf{y}(i, j + 2) & \cdots & \mathbf{y}(i, j + N - 2) \end{bmatrix}
\end{aligned}
$$

and

$$
\begin{aligned}
\mathbf{x}_{ij} &= \begin{bmatrix} x(i, j) & x(i, j + 2) & \cdots & x(i, j + N - 2) \end{bmatrix}^T \\
\mathbf{y}(i, j) &= \begin{bmatrix} y(i, j) & y(i, j + 2) & \cdots & y(i, j + N - 2) \end{bmatrix}.
\end{aligned}
$$

The vectors $\mathbf{X}_{ij}$ and $\mathbf{Y}(i, j)$ are of length $N^2/4$. This computation also requires N^2 multiply-accumulate operations per output sample.

(b) Verify that the computation below is identical to the 2D filtering operation in (a).

$$
\begin{bmatrix}
z(2m, 2n) \\
z(2m+1, 2n) \\
z(2m, 2n+1) \\
z(2m+1, 2n+1)
\end{bmatrix}
$$

$$
= \begin{bmatrix}
(\mathbf{B}(2m, 2n) + \mathbf{B}(2m, 2n+1))\mathbf{X}_{00} \\
(\mathbf{B}(2m+1, 2n) + \mathbf{B}(2m+1, 2n+1))\mathbf{X}_{10} \\
(\mathbf{B}(2m, 2n+1) + \mathbf{B}(2m, 2n+2))\mathbf{X}_{01} \\
(\mathbf{B}(2m+1, 2n+1) + \mathbf{B}(2m+1, 2n+2))\mathbf{X}_{11}
\end{bmatrix}
$$

$$
+ \begin{bmatrix}
-1 & 0 \\
0 & -1 \\
1 & 0 \\
0 & 1
\end{bmatrix}
\begin{bmatrix}
\mathbf{B}(2m, 2n+1)(\mathbf{X}_{00} - \mathbf{X}_{01}) \\
\mathbf{B}(2m+1, 2n+1)(\mathbf{X}_{10} - \mathbf{X}_{11})
\end{bmatrix}
$$

$$
+ \begin{bmatrix}
-1 & 0 \\
1 & 0 \\
0 & -1 \\
0 & 1
\end{bmatrix}
\begin{bmatrix}
(\mathbf{Y}(2m+1, 2n) + \mathbf{Y}(2m+1, 2n+1))\mathbf{A}_0 \\
(\mathbf{Y}(2m+1, 2n+1) + \mathbf{Y}(2m+1, 2n+2))\mathbf{A}_1
\end{bmatrix}
$$

$$
+ \begin{bmatrix}
1 \\
-1 \\
-1 \\
1
\end{bmatrix}
\mathbf{Y}(2m+1, 2n+1)(\mathbf{A}_0 - \mathbf{A}_1),
$$

where

$$
\mathbf{A}_0 = \mathbf{X}_{00} - \mathbf{X}_{10}, \quad \mathbf{A}_1 = \mathbf{X}_{01} - \mathbf{X}_{11}
$$
$$
\mathbf{B}(i, j) = \mathbf{Y}(i, j) + \mathbf{Y}(i+1, j).
$$

(c) Show that computation complexity of the 2D filter is reduced from $N^2 M^2$ to

$$
\tfrac{9}{16}(N^2 \cdot M^2) + [\tfrac{5}{4}N^2 + 2(N + M - 2)(N + M - 1) \\
+ (N + M - 2)^2] + \tfrac{10}{4}M^2,
$$

where the first term $(\tfrac{9}{16}(N^2 \cdot M^2))$ number of operations are required for the 9 filtering operations, the last term $(\tfrac{10}{4}M^2)$ number of operations are required for postprocessing and the middle-term number of operations are required for preprocessing of filter coefficients and filter inputs. In this problem, an operation can be a multiplication, an addition, or a multiply-add operation.

24. This problem considers the implementation of motion estimation using a programmable DSP based on fast filtering approaches [12]. Rather than

the mean absolute difference (MAD) criteria, the mean-square error (MSE) criteria is used for the motion estimation. The MSE is defined as

$$s(m,n) = \sum_{i=0}^{N-1} \sum_{j=0}^{N-1} (x(i,j) - y(i+m,j+n))^2,$$
$$0 \le m, n \le M - 1. \tag{9.90}$$

To reduce the computation complexity, the MSE is expressed as

$$s(m,n) = \sum_{i=0}^{N-1} \sum_{j=0}^{N-1} x(i,j)^2 - 2 \sum_{i=0}^{N-1} \sum_{j=0}^{N-1} x(i,j)y(i+m,j+n)$$
$$+ \sum_{i=0}^{N-1} \sum_{j=0}^{N-1} y(i+m,j+n)^2, \ 0 \le m, n \le M - 1. \tag{9.91}$$

The 1st term of (9.91) is constant for each reference block. This term is unimportant for comparison purposes and need not be computed. The 2nd term can be implemented using the fast 2D filtering approach in Problem 23. The 3rd term in (9.91) can be computed iteratively. Assume an operation can be either an add, a multiply, or a multiply-add operation.

(a) Calculate the total number of operations needed by (9.90) for $N = 16$ and $M = 32$.

(b) Use the result of part (c) of Problem 23 to calculate the number of operations needed for the fast implementation of the 2D filter for $N = 16$ and $M = 32$.

(c) Show that the 3rd term in (9.91)

$$f(m,n) = \sum_{i=0}^{N-1} \sum_{j=0}^{N-1} y(i+m,j+n)^2, \ 0 \le m, n \le M - 1 \tag{9.92}$$

can be expressed as

$$f'(m,n) = \sum_{i=0}^{N-1} y(i+m,n)^2,$$
$$m = 0, \cdots, M - 1; \ n = 0, \cdots, N + M - 2$$
$$f(m,n) = \sum_{j=0}^{N-1} f'(m,j+n)$$
$$0 \le m, n \le M - 1. \tag{9.93}$$

Show that (9.93) can be computed iteratively by

$$f'(m,n) = f'(m-1,n) + y_{m+N-1,n}^2 - y_{m-1,n}^2$$
$$f(m,n) = f(m,n-1) + f'(m,n+N-1) - f'(m,n-1) \tag{9.94}$$

using $N + 2(M - 1)(N + M - 1) + M(N + 2(M - 1))$ operations. Calculate the number of operations for $N = 16$ and $M = 32$.

(d) Compare the number of operations in (a) to the total number of operations in (b) and (c).

25. To derive the IDCT in (9.47) from the DCT in (9.46), use the following steps:

(a) Show that

$$\sum_{k=0}^{N-1} (e^{j\frac{ik\pi}{N}} + e^{-j\frac{ik\pi}{N}}) = \begin{cases} 2N & i = 0 \\ 0 & i \text{ even, but not } 0 \\ 2 & i \text{ odd} \end{cases}$$

(b) Use (a) to show that

$$\sum_{k=0}^{N-1} \cos\frac{(2l + 1)k\pi}{2N} \cos\frac{(2m + 1)k\pi}{2N} = \frac{1}{2} + \frac{N}{2}\delta(l - m).$$

(Hint: First express $\cos\theta$ as $(e^{j\theta} + e^{-j\theta})/2$.)

(c) Use (b) to derive (9.47) from (9.46).

26. Using the definition of rotation in (9.55), prove the transformation of Fig. 9.13(c).

27. Derive an 8-point IDCT architecture by transposing the structure in Fig. 9.14.

28. Derive a 16-point DCT architecture using algorithm-architecture transformations.

29. Derive a scaled structure for an 8-point DCT using algorithm transformation based DCT where every output is scaled by $1/c_4$. Count the number of multiplications in the scaled DCT structure.

30. This problem considers design of a fast 6-point IDCT structure based on decimation-in-frequency approach.

(a) First obtain a 3-point IDCT butterfly for computing

$$x(n) = \sum_{k=0}^{2} X(k) \cos\frac{(2n + 1)k\pi}{6}, \quad n = 0, 1, 2.$$

(b) Using the 3-point IDCT butterfly in (a) implement the 6-point fast IDCT decimation-in-frequency structure. Calculate the total number of multiplication and add operations in this structure.

31. This problem considers the implementation of a scaled 8-point DCT where instead of $X(k)$, $X(k)/c_4$ coefficients are computed. Transform the structure in Fig. 9.17 to obtain a scaled DCT structure using 11 multiplication operations.

32. Derive a 16-point IDCT structure based on the decimation-in-frequency fast algorithm. Calculate the number of multiply and add operations.

33. Consider the implementation of an 8-point DCT in a Programmable DSP that can perform 1 multiply, 1 add, or 1 multiply-add operation in a single clock cycle.

    (a) Consider the DCT implementation using (9.53) for all $X(k)$ except $X(4)$ and $X(0)$ and

    $$\begin{bmatrix} X(0) \\ X(4) \end{bmatrix} = \begin{bmatrix} c_4 & c_4 \\ c_4 & -c_4 \end{bmatrix} \begin{bmatrix} P_{10} \\ P_{11} \end{bmatrix}.$$

    Show that this DCT can be implemented using the programmable DSP in 35 clock cycles.

    (b) Calculate the number of clock cycles needed to implement the DCT based on the fast flow graph in Fig. 9.17.

    (c) Which implementation in (a) and (b) is better? Why?

34. Draw the architectures of 3×5, 4×5 and 2×6 mergers where two presorted sequences are merged to form a completely sorted sequence.

35. Prove that a 2^p by 2^p merger constructed using the odd-even merger approach requires $p2^p + 1$ compare-swap elements and has a critical path of $(p + 1)T_{CS}$, where T_{CS} represents the computation time of a compare-swap unit.

36. Draw the complete architecture of parallel programmable rank-order filter structures for window size 7 and for block sizes 2, 4, and 8. What is the number of compare-swap units needed in these architectures? If the parallel rank-order filters are used for the same sample rate as the sequential one, what would be the power consumption of these architectures as a percentage of the sequential architecture for the threshold voltage of $V_t = 0.6$ V and the supply voltage of $V_0 = 5$ V? Assume that the sequential and parallel filters are pipelined such that the critical path is limited by one compare-swap unit.

37. Repeat Problem 36 for block sizes 3 and 5.

38. A 3-parallel architecture for a rank-order filter with window size 5 has been derived in Example 9.4.6. Design another 3-parallel architecture by considering $y(3k)$, $y(3k+1)$, and $y(3k+2)$ as a group. Draw detailed circuits for all mergers used in this architecture.

39. Calculate the number of compare-swap units required for parallel rank-order filters with window size of 9 and block sizes of 3 and 4.

40. Prove that the number of compare-swap units needed for an L-parallel rank-order filter with window size=5 using substructure sharing is $6L+1$ for even L and $6L + 3$ for odd L.

41. Prove that the number of compare-swap units for a parallel rank-order filter with window size=7 and block size=L is given by

$$\begin{aligned}
10.25L + 2, & \quad L = 4k \\
10.25L + 5.75, & \quad L = 4k + 1 \\
10.25L + 3.5, & \quad L = 4k + 2 \\
10.25L + 4.25, & \quad L = 4k + 3.
\end{aligned} \tag{9.96}$$

What is the asymptotic power reduction factor with respect to block size L for the parallel filter?

42. Consider a sequential implementation of a programmable rank-order digital filter for window size 5. Let the sample period of the system be T. Assume this system is operated with supply voltage of 5 V and assume the threshold voltage of the technology to be 0.75 V. We are interested in designing an implementation that can operate with the sample period $T/2$ (i.e., with 2 times higher speed) and can simultaneously reduce power consumption. To this end, we assume the availability of a voltage supply with variable voltage where the voltage can be varied from 1.5 V to 5 V. We consider the implementation of this system, which combines pipelining by 2 levels and parallel processing with block size L. Assume L can take values of 2, 4, 6, 8, 10, etc. Recall that the pipelined-parallel system cannot be operated with the supply voltage lower than 1.5 V and must achieve sample period of $T/2$. What value of L leads to the least power consumption? What value of L leads to the least *Area* $\times$ *Power* product?

43. Design a parallel rank-order filter for window size $W=7$ and block size $L=6$. Calculate the number of **C&S** units.

44. Design rank-order filter architecture for window size $W=5$ with minimum number of **C&S** units. (Hint: Use both Batcher's merge-sorter and running-order merge-sorter.)

45. Draw the architecture of rank-order filter of window size $W=7$ with minimum number of **C&S** units. Design the corresponding block rank-order filters with block size $L=3$ and $L = 5$ using the running-order sorter and substructure sharing techniques.

REFERENCES

1. P. P. Vaidyanathan, *Multirate Systems and Filter Banks*. Prentice Hall, 1993.

2. S. Winograd, "Arithmetic complexity of computations," in *CBMS-NSF Regional Conference Series in Applied Mathematics*, no. 33, SIAM Publications, 1980.

3. R. E. Blahut, *Fast Algorithms for Digital Signal Processing*. Addison-Wesley, 1985.

4. Z.-J. Mou and P. Duhamel, "Short-length FIR filters and their use in fast non-recursive filtering," *IEEE Trans. on Signal Processing*, vol. 39, pp. 1322–1332, June 1991.

5. Z.-J. Mou and P. Duhamel, "Fast FIR filtering: algorithms and implementations," *Signal Processing*, vol. 13, no. 4, pp. 377–384, Dec. 1987.

6. D. A. Parker and K. K. Parhi, "Low-area/power parallel fir digital filter implementations," *Journal of VLSI Signal Processing*, no. 1/2, pp. 75–92, Sept. 1997.

7. J.-G. Chung, Y.-B. Kim, H.-G. Jeong, K. K. Parhi, and Z. Wang, "Efficient parallel FIR filter implementations using frequency spectrum characteristics," in *IEEE International Symposium on Circuits and Systems*, (Monterey, CA), vol. 5, pp. 354–358, June 1998.

8. J. I. Acha, "Computational structures for fast implementation of L-path and L-block digital filters," *IEEE Transactions on Circuits and Systems*, vol. 36, no. 6, pp. 805–812, June 1989.

9. J. Granata, M. Conner, and R. Tolimieri, "The tensor product: a mathematical programming language for FFTs and other fast DSP operations," *IEEE Signal Processing Magazine*, pp. 40–48, Jan. 1992.

10. O. Rioul and P. Duhamel, "Fast algorithms for discrete and continuous wavelet transforms," *IEEE Trans. on Information Theory*, no. 3, pp. 569–586, March 1992.

11. N. Shanbhag and M. Goel, "Low-power adaptive filter architectures and their application to 51.84 mb/s atm-lan," *IEEE Trans. on Signal Processing*, no. 5, pp. 1276–1290, May 1997.

12. Y. Naito, T. Miyazaki, and I. Kuroda, "A fast full-search motion estimation method for programmable processors with a multiply-accumulator," *IEEE International Conference on Acoustics, Speech, and Signal Processing*, (Atalanta, GA), pp. 3221–3224, 1996.

13. N. Demassieux and F. Jutand, "Orthogonal transforms," in *VLSI Implementations for Image Communications* (P. Pirsch, ed.), pp. 217–250, Elsevier, 1993.

14. C. Loeffler, A. Lightenberg, and G. S. Moschytz, "Algorithm-architecture mapping for custom DSP chips," in *IEEE International Symposium on Circuits and Systems*, pp. 1953–1956, 1988.

15. W. Chen, C. Smith, and S. C. Fralick, "A fast computation algorithm for the discrete cosine transform," *IEEE Trans. on Communication*, pp. 1004–1009, Sept. 1977.

16. B. G. Lee, "A new algorithm to compute the discrete cosine transform," *IEEE Trans. on Acoustics, Speech, and Signal Processing*, pp. 1243–1245, Dec. 1984.

17. K. E. Batcher, "Sorting networks and their applications," in *Proc. AFIPS Spring Joint Comput. Conference*, pp. 307–314, 1968.

18. L. E. Lucke and K. K. Parhi, "Parallel processing architectures for rank order and stack filters," *IEEE Trans. on Signal Processing*, no. 5, pp. 1178–1189, May 1994.

19. I. Pitas, "Fast algorithms for running ordering and max/min calculation," *IEEE Trans. on Circuits and Systems*, no. 6, June 1989.

20. N. Sankarayya, K. Roy, and D. Bhattacharya, "Algorithms for low power and high speed FIR filter realization using differential coefficients," *IEEE Trans. on Circuits and Systems—II*, vol. 44, no. 6, pp. 488–497, June 1997.

21. S. Ramprasad, N. R. Shanbhag, and I. N. Hajj, "Decorrelating (DECOR) transformations for low-power adaptive filters," in *Proc. of 1998 IEEE Symposium on Low-Power Electronics*, (Monterey, CA), pp. 250–255, Aug. 1998.

10

Pipelined and Parallel Recursive and Adaptive Filters

10.1 INTRODUCTION

Any required digital filter spectrum can be realized using finite impulse response (FIR) or infinite impulse response (IIR) digital filters. IIR digital filters are often preferred since a specified spectrum can be implemented using a much lower order IIR filter than FIR. FIR and IIR digital filters are ideal for frequency shaping in deterministic environments, but are not useful in time-varying systems. Adaptive filters are used in these cases for applications such as noise cancellation, echo cancellation, beamforming, system identification, etc. Unlike the fixed coefficients FIR or IIR digital filters, the coefficients of the adaptive digital filters are adapted at each iteration until they converge.

Exploiting concurrency in the form of either pipelining or parallel processing is straightforward for nonrecursive computations. However, recursive and adaptive digital filters cannot be easily pipelined or processed in parallel due to the presence of feedback loops in these filters. This chapter presents approaches for pipelining and parallel processing in recursive digital filters using the *look-ahead computation* and *incremental block processing* techniques and the *relaxed look-ahead* transformations for pipelining of LMS and lattice adaptive filters.

This chapter is organized as follows. Pipelining in IIR digital filters using interleaving of filtering operations for multiple channels and look-ahead computation for single channel are introduced in Section 10.2. Section 10.3 addresses pipelining in first-order IIR digital filters using look-ahead and decomposition techniques. Pipelining of higher-order IIR digital filters using clustered and scattered look-ahead transformation approaches is addressed in Section 10.4. Parallel processing in IIR digital filters using straightforward and incremental computation techniques is addressed in Section 10.5. Pipelined and parallel architectures for IIR digital filters are discussed in Section 10.6. Power reduction of IIR digital filters using pipelining and/or parallel processing and reduced supply voltage is illustrated in Section 10.7. Pipelining of adaptive digital filters using relaxed look-ahead transformation is addressed in Section 10.8.

10.2   PIPELINE INTERLEAVING IN DIGITAL FILTERS

In this section, we review the notion of pipeline interleaving in the context of a simple 1st-order recursive digital filter. Three forms of pipeline interleaving are discussed:

1. Inefficient single/multichannel interleaving.

2. Efficient single-channel interleaving.

3. Efficient multichannel interleaving.

In 1, the loop is pipelined without changing the structure of the algorithm and thus hardware is not fully utilized, since zero-samples need to be interleaved to preserve the integrity of the algorithm. In 2 and 3, the internal structure of the algorithm is changed in a way that the pipeline is maximally or fully utilized.

10.2.1   Inefficient Single/Multichannel Interleaving

Consider a 1st-order linear time-invariant recursion described by

$$y(n+1) = ay(n) + bu(n), \qquad (10.1)$$

and shown in Fig. 10.1(a) in the form of a computation graph. The iteration period of this computation graph is $(T_m + T_a)$, where T_m and T_a, respectively, represent the word-level multiplication time and addition time.

Consider an *M-stage* pipelined version of this implementation obtained by *inserting* $(M - 1)$ additional latches inside the loop as shown in Fig. 10.1(b) (at the appropriate places). Then the clock period of this implementation can, in principle, be reduced by M times, but the latency associated with the loop computation and the sample period of the implementation will increase to M clock periods. As an example for $M = 5$, if we begin with a state $y^1(0)$ in clock period 0, the next state $y^1(1)$ will be available in clock period 5. For the case of a single time series, this array will be useful for only 20% of the time. (Trying to input samples of a single time series each clock period would implement a different algorithm, since the number of logical delays inside the loop has been changed.) Hence the sample rate of this

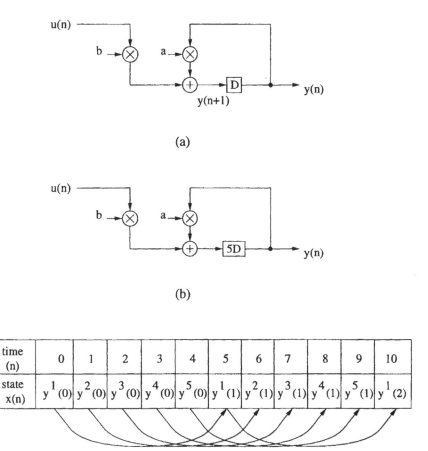

Fig. 10.1 (a) A simple 1st-order recursion. (b) The 1st-order linear time-invariant recursion after inserting $(M - 1)$ delay operations inside the loop (for $M = 5$). This implementation leads to M-way interleaving. (c) A partial schedule for the implementation of (b). The input time series are 5-way interleaved, i.e., 5 independent time series are being filtered simultaneously. The state $y^i(n)$ corresponds to the state of the i-th time series at time index n.

implementation is five times slower than the clock rate, and is no higher than that of the unpipelined version (in fact is worse due to the delay time associated with the additional latches). However if 5 independent time series are available to be filtered by the same hardware, then the hardware can be fully utilized as shown in the schedule of Fig. 10.1(c), although all the independent time series must be filtered at the slow rate. Independent time series can correspond to outputs of each 1st or 2nd-order cascade stage (since these elements can be separated by a feed-forward cutset), or can correspond to independent channels requiring identical filtering operation. As an example, for a 10th order recursive filter implemented as cascaded 2nd-order sections, the 5 section outputs are independent and can be interleaved in the pipeline (of course, each at 5-slow rate). Thus pipeline interleaving approach is well suited for applications requiring nominal concurrency.

To conclude, if a recursive loop with a single delay element is pipelined by M stages by *inserting* $(M - 1)$ additional delay elements, then the input data must be M-way interleaved, i.e., $(M - 1)$ zero time series or independent time series are interleaved with the given data stream (otherwise, the transfer function of the algorithm will be changed), and nothing has been achieved with respect to the sample rate with which a single time series can be filtered. This implementation is also often referred to as *M-slow circuit* in the literature [1]–[3]. The hardware in this slow interleaved implementation is inefficiently utilized if M independent computations are not available to be interleaved (which is often the case).

10.2.2   Efficient Single-Channel Interleaving

Ruling out the interleaving of independent time series, the two problems with M-slow implementations are (1) a sample rate M times slower than the clock rate, and (2) inefficient utilization of processing elements. Now we show that both these problems can be overcome by using the *look-ahead transformation* [4],[5], in which the given linear recursion is first iterated a few times to *create* additional concurrency.

Consider the 1st-order linear time-invariant (LTI) recursion of (10.1). By recasting this recursion, we can express $y(n+2)$ as a function of $y(n)$ to obtain

$$y(n + 2) = a[ay(n) + bu(n)] + bu(n + 1). \qquad (10.2)$$

A realization of this recursion is shown in Fig. 10.2(a). The iteration bound (see Chapter 2) of this recursion is $2(T_m + T_a)/2$ and is the same as that of Fig. 10.1(a), because the amount of computation and the number of logical delays inside the recursive loop are both doubled as compared to that in Fig. 10.1(a) leading to no net improvement. However, another recursion equivalent to that of (10.2) is

$$y(n + 2) = a^2 y(n) + abu(n) + bu(n + 1), \qquad (10.3)$$

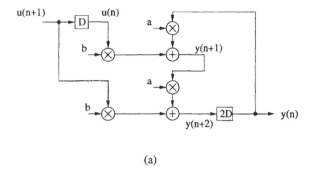

(a)

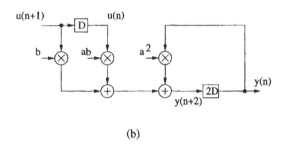

(b)

Fig. 10.2 (a) An equivalent realization of Fig. 10.1(a) obtained without the use of the look-ahead transformation. The iteration bound is the same as that of Fig. 10.1(a). (b) An equivalent 1st-order LTI recursion obtained with the use of look-ahead computation. The iteration bound is improved by a factor of 2 compared to the structure of Fig. 10.2(a).

and is shown in Fig. 10.2(b). The iteration period bound of this realization, $(T_m + T_a)/2$, is a factor of two lower than that of the realizations in Fig. 10.1(a) and Fig. 10.2(a)!

Applying $(M - 1)$ steps of look-ahead to the iteration of (10.1), we can obtain an equivalent implementation described by

$$y(n + M) = a^M y(n) + \sum_{i=0}^{M-1} a^i b u(n + M - 1 - i), \qquad (10.4)$$

and shown in Fig. 10.3(a). Note that the loop delay corresponds to z^{-M} instead of z^{-1}, which implies that the computation must be completed in M clock cycles rather than 1 clock cycle. The iteration bound of this computation graph is $(T_m + T_a)/M$, which corresponds to a sample rate M times higher than that for the original computation graph (although the complexity and system latency are now linearly increased). A portion of the schedule for the realization of Fig. 10.3(a) is shown in Fig. 10.3(b) for $M = 5$. The terms

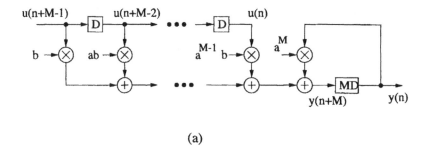

(a)

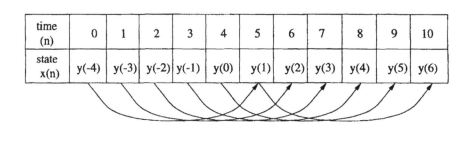

(b)

Fig. 10.3 (a) Equivalent 1st-order LTI recursion obtained using $(M - 1)$ steps of look-ahead. (b) A partial schedule for the structure of Fig. 10.3(a) for $M = 5$.

$ab, a^2b, \cdots, a^{M-1}b, a^M$ in (10.4) can be precomputed and are referred to as the *precomputation terms*. The 2nd term on the right-hand side of (10.4) represents the look-ahead computation term, and its complexity is referred to as the *look-ahead complexity*. Since the look-ahead computation term is nonrecursive, it can be pipelined by placing latches at the appropriate feed-forward cutsets.

The steady-state input-output behavior is not altered by the look-ahead technique. By this it is meant that for sufficiently old inputs, the outputs of the transformed system and the original systems will be identical. However, it is also possible to recast the initial states of the transformed system so that the input-output behavior of the transformed and the original system are identical for *all* inputs, as long as the original system is causal (under infinite precision assumption). Consider the schedule shown in Fig. 10.3(b) corresponding to the implementation of Fig. 10.3(a), where we start with M independent initial states $y(-M + 1), y(-M + 2), \cdots, y(0)$ (for $M = 5$). In the original system of (10.1), the state $y(1)$ is computed in terms of the initial state $y(0)$,

$$y(1) = ay(0) + bu(0). \tag{10.5}$$

For the transformed system of (10.4), the state $y(1)$ is calculated in terms of $y(-M + 1)$,

$$y(1) = a^5 y(-4) + bu(0), \tag{10.6}$$

for $M = 5$ (since $u(-4), \cdots, u(-1)$ are all 0 due to causality). From (10.5) and (10.6),

$$y(-4) = a^{-4} y(0). \tag{10.7}$$

A similar analysis can be carried out to obtain the M initial states

$$y(-i) = a^{-i} y(0), \quad i = 1, 2, \cdots, (M - 1). \tag{10.8}$$

In the transformed system, starting with M initial states, the next M states can be computed in a pipelined interleaved manner (see Fig. 10.3(b)). In this regard, look-ahead computation can be treated as an application of pipeline interleaving. Look-ahead computation has allowed a single serial computation to be transformed into M independent concurrent computations, and to pipeline the feedback loop to achieve high speed filtering of a single time series while maintaining full hardware utilization. Provided the multiplier and the adder can be conveniently pipelined, the iteration bound can be achieved by *retiming* or *cutset transformation* [1]–[3] (see Chapter 4).

10.2.3   Efficient Multichannel Interleaving

Look-ahead can be extended to the case where multiple independent channels require identical filtering operations. Consider the same 1st-order linear recursion of (10.1) for the case of 2 channels, and 6 pipeline stages inside the recursive loop. Then, without use of the look-ahead technique, the hardware will be utilized only one-third of the time. To get full utilization of hardware, we iterate the recursion two times, and interleave the computation of two time series. In general, if P independent time series are available, and the loop is pipelined by M stages (assume $M = PQ$), then the recursion needs to be iterated $(Q - 1)$ times. For this example, the iterated recursion corresponds to

$$y^i(n + 3) = a^3 y^i(n) + a^2 bu^i(n) + abu^i(n + 1) + bu^i(n + 2), \quad i = 1, 2. \tag{10.9}$$

Fig. 10.4 shows a partial schedule for the processing of the states y^1 and y^2 of the two independent time series in an interleaved manner.

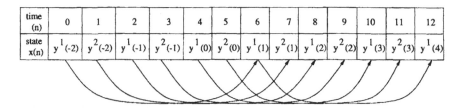

time (n)	0	1	2	3	4	5	6	7	8	9	10	11	12
state x(n)	$y^1(-2)$	$y^2(-2)$	$y^1(-1)$	$y^2(-1)$	$y^1(0)$	$y^2(0)$	$y^1(1)$	$y^2(1)$	$y^1(2)$	$y^2(2)$	$y^1(3)$	$y^2(3)$	$y^1(4)$

Fig. 10.4 A partial schedule for a 2-channel implementation with 6 loop pipelining stages obtained using two steps of look-ahead.

10.3   PIPELINING IN 1ST-ORDER IIR DIGITAL FILTERS

This section presents approaches for pipelining 1st-order recursive digital filter topologies using *look-ahead* techniques. With look-ahead technique, cancelling poles and zeros with equal angular spacing at a distance from the origin the same as that of the original pole are introduced. The pipelined realizations require a linear increase in complexity in the number of loop pipeline stages, and are always guaranteed to be stable for 1st-order IIR filters provided that the original filter is stable. A *decomposition technique* is then presented to implement the nonrecursive portion generated due to the look-ahead process in a decomposed manner to obtain an implementation with logarithmic increase in hardware with respect to the number of loop pipeline stages. The decomposition technique is the key in obtaining area-efficient implementations, and makes pipelined realizations attractive for high speed VLSI IIR filter implementations.

Consider a 1st-order IIR filter designed by the transfer function

$$H(z) = \frac{1}{1 - az^{-1}}. \tag{10.10}$$

The output sample $y(n)$ can be computed using the input sample $u(n)$ and the past output sample as follows:

$$y(n) = ay(n - 1) + u(n). \tag{10.11}$$

The sample rate of this recursive filter is limited by the computation time of one multiply-add operation because there is only one delay element in the critical loop.

10.3.1   Look-Ahead Pipelining for 1st-Order IIR Filters

The basic idea of look-ahead pipelining is to add cancelling poles and zeros to the transfer function such that the coefficients of $z^{-1}, \cdots, z^{-(M-1)}$ in the denominator of the transfer function are zero. The output sample $y(n)$ can then be computed using the inputs and the output sample $y(n - M)$ such that there are M delay elements in the critical loop, which in turn can be used to pipeline the critical loop and hence the sample rate can be increased by a factor M.

Example 10.3.1 *Consider the first-order filter*

$$H(z) = \frac{1}{1 - az^{-1}}, \tag{10.12}$$

which has a pole at $z = a$, $a \leq 1$. A 3-stage pipelined equivalent stable filter can be derived by adding poles and zeros at $z = ae^{\pm(j2\pi/3)}$, and is given by

$$H(z) = \frac{1 + az^{-1} + a^2 z^{-2}}{1 - a^3 z^{-3}}. \blacksquare \tag{10.13}$$

10.3.2   Look-Ahead Pipelining with Power-of-2 Decomposition

With *power-of-2 decomposition*, an M-stage (for power-of-2 M) pipelined implementation for 1st-order IIR filter can be obtained by $log_2 M$ sets of transformations, as illustrated in Example 10.3.2.

Example 10.3.2 *Consider a 1st-order recursive filter transfer function described by*

$$H(z) = \frac{bz^{-1}}{1 - az^{-1}}. \tag{10.14}$$

The equivalent pipelined transfer function can be derived using the decomposition technique, and is described by

$$H(z) = \frac{bz^{-1} \prod_{i=0}^{\log_2 M - 1}(1 + a^{2^i} z^{-2^i})}{1 - a^M z^{-M}}. \tag{10.15}$$

This pipelined implementation has been derived by adding $(M - 1)$ poles and zeros at identical locations. The original transfer function has a single pole at $z = a$ (see Fig. 10.5(a)). The pipelined transfer function has poles at locations a, $ae^{j2\pi/M}$, $ae^{j2(2\pi)/M}$, $ae^{j3(2\pi)/M}$, $\cdots$, $ae^{j(M-1)(2\pi)/M}$ (see Fig. 10.5(b) for $M = 8$). The decomposition of the cancelling zeros is shown in Fig. 10.5(c). The i-th stage of the decomposed nonrecursive portion implements 2^i zeros located at

$$z = ae^{j(2n+1)\pi/2^i}, \quad n = 0, 1, \cdots, (2^i - 1), \tag{10.16}$$

and requires a single pipelined multiplication operation independent of the stage number i. The total complexity of the pipelined implementation is $(\log_2 M + 2)$ multiplications. $\blacksquare$

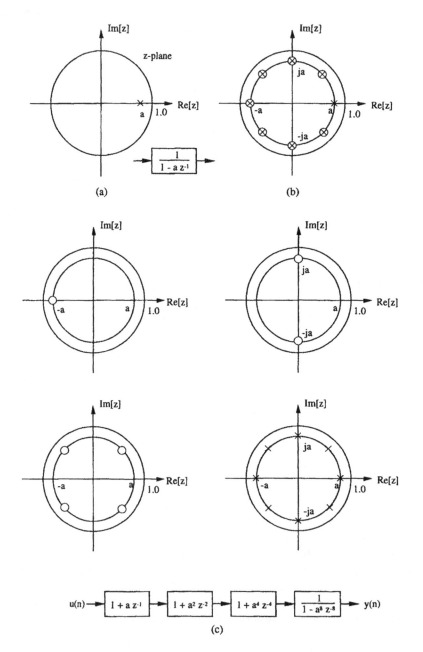

Fig. 10.5 (a) Pole representation of a 1st-order recursive filter. (b) Pole zero representation of a 1st-order LTI recursive system with 8 loop pipelining stages. (c) Decomposition based pipelined implementation of the 1st-order LTI recursive system for $M = 8$.

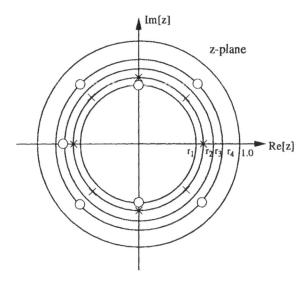

Fig. 10.6 Inexact pole zero cancellation due to finite precision in a 1st-order lookahead filter with 8 loop pipeline stages.

Comments

- The decomposition based pipelined implementation can also be equivalently explained using the time-domain approach. The original recursive filter description is given by

$$y(n + 1) = ay(n) + bu(n), \tag{10.17}$$

and the pipelined realization is given by

$$y(n + M) = a^M y(n) + \sum_{i=0}^{M-1} a^i bu(n + M - 1 - i). \tag{10.18}$$

As an example, for $M = 8$, we have

$$
\begin{aligned}
y(n + 8) &= a^8 y(n) + \sum_{i=0}^{7} a^i bu(n + 7 - i), \\
&= a^8 y(n) + \sum_{i=0}^{7} a^i f_0(n + 7 - i), \\
&= a^8 y(n) + \sum_{i=0}^{3} a^{2i} f_1(n + 7 - 2i),
\end{aligned}
$$

$$= a^8 y(n) + \sum_{i=0}^{1} a^{4i} f_2(n + 7 - 4i), \qquad (10.19)$$

where

$$
\begin{aligned}
f_0(n) &= bu(n), \\
f_1(n) &= a f_0(n - 1) + f_0(n), \\
f_2(n) &= a^2 f_1(n - 2) + f_1(n). \qquad (10.20)
\end{aligned}
$$

- Although the pipelined recursive filter realizations are stable under infinite precision conditions, they are sensitive to filter coefficients under finite precision. In a finite precision implementation, the poles of the 1st-order M-stage pipelined filter are located at

$$p = (a^M + \Delta)^{1/M} \approx a(1 + \frac{\Delta}{M a^M}), \qquad (10.21)$$

where Δ corresponds to the finite precision error in representing a^M. This pole location is more sensitive for smaller values of a (that is when poles are closer to the origin). Fortunately this is not a problem, since the instability problem for the filter with poles closer to origin is not severe.

- In addition to the sensitivity problem, finite precision pipelined filters suffer from inexact pole-zero cancellation (see Fig. 10.6), which leads to magnitude and phase error. These errors can be reduced by increasing the wordlength.

10.3.3   Look-Ahead Pipelining with General Decomposition

We have already explored the power-of-2 decompositions that lead to hardware efficient implementations for power-of-2 stage pipelined 1st-order IIR filters. The idea of decomposition can be extended to any arbitrary number of loop pipelining stages M. If $M = M_1 M_2 \cdots M_p$, then the nonrecursive stages implement $(M_1 - 1)$, $M_1(M_2 - 1)$, $\cdots$, $M_1 M_2 \cdots M_{p-1}(M_p - 1)$ zeros, respectively, totaling $(M - 1)$ zeros.

Example 10.3.3 *Consider the first-order transfer function in (10.12). A 12-stage pipelined decomposed implementation is given by*

$$
\begin{aligned}
H(z) &= \frac{\sum_{i=0}^{11} a^i z^{-i}}{1 - a^{12} z^{-12}}, \\
&= \frac{(1 + a z^{-1})(1 + a^2 z^{-2} + a^4 z^{-4})(1 + a^6 z^{-6})}{1 - a^{12} z^{-12}}. \qquad (10.22)
\end{aligned}
$$

The implementation in (10.22) corresponds to a $2 \times 3 \times 2$ decomposition. The pole-zero configuration of the 12 stage pipelined filter is shown in Fig. 10.7(a). The decomposition of 11 cancelling zeros of this filter is shown in Fig. 10.7(b), where the three sections implement 1, 4, and 6 zeros, respectively. Here the first section implements the zero at $-a$, the second section implements 4 zeros at $ae^{\pm j\pi/3}$ and $ae^{\pm j2\pi/3}$, and the third section implements 6 zeros at $\pm ja$, $ae^{\pm j\pi/6}$, and $ae^{\pm j5\pi/6}$. Another decomposed transfer function is given by

$$H(z) = \frac{(1 + az^{-1})(1 + a^2 z^{-2})(1 + a^4 z^{-4} + a^8 z^{-8})}{1 - a^{12} z^{-12}}, \qquad (10.23)$$

and corresponds to $2 \times 2 \times 3$ decomposition. In this implementation, the 1st nonrecursive section implements 1 zero at $-a$, the 2nd section implements 2 zeros at $\pm ja$, and the 3rd section implements 8 zeros at $ae^{\pm j\pi/6}$, $ae^{\pm j\pi/3}$, $ae^{\pm j2\pi/3}$, and $ae^{\pm j5\pi/6}$. The $3 \times 2 \times 2$ decomposition is given by

$$H(z) = \frac{(1 + az^{-1} + a^2 z^{-2})(1 + a^3 z^{-3})(1 + a^6 z^{-6})}{1 - a^{12} z^{-12}}, \qquad (10.24)$$

and the 3 sections, respectively, implement 2, 3, and 6 zeros. The 1st section implements 2 zeros at $ae^{\pm j2\pi/3}$, the 2nd implements 3 zeros at $-a$ and $ae^{\pm j\pi/3}$, and the 3rd section implements 6 zeros at $ae^{\pm j\pi/6}$, $\pm ja$, and $ae^{\pm j5\pi/6}$.

■

10.4 PIPELINING IN HIGHER-ORDER IIR DIGITAL FILTERS

This section presents approaches for pipelining higher-order recursive digital filter topologies using *clustered* and *scattered look-ahead* techniques. (For 1st-order IIR filters, these two look-ahead approaches reduce to the same form.) With clustered look-ahead, pipelined realizations require a linear complexity in the number of loop pipeline stages and are not always guaranteed to be stable. We illustrate the use of scattered look-ahead approach to derive stable pipelined filters. Then the decomposition technique is revisited in this section for higher-order IIR filters and is used to obtain area-efficient implementations for higher-order filters. In addition to the clustered and the scattered look-ahead techniques, *constrained filter design* techniques that achieve pipelining without pole-zero cancellation are discussed.

Let the transfer function of an N-th order direct-form recursive filter be described by

$$H(z) = \frac{\sum_{i=0}^{N} b_i z^{-i}}{1 - \sum_{i=1}^{N} a_i z^{-i}}. \qquad (10.25)$$

Equivalently, the output sample $y(n)$ can be described in terms of the input

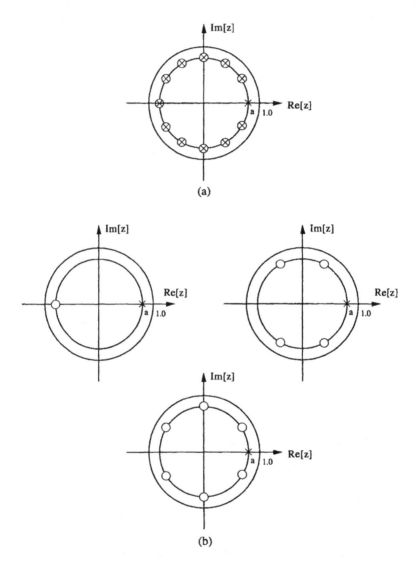

Fig. 10.7 (a) Pole zero location of a 12-stage pipelined 1st-order recursive filter. (b) Decomposition of the zeros of the pipelined filter for a 2 × 3 × 2 decomposition.

sample $u(n)$, and the past input and output samples, and is given by

$$
\begin{aligned}
y(n) &= \sum_{i=1}^{N} a_i y(n-i) + \sum_{i=0}^{N} b_i u(n-i), \\
&= \sum_{i=1}^{N} a_i y(n-i) + z(n).
\end{aligned} \tag{10.26}
$$

Again, the sample rate of this recursive filter realization is limited by the throughput of 1 multiplication and 1 addition since the critical loop contains a single delay operator or latch.

10.4.1   Clustered Look-Ahead Pipelining

The basic idea of clustered look-ahead pipelining is to add cancelling poles and zeros to the filter transfer function such that the coefficients of z^{-1}, $\cdots$, $z^{-(M-1)}$ in the denominator of the transfer function are zero. The output sample $y(n)$ can be described in terms of the *cluster* of N past outputs $y(n - M), y(n - M - 1), \cdots$, and $y(n - M - N + 1)$ [6]. Hence the critical loop of this implementation contains M delay elements and a single multiplication operation. Therefore, this loop can be pipelined by M stages, and the sample rate can be increased by a factor M. This is referred to as M-*stage clustered look-ahead pipelining.*

Example 10.4.1 *Consider the example of an all-pole 2nd-order IIR filter with poles at $z = 1/2$ and $z = 3/4$ (see Fig. 10.8(a)). This original filter is described by the transfer function*

$$
H(z) = \frac{1}{1 - \frac{5}{4}z^{-1} + \frac{3}{8}z^{-2}}. \tag{10.27}
$$

A 2-stage pipelined equivalent recursive digital filter can be derived by eliminating the z^{-1} term in the denominator. In order to do this, one can multiply the numerator and denominator by $(1 + 5/4z^{-1})$, or equivalently introduce a pole and a zero at $z = -5/4$ (see Fig. 10.8(b)). The transformed transfer function is given by

$$
H(z) = \frac{1 + \frac{5}{4}z^{-1}}{1 - \frac{19}{16}z^{-2} + \frac{15}{32}z^{-3}}, \tag{10.28}
$$

where the coefficient of z^{-1} in the denominator is zero. Hence the critical loop of this filter contains 2 delay elements and can be pipelined by 2 stages. Similarly a 3-stage pipelined realization can be derived by eliminating the z^{-1} and z^{-2} terms in the denominator of (10.27), which can be done by multiplying both numerator and denominator by $(1+5/4z^{-1}+19/16z^{-2})$. The new transfer *function is given by*

$$H(z) = \frac{1 + \frac{5}{4}z^{-1} + \frac{19}{16}z^{-2}}{1 - \frac{65}{64}z^{-3} + \frac{57}{128}z^{-4}}. \quad \blacksquare \tag{10.29}$$

In general, an M-stage clustered look-ahead pipelined recursive filter can be obtained by multiplying the numerator and the denominator of the filter transfer function by $\sum_{i=0}^{M-1} r_i z^{-i}$, introducing $M-1$ additional cancelling poles and zeros. The sequence r_i is defined as follows:

$$\begin{aligned}
r_{-i} &= 0, \ for \ i = 1, 2, \cdots, N-1 \\
r_0 &= 1 \\
r_i &= \sum_{k=1}^{N} a_k r_{i-k}, \ i > 0.
\end{aligned} \tag{10.30}$$

Assume that the coefficients of the M-stage pipelined filter are precomputed off-line. Then the numerator or the nonrecursive portion of this pipelined filter can be implemented with $(N+M)$ multiplications, and the denominator or the recursive portion can be implemented with N multiplications. Thus, the total complexity of this pipelined implementation is $(N + N + M)$ multiplications, which is linear with respect to the number of loop pipeline stages M or speedup or increase in the sample rate. So far, the cancelling poles and zeros have been utilized for pipelining recursive filters. However, the additional poles may lie outside the unit circle, which in turn will change the stability property of the original filter.

Example 10.4.2 *The 2nd-order filter in (10.27) has poles at $z = 0.5$ and $z = 0.75$ (see Fig. 10.8(a)). The 2-stage pipelined filter has an additional pole at $z = -1.25$, which lies outside the unit circle (see Fig. 10.8(b)). The 3-stage pipelined filter has 2 additional poles at $z = 0.625 \pm j0.893$ (see Fig. 10.8(c)). Note that the complex conjugate poles are also outside the unit circle. Thus both the 2- and 3-stage equivalent pipelined realizations in (10.28) and (10.29) are unstable, even though the original configuration of (10.27) is stable.* ∎

10.4.2   Stable Clustered Look-Ahead Filter Design

Consider a stable recursive digital filter transfer function given by

$$H(z) = \frac{N(z)}{D(z)}. \tag{10.31}$$

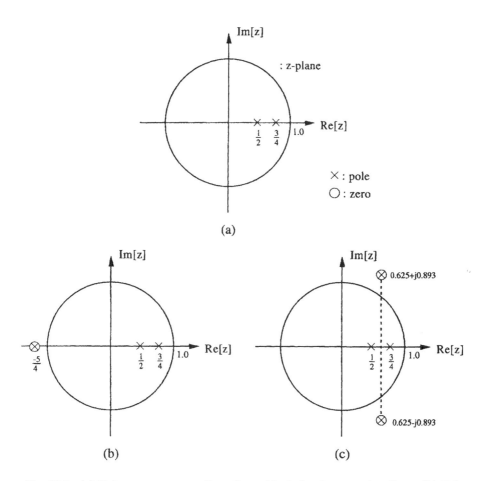

Fig. 10.8 (a) Pole zero representation of a stable 2nd-order recursive filter. (b) Pole zero representation of a 2-stage pipelined equivalent unstable filter derived using clustered look-ahead approach. (c) Pole zero representation of a 3-stage pipelined equivalent unstable filter derived using clustered look-ahead approach.

The clustered look-ahead techniques transform $H(z)$ into the form

$$H(z) = \frac{N(z)P(z)}{D(z)P(z)} = \frac{N(z)P(z)}{1 - z^{-M}Q(z)}, \tag{10.32}$$

where $P(z)$ represents the superfluous poles needed to create the desired pipeline delay M, and $(1 - z^{-M}Q(z))$ is the resulting pipelined denominator. Notice that the denominator of the pipelined filter contains only the terms $z^{-(M+i)}$ (except the constant term), where i can be any nonnegative integer smaller than or equal to the order of $Q(z)$. It has been shown that (10.32) *always* produces a stable filter at some critical delay M_c such that the stability will be assured for $M > M_c$. Therefore, if the desired pipeline delay M does not produce a stable filter, M should be increased until a stable pipelined filter is obtained. To obtain the optimal pipelining level M and $P(z)$, numerical search methods are generally used.

Example 10.4.3 *Consider a 5-level $(M = 5)$ pipelined implementation of the following 2nd-order transfer function*

$$H(z) = \frac{1}{1 - 1.5336z^{-1} + 0.6889z^{-2}}, \tag{10.33}$$

given in [7]. By the stable clustered look-ahead method in [7], it is shown that $(M = 5)$ does not meet the stability condition. Thus M is increased to $M = 6$ to obtain the following stable pipelined filter

$$H(z) = \frac{1 + 1.5336z^{-1} + 1.6630z^{-2} + 1.4939z^{-3} + 1.1454z^{-4} + 0.7275z^{-5}}{1 - 1.3265z^{-6} + 0.5011z^{-7}}. \tag{10.34}$$

Fig. 10.9(a) shows the pole locations of the original filter at $z = 0.7668 \pm j0.3177$. The pipelined filter is derived by adding poles and zeros at $z = 0.9718$, $z = -0.5572 \pm j0.7765$ and $z = 0.2763 \pm j0.862$ and the pole-zero locations are shown in Fig. 10.9(b). ∎

When the number of denominator multipliers is large, the pipelined filter suffers from large roundoff noise, since the filter cannot be implemented using cascade or parallel form structures. (Notice that (10.32) cannot be decomposed into cascade or parallel forms if M level of pipelining is to be maintained.)

10.4.3 Scattered Look-Ahead Pipelining

In scattered look-ahead, the denominator of the transfer function in (10.25) is transformed in a way that it contains the N terms z^{-M}, z^{-2M}, $\cdots$, and z^{-NM} [4]. Equivalently, the state $y(n)$ is computed in terms of N past *scattered* states $y(n-M)$, $y(n-2M)$, $\cdots$, and $y(n-NM)$. In this look-ahead, for each pole in

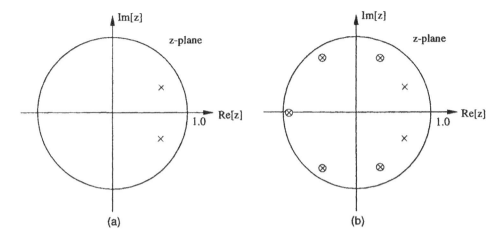

Fig. 10.9 (a) Pole-zero representation of a stable 2nd-order recursive filter. (b) Pole-zero representation of a 6-stage pipelined stable filter derived using a stable clustered look-ahead approach.

the original filter, we introduce $(M-1)$ cancelling poles and zeros with equal angular spacing at a distance from the origin the same as that of the original pole. For example, if the original filter has a pole at $z = p$, we add $(M-1)$ poles and zeros at $z = pe^{j2\pi k/M}$ for $k = 1, 2, \cdots, (M-1)$ to derive a pipelined realization with M loop pipeline stages. Assume that the denominator of the transfer function can be factorized as follows:

$$D(z) = \prod_{i=1}^{N}(1 - p_i z^{-1}). \qquad (10.35)$$

The pipelining process using the scattered look-ahead approach can be described by

$$H(z) = \frac{N(z)}{D(z)} = \frac{N(z)\prod_{i=1}^{N}\prod_{k=1}^{M-1}(1 - p_i e^{j2\pi k/M} z^{-1})}{\prod_{i=1}^{N}\prod_{k=0}^{M-1}(1 - p_i e^{j2\pi k/M} z^{-1})} = \frac{N'(z)}{D'(z^M)}. \qquad (10.36)$$

Now we consider several examples to illustrate scattered look-ahead pipelining for recursive filters.

Example 10.4.4 *Consider the 2nd-order filter transfer function*

$$H(z) = \frac{1}{1 - a_1 z^{-1} - a_2 z^{-2}}. \qquad (10.37)$$

A 3-stage equivalent pipelined filter is given by

$$H(z) = \frac{1 + a_1 z^{-1} + (a_1^2 + a_2)z^{-2} - a_1 a_2 z^{-3} + a_2^2 z^{-4}}{1 - (a_1^3 + 3a_1 a_2)z^{-3} - a_2^3 z^{-6}} \cdot \blacksquare \qquad (10.38)$$

Example 10.4.5 *Consider the 2nd-order filter with complex conjugate poles at $z = re^{\pm j\theta}$. The transfer function of the filter is given by*

$$H(z) = \frac{1}{1 - 2r\cos\theta z^{-1} + r^2 z^{-2}}. \qquad (10.39)$$

We can pipeline this filter by 3 stages by introducing 4 additional poles and zeros at $z = re^{\pm j(\theta + 2\pi/3)}$, and $z = re^{\pm j(\theta - 2\pi/3)}$. The equivalent pipelined filter is given by

$$H(z) = \frac{1 + 2r\cos\theta z^{-1} + (1 + 2\cos 2\theta)r^2 z^{-2} + 2r^3 \cos\theta z^{-3} + r^4 z^{-4}}{1 - 2r^3 \cos 3\theta z^{-3} + r^6 z^{-6}}, \qquad (10.40)$$

when $\theta \neq 2\pi/3$. Note when $\theta = 2\pi/3$, then only 1 additional pole and zero at $z = r$ is required for 3-stage pipelining since $z = re^{\pm j(\theta + 2\pi/3)} = re^{\pm j\theta}$ and $z = re^{\pm j(\theta - 2\pi/3)} = r$. The equivalent pipelined filter is then given by

$$\begin{aligned} H(z) &= \frac{(1 - rz^{-1})}{(1 + rz^{-1} + r^2 z^{-2})(1 - rz^{-1})} \\ &= \frac{1 - rz^{-1}}{1 - r^3 z^{-3}} \cdot \blacksquare \end{aligned} \qquad (10.41)$$

Example 10.4.6 *Consider the 2nd-order filter with real poles at $z = r_1$ and $z = r_2$. The transfer function is given by*

$$H(z) = \frac{1}{1 - (r_1 + r_2)z^{-1} + r_1 r_2 z^{-2}}. \qquad (10.42)$$

A 3-stage pipelined realization is derived by adding poles (and zeros) at $z = r_1 e^{\pm j2\pi/3}$ and $z = r_2 e^{\pm j2\pi/3}$. The pipelined realization is given by

$$H(z) = \frac{1 + (r_1 + r_2)z^{-1} + (r_1^2 + r_1 r_2 + r_2^2)z^{-2} + r_1 r_2(r_1 + r_2)z^{-3} + r_1^2 r_2^2 z^{-4}}{1 - (r_1^3 + r_2^3)z^{-3} + r_1^3 r_2^3 z^{-6}}. \qquad (10.43)$$

The pole-zero locations of a 3-stage pipelined 2nd-order filter with poles at $z = 1/2$ and $z = 3/4$ are shown in Fig. 10.10. $\blacksquare$

The scattered look-ahead approach leads to stable pipelined filters if the original filter is stable, since the distance of the additional poles from the origin is same as that of the original filter. The multiplication complexity of the

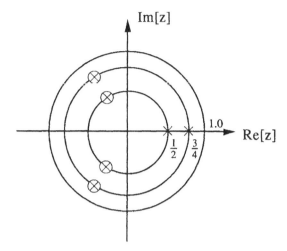

Fig. 10.10 Pole zero representation of a 3-stage pipelined equivalent stable filter derived using scattered look-ahead approach.

nonrecursive portion in (10.36) is $(NM + 1)$, and that of the recursive portion is N, leading to a total complexity $(NM + N + 1)$ pipelined multiplications, a linear complexity with respect to M. Even though this complexity is linear with respect to M, it is much greater than that of clustered look-ahead. Also note that the latch complexity is square in M, since each multiplier is pipelined by M stages.

We now derive another pipelined realization using a *decomposition technique* that leads to a logarithmic increase in hardware with respect to the level of pipelining.

10.4.4 Scattered Look-Ahead Pipelining with Power-of-2 Decomposition

Let the transfer function of a recursive digital filter be described by

$$H'(z) = \frac{\sum_{i=0}^{N} b_i z^{-i}}{1 - \sum_{i=1}^{N} a_i z^{-i}} = \frac{N(z)}{D(z)}. \tag{10.44}$$

A 2-stage pipelined implementation can be obtained by multiplying by $(1 - \sum_{i=1}^{N} (-1)^i a_i z^{-i})$ in the numerator and denominator. The equivalent 2-stage pipelined implementation is described by

$$H'(z) = \frac{\sum_{i=0}^{N} b_i z^{-i}(1 - \sum_{i=1}^{N} (-1)^i a_i z^{-i})}{\left[1 - \sum_{i=1}^{N} a_i z^{-i}\right]\left[1 - \sum_{i=1}^{N} (-1)^i a_i z^{-i}\right]} = \frac{N'(z)}{D'(z^2)}. \tag{10.45}$$

Similarly, subsequent transformations can be applied to obtain 4, 8, and 16 stage pipelined implementations, respectively. Thus to obtain an M-stage pipelined implementation (for power-of-2 M), $\log_2 M$ sets of such transformations need to be applied. Each transformation leads to an increase in multiplication complexity by N while doubling the speed (or sample rate) or the number of pipeline stages inside the critical recursive loop. Series of such transformations lead to a geometric increase in the number of loop pipeline stages or speedup while requiring only an arithmetic increase in hardware complexity!

By applying $(\log_2 M - 1)$ sets of such transformations, an equivalent transfer function (with M pipelining stages inside the recursive loop) can be derived, which requires a complexity of $(2N + N \log_2 M + 1)$ multiplications, a logarithmic complexity with respect to speedup or M. Note that although the number of multiplication operations is logarithmic, the number of delays or latches is linear. The total number of delays or latches is approximately $NM(\log_2 M + 1)$, out of which about NM delays are used for implementation of nonrecursive portions, and about $NM \log_2 M$ delays are required to pipeline each of the $N \log_2 M$ multipliers by M stages. This implementation has been derived by incorporating $N(M - 1)$ additional poles and zeros at identical locations. Instead of implementing the $N(M - 1)$ zeros as a single stage nonrecursive section, we exploit the symmetry of the coefficients and implement it in a decomposed manner. In the decomposed realization, the 1st stage implements an N-th order nonrecursive section, and the subsequent stages respectively implement $2N, 4N, \cdots, NM/2$-order nonrecursive sections. Due to the symmetry of coefficients, each of these nonrecursive sections requires N multiplications independent of the order of that section. Now we consider examples to illustrate scattered look-ahead and decomposition based pipelining in recursive filters.

Example 10.4.7 *Consider a 2nd-order recursive filter described by*

$$H(z) = \frac{Y(z)}{U(z)} = \frac{b_0 + b_1 z^{-1} + b_2 z^{-2}}{1 - 2r \cos \theta z^{-1} + r^2 z^{-2}}. \tag{10.46}$$

The poles of the system are located at $re^{\pm j\theta}$ (see Fig. 10.11(a)). The pipelined function can be described by

$$H(z) = \frac{\left(\sum_{i=0}^{2} b_i z^{-i}\right)}{1 - 2r^M \cos M\theta z^{-M} + r^{2M} z^{-2M}} \times$$

$$\prod_{i=0}^{\log_2 M - 1} \left(1 + 2r^{2^i} \cos 2^i \theta z^{-2^i} + r^{2^{i+1}} z^{-2^{i+1}}\right), \tag{10.47}$$

for the case $\theta \neq 2\pi/M$. (Pipelining for the case $\theta = 2\pi/M$ is addressed in Problem 11.) The 2M poles of the transformed transfer function are located *at*

$$z = re^{\pm j(\theta + i(2\pi/M))}, \quad i = 0,\ 1,\ 2,\ \cdots,\ (M-1), \tag{10.48}$$

and are shown in Fig. 10.11(b). Fig. 10.11(c) shows the decomposition of poles and zeros of the pipelined 2nd-order filter. The decomposed implementation of the pipelined filter is shown in Fig. 10.12. The pipelined filter can be implemented with an implementation complexity of $(2\log_2 M + 5)$ multiplications.

■

10.4.5 Scattered Look-Ahead Pipelining with General Decomposition

Similar to pipelined 1st-order IIR filters, the decomposition of cancelling zeros can also be extended to any arbitrary number of loop pipeline stages for pipelined higher-order IIR filters.

In an N-th order filter with M levels of pipelining, there are $N(M-1)$ cancelling zeros. First consider the simple case of $M = M_1 M_2$ decomposition. In this implementation, the system has $N(M_1 M_2 - 1)$ cancelling zeros. The 1st stage implements $N(M_1 - 1)$ zeros, and the 2nd stage implements $NM_1(M_2 - 1)$ zeros. In a $M_1 M_2 M_3$ decomposition, the 1st stage implements $N(M_1 - 1)$ zeros, the 2nd stage implements $NM_1(M_2 - 1)$ zeros, and the 3rd stage implements $NM_1 M_2(M_3 - 1)$ zeros. In general, in a $M = M_1 M_2 \cdots M_P$ decomposition, the P nonrecursive stages respectively implement $N(M_1 - 1)$, $NM_1(M_2 - 1), \cdots, NM_1 M_2 \cdots M_{P-1}(M_P - 1)$ zeros, totaling $N(M-1)$ zeros. The nonrecursive portion of the general decomposition requires about NM delays and $N \sum_{i=1}^{P}(M_i - 1)$ multipliers (each of these multipliers also requires M latches for pipelining).

The general decomposition techniques for a 1st-order IIR filter has been illustrated in Example 10.3.3. Any higher order recursive filter can be factored in terms of 1st-order sections. General decomposition similar to Example 10.3.3 can be applied to these 1st-order sections, and then the complex conjugate sections can be combined to obtain the decomposed form in terms of real multiplications.

10.4.6 Constrained Filter Design Techniques

The clustered and the scattered look-ahead techniques achieve pipelining by pole-zero cancellation. In addition to the hardware increase due to the cancelling zeros, these pipelined filters suffer from inexact pole-zero cancellations in a finite wordlength implementation. To avoid the drawback of cancelling zeros, the pipelinable transfer function can be designed directly from the filter spectrum while the denominator is constrained to be a polynomial in z^M rather than z, i.e., the denominator can be expressed in scattered look-ahead form. In this section, two constrained filter design techniques are briefly introduced. The constrained filter design approach requires less hardware complex-

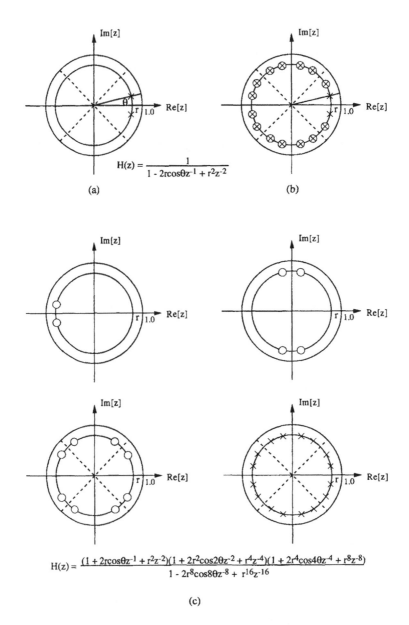

Fig. 10.11 (a) Pole diagram of the 2nd-order filter. The zeros of the filter have not been shown for clarity. (b) Pole zero representation of the pipelined 2nd-order direct-form filter with 8 loop pipelining stages. (c) Decomposition of poles and zeros of the pipelined 2nd-order filter.

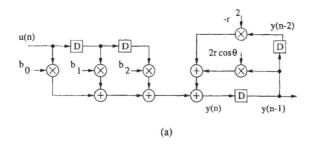

(a)

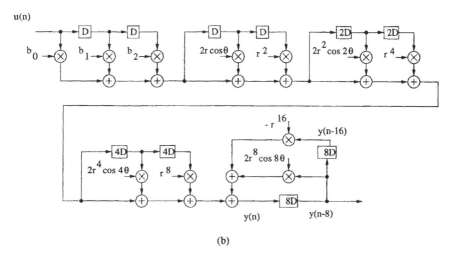

(b)

Fig. 10.12 Implementation of the original 2nd-order filter and the pipelined scattered look-ahead recursive filter using decomposition technique for 8 pipelining stages inside the recursive loop.

ity and leads to less output roundoff noise. Hardware complexity associated with zeros is reduced by placing zeros at -1 which require no multiplication operations and on the unit circle in complex conjugate pairs, which requires 1 multiplication operation.

10.4.6.1 Modified Deczky's Filter Design The design method in [8] first expresses the magnitude and group delay responses of a filter as functions of the radii and angles of the poles and zeros. Then the formulas for the partial derivatives of the magnitude and group delay are obtained with respect to the radius and the angle of a pole and a zero. These derivatives are used in the Fletcher-Powell algorithm to minimize the approximation error [9]. The Fletcher-Powell algorithm finds a local minimum of a function of several variables using only first derivative information.

To obtain an inherently M-level pipelinable filter, the partial derivatives for a denominator are recomputed in powers of z^M rather than z and these equations are used in the Fletcher-Powell algorithm [10]. Then, the denominator of the resulting transfer function is in terms of z^M.

The constrained filter design procedure using modified Deczky's method is summarized as follows:

1. For the given filter specifications (pass-band, stop-band, pass-band ripple, stop-band ripple, and M-level pipelining), we start the filter design with 1-complex pole pair. Then, the order of the denominator is $2M$. We usually start with M unit-circle zero pairs. Some of these zeros are placed on the unit circle in the stop-band to counter the effect of the repeated poles due to the decimating structure.

2. If the filter specifications are not satisfied by 1-complex pole pair, we increase the number of poles and zeros, and adjust initial positions of poles and zeros, and weighting factors for the pass-band and stop-band. The filter is redesigned. This procedure is repeated until the filter specifications are satisfied.

Example 10.4.8 *Consider a 4-stage pipelinable low-pass filter with*

$$pass\text{-}band: 0 - 0.2\pi \ (0.5 \ dB \ ) \ and \ stop\text{-}band: 0.3\pi - \pi \ (20 \ dB).$$

The transfer function obtained by the modified Deczky's method is:

$$
\begin{aligned}
N(z) &= 0.09742(1 - 1.16548z^{-1} + z^{-2})(1 - 0.29069z^{-1} + z^{-2}) \cdot \\
&\quad (1 + 1.19469z^{-1} + z^{-2})(1 + 1.75885z^{-1} + z^{-2}), \\
D(z) &= 1 + 0.63459z^{-4} + 0.10067z^{-8}.
\end{aligned}
$$

Notice that $D(z)$ can be further decomposed as $D(z) = (1 + 0.31729z^{-4})^2$. All the zeros are located on the unit circle at the stop-band and the poles have equal radius of 0.75 and equal angular spacing of 0.5π. The pole-zero plot of the transfer function is shown in Fig. 10.13. Notice that 4-level pipelining is achieved without pole-zero cancellation. ∎

10.4.6.2 Martinez-Parks Decimation Filter Design To obtain inherently pipelinable transfer functions, we can also use the decimation filter design method in [11],[12], which uses equiripple magnitude constraint with the additional constraint that all zeros lie on the unit circle.

The modified Remez exchange algorithm in [11] finds the equiripple solution by repetitively updating the magnitude of the numerator and the squared magnitude of the denominator. This algorithm works as follows: given pass-band ripple, pass-band edge, stop-band edge, and the order of the filter, the stop-band ripple is chosen in such a way that the resulting filter has equiripple behavior.

In [12], the formula for the squared magnitude of the denominator in [11] was slightly changed such that the resulting denominator has only powers of

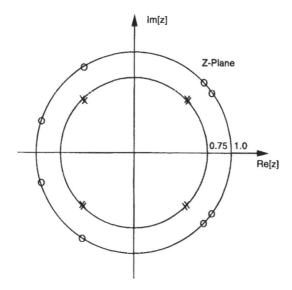

Fig. 10.13 Pole-zero plot of the transfer function in Example 10.4.8.

z^M. Several examples in [12] show that this method is very efficient when the filter spectrum has narrow-band sharp-transition.

10.5   PARALLEL PROCESSING FOR IIR FILTERS

In this section, the techniques for parallel processing of IIR filters is discussed. Parallel processing for a simple 1st-order IIR filter is discussed first. After that, parallel processing for higher order filters is discussed.

Example 10.5.1 *Consider the transfer function of a 1st-order IIR filter given in (10.49)*

$$H(z) = \frac{z^{-1}}{1 - az^{-1}}, \qquad (10.49)$$

where $|a| \leq 1$ for stability. This transfer function has only 1 pole located at $z = a$. The corresponding input output relation can be written as:

$$y(n+1) = ay(n) + u(n). \qquad (10.50)$$

Consider the design of a 4-parallel architecture ($L = 4$) for the foregoing filter. Note that in the parallel system, each delay element is referred to as a block delay, where the clock period of the block system is 4 times the sample period. Therefore, instead of (10.50), the loop update equation should update $y(n+4)$ using inputs and $y(n)$. By iterating the recursion (in (10.50)) or by applying

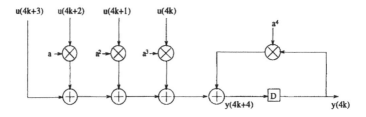

Fig. 10.14 Single state update operation in a 4-parallel filter.

look-ahead technique, we get

$$y(n+4) = a^4 y(n) + a^3 u(n) + a^2 u(n+1) + au(n+2) + u(n+3). \quad (10.51)$$

Substituting $n = 4k$ in (10.51),

$$y(4k+4) = a^4 y(4k) + a^3 u(4k) + a^2 u(4k+1) + au(4k+2) + u(4k+3). \quad (10.52)$$

The corresponding architecture is shown in Fig. 10.14. Notice the pole movement in the parallel filter. The pole of the original system is at $z = a$, whereas the pole for the parallel system is at $z = a^4$, which is closer to the origin since $|a^4|$ is less than or equal to $|a|$ (since $|a| \leq 1$). An important implication of this pole movement is the improved robustness of the system to the roundoff noise. A straightforward block processing structure for $L=4$ obtained by substituting $n = 4k+4$, $4k+5$, $4k+6$ and $4k+7$ in (10.51) is shown in Fig. 10.15.
■

The hardware complexity of this architecture is L^2 multiply-add operations since L multiply-add operations are required for each output and there are L outputs in total.

As can be seen, a straightforward implementation of the block processing architecture is hardware expensive. The square increase in hardware complexity can be reduced by exploiting the concurrency in the computation. Note that the decomposition property in the scattered look-ahead mode cannot be exploited in the block processing mode because one hardware delay element represents L sample delays. However, instead of computing $y(4k+1)$ independently, one can use $y(4k)$ to compute $y(4k+1)$, use $y(4k+1)$ to compute $y(4k+2)$, and use $y(4k+2)$ to compute $y(4k+3)$, at the expense of an increase in the system latency, which leads to a significant reduction in hardware complexity. This is referred to as *incremental block processing* and $y(4k+1)$, $y(4k+2)$, $y(4k+3)$ are computed *incrementally*.

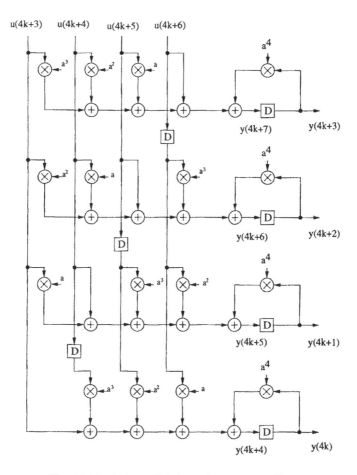

Fig. 10.15   A 4-parallel 1st-order recursive filter.

Example 10.5.2 *Consider the 1st-order filter in Example 10.5.1. To derive its 4-parallel filter structure with the minimum hardware complexity instead of simply repeating the hardware 4 times as in Fig. 10.15, the incremental computation technique can be used to reduce hardware complexity. First, design the circuit for computing $y(4k)$ (same as in Fig. 10.14). Then, derive $y(4k + 1)$ from $y(4k)$ using*

$$y(4k + 1) = ay(4k) + u(4k). \qquad (10.53)$$

Similarly, $y(4k + 2)$ can be computed from $y(4k + 1)$ and $y(4k + 3)$ from $y(4k + 2)$. The complete architecture is shown in Fig. 10.16. Notice that the hardware complexity has been reduced to $2L - 1$ from L^2 at the expense of an increase in the computation time for $y(4k + 1)$, $y(4k + 2)$, and $y(4k + 3)$. ∎

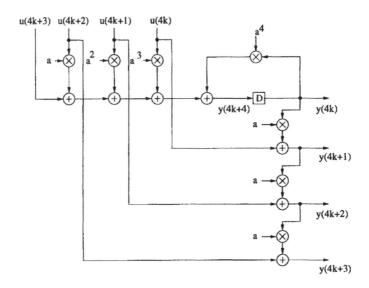

Fig. 10.16   Incremental block filter structure with $L = 4$.

Example 10.5.3 *Consider a 2nd-order IIR filter described by the transfer function shown in (10.54).*

$$H(z) = \frac{(1 + z^{-1})^2}{1 - \frac{5}{4}z^{-1} + \frac{3}{8}z^{-2}} \qquad (10.54)$$

The pole zero locations of this filter are shown in Fig. 10.17. Derive a 3-parallel IIR filter where in every clock cycle 3 inputs are processed and 3 outputs are generated.

Since the filter order is 2, 2 outputs need to be updated independently and the 3rd output can be computed incrementally outside the feedback loop using the 2 updated outputs. Assume that $y(3k)$ and $y(3k + 1)$ are computed using loop update operations and $y(3k + 2)$ is computed incrementally. From the transfer function, we have

$$y(n) = \frac{5}{4}y(n - 1) - \frac{3}{8}y(n - 2) + f(n), \qquad (10.55)$$

where $f(n) = u(n) + 2u(n - 1) + u(n - 2)$. The loop update process for the 3-parallel system is shown in Fig. 10.18 where $y(3k + 3)$ and $y(3k + 4)$ are computed using $y(3k)$ and $y(3k + 1)$. The computation of $y(3k + 3)$ using $y(3k)$ and $y(3k+1)$ can be carried out if $y(n+3)$ can be computed using $y(n)$ and $y(n + 1)$. Similarly $y(3k + 4)$ can be computed using $y(3k)$ and $y(3k + 1)$ if $y(n + 4)$ can be expressed in terms of $y(n)$ and $y(n + 1)$, as illustrated in Fig. 10.19. These state update operations correspond to clustered look-ahead operation for $M = 2$ and 3 cases. The 2-stage and 3-stage clustered look-ahead

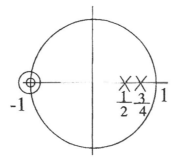

Fig. 10.17   Pole zero plots for the transfer function.

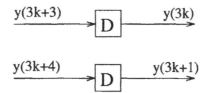

Fig. 10.18   Loop update for block size = 3.

equations are derived as:

$$
\begin{aligned}
y(n) &= \tfrac{5}{4}y(n-1) - \tfrac{3}{8}y(n-2) + f(n) \\
&= \tfrac{5}{4}[\tfrac{5}{4}y(n-2) - \tfrac{3}{8}y(n-3) + f(n-1)] - \tfrac{3}{8}y(n-2) + f(n) \\
&= \tfrac{19}{16}[\tfrac{5}{4}y(n-3) - \tfrac{3}{8}y(n-4) + f(n-2)] - \tfrac{15}{32}y(n-3) \\
&\quad + \tfrac{5}{4}f(n-1) + f(n).
\end{aligned}
\tag{10.56}
$$

Substituting $n = 3k + 3$ and $n = 3k + 4$ into (10.56), we have the following 2 loop update equations:

$$
y(3k+3) = \frac{19}{16}y(3k+1) - \frac{15}{32}y(3k) + \frac{5}{4}f(3k+2) + f(3k+3) \tag{10.57}
$$

$$
y(3k+4) = \frac{65}{64}y(3k+1) - \frac{57}{128}y(3k) + \frac{19}{16}f(3k+2) + \frac{5}{4}f(3k+3) + f(3k+4). \tag{10.58}
$$

The output $y(3k + 2)$ can be obtained incrementally as follows:

$$
y(3k+2) = \frac{5}{4}y(3k+1) - \frac{3}{8}y(3k) + f(3k+2). \tag{10.59}
$$

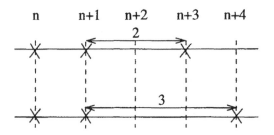

Fig. 10.19   Relationship of the recursion outputs.

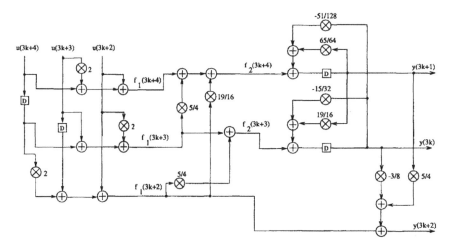

Fig. 10.20   Block structure of the 2nd-order IIR filter ($L = 3$).

The block structure is shown in Fig. 10.20. ∎

Comments

- The original sequential system has 2 poles at $\frac{1}{2}, \frac{3}{4}$. Now consider the pole locations of the new parallel system. Rewrite the 2 state update equations in matrix form:

$$
\begin{pmatrix} y(3k+3) \\ y(3k+4) \end{pmatrix} = \begin{pmatrix} -\frac{15}{32} & \frac{19}{16} \\ -\frac{57}{128} & \frac{65}{64} \end{pmatrix} \begin{pmatrix} y(3k) \\ y(3k+1) \end{pmatrix} + \begin{pmatrix} f_1 \\ f_2 \end{pmatrix} \quad (10.60)
$$

Denote the system matrix as A. The eigenvalues of A are $(\frac{1}{2})^3, (\frac{3}{4})^3$, which are the poles of the new parallel system. Therefore, the parallel system is more stable. Also note that the parallel system has the same number of poles as the original system.

- For a 2nd-order IIR filter (N=2), there are total $3L + [(L - 2) + (L - 1)] + 4 + 2(L - 2) = 7L - 3$ multiplication operations, in which the 1st term is due to the numerator part, the 2nd term is due to the overhead of loop update, the 3rd term is the loop multiplications, and the 4th term is due to the incremental computation. As can be seen, the multiplication complexity is a linear function of block size L. This multiplication complexity can be further reduced by use of fast parallel filter structures and substructure sharing of incrementally computed outputs (see Problems 17 and 18).

In general, for an N-th order IIR filter, its L-level incremental parallel processing architecture can be obtained by computing the first N output samples $y(Lk)$, $y(Lk+1)$, $\cdots$, $y(Lk+N-1)$ independently using loop update equations obtained by clustered look-ahead technique and then computing the remaining $L - N$ samples $y(Lk + N)$, $\cdots$, $y(Lk + L - 1)$ incrementally using the previous N output samples. Note that for the case when $L < N$, the incremental technique is not applicable.

Parallel filters can also be used to reduce the number of multiplications in multirate systems. In a system containing decimators, only one output needs to be computed. This can be achieved either by using an incremental block filter and retaining the first output, or by using scattered look-ahead to update the desired output. Which approach is better depends on the values of the filter order and the decimation ration (see Problem 19). Similarly, in the case of systems containing expanders, no multiplications need to be carried out for 0 inputs.

10.6 COMBINED PIPELINING AND PARALLEL PROCESSING FOR IIR FILTERS

Pipelining and parallel processing can also be combined for IIR filters to achieve a speedup in sample rate by a factor $L \times M$, where L denotes the levels of block processing and M denotes stages of pipelining, or to achieve power reduction at the same speed.

Example 10.6.1 *Consider the 1st-order IIR filter with transfer function*

$$H(z) = \frac{1}{1 - az^{-1}}. \tag{10.61}$$

Derive the filter structure with 4-level pipelining and 3-level block processing, i.e., $M = 4$ and $L = 3$.

Because the filter order is 1, only 1 loop update operation is required. The other 3 outputs can be computed incrementally. Since pipelining level $M = 4$, the loop must contain 4 delay elements, as shown in Fig. 10.21. Since the block

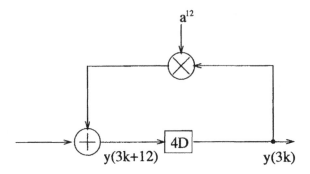

Fig. 10.21   Loop update for the pipelined block system.

size $L=3$, each delay element represents a block delay, which corresponds to 3 sample delays. Therefore, $y(3k + 12)$ needs to be expressed in terms of $y(3k)$ and inputs (see Fig. 10.21). This can be done using look-ahead as follows:

$$
\begin{aligned}
y(n) &= ay(n-1) + u(n) \\
&= a^2 y(n-2) + au(n-1) + u(n) \\
&= \cdots \\
&= a^{12} y(n-12) + a^{11} u(n-11) + a^{10} u(n-10) + \cdots + u(n)
\end{aligned}
\tag{10.62}
$$

Substituting $n = 3k + 12$, we get:

$$
\begin{aligned}
y(3k + 12) =\ & a^{12} y(3k) \\
& + a^{11} u(3k+1) + a^{10} u(3k+2) + a^9 u(3k+3) \\
& + a^8 u(3k+4) + a^7 u(3k+5) + a^6 u(3k+6) \\
& + a^5 u(3k+7) + a^4 u(3k+8) + a^3 u(3k+9) \\
& + a^2 u(3k+10) + au(3k+11) + u(3k+12) \\
=\ & a^{12} y(3k) + a^6 f_2(3k+6) + a^3 f_1(3k+9) + f_1(3k+12),
\end{aligned}
\tag{10.63}
$$

in which

$$
\begin{aligned}
f_1(3k+12) &= a^2 u(3k+10) + au(3k+11) + u(3k+12), \\
f_2(3k+12) &= a^3 f_1(3k+9) + f_1(3k+12).
\end{aligned}
\tag{10.64}
$$

The parallel-pipelined filter structure is shown in Fig. 10.22. ∎

Comments The parallel pipelined filter has 4 poles: $a^3, -a^3, ja^3, -ja^3$. Since the pipelining level is 4 and the filter order is 1, there are total 4 poles in the new system, which are separated by the same angular distance. Since the block size is 3, we expect the distance of the poles from the origin to be $|a^3|$.

It is noted that the decomposition method is used here in the pipelining phase. The multiplication complexity (assuming the level of pipelining M to be power of 2) can be calculated as $(L-1) + \log_2 M + 1 + (L-1) =$

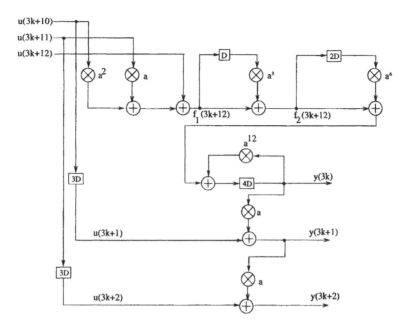

Fig. 10.22   The filter structure of the pipelined block system.

$2L - 1 + \log_2 M$. It is linear with respect to variable L, logarithmic with respect to M and additive with respect to L and M.

Example 10.6.2 *Consider the 2nd-order filter in Example 10.5.3 again. The goal here is to design a pipelined block system for L=3 and M=2. Fig. 10.23 shows the loop update operations for the system. A method similar to clustered look-ahead can be used to update $y(3k + 6)$ and $y(3k + 7)$ using $y(3k)$ and $y(3k + 1)$. Then by index substitution, the final system of equations can be derived. Suppose the system update matrix is A. Since the poles of the original system are $\frac{1}{2}$ and $\frac{3}{4}$, the eigenvalues of A can be verified to be $(\frac{1}{2})^6, (\frac{3}{4})^6$. The poles of the new parallel pipelined second-order filter are the square roots of eigenvalues of A, i.e., $(\frac{1}{2})^3, -(\frac{1}{2})^3, (\frac{3}{4})^3, -(\frac{3}{4})^3$.* ∎

Comments   In general, a systematic approach can be used to compute the pole locations of the new parallel pipelined system following the procedure given here:

1. Write the loop update equations using LM-level look-ahead, where M and L denote the level of pipelining and parallel processing, respectively.

2. Write the state space representation of the parallel pipelined filter, where state matrix A has dimension $N \times N$ and N is the filter order.

3. Compute the eigenvalues λ_i of matrix A, $1 \le i \le N$.

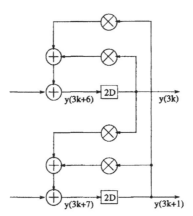

Fig. 10.23   Loop update for the pipelined block system.

4. The NM poles of the new parallel pipelined system correspond to the M-th roots of the eigenvalues of A, $\lambda_i^{\frac{1}{M}}$.

10.7   LOW-POWER IIR FILTER DESIGN USING PIPELINING AND PARALLEL PROCESSING

As illustrated in Chapter 3, pipelining and parallel processing can be used to reduce the power consumption of a system by reducing the supply voltage.

Example 10.7.1 *Consider a low-power implementation of the following 4-th order Chebyshev low-pass filter [13]*

$$H(z) = \frac{0.001836(1+z^{-1})^4}{(1-1.5548z^{-1}+0.6493z^{-2})(1-1.4996z^{-1}+0.8482z^{-2})}.$$

Assume that the capacitance due to the multipliers is dominant and that the capacitance due to the adders can be neglected. Also, assume the supply voltage of the original system to be 5 V and the CMOS threshold voltage to be 1 V. By scattered look-ahead technique with power-of-2 decomposition, the 4-level pipelinable transfer function is given by $N(z)/D(z)$ where

$$
\begin{aligned}
N(z) &= 0.001836(1+z^{-1})^4 \times \\
&\quad (1+1.5548z^{-1}+0.6493z^{-2})(1+1.4996z^{-1}+0.8482z^{-2}) \times \\
&\quad (1+1.1188z^{-2}+0.4216z^{-4})(1+0.5524z^{-2}+0.7194z^{-4}), \\
D(z) &= (1-0.4085z^{-4}+0.1777z^{-8})(1+1.1337z^{-4}+0.5175z^{-8}).
\end{aligned}
$$

Power consumption can be reduced by using pipelining without altering the sample speed. Since the pipelined system has a shorter critical path than the *original system, this smaller amount of charging capacitance can be charged or discharged during the same clock period as the original system. Therefore, the supply voltage of the pipelined system can be reduced to βV_0, where $\beta < 1$ and V_0 is the supply voltage of the original system. The propagation delay for the nonpipelined system is*

$$T_{pd} = \frac{C_{charge} \times 5}{\kappa(5-1)^2}.$$

For the 4-level pipelined system, the propagation delay T_{pd} is

$$T_{pd} = \frac{C_{charge}}{4} \frac{5\beta}{\kappa(5\beta-1)^2}.$$

By equating the previous 2 equations for the propagation time T_{pd}, we obtain $\beta = 0.476$. Therefore, the supply voltage for the pipelined system can be reduced to 2.38 V. Notice that the clock periods for both the original filter and the pipelined filter are the same as T_{pd}. The sample period is also equal to T_{pd}. Therefore, the power for the original system is

$$P_{seq} = \frac{C_{total}^{(seq)} \times 5^2}{T_{pd}} = m_{seq} C_M 5^2 f_s,$$

where $m_{seq} = 5$ represents the number of multiplication operations in the original system and C_M represents the capacitance of a single multiplier. The power consumption for the pipelined system is

$$P_{pip} = \frac{C_{total}^{(pip)} \times 2.38^2}{T_{pd}} = m_{pip} C_M (2.38)^2 f_s,$$

where $m_{pip} = 13$ are the number of multipliers in the 4-level pipelined system. Then,

$$Ratio = \frac{P_{pip}}{P_{seq}} = \left(\frac{13}{5}\right)\left(\frac{2.38}{5}\right)^2 = 0.5891. \tag{10.65}$$

Therefore, the power consumption of the 4-level pipelined system is 58.91% of that of the nonpipelined system. ∎

Example 10.7.2 *Consider the 2nd-order IIR filter in Example 10.5.3. The input output relation is described by*

$$y(n) = \frac{5}{4}y(n-1) - \frac{3}{8}y(n-2) + u(n) + 2u(n-1) + u(n-2). \tag{10.66}$$

The filter structure is shown in Fig. 10.24. Consider the 3-parallel filter derived in Example 10.5.3. Now parallel processing is used to reduce the power consumption. Assume the sample speed remains the same for both the parallel system and the sequential system. Since 3 outputs are generated each clock

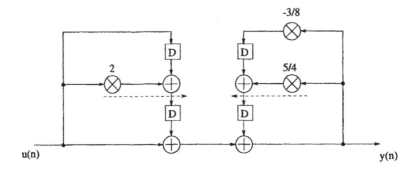

Fig. 10.24   The structure of a 2nd-order IIR filter.

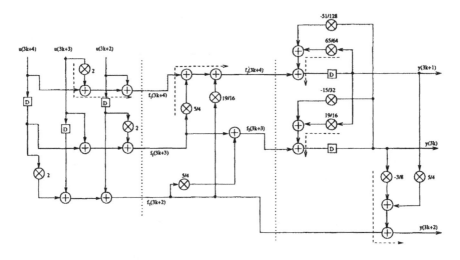

Fig. 10.25   The structure of a pipelined 3-parallel second-order IIR filter.

cycle in the 3-parallel system, in order to maintain the same sample rate, the clock cycle of the parallel system should be 3 times the sample period, or 3 times the clock cycle of the sequential filter. The critical path of the sequential filter is 1 multiply-add time. To maintain the same critical path for the parallel system, some pipelining latches are placed across the feed-forward cutsets denoted by the dashed lines in Fig. 10.25. Then the critical path for the parallel filter is one-multiply-two-add time. Assume both the capacitance and the computation times are dominated by the multiplier. Those for the adders and latches are ignored. This implies that there is three times more time for the parallel filter to charge/discharge the same amount of capacitance (capacitance of 1 multiplier C_M) along the critical path, which in turn indicates that the supply voltage of the 3-parallel IIR filter can drop to βV_0, where $\beta < 1$ and $V_0 = 5.0$ V is the supply voltage of the sequential filter. Assume the *threshold voltage V_t to be 0.6 V. The propagation delay or the clock cycle for the sequential filter is*

$$T_{seq} = \frac{C_M V_0}{k(V_0 - V_t)^2}. \tag{10.67}$$

The propagation delay or the clock cycle of the parallel filter is

$$T_{par} = \frac{C_M \beta V_0}{k(\beta V_0 - V_t)^2}. \tag{10.68}$$

By solving equation $T_{par} = 3T_{seq}$, i.e.,

$$3 \cdot \frac{V_0}{(V_0 - V_t)^2} = \frac{\beta V_0}{(\beta V_0 - V_t)^2}, \tag{10.69}$$

we get $\beta=0.4673$. Therefore, the supply voltage for the 3-parallel filter can be reduced to $\beta V_0 = 2.3365$ V. The total power consumption of the sequential system is

$$P_{seq} = 3C_M V_0^2 f_s. \tag{10.70}$$

The total power consumption of the 3-parallel system is

$$P_{par} = 12C_M(\beta V_0)^2 \frac{f_s}{3} = 4\beta^2 C_M V_0^2 f_s. \tag{10.71}$$

Then we have

$$Ratio = \frac{P_{par}}{P_{seq}} = \frac{4\beta^2}{3} = 29.116\%. \tag{10.72}$$

Therefore, the 3-parallel IIR filter consumes 29.116% power of the original sequential filter. ∎

Comments   Example 10.7.1 illustrates how pipelining itself can be used to reduce the power consumption of an IIR filter. Example 10.7.2 illustrates how parallel processing can be utilized to lower power consumption. These two techniques can also be combined to obtain either faster or lower power IIR filter architectures.

10.8 PIPELINED ADAPTIVE DIGITAL FILTERS

Adaptive digital filters are difficult to pipeline due to the presence of long feedback loops. Techniques such as look-ahead computation can be used to pipeline these filters but the resulting systems are not practical for integrated circuit implementations due to the large increase in hardware [14]. The look-ahead computations maintain exact input-output mapping in frequency shaping filters (such as IIR digital filters), but such exact input-output mapping is not necessary in an adaptive filter, since the coefficients continue to adapt until they converge. However, analysis of the adaptation behavior in adaptive filters as measured by the misadjustment error and adaptation time constant is important. The misadjustment error is an indication of the error between the solution achieved by the adaptive filter and the optimal solution. The adaptation time constant is an indicator of the speed of convergence; the lower the time constant, the faster the convergence.

In this section, *relaxed look-ahead* transformation technique is used to pipeline the adaptive filters with little or no increase in hardware at the expense of marginal degradation in the adaptation behavior. The relaxed look-ahead transformation is based on certain relaxations or approximations of the look-ahead representation. Three forms of relaxed look-ahead are introduced including *product*, *sum*, and *delay* relaxations. Different types of relaxed look-ahead lead to different forms of pipelined topologies. Thus, unlike in look-ahead transformations where the input-output mapping is exact and the transformation is unique, relaxed look-ahead can result in a family of pipelined topologies each with different adaptation behavior. In addition, the approximations used in relaxed look-ahead are typically valid after the filter has converged or in the final stage of convergence but are not valid during the initial convergence period. Therefore, the adaptation behavior of these pipelined adaptive filters should be analyzed using stochastic techniques.

This section addresses the relaxed look-ahead transformation and its application to pipeline the LMS adaptive filter and the stochastic gradient adaptive lattice filter.

10.8.1   Relaxed Look-Ahead

Consider the 1st-order time-varying recursion given by

$$y(n + 1) = a(n)y(n) + u(n) \tag{10.73}$$

with varying coefficients $a(n)$. Using look-ahead, $y(n + M)$ can be expressed in terms of $y(n)$ as follows:

$$\begin{aligned}
y(n + M) &= \prod_{i=0}^{M-1} a(n + M - 1 - i)y(n) \\
&+ \sum_{i=1}^{M-1} [\prod_{j=0}^{i-1} a(n + M - 1 - j)]u(n + M - 1 - i) + u(n + M - 1).
\end{aligned} \tag{10.74}$$

The computation structure corresponding to (10.74) is shown in Fig. 10.26 for $M = 4$. In general, the look-ahead transformation creates $M - 1$ extra delay elements into the recursive loop which can be used to pipeline the multiply-add operation in the loop. For example, the iteration period of the structure in Fig. 10.26 is now limited by $(T_m + T_a)/4$. Note that this transformation does not alter the input-output behavior. This invariance with respect to the input-output behavior has been achieved at the expense of the look-ahead overhead introduced by the 2nd term in the right-hand side (RHS) of (10.74),

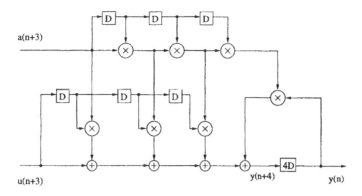

Fig. 10.26 A 4-level look-ahead pipelined 1st-order recursion.

which is dependent on the level of pipelining M. This overhead can be very expensive. However, under certain circumstances we can substitute approximate expressions to simplify the terms in the RHS of (10.74). Depending on the application at hand, different types of approximations (or relaxations) may be employed. This is referred to as *relaxed look-ahead.*

In adaptive filtering, we are more concerned with the stochastic behavior rather than the input-output mapping. As a result, the relaxed look-ahead technique can be applied to pipeline the adaptive filter with marginal hardware penalty at the expense of sacrificing the adaptation behavior to some extent. Three forms of relaxations are used to pipeline the adaptive filters, including product, sum, and delay relaxations. Different relaxations result in different pipelined topologies. Thus, families of pipelined adaptive filters can be obtained by the use of relaxed look-ahead.

10.8.1.1 Product Relaxation If the magnitude of $a(n)$ is close to unity, then $a(n)$ can be replaced by $(1 - \varepsilon(n))$, where $\varepsilon(n)$ is close to zero. Then we have the following approximation

$$\prod_{i=0}^{M-1} a(n + i) \approx a(n + M - 1)^M = (1 - \varepsilon(n + M - 1))^M$$

$$= 1 - M\varepsilon(n + M - 1) = 1 - M(1 - a(n + M - 1)). \quad (10.75)$$

Furthermore, if $u(n + i)$ is close to zero, then $[\prod_{j=0}^{i-1} a(n + M - 1 - j)]u(n + M - 1 - i)$ can be approximated as $u(n + M - 1 - i)$. Therefore, (10.74) can be approximated as

$$y(n + M) = (1 - M(1 - a(n + M - 1)))y(n)$$
$$+ \sum_{i=0}^{M-1} u(n + M - 1 - i). \quad (10.76)$$

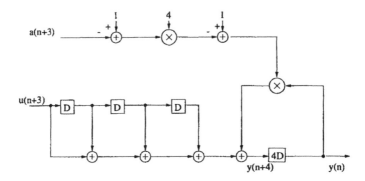

Fig. 10.27 A 4-level product-relaxed look-ahead pipelined 1st-order recursion.

Hence, (10.76) is the result of application of an M-level relaxed look-ahead with product relaxation to (10.73). The computation structure corresponding to the 1st-order recursion in (10.73) with 4-level product-relaxed pipelining is shown in Fig. 10.27. Since $a(n)$ is assumed to be close to 1, then $\prod_{j=0}^{M-1} a(n + M - 1 - j)$ can also be approximated as $a(n + M - 1)$. Then another approximation of (10.74) can be obtained as

$$y(n + M) = a(n + M - 1)y(n)$$
$$+ \sum_{i=0}^{M-1} u(n + M - 1 - i). \tag{10.77}$$

10.8.1.2 *Sum relaxation* If the input $u(n)$ varies slowly over M cycles, then $\sum_{i=0}^{M-1} u(n + M - 1 - i)$ can be approximated as $Mu(n)$. This leads to:

$$y(n + M) = \prod_{i=0}^{M-1} a(n + M - 1 - i)y(n) + Mu(n). \tag{10.78}$$

If $u(n)$ is also close to zero, then $Mu(n)$ can be approximated by $u(n)$ to obtain

$$y(n + M) = \prod_{i=0}^{M-1} a(n + M - 1 - i)y(n) + u(n). \tag{10.79}$$

Thus, equations (10.78) and (10.79) are the results of application of M-level relaxed look-ahead with sum relaxations to (10.73). The computation structure of the 1st-order recursion with 4 levels of sum-relaxed pipelining is shown in Fig. 10.28.

10.8.1.3 *Delay Relaxation* Consider the recursion

$$y(n) = y(n - 1) + a(n)u(n) \tag{10.80}$$

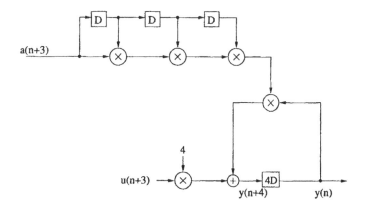

Fig. 10.28 A 4-level sum-relaxed look-ahead pipelined 1st-order recursion.

and its M-level look-ahead pipelined version

$$y(n) = y(n - M) + \sum_{i=0}^{M-1} a(n - i)u(n - i). \tag{10.81}$$

The delay relaxation involves the use of delayed input $u(n - M')$ and delayed coefficient $a(n - M')$ in (10.81). This approximation is based on the assumption that the product $a(n)u(n)$ is more or less constant over M' samples [15]. In general, this assumption is a reasonable approximation for stationary or slowly varying product $a(n)u(n)$. Thus, (10.81) is approximated as:

$$y(n) = y(n - M) + \sum_{i=0}^{M-1} a(n - M' - i)u(n - M' - i). \tag{10.82}$$

These relaxations constitute the relaxed look-ahead technique. The relaxations may be applied individually or in different combinations to derive a rich variety of architectures. (This is in contrast to look-ahead, where there is a one-to-one mapping between the resulting pipelined architecture and the original one.) Each of these architectures would have different convergence characteristics, which depend upon the nature of the approximations made and their validity in the application. The relaxed look-ahead is a transformation technique in the stochastic sense, since the average output profile is maintained while the input-output behavior has been modified.

10.8.2 Pipelined LMS Adaptive Filter

The LMS algorithm can be described as

$$e(n) = \quad d(n) - \hat{d}(n) = d(n) - \mathbf{W}^T(n - 1)\mathbf{U}(n) \tag{10.83}$$

$$\mathbf{W}(n) = \qquad \mathbf{W}(n-1) + \mu e(n)\mathbf{U}(n). \qquad (10.84)$$

The derivation and block diagrams of this adaptive algorithm can be found in Chapter 1 (see Section 1.2.4.1). There are two recursive loops in the LMS architecture: the weight update loop and the error feedback loop. To derive the pipelined adaptive filter, we start with the LMS equations and attempt to apply look-ahead directly. This leads to

$$
\begin{aligned}
\mathbf{W}(n) &= \mathbf{W}(n-1) + \mu e(n)\mathbf{U}(n) \\
&= \mathbf{W}(n - M_2) + \sum_{i=0}^{M_2-1} \mu e(n-i)\mathbf{U}(n-i) \qquad (10.85)
\end{aligned}
$$

where M_2 is the number of delays in the weight update loop. This transformation results in M_2 latches in the weight update loop, which can be retimed to pipeline the add operation at any desired level. However, in order to apply look-ahead exactly, $e(n)$ needs to be expressed as a function of $\mathbf{W}(n - M_2)$ and substituted into (10.85), which would make the resulting equation complicated and therefore very hardware expensive. This overhead can be reduced by applying relaxed look-ahead.

The delay relaxation introduces M_1 delays in the error feedback loop (EFP). Applying the delay relaxation to (10.85), we get the following equation:

$$\mathbf{W}(n) = \mathbf{W}(n - M_2) + \mu \sum_{i=0}^{M_2-1} e(n - M_1 - i)\mathbf{U}(n - M_1 - i). \qquad (10.86)$$

The validity of this summation is based on the assumption that the gradient estimate $e(n)\mathbf{U}(n)$ does not change much over M_1 samples. The hardware overhead in (10.86) is $N(M_2 - 1)$ adders and it can be further reduced using sum relaxation by taking M_2' terms, where $M_2' \leq M_2$. Thus, we get

$$\mathbf{W}(n) = \mathbf{W}(n - M_2) + \sum_{i=0}^{M_2'-1} \mu e(n - M_1 - i)\mathbf{U}(n - M_1 - i). \qquad (10.87)$$

This relaxation is valid for a slowly varying product $e(n)\mathbf{U}(n)$. Therefore, $e(n)$ can be written as

$$
\begin{aligned}
e(n) &= d(n) - \mathbf{W}^T(n-1)\mathbf{U}(n) \\
&= d(n) - [\mathbf{W}^T(n - M_2 - 1) \\
&\quad + \mu \sum_{i=0}^{M_2'-1} e(n - M_1 - i - 1)\mathbf{U}(n - M_1 - i - 1)]\mathbf{U}(n). \quad (10.88)
\end{aligned}
$$

Assuming μ is sufficiently small and replacing $\mathbf{W}(n - M_2 - 1)$ by $\mathbf{W}(n - M_2)$,

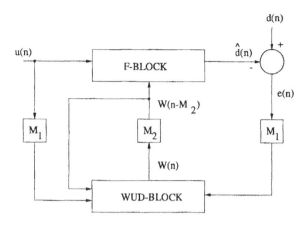

Fig. 10.29 System diagram of the PIPLMS architecture.

(10.88) can be approximated as

$$e(n) = d(n) - \mathbf{W}^T(n - M_2)\mathbf{U}(n). \tag{10.89}$$

The pipelined LMS filter (PIPLMS) is completely described by (10.87) and (10.89) and its hardware overhead is $N(M_2' - 1)$ adders [16]. The system diagram of this PIPLMS architecture is shown in Fig. 10.29. The pipelined LMS filters can also be used to design pipelined adaptive decision-feedback equalizers [17].

10.8.3 Pipelining of Stochastic-Gradient Lattice Architecture

10.8.3.1 Pipelined Stochastic-Gradient Lattice Architecture (PIPSGLA) The stochastic-gradient adaptive algorithm can be completely described by the following equations:

$$
\begin{aligned}
k_m(n + 1) = &\ [1 - \beta_m(e_f^2(n|m - 1) + e_b^2(n - 1|m - 1))]k_m(n) \\
&+ 2\beta_m e_f(n|m - 1)e_b(n - 1|m - 1)
\end{aligned} \tag{10.90}
$$

$$
\begin{aligned}
S(n + 1|m - 1) = &\ (1 - \beta)S(n|m - 1) \\
&+ e_f^2(n|m - 1) + e_b^2(n - 1|m - 1)
\end{aligned} \tag{10.91}
$$

$$\beta_m = \frac{1}{S(n|m-1)} \tag{10.92}$$

$$e_f(n|m) = e_f(n|m - 1) - k_m(n)e_b(n - 1|m - 1) \tag{10.93}$$

$$e_b(n|m) = e_b(n-1|m-1) - k_m(n)e_f(n|m-1). \qquad (10.94)$$

Equations (10.90)–(10.92) and (10.93)–(10.94) are referred to as the adaptation and order-update equations, respectively. The block diagram of the stochastic-gradient lattice architecture (SGLA) is shown in Fig. 1.4 in Chapter 1. Readers may refer to Section 1.2.4.2 for detailed derivations. The SGLA contains 2 recursive loops, the recursions to compute k_m and S, with computation times $T_m + T_a$. Therefore, the pipelining of the SGLA proceeds in 2 steps. The 1st step involves interstage pipelining where delay elements are placed across the feed-forward cutsets along the lattice stages. The 2nd step addresses loop pipelining where relaxed look-ahead is applied to pipeline the recursive loops in the adaptive filter. As the lattice stages are connected in a nonrecursive fashion, the interstage pipelining is trivial and does not change the input-output behavior. Therefore, this step is omitted and the PIPSGLA architectures are derived by applying relaxed look-ahead to the 2 recursive loops in SGLA.

We first apply an M-stage relaxed look-ahead with sum relaxation of (10.79) to (10.91), which describes the recursive computation of the input power, to obtain

$$
\begin{aligned}
S(n+M|m-1) &= (1-\beta)^M S(n|m-1) \\
&\quad + e_f^2(n|m-1) + e_b^2(n|m-1), \qquad (10.95)
\end{aligned}
$$

where $(1-\beta)^M$ can be precomputed. Similarly, the application of an M-stage relaxed look-ahead with sum relaxation of (10.78) to (10.90) leads to

$$
\begin{aligned}
k_m(n+M) = {}& [1 - \beta_m(n)(e_f^2(n|m-1) + e_b^2(n-1|m-1))]^M k_m(n) \\
&+ 2M\beta_m(n)e_f(n|m-1)e_f(n-1|m-1). \qquad (10.96)
\end{aligned}
$$

It can be proved that the bracketed part in the first term is close to unity during the final stage of convergence. Therefore, product relaxation (10.75) can be applied to (10.96) to obtain

$$
\begin{aligned}
k_m(n+M) = {}& [1 - M\beta_m(n)(e_f^2(n|m-1) + e_b^2(n-1|m-1))]k_m(n) \\
&+ 2M\beta_m(n)e_f(n|m-1)e_f(n-1|m-1). \qquad (10.97)
\end{aligned}
$$

Assuming that the inputs to an m-th lattice stage are $e_f(n|m-1)$ and $e_b(n|m-1)$, the following equations describe the time update equations of the 1st PIPSGLA architecture, referred to as PIPSGLA1:

PIPSGLA1

$$
\begin{aligned}
k_m(n+M) = {}& [1 - M\beta_m(n)(e_f^2(n|m-1) + e_b^2(n-1|m-1))]k_m(n) \\
&+ 2M\beta_m(n)e_f(n|m-1)e_b(n-1|m-1) \qquad (10.98)
\end{aligned}
$$

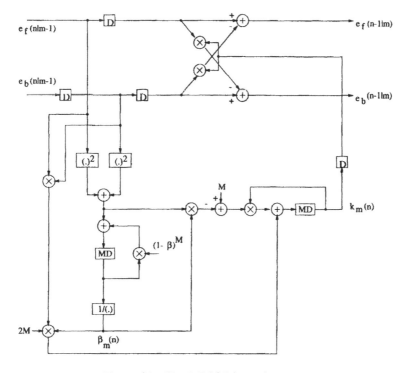

Fig. 10.30 The PIPSGLA1 architecture.

$$S(n + M|m - 1) = \begin{aligned} &(1 - \beta)^M S(n|m - 1) \\ &+ e_f^2(n|m - 1) + e_b^2(n - 1|m - 1). \end{aligned} \tag{10.99}$$

The PIPSGLA1 architecture is shown in Fig. 10.30 [18].

An alternative pipelined architecture PIPSGLA2 can be obtained by simply introducing M latches into the recursive loops in (10.90) and (10.91). This corresponds to the application of the sum relaxation defined in (10.79) and the product relaxation defined in (10.77) to both (10.90) and (10.91). The 2 time update equations for PIPSGLA2 are given as follows:

PIPSGLA2

$$k_m(n + M) = \begin{aligned} &[1 - \beta_m(n)(e_f^2(n|m - 1) + e_b^2(n - 1|m - 1))]k_m(n) \\ &+ 2\beta_m(n)e_f(n|m - 1)e_b(n - 1|m - 1) \end{aligned} \tag{10.100}$$

$$S(n + M|m - 1) = \begin{aligned} &(1 - \beta)S(n|m - 1) \\ &+ e_f^2(n|m - 1) + e_b^2(n - 1|m - 1). \end{aligned} \tag{10.101}$$

10.8.3.2 Convergence Analysis of PIPSGLA As mentioned before, convergence analysis needs to be carried out for the pipelined architectures obtained from relaxed look-ahead technique. The convergence analysis of PIPSGLA1 and PIPSGLA2 is presented briefly in this section. We analyze a single lattice stage assuming its inputs are stationary. It is also assumed that the reflection coefficient $k_m(n_1)$ at time instance n_1 is independent of $e_f(n|m-1)$ and $e_b(n|m-1)$ for all $n < n_1$. This is known as the independence assumption. In order to evaluate the higher order statistical expectations, we also assume that $e_f(n|m-1)$ and $e_b(n|m-1)$ are jointly Gaussian. Based on the foregoing assumptions, the adaptive behavior of the various architectures are analyzed and compared with respect to the following quantities:

- Range of β for convergence/stability

- Rate of convergence, τ

- Misadjustment error.

Expressions of these quantities are derived for PIPSGLA1. Expressions for SGLA and PIPSGLA2 can be obtained similarly. Notice that due to the assumption made, our aim is to obtain a comparative analysis of the various architectures and not to provide an absolute measure of their performance.

Range of β for Convergence   Taking the expectation of (10.98) of PIPSGLA1, we get

$$E[k_m(n+M)] = [1 - M\frac{E(e_f^2 + e_b^2)}{E(S)}]E(k_m) + \frac{2ME(e_f e_b)}{E(S)} \qquad (10.102)$$

where $E[\cdot]$ represents the expectation operation. To find the optimum value $k_{m,opt}$ which minimizes the error, consider the forward and backward error update equations,

$$\begin{aligned} e_f(n|m) &= e_f(n|m-1) - k_m(n)e_b(n-1|m-1) \\ e_b(n|m) &= e_b(n-1|m-1) - k_m(n)e_f(n|m-1). \end{aligned} \qquad (10.103)$$

In what follows, the time index and the stage number are dropped for simplicity. Note that the quantities on the left side correspond to stage m while quantities on the right side correspond to stage $m-1$. Summing the square of the 2 equations in (10.103), we get

$$e_f^2 + e_b^2 = e_f^2 + e_b^2 - 4e_f e_b k_m + k_m^2(e_f^2 + e_b^2). \qquad (10.104)$$

Now, we can compute the gradient of $E[e_f^2(n|m) + e_b^2(n|m)]$ with respect to $k_m(n)$. The optimum value of k_m (denoted as $k_{m,opt}$) is obtained by equating this gradient to zero:

$$\frac{\partial E(e_f^2 + e_b^2)}{\partial k_m} = -4E(e_f e_b) + 2k_m E[e_f^2 + e_b^2] = 0$$

$$\Rightarrow \qquad k_{m,opt} = \frac{2E(e_f e_b)}{E(e_f^2 + e_b^2)}. \qquad (10.105)$$

Taking the expectation of (10.99), we get

$$
\begin{aligned}
E[S] &= (1 - \beta)^M E[S] + E(c_f^2 + e_b^2) \\
\frac{E(e_f^2 + e_b^2)}{E(S)} &= 1 - (1 - \beta)^M \\
&= (1 - (1 - M\beta)) \qquad \text{if } \beta \text{ is small} \\
&= M\beta = \gamma. \qquad (10.106)
\end{aligned}
$$

Multiply both sides of the above equation by $k_{m,opt}$ to get

$$
\begin{aligned}
\frac{E(e_f^2 + e_b^2)}{E(S)} k_{m,opt} &= \gamma k_{m,opt} \\
&= \frac{2E(e_f e_b)}{E(S)}. \qquad (10.107)
\end{aligned}
$$

Substituting (10.106) and (10.107) into (10.102), we obtain

$$
\begin{aligned}
E[k_m(n + M)] &= (1 - M\gamma)E(k_m) + M\gamma k_{m,opt} \\
E[k_m(n + M) - k_{m,opt}] &= (1 - M\gamma)E(k_m) + (M\gamma - 1)k_{m,opt} \\
&= (1 - M\gamma)E[k_m(n) - k_{m,opt}]. \qquad (10.108)
\end{aligned}
$$

Let $v(n) = E[k_m(n) - k_{m,opt}]$ and rewrite (10.108) as

$$v(n + M) = (1 - M\gamma)v(n). \qquad (10.109)$$

Substituting $n = 0$ and $n = M$,

$$
\begin{aligned}
v(M) &= (1 - M\gamma)v(0) \qquad \text{for } n = 0 \\
v(2M) &= (1 - M\gamma)^2 v(0) \qquad \text{for } n = M. \qquad (10.110)
\end{aligned}
$$

Iterating repeatedly, we obtain

$$v(kM) = (1 - M\gamma)^k v(0), \ for \ n = kM. \qquad (10.111)$$

For the LHS (left-hand side) of (10.111) to converge to zero, it is sufficient that

$$
\begin{aligned}
|1 - M\gamma| &< 1 \\
-1 < 1 - M\gamma &< 1 \\
-2 < -M\gamma \qquad \text{and} \qquad -M\gamma &< 0 \\
0 < M\gamma &< 2
\end{aligned}
$$

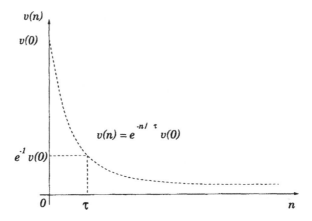

Fig. 10.31   Exponential decaying discrete sequence.

$$0 < M^2\beta < 2$$
$$0 < \beta < \frac{2}{M^2}. \tag{10.112}$$

Convergence Time Constant   Substituting $n = kM$ in (10.111), we have

$$
\begin{aligned}
v(n) &= (1 - M\gamma)^{n/M} v(0) \\
&= [(1 - M\gamma)^{1/M}]^n v(0). \tag{10.113}
\end{aligned}
$$

Consider the exponential decay curve shown in Fig. 10.31. When $n = \tau$, $v(\tau) = e^{-1}v(0)$. Therefore, equating the RHS of (10.113) to a decaying exponential with time-constant τ, we get

$$
\begin{aligned}
\frac{1}{e}v(0) &= [(1 - M\gamma)^{1/M}]^\tau v(0) \\
\ln\frac{1}{e} &= \ln[(1 - M\gamma)^{1/M}]^\tau \\
\tau &= \frac{-\ln e}{\ln(1 - M\gamma)^{1/M}} \\
&= \frac{-1}{\ln(1 - M\gamma)^{1/M}}. \tag{10.114}
\end{aligned}
$$

Using the approximation

$$(1 - M\gamma)^{1/M} \approx 1 - (\frac{1}{M})M\gamma \approx 1 - \gamma \tag{10.115}$$

and

$$\ln(1 - x) \approx -x - \frac{x^2}{2} - \frac{x^3}{3} - \cdots \approx -x \tag{10.116}$$

(10.114) can be simplified as

$$
\begin{aligned}
\tau &= \frac{-1}{\ln(1 - M\gamma)^{1/M}} \approx \frac{-1}{-\gamma} \\
&= \frac{1}{\gamma} = \frac{1}{M\beta}.
\end{aligned} \tag{10.117}
$$

So, the speed of convergence increases as M increases.

Misadjustment Error The adaptation accuracy of an adaptive algorithm is defined in terms of its misadjustment error, which is defined as follows:

$$\mathcal{M} = \frac{E(J(\infty)) - J_{min}}{J_{min}} = \frac{E(J_{ex}(\infty))}{J_{min}}, \tag{10.118}$$

where $J(n)$ is the mean-squared error at time instance n and is defined as

$$J(n) = e_f^2(n|m) + e_b^2(n|m), \tag{10.119}$$

and $E(J(n))$ is its average and J_{ex} denotes the excess error. The notation J_{min} refers to the minimum mean-squared error, which would be obtained if the reflection coefficient $k_m(n)$ equalled the optimal value $k_{m,opt}$.

In order to get the closed form expressions for the misadjustment of SGLA, PIPSGLA1 and PIPSGLA2, certain simplifying assumptions need to be made. In particular, the assumptions made at the beginning of this section, the independence assumptions and the jointly Gaussian assumptions are often invoked. In addition, let

$$\sigma_e^2 = E[e_f^2(n|m - 1)] = E[e_b^2(n|m - 1)] \tag{10.120}$$

represent the input signal power. Next we first derive the expression for $E(J(n))$ or $E(J_{ex}(n))$, then derive some preliminary expressions and finally derive the expression for the misadjustment of PIPSGLA1.

It is known that if X_1, X_2, X_3, and X_4 are jointly Gaussian variables then

$$
\begin{aligned}
E[X_1 X_2 X_3 X_4] = {}& E[X_1 X_2]E[X_3 X_4] \\
& + E[X_1 X_3]E[X_2 X_4] + E[X_1 X_4]E[X_2 X_3].
\end{aligned} \tag{10.121}
$$

Using (10.122) and the expression for $k_{m,opt}$ in (10.105), it is trivial to show the validity of the following equations:

$$E[e_f(n|m - 1)e_b(n - 1|m - 1)] = k_{m,opt}\sigma_e^2 \tag{10.122}$$

$$E[e_f^2(n|m-1)e_b^2(n-1|m-1)] = (1 + 2k_{m,opt}^2)\sigma_e^4 \qquad (10.123)$$

$$E[e_f^3(n|m-1)e_b(n-1|m-1) + e_f(n|m-1)e_b^3(n-1|m-1)] = 6k_{m,opt}\sigma_e^4 \qquad (10.124)$$

$$E[(e_f^2(n|m-1) + e_b^2(n-1|m-1))^2] = (8 + 4k_{m,opt}^2)\sigma_e^4. \qquad (10.125)$$

From (10.106), it is known that

$$\frac{E[e_f^2 + e_b^2]}{E[S]} = \gamma \qquad (10.126)$$

and from (10.105)

$$k_{m,opt} = \frac{2E[e_f e_b]}{E[e_f^2 + e_b^2]}. \qquad (10.127)$$

Therefore, we have

$$\frac{E[e_f e_b]}{E[S]} = \frac{\gamma}{2}k_{m,opt}. \qquad (10.128)$$

Finally, we need to derive the expression for $E[S^2(n|m-1)]$. Squaring (10.99) and taking its expectation, we have

$$E[S^2] = (1-\beta)^{2M}E[S^2] + 2(1-\beta)^M E[S(e_f^2 + e_b^2)] + E[(e_f^2 + e_b^2)^2]. \qquad (10.129)$$

Multiplying both sides of (10.99) by $S(n|m-1)$ and taking its expectation, we get

$$E[S^2] = (1-\beta)^M E[S^2] + E[S(e_f^2 + e_b^2)], \qquad (10.130)$$

i.e.,

$$E[S(e_f^2 + e_b^2)] = [1 - (1-\beta)^M]E[S^2] \approx \gamma E[S^2]. \qquad (10.131)$$

Substituting (10.131) and (10.125) into (10.129), we get the desired expression

$$E[S^2] = \frac{(8 + 4k_{m,opt}^2)\sigma_e^4}{\gamma^2}. \qquad (10.132)$$

So far, we have derived all the preliminary expressions. Next we derive the expression for $E[J(n)]$. Notice that

$$\begin{aligned}
J(n) &= e_f^2(n|m) + e_b^2(n|m) \\
&= (e_f^2(n|m-1) + e_b^2(n-1|m-1))(1 + k_m^2(n)) \\
&\quad -4k_m(n)e_f(n|m-1)e_b(n-1|m-1). \qquad (10.133)
\end{aligned}$$

Therefore,

$$
\begin{aligned}
E[J(n)] &= E[e_f^2(n|m-1) + e_b^2(n-1|m-1)](1 + E[k_m^2(n)]) \\
&\quad -2E[k_m(n)] \cdot 2E[e_f(n|m-1)e_b(n-1|m-1)] \\
&= (1 + E[k_m^2(n)] - 2E[k_m(n)]k_{m,opt}) \\
&\quad \cdot E[e_f^2(n|m-1) + e_b^2(n-1|m-1)] \\
&= (1 + (E[k_m(n)] - k_{m,opt})^2 - k_{m,opt}^2 + E[k_m^2(n)] - E^2[k_m(n)]) \\
&\quad \cdot E[e_f^2(n|m-1) + e_b^2(n-1|m-1)] \\
&= (1 + v^2(n) - k_{m,opt}^2 + var(k_m(n))) \\
&\quad \cdot E[e_f^2(n|m-1) + e_b^2(n-1|m-1)].
\end{aligned}
\tag{10.134}
$$

Considering the limit as $n \to \infty$ ($v^2(n)$ approaches zero), we have

$$
\begin{aligned}
E[J(\infty)] &= (1 - k_{m,opt}^2 + var(k_m(\infty))) \cdot 2\sigma_e^2 \\
&= (1 - k_{m,opt}^2) \cdot 2\sigma_e^2 + var(k_m(\infty)) \cdot 2\sigma_e^2 \\
&= J_{min} + E[J_{ex}(\infty)],
\end{aligned}
\tag{10.135}
$$

where J_{min} represents the minimum error and J_{ex} represents the excess error. Therefore, the misadjustment error $\mathcal{M}$ for a lattice stage is given by

$$
\mathcal{M} = \frac{E[J_{ex}(\infty)]}{J_{min}} = \frac{var(k_m(\infty))}{(1 - k_{m,opt}^2)}.
\tag{10.136}
$$

Hence, all that remains to be done is to calculate the steady-state variance of the reflection coefficient $var(k_m(\infty))$. Subtracting $k_{m,opt}$ from both sides of (10.98) and squaring, we get

$$
\begin{aligned}
(k_m(n+M) - k_{m,opt})^2 &= (1 - \frac{M(e_f^2 + e_b^2)}{S})^2 k_m^2(n) + \frac{4M^2 e_f^2 e_b^2}{S^2} \\
&\quad + k_{m,opt}^2 + \frac{4M e_f e_b}{S}(1 - \frac{M(e_f^2 + e_b^2)}{S})k_m(n) \\
&\quad - 2k_{m,opt}(1 - \frac{M(e_f^2 + e_b^2)}{S})k_m(n) - \frac{4M e_f e_b}{S}k_{m,opt}.
\end{aligned}
\tag{10.137}
$$

In what follows, all the expectations are in the limit as $n \to \infty$. Notice that when $n \to \infty$, $E[k_m(n)] = k_{m,opt}$. Taking the expectation of (10.137) and simplifying it using equations (10.122)−(10.132), we get

$$
\begin{aligned}
var(k_m(\infty)) &= E[(k_m(n+M) - k_{m,opt})^2] \\
&= (1 - 2M\gamma + M^2\gamma^2)E[k_m^2(n)] - (1 - 2M\gamma)k_{m,opt}^2 \\
&\quad + \frac{M^2\gamma^2(1 - 4k_{m,opt}^2)}{2 + k_{m,opt}^2}.
\end{aligned}
$$

$$= (1 - 2M\gamma + M^2\gamma^2)(E[k_m^2(n)] - k_{m,opt}^2)$$

$$M^2\gamma^2 k_{m,opt}^2 + \frac{M^2\gamma^2(1 - 4k_{m,opt}^2)}{2 + k_{m,opt}^2}. \tag{10.138}$$

Notice that

$$var(k_m(\infty)) = E[(k_m(n + M) - k_{m,opt})^2] = E[k_m^2(n)] - k_{m,opt}^2. \tag{10.139}$$

Therefore, we have

$$var(k_m(\infty)) = \frac{M\gamma(1 - k_{m,opt}^2)^2}{(2 - M\gamma)(2 + k_{m,opt}^2)}, \tag{10.140}$$

and the misadjustment error for PIPSGLA1 is given by

$$\mathcal{M} = \frac{M\gamma(1 - k_{m,opt}^2)}{(2 - M\gamma)(2 + k_{m,opt}^2)}. \tag{10.141}$$

A comparison of the convergence behavior for different architectures is given in Table 10.1. In order to obtain a more closer comparison, we assume

Table 10.1   Comparison of Misadjustment Errors for Different SGLA Architectures

	τ	Misadj. Error
SGLA	$\frac{1}{\beta}$	$\frac{\beta(1-k_{m,opt}^2)}{(2-\beta)(2+k_{m,opt}^2)}$
PIPSGLA1	$\frac{1}{M\beta}$	$\frac{M^2\beta(1-k_{m,opt})}{(2-M^2\beta)(2+k_{m,opt}^2)}$
PIPSGLA2	$\frac{M}{\beta}$	$\frac{\beta(1-k_{m,opt}^2)}{(2-\beta)(2+k_{m,opt}^2)}$

that β is much smaller than 1 and approximate both $(2 - \beta)$ and $(2 - M^2\beta)$ as 2. This leads to the new comparison results in Table 10.2, from where it is clear that the product of misadjustment error and time constant is degraded M times for M-level pipelined lattice adaptive filters. On the other hand, relaxed look-ahead pipelined lattice filters provide a tradeoff with respect to the misadjustment error and the convergence time constant. Various types of relaxations can provide different tradeoffs between these 2 parameters.

10.9 CONCLUSIONS

In this chapter, the clustered and scattered look-ahead pipelining methodologies have been applied to pipeline the 1st-order and higher order IIR digital

Table 10.2   Comparison of Misadjustment Errors for Different SGLA Architectures

	τ	Misadj. Error	$\tau \times$ Misadj. Error
SGLA	$\frac{1}{\beta}$	$\frac{\beta}{2}\frac{1-k_{m,opt}^2}{2+k_{m,opt}^2}$	$\frac{1}{2}\frac{1-k_{m,opt}^2}{2+k_{m,opt}^2}$
PIPSGLA1	$\frac{1}{M\beta}$	$\frac{M^2\beta}{2}\frac{1-k_{m,opt}^2}{2+k_{m,opt}^2}$	$\frac{M}{2}\frac{1-k_{m,opt}^2}{2+k_{m,opt}^2}$
PIPSGLA2	$\frac{M}{\beta}$	$\frac{\beta}{2}\frac{1-k_{m,opt}^2}{2+k_{m,opt}^2}$	$\frac{M}{2}\frac{1-k_{m,opt}^2}{2+k_{m,opt}^2}$

filters. This chapter also addressed the design of parallel IIR filters. The incremental block processing approach has been used to design low-area parallel architectures for higher order IIR filters. Pipelining of lattice recursive digital filters is addressed in Chapter 12. Pipelining and parallel processing can be exploited to either increase the sampling speed or lower the supply voltage at the same speed to reduce power consumption. Look-ahead can also be used for concurrent implementations of dynamic programming problems [19] (see Problem 25), Viterbi decoders [20], and quantizer loops [21]. Different forms of relaxations of the look-ahead including sum, product, and delay relaxations, were used to derive a family of pipelined topologies for LMS and stochastic-gradient lattice adaptive digital filters. Pipelining of few other types of adaptive digital filters is addressed in [22]. Pipelining of recursive least square (RLS) adaptive digital filters using *scaled tangent rotation* (STAR) is addressed in [23] and using *annihilation-reordering look-ahead* is addressed in [24].

10.10   PROBLEMS

1. Consider the direct-form 3rd-order IIR filter

$$H(z) = \frac{0.5 + 0.25z^{-1}}{1 - \frac{3}{2}z^{-1} + \frac{11}{16}z^{-2} - \frac{3}{32}z^{-3}}. \tag{10.142}$$

Pipeline this structure using clustered look-ahead pipelining for (a) 2-level, and (b) 4-level pipelining of each multiply-add operation. For each case, what are the poles of the new system? Are these pipelined systems stable?

2. Pipeline the IIR filter of Problem 1 using scattered look-ahead such that each multiply-add can be pipelined by 2 stages. Draw the complete structure, and pipeline this structure by placing latches at appropriate locations (you will need to break up multipliers into 2 segments). What

are the poles of this system?

3. Consider the 2nd-order IIR filter with transfer function:

$$H(z) = \frac{0.13021(1 + z^{-1})}{1 - \frac{13}{24}z^{-1} + \frac{1}{16}z^{-2}}. \tag{10.143}$$

Obtain a 3-stage pipelined transfer function using scattered look-ahead transformation. Specify the poles and zeros of this pipelined filter.

4. Consider the IIR digital filter transfer function

$$H(z) = \frac{1}{1 - \frac{4}{3}z^{-1} + \frac{5}{12}z^{-2}}. \tag{10.144}$$

Obtain an equivalent 4-level pipelined transfer function using (a) Clustered look-ahead and (b) Scattered look-ahead and decomposition approaches.

5. Consider the 2nd-order all-pole recursive filter

$$H(z) = \frac{1}{1 - 0.6z^{-1} + 0.25z^{-2}}. \tag{10.145}$$

This filter needs to be pipelined by 9 stages using scattered look-ahead and decomposition technique. Derive transfer function and structure using a 3×3 decomposition. Clearly show the locations of the zeros represented by each section and the poles of filter using pole-zero plots. (Hint: $\frac{1}{1-a} = \frac{(1+a+a^2)(1+a^3+a^6)}{1-a^9}$.)

6. The filter in Problem 5 needs to be pipelined by 6 stages using scattered look-ahead and decomposition approaches. Derive pipelined transfer functions and corresponding structures for 3×2 and 2×3 decompositions. Show the zero locations of each section in this filter.

7. A 2nd-order IIR digital filter with transfer function

$$H(z) = \frac{1}{1 - 2r\cos\theta z^{-1} + r^2 z^{-2}} \tag{10.146}$$

is realized using these 2 alternate transfer functions:

$$H_1(z) = \frac{1 + 2r\cos\theta z^{-1} + r^2 z^{-2}}{1 - 2r^2 \cos 2\theta z^{-2} + r^4 z^{-4}}$$
$$(2 - level\ pipelined)$$

$$H_2(z) = \frac{(1 + 2r\cos\theta z^{-1} + r^2 z^{-2})(1 + 2r^2 \cos 2\theta z^{-2} + r^4 z^{-4})}{1 - 2r^4 \cos 4\theta z^{-4} + r^8 z^{-8}}$$
$$(4 - level\ pipelined). \tag{10.147}$$

Our objective is to examine which realization achieves less $area \times power$ product if the sample period is a known constant. The structures $H_1(z)$ and $H_2(z)$ can be operated with lower supply voltages. Assume that $H(z)$ is implemented with supply voltage of 5 V and the threshold voltage is 0.6 V. Assume the area required by the adders and capacitance of the adders to be negligible compared to those of the multipliers, respectively. Calculate the $area \times power^2$ product of $H_1(z)$ and $H_2(z)$ normalized with respect to $H(z)$. Which realization has the least $area \times power^2$ product?

8. Consider the implementation of a 1-pole IIR digital filter with transfer function $1/(1-az^{-1})$. This filter needs to be implemented with a sample period of one-third multiply-add time, which can be achieved either by 3-stage pipelining or by block processing with block size 3. Which realization is more useful for power reduction?

9. Repeat Problem 8 for the case when sample period is one-fourth multiply-add time.

10. The 1-pole IIR filter with transfer function $1/(1-az^{-1})$ needs to be implemented with a speedup of 15 as compared with a sequential implementation. This can be achieved with several approaches such as 15-level pipelining, 15-level block processing, 3-level of pipelining and 5-level block processing, or 5-level of pipelining and 3-level block processing. Assume the sequential and concurrent systems to be operated at the same sample rate. Which of all such possible configurations is best suited for the lowest area implementation assuming power consumption is not an issue? Which is best suited for lowest power implementation assuming area is not an issue? Which implementation achieves the least $area \times power$ product?

11. Consider the transfer function

$$H(z) = \frac{(1 + z^{-1})^2}{1 - \frac{3}{2\sqrt{2}}z^{-1} + \frac{9}{16}z^{-2}}. \qquad (10.148)$$

This system has poles at $3/4e^{\pm j\pi/4}$. Obtain an equivalent 4-level pipelined filter for this IIR filter. Also obtain a 4-parallel version of this filter.

12. Design a block filter architecture for the filter in Problem 4 for block size 4. Obtain the poles of the system using systematic approaches.

13. Consider the direct-form 3rd-order IIR filter

$$H(z) = \frac{1}{1 - \frac{3}{2}z^{-1} + \frac{11}{16}z^{-2} - \frac{3}{32}z^{-3}}. \qquad (10.149)$$

Draw a block processing architecture for this filter for block size 2. Compute the poles of the block filter using a state representation.

14. Repeat Problem 13 for block size 4.

15. A 4-th order IIR digital filter has poles at 0.6, $0.3 \pm j0.4$ and -0.8. Where are the poles for the following filters derived from this filter using scattered look-ahead pipelining and/or block processing?

    (a) 3-level pipelining
    (b) 4-level parallel processing
    (c) 2-level pipelining, 3-level parallel processing
    (d) 4-level pipelining, 2-level parallel processing.

16. Calculate the power reduction obtained by the 4-parallel IIR filter in Problem 12 as compared with the sequential realization. Use the initial supply voltage of 3.3 V for the original system and a device threshold voltage of 0.45 V. If the block size is assumed to be variable, what block size can be used for least *area* × *power* product for this filter? Assume the supply voltage lower bound to be 1.0 V.

17. Consider the design of a 3-parallel IIR filter for the second-order transfer function

    $$\frac{Y(z)}{U(z)} = H(z) = \frac{b_0 + b_1 z^{-1} + b_2 z^{-2}}{1 - a_1 z^{-1} - a_2 z^{-2}}. \tag{10.150}$$

    Let $f(n) = b_0 u(n) + b_1 u(n-1) + b_2 u(n-2)$. Then this filter requires computation of $f(3k)$, $f(3k+1)$ and $f(3k+2)$. These 3 outputs can be computed using fewer multipliers based on the fast parallel FIR filtering approaches described in Chapter 9. Design this architecture using 15 multipliers. Calculate the number of adders in your architecture.

18. What is the minimum number of multiplications needed for a 6-parallel implementation of the 2nd-order IIR digital filter in Problem 17? The number of multiplications can be reduced by use of fast parallel FIR filters and strength reduction in the incrementally computed outputs. Explain how an architecture using these minimum number of multiplications can be designed. You do not need to complete the design of this filter. (Hint: Design an architecture using 31 multiplications.)

19. Implement the system in Fig. 10.32 using the fewest multiplication operations.

20. For the system identification problem shown in Fig. 10.33, consider a linear time-invariant discrete-time plant with "unknown" system unit-sample response h(n)=[0.3208, 0.1535, 0.2133, 0.1964, 0.1859, 0.1694, 0.1579, 0.1457, 0.1367, 0.1281].

    The input $u(n)$ is an independent and identically-distributed (IID) random sequence that takes values $+1$ or -1 with equal probabilities. Apply the LMS algorithm to find the unknown filter coefficients. Plot the squared error output in dB, as a function of time, for the following cases:

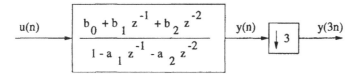

Fig. 10.32 Figure for Problem 19.

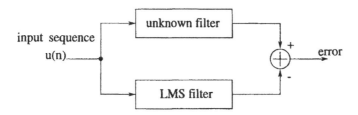

Fig. 10.33 System Identification Diagram for Problem 20.

(a) Normal LMS, with 10 taps and weight update coefficient $\mu=0.1$. Perform the experiment for 1000 iterations.

(b) Pipelined LMS filter with (i) delay relaxation with $M_1=10$, (ii) with sum and delay relaxation with $M_1=10$ and $M_2=5$. Use the same μ as in part (a) and perform the experiment for 5000 iterations.

(c) To examine the effect of $(M_2' - 1)$ adders, use $M_1=20$, $M_2=6$, and $\mu=0.003$ and compare the results of $M_2'=1$ and 5.

(d) Define

$$R = E[\mathbf{U}(n)\mathbf{U}^T(n)] \tag{10.151}$$

$$M_1 = KM_2 \tag{10.152}$$

$$\lambda_{rms}^2 = \frac{\sum_{i=1}^{N} \lambda_i^2}{N} \tag{10.153}$$

$$\lambda_{av} = \frac{\sum_{i=1}^{N} N\lambda_i}{N} = \sigma^2 \tag{10.154}$$

$$\alpha = \frac{\lambda_{rms}^2}{\lambda_{av}^2} \tag{10.155}$$

$$v = \frac{E[(u(n))^4]}{(E[(u(n))^2])^2} \tag{10.156}$$

$$P = N + v - 1 \tag{10.157}$$

$$b = \mu\sigma^2 \tag{10.158}$$

and consider the bound on μ for the convergence of PIPLMS filter given by

$$0 \leq \mu \leq \frac{\alpha P + 2K - \sqrt{(\alpha P + 2K)^2 - 8K(K+1)}}{2K(K+1)\sigma^2}. \quad (10.159)$$

Compute the range of μ for filter convergence using above formulas. Set $M_1 = 20$, $M_2 = M_2' = 5$ and let μ take values of 0.01, 0.05, 0.1 and perform the experiments. Comment on your graphs.

21. Prove the expressions of misadjustment error for SSGLA and PIPSGLA2 architectures described in Table 10.1.

22. Consider the following 2 state update equations of the stochastic gradient lattice filter. These have been derived using various sum and product relaxations on the original lattice filter. For each of these representations, obtain the limits on β for stability and derive the time constant and misadjustment parameters. In these equations, the stage number m notation has been omitted. Other lattice filter equations remain the same as in the sequential filter.

$$\begin{aligned}
k(n+M) = \quad & [1 - \beta(n)(e_f^2(n) + e_b^2(n-1))]k(n) \\
& + 2\beta(n)e_f(n)e_b(n-1) \\
S(n+M) = \quad & (1-\beta)^M S(n) + M(e_f^2(n) + e_b^2(n-1)). \quad (10.160)
\end{aligned}$$

23. Repeat Problem 22 with

$$\begin{aligned}
k(n+M) = \quad & [1 - \beta(n)(e_f^2(n) + e_b^2(n-1))]k(n) \\
& + 2\beta(n)e_f(n)e_b(n-1) \\
S(n+M) = \quad & (1-\beta)^M S(n) + (e_f^2(n) + e_b^2(n-1)). \quad (10.161)
\end{aligned}$$

24. Repeat Problem 22 with

$$\begin{aligned}
k(n+M) = \quad & [1 - \beta(n)(e_f^2(n) + e_b^2(n-1))]k(n) \\
& + 2\beta(n)e_f(n)e_b(n-1) \\
S(n+M) = \quad & (1-\beta)^{\sqrt{M}} S(n) + (e_f^2(n) + e_b^2(n-1)). \quad (10.162)
\end{aligned}$$

25. Consider a 2-state dynamic programming computation (see Section 1.2.8)

$$x_i(n+1) = \max_j [x_j(n) + a_{ji}(n)], \quad i, j = 1, 2. \quad (10.163)$$

The iteration bound of this computation is limited by an addition-comparison-selection (ACS) operation.

time n-1   **time n**

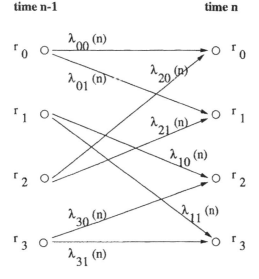

Fig. 10.34   Trellis diagram for Problem 26.

(a) Use look-ahead to obtain an equivalent implementation where the ACS operation can be pipelined by 4-levels. Use decomposition to reduce the hardware complexity overhead.

(b) Design a 4-parallel implementation of this computation using look-ahead.

26. Consider the implementation of a 4-state, rate-1/2 Viterbi decoder (see Section 1.2.8) described by the trellis in Fig. 10.34.

Each node in the trellis represents an ACS operation. For example, the node at the top (corresponding to state 0) performs the computation

$$r_0(n) = \min[r_0(n-1) + \lambda_{00}(n), r_2(n-1) + \lambda_{20}(n)]. \quad (10.164)$$

The iteration bound of this architecture is limited by the throughput of one ACS operation.

(a) Use look-ahead to design the Viterbi decoder such that the ACS unit can be pipelined by 2 stages.

(b) Repeat (a) for 4-stage pipelining of the ACS unit.

REFERENCES

1. S. Y. Kung, "On supercomputing with systolic/wavefront array processors," *Proc. IEEE*, vol. 72, pp. 867–884, July 1984.

2. C. E. Leiserson, F. Rose, and J. Saxe, "Optimizing synchronous circuitry by retiming," in *3rd Caltech Conference on VLSI*, (Pasadena, CA), pp. 87–116, March 1983.

3. D. A. Schwartz and T. P. Barnwell, III, "A graph theoretic technique for the generation of systolic implementations for shift invariant flow graphs," in *Proc of ICASSP-84*, (San Diego), Mar. 1984.

4. K. K. Parhi and D. G. Messerschmitt, "Pipeline interleaving and parallelism in recursive digital filters—part I: pipelining using scattered look-ahead and decomposition," *IEEE Trans. on Acoustics, Speech, and Signal Processing*, pp. 1099–1117, July 1989.

5. K. K. Parhi and D. G. Messerschmitt, "Pipeline interleaving and parallelism in recursive digital filters—part II: pipelined incremental block filtering," *IEEE Trans. on Acoustics, Speech, and Signal Processing*, pp. 1118–1134, July 1989.

6. H. H. Loomis, Jr. and B. Sinha, "High speed recursive digital filter realization," *Circuits, Systems, Signal Process.*, vol. 3, no. 3, pp. 267–294, 1984.

7. M. A. Soderstrand, A. E. de la Serna, and H. H. Loomis, Jr., "New approach to clustered look-ahead pipelined IIR digital filters," *IEEE Trans. on Circuits and Systems, Part II: Analog and Digital Signal Processing* , vol. 42, pp. 269–274, April 1995.

8. A. G. Deczky, "Synthesis of recursive digital filters using the minimum p-error criterion," *IEEE Trans. on Audio and Electroacoustics*, vol. AU-20, pp. 257–263, Oct. 1972.

9. R. Fletcher and M. J. D. Powell, "A rapidly convergent descent method for minimization," *Comput. Journal*, vol. 6, pp. 163–168, 1963.

10. M. A. Richards, "Application of Deczky's program for recursive filter design to the design of recursive decimators," *IEEE Trans. on Acoustics, Speech, and Signal Processing*, pp. 811–814, Oct. 1982.

11. H. G. Martinez and T. W. Parks, "Design of recursive digital filters with optimum magnitude and attenuation poles on the unit circle," *IEEE Trans. on Acoustics, Speech, and Signal Processing*, vol. ASSP-26, pp. 150–157, April 1978.

12. H. G. Martinez and T. W. Parks, "A class of infinite-duration impulse response digital filters for sampling rate reduction," *IEEE Trans. on Acoustics, Speech, and Signal Processing*, vol. ASSP-27, pp. 154–162, April 1979.

13. A. V. Oppenheim and R. W. Schafer, *Discrete Time Signal Processing*. Prentice-Hall, 1989.

14. T. Meng and D. G. Messerschmitt, "Arbitrarily high sampling rate adaptive filters," *IEEE Trans. on Acoustics, Speech, and Signal Processing*, vol. 35, no. 4, pp. 455–470, 1987.

15. G. Long, F. Ling, and J. G. Proakis, "The LMS algorithm with delayed coefficient adaptation," *IEEE Trans. on Acoustics, Speech, and Signal Processing*, vol. 37, no. 9, pp. 1397−1405, 1989.

16. N. R. Shanbhag and K. K. Parhi, "Relaxed look-ahead pipelined LMS adaptive filters and their application to ADPCM coder," *IEEE Trans. on Circuits and Systems, Part II: Analog and Digital Signal Processing*, vol. 40, no. 12, pp. 753−766, 1993.

17. N. R. Shanbhag and K. K. Parhi, "Pipelined adaptive DFE architectures using relaxed look-ahead," *IEEE Trans. on Signal Processing*, vol. 43, no. 6, pp. 1368−1385, 1995.

18. N. R. Shanbhag and K. K. Parhi, "A pipelined adaptive lattice filter architecture," *IEEE Transactions on Signal Processing*, vol. 41, no. 5, pp. 1925−1939, May 1993.

19. K. K. Parhi, "High speed VLSI architectures for Huffman and Viterbi decoders," *IEEE Trans. on Circuits and Systems, Part II: Analog and Digital Signal Processing*, vol. 39, no. 6, pp. 385−391, 1992.

20. G. Fettweis and H. Meyr, "Parallel Viterbi algorithm implementation: Breaking the ACS-bottleneck," *IEEE Trans. on Communications*, vol. 37, no. 8, pp. 785−789, 1989.

21. K. K. Parhi, "Pipelining in algorithms with quantizer loops," *IEEE Trans. on Circuits and Systems*, vol. 38, no. 7, pp. 745−754, 1991.

22. N. R. Shanbhag and K. K. Parhi, *Pipelined Adaptive Digital Filters*. Kluwer, 1994.

23. K. J. Raghunath, and K. K. Parhi, "Pipelined RLS adaptive filtering using scaled tangent rotations (STAR)," *IEEE Trans. on Signal Processing*, vol. 44, no. 10, pp. 2591−2604, Oct. 1996.

24. J. Ma, E. F. Deprettere and K. K. Parhi, "Pipelined CORDIC based QRD-RLS adaptive filtering using matrix look-ahead," *Proc. of 1997 IEEE Workshop on Signal Processing Systems: Design and Implementation*, (Leicester, U.K.), pp. 131-140, Nov. 1997.

11

Scaling and Roundoff Noise

11.1 INTRODUCTION

When a digital filter transfer function is implemented using a digital system, it invariably involves quantization of signals and coefficients in the system. As a result, the overall input-output behavior is not ideal. There are two basic types of quantization effects in any implementation [1],[2]. The first is due to parameter (coefficient) quantization. The result of parameter quantization is that the actual implemented transfer function is different from the ideal transfer function. In fixed-point VLSI implementations or software implementations using fixed-point programmable DSPs, study of finite wordlength behavior in digital filters is extremely important.

The second type of quantization is due to signal rounding. The internal signals in a digital filter are invariably subject to quantization, causing an error in the computed output. Such quantization is clearly a nonlinear phenomenon and can be further subdivided into two types of effects, i.e., limit-cycle oscillations and roundoff noise. Limit-cycle oscillations can be defined as undesirable periodic components at the filter output and are due to the fact that quantization is a nonlinear operation. Notice that oscillations are always possible when there exist nonlinear operations in feedback paths. Conversely, roundoff noise affects the filter output in the form of a random disturbance and can be analyzed by suitable noise modeling and by the use of linear system theory.

In addition to the parameter quantization and signal rounding, internal overflows must be prevented since they cause much larger errors. This is accomplished by properly scaling the realization. Scaling constrains the numerical values of the internal filter variables to remain in a range appropriate to the hardware.

State variable description of a linear filter is most useful when it becomes necessary to compute quantities that depend on the internal structure of the filter. This representation provides a mathematical formulation for studying various structures not feasible with any other description. Due to simple computing algorithms available, the power at each internal node and the output roundoff noise of a digital filter can be easily computed once the digital filter is described in state variable form. The techniques presented in this chapter are also applicable to FIR digital filters.

This chapter is organized as follows. Scaling and roundoff noise concepts are introduced in Section 11.2. The state variable description, the state covariance matrix, $\mathbf{K}$, and the output covariance matrix, $\mathbf{W}$, are discussed in Section 11.3. Approaches to computation of scaling transformation and roundoff noise are introduced in Section 11.4 and are applied to pipelined recursive digital filters in Section 11.5. Fast computation of $\mathbf{K}$ and $\mathbf{W}$ matrices is addressed in Section 11.6 [3]. Section 11.7 addresses slow-down, retiming and pipelining transformation to convert nonstate variables to state variable nodes.

11.2   SCALING AND ROUNDOFF NOISE

11.2.1   Scaling Operation

Scaling is a process of readjusting certain internal gain parameters in order to constrain internal signals to a range appropriate to the hardware with the constraint that the transfer function from input to output should not be changed.

The filter in Fig. 11.1(a) with unscaled node x has the transfer function

$$H(z) = D(z) + F(z)G(z). \tag{11.1}$$

To scale the node x, we divide $F(z)$ by some number β and multiply $G(z)$ by the same number as in Fig. 11.1(b). Although the transfer function does not change by this operation, the signal level at node x has been changed. The scaling parameter β can be chosen to meet any specific scaling rule such as

$$l_1 \text{ scaling}: \quad \beta \;=\; \sum_{i=0}^{\infty} |f(i)|, \tag{11.2}$$

$$l_2 \text{ scaling}: \quad \beta \;=\; \delta\sqrt{\sum_{i=0}^{\infty} f^2(i)}, \tag{11.3}$$

where $f(i)$ is the unit-sample response from input to the node x and the parameter δ can be interpreted to represent the number of standard deviations

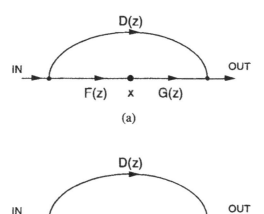

Fig. 11.1   (a) A filter with unscaled node x and (b) A filter with scaled node x'.

representable in the register at node x if the input is unit-variance white noise. If the input is bounded by $|u(n)| \leq 1$, then

$$|x(n)| = \left| \sum_{i=0}^{\infty} f(i)u(n-i) \right| \leq \sum_{i=0}^{\infty} |f(i)|. \tag{11.4}$$

Equation (11.4) represents the true bound on the range of x and overflow is completely avoided by l_1 scaling in (11.2), which is the most stringent scaling policy.

In many cases, input can be assumed to be white noise. Although we cannot compute a true bound on the signal at x under this assumption, we can compute the variance at node x. For unit-variance white noise input,

$$E\left[x^2(n)\right] = \sum_{i=0}^{\infty} f^2(i). \tag{11.5}$$

Since most input signals can be assumed to be white noise, l_2 scaling is commonly used. In addition, (11.5) can be easily computed. Since (11.5) is the variance (not a strict bound), there is a possibility of overflow, which can be reduced by increasing δ in (11.3). For large values of δ, the internal variables are scaled conservatively so that no overflow occurs. However, there is a trade-off between overflow and roundoff noise, since increasing δ deteriorates the output SNR (signal to noise ratio).

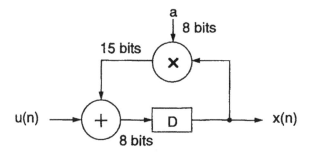

Fig. 11.2   A 1st-order IIR filter ($W = 8$).

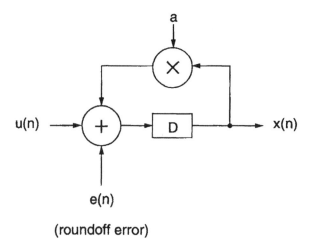

Fig. 11.3   Model of roundoff error.

11.2.2   Roundoff Noise

If two W-bit fixed-point fraction numbers are multiplied together, the product is $(2W - 1)$ bits long. This product must eventually be quantized to W-bits by rounding or truncation. For example, consider the 1st-order IIR filter shown in Fig. 11.2. Assume that the input wordlength is $W = 8$ bits. If the multiplier coefficient wordlength is also the same, then to maintain full precision in the output we need to increase the output wordlength by 8 bits per iteration. This is clearly infeasible. The alternative is to round off (or truncate) the output to its nearest 8-bit representation.

The result of such quantization introduces roundoff noise $e(n)$. For mathematical ease a system with roundoff can be modeled as an infinite precision system with an external error input. For example in the previous case (shown in Fig. 11.2) we round off the output of the multiply add operation and an equivalent model is shown in Fig. 11.3.

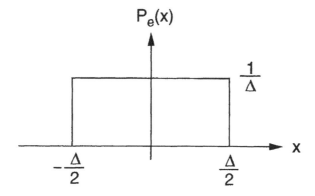

Fig. 11.4 Error probability distribution.

Although rounding is not a linear operation, its effect at the output can be analyzed using linear system theory with the following assumptions about $e(n)$:

1. $e(n)$ is uniformly distributed white noise.

2. $e(n)$ is a wide-sense stationary random process, i.e., mean and co-variance of $e(n)$ are independent of the time index n.

3. $e(n)$ is uncorrelated to all other signals such as input and other noise signals.

Let the wordlength of the output be W-bits, then the roundoff error $e(n)$ can be given by

$$\frac{-2^{-(W-1)}}{2} \le e(n) \le \frac{2^{-(W-1)}}{2}. \tag{11.6}$$

Since the error is assumed to be uniformly distributed over the interval given in (11.6), the corresponding probability distribution is shown in Fig. 11.4, where Δ is the length of the interval (i.e., $2^{-(W-1)}$).

Let us compute the mean $E[e(n)]$ and variance $E[e^2(n)]$ of this error function.

$$E[e(n)] = \int_{\frac{-\Delta}{2}}^{\frac{\Delta}{2}} x P_e(x) dx = \frac{1}{\Delta} \frac{x^2}{2} \Big]_{\frac{-\Delta}{2}}^{\frac{\Delta}{2}} = 0. \tag{11.7}$$

Note that since mean is zero, variance is simply $E[e^2(n)]$.

$$E[e^2(n)] = \int_{\frac{-\Delta}{2}}^{\frac{\Delta}{2}} x^2 P_e(x) dx = \frac{1}{\Delta} \frac{x^3}{3} \Big]_{\frac{-\Delta}{2}}^{\frac{\Delta}{2}} = \frac{\Delta^2}{12} = \frac{2^{-2W}}{3}. \tag{11.8}$$

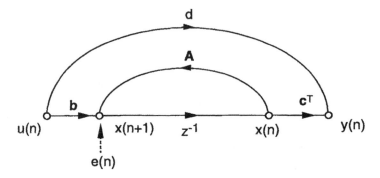

Fig. 11.5 Signal flow graph of IIR filter.

In other words, (11.8) can be rewritten as,

$$\sigma_e^2 = \frac{2^{-2W}}{3},$$ (11.9)

where σ_e^2 is the variance of the roundoff error in a finite precision, W-bit wordlength system. Since the variance is proportional to 2^{-2W}, increase in wordlength by 1 bit decreases the error by a factor of 4.

The purpose of analyzing roundoff noise is to determine its effect at the output signal. If the noise variance at the output is not negligible in comparison to the output signal level, the wordlength should be increased or some low-noise structures should be used. Therefore, we need to compute SNR at the output, not just the noise gain to the output. In the noise analysis, we use a double-length accumulator model, which means rounding is performed after two $(2W - 1)$-bit products are added. Also, notice that multipliers are the sources for roundoff noise.

11.3   STATE VARIABLE DESCRIPTION OF DIGITAL FILTERS

Consider the signal flow graph (SFG) of an N-th order digital filter in Fig. 11.5. We can represent this filter in the following recursive matrix form,

$$\mathbf{x}(n+1) = \mathbf{A}\mathbf{x}(n) + \mathbf{b}u(n),$$ (11.10)

$$y(n) = \mathbf{c}^T\mathbf{x}(n) + du(n).$$ (11.11)

The boldfaced letters imply a vector or a matrix. In the above representation $\mathbf{x}$ is the state vector, u is the input, and y is the output of the filter; $\mathbf{x}$, $\mathbf{b}$, and $\mathbf{c}$ are $N \times 1$ column vectors; $\mathbf{A}$ is $N \times N$ matrix; d, u and y are scalars. Let $\mathbf{f}_i(n)$ be the unit-sample response from the input $u(n)$ to the state $\mathbf{x}_i(n)$ and let $\mathbf{g}_i(n)$ be the unit-sample response from the state $\mathbf{x}_i(n)$ to

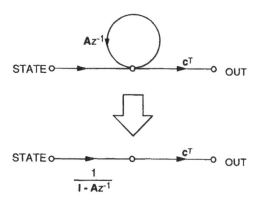

Fig. 11.6 Signal flow graph of $\mathbf{g}(n)$.

the output $\mathbf{y}_i(n)$. To avoid internal overflow, it is necessary to scale the inputs to multipliers. Since the signals $\mathbf{x}(n)$ are inputs to multipliers in Fig. 11.5, we need to compute $\mathbf{f}(n)$ for scaling. Conversely, to find the noise variance at the output, it is necessary to find the unit-sample response from the location of the noise source $e(n)$ to $y(n)$. Thus $\mathbf{g}(n)$ represents the unit-sample response of the noise transfer function except for a delay, which has no effect on the output noise variance.

From the SFG of Fig. 11.5 we can write,

$$\frac{\mathbf{X}(z)}{U(z)} = \frac{\mathbf{b}z^{-1}}{\mathbf{I} - z^{-1}\mathbf{A}}. \tag{11.12}$$

Then we can write the z-transform of $\mathbf{f}(n)$, $\mathbf{F}(z)$ as,

$$\mathbf{F}(z) = \frac{\mathbf{X}(z)}{U(z)} = (\mathbf{I} + \mathbf{A}z^{-1} + \mathbf{A}^2 z^{-2} + \cdots)\mathbf{b}z^{-1}, \tag{11.13}$$

$$\Rightarrow \mathbf{f}(n) = \mathbf{A}^{n-1}\mathbf{b}, \ \ n \geq 1. \tag{11.14}$$

We could have computed $\mathbf{f}(n)$ by substituting $u(n)$ by $\delta(n)$ and using the recursion,

$$\mathbf{f}(n+1) = \mathbf{A}\mathbf{f}(n) + \mathbf{b}\delta(n). \tag{11.15}$$

with initial condition $\mathbf{f}(0) = 0$. The unit-sample response $\mathbf{g}(n)$ from the state $\mathbf{x}(n)$ to the output $y(n)$ can be computed similarly with $u(n) = 0$. The corresponding SFG is shown in Fig. 11.6, which represents the following transfer function $\mathbf{G}(z)$,

$$\mathbf{G}(z) = \frac{\mathbf{c}^T}{\mathbf{I} - \mathbf{A}z^{-1}}, \tag{11.16}$$

$$\Rightarrow \mathbf{g}(n) = \mathbf{c}^T \mathbf{A}^n, \ \ n \geq 0. \tag{11.17}$$

Consider the state covariance matrix $\mathbf{K}$ defined as,

$$\mathbf{K} = E[\mathbf{x}(n)\mathbf{x}^T(n)]. \tag{11.18}$$

Since $\mathbf{x}$ is an $N \times 1$ vector, $\mathbf{K}$ will be an $N \times N$ matrix. Let x_i's denote the individual elements of $\mathbf{x}$, i.e.,

$$\mathbf{x}(n) = [x_1(n) \ x_2(n) \ \cdots \ x_N(n)]^T. \tag{11.19}$$

To understand the significance of $\mathbf{K}$, let us consider K_{11}, i.e., the 1st diagonal entry in matrix $\mathbf{K}$. Note that K_{11} is simply $E[x_1^2(n)]$, which is nothing but the energy of the error signal at state $x_1(n)$ due to the input white noise. This indicates that $\mathbf{K}$, in some sense, is a measure of error power at various states. To continue our discussion, let us try to express $\mathbf{K}$ in a form that reflects the error properties of the filter. Note that $\mathbf{x}(n)$ in (11.18) can be written as a convolution of input $u(n)$ with unit-sample response $\mathbf{f}(n)$. Further substituting for $\mathbf{f}(n)$ from (11.14) we get,

$$\mathbf{x}(n) = \mathbf{f}(n) * u(n) = \sum_{l=0}^{\infty} \mathbf{A}^l \mathbf{b} u(n-l-1). \tag{11.20}$$

Therefore,

$$
\begin{aligned}
\mathbf{K} &= E\left[\sum_{l=0}^{\infty} \mathbf{A}^l \mathbf{b} u(n-l-1) \sum_{m=0}^{\infty} u(n-m-1)(\mathbf{A}^m \mathbf{b})^T \right], \\
&= E\left[\sum_{l=0}^{\infty} \sum_{m=0}^{\infty} \mathbf{A}^l \mathbf{b} u(n-l-1)u(n-m-1)(\mathbf{A}^m \mathbf{b})^T \right], \\
&= \sum_{l=0}^{\infty} \sum_{m=0}^{\infty} \mathbf{A}^l \mathbf{b} E\left[u(n-l-1)u(n-m-1) \right] (\mathbf{A}^m \mathbf{b})^T. \tag{11.21}
\end{aligned}
$$

If the input $u(n)$ is assumed to be zero mean unit variance white noise then,

$$
\begin{aligned}
E[u^2(n)] &= 1, \tag{11.22} \\
E[u(n)u(n-k)] &= 0, \text{ for } k \neq 0. \tag{11.23}
\end{aligned}
$$

Substituting these values from (11.22) and (11.23) into (11.21) we obtain,

$$
\begin{aligned}
\mathbf{K} &= \sum_{l=0}^{\infty} \sum_{m=0}^{\infty} \mathbf{A}^l \mathbf{b} \delta_{lm} (\mathbf{A}^m \mathbf{b})^T, \\
&= \sum_{l=0}^{\infty} \mathbf{f}(l)\mathbf{f}^T(l),
\end{aligned}
$$

$$= \sum_{l=0}^{\infty} \mathbf{A}^l \mathbf{b}(\mathbf{A}^l \mathbf{b})^T,$$

$$= \mathbf{b}\mathbf{b}^T + \sum_{l=1}^{\infty} \mathbf{A}^l \mathbf{b}(\mathbf{A}^l \mathbf{b})^T,$$

$$= \mathbf{b}\mathbf{b}^T + \sum_{k=0}^{\infty} \mathbf{A}^{k+1} \mathbf{b}(\mathbf{A}^{k+1} \mathbf{b})^T,$$

$$= \mathbf{b}\mathbf{b}^T + \sum_{k=0}^{\infty} \mathbf{A}[\mathbf{A}^k \mathbf{b}(\mathbf{A}^k \mathbf{b})^T]\mathbf{A}^T,$$

$$= \mathbf{b}\mathbf{b}^T + \mathbf{A} \left[\sum_{k=0}^{\infty} \mathbf{A}^k \mathbf{b}(\mathbf{A}^k \mathbf{b})^T \right] \mathbf{A}^T, \qquad (11.24)$$

$$\Rightarrow \mathbf{K} = \mathbf{b}\mathbf{b}^T + \mathbf{A}\mathbf{K}\mathbf{A}^T. \qquad (11.25)$$

Equation (11.25) is also known as the *Lyapunov equation*. Note that if for some state x_i, $E[x_i^2]$ has a higher value than another state, then x_i needs to be assigned more bits. But then we have differing wordlengths at each state which leads to extra hardware and an irregular design. If somehow we can ensure that all nodes have equal power (i.e., $E[x_i^2]$ is the same for all i's), the same wordlength can be assigned to all the nodes. This can be achieved by scaling.

A filter structure is *orthogonal* if all internal variables are uncorrelated and have unit variance, assuming a white noise input [3]. In other words, a filter structure is orthogonal if it satisfies the following:

$$\mathbf{K} = \mathbf{I} = \mathbf{A}\mathbf{A}^T + \mathbf{b}\mathbf{b}^T. \qquad (11.26)$$

Orthogonal filter structures have the following advantages:

- The scaling rule is automatically satisfied.

- The roundoff noise gain is low and invariant under frequency transformations.

- Overflow oscillations are impossible.

Similarly we define the output covariance matrix $\mathbf{W}$ as follows:

$$\mathbf{W} = \sum_{n=0}^{\infty} \mathbf{g}^T(n)\mathbf{g}(n) = \sum_{n=0}^{\infty} (\mathbf{c}^T \mathbf{A}^n)^T \mathbf{c}^T \mathbf{A}^n. \qquad (11.27)$$

Proceeding in a similar manner as before, we can show

$$\mathbf{W} = \mathbf{A}^T \mathbf{W} \mathbf{A} + \mathbf{c}\mathbf{c}^T. \qquad (11.28)$$

11.4 SCALING AND ROUNDOFF NOISE COMPUTATION

11.4.1 Scaling Operation

As mentioned before, the same wordlength can be assigned to all the variables of the system only if all the states have equal power. The way to achieve this is called *scaling*. The state vector is premultiplied by inverse of the scaling matrix $\mathbf{T}$. If we denote the scaled states by $\mathbf{x}_s$, we can write,

$$\mathbf{x}_s(n) = \mathbf{T}^{-1}\mathbf{x}(n) \;\Rightarrow\; \mathbf{x}(n) = \mathbf{T}\mathbf{x}_s(n). \tag{11.29}$$

Substituting for $\mathbf{x}$ from (11.29) into the state update equation (11.10) and solving for $\mathbf{x}_s$ we get,

$$\begin{aligned}
\mathbf{T}\mathbf{x}_s(n+1) &= \mathbf{A}\mathbf{T}\mathbf{x}_s(n) + \mathbf{b}u(n), & (11.30) \\
\Rightarrow \mathbf{x}_s(n+1) &= \mathbf{T}^{-1}\mathbf{A}\mathbf{T}\mathbf{x}_s(n) + \mathbf{T}^{-1}\mathbf{b}u(n), & (11.31) \\
\Rightarrow \mathbf{x}_s(n+1) &= \mathbf{A}_s\mathbf{x}_s(n) + \mathbf{b}_su(n), & (11.32)
\end{aligned}$$

where $\mathbf{A}_s = \mathbf{T}^{-1}\mathbf{A}\mathbf{T}$ and $\mathbf{b}_s = \mathbf{T}^{-1}\mathbf{b}$.

Similarly the output equation (11.11) can be derived as follows,

$$\begin{aligned}
y(n) &= \mathbf{c}^T\mathbf{T}\mathbf{x}_s(n) + du(n), \\
&= \mathbf{c}_s^T\mathbf{x}_s(n) + d_su(n), \\
\Rightarrow \mathbf{c}_s^T &= \mathbf{c}^T\mathbf{T} \text{ and } d_s = d. & (11.33)
\end{aligned}$$

The scaled $\mathbf{K}$ matrix is given by

$$\begin{aligned}
\mathbf{K}_s &= E[\mathbf{x}_s\mathbf{x}_s^T], \\
&= E[\mathbf{T}^{-1}\mathbf{x}\mathbf{x}^T(\mathbf{T}^{-1})^T], \\
&= \mathbf{T}^{-1}E[\mathbf{x}\mathbf{x}^T](\mathbf{T}^{-1})^T, \\
\Rightarrow \mathbf{K}_s &= \mathbf{T}^{-1}\mathbf{K}(\mathbf{T}^{-1})^T. & (11.34)
\end{aligned}$$

Since it is desirable to have equal power at all states, a transformation matrix $\mathbf{T}$ is chosen such that the $\mathbf{K}_s$ matrix of the scaled system has all diagonal entries as 1. Further assume $\mathbf{T}$ to be diagonal, i.e.,

$$\mathbf{T} = diag\,[t_{11}\; t_{22}\; \cdots\; t_{NN}], \tag{11.35}$$

$$\Rightarrow \mathbf{T}^{-1} = diag\,[\frac{1}{t_{11}}\; \frac{1}{t_{22}}\; \cdots\; \frac{1}{t_{NN}}] = (\mathbf{T}^{-1})^T. \tag{11.36}$$

From (11.34) we can write the diagonal entries of $\mathbf{K}_s$ in terms of those of $\mathbf{K}$

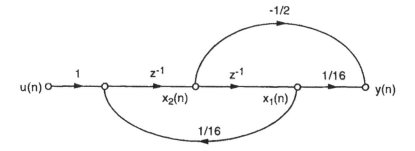

Fig. 11.7 An SFG of an unscaled 2nd-order filter.

and if we equate $(K_s)_{ii}$ to 1 then we can obtain the scaling matrix $\mathbf{T}$:

$$(K_s)_{ii} = \frac{K_{ii}}{t_{ii}^2} = 1, \tag{11.37}$$

$$\Rightarrow t_{ii} = \sqrt{K_{ii}}. \tag{11.38}$$

To conclude, by choosing i-th diagonal entry in $\mathbf{T}$ to be equal to the square root of the i-th diagonal element of $\mathbf{K}$ matrix, all the states can be guaranteed to have equal unity power.

Example 11.4.1 *Consider the unscaled 2nd-order filter shown in Fig. 11.7. The state variable matrices are*

$$\mathbf{A} = \begin{bmatrix} 0 & 1 \\ \frac{1}{16} & 0 \end{bmatrix},$$

$$\mathbf{b} = \begin{bmatrix} 0 \\ 1 \end{bmatrix},$$

$$\mathbf{c} = \begin{bmatrix} \frac{1}{16} \\ -\frac{1}{2} \end{bmatrix},$$

$$d = 0.$$

The state covariance matrix $\mathbf{K}$ *can be computed using (11.25) as*

$$\begin{bmatrix} K_{11} & K_{12} \\ K_{21} & K_{22} \end{bmatrix} = \begin{bmatrix} 0 & 1 \\ \frac{1}{16} & 0 \end{bmatrix} \begin{bmatrix} K_{11} & K_{12} \\ K_{21} & K_{22} \end{bmatrix} \begin{bmatrix} 0 & \frac{1}{16} \\ 1 & 0 \end{bmatrix} + \begin{bmatrix} 0 & 0 \\ 0 & 1 \end{bmatrix},$$

$$= \begin{bmatrix} K_{22} & \frac{1}{16}K_{21} \\ \frac{1}{16}K_{12} & \frac{1}{256}K_{11} + 1 \end{bmatrix}.$$

Thus

$$K_{11} = K_{22} = \frac{256}{255}, \quad K_{12} = K_{21} = 0.$$

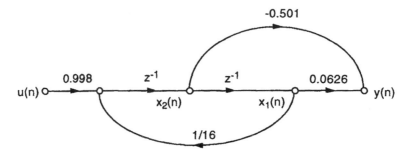

Fig. 11.8 A SFG of a scaled 2nd-order filter.

For l_2 scaling with $\delta = 1$, the transformation matrix is

$$\mathbf{T} = \begin{bmatrix} \frac{16}{\sqrt{255}} & 0 \\ 0 & \frac{16}{\sqrt{255}} \end{bmatrix}.$$

Thus the scaled filter is described by

$$\mathbf{A}_s = \mathbf{T}^{-1}\mathbf{AT} = \begin{bmatrix} 0 & 1 \\ \frac{1}{16} & 0 \end{bmatrix},$$

$$\mathbf{b}_s = \mathbf{T}^{-1}\mathbf{b} = \begin{bmatrix} 0 \\ \frac{\sqrt{255}}{16} \end{bmatrix},$$

$$\mathbf{c}_s = \mathbf{T}^T\mathbf{c} = \begin{bmatrix} \frac{1}{\sqrt{255}} \\ -\frac{8}{\sqrt{255}} \end{bmatrix},$$

$$d_s = 0,$$

and is shown in Fig. 11.8. Notice that the state covariance matrix $\mathbf{K}_s$ of the scaled filter is

$$
\begin{aligned}
\mathbf{K}_s &= \begin{bmatrix} \frac{\sqrt{255}}{16} & 0 \\ 0 & \frac{\sqrt{255}}{16} \end{bmatrix} \begin{bmatrix} \frac{256}{255} & 0 \\ 0 & \frac{256}{255} \end{bmatrix} \begin{bmatrix} \frac{\sqrt{255}}{16} & 0 \\ 0 & \frac{\sqrt{255}}{16} \end{bmatrix}, \\
&= \begin{bmatrix} 1 & 0 \\ 0 & 1 \end{bmatrix}. \blacksquare
\end{aligned}
$$

11.4.2   Roundoff Noise Computation

Let $e_i(n)$ be the error due to roundoff at state x_i. Then the output roundoff noise $y_i(n)$, due to this error, can be written as the convolution of the error input $e_i(n)$ with the state-to-output unit-sample response $g_i(n)$:

$$y_i(n) = e_i(n) * g_i(n) = \sum_{l=0}^{\infty} e_i(l)g_i(n-l). \tag{11.39}$$

Consider the mean and the variance of $y_i(n)$. Since $e_i(n)$ is white noise with zero mean, the mean of $y_i(n)$ is also zero.

$$
\begin{aligned}
E[y_i(n)] &= 0, & \text{(11.40)} \\
E[y_i^2(n)] &= E\left[\sum_l e_i(l)g_i(n-l) \sum_m e_i(m)g_i(n-m)\right], \\
&= \sum_l \sum_m g_i(n-l)E[e_i(l)e_i(m)]g_i(n-m), \\
&= \sum_l \sum_m g_i(n-l)\sigma_e^2 \delta_{lm} g_i(n-m), \\
&= \sigma_e^2 \sum_l g_i^2(n-l) = \sigma_e^2 \sum_n g_i^2(n), & \text{(11.41)}
\end{aligned}
$$

where σ_e^2 is the variance of $e_i(n)$. If we expand $\mathbf{W}$ and write it in its explicit matrix form we observe that all the diagonal entries are of the form $\sum_n g_i^2(n)$.

$$
\begin{aligned}
\mathbf{W} &= \sum_n \mathbf{g}^T(n)\mathbf{g}(n), \\
&= \sum_n \begin{bmatrix} g_1(n) \\ g_2(n) \\ \vdots \\ g_N(n) \end{bmatrix} [g_1(n)\ g_2(n)\ \cdots\ g_N(n)], & \text{(11.42)} \\
&= \begin{bmatrix} \sum_n g_1^2(n) & \sum_n g_1(n)g_2(n) & \cdots & \sum_n g_1(n)g_N(n) \\ \sum_n g_2(n)g_1(n) & \sum_n g_2^2(n) & \cdots & \sum_n g_2(n)g_N(n) \\ \vdots & \vdots & \vdots & \vdots \\ \sum_n g_N(n)g_1(n) & \sum_n g_N(n)g_2(n) & \cdots & \sum_n g_N^2(n) \end{bmatrix}. & \text{(11.43)}
\end{aligned}
$$

Using (11.41) we can write the expression for the total output roundoff noise in terms of trace of $\mathbf{W}$:

$$\text{total roundoff noise} = \sigma_e^2 \sum_{i=1}^N \sum_n g_i^2(n) = \sigma_e^2 \sum_{i=1}^N W_{ii} = \sigma_e^2\ \text{Trace}(\mathbf{W}). \tag{11.44}$$

Though the expression given in (11.44) is valid for all cases, one must keep in mind that if there is no roundoff operation at any node then the W_{ii} term corresponding to that node should not be included while computing noise power.

From (11.44) we can also compute the total roundoff noise for the scaled system, which will simply be the trace of scaled $\mathbf{W}$ matrix. We can write,

$$\text{total roundoff noise (scaled system)} = \sigma_e^2 \, \text{Trace}(\mathbf{W}_s). \tag{11.45}$$

Replacing the filter parameters with the scaled parameters in (11.27), we can show

$$\mathbf{W}_s = \mathbf{T}^T \mathbf{W} \mathbf{T}. \tag{11.46}$$

Also, for a diagonal $\mathbf{T}$ we can write,

$$\text{Trace}(\mathbf{W}_s) = \sum_{i=1}^{N} (W_s)_{ii} = \sum_{i=1}^{N} t_{ii}^2 W_{ii}. \tag{11.47}$$

Since t_{ii} is defined as $\sqrt{K_{ii}}$, (11.47) can be rewritten as

$$\text{Trace}(\mathbf{W}_s) = \sum_{i=1}^{N} (K_{ii} W_{ii}),$$

$$\Rightarrow \text{total roundoff noise (scaled system)} \ = \ \sigma_e^2 \sum_{i=1}^{N} (K_{ii} W_{ii}). \tag{11.48}$$

The roundoff noise of the scaled system can be computed using K_{ii} and W_{ii}.

Example 11.4.2 *To find the output roundoff noise for the l_2 scaled filter in Fig. 11.8, $\mathbf{W}$ can be calculated using (11.28) as*

$$\begin{bmatrix} W_{11} & W_{12} \\ W_{21} & W_{22} \end{bmatrix} = \begin{bmatrix} 0 & \frac{1}{16} \\ 1 & 0 \end{bmatrix} \begin{bmatrix} W_{11} & W_{12} \\ W_{21} & W_{22} \end{bmatrix} \begin{bmatrix} 0 & 1 \\ \frac{1}{16} & 0 \end{bmatrix} +$$

$$\begin{bmatrix} \frac{1}{255} & -\frac{8}{255} \\ -\frac{8}{255} & \frac{64}{255} \end{bmatrix} = \begin{bmatrix} \frac{1}{256} W_{22} + \frac{1}{255} & \frac{1}{16} W_{21} - \frac{8}{255} \\ \frac{1}{16} W_{12} - \frac{8}{255} & W_{11} + \frac{64}{255} \end{bmatrix}.$$

Thus

$$\begin{bmatrix} W_{11} & W_{12} \\ W_{21} & W_{22} \end{bmatrix} = \begin{bmatrix} 0.0049 & -0.0332 \\ -0.0332 & 0.2559 \end{bmatrix}.$$

The total output roundoff noise for the scaled filter is

$$(W_{11} + W_{22})\sigma_e^2 = 0.2608 \sigma_e^2.$$

For the unscaled filter in Fig. 11.7,

$$
\begin{bmatrix} W_{11} & W_{12} \\ W_{21} & W_{22} \end{bmatrix} = \begin{bmatrix} 0 & \frac{1}{16} \\ 1 & 0 \end{bmatrix} \begin{bmatrix} W_{11} & W_{12} \\ W_{21} & W_{22} \end{bmatrix} \begin{bmatrix} 0 & 1 \\ \frac{1}{16} & 0 \end{bmatrix} + \begin{bmatrix} \frac{1}{256} & -\frac{1}{32} \\ -\frac{1}{32} & \frac{1}{4} \end{bmatrix}
$$

$$
= \begin{bmatrix} \frac{1}{256}W_{22} + \frac{1}{256} & \frac{1}{16}W_{21} - \frac{1}{32} \\ \frac{1}{16}W_{12} - \frac{1}{32} & W_{11} + \frac{1}{4} \end{bmatrix}.
$$

Thus

$$
\begin{bmatrix} W_{11} & W_{12} \\ W_{21} & W_{22} \end{bmatrix} = \begin{bmatrix} 0.0049 & -0.0333 \\ -0.0333 & 0.2549 \end{bmatrix}.
$$

The total output roundoff noise for the unscaled filter is

$$
(W_{11} + W_{22})\sigma_e^2 = 0.2598\sigma_e^2.
$$

Notice that the scaled filter suffers from larger roundoff noise, i.e.,

$$
\frac{\text{roundoff noise (unscaled)}}{\text{roundoff noise (scaled)}} = \frac{0.2598}{0.2608},
$$

which can be also observed by comparing the unscaled and scaled filter structures. In the scaled filter, input is scaled down by multipling 0.998 to the input to avoid overflow (refer to Fig. 11.8). Therefore, to keep the transfer functions the same in both filters, the output path of the scaled filter should have a gain which is $1/0.998$ times the gain of the output path of the unscaled filter. Thus the roundoff noise of the scaled filter is $1/0.998^2$ times that of the unscaled filter.

The above observation represents the tradeoff between overflow and roundoff noise. More stringent scaling reduces the possibility of overflow but increases the effect of roundoff noise.

In addition, notice that for the unscaled filter,

$$
K_{11}W_{11} + K_{22}W_{22} = \frac{256}{255}(0.0049 + 0.2549) = 0.2608,
$$

which is equal to $(W_{11} + W_{22})$ of the scaled filter. Thus (11.48) is confirmed.

■

11.5   ROUNDOFF NOISE IN PIPELINED IIR FILTERS

In this section, roundoff noise properties in pipelined 1st-order and 2nd-order direct-form IIR filters are discussed [4],[5]. Roundoff noise of the scaled pipelined versions are also considered.

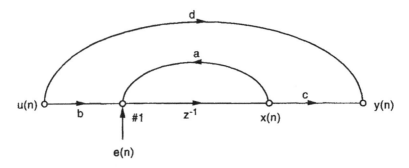

Fig. 11.9 Signal flow graph of 1st-order nonpipelined IIR filter.

11.5.1   First-Order IIR Filter

Consider the 1-pole IIR filter transfer function

$$H(z) = \frac{bcz^{-1}}{1 - az^{-1}} + d. \tag{11.49}$$

We are interested in the total roundoff noise of this filter for different levels of pipelining (i.e., different values of M) with and without l_2 scaling. The SFG of the filter is shown in Fig. 11.9.

$M = 1$ **Unscaled system:**

As we can see in Fig. 11.9 there is just one rounding operation in the filter (at node 1); therefore, there is just one error contribution $e(n)$ and just one state. As we have shown in (11.44), the roundoff noise is $\sigma_e^2 \sum_n g^2(n)$, where $g(n)$ is the unit-sample response from the state to the output $y(n)$. From the SFG of Fig. 11.9 we can write the transfer function $G(z)$, from the roundoff input to the output:

$$G(z) = \frac{cz^{-1}}{1 - az^{-1}} = cz^{-1}(1 + az^{-1} + a^2 z^{-2} + \cdots),$$

$$\Rightarrow G(z) = cz^{-1} + caz^{-2} + ca^2 z^{-3} + \cdots, \tag{11.50}$$

$$\Rightarrow \text{time series } g(n) = \{0, \ c, \ ac, \ a^2 c, \ \cdots\}. \tag{11.51}$$

The roundoff noise can be computed as

$$\text{roundoff noise} = \sigma_e^2 \sum_n g^2(n) = \sigma_e^2 \frac{c^2}{1 - a^2}. \tag{11.52}$$

$M = 1$ **Scaled system:**

To compute the roundoff noise in the scaled system we need to compute K first. Since K is defined as $\sum_n f^2(n)$ we need to compute $f(n)$, the unit-

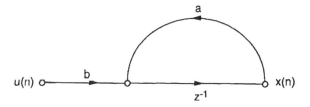

Fig. 11.10 Signal flow graph of f(n).

sample response from the input to the state node. The SFG representing the corresponding transfer function $F(z)$ is shown in Fig. 11.10, from which we can write down the expression for $F(z)$ and from there we can obtain the time series $f(n)$. Then K and t can be used to obtain all the scaled parameters.

$$F(z) = \frac{b}{1 - az^{-1}} = b(1 + az^{-1} + a^2 z^{-2} + \cdots), \quad (11.53)$$

$$\Rightarrow \quad f(n) = \{b, \ ab, \ a^2 b, \cdots\}, \quad (11.54)$$

$$\Rightarrow \quad K = \sum_n f^2(n) = \frac{b^2}{1 - a^2}, \quad (11.55)$$

$$\Rightarrow \quad t = \sqrt{K} = \frac{b}{\sqrt{1 - a^2}}. \quad (11.56)$$

Therefore,

$$a_s = \mathbf{T}^{-1}a\mathbf{T} = \frac{1}{t}at = a,$$

$$b_s = \mathbf{T}^{-1}b = \frac{\sqrt{1 - a^2}}{b}b = \sqrt{1 - a^2},$$

$$c_s = \mathbf{T}^T c = \frac{bc}{\sqrt{1 - a^2}},$$

$$d_s = d. \quad (11.57)$$

The reader can verify that $K_s = b_s^2/(1-a_s^2) = 1$ for the scaled system. Just like (11.52) we can write the roundoff noise in terms of the scaled parameters a_s, b_s, and c_s, as

$$\text{roundoff noise} = \sigma_e^2 \sum_n g^2(n) = \sigma_e^2 \frac{c_s^2}{1 - a_s^2} = \sigma_e^2 \frac{b^2 c^2}{(1 - a^2)^2}. \quad (11.58)$$

Alternatively one can also obtain the roundoff noise by computing KW of

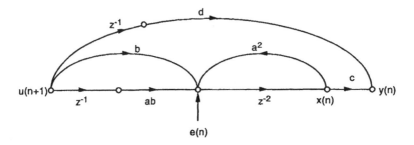

Fig. 11.11 Signal flow graph of 2-level pipelined IIR filter.

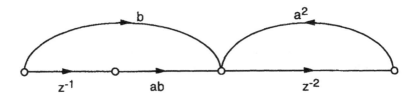

Fig. 11.12 Signal flow graph of f(n).

the original system as shown below,

$$\text{roundoff noise} = \sigma_e^2(KW) = \sigma_e^2 \frac{b^2}{(1-a^2)} \frac{c^2}{(1-a^2)}. \tag{11.59}$$

$M = 2$ Case:

The transfer function for this case is

$$H(z) = \frac{(bcz^{-1})(1+az^{-1})}{1-a^2z^{-2}} + d. \tag{11.60}$$

Fig. 11.11 shows the SFG corresponding to $z^{-1}H(z)$. To analyze the roundoff noise, let us first compute K for this filter. Notice that again we have just one roundoff operation and therefore we have just one state. The SFG for finding the $F(z)$ is shown in Fig. 11.12.

$$F(z) = \frac{b+abz^{-1}}{1-a^2z^{-2}} = \frac{b}{1-az^{-1}}, \tag{11.61}$$

$$\Rightarrow K = \frac{b^2}{1-a^2}. \tag{11.62}$$

Similarly we can compute W from $G(z)$. The SFG for finding out $G(z)$ is shown in Fig. 11.13.

$$G(z) = \frac{z^{-2}c}{1-a^2z^{-2}} = cz^{-2}(1+a^2z^{-2}+a^4z^{-4}+\cdots), \tag{11.63}$$

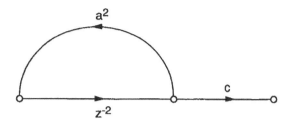

Fig. 11.13 Signal flow graph of g(n).

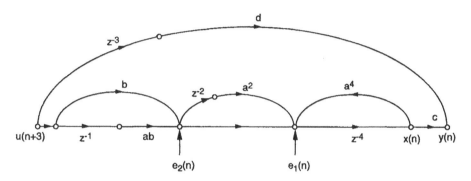

Fig. 11.14 Signal flow graph of 4-level pipelined IIR filter.

$$\Rightarrow g(n) = \{0, 0, c, 0, a^2c, 0, a^4c, \cdots \}, \tag{11.64}$$

$$\Rightarrow W = \sum_n g^2(n) = \frac{c^2}{1 - a^4}. \tag{11.65}$$

Since now we have both K and W available we can compute the roundoff noise for scaled as well as unscaled system.

$$\text{roundoff noise (unscaled)} = \sigma_e^2 \, \text{Trace} \, (W) = \sigma_e^2 \frac{c^2}{1 - a^4}, \tag{11.66}$$

$$\text{roundoff noise (scaled)} = \sigma_e^2 \sum_i K_{ii}W_{ii} = \sigma_e^2 \frac{b^2c^2}{(1 - a^2)(1 - a^4)}. \tag{11.67}$$

$M = 4$ Case:

The 4-level pipelined transfer function $H(z)$ is given by

$$H(z) = \frac{(bcz^{-1})(1 + az^{-1})(1 + a^2z^{-2})}{1 - a^4z^{-4}} + d. \tag{11.68}$$

The SFG, shown in Fig. 11.14, implements $z^{-3}H(z)$. Note that now we have two noise sources $e_1(n)$ and $e_2(n)$, as there are two roundoff operations being performed. Therefore, $\mathbf{K}$ and $\mathbf{W}$ are 2×2 matrices and all the diagonal elements of $\mathbf{K}$ and $\mathbf{W}$ need to be computed.

$\underline{K_{11}}$:

$$
\begin{aligned}
F_1(z) &= \frac{(b + abz^{-1})(1 + a^2 z^{-2})}{1 - a^4 z^{-4}} = \frac{b}{1 - az^{-1}}, \\
&= b(1 + az^{-1} + a^2 z^{-2} + \cdots), \\
\Rightarrow f_1(n) &= \{b,\ ab,\ a^2 b,\ \cdots\}, \qquad\qquad (11.69) \\
\Rightarrow K_{11} &= \sum_{n=0}^{\infty} f_1^2(n) = \frac{b^2}{1 - a^2}. \qquad\qquad (11.70)
\end{aligned}
$$

$\underline{K_{22}}$:

$$
\begin{aligned}
F_2(z) &= b + abz^{-1}, \\
\Rightarrow f_2(n) &= \{b,\ ab,\ 0,\ 0,\ \cdots\}, \qquad\qquad (11.71) \\
\Rightarrow K_{22} &= \sum_{n=0}^{\infty} f_2^2(n) = b^2(1 + a^2). \qquad\qquad (11.72)
\end{aligned}
$$

$\underline{W_{11}}$:

$$
\begin{aligned}
G_1(z) &= \frac{cz^{-4}}{1 - a^4 z^{-4}} = cz^{-4}(1 + a^4 z^{-4} + a^8 z^{-8} + \cdots), \\
\Rightarrow g_1(n) &= \{0,\ 0,\ 0,\ 0,\ c,\ 0,\ 0,\ 0,\ a^4 c,\ \cdots\}, \qquad (11.73) \\
\Rightarrow W_{11} &= \sum_{n=0}^{\infty} g_1^2(n) = \frac{c^2}{1 - a^8}. \qquad\qquad (11.74)
\end{aligned}
$$

$\underline{W_{22}}$:

$$
\begin{aligned}
G_2(z) &= \frac{cz^{-4}(1 + a^2 z^{-2})}{1 - a^4 z^{-4}} = \frac{cz^{-4}}{1 - a^2 z^{-2}}, \\
&= cz^{-4}(1 + a^2 z^{-2} + a^4 z^{-4} + \cdots), \\
\Rightarrow g_2(n) &= \{0,\ 0,\ 0,\ 0,\ c,\ 0,\ a^2 c,\ \cdots\}, \qquad (11.75) \\
\Rightarrow W_{22} &= \sum_{n=0}^{\infty} g_2^2(n) = \frac{c^2}{1 - a^4}. \qquad\qquad (11.76)
\end{aligned}
$$

Now we have all the parameters needed for computing the system roundoff noise.

$$
\text{roundoff noise (unscaled)} = \sigma_e^2 \sum_{i=1}^{2} W_{ii} = \sigma_e^2 \frac{c^2(2 + a^4)}{1 - a^8}, \qquad (11.77)
$$

Table 11.1   Roundoff Noise for Two Special Cases ($\sigma_e^2 = 1$)

Case	Unscaled	Scaled
$a \to 0$	$c^2 \log_2 M$	$b^2 c^2 \log_2 M$
$a = 1 - \epsilon$	$\frac{c^2(M-1)}{2M\epsilon}$	$\frac{b^2 c^2}{4M\epsilon^2}$

Table 11.2   Roundoff Noise as a Function of M and ϵ ($\sigma_e^2 = 1$)

M	Unscaled			Scaled		
	$\epsilon = 0.1$	$\epsilon = 0.2$	$\epsilon = 0.3$	$\epsilon = 0.1$	$\epsilon = 0.2$	$\epsilon = 0.3$
1	5.00	2.50	1.67	25.0	6.25	2.78
2	2.50	1.25	0.83	12.5	3.12	1.39
4	3.75	1.87	1.25	6.25	1.56	0.69

$$\text{roundoff noise (scaled)} = \sigma_e^2 \sum_{i=1}^{2} K_{ii} W_{ii} = \sigma_e^2 \frac{b^2 c^2 (2 - a^8)}{(1 - a^2)(1 - a^8)}. \tag{11.78}$$

In fact we can write a general expression for the roundoff noise for any arbitrary M which is a power-of-2. The roundoff noise values for unscaled and scaled systems are given by

$$\text{roundoff noise (unscaled)} = \sigma_e^2 c^2 \sum_{j=1}^{\log_2 M} \frac{1}{1 - a^{2j+1}}, \tag{11.79}$$

$$\text{roundoff noise (scaled)} = \sigma_e^2 b^2 c^2 \frac{\log_2 M - (\log_2 M - 1)a^{2M}}{(1 - a^2)(1 - a^{2M})}, \tag{11.80}$$

where M is a power-of-2 and $M > 1$.

If the value of a in (11.79) and (11.80) is very close to 1 or 0 then we need to deal with them separately. As $a \to 0$ both the denominators in (11.79) and (11.80) become unity and the roundoff noise for the scaled and unscaled system will be $\sigma_e^2 b^2 c^2 \log_2 M$ and $\sigma_e^2 c^2 \log_2 M$, respectively. To perform the analysis for $a \to 1$ case, let us assume that $a = 1 - \epsilon$ where $\epsilon \ll 1$. Substituting this in (11.79) and (11.80), we obtain the expressions shown in Table 11.1.

To illustrate it further, consider the case $b = c = 1$ and $a = 1 - \epsilon$. Table 11.2 shows the roundoff noise values for various M and ϵ. The important point to note here is that scaling should not be confused with reduction in roundoff noise. Scaling is a method to assign equal wordlengths to all the states in the system. This point is clearly brought out in Table 11.2. Notice that in some cases the total roundoff noise has increased as a result of scaling. Furthermore, the roundoff noise of the scaled filter decreases linearly with M for poles close to unity whereas the unscaled filter roundoff noise for this case remains approximately constant.

To determine the wordlength or SNR of a pipelined filter, the output signal power of the pipelined filter needs to be computed. When a filter is pipelined by the scattered look-ahead technique, the output signal power of the pipelined filter is the same as that of the nonpipelined filter. From (11.49), output signal power of the nonpipelined filter is computed using Parseval's relation as

$$\sum_n h^2(n) = \frac{1}{2\pi j} \oint_C H(z)H(z^{-1})z^{-1}dz, \tag{11.81}$$

$$= \frac{b^2 c^2}{1 - a^2} + d^2, \tag{11.82}$$

where C is a counterclockwise contour and the contour integral in (11.81) can be easily evaluated using Cauchy's residue theorem [1],[3].

For convenience, d in (11.82) can be set to zero, since d in (11.49) does not cause *internal* rounding operation (see Fig. 11.9, also notice that (11.79) and (11.80) do not depend on d). Then, for nonpipelined filter ($M = 1$), we can compute the noise to signal ratio (NSR) as:

$$\text{NSR (unscaled)} = \frac{\sigma_e^2}{b^2}, \tag{11.83}$$

$$\text{NSR (scaled)} = \frac{\sigma_e^2}{1 - a^2}. \tag{11.84}$$

For $M > 1$,

$$\text{NSR (unscaled)} = \sigma_e^2 \frac{1 - a^2}{b^2} \sum_{j=1}^{\log_2 M} \frac{1}{1 - a^{2^{j+1}}}, \tag{11.85}$$

$$\text{NSR (scaled)} = \sigma_e^2 \frac{\log_2 M - (\log_2 M - 1)a^{2M}}{1 - a^{2M}}. \tag{11.86}$$

11.5.2   Second-Order IIR Filter

Consider the following 2nd-order IIR filter

$$H(z) = \frac{1}{1 - 2r\cos\theta z^{-1} + r^2 z^{-2}}. \tag{11.87}$$

The SFG of the filter is shown in Fig. 11.15. We are interested in the total roundoff noise of this filter for different levels of pipelining *with* l_2 scaling.

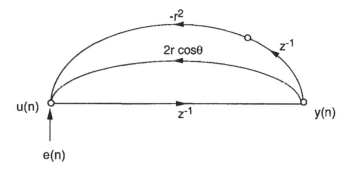

Fig. 11.15   Signal flow graph of 2nd-order nonpipelined IIR filter.

The computation of the roundoff noise without scaling is left to the reader.

$M = 1$ **Case:**

As can be seen in Fig. 11.15, only one rounding operation is performed in this filter. Therefore, there is just one error contribution $e(n)$. From Fig. 11.15,

$$F(z) = \frac{1}{1 - 2r\cos\theta z^{-1} + r^2 z^{-2}}. \tag{11.88}$$

Then, using Parseval's relation,

$$\sum_n f^2(n) = \frac{1}{2\pi j} \oint_C \frac{z\,dz}{(z - re^{j\theta})(z - re^{-j\theta})(1 - re^{j\theta}z)(1 - re^{-j\theta}z)}. \tag{11.89}$$

By Cauchy's residue theorem, (11.89) can be expressed as

$$
\begin{aligned}
K &= \sum_n f^2(n), \\
&= \frac{re^{j\theta}}{(re^{j\theta} - re^{-j\theta})(1 - r^2 e^{j2\theta})(1 - r^2)} + \\
&\quad \frac{re^{-j\theta}}{(re^{-j\theta} - re^{j\theta})(1 - r^2 e^{-j2\theta})(1 - r^2)}, \\
&= \frac{1 + r^2}{1 - r^2} \frac{1}{1 - 2r^2\cos 2\theta + r^4}. \tag{11.90}
\end{aligned}
$$

Since $K = W$ as can be seen in Fig. 11.15, the roundoff noise of the 2nd-order nonpipelined system is

$$
\begin{aligned}
\text{roundoff noise} &= \sigma_e^2(KW), \\
&= \sigma_e^2 K^2, \\
&= \sigma_e^2 \left(\frac{1 + r^2}{1 - r^2}\right)^2 \frac{1}{(1 - 2r^2\cos 2\theta + r^4)^2}. \tag{11.91}
\end{aligned}
$$

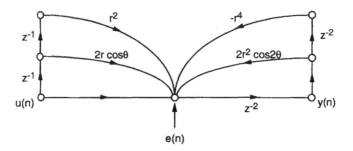

Fig. 11.16   Signal flow graph of 2-level pipelined IIR filter.

From (11.91), we observe the relationship between the pole locations and the roundoff noise as

$$r \to 0 \quad : \quad \text{roundoff noise} \to \sigma_e^2,$$

$$r \to 1 \quad : \quad \text{roundoff noise} \to \frac{\sigma_e^2}{(4\epsilon \sin^2 \theta)^2}, \tag{11.92}$$

where $\epsilon \to 0$.

$\underline{M = 2 \text{ Case:}}$

The 2-level pipelined transfer function is

$$H(z) = \frac{1 + 2r \cos \theta z^{-1} + r^2 z^{-2}}{1 - 2r^2 \cos 2\theta z^{-2} + r^4 z^{-4}}, \tag{11.93}$$

and the corresponding SFG is shown in Fig. 11.16. There is just one error contribution $e(n)$ in Fig. 11.16. Thus, $F(z)$ is computed as

$$
\begin{aligned}
F(z) &= \frac{1 + 2r \cos \theta z^{-1} + r^2 z^{-2}}{1 - 2r^2 \cos 2\theta z^{-2} + r^4 z^{-4}}, \\
&= \frac{1}{1 - 2r \cos \theta z^{-1} + r^2 z^{-2}}. \tag{11.94}
\end{aligned}
$$

Notice that $F(z)$ in (11.94) is the same as $F(z)$ in (11.88). Thus K is given by (11.90).

From Fig. 11.16 with input $= 0$, $G(z)$ is computed as

$$G(z) = \frac{1}{1 - 2r^2 \cos 2\theta z^{-2} + r^4 z^{-4}}, \tag{11.95}$$

which leads to

$$W = \frac{1 + r^4}{1 - r^4} \frac{1}{1 - 2r^4 \cos 4\theta + r^8}. \tag{11.96}$$

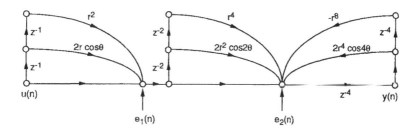

Fig. 11.17 Signal flow graph of 4-level pipelined IIR filter.

Therefore,

$$
\begin{aligned}
\text{roundoff noise} \;=\;& \sigma_e^2 (KW), \\
=\;& \sigma_e^2 \frac{(1+r^2)(1+r^4)}{(1-r^2)(1-r^4)} \times \\
& \frac{1}{(1-2r^2 \cos 2\theta + r^4)(1-2r^4 \cos 4\theta + r^8)}. \quad (11.97)
\end{aligned}
$$

From (11.97), we observe the relationship between the pole locations and the roundoff noise as

$$
r \to 0 \;:\; \text{roundoff noise} \to \sigma_e^2,
$$

$$
r \to 1 \;:\; \text{roundoff noise} \to \frac{\sigma_e^2}{(4\epsilon \sin^2 \theta)(8\epsilon \sin^2 2\theta)}. \quad (11.98)
$$

$M = 4$ Case:

After pipelining by 4 levels, the transfer function $H(z)$ becomes

$$
H(z) = \frac{(1 + 2r \cos \theta z^{-1} + r^2 z^{-2})(1 + 2r^2 \cos 2\theta z^{-2} + r^4 z^{-4})}{1 - 2r^4 \cos 4\theta z^{-4} + r^8 z^{-8}}. \quad (11.99)
$$

The SFG of the filter is shown in Fig. 11.17. Note that we have two noise sources $e_1(n)$ and $e_2(n)$. By the same procedure as before, the following results are obtained:

$e_1(n)$:

$$
r \to 0 \;:\; K_{11}W_{11} \to 1,
$$

$$
r \to 1 \;:\; K_{11}W_{11} \to \frac{2 + 4\cos^2 \theta}{8\epsilon \sin^2 2\theta}. \quad (11.100)
$$

$e_2(n)$:

$$
r \to 0 \;:\; K_{22}W_{22} \to 1,
$$

$$r \to 1 \quad : \quad K_{22}W_{22} \to \frac{1}{(4\epsilon \sin^2 \theta)(16\epsilon \sin^2 4\theta)}. \qquad (11.101)$$

From (11.100) and (11.101), the total roundoff noise is obtained as

$$r \to 0 \quad : \quad \sigma_e^2 \sum_i K_{ii}W_{ii} \to 2\sigma_e^2$$

$$r \to 1 \quad : \quad \sigma_e^2 \sum_i K_{ii}W_{ii} \to \frac{\sigma_e^2}{(4\epsilon \sin^2 \theta)(16\epsilon \sin^2 4\theta)}. \qquad (11.102)$$

In general, when M is a power-of-2, roundoff noise of M-level pipelined filter can be expressed as

$$r \to 0 \quad : \quad \sigma_e^2 \sum_i K_{ii}W_{ii} \to \sigma_e^2 \log_2 M,$$

$$r \to 1 \quad : \quad \sigma_e^2 \sum_i K_{ii}W_{ii} \to \frac{\sigma_e^2}{(4\epsilon \sin^2 \theta)(4M\epsilon \sin^2 M\theta)}. \qquad (11.103)$$

To compute NSR, we need to compute output signal power, which is given by (11.90). (Notice that $H(z) = F(z)$ for $M = 1$ case.) From (11.90), at the output node,

$$r \to 0 \quad : \quad \text{signal power} \to 1,$$

$$r \to 1 \quad : \quad \text{signal power} \to \frac{1}{4\epsilon \sin^2 \theta}. \qquad (11.104)$$

Thus,

$$r \to 0 \quad : \quad \text{NSR} \to \log_2 M,$$

$$r \to 1 \quad : \quad \text{NSR} \to \frac{1}{4M\epsilon \sin^2 M\theta}. \qquad (11.105)$$

As the poles approach the origin, the NSR becomes independent of M and θ. However, the NSR increases rapidly as the poles approach the unit circle. The effect of roundoff noise is most severe when the poles simultaneously satisfy the following two conditions:

$$r \quad \to \quad 1,$$

$$\theta \quad \to \quad \frac{n\pi}{M}, \quad n = 0, \pm 1, \cdots, \pm M. \qquad (11.106)$$

Note that the NSR expressions in (11.105) are not valid when $\theta = n\pi/M$, $n = 0, \pm 1, \cdots, \pm M$. The calculation of roundoff noise for this case is left as an exercise (see Problem 11).

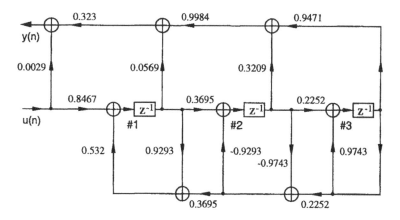

Fig. 11.18 A 3rd-order scaled-normalized lattice filter.

11.6 ROUNDOFF NOISE COMPUTATION USING STATE VARIABLE DESCRIPTION

Parseval's relation and Cauchy's residue theorem are useful for finding signal power or roundoff noise of digital filters. However, it is not easy to apply Parseval's relation to a filter with complex structure. (For example, see the 3rd-order scaled-normalized lattice filter in Fig. 11.18.)

However, due to simple computing algorithms available [3], the power at each internal node and the output roundoff noise of a digital filter can be easily computed once the digital filter is described in state variable form. Using (11.24), $\mathbf{K}$ can be computed efficiently by the following algorithm [3].

Algorithm for Computing $\mathbf{K}$:

- Initialize:
$$\mathbf{F} \longleftarrow \mathbf{A},$$
$$\mathbf{K} \longleftarrow \mathbf{b}\mathbf{b}^T.$$
- Loop:
$$\mathbf{K} \longleftarrow \mathbf{F}\mathbf{K}\mathbf{F}^T + \mathbf{K},$$
$$\mathbf{F} \longleftarrow \mathbf{F}^2.$$
- Continue until $\mathbf{F} = 0$.

After 1st loop iteration,

$$\mathbf{K} = \mathbf{A}\mathbf{b}\mathbf{b}^T\mathbf{A}^T + \mathbf{b}\mathbf{b}^T,$$
$$\mathbf{F} = \mathbf{A}^2. \tag{11.107}$$

After 2nd loop iteration,

$$\mathbf{K} = \mathbf{A}^3 \mathbf{bb}^T (\mathbf{A}^3)^T + \mathbf{A}^2 \mathbf{bb}^T (\mathbf{A}^2)^T + \mathbf{Abb}^T \mathbf{A}^T + \mathbf{bb}^T,$$
$$\mathbf{F} = \mathbf{A}^4. \tag{11.108}$$

Thus, each execution of the loop doubles the number of terms in the sum of (11.24). The above algorithm converges as long as the filter is stable since the eigenvalues of the matrix $\mathbf{A}$ are the poles of the transfer function. (It is well-known from linear algebra theory that the matrix powers $\mathbf{A}^i$ tend to the zero matrix as i approaches infinity if and only if all eigenvalues of the matrix $\mathbf{A}$ are less than one in magnitude.) Notice that the algorithm for computing $\mathbf{K}$ also computes $\mathbf{W}$ by substituting $\mathbf{A}^T$ for $\mathbf{A}$ and $\mathbf{c}$ for $\mathbf{b}$ in the initialization step.

Algorithm for Computing $\mathbf{W}$:

- Initialize:
$$\mathbf{F} \longleftarrow \mathbf{A}^T,$$
$$\mathbf{W} \longleftarrow \mathbf{cc}^T.$$
- Loop:
$$\mathbf{W} \longleftarrow \mathbf{FWF}^T + \mathbf{W},$$
$$\mathbf{F} \longleftarrow \mathbf{F}^2.$$
- Continue until $\mathbf{F} = 0$.

Example 11.6.1 *Consider the scaled-normalized lattice filter in Fig. 11.18. Assume that it is desired to compute signal powers at nodes 1, 2, and 3. Since there are three states $(1 - 3)$, the dimensions of the matrices $\mathbf{A}$, $\mathbf{b}$, $\mathbf{c}$, and $\mathbf{d}$ are 3×3, 3×1, 3×1, and 1×1, respectively. From Fig. 11.18, state equations can be written as*

$$\begin{aligned}
x_1(n+1) &= 0.4944x_1(n) - 0.1915x_2(n) + 0.0443x_3(n) + 0.8467u(n), \\
x_2(n+1) &= 0.3695x_1(n) + 0.9054x_2(n) - 0.2093x_3(n), \\
x_3(n+1) &= 0.2252x_2(n) + 0.9743x_3(n), \\
y(n) &= 0.0184x_1(n) + 0.1035x_2(n) + 0.3054x_3(n) + 0.0029u(n).
\end{aligned}$$

From the foregoing equations, matrices $\mathbf{A}$, $\mathbf{b}$, $\mathbf{c}$, and $\mathbf{d}$ can be obtained in a straightforward manner. By substituting these matrices to the $\mathbf{K}$-computing algorithm, we obtain

$$\mathbf{K} = \begin{bmatrix} 1 & 0 & 0 \\ 0 & 1 & 0 \\ 0 & 0 & 1 \end{bmatrix}.$$

Since $K_{11} = K_{22} = K_{33} = 1$, we conclude that no scaling is needed for nodes $1 - 3$. In addition, the $\mathbf{K}$ matrix shows that the signals at nodes $1 - 3$ are orthogonal to each other since all off-diagonal elements are zeros.

By the $\mathbf{W}$-computing algorithm, we obtain $W_{11} = 0.1455$, $W_{22} = 0.2952$,

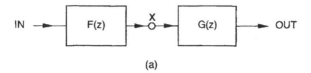

(a)

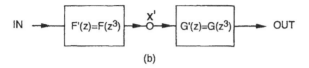

(b)

Fig. 11.19 (a) A filter with transfer function $H(z) = F(z)G(z)$. (b) Transformed filter obtained by 3 slow-down transformation ($H'(z) = F(z^3)G(z^3)$).

and $W_{33} = 0.3096$. ∎

Example 11.6.1 shows that it is straightforward to compute signal power or roundoff noise of a digital filter once the filter is described in state variable form. However, it is difficult to compute signal power or roundoff noise at nodes that are not connected to unit-delay branches, since these nodes do not appear in the state variable description. For example, signal powers at the nodes on top or bottom edges in Fig. 11.18 cannot be computed directly.

11.7 SLOW-DOWN, RETIMING, AND PIPELINING

Many useful realizations contain nodes that are not connected to unit-delay branches. These nodes or variables thus do not appear in a state variable description and the scaling and noise computation methods cannot be applied directly. To overcome this difficulty, the SRP (slow-down and retiming/pipelining) transformation technique (see chapters 4 and 3) can be used as a preprocessing step.

Consider the filter in Fig. 11.19(b) which is obtained by applying slow-down transformation ($M = 3$) to the filter in Fig. 11.19(a). By 3 slow-down transformation, every z-variable in Fig. 11.19(a) is changed into z^3. Thus the transfer function of the transformed filter $H'(z)$ is related to the original transfer function $H(z)$ as

$$H'(z) = F'(z)G'(z) = F(z^3)G(z^3) = H(z^3). \tag{11.109}$$

Thus, if the unit-sample response from the input to the internal node x in Fig. 11.19(a) is defined by

$$f(n) = \{f(0),\ f(1),\ f(2), \cdots\}, \tag{11.110}$$

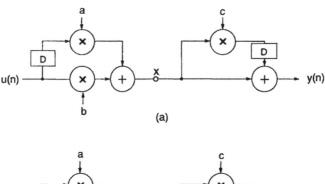

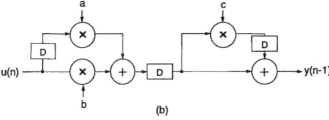

Fig. 11.20 (a) A filter with a nonstate variable node on a feed-forward path. (b) Nonstate variable node is converted into state variable node by pipelining.

the unit-sample response from the input to the internal node x' in Fig. 11.19(b) is

$$f'(n) = \{f(0),\ 0,\ 0,\ f(1),\ 0,\ 0,\ f(2),\ 0,\ 0,\cdots\}. \tag{11.111}$$

Then,

$$K'_{xx} = \sum_n (f'(n))^2 = \sum_n f(n)^2 = K_{xx}. \tag{11.112}$$

Similarly, it can be shown that

$$W'_{xx} = W_{xx}. \tag{11.113}$$

The foregoing analysis shows that slow-down transformation does not alter the finite wordlength behavior.

Consider the filter in Fig. 11.20(a), which has a nonstate variable node x on the feed-forward path. It is obvious that the nonstate variable node cannot be converted into the state variable node by slow-down transformation. However, since x is on the feed-forward path, a delay can be placed on a proper cutset location as shown in Fig. 11.20(b). This pipelining operation converts the nonstate variable node x into state variable node. The output sequence of the pipelined filter is equal to that of the original filter except one clock cycle delay. This means the pipelined filter undergoes the same possibility of overflow and the same effect of roundoff noise as in the original filter. Thus it is clear that pipelining does not alter the finite wordlength behavior.

In a linear array, if either all the left-directed or all the right-directed edges

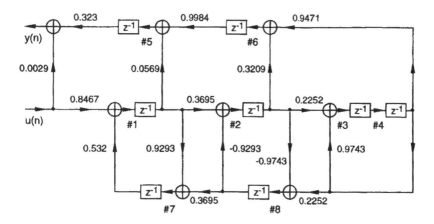

Fig. 11.21 A transformed filter of the 3rd-order scaled-normalized lattice filter in Fig. 11.18.

between modules carry at least one delay on each edge, the cutset localization procedure can be applied to transfer some delays or a fraction of a delay to the opposite directed edges (see Chapter 4) [6],[7]. Based on this property and the foregoing observations, the SRP transformation technique is summarized as follows:

1. Apply slow-down transformation by a factor of M to a linear array, i.e., replace z by z^M. Also, apply pipelining technique to appropriate locations.

2. Distribute the additional delays to proper locations such that non-state variable nodes are converted to state variable nodes.

3. Apply the scaling and noise computation method using state variable description.

Example 11.7.1 *Consider the filter shown in Fig. 11.21. This filter is the same as the 3rd-order scaled-normalized lattice filter in Fig. 11.18 except that it has five more delays. The SFG in Fig. 11.21 is obtained by using a 2-slow transformation followed by retiming or cutset transformation. Notice that signal power or roundoff noise at every internal node in this filter can be computed using state variable description since each node is connected to a unit delay branch. Since there are 8 states $(1 - 8)$, the dimensions of the matrices $\mathbf{A}$, $\mathbf{b}$, $\mathbf{c}$, and d are 8×8, 8×1, 8×1, and 1×1, respectively. From Fig. 11.21, state equations can be written as*

$$
\begin{aligned}
x_1(n+1) &= 0.532x_7(n) + 0.8467u(n), \\
x_2(n+1) &= 0.3695x_1(n) - 0.9293x_8(n), \\
x_3(n+1) &= 0.2252x_2(n) + 0.9743x_4(n),
\end{aligned}
$$

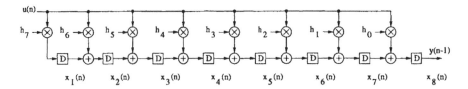

Fig. 11.22   The 8-tap FIR filter in Example 11.7.2.

$$
\begin{aligned}
x_4(n+1) &= x_3(n), \\
x_5(n+1) &= 0.0569x_1(n) + 0.9984x_6(n), \\
x_6(n+1) &= 0.3209x_2(n) + 0.9471x_4(n), \\
x_7(n+1) &= 0.9293x_1(n) + 0.3695x_8(n), \\
x_8(n+1) &= -0.9743x_2(n) + 0.2252x_4(n), \\
y(n) &= 0.323x_5(n) + 0.0029u(n).
\end{aligned}
$$

From the above equations, matrices $\mathbf{A}$, $\mathbf{b}$, $\mathbf{c}$, and d can be obtained in a straightforward manner. Notice that the number of nonzero elements in each row of $\mathbf{A}$ is at most two although the matrix dimension has been increased. Furthermore, each of the parameters in Fig. 11.21 appears directly in the above equations without any additional computations. (In Example 11.6.1, additional computations are needed.) In fact, matrices $\mathbf{A}$, $\mathbf{b}$, $\mathbf{c}$, and d can be obtained directly from Fig. 11.21 by simple inspection. Using the $\mathbf{K}$-computing algorithm, we obtain $\{K_{ii}=1, i=1, 2, \cdots, 8\}$, which means that every internal node has been scaled perfectly. Similarly, we obtain $W_{11} - W_{88}$ as $\{0.1455, 0.2952, 0.3096, 0.3096, 0.1043, 0.104, 0.0412, 0.1912\}$. Thus the total output roundoff noise is $1.191\sigma_e^2$. Note that no roundoff operation is associated with node 4 or state $x_4(n)$. Therefore, W_{44} is not included in $\mathrm{Trace}(\mathbf{W})$ for roundoff noise computation. ∎

Example 11.7.2 Consider the 8-tap low-pass data-broadcast FIR filter shown in Fig. 11.22 and its frequence response shown in Fig. 11.23.   The signal power at every internal node in this filter can be computed using state variable descriptions. Here one more state variable is introduced by adding one delay element before the output signal $y(n)$. This structure is described by the state variable description:

$$
\begin{aligned}
x_1(n+1) &= h_7 u(n), \\
x_2(n+1) &= x_1(n) + h_6 u(n), \\
x_3(n+1) &= x_2(n) + h_5 u(n), \\
x_4(n+1) &= x_3(n) + h_4 u(n), \\
x_5(n+1) &= x_4(n) + h_3 u(n), \\
x_6(n+1) &= x_5(n) + h_2 u(n),
\end{aligned}
$$

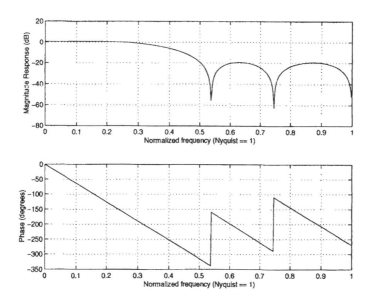

Fig. 11.23 The frequence response of the 8-tap FIR filter in Example 11.7.2.

$$
\begin{aligned}
x_7(n+1) &= x_6(n) + h_1 u(n), \\
x_8(n+1) &= x_7(n) + h_0 u(n), \\
y(n-1) &= x_8(n).
\end{aligned}
$$

From the foregoing equations, matrices $\mathbf{A}$, $\mathbf{b}$, $\mathbf{c}$, *and* d *can be obtained in a straightforward manner. The dimension of the matrices* $\mathbf{A}$, $\mathbf{b}$, $\mathbf{c}$, *and* d *are* 8×8, 8×1, 8×1, *and* 1×1, *respectively. Using* $\mathbf{K}$ *and* $\mathbf{W}$*-computing algorithms, we obtain*

$$
\mathbf{K} = \begin{bmatrix}
0.407 & 0.322 & 0.147 & -0.002 & -0.054 & -0.034 & -0.003 & 0.007 \\
0.322 & 0.401 & 0.324 & 0.164 & 0.029 & -0.023 & -0.017 & -0.002 \\
0.147 & 0.324 & 0.401 & 0.320 & 0.1560 & 0.021 & -0.027 & -0.017 \\
-0.002 & 0.164 & 0.320 & 0.356 & 0.237 & 0.073 & -0.024 & -0.031 \\
-0.054 & 0.029 & 0.156 & 0.237 & 0.204 & 0.085 & -0.009 & -0.031 \\
-0.034 & -0.023 & 0.021 & 0.073 & 0.085 & 0.052 & 0.003 & -0.017 \\
-0.003 & -0.017 & -0.027 & -0.024 & -0.009 & 0.003 & 0.007 & -0.002 \\
0.007 & -0.002 & -0.017 & -0.031 & -0.031 & -0.017 & -0.002 & 0.007
\end{bmatrix}
$$

and $\mathbf{W}$ *is the same as* $\mathbf{I}_{8 \times 8}$, *i.e., the identity matrix of dimension* 8×8. *Thus, the roundoff noise of this structure is* $8\sigma_e^2$. *The* $\mathbf{K}$ *matrix can be used to obtain the scaled structure shown in Fig. 11.24. The total roundoff noise*

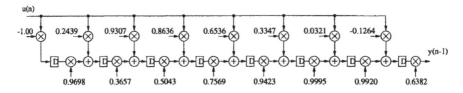

Fig. 11.24   The scaled FIR filter in Example 11.7.2.

of the scaled structure is

$$\sum_{i=1}^{8} K_{ii}W_{ii} = \sum_{i=1}^{8} K_{ii} = 1.835\sigma_e^2.$$

The roundoff noise of the scaled FIR filter can also be obtained by computing the trace of the **W** *matrix for the scaled system.* ■

11.8   CONCLUSIONS

Approaches to scaling and roundoff noise in state variable description based IIR and FIR digital filters have been addressed. In many digital filters, all roundoff noise nodes cannot be modeled as state variable nodes. These filters can be preprocessed using pipelining and/or M-slow transformation and re-timing so that the output of every roundoff noise node can be described by a state variable. Fast algorithms for computation of state and output covariance matrices have also been presented. These matrices can be used to perform scaling and to compute roundoff noise.

11.9   PROBLEMS

1. Consider the SFG in Fig. 11.25 which corresponds to the all-pole transfer function

$$H(z) = \frac{z^{-1}}{1 - az^{-1}},$$

where $-1 < a < 1$ for stability.

   (a) Calculate the output roundoff noise. Show that the noise variance σ_e^2 gets amplified through the *feedback* section, i.e., even though $e(n)$ may be *small*, its effect on $y(n)$ can be *large*.

   (b) Compute roundoff noise for (i) $a = 0.1$, (ii) $a = 0.5$, and (iii) $a = 0.998$. Comment on the relation between roundoff noise and pole locations.

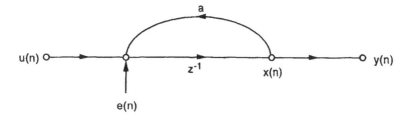

Fig. 11.25 Signal flow graph of an all-pole IIR filter.

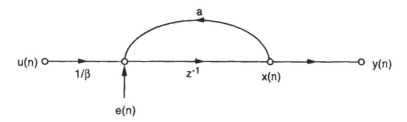

Fig. 11.26 Signal flow graph of a scaled all-pole IIR filter.

(c) For narrowband filters, $|a|$ is typically very close to 1. For example, $a = 0.998$ is not uncommon. For such filters, the noise variance σ_e^2 gets amplified enormously. (In that case, low-noise/sensitivity filter structures such as lattice filters and wave digital filters need to be considered.) Explain conceptually why poles are located very close to the unit circle for narrowband filters.

2. Assume that the input signal $u(n)$ in Fig. 11.25 is a zero mean white wide sense stationary random process with variance σ_u^2.

   (a) Compute the variance of the output signal $y(n)$ for the input $u(n)$.

   (b) Show that NSR (noise-to-signal ratio) is

   $$\frac{N}{S} = \frac{\sigma_e^2}{\sigma_u^2}.$$

   (c) From (b), NSR is apparently independent of pole location. What makes this a false conclusion? *Hint:* For $a \to 1$, the signal gain from the input to the output is very large. Then $y(n)$ suffers from possible overflow.

3. The all-pole filter in Fig. 11.25 can be scaled using l_1 scaling scheme as shown in Fig. 11.26.

   Assume input $u(n)$ is a wide sense stationary random process with a uniform probability density function and $|u(n)| \leq 1$.

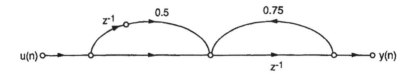

Fig. 11.27 Signal flow graph of $H(z)$ for Problem 6.

(a) Show that $\beta > 1$. (To avoid the use of an expensive multiplier $1/\beta$, it can be replaced with the nearest power of 2 or merged with a multiplier of the preceding filter stage.)

(b) Compute the variance of the input.

(c) Compute the output signal variance σ_y^2, i.e., variance of $y(n)$ without noise.

(d) Show that output NSR is

$$\frac{N}{S} = \frac{3\sigma_e^2}{(1 - |a|)^2}.$$

Notice that for a given a, the only way to decrease this ratio is to decrease σ_e^2 by increasing the wordlength.

4. For a standard state variable representation of an N-th order IIR filter, prove the following:

(a) $\mathbf{W} = \sum_{n=0}^{\infty} (\mathbf{c}^T \mathbf{A}^n)^T \mathbf{c}^T \mathbf{A}^n$.

(b) $\mathbf{W} = \mathbf{A}^T \mathbf{W} \mathbf{A} + \mathbf{c}\mathbf{c}^T$.

(c) For a scaled system, $\mathbf{W}_s = \mathbf{T}^T \mathbf{W} \mathbf{T}$.

5. Show that each execution of the loop of the $\mathbf{W}$-computing algorithm doubles the number of terms in the sum of (11.27).

6. Consider the SFG in Fig. 11.27 that corresponds to the transfer function

$$H(z) = \frac{z^{-1} + 0.5z^{-2}}{1 - 0.75z^{-1}}.$$

(a) Calculate its roundoff noise.

(b) The 2-level pipelined implementation of this structure can be realized in two ways as shown in Fig. 11.28. Calculate the roundoff noise of both these structures.

(c) Repeat (a) and (b) for scaled structures without deriving scaled versions of structures in (a) and (b).

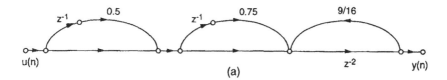

(a)

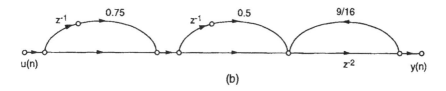

(b)

Fig. 11.28 A 2-level pipelined implementations of the filter in Problem 6.

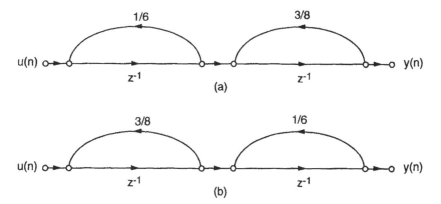

Fig. 11.29 Two different realizations of a 2nd-order filter for Problem 7.

7. Consider the two different realizations of a 2nd-order filter shown in Fig. 11.29.

   (a) Obtain l_2 scaled versions of the two filter structures.

   (b) Calculate NSRs for the scaled filters obtained in a). Compare the NSRs.

8. Consider the 2nd-order filter shown in Fig. 11.30.

   (a) Calculate the transfer function.

   (b) Calculate **K** by solving (11.25).

   (c) For l_2 scaling, choose a diagonal transformation matrix **T** such that $t_i = \sqrt{K_{ii}}$.

   (d) Draw the SFG of the scaled filter. Find the output roundoff noise by calculating the **W** matrix for this scaled structure.

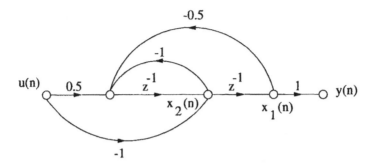

Fig. 11.30   A 2nd-order direct form filter.

9. Consider a 2-level pipelined implementation of the 2nd-order filter in Fig. 11.30.

   (a) Find a 2-level pipelinable transfer function of the filter in Fig. 11.30 using scattered look-ahead transformation. Draw an SFG corresponding to the obtained transfer function.

   (b) Calculate **K** (i) with **K**-computing algorithm, and (ii) by solving (11.25).

   (c) For l_2 scaling, choose a diagonal transformation matrix **T** such that $t_i = \sqrt{K_{ii}}$.

   (d) Draw an SFG of the scaled filter. Find the output roundoff noise by calculating the **W** matrix for this scaled structure.

10. Calculate **K** and **W** matrices of the filter structure in Fig. 11.21 using **K**-computing algorithm.

11. The NSR expression in (11.105) is not valid when $\theta = n\pi/M$, $n = 0, \pm1, \cdots, \pm M$. Derive a valid NSR expression for the case of $M = 4$ and $\theta = \pi/4$.

12. Consider the SFG in Fig. 11.31 obtained by replacing each z^{-1} in Fig. 11.30 by z^{-2}.

   (a) Show that $K_{11} = K_{33}$ and $K_{22} = K_{44}$.

   (b) Find $F_1(z)$ and $F_2(z)$.

   (c) Express $F_1(z)$ and $F_2(z)$ in Fig. 11.31 in terms of $F_1(z)$ and $F_2(z)$ in Fig. 11.30.

   (d) Show the following:

$$K_{11} \text{ in Fig. 11.30} = K_{11} \text{ in Fig. 11.31},$$
$$K_{22} \text{ in Fig. 11.30} = K_{22} \text{ in Fig. 11.31}.$$

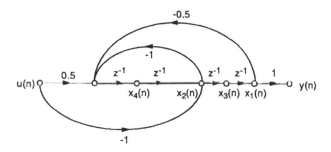

Fig. 11.31 The filter structure obtained by replacing z^{-1} in Fig. 11.30 by z^{-2}.

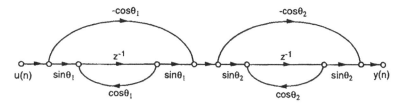

Fig. 11.32 An orthogonal filter structure with a nonstate variable node.

13. Derive the relation between **W** in Fig. 11.30 and **W** in Fig. 11.31.

14. Show that the original filter and the pipelined filter in Fig. 11.20 exhibit the same finite wordlength behavior by calculating **K** and **W** matrices for both filters. Assume that $a = 2$, $b = 3$, and $c = 4$.

15. Consider the filter structure shown in Fig. 11.32. Notice that the filter has a nonstate variable node.

    (a) Modify the filter in Fig. 11.32 such that every node of the new structure is a state variable node while the finite wordlength behavior remains the same as the original filter.

    (b) Find state variable matrices **A**, **b**, **c**, and d of the modified filter.

    (c) Compute **K** for this filter and show that **K** = **I**. This filter is, therefore, an orthogonal filter.

    (d) Verify that $\mathbf{AA}^T + \mathbf{bb}^T = \mathbf{I}$.

16. Consider the 1st-order filters shown in Fig. 11.33.

    (a) Find the transfer function of the filter in Fig. 11.33(a). What is the output signal power?

    (b) Assume that the pole of the 1st-order filter is located at $z = r$. Show that $\alpha = 1 - r$.

    (c) Show that the filter in Fig. 11.33(b) can be obtained from that in Fig. 11.33(a) by SRP transformation.

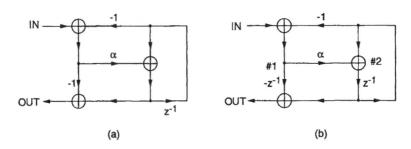

Fig. 11.33   (a) A 1st-order filter. (b) Transformed filter by SRP transformation.

(d) Calculate $\mathbf{K}$ and $\mathbf{W}$ of the filter in Fig. 11.33(b). Derive the relation between pole location r and NSR of the scaled filter. (Notice that only node 2 generates roundoff noise.)

17. Consider two possible implementations of the symmetric 8-tap low-pass FIR filter in Example 11.7.2 with coefficients

$$
\begin{aligned}
h_0 &= \quad h_7 = -0.0807 \\
h_1 &= \quad h_6 = 0.0203 \\
h_2 &= \quad h_5 = 0.2118 \\
h_3 &= \quad h_4 = 0.3897
\end{aligned}
$$

using 4 multipliers as shown in Fig. 11.34. Assume that rounding is performed by multiply or multiply-add nodes, and no rounding is performed due to only addition operations.

(a) Calculate the roundoff noise in these two structures.

(b) Express these 2 structures in state variable form. Retime the structure in Fig. 11.34(b) by selecting appropriate cutsets so that the outputs of all roundoff nodes can be modeled as state variables. Compute $\mathbf{K}$ and $\mathbf{W}$ matrices using the $\mathbf{K}$ and $\mathbf{W}$ computing algorithms and obtain l_2 scaled versions of these 2 structures.

(c) Calculate the roundoff noise of the scaled structures using $\mathbf{K}$ and $\mathbf{W}$ matrices computed in (b).

(d) Compute $\mathbf{W}$ matrix for the scaled structures in (b) and use these to compute the roundoff noise of these structures.

(e) Verify that the results obtained in (c) and (d) are the same.

18. Consider the 8-tap low-pass filter with coefficients

$$
h_0 = \quad h_7 = -0.0807
$$

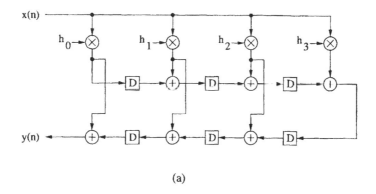

(a)

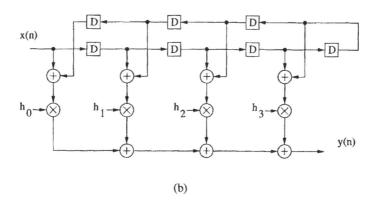

(b)

Fig. 11.34 Two implementations of the FIR filter in Problem 17.

$$h_1 = \quad h_6 = 0.0203$$
$$h_2 = \quad h_5 = 0.2118$$
$$h_3 = \quad h_4 = 0.3897$$

implemented using the structure in Fig. 11.35. Assume that rounding is performed after 1 multiply-add operation or after 1 multiplication followed by 2 addition operations.

(a) Calculate the roundoff noise of this structure.

(b) Compute $\mathbf{K}$ and $\mathbf{W}$ using the $\mathbf{K}$ and $\mathbf{W}$ computing algorithms. Obtain the scaled version of this structure. Calculate the roundoff noise of the scaled version of this filter.

(c) Calculate the $\mathbf{K}$ and $\mathbf{W}$ matrices of the scaled filter.

19. Consider a low-noise 2-parallel implementation of the 8-tap low-pass FIR filter described by the coefficients

$$h_0 = \quad h_7 = -0.0807$$

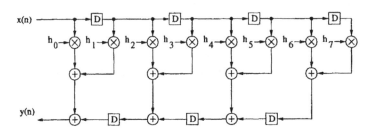

Fig. 11.35 Two FIR filter implementations in Problem 18.

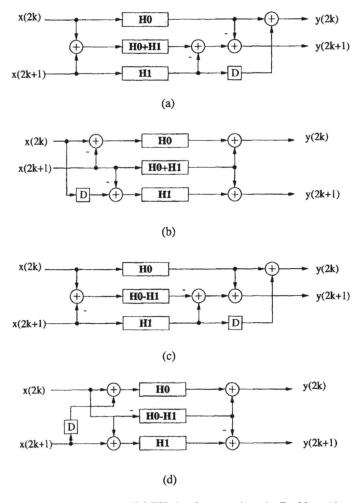

(a)

(b)

(c)

(d)

Fig. 11.36 Four parallel FIR implementations in Problem 19.

$$h_1 = \quad h_6 = 0.0203$$
$$h_2 = \quad h_5 = 0.2118$$
$$h_3 = \quad h_4 = 0.3897.$$

With l_2 scaling, 4 possible parallel structures are shown in Fig. 11.36.

Which of these structures has the least average roundoff noise when scaled using l_2 scaling? The average roundoff noise of the scaled filter is defined as half of the sum of the roundoff noise at both outputs in the scaled structure. Compute average roundoff noise for scaled versions of all 4 structures using **K**- and **W**-computing algorithms. Assume that roundoff is only introduced due to multiply-add operations and that no roundoff error is introduced due to the adders. Assume use of data-broadcast FIR subfilters in the parallel structures.

REFERENCES

1. A. V. Oppenheim and R. W. Schafer, *Digital Signal Processing*. Prentice Hall, 1975.

2. P. P. Vaidyanathan, "Low-noise and low-sensitivity digital filters," in *Handbook of Digital Signal Processing* (D. F. Elliott, ed.), pp. 359–479, Academic Press, 1987.

3. R. A. Roberts and C. T. Mullis, *Digital Signal Processing*. Addison-Wesley, 1987.

4. K. H. Chang and W. G. Bliss, "Finite word-length effects of pipelined recursive digital filters," *IEEE Trans. on Signal Processing*, vol. 42, no. 8, pp. 1983–1995, Aug. 1994.

5. J. G. Chung and K. K. Parhi, *Pipelined Lattice and Wave Digital Recursive Filters*. Kluwer, 1996.

6. S. Y. Kung, "On supercomputing with systolic/wavefront array processors," *Proc. IEEE*, vol. 72, pp. 867–884, July 1984.

7. C. E. Leiserson, F. Rose, and J. Saxe, "Optimizing synchronous circuitry by retiming," in *3rd Caltech Conference on VLSI*, (Pasadena, CA), pp. 87–116, March 1983.

12

Digital Lattice Filter Structures

12.1 INTRODUCTION

This chapter addresses the design of lattice digital filters. Four types of lattice digital filters are presented: basic, 1-multiplier, normalized and scaled-normalized. Although the major emphasis of this chapter is on design of IIR lattice filters, the techniques can also be used to design FIR lattice filters. Design of FIR lattice filters is illustrated only in the context of basic lattice digital filters.

The simplest form of the IIR digital filter structures is the direct-form structure, where the numerator and the denominator coefficients are directly used as multiplier coefficients in the implementation. However, this structure has very high sensitivity, because the roots of a polynomial are very sensitive to the coefficients, so the poles and zeros of the given transfer function are very sensitive to the quantized multiplier coefficients [1]. With standard filters such as low-pass, high-pass, and band-pass, the poles are generally crowded at angles close to the band edge. Sensitivity of the structure becomes worse as the number of crowded poles increases. This sensitivity problem can be avoided by implementing the transfer function as a sum or product of 1st and 2nd-order sections, i.e., parallel or cascade form structures. However, for complex conjugate poles with small angles (e.g., narrow-band sharp-transition filters), we still have high sensitivity problems even with 2nd-order sections.

However, the lattice digital filters have good numerical properties since the denominator of a given transfer function is synthesized in a robust way. In addition, lattice digital filters are implemented as a cascade of regular modules so that these filters are suitable for VLSI implementation.

The lattice structure is motivated by the theory of autoregressive signal modeling [2]. However, much insight into the numerical properties of the lattice structure can be obtained by deriving the lattice structure using the Schur algorithm. This chapter presents the design and pipelining techniques of various types of lattice digital filters using the Schur algorithm. An approach to computation of roundoff noise using the polynomial expansion algorithm and the transposition theorem is also presented.

12.2   SCHUR ALGORITHM

The Schur algorithm was originally used to test if a power series is analytic and bounded in the unit disk [3]. If an N-th order polynomial $\Phi_N(z)$ has all zeros inside the unit circle, $N+1$ polynomials $\{\Phi_i(z), i = N, N-1, \cdots, 0\}$ can be generated by the Schur algorithm. One of the most important properties of the Schur algorithm is that these $N+1$ polynomials are orthonormal to each other and can be used as orthonormal basis functions to expand any N-th order polynomial. This orthonormality of the Schur algorithm has been exploited to synthesize various types of lattice filters.

To illustrate the orthonormality of the Schur algorithm, we propose an inner product formulation, which is based on the power computation at an internal node of a filter structure. Although the inner product formulation includes complex integration in the definition, no actual complex integration is needed for the evaluation of the inner product due to some useful properties of the inner product.

12.2.1   Computation of Schur Polynomials

The Schur polynomial is a polynomial that does not have zeros on or outside the unit circle. Therefore, the denominator of a stable IIR filter is a Schur polynomial. Let a real polynomial with all zeros inside the unit circle be defined by

$$D_N(z) = \sum_{i=0}^{N} d_i z^i. \tag{12.1}$$

Then, initialize the N-th order Schur polynomial $\Phi_N(z)$ as

$$\Phi_N(z) = D_N(z), \tag{12.2}$$

where

$$\Phi_N(z) = \sum_{i=0}^{N} \phi_i z^i. \tag{12.3}$$

From $\Phi_N(z)$, form the polynomial $\Phi_{N-1}(z)$ as follows:

$$
\begin{aligned}
\Phi_{N-1}(z) &= \frac{z^{-1}\{\phi_N \Phi_N(z) - \phi_0 \Phi_N^*(z)\}}{\sqrt{\phi_N^2 - \phi_0^2}}, \\
&= \frac{z^{-1}\{\Phi_N(z) - k_N \Phi_N^*(z)\}}{\sqrt{1 - k_N^2}},
\end{aligned}
\tag{12.4}
$$

where $k_N = \phi_0/\phi_N$ and $\Phi_N^*(z)$ is the reverse polynomial of $\Phi_N(z)$ and is defined by

$$
\Phi_N^*(z) = z^N \Phi_N(z^{-1}).
\tag{12.5}
$$

Note that the degree of $\Phi_{N-1}(z)$ is reduced by 1 when compared with that of $\Phi_N(z)$. Each of the polynomials $\Phi_{N-i}(z)$ can be generated from $\Phi_{N-i+1}(z)$, for $i = 1, 2, \cdots, N$, in the same manner as $\Phi_{N-1}(z)$ is generated from $\Phi_N(z)$. For $\Phi_N(z)$ to be a Schur polynomial, it is required that the absolute value of the constant term be less than the absolute value of the coefficient of the highest power in z for each of the polynomials in the set $\{\Phi_N(z), \Phi_{N-1}, \cdots, \Phi_1(z)\}$.

It may be noted that the coefficients of increasing powers of z in $\Phi_{N-1}(z)$ are $1/\sqrt{\phi_N^2 - \phi_0^2}$ times the N determinants of the 2×2 submatrices formed by the 1st column and each succeeding column in the following matrix:

$$
\begin{bmatrix}
\phi_N & \phi_{N-1} & \phi_{N-2} & \cdots & \phi_2 & \phi_1 & \phi_0 \\
\phi_0 & \phi_1 & \phi_2 & \cdots & \phi_{N-2} & \phi_{N-1} & \phi_N
\end{bmatrix}.
\tag{12.6}
$$

The matrix representation of the Schur algorithm in (12.6) is very useful for pipelining lattice filters, as described in Section 12.8.

Example 12.2.1 *Consider the following 3rd-order polynomial*

$$
D_3(z) = 345.1z^3 - 819.3z^2 + 665.8z - 183.6.
$$

Using the Schur algorithm, we obtain

$$
\begin{aligned}
\Phi_3(z) &= 345.1z^3 - 819.3z^2 + 665.8z - 183.6, \\
\Phi_2(z) &= 292.2072z^2 - 549.2662z + 271.5337, \\
\Phi_1(z) &= 107.956z - 105.1841, \\
\Phi_0(z) &= 24.3064.
\end{aligned}
$$

For each of the polynomials in the set $\{\Phi_3(z), \Phi_2(z), \Phi_1(z)\}$, *the coefficient of the highest power in z is larger than the constant. Therefore, we conclude that $D_3(z)$ is a Schur polynomial.* ∎

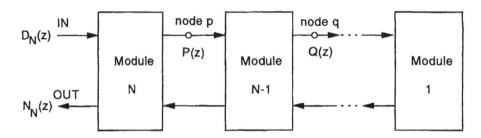

Fig. 12.1 A filter structure implementing $H(z) = N_N(z)/D_N(z)$.

12.2.2 Orthonormality of Schur Polynomials

Consider the filter structure in Fig. 12.1, which implements a real, causal, stable transfer function $H(z) = N_N(z)/D_N(z)$. If the polynomials associated with node p and the input node are $P(z)$ and $D_N(z)$, respectively, then the transfer function from the input to the node p is $P(z)/D_N(z)$. If the input signal is modeled as random and white with unit power, the average power at the node p is given by

$$
\begin{aligned}
P_p &= \frac{1}{2\pi} \int_{-\pi}^{\pi} \left| \frac{P(e^{j\omega})}{D_N(e^{j\omega})} \right|^2 d\omega, \\
&= \frac{1}{2\pi} \int_{-\pi}^{\pi} \frac{P(e^{j\omega})P(e^{-j\omega})}{D_N(e^{j\omega})D_N(e^{-j\omega})} d\omega.
\end{aligned}
\tag{12.7}
$$

On the unit circle, i.e., for $z = e^{j\omega}$,

$$
dz = je^{j\omega} d\omega.
\tag{12.8}
$$

Then, the average power can be computed in z-domain using

$$
P_p = \frac{1}{2\pi j} \oint_C \frac{P(z)P(z^{-1})z^{-1}}{D_N(z)D_N(z^{-1})} dz.
\tag{12.9}
$$

where C is a counterclockwise contour. Notice that the unit circle can be chosen as the contour since all zeros of $D_N(z)$ are inside the unit circle. Using (12.9) of average power, we define an inner product of 2 internal polynomials $P(z)$ and $Q(z)$ in Fig. 12.1 as

$$
\langle P(z), Q(z) \rangle = \frac{1}{2\pi j} \oint_C \frac{P(z)Q(z^{-1})z^{-1}}{D_N(z)D_N(z^{-1})} dz.
\tag{12.10}
$$

The average power in (12.9) can now be calculated as $P_p = \langle P(z), P(z) \rangle$. To show that (12.10) is a valid inner product definition, it is sufficient to show that the following 3 properties are satisfied:

1. Conjugate symmetry:

$$\langle P(z), Q(z) \rangle = \langle Q(z), P(z) \rangle^*,$$

where $(*)$ represents complex conjugate operation. In this chapter, $P(z)$ and $Q(z)$ are assumed to contain only real coefficients and

$$\langle P(z), Q(z) \rangle = \langle Q(z), P(z) \rangle.$$

2. Linearity: for any real constants α, β, and γ,

$$\langle \alpha P(z), \beta Q(z) + \gamma R(z) \rangle = \alpha\beta \langle P(z), Q(z) \rangle + \alpha\gamma \langle P(z), R(z) \rangle.$$

3. Positive norm:
$$\langle P(z), P(z) \rangle \geq 0,$$

where equality holds if and only if $P(z) = 0$.

It is easy to verify that the inner product in (12.10) satisfies all **3** properties. The commutative property of the inner product, i.e., $\langle P(z), Q(z) \rangle = \langle Q(z), P(z) \rangle$ can be proved as follows:

$$\langle P(z), Q(z) \rangle = \frac{1}{2\pi j} \oint_{C_0} \frac{P(z)Q(z^{-1})z^{-1}}{D_N(z)D_N(z^{-1})} dz, \tag{12.11}$$

$$= \frac{-1}{2\pi j} \oint_{C_1} \frac{P(t^{-1})Q(t)t}{D_N(t)D_N(t^{-1})t^2} dt, \quad (t = z^{-1}) \tag{12.12}$$

$$= \frac{1}{2\pi j} \oint_{C_0} \frac{Q(t)P(t^{-1})t^{-1}}{D_N(t)D_N(t^{-1})} dt, \tag{12.13}$$

$$= \langle Q(z), P(z) \rangle. \tag{12.14}$$

In the foregoing equations, C_0 represents a counterclockwise contour that encircles the origin and C_1 represents a clockwise contour.

Contour integrals are often conveniently evaluated using the Cauchy's residue theorem [1],[4]:

$$\frac{1}{2\pi j} \oint_C X(z) dz = \sum [\text{residues of } X(z) \text{ at the poles inside } C]. \tag{12.15}$$

Any rational function $X(z)$ can be expressed as

$$X(z) = \frac{\Theta(z)}{(z - d_0)^s}, \tag{12.16}$$

where $X(z)$ has s poles at $z = d_0$ and $\Theta(z)$ has no poles at $z = d_0$. Then, the residue of $X(z)$ at $z = d_0$ is given by

$$\text{Res}[X(z) \text{ at } z = d_0] = \frac{1}{(s-1)!} \left[\frac{d^{s-1} \Theta(z)}{dz^{s-1}} \right]_{z=d_0}. \qquad (12.17)$$

For example, if $X(z) = z^{-i}$,

$$\frac{1}{2\pi j} \oint_C z^{-i} dz = \begin{cases} 1 & \text{for } i = 1, \\ 0 & \text{otherwise.} \end{cases} \qquad (12.18)$$

Then, with $D_N(z) = \Phi_N(z)$,

$$\begin{aligned}
\langle \Phi_N(z), z^i \rangle &= \frac{1}{2\pi j} \oint_C \frac{\Phi_N(z) z^{-i}}{\Phi_N(z) \Phi_N(z^{-1}) z} dz, \\
&= \frac{1}{2\pi j} \oint_C \frac{z^{N-i-1}}{\Phi_N^*(z)} dz, \\
&= \begin{cases} 1/\phi_N & \text{for } i = N, \\ 0 & \text{for } i \le N-1. \end{cases}
\end{aligned} \qquad (12.19)$$

Note that $\Phi_N^*(z) = z^N \Phi_N(z^{-1})$ is referred to as the reverse Schur polynomial. In the derivation of (12.19), we used the fact that $\Phi_N^*(z)$ has all roots outside the unit circle. Similarly, using (12.3) and (12.5)

$$\begin{aligned}
\langle \Phi_N^*(z), z^i \rangle &= \langle z^i, \Phi_N^*(z) \rangle, \\
&= \frac{1}{2\pi j} \oint_C \frac{z^i z^{-N} \Phi_N(z)}{\Phi_N(z) \Phi_N(z^{-1}) z} dz, \\
&= \frac{1}{2\pi j} \oint_C \frac{z^{i-1}}{\Phi_N^*(z)} dz, \\
&= \begin{cases} 1/\phi_N & \text{for } i = 0, \\ 0 & \text{for } i \ge 1. \end{cases}
\end{aligned} \qquad (12.20)$$

Using (12.19) and (12.20), the following two useful relations are obtained:

$$\begin{aligned}
\langle \Phi_N(z), P(z) \rangle &= p_N/\phi_N, & (12.21) \\
\langle \Phi_N^*(z), P(z) \rangle &= p_0/\phi_N, & (12.22)
\end{aligned}$$

where p_N is the coefficient of z^N of the N-th order polynomial $P(z)$, and p_0 is the constant term in $P(z)$. As a simple application of (12.21–12.22), we obtain the following relations :

$$\begin{aligned}
\langle \Phi_N(z), \Phi_N(z) \rangle &= \phi_N/\phi_N &= 1, & (12.23) \\
\langle \Phi_N^*(z), \Phi_N^*(z) \rangle &= \phi_N/\phi_N &= 1, & (12.24) \\
\langle \Phi_N(z), \Phi_N^*(z) \rangle &= \phi_0/\phi_N. & & (12.25)
\end{aligned}$$

In addition to (12.21) and (12.22), the following 2 useful equations can be derived easily from (12.10):

$$\langle z^{-j}\Phi_N(z), z^i \rangle = \langle \Phi_N(z), z^{i+j} \rangle, \tag{12.26}$$

$$\langle z^{-j}\Phi_N^*(z), z^i \rangle = \langle \Phi_N^*(z), z^{i+j} \rangle. \tag{12.27}$$

Using the properties of the inner product, it can be shown that the Schur polynomials satisfy the following orthonormality condition:

$$\langle \Phi_i(z), \Phi_j(z) \rangle = \begin{cases} 1, & i = j, \\ 0, & i \neq j, \end{cases} \tag{12.28}$$

where $0 \leq i, j \leq N$. (For detailed proof of (12.28), refer to Appendix D.)

As opposed to the Schur polynomials, the reverse Schur polynomials are not orthogonal to each other. As an example,

$$\langle \Phi_N^*(z), \Phi_i^*(z) \rangle = \Phi_i^*(0)/\phi_N \neq 0, \quad \text{for } 0 \leq i \leq N - 1, \tag{12.29}$$

since the constant of $\Phi_i^*(z)$ is generally nonzero. However, if some conditions are met, the reverse Schur polynomials can be used as orthonormal basis functions. Consider the inner product

$$\begin{aligned}
\langle \Phi_i^*(z), z^{i-j}\Phi_j^*(z) \rangle &= \langle z^{j-i}\Phi_j^*(z^{-1}), \Phi_i^*(z^{-1}) \rangle, \quad \text{(by conjugate symmetry)} \\
&= \langle z^j \Phi_j^*(z^{-1}), z^i \Phi_i^*(z^{-1}) \rangle, \\
&= \langle \Phi_j(z), \Phi_i(z) \rangle, \\
&= 0, \tag{12.30}
\end{aligned}$$

where $0 \leq j < i \leq N$. The relationship in (12.30) can be referred to as $(i-j)$ *orthonormality of the reverse Schur polynomials.* Therefore, the polynomials $\{\Phi_N^*(z), z\Phi_{N-1}^*(z), z^2\Phi_{N-2}^*(z), \cdots, z^N\Phi_0(z)\}$ form an orthonormal basis. The $(i-j)$ orthonormality of the reverse Schur polynomials is useful when we discuss the various lattice filter structures.

12.2.3   Polynomial Expansion Algorithm

Since the Schur polynomials in the set $\{\Phi_N(z), \Phi_{N-1}(z), \cdots, \Phi_0(z)\}$ are orthonormal to each other, they can be used as orthonormal basis functions. Therefore, any N-th order polynomial $N_N(z)$ can be expanded using those polynomials as

$$N_N(z) = \sum_{i=0}^{N} c_i \Phi_i(z), \tag{12.31}$$

where c_i's, for $i = 0$ to N, are called the expansion coefficients. The expansion coefficients can be calculated by the polynomial expansion algorithm [5]:

Polynomial Expansion Algorithm:

- For any polynomial $N_m(z)$ of degree m $(0 < m \leq N)$,
  initialize $Q(z) = N_m(z)$ with $c_i = 0$, for $m < i \leq N$.

- For $i = m, m - 1, \cdots, 0$,
  (a) compute c_i by $c_i = Q^*(0)/\Phi_i^*(0)$,
  (b) update $Q(z)$ by $Q(z) = Q(z) - c_i \Phi_i(z)$.

In the above algorithm, $Q^*(z)$ and $\Phi_i^*(z)$ are the reverse polynomials of $Q(z)$ and $\Phi_i(z)$. Thus, $Q^*(0)$ and $\Phi_i^*(0)$ are the leading coefficients of $Q(z)$ and $\Phi_i(z)$, respectively

Example 12.2.2 *Consider expanding the following 3rd-order polynomial*

$$N_3(z) = z^3 + 3z^2 + 3z + 1$$

using the Schur polynomials $\{\Phi_3(z), \cdots, \Phi_0(z)\}$ *obtained in Example 12.2.1. Each step required for the expansion is summarized as follows:*

1. *Initialize* $Q(z) = N_3(z) = z^3 + 3z^2 + 3z + 1$.
   Then, $c_3 = 1/345.1 = 0.0029$.

2. $Q(z)$ *is updated as* $Q(z) = 5.3741z^2 + 1.0707z + 1.532$.
   Then $c_2 = 5.3741/292.2072 = 0.0184$.

3. $Q(z)$ *is updated as* $Q(z) = 11.1725z - 3.4619$.
   Then $c_1 = 11.1725/107.956 = 0.1035$.

4. $Q(z)$ *is updated as* $Q(z) = 7.4238$.
   Then $c_0 = 7.4238/24.3064 = 0.3054$. ∎

In lattice filters, the denominator is synthesized using the Schur algorithm. The numerator part is synthesized using the polynomial expansion algorithm with orthogonal basis functions obtained from the denominator by the Schur algorithm.

12.2.4   Power Calculation Using Schur Algorithm

Consider again the filter structure in Fig. 12.1. If the input signal is modeled as random and white with unit power then, using the definition of the inner product in (12.10), the average power at the internal node p can be written as

$$P_p = \langle P(z), P(z) \rangle. \tag{12.32}$$

Since the denominator $D_N(z)$ is a Schur polynomial, $P(z)$ can be expressed by the polynomial expansion algorithm as

$$P(z) = \sum_i c_i \Phi_i(z). \tag{12.33}$$

By substituting (12.33) into (12.32),

$$P_p = \left\langle \sum_i c_i \Phi_i(z), \sum_i c_i \Phi_i(z) \right\rangle. \tag{12.34}$$

Then, from the linearity of the inner product and the orthonormality of the Schur algorithm, (12.34) reduces to

$$P_p = \sum_i c_i^2. \tag{12.35}$$

Thus the average signal power at the internal node or output node associated with $P(z)$ can be simply computed by the sum of the square of the expansion coefficients obtained from $P(z)$.

Example 12.2.3 *Consider computation of the output signal power of the filter*

$$H(z) = \frac{z^3 + 3z^2 + 3z + 1}{345.1z^3 - 819.3z^2 + 665.8z - 183.6}.$$

From Example 12.2.2, the expansion coefficients calculated by the polynomial expansion algorithm are $\{0.0029, 0.0184, 0.1035, 0.3054\}$. *Then, by adding the square of the expansion coefficients, the output signal power is 0.1043.* ∎

12.3 DIGITAL BASIC LATTICE FILTERS

Digital lattice filters are composed of regular modules. If the order of a filter is N, then N modules are needed. The lattice filter that realizes any transfer function can be viewed as a filter with the property that if the denominator polynomial is fed into the filter, the numerator polynomial is obtained at the output node. The essence of this synthesis procedure is based on the *polynomial degree reduction*, which means that the degree of these polynomials will be reduced by one after passing through each module. After N modules, the polynomials have degree zero and are just constants. By matching these constants, we can simply interconnect them by appropriate multipliers.

In this section, 2 slightly different basic lattice filter structures are derived. The 1st one is derived using the Schur polynomials and the 2nd one is derived using the reverse Schur polynomials.

12.3.1 Derivation of Basic Lattice Filters

The Schur polynomials are obtained by using the degree reduction procedure

$$\Phi_{i-1}(z) = \frac{z^{-1}\{\Phi_i(z) - k_i\Phi_i^*(z)\}}{s_i}, \tag{12.36}$$

where s_i is any nonzero scaling factor and

$$k_i = \Phi_i(0)/\Phi_i^*(0). \tag{12.37}$$

If we choose

$$s_i = \sqrt{1 - k_i^2}, \tag{12.38}$$

then the Schur polynomials $\{\Phi_N(z), \Phi_{N-1}(z), \cdots, \Phi_0(z)\}$ are orthonormal to each other and can be used for designing normalized and scaled-normalized lattice filters. On the other hand, the basic lattice filter is designed by choosing s_i as

$$s_i = 1 - k_i^2. \tag{12.39}$$

In this chapter, the i-th order Schur polynomial with the choice of s_i in (12.39) is referred to as $\Psi_i(z)$ and $\Phi_i(z)$ is used when s_i is chosen by (12.38).

Consider an N-th order IIR transfer function $H_N(z) = N_N(z)/D_N(z)$. Then, initialize the N-th order Schur polynomial $\Psi_N(z)$ as $\Psi_N(z) = D_N(z)$, where

$$\Psi_N(z) = \sum_{i=0}^{N} \psi_i z^i. \tag{12.40}$$

From $\Psi_N(z)$, form the polynomial $\Psi_{N-1}(z)$ by the degree reduction procedure as

$$\Psi_{N-1}(z) = \frac{z^{-1}\{\Psi_N(z) - k_N\Psi_N^*(z)\}}{1 - k_N^2}. \tag{12.41}$$

Also, $\Psi_{N-1}^*(z)$, the reverse polynomial of $\Psi_{N-1}(z)$ is defined by

$$\Psi_{N-1}^*(z) = z^{N-1}\Psi_{N-1}(z^{-1}) = \frac{\Psi_N^*(z) - k_N\Psi_N(z)}{1 - k_N^2}. \tag{12.42}$$

From (12.42),

$$\Psi_N^*(z) = (1 - k_N^2)\Psi_{N-1}^*(z) + k_N\Psi_N(z). \tag{12.43}$$

Using (12.41) and (12.43), $\Psi_{N-1}(z)$ can be expressed as a function of $\Psi_N(z)$ and $\Psi_{N-1}^*(z)$ as

$$\Psi_{N-1}(z) = z^{-1}\{\Psi_N(z) - k_N\Psi_{N-1}^*(z)\}. \tag{12.44}$$

Also, from (12.43) and (12.44)

$$\begin{aligned}
\Psi_N^*(z) &= \Psi_{N-1}^*(z) + k_N\{\Psi_N(z) - k_N\Psi_{N-1}^*(z)\}, \\
&= \Psi_{N-1}^*(z) + k_N z\Psi_{N-1}(z). \qquad (12.45)
\end{aligned}$$

An implementation of (12.44) and (12.45) is shown in Fig. 12.2(a). By repeatedly applying the foregoing procedure with replacing $\Psi_i(z)$ by $\Psi_{i-1}(z)$, for $i = N, N-1, \cdots, 1$, the denominator $D_N(z)$ can be synthesized as shown in Fig. 12.2(b). This structure can be used to implement an all-pole filter with transfer function $\Psi_0(z)/\Psi_N(z)$ or an *all-pass* filter with transfer function $\Psi_N^*(z)/\Psi_N(z)$.

From (12.36-12.39), the relation between $\Psi_i(z)$ and $\Phi_i(z)$ can be shown to be

$$\begin{aligned}
\Psi_N(z) &= \Phi_N(z), \\
\Psi_i(z) &= \frac{\Phi_i(z)}{\sqrt{(1 - k_N^2)(1 - k_{N-1}^2)\cdots(1 - k_{i+1}^2)}}, \quad 0 \le i < N. \quad (12.46)
\end{aligned}$$

Notice that $\Psi_i(z)$ is different from $\Phi_i(z)$ only by a scale factor. Therefore, the k-parameter computed from $\Psi_i(z)$ is equal to the k-parameter computed from $\Phi_i(z)$ as

$$k_i = \Psi_i(0)/\Psi_i^*(0) = \Phi_i(0)/\Phi_i^*(0). \qquad (12.47)$$

Also, it is easily seen from (12.46) that $\{\Psi_N(z), \Psi_{N-1}(z), \cdots, \Psi_0(z)\}$ are orthogonal but not orthonormal since

$$\begin{aligned}
\langle \Psi_i(z), \Psi_i(z) \rangle &= \langle \Psi_i^*(z), \Psi_i^*(z) \rangle, \\
&= \frac{1}{(1 - k_N^2)(1 - k_{N-1}^2)\cdots(1 - k_{i+1}^2)}. \qquad (12.48)
\end{aligned}$$

From (12.48), notice that $\langle \Psi_i(z), \Psi_i(z) \rangle$ increases as i decreases since all of the k-parameters are less than one in magnitude. When most of the k-parameters are close to one, the difference of powers among the nodes in Fig. 12.2(b) is very large and the input needs to be scaled down by a large factor to prevent overflow at a critical node. As a result, the effect of roundoff noise increases significantly. In normalized lattice filter, however, input scaling is not necessary since all of the nodes on the feedback portion have the same power as can be seen later in this Chapter.

Since the polynomials $\{\Psi_N(z), \Psi_{N-1}(z), \cdots, \Psi_1(z), \Psi_0(z)\}$ on the top line of Fig. 12.2(b) are orthogonal, they can be used as basis functions to expand the numerator $N_N(z)$ by the polynomial expansion algorithm as

$$N_N(z) = \sum_{i=0}^{N} c_i \Psi_i(z). \qquad (12.49)$$

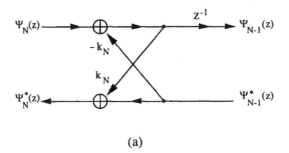

(a)

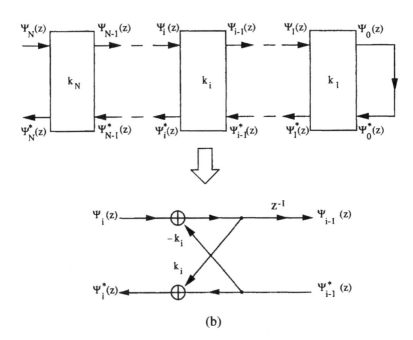

(b)

Fig. 12.2 (a) Implementation of (12.44) and (12.45) and (b) implementation of the denominator $D_N(z)$.

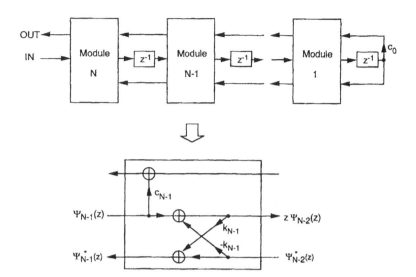

Fig. 12.3   The structure of an N-th order basic lattice filter.

By combining these tap-gain parameters $\{c_N, c_{N-1}, \cdots, c_0\}$ to the all-pole portion in Fig. 12.2(b), the basic lattice filter structure is obtained as shown in Fig. 12.3.

Example 12.3.1   *Consider the 3rd-order Butterworth low-pass filter*

$$H(z) = \frac{(1+z)^3}{345.1z^3 - 819.3z^2 + 665.8z - 183.6}.$$

From (12.40) and (12.41),

$$
\begin{aligned}
\Psi_3(z) &= 345.1z^3 - 819.3z^2 + 665.8z - 183.6, \\
\Psi_2(z) &= 345.1z^2 - 648.6896z + 320.6843, \\
\Psi_1(z) &= 345.1z - 336.2392, \\
\Psi_0(z) &= 345.1.
\end{aligned}
$$

Thus k-parameters are computed as

$$k_3 = -0.532, \ k_2 = 0.9293, \ and \ k_1 = -0.9743.$$

By (12.49), the expansion coefficients computed using $\Psi_i(z)$'s are

$$c_3 = 0.0029, \ c_2 = 0.0156, \ c_1 = 0.0324, \ and \ c_0 = 0.0215.$$

Fig. 12.4 shows the basic lattice filter synthesized using the Schur polynomials.

■

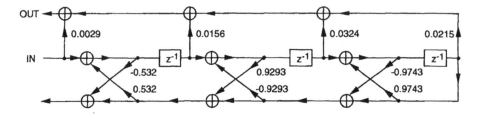

Fig. 12.4   A 3rd-order basic lattice filter designed using Schur polynomials.

12.3.2   Derivation of Basic Lattice Filters Using Reverse Schur Polynomials

In Fig. 12.2(a), the delay on the top edge can be moved to the bottom edge without altering the input-output relation as shown in Fig. 12.5(a). Notice that the polynomials on the right side in Fig. 12.5(a) are $z\Psi_{N-1}(z)$ and $z\Psi_{N-1}^{*}(z)$ instead of $\Psi_{N-1}(z)$ and $\Psi_{N-1}^{*}(z)$ since we moved the delay from top to bottom edge. Fig. 12.5(b) shows the implementation of the denominator with all delays on the bottom edge. From the $(i - j)$ orthonormality of the reverse Schur polynomials, $\{\Phi_{N}^{*}(z), z\Phi_{N-1}^{*}(z), z^{2}\Phi_{N-2}^{*}(z), \cdots, z^{N}\Phi_{0}(z)\}$ are orthonormal. Thus the polynomials $\{\Psi_{N}^{*}(z), z\Psi_{N-1}^{*}(z), z^{2}\Psi_{N-2}^{*}(z), \cdots, z^{N}\Psi_{0}(z)\}$, obtained from each node on the bottom line in Fig. 12.5(b), are orthogonal and the polynomials can be used as a basis to expand the numerator as

$$N_{N}(z) = \sum_{i=0}^{N} c_{i}z^{N-i}\Psi_{i}^{*}(z). \qquad (12.50)$$

In (12.50), notice that the order of each polynomial $z^{N-i}\Psi_{i}^{*}(z)$, for $i = N$ to 0, is N, and we cannot directly use the polynomial expansion algorithm. However, from (12.50),

$$
\begin{aligned}
N_{N}^{*}(z) &= z^{N}\left\{\sum_{i=0}^{N} c_{i}z^{-(N-i)}\Psi_{i}^{*}(z^{-1})\right\}, \\
&= \sum_{i=0}^{N} c_{i}\Psi_{i}(z). \qquad (12.51)
\end{aligned}
$$

It is obvious that the polynomial expansion algorithm can be applied to (12.51). Therefore, the expansion coefficients in (12.50) are the same as the expansion coefficients obtained by expanding the reverse polynomial of the numerator using $\{\Psi_{N}(z), \Psi_{N-1}(z), \cdots, \Psi_{0}(z)\}$. The basic lattice filter structure obtained by the foregoing procedure is shown in Fig. 12.6.

Example 12.3.2 *Consider again the 3rd-order Butterworth low-pass filter given in Example 12.3.1. From (12.51), the expansion coefficients computed*

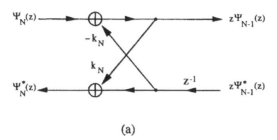

(a)

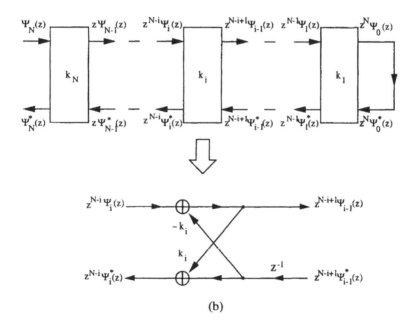

(b)

Fig. 12.5 (a) Implementation of (12.44) and (12.45) with the delay on the bottom edge and (b) implementation of the denominator $D_N(z)$.

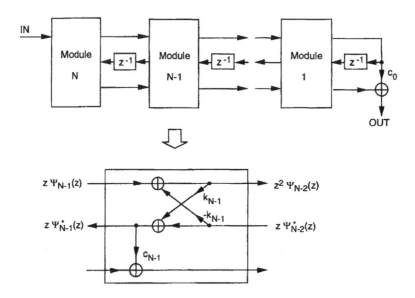

Fig. 12.6 The structure of an N-th order basic lattice filter obtained using the reverse Schur polynomials.

using reverse Schur polynomials ($\Psi_i^*(z)$'s) are

$$c_3 = 0.0029, \quad c_2 = 0.0156, \quad c_1 = 0.0324, \quad \text{and} \quad c_0 = 0.0215.$$

Notice that the expansion coefficients computed in this example are the same as those computed in Example 12.3.1 due to the symmetric numerator, i.e., $N(z) = N^*(z)$. Fig. 12.7 shows the basic lattice filter synthesized using the reverse Schur polynomials. ■

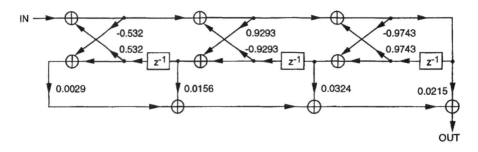

Fig. 12.7 A 3rd-order basic lattice filter designed using reverse Schur polynomials.

12.3.3 Derivation of FIR Lattice Filters

In this section, FIR lattice filter structure corresponding to an N-th order FIR transfer function $H_N(z) = \Psi_N(z)$ is considered. (The coefficient of the highest power in z of $\Psi_N(z)$ is assumed to be unity.) From (12.44) and (12.45),

$$
\begin{aligned}
\Psi_N(z) &= z\Psi_{N-1}(z) + k_N\Psi_{N-1}^*(z), \\
\Psi_N^*(z) &= \Psi_{N-1}^*(z) + k_N z\Psi_{N-1}(z).
\end{aligned}
\tag{12.52}
$$

An implementation of (12.52) is shown in Fig. 12.8(a). By repeatedly applying the above procedure with replacing $\Psi_i(z)$ by $\Psi_{i-1}(z)$, for $i = N, N-1, \cdots, 1$, $H_N(z)$ can be synthesized as shown in Fig. 12.8(b). Notice that the FIR lattice filter in Fig. 12.8(b) has $2N$ multipliers, although its unit-sample response has only N nonunity coefficients. Thus, such structures are not as efficient as the direct-form FIR structure. However, the structure has some desirable properties for implementing adaptive filters (see Section 1.2) and it plays a central role in the theory of autoregressive signal modeling.

Example 12.3.3 *Consider the 3rd-order FIR filter transfer function*

$$
H(z) = z^3 - 2.3741z^2 + 1.9293z - 0.532,
$$

which was obtained from the denominator of the 3rd-order Butterworth filter in Example 12.3.1 by scaling the coefficient of the highest power in z to unity. Thus,

$$
\begin{aligned}
\Psi_3(z) &= z^3 - 2.3741z^2 + 1.9293z - 0.532, \\
\Psi_2(z) &= z^2 - 1.8797z + 0.9293, \\
\Psi_1(z) &= z - 0.9743, \\
\Psi_0(z) &= 1,
\end{aligned}
$$

and k-parameters are

$$
k_3 = -0.532, \ k_2 = 0.9293, \ and \ k_1 = -0.9743.
$$

Fig. 12.9 shows the FIR lattice filter implementation of $H(z)$. ∎

12.4 DERIVATION OF ONE-MULTIPLIER LATTICE FILTER

By choosing $s_i = 1 - \epsilon_i k_i$ in (12.36), the Schur algorithm can be expressed as

$$
\Lambda_{i-1}(z) = \frac{z^{-1}\{\Lambda_i(z) - k_i\Lambda_i^*(z)\}}{1 - \epsilon_i k_i},
\tag{12.53}
$$

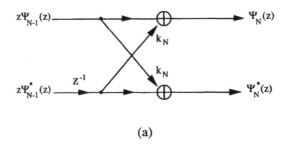

(a)

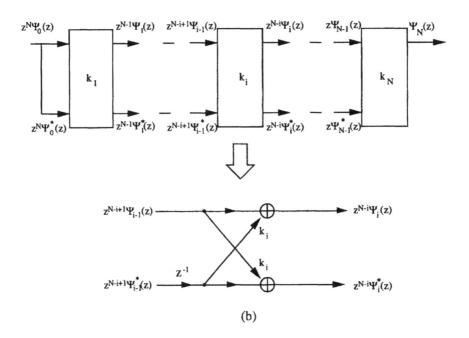

(b)

Fig. 12.8 (a) Implementation of (12.52) and (b) implementation of $H_N(z) = \Psi_N(z)$.

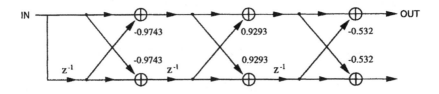

Fig. 12.9 A 3rd-order FIR lattice filter in Example 12.3.3.

where ϵ_i is called a sign parameter and is either 1 or -1. Consider an N-th order IIR transfer function $H_N(z) = N_N(z)/D_N(z)$. Then, initialize the N-th order Schur polynomial $\Lambda_N(z)$ as $\Lambda_N(z) = D_N(z)$. From $\Lambda_N(z)$, form the polynomial $\Lambda_{N-1}(z)$ by the Schur algorithm as

$$\Lambda_{N-1}(z) = \frac{z^{-1}\{\Lambda_N(z) - k_N\Lambda_N^*(z)\}}{1 - \epsilon_N k_N}, \tag{12.54}$$

where

$$k_i = \Lambda_i(0)/\Lambda_i^*(0). \tag{12.55}$$

With $i = N$,

$$\Lambda_{N-1}^*(z) = \frac{\Lambda_N^*(z) - k_N\Lambda_N(z)}{1 - \epsilon_N k_N}. \tag{12.56}$$

From (12.56),

$$\Lambda_N^*(z) = k_N\Lambda_N(z) + (1 - \epsilon_N k_N)\Lambda_{N-1}^*(z). \tag{12.57}$$

Using (12.54) and (12.57),

$$\Lambda_{N-1}(z) = z^{-1}\{(1 + \epsilon_N k_N)\Lambda_N(z) - k_N\Lambda_{N-1}^*(z)\}. \tag{12.58}$$

An implementation of (12.57) and (12.58) is shown in Fig. 12.10(a). By repeatedly applying the foregoing procedure with replacing $\Lambda_i(z)$ by $\Lambda_{i-1}(z)$, for $i = N, N-1, \cdots, 1$, the denominator $D_N(z)$ can be synthesized as shown in Fig. 12.10(b).

The relation between $\Lambda_i(z)$ and $\Phi_i(z)$ can be shown to be

$$\Lambda_N(z) = \Phi_N(z),$$
$$\Lambda_i(z) = \Phi_i(z)\sqrt{\frac{(1 + \epsilon_N k_N)(1 + \epsilon_{N-1}k_{N-1})\cdots(1 + \epsilon_{i+1}k_{i+1})}{(1 - \epsilon_N k_N)(1 - \epsilon_{N-1}k_{N-1})\cdots(1 - \epsilon_{i+1}k_{i+1})}}, \tag{12.59}$$

where $0 \leq i < N$. Notice that the k-parameter computed from $\Lambda_i(z)$ is the same as the k-parameter computed from $\Phi_i(z)$ since

$$k_i = \Lambda_i(0)/\Lambda_i^*(0) = \Phi_i(0)/\Phi_i^*(0). \tag{12.60}$$

Also, it is easily seen from (12.59) that $\{\Lambda_N(z), \Lambda_{N-1}, \cdots, \Lambda_0(z)\}$ are orthogonal but not orthonormal since

$$\langle\Lambda_i(z), \Lambda_i(z)\rangle = \langle\Lambda_i^*(z), \Lambda_i^*(z)\rangle,$$
$$= \frac{(1 + \epsilon_N k_N)(1 + \epsilon_{N-1}k_{N-1})\cdots(1 + \epsilon_{i+1}k_{i+1})}{(1 - \epsilon_N k_N)(1 - \epsilon_{N-1}k_{N-1})\cdots(1 - \epsilon_{i+1}k_{i+1})}. \tag{12.61}$$

From (12.61), notice that the magnitude of $\langle\Lambda_i(z), \Lambda_i(z)\rangle$ can be adjusted by properly choosing the sign parameters. Therefore, the 1-multiplier lattice

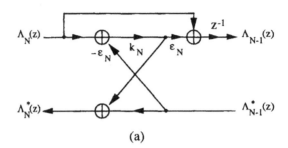

(a)

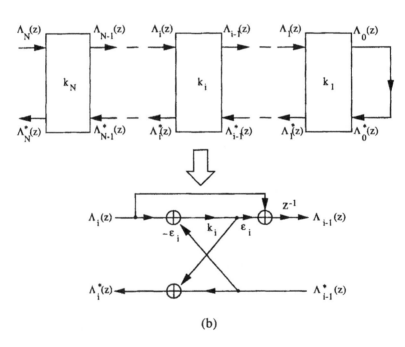

(b)

Fig. 12.10 (a) Implementation of (12.57) and (12.58) and (b) implementation of the denominator $D_N(z)$.

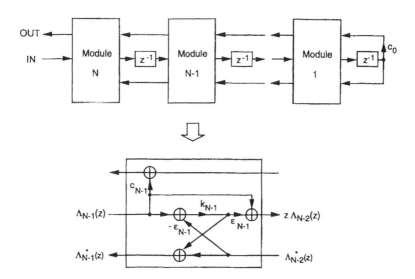

Fig. 12.11 The structure of an N-th order 1-multiplier lattice filter.

filter can avoid severe input scaling and has better roundoff noise property than the basic lattice filter.

One optimization criterion for choosing the sign parameters is to require that the node associated with the largest k-parameter in magnitude have the largest power. Then the sign parameters are recursively found by requiring that the powers at other nodes be as large as possible without exceeding the maximum value [6]. This procedure is explained in Example 12.4.1.

Since the polynomials $\{\Lambda_N(z), \Lambda_{N-1}(z), \cdots, \Lambda_1(z), \Lambda_0(z)\}$ on the top line of Fig. 12.10(b) are orthogonal, they can be used as an orthogonal basis to expand the numerator $N_N(z)$ by the polynomial expansion algorithm as

$$N_N(z) = \sum_{i=0}^{N} c_i \Lambda_i(z). \tag{12.62}$$

By combining these tap-gain parameters $\{c_N, c_{N-1}, \cdots, c_0\}$ to the all-pole portion in Fig. 12.10(b), the 1-multiplier lattice filter structure is obtained as shown in Fig. 12.11.

By the same procedure as in the previous section, the delays on the top edges in Fig. 12.10(b) can be moved to the bottom edges. Then, the tap-gain parameters are computed as

$$N_N^*(z) = \sum_{i=0}^{N} c_i \Lambda_i(z). \tag{12.63}$$

Fig. 12.12 shows the 1-multiplier lattice filter structure obtained by the reverse

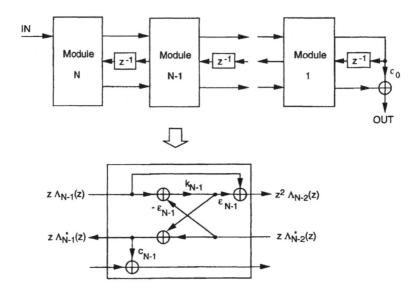

Fig. 12.12 The structure of an N-th order 1-multiplier lattice filter obtained using the reverse Schur polynomials.

Schur polynomials.

Example 12.4.1 *From the 3rd-order Butterworth filter in Example 12.3.1, the following Schur polynomials are computed:*

$$
\begin{aligned}
\Phi_3(z) &= 345.1z^3 - 819.3z^2 + 665.8z - 183.6, \\
\Phi_2(z) &= 292.2072z^2 - 549.2662z + 271.5337, \\
\Phi_1(z) &= 107.956z - 105.1841, \\
\Phi_0(z) &= 24.3064.
\end{aligned}
$$

By (12.60), the k-parameters are computed as

$$
k_3 = -0.532, \quad k_2 = 0.9293, \quad k_1 = -0.9743.
$$

Using (12.61), the power of each internal polynomial is computed as

$$
\begin{aligned}
\langle \Lambda_3(z), \Lambda_3(z) \rangle &= 1, \\
\langle \Lambda_2(z), \Lambda_2(z) \rangle &= \frac{(1 + \epsilon_3 k_3)}{(1 - \epsilon_3 k_3)}, \\
\langle \Lambda_1(z), \Lambda_1(z) \rangle &= \frac{(1 + \epsilon_3 k_3)(1 + \epsilon_2 k_2)}{(1 - \epsilon_3 k_3)(1 - \epsilon_2 k_2)}, \\
\langle \Lambda_0(z), \Lambda_0(z) \rangle &= \frac{(1 + \epsilon_3 k_3)(1 + \epsilon_2 k_2)(1 + \epsilon_1 k_1)}{(1 - \epsilon_3 k_3)(1 - \epsilon_2 k_2)(1 - \epsilon_1 k_1)}.
\end{aligned}
$$

Since k_1 is largest in magnitude, $\langle \Lambda_0(z), \Lambda_0(z) \rangle$ is required to have the maximum value. Also, it is desired that the powers at other nodes be as large as possible without exceeding $\langle \Lambda_0(z), \Lambda_0(z) \rangle$. To determine ϵ_1, consider the following ratio:

$$\frac{\langle \Lambda_1(z), \Lambda_1(z) \rangle}{\langle \Lambda_0(z), \Lambda_0(z) \rangle} = \frac{1 - \epsilon_1 k_1}{1 + \epsilon_1 k_1},$$

which is required to be less than one and which is satisfied by

$$\epsilon_1 = sign(k_1) = -1.$$

Then, $\langle \Lambda_1(z), \Lambda_1(z) \rangle / \langle \Lambda_0(z), \Lambda_0(z) \rangle = 0.013$. Next, the following condition also needs to be satisfied

$$\frac{\langle \Lambda_2(z), \Lambda_2(z) \rangle}{\langle \Lambda_0(z), \Lambda_0(z) \rangle} = \frac{1 - \epsilon_2 k_2}{1 + \epsilon_2 k_2} (0.013) < 1.$$

This value needs to be as large as possible without exceeding one. Thus, we choose

$$\epsilon_2 = -sign(k_2) = -1,$$

which gives

$$\frac{(1 - \epsilon_2 k_2)(1 - \epsilon_1 k_1)}{(1 + \epsilon_2 k_2)(1 + \epsilon_1 k_1)} = 0.3548.$$

Finally, from the following condition

$$\frac{\langle \Lambda_3(z), \Lambda_3(z) \rangle}{\langle \Lambda_0(z), \Lambda_0(z) \rangle} = \frac{1 - \epsilon_3 k_3}{1 + \epsilon_3 k_3} (0.3548) < 1,$$

ϵ_3 is chosen as

$$\epsilon_3 = sign(k_3) = -1.$$

By substituting ϵ_1, ϵ_2, and ϵ_3 into (12.59), we obtain

$$
\begin{aligned}
\Lambda_3(z) &= 345.1z^3 - 819.3z^2 + 665.8z - 183.6, \\
\Lambda_2(z) &= 528.7z^2 - 993.8053z + 491.2947, \\
\Lambda_1(z) &= 37.4053z - 36.448, \\
\Lambda_0(z) &= 73.8501.
\end{aligned}
$$

From (12.63) and the polynomial expansion algorithm, the expansion coefficients of the numerator with respect to the reverse Schur polynomials ($\Lambda_i^*(z)$'s) are

$$c_3 = 0.0029, \quad c_2 = 0.0102, \quad c_1 = 0.2987, \quad c_0 = 0.1005.$$

Fig. 12.13 shows the 1-multiplier lattice filter synthesized using the reverse Schur polynomials. ∎

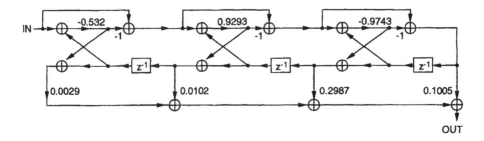

Fig. 12.13 A 3rd-order 1-multiplier lattice filter in Example 12.4.1.

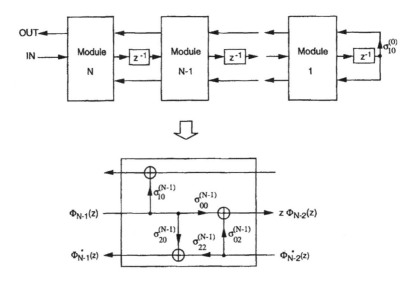

Fig. 12.14 The structure of an N-th order normalized lattice filter.

12.5 DERIVATION OF NORMALIZED LATTICE FILTER

The structure of an N-th order normalized lattice filter is shown in Fig. 12.14. Consider an N-th order IIR transfer function $H_N(z) = N_N(z)/D_N(z)$. Then, initialize the N-th order Schur polynomial $\Phi_N(z)$ as $\Phi_N(z)=D_N(z)$, where

$$\Phi_N(z) = \sum_{i=0}^{N} \phi_i z^i. \qquad (12.64)$$

From $\Phi_N(z)$, form the polynomial $\Phi_{N-1}(z)$ by the Schur algorithm as

$$\Phi_{N-1}(z) = \frac{z^{-1}\{\Phi_N(z) - k_N \Phi_N^*(z)\}}{\sqrt{1 - k_N^2}}, \qquad (12.65)$$

where

$$k_i = \Phi_i(0)/\Phi_i^*(0), \tag{12.66}$$

with $i = N$. Also, $\Phi_{N-1}^*(z)$, the reverse polynomial of $\Phi_{N-1}(z)$ is

$$\Psi_{N-1}^*(z) = z^{N-1}\Phi_{N-1}(z^{-1}) = \frac{\Phi_N^*(z) \cdot k_N \Phi_N(z)}{\sqrt{1 - k_N^2}}. \tag{12.67}$$

From (12.67),

$$\Phi_N^*(z) = \sqrt{1 - k_N^2}\,\Phi_{N-1}^*(z) + k_N \Phi_N(z). \tag{12.68}$$

Using (12.65) and (12.68), $\Phi_{N-1}(z)$ can be expressed as a function of $\Phi_N(z)$ and $\Phi_{N-1}^*(z)$ as

$$\Phi_{N-1}(z) = z^{-1}\{\sqrt{1 - k_N^2}\,\Phi_N(z) - k_N \Phi_{N-1}^*(z)\}. \tag{12.69}$$

An implementation of (12.68) and (12.69) is shown in Fig. 12.15(a), which is the same as the feedback part of module N of the normalized lattice filter in Fig. 12.14 if

$$\sigma_{20}^{(N)} = -\sigma_{02}^{(N)} = k_N, \quad \sigma_{00}^{(N)} = \sigma_{22}^{(N)} = \sqrt{1 - k_N^2}. \tag{12.70}$$

By repeatedly applying the above procedure with replacing $\Phi_i(z)$ by $\Phi_{i-1}(z)$ for $i = N, N-1, \cdots, 1$, the denominator $D_N(z)$ can be synthesized as shown in Fig. 12.15(b). For module i in Fig. 12.15(b),

$$\sigma_{20}^{(i)} = -\sigma_{02}^{(i)} = k_i, \quad \sigma_{00}^{(i)} = \sigma_{22}^{(i)} = \sqrt{1 - k_i^2}. \tag{12.71}$$

Notice that each module in Fig. 12.15(b) forms a Givens rotation, which is known to exhibit good numerical properties. Also, in Fig. 12.15(b), the polynomials along the top line are the polynomials $\{\Phi_N(z), \Phi_{N-1}, \cdots, \Phi_0(z)\}$, which can be used as orthonormal basis functions to expand any N-th order polynomial. If the numerator $N_N(z)$ is expanded using the polynomial expansion algorithm using

$$N_N(z) = \sum_{i=0}^{N} c_i \Phi_i(z), \tag{12.72}$$

then the numerator can be synthesized as in Fig. 12.14 by choosing

$$\sigma_{10}^{(i)} = c_i. \tag{12.73}$$

Therefore, by choosing the filter parameters as in (12.71) and (12.73), the numerator $N_N(z)$ is obtained at the filter output if the input to the filter is $D_N(z)$. This means that the normalized lattice filter in Fig. 12.14 implements

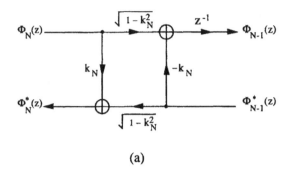

(a)

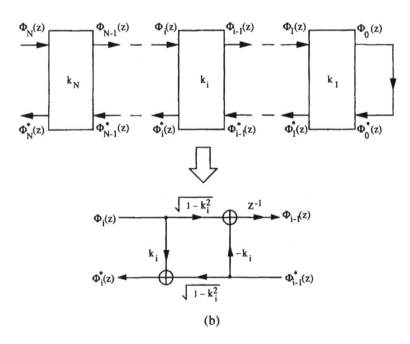

(b)

Fig. 12.15 (a) Implementation of (12.68) and (12.69) and (b) implementation of the denominator $D_N(z)$.

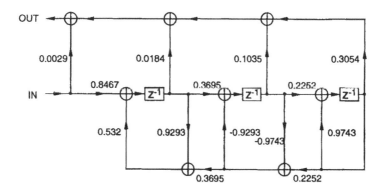

Fig. 12.16 Third-order normalized lattice filter in Example 12.5.1.

$H_N(z) = N_N(z)/D_N(z)$. Notice that every node on the feedback path, i.e., every node in Fig. 12.15(b), has unit power since

$$\langle \Phi_i(z), \Phi_i(z) \rangle = \langle \Phi_i^*(z), \Phi_i^*(z) \rangle = 1. \tag{12.74}$$

Therefore, the state covariance matrix, $\mathbf{K}$, for an all-pole normalized lattice filter is an identity matrix, i.e., $\mathbf{K} = \mathbf{I}$, and this structure is an orthonormal filter. However, the pole-zero normalized lattice filter is not an orthonormal filter, since the variance of the states corresponding to the numerator part are not unity. By the same procedure as in the previous sections, the structure of a normalized lattice filter can be derived using the reverse Schur polynomials.

Example 12.5.1 *Consider the normalized lattice filter implementation of the transfer function given in Example 12.3.1. Using (12.47) and the results of Example 12.3.1, the k-parameters for the normalized lattice filter are*

$$k_3 = -0.532, \ k_2 = 0.9293, \ k_1 = -0.9743.$$

Using (12.72), the expansion coefficients of the numerator with respect to the Schur polynomials are

$$c_3 = 0.0029, \ c_2 = 0.0184, \ c_1 = 0.1035, \ c_0 = 0.3054.$$

Then the normalized lattice filter is synthesized as shown in Fig. 12.16. ∎

12.6   DERIVATION OF SCALED-NORMALIZED LATTICE FILTER

By applying the slow-down and retiming/pipelining (SRP) transformation (see Section 11.7) with $M = 2$ to a 3rd-order normalized lattice filter, we obtain the filter structure in Fig. 12.17. In Fig. 12.17, each delay element is

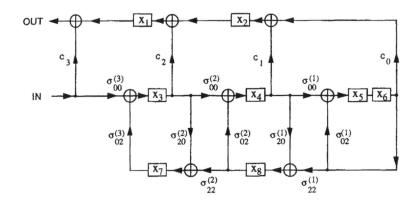

Fig. 12.17 A 3rd-order normalized lattice filter after upsampling and retiming with $M = 2$.

represented by x_i, for $i = 1$ to 8, and $\sigma_{10}^{(i)}$ is denoted by c_i, for $i = 0$ to 3. From (12.74), each $x_i(n)$, for $i = 3$ to 8, has unit power. In terms of the state covariance matrix, $K_{ii} = 1$, for $i = 3$ to 8, where K_{ii} is the i-th diagonal element of $\mathbf{K}$. Then, to scale the filter, we only need to compute the powers of $x_1(n)$ and $x_2(n)$, which can be computed from (11.25). In the case of the normalized lattice filter, K_{11} and K_{22} can be computed more efficiently using the orthonormality of the Schur polynomials. From Fig 12.17, the polynomial at the state x_1 is given by:

$$\Phi^{(x_1)}(z) = c_2 \Phi_2(z) + c_1 \Phi_1(z) + c_0 \Phi_0(z). \tag{12.75}$$

Therefore, using the orthonormality of the Schur polynomials,

$$
\begin{aligned}
K_{11} &= \langle \Phi^{(x_1)}(z), \Phi^{(x_1)}(z) \rangle, \\
&= c_2^2 + c_1^2 + c_0^2. \tag{12.76}
\end{aligned}
$$

By the same way,

$$K_{22} = c_1^2 + c_0^2. \tag{12.77}$$

In general, for the summing node on the top line of module i, the power is $\sum_{j=0}^{i} c_j^2$. To have unit power at each of the internal nodes, the elements of the diagonal transformation matrix $\mathbf{T}$ of the 3rd-order normalized lattice filter are computed using (11.38) as

$$
\begin{aligned}
t_1 &= \sqrt{c_2^2 + c_1^2 + c_0^2}, \\
t_2 &= \sqrt{c_1^2 + c_0^2}, \\
t_i &= 1, \ i = 3 \text{ to } 8. \tag{12.78}
\end{aligned}
$$

Fig. 12.18 Transformation using transformation rule of $\mathbf{x}' = \mathbf{T}^{-1}\mathbf{x}$.

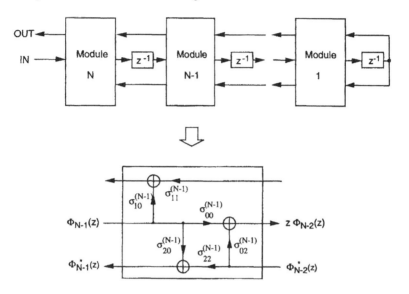

Fig. 12.19 The structure of an N-th order scaled-normalized lattice filter.

From the transformation rule $\mathbf{x}' = \mathbf{T}^{-1}\mathbf{x}$, we observe that $x_i' = x_i/t_i$. Therefore to scale the system, all coefficients associated with edges input to the state x_i should be multiplied by $1/t_i$ and the coefficients associated with edges outgoing from state x_i should be multiplied by t_i (see Fig. 12.18).

Applying the foregoing observations to the general N-th order normalized lattice filter, we obtain the N-th order scaled-normalized lattice filter structure shown in Fig. 12.19, where

$$\text{Module } N \quad : \quad \sigma_{10}^{(N)} = c_N, \ \sigma_{11}^{(N)} = \sqrt{\sum_{j=0}^{N-1} c_j^2},$$

$$\text{Module } i \ (i = N-1 \text{ to } 1) \quad : \quad \sigma_{10}^{(i)} = \frac{c_i}{\sqrt{\sum_{j=0}^{i} c_j^2}}, \ \sigma_{11}^{(i)} = \frac{\sqrt{\sum_{j=0}^{i-1} c_j^2}}{\sqrt{\sum_{j=0}^{i} c_j^2}},$$

$$\text{Any module } i \ (i = N \text{ to } 1) \quad : \quad \sigma_{20}^{(i)} = -\sigma_{02}^{(i)} = k_i,$$

$$\sigma_{00}^{(i)} = \sigma_{22}^{(i)} = \sqrt{1 - k_i^2}. \tag{12.79}$$

The foregoing equations describe the scaled-normalized lattice filter. Thus this lattice filter is derived from scaling considerations [7] as opposed to the local optimization approach used in [5].

In (12.79), the parameters k_i and c_i are computed by the same method as in the normalized lattice filter. Notice that the feedback parts $\{\sigma_{20}^{(i)},\ \sigma_{02}^{(i)},\ \sigma_{00}^{(i)}$ and $\sigma_{22}^{(i)}\}$ of the normalized and the scaled-normalized lattice filters are the same.

In finite wordlength arithmetic, it is desirable that all numerical values be as large as possible without causing overflow at critical nodes, so that the number of significant figures in the respective calculations can also be as large as possible [8]. In addition, if every internal node has the same power, each of the calculations is carried out (on the average) with the same number of significant figures. If l_2 scaling is chosen such that the power of each internal node is bounded by unity, then the input to the filter is usually scaled down by the largest norm of the nodes on the feedback path. This scaling down reduces the dynamic range of the input and increases the effect of rounding errors to the output signal.

The scaled-normalized lattice filter is perfectly scaled such that every internal node has unit power. Also, no input scaling is needed since the largest norm is unity. As a result, the scaled-normalized lattice filter has good finite wordlength properties. In addition, the filter has suitable properties for VLSI design such as regularity, modularity, local connection, and pipelinability. Also, the Givens rotation of each module can be efficiently implemented using the CORDIC algorithm [9],[10].

When the poles of the filter are not clustered, there is little difference in roundoff noise between a scaled-normalized lattice filter and a parallel/cascade form filter. However, for clustered poles, normalized or scaled-normalized lattice filters have much better roundoff noise characteristics than the standard parallel/cascade form filters. In [11], a band-pass filter with clustered poles was simulated using a 36-bit PDP-10 computer, and the normalized lattice filter was superior to the parallel form filter by approximately 10 bits. Since the scaled-normalized lattice filter has smaller roundoff noise than the normalized lattice filter [5], we conclude that the scaled-normalized lattice filter also requires at least 10 bits less than the parallel form filter for the same specifications.

The scaled-normalized lattice filters require more number of multipliers than the standard parallel/cascade form filters. However, as was discussed in the previous paragraph, it is meaningless to compare just the number of multipliers between different filter structures. Since the hardware complexity of a multiplier is proportional to the square of the wordlength, a filter with more multipliers and smaller wordlength can sometimes be implemented with less hardware than a filter with fewer multipliers and larger wordlength. Therefore, the hardware complexity of a digital filter should be determined carefully depending upon the frequency specifications.

The design procedure for the scaled-normalized lattice filter is summarized

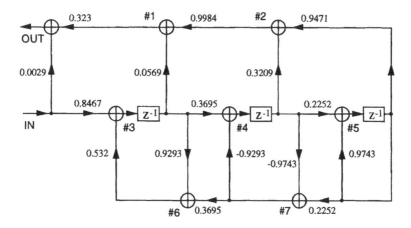

Fig. 12.20 Third-order scaled-normalized lattice filter in Example 12.6.1.

as follows:

1. Compute the Schur polynomials $\{\Phi_N(z),\ \Phi_{N-1}(z),\ \cdots,\ \Phi_0(z)\}$ from the denominator $D_N(z)$.

2. For $i = N,\ N-1,\ \cdots,\ 1$, compute k-parameters $k_i = \Phi_i(0)/\Phi_i^*(0)$.

3. Expand the numerator $N_N(z)$ by the polynomial expansion algorithm such that $N_N(z) = \sum_{i=0}^{N} c_i \Phi_i(z)$.

4. By (12.79), the scaled-normalized lattice filter is synthesized using the parameters computed in steps 2 and 3.

Example 12.6.1 *Consider a scaled-normalized lattice filter implementation of the transfer function given in Example 12.3.1. Using (12.79) and the expansion coefficients of the numerator obtained in Example 12.5.1, the scaled-normalized lattice filter is synthesized as shown in Fig. 12.20.* ∎

In Fig. 12.15(a), the delay on the top edge can be moved to the bottom edge without altering the input-output relation as shown in Fig. 12.21(a). Notice that the polynomials on the right side in Fig. 12.21(a) are $z\Phi_{N-1}(z)$ and $z\Phi_{N-1}^*(z)$ instead of $\Phi_{N-1}(z)$ and $\Phi_{N-1}^*(z)$. Fig. 12.21(b) shows the implementation of the denominator with all delays on the bottom edge. From the $(i - j)$ orthonormality of the reverse Schur polynomials, the polynomials obtained from each node on the bottom line in Fig. 12.21(b) are orthonormal and can be used as an orthonormal basis to expand the numerator as

$$N_N(z) = \sum_{i=0}^{N} c_i z^{N-i} \Phi_i^*(z). \tag{12.80}$$

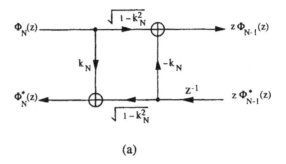

(a)

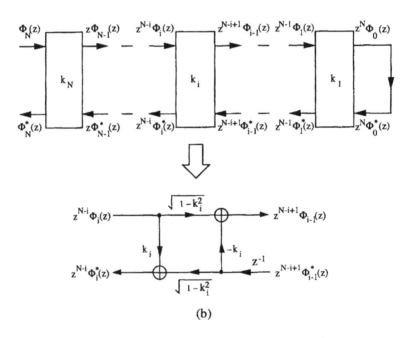

(b)

Fig. 12.21 (a) Implementation of (12.68) and (12.69) with the delay on the bottom edge and (b) implementation of the denominator $D_N(z)$.

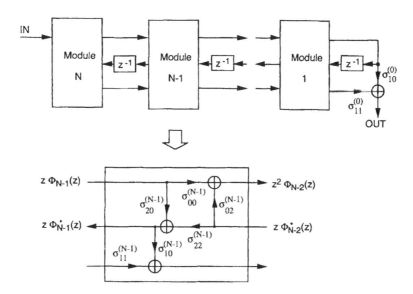

Fig. 12.22 The structure of an N-th order reverse scaled-normalized lattice filter.

In (12.80), notice that the order of each polynomial $z^{N-i}\Phi_i^*(z)$, for $i = N$ to 0, is N, and we cannot directly apply the polynomial expansion algorithm. However, from (12.80),

$$
\begin{aligned}
N_N^*(z) &= z^N \left\{ \sum_{i=0}^{N} c_i z^{-(N-i)} \Phi_i^*(z^{-1}) \right\}, \\
&= \sum_{i=0}^{N} c_i \Phi_i(z).
\end{aligned}
\tag{12.81}
$$

It is obvious that the polynomial expansion algorithm can be applied to (12.81). Therefore, the expansion coefficients in (12.80) can be computed by expanding the reverse polynomial of the numerator using $\{\Phi_N(z), \Phi_{N-1}(z), \cdots, \Phi_0(z)\}$. The reverse scaled-normalized lattice filter (the scaled-normalized lattice filter structure whose tap gain parameters are obtained by the reverse Schur polynomials) is shown in Fig. 12.22. In Fig. 12.22, the parameters $\{\sigma_{00}^{(i)}, \sigma_{20}^{(i)}, \sigma_{02}^{(i)}, \sigma_{22}^{(i)}\}$ are the same as in (12.79). By the same procedure as in the previous section, the tap-gain parameters are computed such that every internal node has unit power. The computed tap-gain parameters are

$$\text{Module } N \quad : \quad \sigma_{10}^{(N)} = 1, \ \sigma_{11}^{(N)} = 0,$$

$$\text{Module } i \ (i = N-1 \text{ to } 1) \quad : \quad \sigma_{10}^{(i)} = \frac{c_i}{\sqrt{\sum_{j=i}^{N} c_j^2}}, \ \sigma_{11}^{(i)} = \frac{\sqrt{\sum_{j=i+1}^{N} c_j^2}}{\sqrt{\sum_{j=i}^{N} c_j^2}},$$

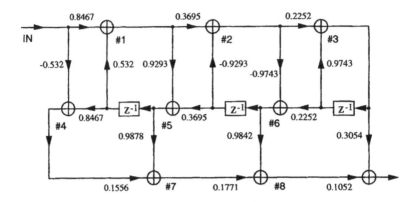

Fig. 12.23 Third-order reverse scaled-normalized lattice filter in Example 12.6.2.

$$\text{Others} \quad : \quad \sigma_{10}^{(0)} = c_0, \ \sigma_{11}^{(0)} = \sqrt{\sum_{j=1}^{N} c_j^2}. \tag{12.82}$$

Example 12.6.2 *The transfer function used in Example 12.3.1 is implemented using the reverse scaled-normalized lattice filter as shown in Fig. 12.23. Notice that the tap-gain parameters of Fig. 12.23 are the same as those in Fig. 12.20 since* $N^*(z) = N(z)$. ■

12.7   ROUNDOFF NOISE CALCULATION IN LATTICE FILTERS

In addition to the computation of **K** and **W** matrices based on the state variable description method, roundoff noise of lattice filters can be conveniently computed by the method proposed in [5]. This method is based upon the Schur algorithm and the transposition theorem [1],[12] and is explained in this section. Roundoff noise properties of the scaled-normalized and the reverse scaled-normalized lattice filters are also compared.

12.7.1   Roundoff Noise Computation Using Transposition Theorem

To compute the output roundoff noise, the transfer functions from the internal nodes to the output node are needed and can be found by the transposition theorem. According to the transposition theorem, the transfer functions from input to the internal nodes of transposed graph are also the transfer functions from those corresponding internal nodes to the output node in the original graph. Fig. 12.24 shows a module of the transposed graph of scaled-normalized lattice filter. (For notational convenience, superscripts are omitted. Also, using (12.79), the following notations are used: $k = \sigma_{20} = -\sigma_{02}$,

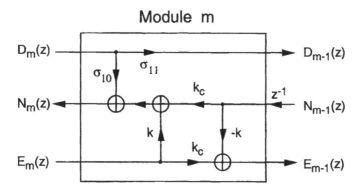

Fig. 12.24 Module m of transposed graph of the scaled-normalized lattice filter.

$k_c = \sqrt{1 - k^2} = \sigma_{00} = \sigma_{22}.$)

From the transposed graph, the following equations can be derived:

$$
\begin{aligned}
N_m(z) &= \sigma_{10} D_m(z) + k E_m(z) + k_c z^{-1} N_{m-1}(z), \\
D_{m-1}(z) &= \sigma_{11} D_m(z), \\
E_{m-1}(z) &= k_c E_m(z) - k z^{-1} N_{m-1}(z).
\end{aligned}
\tag{12.83}
$$

After simple algebraic manipulations, $z^{-1} N_{m-1}(z)$, $D_{m-1}(z)$, and $E_{m-1}(z)$ can be represented in terms of $N_m(z)$, $D_m(z)$ and $E_m(z)$ as

$$
\begin{bmatrix}
z^{-1} N_{m-1}(z) \\
D_{m-1}(z) \\
E_{m-1}(z)
\end{bmatrix}
= \frac{1}{k_c}
\begin{bmatrix}
1 & -\sigma_{10} & -k \\
0 & k_c \sigma_{11} & 0 \\
-k & k \sigma_{10} & k_c^2 + k^2
\end{bmatrix}
\begin{bmatrix}
N_m(z) \\
D_m(z) \\
E_m(z)
\end{bmatrix}.
\tag{12.84}
$$

This relation can be applied directly to the normalized lattice filter if σ_{11} is replaced by 1. By similar procedures, the relations for basic and 1-multiplier lattice filters can be derived.

Consider a lattice filter implementing an N-th order transfer function $H(z) = N_N(z)/D_N(z)$. If the input to the filter is $D_N(z)$, then the output should be $N_N(z)$. Therefore, for module N, $N_N(z)$ and $D_N(z)$ are determined from the transfer function. Also, note that $E_N(z)$ is zero for module N. Then the polynomials of the right side of module N are calculated by the foregoing matrix multiplication. By the same procedure, all of the polynomials are calculated for each module m, for $m = N, N - 1, \cdots, 1$. Once the polynomials associated with the internal nodes are obtained, the output roundoff noise gains are computed by the method discussed in Section 12.2.4.

Example 12.7.1 *Consider again the normalized lattice filter discussed in Example 12.5.1. Fig. 12.25 shows the transposed graph of the normalized lattice filter in Fig. 12.16. The transfer functions from input to internal nodes 1 − 9 of the transposed graph are also the transfer functions from those correspond-*

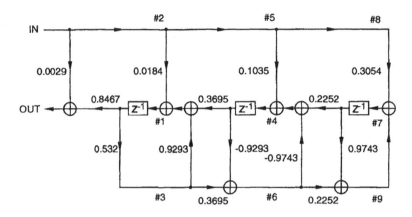

Fig. 12.25 Transposed graph of the normalized lattice filter in Fig. 12.16.

ing internal nodes to the output node in the original graph in Fig. 12.16. The polynomials associated with each node $1 - 9$ of the transposed graph are:

$$1 \quad : \quad 6.3469z^3 + 1.2645z^2 + 1.8093z,$$
$$2,5,8 \quad : \quad 345.1z^3 - 819.3z^2 + 665.8z - 183.6,$$
$$3 \quad : \quad 3.3767z^2 + 0.6727z + 0.9626,$$
$$4 \quad : \quad 35.7147z^3 - 29.9385z^2 + 6.7185z,$$
$$6 \quad : \quad -31.9404z^2 + 28.0689z - 5.8876,$$
$$7 \quad : \quad 105.4016z^3 - 154.7295z^2 + 58.914z,$$
$$9 \quad : \quad 95.5039z^2 - 144.4369z - 56.0758.$$

By applying polynomial expansion algorithm to each of the polynomials, the output roundoff noise gains from the internal nodes $1 - 9$ are $\{0.1455, 1, 0.0412, 0.2952, 1, 0.1912, 0.3096, 1, 0.2163\}$, respectively. By summing the noise gains from nodes $1 - 7$, the total output roundoff noise gain of the normalized lattice filter in Fig. 12.16 is 2.9827. (Notice that node 9 does not generate roundoff noise (see Fig. 12.16). Since double-length accumulator model is used, the roundoff noise of node 8 is counted at node 5.) ■

12.7.2   Roundoff Noise Comparisons

Any stable transfer function can be implemented by the scaled-normalized lattice filter or by the reverse scaled-normalized lattice filter. In addition to these structures, it is also possible to compute the tap-gain parameters using linear combination of the Schur polynomials and the reverse Schur polynomials. In this case, the tap-gain parameters are connected both to the Schur polynomial side and to the reverse Schur polynomial side. Therefore, it is necessary to examine the roundoff noise properties of these diverse structures.

In [13], it is shown that the best roundoff noise property is obtained if the tap-gain parameters are connected to the Schur polynomial side. Consider the pure lattice section without tap-gain parameters in Fig. 12.21(b). Let $S_{ij}(z)$ be the transfer function from state x_j to x_i, where x_j is the delay at module j. Then, the effect of the noise injected at the j-th node to the i-th node is represented by the norm

$$\|S_{ij}\|^2 = \frac{1}{2\pi} \int_0^{2\pi} |S_{ij}(e^{j\omega})|^2 d\omega. \tag{12.85}$$

Next, consider the same structure except that the i-th delay is transferred from the bottom to the top edge. The transfer function from x_j to x_i of this new structure is represented by $T_{ij}(z)$. Then, using the state variable description, the following identity is derived in [13]:

$$\|S_{ij}\|^2 - \|T_{ij}\|^2 = \begin{cases} 1, & 1 \le j \le i - 1, \\ 0, & i \le j \le n. \end{cases} \tag{12.86}$$

The implication of (12.86) is as follows. Take an arbitrary cutset in the pure lattice section that is composed of two edges. The variable associated with the upper edge of the cutset is less influenced than the one associated with the lower edge by the roundoff noise generated at the state node to the right of the cutset. As for the noise sources located to the left of the cutset, their effects on the upper and the lower variables are the same. This implies that taking the tap-gain parameters from the Schur polynomial side can improve the roundoff error.

Example 12.7.2 *From the scaled-normalized lattice filter in Fig. 12.20, the output roundoff noise gains from nodes $1 - 7$ are computed as $\{0.1043, 0.104,$ $0.1455, 0.2952, 0.3096, 0.0412, 0.1912\}$. (Refer to Example 12.6.1.) By summing the noise gains from each node, the total output roundoff noise gain of the scaled-normalized lattice filter is 1.191. Since the output signal can be expressed as $\sum_{i=0}^{3} c_i \Phi_i(z)$, the output signal power is $\sum_{i=0}^{3} c_i^2 = 0.10434$. Therefore, the noise-to-signal ratio (NSR) of the filter is $1.191/0.10434 = 11.4146$.*

The transfer function used for the scaled-normalized lattice filter is implemented using the reverse scaled-normalized lattice filter in Fig. 12.23. (Refer to Example 12.6.2.) The output roundoff noise gains from nodes $1 - 8$ are $\{0.1432, 0.19, 0.2057, 0.0933, 0.1428, 0.19, 0.104, 0.1043\}$. By summing the noise gains from each node, the total output roundoff noise gain of the reverse scaled-normalized lattice filter is 1.1734. Since the output signal power is 0.10434, the NSR of the reverse scaled-normalized lattice filter is $1.1734/0.10434 = 11.246$. ■

In Example 12.7.2, the NSR of the reverse scaled-normalized lattice filter is almost the same as that of the scaled-normalized lattice filter. The following

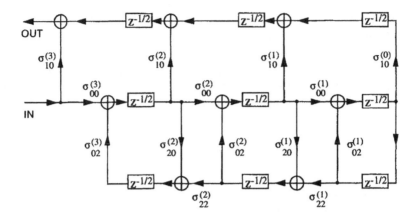

Fig. 12.26 A 3rd-order normalized lattice filter with transferred half delays.

example clearly shows the validity of (12.86).

Example 12.7.3 *Consider a 3rd-order elliptic low-pass filter*

$$H(z) = \frac{0.3296(z^3 + 1.61165z^2 + 1.61165z + 1)}{z^3 + 0.0522z^2 + 0.7139z - 0.0445}.$$

The k-parameters and the tap-gain parameters are computed as

$$k_3 = -0.0445, \quad k_2 = 0.71766, \quad k_1 = -0.049,$$
$$\sigma_{10}^{(3)} = 0.3296, \quad \sigma_{10}^{(2)} = 0.8141 \quad \sigma_{10}^{(1)} = 0.9894,$$
$$\sigma_{11}^{(3)} = 0.632, \quad \sigma_{11}^{(2)} = 0.5807, \quad \sigma_{11}^{(1)} = 0.145.$$

The signal power at the output is 0.508. The NSR of the scaled-normalized lattice filter is 2.863 and that of the reverse scaled-normalized lattice filter is 5.441. Therefore, the NSR of the scaled-normalized lattice filter is only 52.8% of that of the reverse scaled-normalized lattice filter. ∎

12.8 PIPELINING OF LATTICE IIR DIGITAL FILTERS

Although the lattice filters can be pipelined by the cutset localization procedure, the maximum sample rate of these pipelined filters is limited by the feedback loop computations. For example, in normalized lattice filters, the cutset localization procedure (see Chapter 4) can be applied to transfer one half of each delay on the right directed edges to the left directed edges as shown in Fig. 12.26. The half delays can be implemented by time rescaling. For example, using 1 clock cycle to represent a half delay, we can input 1 sample every 2 clock cycles and generate the output samples once every 2 clock cycles. The maximum sample rate of this structure is limited by the feedback loop computation, which involves 2 multiplications and 2 additions.

Using the Schur algorithm, we show that if the denominator of the transfer function is in scattered look-ahead form, then the transfer function satisfies the pipelining property of lattice digital filters [14],[15]. One drawback of the scattered look-ahead technique is the introduction of the cancelling zeros. These zeros increase the number of multiplication operations needed to implement the digital filter and lead to inexact pole-zero cancellation in fixed point implementations. To avoid the drawback of cancelling zeros, we use pipelined transfer functions designed using constrained filter design approaches. One approach is to use the filter design procedure used for decimation filter design [16]–[19]. Another approach also used for decimation filter design can be found in [20],[21].

12.8.1   Pipelining Property of the Schur Algorithm

An i-th order real Schur polynomial is expressed as

$$\Phi_i(z) = \sum_{m=0}^{i} \phi_m^{(i)} z^m. \qquad (12.87)$$

To compute the k-parameters of basic, 1-multiplier, normalized, and scaled-normalized lattice filters, we need to compute the Schur polynomials $\{\Phi_{N-1}(z), \Phi_{N-2}(z), \cdots, \Phi_0(z)\}$ from $\Phi_N(z) = D_N(z)$ by the Schur algorithm. The coefficients of increasing powers of z in $\Phi_{i-1}(z)$ are $\left\{ (\phi_i^{(i)})^2 - (\phi_0^{(i)})^2 \right\}^{-\frac{1}{2}}$ times the i determinants of the 2×2 submatrices formed by the 1st column and each succeeding column in the following matrix:

$$\begin{bmatrix} \phi_i^{(i)} & \phi_{i-1}^{(i)} & \phi_{i-2}^{(i)} & \cdots & \phi_2^{(i)} & \phi_1^{(i)} & \phi_0^{(i)} \\ \phi_0^{(i)} & \phi_1^{(i)} & \phi_2^{(i)} & \cdots & \phi_{i-2}^{(i)} & \phi_{i-1}^{(i)} & \phi_i^{(i)} \end{bmatrix}. \qquad (12.88)$$

For each 2×2 submatrix, if a column is composed of all zero elements, the determinant of the corresponding submatrix is zero. Using this property of determinant, we observe an useful property for pipelining lattice filters.

Zero Coefficient Property of the Schur Algorithm:
If $\Phi_N(z)$ is a Schur polynomial of order N, and has j-consecutive zero coefficients between each 2 nonzero coefficients of nearest degree, then the polynomial $\Phi_{N-i}(z)$ of order $(N-i)$ also has j-consecutive zero coefficients between each 2 nonzero coefficients of nearest degree for $i = 1$ to $N - j - 1$ and has only one nonzero coefficient for $i = N - j$ to N.

Example 12.8.1 *Consider the polynomial*

$$D_8(z) = z^8 + 0.63459z^4 + 0.10067.$$

Notice that $D_8(z)$ has 3 consecutive zero coefficients between each 2 nonzero coefficients ($j = 3$). Using the Schur algorithm, the Schur polynomials are computed as

$$\Phi_8(z) = z^8 + 0.63459z^4 + 0.10067,$$
$$\Phi_7(z) = 0.99492z^7 + 0.57362z^3,$$
$$\Phi_6(z) = 0.99492z^6 + 0.57362z^2,$$
$$\Phi_5(z) = 0.99492z^5 + 0.57362z,$$
$$\Phi_4(z) = 0.99429z^4 + 0.57362,$$
$$\Phi_3(z) = 0.81291z^3,$$
$$\Phi_2(z) = 0.81291z^2,$$
$$\Phi_1(z) = 0.81291z,$$
$$\Phi_0(z) = 0.81291.$$

Polynomials $\Phi_8(z), \Phi_7(z), \Phi_6(z), \Phi_5(z), \Phi_4(z)$ have 3 consecutive zero coefficients between each 2 nonzero coefficients of nearest degree and the other polynomials have only 1 nonzero coefficient. ∎

Consider $\Phi_N(z)$, which has a *nonzero constant term* and has j consecutive zero coefficients between each 2 nonzero coefficients of nearest degree. Then, the degree of $\Phi_{N-1}(z)$ is reduced only by one compared with that of $\Phi_N(z)$ but $\Phi_{N-1}(z)$ should have j consecutive zero coefficients between each 2 nonzero coefficients of nearest degree. Therefore, $\Phi_{N-1}(z)$ should have zero constant term if $j \geq 1$. This observation is generalized as follows.

Zero Constant Term Property of the Schur Algorithm:
If $\Phi_N(z)$ is a Schur polynomial of order N with a nonzero constant term and has j consecutive zero coefficients between each 2 nonzero coefficients of nearest degree, then the polynomial $\Phi_{N-i}(z)$ has zero constant term if i is not a multiple of $(j + 1)$.

Example 12.8.2 *Consider the Schur polynomials in Example 12.8.1. $\Phi_8(z)$ has a nonzero constant term with $j = 3$. Then, the polynomials which have nonzero constant terms are (1) $\Phi_{8-0\cdot4}(z) = \Phi_8(z)$, (2) $\Phi_{8-1\cdot4}(z) = \Phi_4(z)$, and (3) $\Phi_{8-2\cdot4}(z) = \Phi_0(z)$.* ∎

12.8.2 Pipelining of Basic Lattice Filter

The structure of a 2nd-order basic lattice filter is shown in Fig 12.27. Notice that the tap-gain parameters $\{c_2, c_1, c_0\}$ constitute the feed-forward section and the feedback section is described by the k-parameters only. The iteration bound of this structure is limited by the time required for 2 multiplications and 3 addition operations. In Fig 12.27, if the k-parameter of module 1 (i.e.

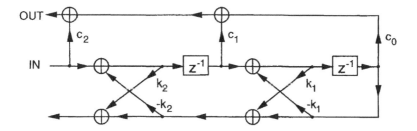

Fig. 12.27   Second-order basic lattice filter.

k_1) is zero, then the feedback loop of the module 1 is removed. Then the delay of module 1 is shared with module 2 and consequently there are 2 delays in the feedback loop, which leads to 2-level pipelining of the basic lattice filter.

By the same way, if the k-parameters of $(M - 1)$ consecutive modules of an N-th order basic lattice filter are zero, then the feedback loops of those modules are removed and consequently there are M delays in each loop, which leads to M-level pipelining of the basic lattice filter.

The k-parameters of an N-th order basic lattice filter are computed by

$$k_i = \frac{\Psi_i(0)}{\Psi_i^*(0)} = \frac{\Phi_i(0)}{\Phi_i^*(0)}, \quad i = N, \ N - 1, \ \cdots, \ 1. \tag{12.89}$$

Therefore, to obtain zero k-parameter for module i, the constant term of $\Phi_i(z)$ should be zero. From the zero constant term property of the Schur algorithm, if $D_N(z)$ has a nonzero constant term and has $(M - 1)$ consecutive zero coefficients between each 2 nonzero coefficients of nearest degree, then only $\{\Phi_N(z), \ \Phi_{N-M}(z), \ \Phi_{N-2M}(z), \ \cdots, \ \Phi_0(z)\}$ have nonzero constant terms. Therefore, we have $(M - 1)$ consecutive zero k-parameters and consequently there are M delays in each loop, which leads to M-level pipelining of basic lattice filter [14].

The M delays in each loop can be redistributed at appropriate locations to pipeline the loop multiply-add operations. Also, notice that the multiply-add operations in the feed-forward section can be pipelined at any desired level by placing latches at appropriate feed-forward cutset locations. Since the number of multiply-add operations in every loop remains constant, the M-level pipelined filter can be clocked at M times faster rate, as compared with the nonpipelined filter.

Example 12.8.3 *Consider the following transfer function*

$$H(z) = \frac{z^4 + 3.9z^3 + 5.7z^2 + 3.7z + 0.9}{z^4 - 0.17z^2 - 0.5184}.$$

Notice that the denominator has one zero coefficient between each 2 nonzero coefficients of nearest degree. From the denominator, k-parameters are com-

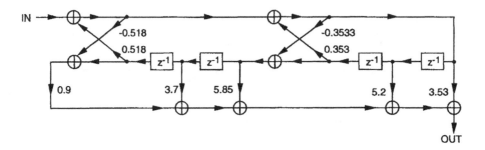

Fig. 12.28 Two-level pipelined basic lattice filter in Example 12.8.3.

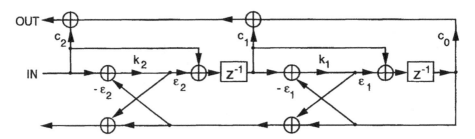

Fig. 12.29 Second-order 1-multiplier lattice filter.

puted as

$$k_4 = -0.518, \ k_3 = 0, \ k_2 = -0.353, \ k_1 = 0.$$

The computed k-parameters clearly show that this transfer function can be implemented by a 2-level pipelined basic lattice filter. Fig. 12.28 shows the 2-level pipelined basic lattice filter designed using reverse Schur polynomials. In the nonpipelined filter, there is only one delay in every loop. However, the 2-level pipelined filter contains 2 delays in every loop and can be clocked at a twice faster rate as compared with the nonpipelined filter. ∎

12.8.3   Pipelining of One-Multiplier Lattice Filter

The structure of a 2nd-order 1-multiplier lattice filter is shown in Fig 12.29. Notice that the tap-gain parameters $\{c_2, c_1, c_0\}$ constitute the feed-forward section and the feedback section is described by the k-parameters and the sign parameters $\{\epsilon_2, \epsilon_1, \epsilon_i = \pm 1\}$ only. The iteration bound (see Chapter 2) of this structure is limited by 2 multiplications and 4 addition operations. As can be seen from Fig 12.29, the feedback loop of the module i is removed if the k-parameter of module i is zero. Therefore, by removing $(M-1)$ consecutive k-parameters, the 1-multiplier lattice filter can be pipelined by M-levels.

The k-parameters of an N-th order one-multiplier lattice filter are com-

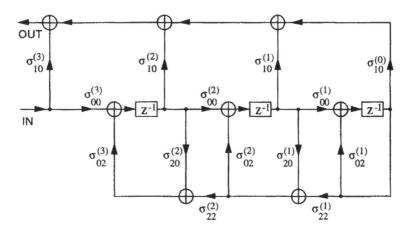

Fig. 12.30 Third-order normalized lattice filter.

puted by

$$k_i = \frac{\Lambda_i(0)}{\Lambda_i^*(0)}, \quad i = N, \ N-1, \ \cdots, \ 1. \tag{12.90}$$

Note that $\Lambda_i(z)$ is different from $\Phi_i(z)$ only by a scale factor. As a result, the k-parameter computed from $\Lambda_i(z)$ is equal to the k-parameter computed from $\Phi_i(z)$. Therefore, it is clear that the feedback section of the one-multiplier lattice filter can be pipelined by the same method as in the basic lattice filter. The multiply-add operations in the feed-forward section can be pipelined at any desired level by placing latches at appropriate feed-forward cutset locations.

12.8.4 Pipelining of Normalized Lattice Filters

The structure of a 3rd-order normalized lattice filter is shown in Fig 12.30. Notice that the tap-gain parameters $\{\sigma_{10}^{(3)}, \ \sigma_{10}^{(2)}, \ \sigma_{10}^{(1)}, \ \sigma_{10}^{(0)}\}$ constitute the feed-forward section and the feedback section is described by the parameters $\{\sigma_{00}^{(i)}, \ \sigma_{02}^{(i)}, \ \sigma_{20}^{(i)}, \ \sigma_{22}^{(i)}\}$, for $i = 1$ to 3. Recall that from (12.71),

$$\sigma_{20}^{(i)} = -\sigma_{02}^{(i)} = k_i, \ \sigma_{00}^{(i)} = \sigma_{22}^{(i)} = \sqrt{1 - k_i^2}. \tag{12.91}$$

Therefore, the feedback section is described by the k-parameters only.

If the k-parameter of module i is zero, then $\sigma_{20}^{(i)} = -\sigma_{02}^{(i)} = 0$, and $\sigma_{00}^{(i)} = \sigma_{22}^{(i)} = 1$. Therefore, the feedback loop of the module i is removed, and the delay of the module is shared with the adjacent modules. By the same way, if the k-parameters of $(M-1)$ consecutive modules are zero, then the feedback loops of those modules are removed and consequently there are M delays in each loop, which leads to M-level pipelining of the normalized lattice filter. Since the k-parameter of module i is computed from $\Phi_i(z)$, the normalized lattice filter can be pipelined by the same method as in the basic lattice filter.

12.8.5 Pipelining of Scaled-Normalized Lattice Filter

The feedback section of the scaled-normalized lattice filter is exactly the same as that of the normalized lattice filter. Therefore, if the denominator has $(M - 1)$ consecutive zero coefficients between each 2 nonzero coefficients of nearest degree, then the feedback section can be pipelined by M levels. The multiply-add operations in the feed-forward section can be pipelined at any desired level by placing latches at appropriate feed-forward cutset locations.

12.8.6 Retimed Pipelined Lattice Filter

From the previous discussion, it is clear that basic, 1-multiplier, normalized and scaled-normalized lattice filters can be pipelined by M levels if the denominator of the filter has $(M - 1)$ consecutive zero coefficients between each 2 nonzero coefficients of nearest degree. The M delays in each loop can be redistributed at appropriate locations to pipeline the loop multiply-add locations.

As an example, consider a 4-level pipelined normalized lattice filter in Fig 12.31(a). Since each feedback loop has 4 delays, the clock period T_{clk} is limited by

$$T_{clk} \geq \frac{2(\text{multiply-add})}{4} = \frac{\text{multiply-add}}{2}. \tag{12.92}$$

Thus the multiply-add operation in Fig 12.31(a) can be divided into two parts m_1 and m_2 such that Computation_Time(m_1) = Computation_Time(m_2) = Computation_Time(multiply-add)/2. Fig 12.31(b) shows the circuit obtained by retiming (see Chapter 4) which can be operated four times faster than the nonpipelined circuit since the clock period of the nonpipelined circuit is limited by 2 multiply-add operations.

12.9 DESIGN EXAMPLES OF PIPELINED LATTICE FILTERS

To pipeline basic, 1-multiplier, normalized, and scaled-normalized lattice filters by M levels, the denominator of a transfer function is required to have $(M - 1)$ consecutive zero coefficients between each 2 nonzero coefficients of nearest degree. The pipelinable transfer functions can be obtained by applying the scattered look-ahead method to the nonpipelined filter transfer functions. To avoid the drawbacks of the cancelling zeros such as hardware increase and inexact pole-zero cancellations in a finite wordlength implemen-

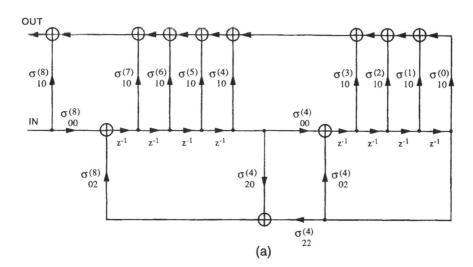

(a)

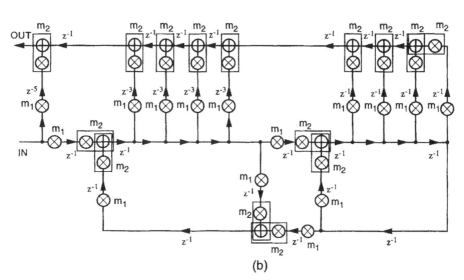

(b)

Fig. 12.31 (a) A 4-level pipelined normalized lattice filter before retiming. (b) The 4-level pipelined normalized lattice filter after retiming. Computation_Time(m_1) = Computation_Time(m_2) = Computation_Time(multiply & add)/2.

tation, a pipelinable transfer function can also be designed directly from the filter spectrum while the denominator is constrained to be a polynomial in z^M rather than z.

In this section, two design examples of pipelined lattice filters are presented. The pipelinable transfer functions have been obtained by the modified Deczky's method [19].

Example 12.9.1 *Consider a 4-stage pipelinable low-pass filter with*

$$pass\text{-}band : 0 - 0.2\pi \ (0.5 \ dB) \ and \ stop\text{-}band : 0.3\pi - \pi \ (20 \ dB).$$

The transfer function obtained by the modified Deczky's method is:

$$
\begin{aligned}
N(z) &= 0.09742(1 - 1.16548z^{-1} + z^{-2})(1 - 0.29069z^{-1} + z^{-2}) \cdot \\
&\quad (1 + 1.19469z^{-1} + z^{-2})(1 + 1.75885z^{-1} + z^{-2}), \\
D(z) &= 1 + 0.63459z^{-4} + 0.10067z^{-8}.
\end{aligned}
$$

Notice that $D(z)$ can be further decomposed as $D(z) = (1 + 0.31729z^{-4})^2$. All the zeros are located on the unit circle at the stop-band and the poles have equal radius of 0.75 and equal angular spacing of 0.5π. The pole-zero plot of the transfer function is shown in Fig. 12.32(a). Note that $D(z)$ was used as the Schur polynomial in Example 12.8.1. Since the Schur polynomials $\Phi_m(z)$, $m = 1$ to 3 and 5 to 7 have no constant terms, $k^{(m)} = 0$ for $m = 1$ to 3 and 5 to 7. Therefore, each loop has 4 delays. The implementation of the transfer function by a scaled-normalized lattice filter is shown in Fig. 12.32(b). While the number of multiply-add operations in each loop remains the same compared with the nonpipelined filter, the number of delays in each loop has increased to 4. Therefore, the 4-stage pipelined filter can be operated at a four times faster rate by redistributing the delays at appropriate locations. ∎

Example 12.9.2 *Consider a low-pass filter with*

$$pass\text{-}band : 0 - 0.3\pi \ (0.2 \ dB) \ and \ stop\text{-}band : 0.36\pi - \pi \ (40 \ dB).$$

This specification can be met by a 6th-order elliptic filter. The pipelinable transfer functions for $M = 1$, 2, and 4 are obtained by the modified Deczky's method. Since the degree of the numerator is larger than that of the denominator for each M, the numerator is represented by $N_f(z) \cdot N_i(z)$, where $N_f(z)$ is implemented by an FIR filter and $N_i(z)/D(z)$ is implemented by a scaled-normalized lattice filter. In our implementation, the FIR filter output is connected to the input of the IIR lattice filter.
1) $M = 1$

$$
\begin{aligned}
N_f(z) &= 0.11 + 0.3624z^{-1} + 0.5972z^{-2} + 0.5972z^{-3} + 0.3624z^{-4} + \\
&\quad 0.11z^{-5}, \\
N_i(z) &= 0.1282 - 0.1739z^{-1} + 0.3117z^{-2} - 0.1739z^{-3} + 0.1282z^{-4},
\end{aligned}
$$

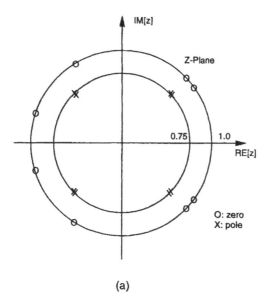

(a)

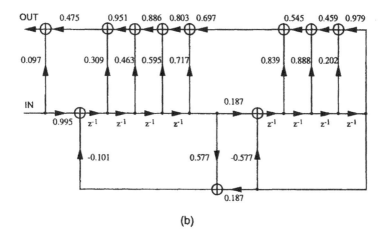

(b)

Fig. 12.32 (a) Pole-zero plot of the transfer function in Example 12.9.1. (b) The 4-stage pipelined structure of the scaled-normalized lattice filter in Example 12.9.1.

Table 12.1 Number of Multiply/Add Operations and Roundoff Noise of Scaled-Normalized Lattice Filters for $M = 1$, 2, and 4

	Constrained Filters			Pipelined Elliptic Filters		
M	Multiply	Add	Noise	Multiply	Add	Noise
1	31	15	2.2850	34	17	3.6477
2	37	18	2.8899	46	23	2.7247
4	53	26	1.0527	70	35	2.3608

$$D(z) = 1 - 2.0874z - 1 + 2.5698z^{-2} - 1.533z^{-3} + 0.5227z^{-4}.$$

2) M = 2

$$N_f(z) = 0.4539 + 0.5311z^{-1} + 0.1543z^{-2} + 0.5311z^{-3} + 0.4539z^{-4},$$
$$N_i(z) = 0.0434 + 0.1042z^{-1} + 0.223z^{-2} + 0.2864z^{-3} + 0.3448z^{-4} +$$
$$0.2864z^{-5} + 0.223z^{-6} + 0.1042z^{-7} + 0.0434z^{-8},$$
$$D(z) = 1 + 0.7802z^{-2} + 1.2014z^{-4} + 0.3109z^{-6} + 0.2418z^{-8}.$$

3) M = 4

$$N_f(z) = 0.1436 + 0.4896z^{-1} + 0.6923z^{-2} + 0.4896z^{-3} + 0.1436z^{-4},$$
$$N_i(z) = 0.1365 + 0.0232z^{-1} + 0.2879z^{-2} + 0.0557z^{-3} + 0.3954z^{-4} +$$
$$0.0443z^{-5} + 0.4058z^{-6} + 0.0472z^{-7} + 0.3867z^{-8} + 0.0532z^{-9} +$$
$$0.2952z^{-10} + 0.0229z^{-11} + 0.1717z^{-12} + 0.0106z^{-13} +$$
$$0.0528z^{-14} + 0.0056z^{-15} + 0.0329z^{-16},$$
$$D(z) = 1 + 1.794z^{-4} + 1.4404z^{-8} + 0.483z^{-12} + 0.0582z^{-16}.$$

Due to the symmetry of the coefficients in each $N_f(z)$, FIR sections are efficiently implemented based on the direct-form structure. In addition, to preserve the unit internal power property of the scaled-normalized lattice filter, all the internal nodes of the FIR sections are scaled to have unit power. The number of multiply/add operations and roundoff noises of constrained filters and those of the pipelined elliptic filters obtained by applying the scattered look-ahead transformation on the 6th-order elliptic filter are compared in Table 12.9.2. While there is little difference in the roundoff noises, which depend on pole locations, the hardware complexity is greatly reduced by the constrained design method as the value of M increases. ∎

12.10   LOW-POWER CMOS LATTICE IIR FILTERS

As explained in Chapter 3, pipelining can be used to achieve dramatic power reductions at same sample speed. In the following example, it is shown that pipelining can be used for low-power implementation of scaled-normalized lattice filters.

Example 12.10.1 *This example considers the low-power implementation of the scaled-normalized lattice filter that satisfies the specifications of Example 12.9.2. Assume that the capacitance due to the multipliers is dominant and that the capacitance due to the adders can be neglected. Also, assume that the supply voltage of the original system $(M = 1)$ to be 5 V and the CMOS threshold voltage to be 0.5 V. Then the propagation delay for the original system is*

$$T_o = \frac{C_l \times 5}{\kappa(5 - 0.5)^2}. \tag{12.93}$$

Next, consider the pipelined system by 4 stages $(M = 4)$. For low-power implementation, we keep the clock speed the same as in the original system. Therefore, for the pipelined system,

$$T_o = \frac{1}{4} \frac{C_l V_p}{\kappa(V_p - 0.5)^2}. \tag{12.94}$$

From (12.93) and (12.94), $V_p = 1.879$ V. Therefore, the supply voltage for the pipelined system can be reduced to 1.879 V.

The power for the original system is

$$P_o = \frac{C_t V_o^2}{T_o}. \tag{12.95}$$

On the other hand, the power for the pipelined system is

$$P_p = \frac{m_P}{m_o} \frac{C_t V_p^2}{T_o}. \tag{12.96}$$

where m_p and m_o are the number of multipliers for the 4-stage pipelined system and the original system, respectively (Refer to Table 12.9.2). Then,

$$power\ saving = \frac{P_p}{P_o} = \left(\frac{m_P}{m_o}\right)\left(\frac{V_p}{V_o}\right)^2 = 0.2414. \tag{12.97}$$

Therefore, the power consumption of the 4-stage pipelined system is only 24.14% of the original system. Note that this reduction of power consumption is achieved at the expense of 70% increase in area. ■

12.11   CONCLUSIONS

Design of 4 types of lattice digital filters, which include basic, one-multiplier, normalized, and scaled-normalized, have been presented. It has been shown that the scattered look-ahead pipelined transfer functions always leads to pipelined lattice IIR digital filters. An approach to computation of roundoff noise in lattice digital filters using the polynomial expansion principle and the use of transposition has also been presented. The lattice filter design procedure is applicable to design of both IIR and FIR digital filters.

12.12   PROBLEMS

1. Consider the orthonormal Schur polynomial basis $\{\Phi_i(z)\}$. Starting with definitions, prove the following:

   (a) $\langle \Phi_{N-1}(z), \Phi_{N-1}(z) \rangle = 1$,

   (b) $\langle \Phi_N(z), \Phi_{N-1}(z) \rangle = 0$,

   (c) $\langle \Phi_N(z), \Phi_{N-2}(z) \rangle = 0$.

2. Prove the following inner product identities:

   (a) $\langle \Phi_N^*(z), \Phi_{N-1}^*(z) \rangle = \sqrt{1 - k_N^2}$,

   (b) $\langle \Phi_N^*(z), \Phi_{N-2}^*(z) \rangle = \sqrt{(1 - k_N^2)(1 - k_{N-1}^2)}$.

3. Consider the following transfer function

$$H(z) = \frac{1 + 3z^{-1} + 3z^{-2} + z^{-3}}{1 - 0.9z^{-1} + 0.64z^{-2} - 0.576z^{-3}}.$$

   (a) Obtain orthonormal basis functions from the denominator using the Schur algorithm.

   (b) Expand the numerator using the orthonormal polynomials obtained in (a).

   (c) Calculate the output signal power when the input is a white wide-sense stationary random process with unit power.

   (d) Determine a scaling constant α such that the scaled transfer function $\alpha H(z)$ has unit output signal power.

4. Consider the following transfer function

$$H(z) = \frac{1 + 5/12z^{-1} + 1/24z^{-2}}{1 - 9/8z^{-1} + 5/16z^{-2}}.$$

(a) Derive 2 basic lattice filter structures for $H(z)$ where the numerator is expanded using Schur polynomials and reverse Schur polynomials.

(b) Transform $H(z)$ to a 2-level pipelined form using scattered look-ahead. Derive both types of basic lattice filters for the 2 level pipelined filter.

(c) Calculate the roundoff noise values for all 4 lattice filters designed in (a) and (b) using (i) **W** matrix method based on the state variable description and (ii) polynomial expansion approaches.

(d) Assuming the 2-level pipelined lattice filter and the original non-pipelined lattice filter are to be used for the same application with identical sample speed, what would be the power reduction using the pipelined architecture? For power calculations, assume the supply voltage of the original sequential system to be 5 V and the CMOS threshold voltage to be 0.5 V. Assume the capacitance and critical path due to the multipliers to be dominant and assume that the capacitance and critical path due to the adders can be neglected.

5. Obtain basic, 1-multiplier, normalized, and scaled-normalized lattice filter structures for $H(z)$ in Problem 3.

6. Use scattered look-ahead transformation to obtain a 2-level pipelinable transfer function for $H(z)$ in Problem 3. For the pipelined transfer function, obtain basic, 1-multiplier, normalized, and scaled-normalized lattice filter structures.

7. Obtain a 1-multiplier lattice structure for the 2nd-order transfer function

$$H(z) = \frac{(1+z^{-1})^2}{1 - 3/(2\sqrt{2})z^{-1} + 9/16z^{-2}}.$$

This filter should be designed such that the numerator is expanded from the reverse Schur polynomial side.

8. Consider the following transfer function

$$H(z) = \frac{1/2 + 1/4z^{-1} + z^{-2}}{1 + 1/4z^{-1} + 1/2z^{-2}}.$$

(a) Obtain Schur polynomials $\Phi_2(z)$, $\Phi_1(z)$ and $\Phi_0(z)$.

(b) Expand the numerator using the Schur polynomials obtained in (a). With the expansion coefficients, implement $H(z)$ using normalized lattice filter structure.

(c) Show that the structure obtained in (b) is not efficient. In other words, show that correct output can be obtained without tap-gain parameters.

(d) Modify the structure obtained in (b) such that the implemented transfer function is

$$H(z) = \frac{1}{1 + 1/4z^{-1} + 1/2z^{-2}}.$$

9. Derive basic, 1-multiplier, normalized, and scaled-normalized lattice filter structures for the following transfer function:

$$H(z) = \frac{1 + 3z^{-1} + 3z^{-2} + z^{-3}}{1 - \frac{3}{2}z^{-1} + \frac{11}{16}z^{-2} - \frac{3}{32}z^{-3}}.$$

10. Use scattered look-ahead transformation to obtain a 2-level pipelinable transfer function for $H(z)$ in Problem 9. For the pipelined transfer function, derive basic, 1-multiplier, normalized, and scaled-normalized lattice filter structures.

11. For $H(z)$ in Problem 9 and the 2-level pipelined transfer function in Problem 10, derive reverse scaled-normalized lattice filter structures.

12. For the scaled-normalized lattice filter in Problem 9 and the reverse scaled-normalized lattice filter in Problem 11, calculate NSRs. Compare the two NSRs.

13. Obtain reverse normalized lattice filter implementation of the transfer function given in Problem 3.

14. For the following 2-stage pipelinable transfer function

$$H(z) = \frac{1}{1 - 2r^2 \cos 2\theta z^{-2} + r^4 z^{-4}}. \tag{12.98}$$

(a) Derive the scaled-normalized lattice filter structure.

(b) Calculate the output signal power.

(c) Calculate the NSR.

(d) Plot the NSR obtained in (c) as a function of r.

15. Design a 3rd order *all-pass* transfer function with poles at $z = -0.9$ and $z = 0.9e^{\pm j\pi/4}$. Implement the all-pass transfer function using normalized lattice filter structure. The implemented normalized lattice filter should have no tap-gain parameters.

16. A wide family of practical transfer functions including Butterworth, Chebyshev, and elliptic filters can be represented as

$$H(z) = \frac{1}{2}\{A_0(z) + A_1(z)\},$$

where $A_0(z)$ and $A_1(z)$ are stable unit-magnitude all-pass filters. For an odd order Butterworth, Chebyshev and elliptic filters, the all-pass decomposition can be done very efficiently by using the following pole interlace property [22].

Pole Interlace Property: Let the poles of $H(z)$ be $z_0, z_1, \cdots, z_{N-1}$ with pole angles $\theta_0, \theta_1, \cdots, \theta_{N-1}$, where $\theta_i < \theta_{i+1}$. Then, the poles of $A_0(z)$ are given by z_{2k} and those of $A_1(z)$ by z_{2k+1}. From these poles, $A_0(z)$ and $A_1(z)$ can be computed.

Consider a 3rd-order elliptic low-pass filter

$$H(z) = \frac{0.3296(1 + 1.61165z^{-1} + 1.61165z^{-2} + z^{-3})}{1 + 0.0522z^{-1} + 0.7139z^{-2} - 0.0445z^{-3}}.$$

(a) Decompose $H(z)$ into two all-pass functions using pole interlace property.

(b) Implement the decomposed transfer function using one-multiplier lattice filter structure. How many multipliers and adders are needed for the implementation?

17. Consider the narrow-band low-pass specifications shown in Fig. 12.33(a). Since the poles of a typical narrow-band filter are located close to the unit circle, this filter suffers from large roundoff noise and consequently large wordlength is required for the implementation. Thus, instead of meeting the specifications in Fig. 12.33(a), a twofold stretched IIR filter $G_2(z)$ can be designed. Fig. 12.33(b) shows the magnitude response of $G_2(z^2)$, where the passband around π is unwanted and can be suppressed by cascading $G_2(z^2)$ with a FIR filter $I_1(z)$ shown in Fig. 12.33(c). $I_1(z)$ can be designed efficiently due to its wide transition bandwidth. The desired response is obtained by cascading $G_2(z^2)$ and $I_1(z)$. Notice that the implemented filter $G_2(z^2)I_1(z)$ is 2-stage pipelinable since FIR filter $I_1(z)$ can be pipelined at any desired level. Assume that the low-pass filter in Fig. 12.33(a) has the following specifications: $\omega_p = 0.0625\pi$, $\omega_s = 0.075\pi$, passband ripple = 0.5 dB, and stopband attenuation = 50 dB. In this problem, all IIR filters are designed using elliptic filter design method and implemented using 1-multiplier lattice filter structure. FIR filters are designed using McClellan-Parks algorithm and implemented using direct-form structure.

(a) Design an IIR filter satisfying the specifications in Fig. 12.33(a). Draw the SFG of the filter and calculate its NSR.

(b) Design a twofold stretched IIR filter $G_2(z)$. Design an FIR filter satisfying the specifications in Fig. 12.33(c). Draw the magnitude response and the SFG of the cascaded system $G_2(z^2)I_1(z)$. Calculate its NSR and compare with the NSR in a).

(c) Design a 4-fold stretched filter $G_4(z)$. The magnitude response of $G_4(z^4)$ should look like Fig. 12.33(d). Assume that the unwanted

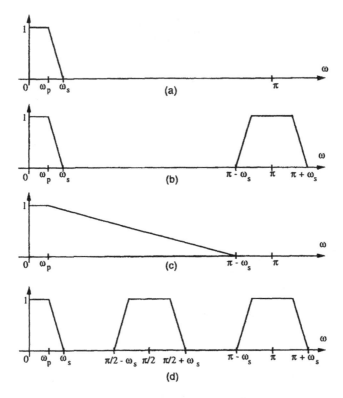

Fig. 12.33 (a) Desired response. (b) Response of $G_2(z^2)$. (c) Response of FIR filter $I_1(z)$. (d) Response of $G_4(z^4)$.

passbands are suppressed by a cascade of 2 FIR filters $I_1(z)I_2(z^2)$, where $I_1(z)$ has the specifications shown in Fig. 12.33(c). Then, what should be the magnitude response for $I_2(z)$? Draw magnitude response of the cascaded system $G_4(z^4)I_1(z)I_2(z^2)$. Calculate NSR of the cascaded system and compare with the NSRs in (a) and (b).

REFERENCES

1. A. V. Oppenheim and R. W. Schafer, *Digital Signal Processing.* Prentice Hall, 1975.

2. J. D. Markel and A. H. Gray, Jr., "On autocorrelation equations as applied to speech analysis," *IEEE Trans. on Acoustics, Speech, and Signal Processing,* vol. AU-21, pp. 69–79, April 1973.

3. J. Schur, "Ueber Potenzreihen die im Innern des Einheitslreises beschrankt sind," in *J. Reine Angewandte Mathematik,* vol. 147, pp. 205–232, (Berlin

Germany), 1917.

4. R. A. Roberts and C. T. Mullis, *Digital Signal Processing*. Addison-Wesley, 1987.

5. S. M. Lei and K. Yao, "A class of systolizable IIR digital filters and its design for proper scaling and minimum output roundoff noise," *IEEE Trans. on Circuits and Systems*, pp. 1217–1230, Oct. 1990.

6. A. H. Gray, Jr., and J. D. Markel, "Digital lattice and ladder filter synthesis," *IEEE Trans. on Audio and Electroacoustics*, vol. AU-21, pp. 491–500, Dec. 1973.

7. J. G. Chung and K. K. Parhi, "Scaled normalized lattice digital filter structures," *IEEE Transactions on Circuits and Systems, Part II: Analog and Digital Signal Processing*, pp. 278–282, April 1995.

8. A. H. Gray, Jr., and J. D. Markel, "A normalized digital filter structure," *IEEE Trans. on Acoustics, Speech, and Signal Processing*, vol. ASSP-23, pp. 268–277, June 1975.

9. J. E. Volder, "The CORDIC trigonometric computing technique," *IRE Trans. on Electronic Computers*, vol. EC-8, pp. 330–334, Sept. 1959.

10. P. Dewilde, E. Deprettere, and R. Nouta, "Parallel and pipelined VLSI implementation of signal processing algorithms," in *VLSI and Modern Signal Processing* (S. Kung, H. Whitehouse, and T. Kailath, eds.), Prentice Hall, 1984.

11. J. D. Markel and A. H. Gray, Jr., "Roundoff noise characteristics of a class of orthogonal polynomial structures," *IEEE Trans. on Acoustics, Speech, and Signal Processing*, vol. ASSP-23, pp. 473–486, Oct. 1975.

12. S. J. Mason and H. J. Zimmermann, *Electronic Circuits, Signals and Systems*. Wiley, 1960.

13. H. Kimura and T. Osada, "Canonical pipelining of lattice filters," *IEEE Trans. on Acoustics, Speech, and Signal Processing*, vol. ASSP-35, pp. 878–887, June 1987.

14. J. G. Chung and K. K. Parhi, "Pipelining of lattice IIR digital filters," *IEEE Trans. on Signal Processing*, vol. 42, pp. 751–761, April 1994.

15. J. G. Chung and K. K. Parhi, *Pipelined Lattice and Wave Digital Recursive Filters*. Kluwer, 1996.

16. A. G. Deczky, "Synthesis of recursive digital filters using the minimum p-error criterion," *IEEE Trans. Audio Electroacoustics*, vol. AU-20, pp. 257–263, Oct. 1972.

17. A. G. Deczky, "Program for minimum-p synthesis of recursive digital filters," in *Programs for Digital Signal Processing*, IEEE Press, 1979.

18. R. Fletcher and M. J. D. Powell, "A rapidly convergent descent method for minimization," *Comput. Journal*, vol. 6, pp. 163–168, 1963.

19. M. A. Richards, "Application of Deczky's program for recursive filter design to the design of recursive decimators," *IEEE Trans. on Acoustics, Speech, and Signal Processing*, pp. 811–814, Oct. 1982.

20. H. G. Martinez and T. W. Parks, "Design of recursive digital filters with optimum magnitude and attenuation poles on the unit circle," *IEEE Trans. on*

Acoustics, Speech, and Signal Processing, vol. ASSP-26, pp. 150–157, April 1978.

21. H. G. Martinez and T. W. Parks, "A class of infinite-duration impulse response digital filters for sampling rate reduction," *IEEE Trans. on Acoustics, Speech, and Signal Processing*, vol. ASSP-27, pp. 154–162, April 1979.

22. L. Gazsi, "Explicit formulas for lattice wave digital filters," *IEEE Trans. on Circuits and Systems*, vol. CAS-32, pp. 68–88, Jan. 1985.

13

Bit-Level Arithmetic Architectures

13.1 INTRODUCTION

This chapter addresses the design of bit-level architectures for addition and multiplication frequently encountered in DSP algorithms. Three implementation styles, bit-parallel, bit-serial, and digit-serial are addressed. *Bit-parallel* systems process one whole word of the input sample each clock cycle and are ideal for high-speed applications. *Bit-serial* systems process 1 bit of the input sample every clock cycle. These systems can be synthesized using integer linear programming based scheduling approach (see Appendix F). Bit-serial systems are area-efficient and suitable for low-speed applications [1] −[3]. Bit-serial arithmetic is used for the implementation of data-flow algorithms of medium complexity and low to medium data rate, whereas bit-parallel operators may be used for the implementation of data-flow algorithms of low complexity and high data rate. *Digit-serial* systems [4],[5] process multiple number of bits (referred to as *digit-size*) every clock cycle and are best suited for applications requiring moderate sample rate, where area and power consumption are critical.

This chapter considers the design of bit-parallel and bit-serial multipliers, bit-serial digital filter design and implementations, and bit-level implementation schemes for vector-vector multiplications. The major emphasis is on architecture design based on design methodologies for mapping algorithms to arithmetic architectures at bit-level. Basic knowledge of computer arithmetic, such as number representations, and addition and multiplication algorithms are assumed, as they are covered in many VLSI design and computer arithmetic books [6]−[8]. In this chapter, all numbers are assumed to be represented in fixed-point two's complement representation. A W-bit number A is represented as:

$$A = a_{W-1}.a_{W-2}\cdots a_1 a_0 \tag{13.1}$$

where the bits a_i, $0 \le i \le W - 1$, are either 0 or 1, and the most significant bit (msb) a_{W-1} is the *sign bit* with value of 0 denoting positive number and 1 denoting negative number. The value of this number is in the range of $[-1, 1 - 2^{-W+1}]$ and is given by:

$$A = -a_{W-1} + \sum_{i=1}^{W-1} a_{W-1-i} 2^{-i}. \tag{13.2}$$

A main advantage of two's complement arithmetic is the ability to generate a correct final result in spite of intermediate overflow. Thus, in a chain of additions or subtractions, the final result is correct if it is known to lie in the range $[-(1 - 2^{-W+1}), 1 - 2^{-W+1}]$ even though intermediate operations lead to overflow. For bit-serial implementations, constant wordlength multipliers are considered, where a constant wordlength of W-bit is maintained for all the signals in the architecture. Although a $W \times W$-bit multiplication generates $(2W - 1)$-bit product, only the W most-significant bits are retained.

This chapter is organized as follows: Section 13.2 discusses bit-parallel multiplier design, including carry-ripple array multiplication, carry-save array multiplication, Baugh-Wooley multiplication, and Booth-recoded multiplications. The two efficient layout strategies, *interleaved floor-plan* and *bit-plane*, for digital filters are discussed in Section 13.3. Design of bit-serial multipliers using systolic mapping as well as Horner's rule are addressed in Section 13.4. Section 13.5 addresses the design methodologies for bit-level pipelined bit-serial FIR and IIR filters with constant coefficients. This section also addresses issues related to delay management and synchronization in bit-serial implementations. Section 13.6 addresses the design of low-cost, high-speed constant multipliers using the canonic signed digit (CSD) representation. Section 13.7 addresses the bit-level implementation schemes for vector-vector multiplication based on the distributed arithmetic approach.

13.2   PARALLEL MULTIPLIERS

This section considers multipliers that can perform two's complement multiplication in time $O(W)$ using regular structures, including multiplication with sign extension (derived from Horner's rule) and Baugh-Wooley multiplication [9]. Two regular implementation styles, carry-ripple and and carry-save array, are introduced.

It has been proved that multiplications cannot be performed in a time smaller than $O(log_2 W)$. Such a bound is attainable by the *binary-tree* and

Wallace-tree multipliers (see Appendix E) [10]. However, their corresponding architectures are very irregular.

Let the multiplicand and multiplier be A and B:

$$A = a_{W-1}.a_{w-2} \cdots a_1 a_0 = -a_{W-1} + \sum_{i=1}^{W-1} a_{W-1-i} 2^{-i}$$

$$B = b_{W-1}.b_{w-2} \cdots b_1 b_0 = -b_{W-1} + \sum_{i=1}^{W-1} b_{W-1-i} 2^{-i},$$

where $-1 < A, B < 1$ and the case when both A and B is equal to -1 is excluded. The value of their product $P = A \times B$ is given by:

$$P = -p_{2W-2} + \sum_{i=1}^{2W-2} p_{2W-2-i} 2^{-i},$$

(13.3)

where the radix point is to the right of the msb p_{2W-2}. Since the product of 2 numbers within $[-1, 1)$ is also in this range, all higher order bits to the left of bit-position $2W - 2$ in the result are ignored.

In constant wordlength multiplication, the $W - 1$ lower order bits in the product P are discarded, and the product is denoted as $X \Leftarrow P = A \times B$, where

$$X = -x_{W-1} + \sum_{i=1}^{W-1} x_{W-1-i} 2^{-i}.$$

(13.4)

The product X is used when a constant wordlength multiplier is considered and P is used when a full-precision product is required.

13.2.1 Parallel Multiplication with Sign Extension

Using *Horner's rule*, multiplication of A and B can be written as

$$
\begin{aligned}
P &= A \times (-b_{W-1} + \sum_{i=1}^{W-1} b_{W-1-i} 2^{-i}) \\
&= -A \cdot b_{W-1} + [A \cdot b_{W-2} + [A \cdot b_{W-3} + [\cdots + [A \cdot b_1 \\
&\quad + A \cdot b_0 2^{-1}] 2^{-1}] \cdots] 2^{-1}] 2^{-1},
\end{aligned}
$$

(13.5)

where 2^{-1} denotes a *scaling* operation. In two's complement system, negating a number is equivalent to taking its one's complement and then adding a 1 to

p_6	p_5	p_4	p_3	p_2	p_1	p_0
			a_3	a_2	a_1	a_0
			b_3	b_2	b_1	b_0
			$-a_3b_0$	a_2b_0	a_1b_0	a_0b_0
		$-a_3b_1$	a_2b_1	a_1b_1	a_0b_1	
	$-a_3b_2$	a_2b_2	a_1b_2	a_0b_2		
$-\bar{a}_3b_3$	$\bar{a}_2b_3$	$\bar{a}_1b_3$	$\bar{a}_0b_3$			
			b_3			
p_6	p_5	p_4	p_3	p_2	p_1	p_0

Fig. 13.1 Tabular form of bit-level array multiplication.

the least significant bit (lsb) position, as shown below:

$$
\begin{aligned}
-A &= a_{W-1} - \sum_{i=1}^{W-1} a_{W-1-i}2^{-i} \\
&= a_{W-1} + \sum_{i=1}^{W-1} (1 - a_{W-1-i})2^{-i} - \sum_{i=1}^{W-1} 2^{-i} \\
&= a_{W-1} + \sum_{i=1}^{W-1} (1 - a_{W-1-i})2^{-i} - 1 + 2^{-W+1} \\
&= -(1 - a_{W-1}) + \sum_{i=1}^{W-1} (1 - a_{W-1-i})2^{-i} + 2^{-W+1} \\
&= -\bar{a}_{W-1} + \sum_{i=1}^{W-1} \bar{a}_{W-1-i}2^{-i} + 2^{-W+1},
\end{aligned}
\tag{13.6}
$$

where $(1 - a_i)$ is the one's complement of a_i and denoted as $\bar{a}_i$, for $0 \leq i \leq W - 1$. Therefore, the term $-A \cdot b_{W-1}$ in 4-bit multiplication can be written as

$$
-A \times b_3 = -\bar{a}_3b_3 + \bar{a}_2b_32^{-1} + \bar{a}_1b_32^{-2} + \bar{a}_0b_32^{-3} + b_32^{-3}.
$$

The multiplication operation can be carried out using the table shown in Fig. 13.1. In Fig. 13.1, the additions cannot be carried out directly due to the terms with negative weight. *Sign extension* can be used to solve this problem. For example,

$$
\begin{aligned}
A &= -a_3 + a_22^{-1} + a_12^{-2} + a_02^{-3} \\
&= -a_32 + a_3 + a_22^{-1} + a_12^{-2} + a_02^{-3} \\
&= -a_32^2 + a_32 + a_3 + a_22^{-1} + a_12^{-2} + a_02^{-3}
\end{aligned}
$$

			$a_3.$	a_2	a_1	a_0
			$b_3.$	b_2	b_1	b_0
		$a_3 b_0$	$\leftarrow a_3 b_0$	$a_2 b_0$	$a_1 b_0$	$\boxed{a_0 b_0}$
		$a_3 b_1$	$a_2 b_1$	$a_1 b_1$	$a_0 b_1$	
	pp^1_3	$\leftarrow pp^1_3$	pp^1_2	pp^1_1	$\boxed{pp^1_0}$	
	$a_3 b_2$	$a_2 b_2$	$a_1 b_2$	$a_0 b_2$		
pp^2_3	$\leftarrow pp^2_3$	pp^2_2	pp^2_1	$\boxed{pp^2_0}$		
$\bar{a}_3 b_3$	$\bar{a}_2 b_3$	$\bar{a}_1 b_3$	$\bar{a}_0 b_3$			
			b_3			
$x_3.$	x_2	x_1	x_0			

Fig. 13.2 Tabular form of bit-level two's complement array multiplication.

describes sign extension of A by 1 and 2 bits, and its value remains unchanged. In two's complement representation, the scaling operation 2^{-i} is always carried out as shift right with sign extension. For example, scaling of A by 2^{-1} is performed as follows:

$$
\begin{aligned}
A \cdot 2^{-1} &= (-a_3 + a_2 2^{-1} + a_1 2^{-2} + a_0 2^{-3})2^{-1} \\
&= -a_3 2^{-1} + a_2 2^{-2} + a_1 2^{-3} + a_0 2^{-4} \\
&= -a_3 + a_3 2^{-1} + a_2 2^{-2} + a_1 2^{-3} + a_0 2^{-4} \\
&\Rightarrow -a_3 + a_3 2^{-1} + a_2 2^{-2} + a_1 2^{-3},
\end{aligned}
\tag{13.7}
$$

where all the bits are shifted right by 1 bit position, the extended sign bit a_3 of the multiplicand A remains at the msb position and the a_0 bit is eliminated. The scaled number is represented using the same wordlength of 4 bits.

The multiplication with sign extension can now be described at bit level. A 4×4-bit multiplication is illustrated in tabular form in Fig. 13.2, where pp^i_j is the j th bit of the partial product PP^i. The lsbs in the boxes of the right-shifted partial products are eliminated to maintain a constant wordlength. Since the partial products are accumulated step by step, sign extension by 1 bit is sufficient to align the sign bits for the partial products at each step.

Unfortunately, sign extension by 1 bit at each step cannot eliminate *overflow*. To get the correct product, the msb of the W-bit multiplicand, a_{W-1}, is defined as the *guard* bit in the multiplicand and is set equal to a_{W-2}. In other words, the multiplicands of these multipliers must lie in the range $[-1/2, 1/2)$. Otherwise, 2-bit sign extension can be used at each step to get the correct product.

13.2.1.1 Parallel Carry-Ripple Array Multipliers

In the carry-ripple array multiplier, the carry output of an adder is rippled to the adder to the left in the

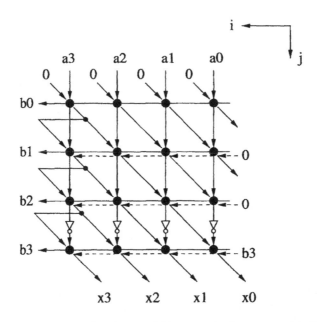

Fig. 13.3 Dependence graph for the 4 × 4-bit carry-ripple array multiplication.

same row. The bit-level dependence graph (DG) for this multiplication operation is shown in Fig. 13.3.

A parallel array multiplier can be derived directly from the DG in Fig. 13.3, as shown in Fig. 13.4. Pipelining by placing delay elements at the cutsets shown in Fig. 13.4 can reduce the critical path of this multiplier from $2W$ to W. Bit-level pipelining can be achieved by two-dimensional (2D) pipelining (not shown in Fig. 13.4).

13.2.1.2 Parallel Carry-Save Array Multipliers

In carry-ripple multipliers, carries are propagated during each additions. This carry-propagation limits the speed of multiplication. In a case involving several additions, such as partial product accumulation in multiplication, it is not strictly necessary to propagate these carries during each cycle. Instead, the carries generated during the addition of a pair of operands can be *saved* and added, with proper alignment, to the next operands. This leads to the concept of *carry-save* addition. In the carry-save array multiplier, the carry outputs are saved and used in the adder in the next row. In this case, the partial product is replaced by a *partial sum* and a *partial carry*, which are saved and passed on to the next row. The advantage of carry-save addition is that the additions at different bit positions in the same row are now independent of each other and can be carried out in parallel, which essentially speeds up the addition phase of each cycle, and hence speeds up the multiplication. This carry-save addition can be applied to all but the last step, where there is no more multiplicand-multiple

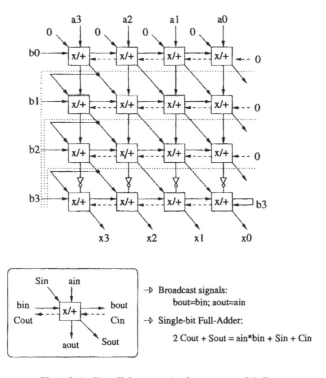

Fig. 13.4 Parallel carry-ripple array multiplier.

to be added, but the partial sum and partial carry. The addition of partial sum and partial carry is performed by a *vector merging adder* (VMA). The dependence graph of bit-level carry-save multiplication is shown in Fig. 13.5. A parallel carry-save array multiplier can be designed from this dependence graph, as shown in Fig. 13.6, which can be pipelined at bit-level by placing delay elements across the cutsets shown in dotted lines in the figure.

The VMA can be implemented either as a 4×4 carry-save array as shown in Fig. 13.7(a) which contains only half-adders and has a more regular and easier-to-pipeline structure, but requires more half adders; or as a 4-bit carry-ripple adder as shown in Fig. 13.7(b). When bit-level pipelining is not required, the carry-ripple and carry-save principles can also be combined into a single structure as shown in Fig. 13.7(c), where the carry output can ripple through at most 1 bit in the same row, and the resulting carry from each carry-ripple portion is passed on to the next row like the carry-save architecture. The number of adders required in this combined vector merging part is between that of the carry-save and the carry-ripple vector merging structures.

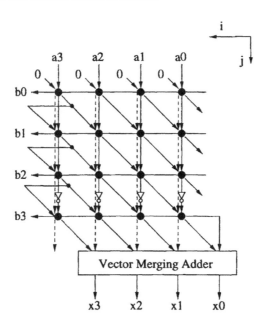

Fig. 13.5 Dependence graph for the 4 × 4-bit carry-save array multiplication.

13.2.2 Baugh-Wooley Multipliers

The difficulty of two's complement multiplication lies in handling the sign bits of the multiplicand and multiplier. An efficient way to overcome this problem is provided by the Baugh-Wooley multiplication algorithm [9]. This multiplication algorithm is illustrated by the multiplication table shown in Fig. 13.8 for a 4 × 4-bit multiplication, where all the bits have positive weight and can be accumulated directly. The derivation of this algorithm is left as an exercise at the end of this chapter (see Problem 4).

The Baugh-Wooley multiplication table in Fig. 13.8 can be implemented either as a carry-ripple array or a carry-save array. A carry-save Baugh-Wooley multiplier is shown in Fig. 13.9, where $P = p_6.p_5p_4p_3p_2p_1p_0$ is the product with full precision. Note that the product of two 4-bit numbers in the range $(-1, 1)$ lies in the same range. Since the radix point is to the right of the bit p_6, any higher order bits are ignored. The truncated result is represented as $X = x_3.x_2x_1x_0$.

13.2.3 Parallel Multipliers with Modified Booth Recoding

Multiplication involves two basic operations: the generation of partial products and their accumulation. Consequently, there are two ways to speed up the multiplication: reduce the number of partial products or accelerate their accumulation. Carry-save addition can be used to accelerate the accumulation

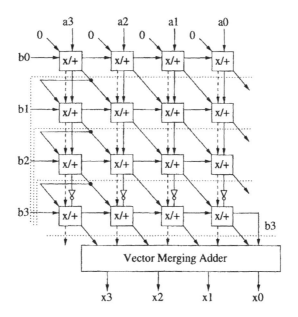

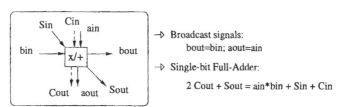

Fig. 13.6 Parallel carry-save array multiplier.

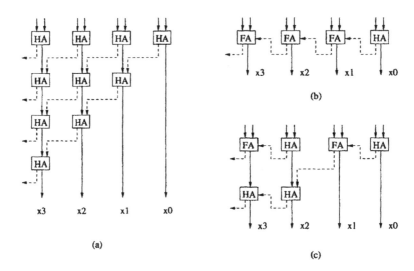

Fig. 13.7 Vector merging for 4 × 4-bit parallel carry-save multiplication: (a) carry-save vector merging, (b) carry-ripple vector merging, (c) combined carry-save and carry-ripple vector merging.

				a_3	a_2	a_1	a_0
				b_3	b_2	b_1	b_0
				$\overline{a_3 b_0}$	$a_2 b_0$	$a_1 b_0$	$a_0 b_0$
			$\overline{a_3 b_1}$	$a_2 b_1$	$a_1 b_1$	$a_0 b_1$	
		$\overline{a_3 b_2}$	$a_2 b_2$	$a_1 b_2$	$a_0 b_2$		
	$a_3 b_3$	$\overline{a_2 b_3}$	$\overline{a_1 b_3}$	$\overline{a_0 b_3}$			
			1				
	x_3	x_2	x_1	x_0			

Fig. 13.8 Tabular form of bit-level Baugh-Wooley multiplication.

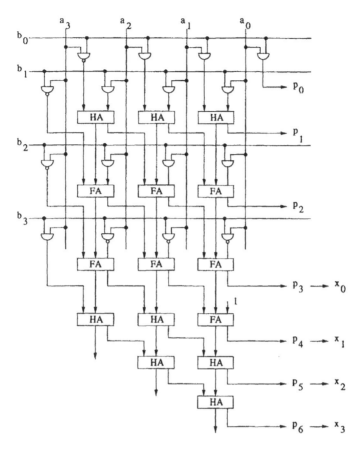

Fig. 13.9 A 4 × 4-bit Baugh-Wooley carry-save multiplier.

of the partial products. To reduce the number of partial products, a straight-forward approach is to examine 2 or more bits of the multiplier at a time. The reduction in the number of partial products can reduce the latency of the multiplication operation. However, this requires the generation of multiples A, $2A$, $3A$, etc., where A is the multiplicand.

The number of partial products can be reduced by the *modified Booth recoding*. This algorithm is based on the fact that fewer partial products need to be generated for groups of consecutive zeros and ones. For a group of consecutive zeros, there is no need to generate any new partial products. For a group of, say m, consecutive ones in the multiplier, i.e.,

$$\cdots 0\{11 \cdots 1\}0 \cdots = \cdots 1\{00 \cdots 0\}0 \cdots - \cdots 0\{00 \cdots 1\}0 \cdots$$
$$= \cdots 1\{00 \cdots \bar{1}\}0 \cdots, \tag{13.8}$$

instead of m partial products, only 2 partial products need to be generated

Table 13.1   Radix-4 Modified Booth Recoding Algorithm

b_{2i+1}	b_{2i}	b_{2i-1}	b'_i	Operation	Comments
0	0	0	0	$+0$	string of zeros
0	0	1	1	$+A$	end of 1's
0	1	0	1	$+A$	a single 1
0	1	1	2	$+2A$	end of 1's
1	0	0	-2	$-2A$	beginning of 1's
1	0	1	-1	$-A$	a single 0
1	1	0	-1	$-A$	beginning of 1's
1	1	1	0	-0	string of 1's

if *signed-digit* representation is used. Hence, in this multiplication scheme, the multiplier bits are first *recoded* into signed-digit representation with fewer number of nonzero digits; the partial products are then generated using the recoded multiplier digits and accumulated.

In the modified Booth recoding algorithm, the signed-digit set $\{-2,-1,0,1,2\}$ is used, and it is, therefore, also referred to as *5-level* Booth recoding. In this recoding algorithm, the multiplier bits b_{2i+1} and b_{2i} are recoded into signed digit b'_i, with b_{2i-1} serving as a reference bit. For example, an 8-bit number can be recoded as follows:

$$b_7 \quad b_6 \quad b_5 \quad b_4 \quad b_3 \quad b_2 \quad b_1 \quad b_0 \quad b_{-1} \tag{13.9}$$

$$b'_3 \qquad b'_2 \qquad b'_1 \qquad b'_0$$

where $b_{-1} = 0$ is appended after the lsb of this multiplier as a reference bit. The modified Booth recoding algorithm to generate b'_i from b_{2i+1}, b_{2i}, and b_{2i-1} is shown in Table 13.1.

A simple way to describe the recoding operation is to calculate

$$b'_i = -2b_{2i+1} + b_{2i} + b_{2i-1}. \tag{13.10}$$

The reader can verify that

$$-b_7 + \sum_{i=1}^{7} b_{7-i}2^{-i} = \sum_{i=0}^{3} b'_{3-i}2^{-(2i+1)}. \tag{13.11}$$

The Booth recoded multiplier consists of 3 parts, the recoding (control) circuitry for multiplier bits, the partial product generation, and accumulation. Design of fast multipliers using 5-level modified Booth recoding is left as an exercise at the end of this chapter (see Problem 11). Conventional Booth recoding circuitry has *race* problem due to the unbalanced paths from inputs to outputs and leads to higher power consumption. A low-power Booth-recoding circuitry is presented in [11], which reduces glitches and power consumption by using a redundant recoding scheme. Design of low-power Booth recoding circuitry is explored in Problem 12.

13.3 INTERLEAVED FLOOR-PLAN AND BIT-PLANE-BASED DIGITAL FILTERS

This section is concerned with efficient implementation and floor-plan techniques for bit-parallel FIR digital filters. These techniques can be adapted for implementations of IIR filters as well.

Consider the constant-coefficient FIR filtering operation

$$y(n) \quad = \quad x(n) + f \cdot x(n-1) + g \cdot x(n-2), \tag{13.12}$$

where $x(n)$ is the input signal, and f and g are filter coefficients. Assume the signal and coefficient wordlengths to be 6 and 4 bits, respectively, and both are represented in two's complement format.

An *interleaved* approach [12] for high-speed filtering is presented. The main idea behind the interleaved approach is to perform the computation and accumulation of partial products associated with f and g simultaneously, which leads to dramatic reduction in the routing complexity. Another advantage is that since the truncation is performed only at the final step, it also leads to better accuracy. The multiplication chart, based on the Baugh-Wooley algorithm, for computing the output $y(n)$ using this interleaved approach is shown in Fig. 13.10, which is the result of interleaving of 2 parallel Baugh-Wooley multiplications. Note that only the most significant 4 bits of $x(n)$ are considered since a 6-bit result is desired at the output.

The final interleaved architecture is shown in Fig. 13.11, where the vector merging portion is a combination of carry-ripple and carry-save implementations, which permits carry-ripple operation under the constraint that the architecture can be pipelined at 2-bit level (the pipelining latches are not shown in Fig. 13.11). As a result, after carry has rippled through 2 adders, it is saved and passed to the adder in next row.

If the coefficients are interleaved in such a way that their partial product terms are computed in different rows, the resulting architecture is referred to as the *bit-plane* architecture [13] and is shown in Fig. 13.12, where a row of flip-flops has been added after every row of adders in the array thereby enabling processing at high speed. In order to permit the interleaving operation, the direction of the sum and carry-out signals alternate. If the digital filter implementation needs to be pipelined at p-bit-level, then each bit-plane in the

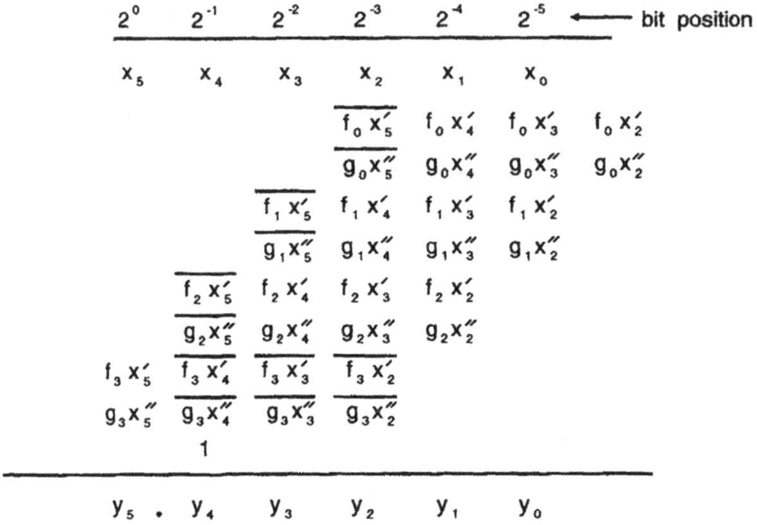

2^0	2^{-1}	2^{-2}	2^{-3}	2^{-4}	2^{-5}		bit position
x_5	x_4	x_3	x_2	x_1	x_0		
			$\overline{f_0 x_5'}$	$f_0 x_4'$	$f_0 x_3'$	$f_0 x_2'$	
			$g_0 x_5''$	$g_0 x_4''$	$g_0 x_3''$	$g_0 x_2''$	
		$\overline{f_1 x_5'}$	$f_1 x_4'$	$f_1 x_3'$	$f_1 x_2'$		
		$g_1 x_5''$	$g_1 x_4''$	$g_1 x_3''$	$g_1 x_2''$		
	$\overline{f_2 x_5'}$	$f_2 x_4'$	$f_2 x_3'$	$f_2 x_2'$			
	$\overline{g_2 x_5''}$	$g_2 x_4''$	$g_2 x_3''$	$g_2 x_2''$			
$f_3 x_5'$	$\overline{f_3 x_4'}$	$\overline{f_3 x_3'}$	$\overline{f_3 x_2'}$				
$g_3 x_5''$	$g_3 x_4''$	$g_3 x_3''$	$g_3 x_2''$				
	1						
y_5 .	y_4	y_3	y_2	y_1	y_0		

Fig. 13.10 Multiplication chart for the illustration of the interleaved approach. Here, x_i represents $x_i(n)$, x_i' represents $x_i(n-1)$, and x_i'' represents $x_i(n-2)$.

bit-plane architecture can be replaced by a *modified bit-plane* where each bit is replaced by a group of p consecutive bits. For $p = 2$, the modified bit-plane architecture can be designed using the multiplication chart of Fig. 13.13.

13.4 BIT-SERIAL MULTIPLIERS

This section addresses the derivation of Lyon's bit-serial multiplier [14] using Horner's rule. Several other bit-serial multipliers are then derived using systolic mapping techniques.

13.4.1 Design of Lyon's Bit-Serial Multipliers Using Horner's Rule

The multiplication rule in (13.5) can be used to derive bit-serial multipliers. The architecture for a 4×4-bit bit-serial multiplication is shown in Fig. 13.14(a), where the $\boxed{2^{-1}}$ is a bit-serial zero-latency scaling operator and its functionality is illustrated in Fig. 13.14(b). For a bit-serial zero-latency system, the first output bit needs to be generated in the same clock cycle as the first input bit entering the system. For the scaling operator, the first output bit a_1 should be generated at the same time instance when the first input a_0 enters the operator. Since input a_1 has not entered the system yet, the scaling operator is a noncausal or advance operation, and cannot be implemented in hardware.

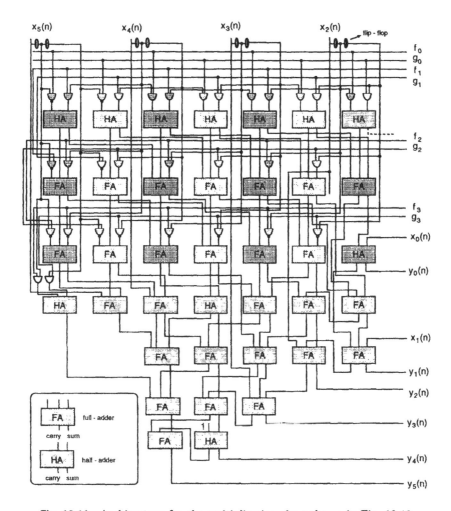

Fig. 13.11 Architecture for the multiplication chart shown in Fig. 13.10.

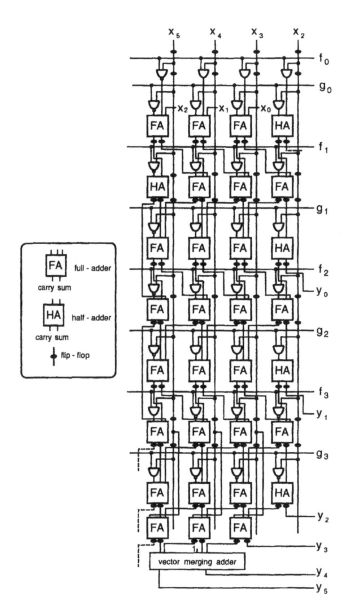

Fig. 13.12 Bit-plane architecture for the multiplication chart shown in Fig. 13.10.

2^0	2^{-1}	2^{-2}	2^{-3}	2^{-4}	2^{-5}	← bit position
x_5	x_4	x_3	x_2	x_1	x_0	
			$\overline{f_0 x_5'}$	$f_0 x_4'$	$f_0 x_3'$	$f_0 x_2'$
		$\overline{f_1 x_5'}$	$f_1 x_4'$	$f_1 x_3'$	$f_1 x_2'$	
			$g_0 x_5''$	$g_0 x_4''$	$g_0 x_3''$	$g_0 x_2''$
		$\overline{g_1 x_5''}$	$g_1 x_4''$	$g_1 x_3''$	$g_1 x_2''$	
	$\overline{f_2 x_5'}$	$f_2 x_4'$	$f_2 x_3'$	$f_2 x_2'$		
$f_3 x_5'$	$\overline{f_3 x_4'}$	$\overline{f_3 x_3'}$	$\overline{f_3 x_2'}$			
	$g_2 x_5''$	$g_2 x_4''$	$g_2 x_3''$	$g_2 x_2''$		
$g_3 x_5''$	$\overline{g_3 x_4''}$	$\overline{g_3 x_3''}$	$\overline{g_3 x_2''}$			
	1					
y_5 .	y_4	y_3	y_2	y_1	y_0	

Fig. 13.13 Multiplication chart for the modified bit-plane architecture.

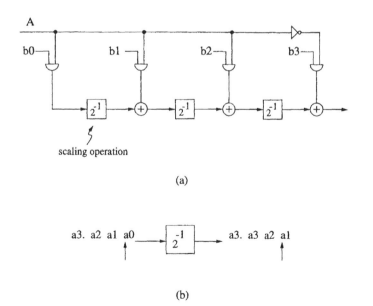

(a)

(b)

Fig. 13.14 (a) Bit-serial two's complement multiplication derived from Horner's rule. This architecture is not implementable due to the presence of the scaling operation. (b) The scaling operator is a zero-latency advance operation.

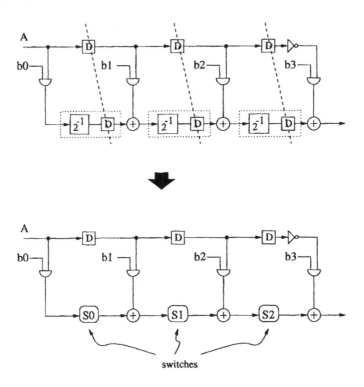

Fig. 13.15   Derivation of implementable bit-serial two's complement multiplier.

It is possible to implement the architecture in Fig. 13.14(a) using pipelining and placing delay elements at the feed-forward cutsets shown in Fig. 13.15. This combination of a delay element and a zero-delay scaling operator can now be realized in hardware. In Fig. 13.15, switching elements $S0$, $S1$, and $S2$ replace the combined scaling operators and delay elements at their corresponding positions, respectively. Their switching time instances can be found by scheduling the operations in the array multiplication as shown in Fig. 13.16, where the number in the box to the right of each computation indicates the time instance when this computation can be performed. Note that the switches eliminate the lsb of the current partial remainder and extend the sign of the previous partial remainder at the same time. Therefore, scaling operators are also referred to as *bit-repeaters* as these repeat the msb. The multiplier bits are input at time 0 to the corresponding AND gates; the multiplicand bits are input bit-serially lsb-first. The first bit (lsb) of the 4-bit product is generated at time instance 3. The complete diagram of the bit-serial two's complement multiplier is shown in Fig. 13.17. This multiplier is also referred to as *Lyon's multiplier* [14]. This system has a latency of 3 clock cycles. If the time for AND and multiplexing operations are ignored, the critical path computation time of this bit-serial multiplier is equal to $3T_a$, where T_a is the time for single-bit addition. Generally, a $W \times W$-bit bit-

			$a_3 \boxed{3}$	$a_2 \boxed{2}$	$a_1 \boxed{1}$	$a_0 \boxed{0}$
			$b_3 \boxed{0}$	$b_2 \boxed{0}$	$b_1 \boxed{0}$	$b_0 \boxed{0}$
		$a_3 b_0 \boxed{4}$	$\leftarrow a_3 b_0 \boxed{3}$	$a_2 b_0 \boxed{2}$	$a_1 b_0 \boxed{1}$	$\boxed{a_0 b_0}$
		$a_3 b_1 \boxed{4}$	$a_2 b_1 \boxed{3}$	$a_1 b_1 \boxed{2}$	$a_0 b_1 \boxed{1}$	
	$pp_3^1 \boxed{5}$	$\leftarrow pp_3^1 \boxed{4}$	$pp_2^1 \boxed{3}$	$pp_1^1 \boxed{2}$	$\boxed{pp_0^1}$	
	$a_3 b_2 \boxed{5}$	$a_2 b_2 \boxed{4}$	$a_1 b_2 \boxed{3}$	$a_0 b_2 \boxed{2}$		
$pp_3^2 \boxed{6}$	$\leftarrow pp_3^2 \boxed{5}$	$pp_2^2 \boxed{4}$	$pp_1^2 \boxed{3}$	$\boxed{pp_0^2}$		
$\bar{a}_3 b_3 \boxed{6}$	$\bar{a}_2 b_3 \boxed{5}$	$\bar{a}_1 b_3 \boxed{4}$	$\bar{a}_0 b_3 \boxed{3}$			
			b_3			
$x_3 \boxed{6}$	$x_2 \boxed{5}$	$x_1 \boxed{4}$	$x_0 \boxed{3}$			

Fig. 13.16 Scheduling instances for operations in bit-serial two's complement array multiplication.

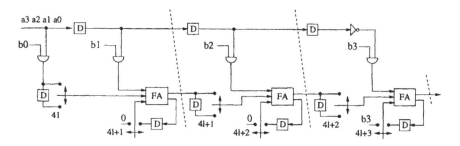

Fig. 13.17 Lyon's bit-serial two's complement multiplier.

serial multiplier has a latency equal to $W - 1$ clock cycles with the cycle time $T_{clk} \geq (W - 1)T_a$. Pipelining can be used to reduce the critical path and hence the clock period. For example, by placing delay elements across the feed-forward cutsets (shown by dashed lines) in Fig. 13.17, the critical path of the 4×4 bit-serial multiplier is reduced to 1 single-bit addition at the expense of an increase in the latency. The critical path of a W-bit Lyon's multiplier can be reduced to $2T_a$ without introducing extra pipelining latches, by using associativity and retiming [15] (see Problem 18).

13.4.2   Design of Bit-Serial Multipliers Using Systolic Mappings

Bit-serial multipliers can be designed by using systolic mapping methodology (see Chapter 7) of the 2D DGs to one-dimension (1D) array.

Example 13.4.1 *This example considers the design of Lyon's bit-serial multiplier by systolic mapping using the DG of ripple-carry multiplication in*

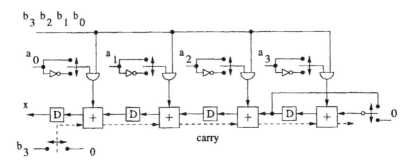

Fig. 13.18 Bit-serial carry-ripple multiplier in Example 13.4.2.

Fig. 13.3. Using the projection vector $\mathbf{d}^T = [1\ 0]$, the scheduling vector $\mathbf{s}^T = [1\ 1]$, and the processor space vector $\mathbf{p}^T = [0\ 1]$, we have the following edge mappings:

e^T	$\mathbf{p}^T\mathbf{e}$	$\mathbf{s}^T\mathbf{e}$
$a\ (0,\ 1)$	1	1
$b\ (1,\ 0)$	0	1
carry $(1,\ 0)$	0	1
$x\ (-1,\ 1)$	1	0

With additional sign-extension circuitry, the resulting bit-serial multiplier in Fig. 13.17 is obtained. Bit-level pipelined version of Lyon's multiplier can also be designed directly from the ripple-carry multiplication DG by systolic mapping techniques (see Problem 10).

Example 13.4.2 *Consider the DG for the carry-ripple array multiplication in Fig. 13.3. Using the projection vector, processor space vector, and scheduling vector*

$$\mathbf{d} = \begin{pmatrix} 0 \\ 1 \end{pmatrix}, \quad \mathbf{p}^T = (\ 1\quad 0\ ), \quad \mathbf{s}^T = (\ 0\quad 1\ ), \qquad (13.13)$$

we have the following edge mappings:

e^T	$\mathbf{p}^T\mathbf{e}$	$\mathbf{s}^T\mathbf{e}$
$a\ (0,\ 1)$	0	1
$b\ (1,\ 0)$	1	0
carry $(1,\ 0)$	1	0
$x\ (-1,\ 1)$	-1	1

The resulting bit-serial carry-ripple multiplier is shown in Fig. 13.18, where the switching instances for the multiplexers are omitted for clarity. ∎

Example 13.4.3 *Consider the DG for the carry-save array multiplication in Fig. 13.5. Suppose a carry-ripple adder is used in the vector merging portion.*

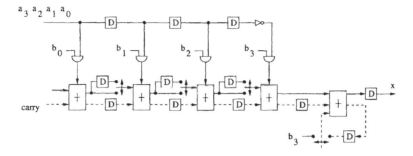

Fig. 13.19 Bit-serial carry-save multiplier in Example 13.4.3.

Using the projection vector, processor vector, and scheduling vector

$$\mathbf{d} = \begin{pmatrix} 1 \\ 0 \end{pmatrix}, \quad \mathbf{p}^T = (\ 0 \quad 1\ ), \quad \mathbf{s}^T = (\ 1 \quad 1\ ), \tag{13.14}$$

we have the following edge mappings:

$\mathbf{e}^T$	$\mathbf{p}^T\mathbf{e}$	$\mathbf{s}^T\mathbf{e}$
$a\ (0,\ 1)$	1	1
$carry\ (0,\ 1)$	1	1
$b\ (1,\ 0)$	0	1
$x\ (-1,\ 1)$	1	0

The resulting bit-serial carry-save multiplier is shown in Fig. 13.19. The control signals of the multiplexers in this figure are omitted for clarity. ∎

Example 13.4.4 *Consider the multiplication table for Baugh-Wooley multiplication shown in Fig. 13.8. Suppose a carry-save addition is used to accumulate the partial products and a carry-ripple adder is used in the vector merging portion. The DG for this computation is shown in Fig. 13.20.*

The projection with the following projection vector, processor space vector and scheduling vector

$$\mathbf{d} = \begin{pmatrix} 0 \\ 1 \end{pmatrix}, \quad \mathbf{p}^T = (\ 1 \quad 0\ ), \quad \mathbf{s}^T = (\ 0 \quad 1\ ) \tag{13.15}$$

leads to the following edge mappings:

$\mathbf{e}^T$	$\mathbf{p}^T\mathbf{e}$	$\mathbf{s}^T\mathbf{e}$
$a\ (0,\ 1)$	0	1
$carry\ (0,\ 1)$	0	1
$b\ (1,\ 0)$	1	0
$x\ (1,\ 1)$	1	1
$carry\text{-}vm\ (-1,\ 0)$	-1	0

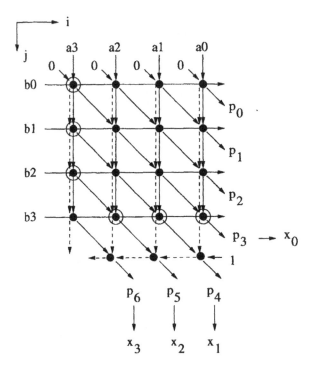

Fig. 13.20 Dependence graph for carry-save Baugh-Wooley multiplication with carry-ripple vector merging.

where carry−vm denotes the carry outputs in the vector merging portion. The resulting bit-serial carry-save Baugh-Wooley multiplier is shown in Fig. 13.21, where blocks $\boxed{C}$ perform inversion operations at some clock cycles to generate the appropriate partial products and these control details have been omitted for simplicity. Note that in this design, the computation at node (i, j) is scheduled at time j, for $j = 0, 1, 2, 3, 4$. Therefore, the result bit x_0 is generated at time $5l + 3$ and x_3, x_2, and x_1 are generated at time $5l + 4$ in parallel format. A parallel-to-serial converter is used such that these result bits are output in serial at time instance $5l$, $5l + 1$, $5l + 2$, $5l + 3$, and $5l + 4$, respectively. The control signal $T_0 = 1$ at time $5l$ when a new multiplication starts, and $T_0 = 0$ otherwise. Hence the architecture has latency equal to 5 cycles and is able to generate 1 output word every 5 cycles. In addition to inherent hardware utilization inefficiency, a major drawback of this design is the long critical path (shown in dashed line in Fig. 13.21) proportional to the wordlength.

Another design can be obtained by using the modified DG shown in Fig. 13.22, with the same projection vector, processor vector, and scheduling vector as in (13.15). In this case, the carry-save array and the vector merging portion are treated as two separate planes during systolic mapping, and the carry-ripple addition in vector merging portion is performed by a separate adder and result

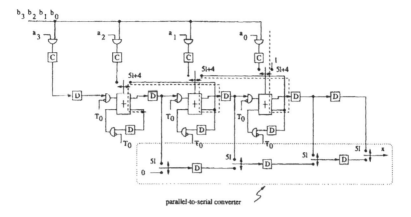

Fig. 13.21 Bit-serial Baugh-Wooley multiplier 1 in Example 13.4.4.

bits are generated in serial. This bit-serial design is shown in Fig. 13.23. It has a latency equal to four clock cycles and is able to generate one output every four clock cycles. Note that the critical path of this design is limited by one binary adder delay. ∎

13.5 BIT-SERIAL FILTER DESIGN AND IMPLEMENTATION

FIR and IIR filters are the two most basic structures used in DSP. This section considers design of bit-serial FIR and IIR digital filters with fixed constant coefficients, where the multiplications with constant coefficients are decomposed and implemented using bit-serial shifts and adds.

13.5.1 Bit-Serial FIR Filter

Consider the implementation of the FIR filter

$$y(n) = -\frac{7}{8}x(n) + \frac{1}{2}x(n-1),$$ (13.16)

with a signal wordlength of 8. Equation (13.16) can be rewritten in terms of shifts and adds as follows:

$$y(n) = -x(n) + x(n)2^{-3} + x(n-1)2^{-1}.$$ (13.17)

The word-level signal flow graph of the shift-add based FIR filter is shown in Fig. 13.24(a). Due to the presence of noncausal scaling operators, this is not a feasible design. Pipelining cutsets, shown in dashed lines in Fig. 13.24(a), can be used to delay the advance scaling operations. By placing delay elements

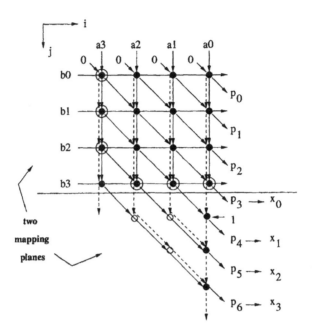

Fig. 13.22 Bit-serial Baugh-Wooley multiplier DG in Example 13.4.4.

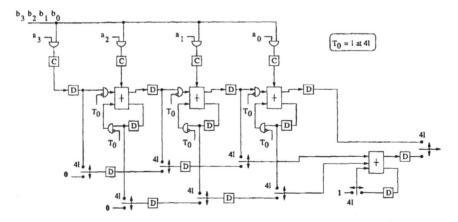

Fig. 13.23 Bit-serial Baugh-Wooley multiplier # 2 in Example 13.4.4.

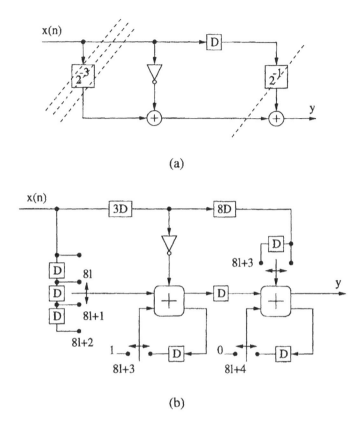

(a)

(b)

Fig. 13.24 Bit-level pipelined bit-serial FIR filter where constant coefficient multiplications are implemented as shifts and adds. (a) Filter architecture with scaling operators; (b) feasible bit-level pipelined architecture.

along the cutsets and replacing the delayed scaling operators with switches, a feasible bit-level pipelined bit-serial FIR filter can be derived, as shown in Fig. 13.24(b). Note that a word-level delay is equivalent to W bit-level delays for a signal wordlength of W. Therefore, the one word delay in Fig. 13.24(a) is replaced by 8 bit-level delays in Fig. 13.24(b). The switching time instances can be derived by scheduling the bit-level computations.

13.5.2 Bit-Serial IIR Filter

Consider the implementation of the IIR filter

$$y(n) = -\frac{7}{8}y(n-1) + \frac{1}{2}y(n-2) + x(n), \tag{13.18}$$

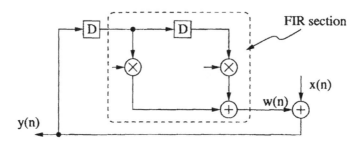

Fig. 13.25   IIR filter can be obtained from a FIR section as shown in this figure.

where the signal wordlength is assumed to be 8. This IIR filter equation can be rewritten as

$$w(n) \;=\; -\frac{7}{8}y(n-1) + \frac{1}{2}y(n-2),$$
$$y(n) \;=\; w(n) + x(n),$$

which can be implemented as an FIR section (computing $w(n)$ from $y(n-1)$) with an addition and a feedback loop, as shown in Fig. 13.25. A bit-level pipelined bit-serial IIR filter architecture can be derived by going through the following steps.

First, a bit-level pipelined bit-serial implementation of the FIR section needs to be derived. (For this example, this has already been carried out in the previous subsection.) The 2nd step is an intermediate design stage. In this step, the input signal $x(n)$ is added to the output of the bit-serial FIR section $w(n)$. The resulting signal $y(n)$ is connected with the signal $y(n-1)$. The number of delay elements on this edge, marked by $\boxed{?D}$ in Fig. 13.26(a), is yet to be determined. The resulting structure is shown in Fig. 13.26(a), which contains 2 loops shown in dashed lines. This completes all the interconnections in the bit-serial system. However, for systems containing loops, the total number of delay elements in the loops should be consistent with that in the original signal-flow graph (SFG), in order to maintain synchronization as well as correct functionality. In this case, the number of bit-level delay elements in the bit-serial loops should equal $W \times N_D$, where W is the signal wordlength and N_D denotes the number of (word-level) delay elements in the loops of the original word-level SFG. Matching the number of word-level loop delay elements and that in the bit-serial architecture is referred to as *loop delay synchronization*. For this IIR filtering example, originally, the inner loop contains 1 word delay and the outer loop contains 2 word delays. Hence, in the resulting architecture, the inner loop and outer loop should contain 8 and 16 delay elements, respectively. To compute the total number of delays in the bit-level architecture, the paths with the *largest number of delay elements* in the switching elements should be counted. For this example, there are 6 delay elements and 14 delay elements in the inner loop and outer loop of the intermediate architecture, respectively. Therefore, 2 *synchronization delays* are added to the common part of inner and outer loop and the final architecture is shown in Fig. 13.26(b). Five input synchronizing delay elements are added to the input, which are also referred to as *shimming* delays or *skewing* delays. This bit-level pipelined bit-serial IIR filter has a critical path containing 1 single-bit adder, and has a throughput of 1 output word every 8 clock cycles. Note that it is also possible that the loops in the intermediate bit-level pipelined architecture may contain more than $W \times N_D$ number of bit-level delay elements. In this case, the wordlength needs to be increased.

Note that the architecture without the 2 loop synchronizing delays (in shaded region) can function correctly with a signal wordlength of 6, which is the *minimum wordlength* for the bit-level pipelined bit-serial architecture in Fig. 13.26(b). (In the case of signal wordlength 6, the $\boxed{8D}$ delays in the outer loop should be changed to $\boxed{6D}$ delays.) The minimum feasible wordlength of a bit-level pipelined bit-serial system decides its maximum throughput. In this case, the throughput corresponds to 1 output (word) every 6 clock cycles.

The IIR filter architecture in Fig. 13.26(b) is derived from the signal-flow graph shown in Fig. 13.27(a). Its minimum wordlength of 6 is constrained by the loop iteration period of one-multiply-two-add (inner loop) time in the signal flow graph of Fig. 13.27(a). This iteration bound (see Chapter 2) can be reduced to one-multiply-add by using *associativity* which leads to the structure shown in Fig. 13.27(b). A bit-serial implementation of the structure in Fig. 13.27(b) is shown in Fig. 13.28, which requires a minimum feasible wordlength of 5.

Example 13.5.1 *Consider the implementation of the equation:*

$$x(n) = -\frac{7}{32}x(n-1) + \frac{3}{4}x(n-2) + u(n). \tag{13.19}$$

Assume the signal wordlength to be 8 (i.e., the wordlengths for x and u are 8 bits). Assume the coefficient $-7/32 = -1 + 1/2 + 1/4 + 1/32$ is encoded as 1.11001 and $3/4 = 1/2 + 1/4$ is encoded as 0.11 in two's complement format.

A bit-serial architecture based on the block diagram of Fig. 13.27(b) is shown in Fig. 13.29, where the notation $(8l + i)$ represents the time instance $\{8l+i\}$ and 7/8 represents the remaining 7 time slots in a period of periodicity 8. Note that the number of loop delay elements equals 8 in the inner loop and 16 in the outer loop (while counting the number of loop delay elements, the maximum number of delay elements in the switches should be included), which is consistent with the word-level architecture. ∎

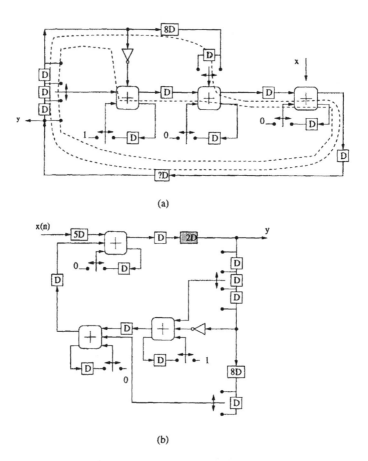

(a)

(b)

Fig. 13.26 Design of bit-level pipelined bit-serial IIR filter. (a) Bit-level pipelined bit-serial architecture, without synchronization delay elements. (b) Bit-serial IIR filter. Note that this implementation requires a minimum feasible wordlength of 6.

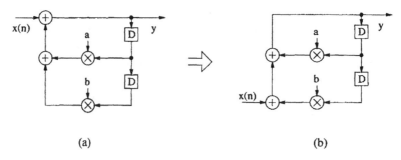

(a)   (b)

Fig. 13.27 Loop iteration bound of IIR filter can be reduced from one-multiply-two-add to one-multiply-add by associative transformation.

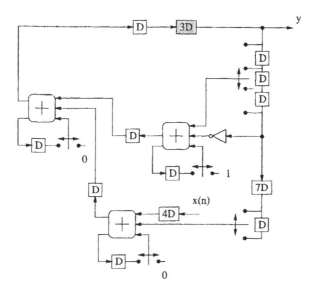

Fig. 13.28 Bit-serial IIR filter after associative transformation. This implementation requires a minimum feasible wordlength of 5.

13.6 CANONIC SIGNED DIGIT ARITHMETIC

The number of add operations required in a constant coefficient multiplication equals one less than the number of nonzero bits in the constant coefficient. In order to further reduce the area and power consumption, the constant coefficient can be encoded such that it contains the fewest number of nonzero bits, which can be accomplished using *canonic signed digit* (CSD) representation. Quantization of FIR digital filters using a specified number of signed power-of-two (SPT) terms is described in Appendix G.

This section addresses the CSD number representation and its applications for the design of bit-serial and bit-parallel constant multipliers.

13.6.1 CSD Representation

Consider the number $A = a_{W-1}.a_{W-2} \cdots a_1 a_0$, where each a_i $(W-1 \geq i \geq 0)$ is in the set $\{-1, 0, 1\}$. Two's complement representation may be considered as a special case, in which the bit a_{W-1} is equal to 0 or -1, whereas $a_i=0$ or 1 for $0 \leq i \leq W - 2$. Now the multiplication $A \times X$, where X is a variable, can be expressed as

$$A \times X = \sum_{i=0}^{W-1} a_{W-1-i} X 2^{-i},$$

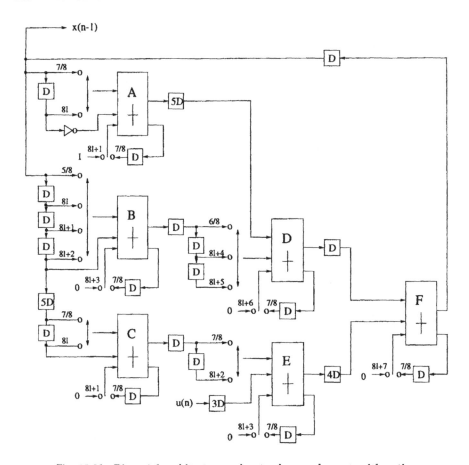

Fig. 13.29 Bit-serial architecture using two's complement arithmetic.

where the number of additions/subtractions required equals one less than the number of nonzero bits in A. CSD representation is another special case, where no 2 consecutive a_i's are nonzero.

The properties of CSD number representations have been considered in [16] and are summarized as follows.

- No 2 consecutive bits in a CSD number are nonzero.

- The CSD representation of a number contains the minimum ˙possible number of nonzero bits, thus the name *canonic*.

- The CSD representation of a number is unique.

- CSD numbers cover the range $(-4/3, 4/3)$, out of which the values in the range $[-1, 1)$ are of greatest interest.

- Among the W-bit CSD numbers in the range $[-1, 1)$, the average number of nonzero bits is $W/3 + 1/9 + O(2^{-W})$. Hence, on average, CSD numbers contains about 33% fewer nonzero bits than two's complement numbers.

An algorithm for computing the CSD format of a W-bit number is presented in [16]. Denote the two's complement representation of the number A as $A = \hat{a}_{W-1}.\hat{a}_{W-2}\cdots\hat{a}_1\hat{a}_0$ and its CSD representation $A = a_{W-1}.a_{W-2}...a_1a_0$. The conversion is illustrated using the following iterative algorithm:

$$\hat{a}_{-1} = 0$$
$$\gamma_{-1} = 0$$
$$\hat{a}_W = \hat{a}_{W-1}$$
$$\text{for } (i = 0 \text{ to } W - 1)$$
$$\{$$
$$\theta_i = \hat{a}_i \oplus \hat{a}_{i-1}$$
$$\gamma_i = \overline{\gamma_{i-1}}\,\theta_i$$
$$a_i = (1 - 2\hat{a}_{i+1})\gamma_i$$
$$\}$$

Here, the symbol $\oplus$ denotes exclusive OR, and the overbar indicates complementation.

Example 13.6.1 *The input is the number* 1.01110011. *Its CSD representation is computed as follows:*

i	W	$W-1$				$\cdots$				0	-1
$\hat{a}_i$	1	1	0	1	1	1	0	0	1	1	0
θ_i		1	1	0	0	1	0	1	0	1	
γ_i		0	1	0	0	1	0	1	0	1	0
$1 - 2\hat{a}_{i+1}$		-1	-1	1	-1	-1	-1	1	1	-1	
a_i		0	-1	0	0	-1	0	1	0	-1	

13.6.2 CSD Multiplication

As mentioned previously, constant multiplication can be carried out by adding or subtracting a number of partial product terms corresponding to the nonzero bit positions in the constant multiplier. A CSD-encoded multiplier contains the least number of nonzero bits and, hence, requires the minimum number of addition/subtraction operations. In CSD representation, the multiplication $x \times 0.1010010010\bar{1}00\bar{1}$ can be computed as shown in Fig. 13.30, where the partial products are accumulated in a linear arrangement. However, this is not an efficient implementation in terms of either computation time or accuracy. This section introduces Horner's rule based multiplication and tree-height reduction to overcome these problems. Note that these two techniques are also applicable to two's complement arithmetic.

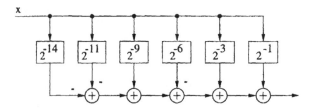

Fig. 13.30   A CSD multiplier using linear arrangement of adders.

13.6.2.1 Horner's Rule for Precision Improvement

In a constant wordlength multiplier, the extra bits in the partial sums as well as the final product are truncated, and the number of binary adders required for accumulating 2 partial products equals the wordlength W. This causes truncation errors, whose value not only depends on the multiplicand and multiplier, but also on the arrangement of the partial product accumulation.

For example, consider the addition of $x \cdot 2^{-5} + x \cdot 2^{-3}$, assuming a wordlength of 8 for the variable x. This can be carried out as shown in Fig. 13.31(a), where the 2 partial products are $x \cdot 2^{-5}$ and $x \cdot 2^{-3}$; the accumulation only includes those bits in the rectangular box, and the lower order bits are truncated. This addition can also be computed as $(x \cdot 2^{-2} + x)2^{-3}$, where the 2 partial products are $x \cdot 2^{-2}$ and x, as shown in Fig. 13.31(b). In this case, the same number of adders are required; however, the accumulation involves more lower order bits and has less truncation error as compared with the computation in Fig. 13.31(a). Thus, by delaying the scaling operation common to the 2 partial products, the accuracy of the final result is improved. However, some scaling operation may need to be performed before addition due to dynamic range considerations. For example, to achieve dynamic arrange $[-1, 1)$ for the operand x, $x \cdot 2^{-5} + x \cdot 2^{-3}$ should be rewritten as $(x \cdot 2^{-3} + x \cdot 2^{-1})2^{-2}$. In this representation, the output of the adder cannot overflow. Note that for no overflow in $(x \cdot 2^{-2} + x)$, the dynamic range of x is limited to $(-0.8, 0.8)$. This dynamic range issue is not considered any further.

Similarly, the computation of $x \times 0.1010010010\overline{1}00\overline{1}$ in Fig. 13.30 can be rearranged as

$$
\begin{aligned}
& x \times 0.1010010010\overline{1}00\overline{1} \\
={} & x \cdot (2^{-1} + 2^{-3} - 2^{-6} + 2^{-9} - 2^{-11} - 2^{-14}) \\
={} & 2^{-1}(x + 2^{-2}(x + 2^{-3}(-x + 2^{-3}(x + 2^{-2}(-x - 2^{-3}x))))) \\
={} & 2^{-1}(x + 2^{-2}(x + 2^{-3}(-x + 2^{-3}(x - 2^{-2}(x + 2^{-3}x)))))
\end{aligned}
$$

where the computation starts from the innermost bracket, and the scaling operations common to the 2 partial products in a bracket are delayed, as shown in Fig. 13.32. This expansion using Horner's rule reduces the truncation error and improves the precision of the multiplication.

Note that in order to prevent overflow, at least 1 scaling operation is re-

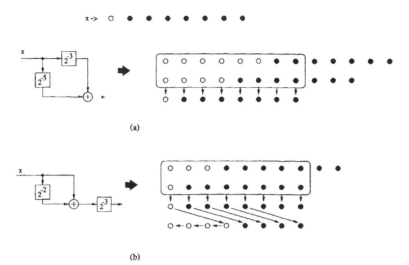

(a)

(b)

Fig. 13.31 Using Horner's rule for partial product accumulation to reduce the truncation error.

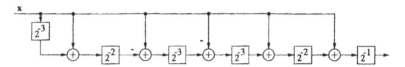

Fig. 13.32 Rearrangement of the CSD multiplication in Fig. 13.30 using Horner's rule for partial product accumulation to reduce the truncation error.

quired for each operand before addition. Here, a guard bit is assumed in the variable x, as discussed in Section 13.2. This excludes the necessity of appropriate scaling operation before addition.

13.6.2.2 Use of Tree-Height Reduction for Latency Reduction

Accumulation of N values can be arranged either in a linear array or in a tree-type structure, as shown in Fig. 13.33 for $N = 4$. With the same hardware requirement, the tree type arrangement can reduce the latency from $(N - 1)T_a$ to $\lceil \log_2 N \rceil T_a$, where T_a denotes the computation time for 1 addition operation.

The partial products in CSD multiplication in Figs. 13.30 and 13.32 are accumulated in a linear arrangement. Their latency can be reduced by using a tree of adders. In this case, the multiplication is performed as

$$
\begin{aligned}
&x \times 0.101001001010\bar{1}00\bar{1} \\
&= \ x \cdot (2^{-1} + 2^{-3} - 2^{-6} + 2^{-9} - 2^{-11} - 2^{-14}) \\
&= \ 2^{-1}((x + 2^{-2}x) + 2^{-5}((-x + 2^{-3}x) - 2^{-5}(x + 2^{-3}x)))
\end{aligned}
$$

as illustrated in Fig. 13.34.

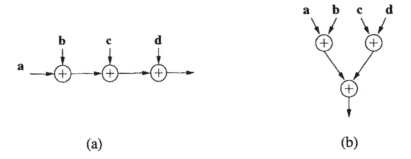

(a)   (b)

Fig. 13.33   (a) Linear arrangement; (b) tree arrangement.

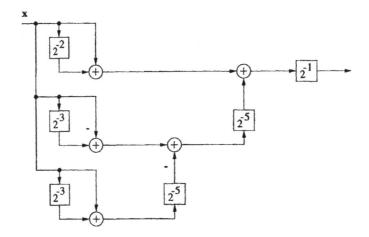

Fig. 13.34   Combination of tree-type arrangement and Horner's rule for the accumulation of partial products in CSD multiplication.

It has been shown that use of Horner's rule and tree-height reduction transformation can reduce the truncation error and the computation latency for constant wordlength multiplications. For full-precision multiplications, these two schemes can be used to save the number of adders required.

Example 13.6.2 *In this example, the IIR filter in Example 13.5.1 is being redesigned using canonic signed digit representation. In this case, the coefficient* $-7/32 = -1/4 + 1/32$ *is encoded as* $0.0\bar{1}001$ *and* $3/4 = 1 - 1/4$ *is encoded as* $1.0\bar{1}$ *in CSD format. The bit-serial architecture using CSD representation is shown in Fig. 13.35. Note that the number of adders is reduced from 6 to 4. Furthermore, since the inner loop multiplication latency is now 6 time units, the minimum feasible wordlength is reduced to* $6 + 1 = 7$ *bits compared to the 8 bits in two's complement representation.* ■

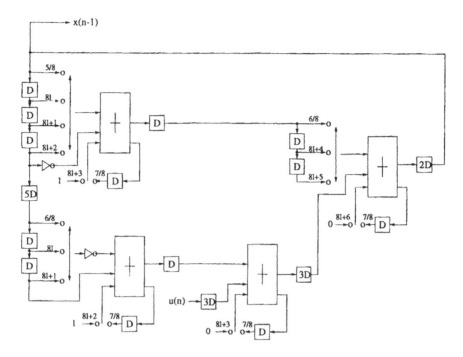

Fig. 13.35 Bit-serial architecture using CSD arithmetic.

13.7 DISTRIBUTED ARITHMETIC

Distributed arithmetic is used to design bit-level architectures for vector-vector multiplications. In distributed arithmetic, each word in the vectors is represented as a binary number, the multiplications are reordered and mixed such that the arithmetic becomes "distributed" through the structure. Distributed arithmetic is commonly used for implementation of convolution operations and discrete cosine transforms (DCT) commonly used in video compression systems [17],[18].

13.7.1 Conventional Distributed Arithmetic

Consider an inner product between 2 length-N vectors C and X:

$$Y = \sum_{i=0}^{N-1} c_i x_i, \tag{13.20}$$

where $\{c_i\}$'s are M-bit constants and $\{x_i\}$'s are coded as W-bit 2's complement numbers

$$x_i = -x_{i,W-1} + \sum_{j=1}^{W-1} x_{i,W-1-j} 2^{-j}. \tag{13.21}$$

Substituting (13.21) in (13.20),

$$
\begin{aligned}
Y &= \sum_{i=0}^{N-1} c_i \left(-x_{i,W-1} + \sum_{j=1}^{W-1} x_{i,W-1-j} 2^{-j} \right) \\
&= -\sum_{i=0}^{N-1} c_i x_{i,W-1} + \sum_{j=1}^{W-1} \left(\sum_{i=0}^{N-1} c_i x_{i,W-1-j} \right) 2^{-j}.
\end{aligned}
\tag{13.22}
$$

Define

$$C_{W-1-j} = \sum_{i=0}^{N-1} c_i x_{i,W-1-j} \ (j \neq 0), \quad C_{W-1} = -\sum_{i=0}^{N-1} c_i x_{i,W-1}. \tag{13.23}$$

Then,

$$Y = \sum_{j=0}^{W-1} C_{W-1-j} 2^{-j}. \tag{13.24}$$

Therefore, by interchanging the summing order of i and j, the initial multiplications in (13.20) are now *distributed* to another computation pattern [19],[20].

Since the term C_j depends on the $x_{i,j}$ values and has only 2^N possible values, it is possible to precompute them and store them in a read only memory (ROM). An input set of N bits $(x_{0j}, x_{1j}, \cdots, x_{N-1,j})$ is used as an address to retrieve the corresponding C_j values. These intermediate results are accumulated in W clock cycles to produce one Y value. This leads to a multiplier-free realization of vector multiplication. Table 13.2 shows the content of the ROM for $N=4$. Fig. 13.36 shows a typical architecture for the computation of the inner product of two length-N vectors. The shift-accumulator is a bit-parallel carry-propagate adder that adds the ROM content to the previous accumulated result. The inverter and the MUX are used for inverting the output of the ROM in order to compute C_{W-1} and the control signal S is 1 when $j = W - 1$ and 0 otherwise. The computation runs from $j = 0$ to $j = W - 1$ and the result is available in bit-parallel format after W clock cycles. This approach corresponds to a bit-serial distributed arithmetic. The speed of a traditional bit-serial distributed arithmetic implementation can be limited for certain real-time applications such as DCT implementation for video compression in a digital TV system. The speed of these systems can be improved by a digit-serial distributed arithmetic [21],[22] where a digit containing multiple bits is processed in a clock cycle. For example, if J consecutive bits are

Table 13.2 Content of the ROM ($N=4$)

$x_{0,j}$	$x_{1,j}$	$x_{2,j}$	$x_{3,j}$	Content of the ROM
0	0	0	0	0
0	0	0	1	c_3
0	0	1	0	c_2
0	0	1	1	$c_2 + c_3$
0	1	0	0	c_1
0	1	0	1	$c_1 + c_3$
0	1	1	0	$c_1 + c_2$
0	1	1	1	$c_1 + c_2 + c_3$
1	0	0	0	c_0
1	0	0	1	$c_0 + c_3$
1	0	1	0	$c_0 + c_2$
1	0	1	1	$c_0 + c_2 + c_3$
1	1	0	0	$c_0 + c_1$
1	1	0	1	$c_0 + c_1 + c_3$
1	1	1	0	$c_0 + c_1 + c_2$
1	1	1	1	$c_0 + c_1 + c_2 + c_3$

processed in a single clock cycle using J ROMs, then the input words are processed in W/J clock cycles. A multi-input shift-accumulator adds the contents of J ROMs and the previous accumulated result, and generates the output in bit-parallel format. The detailed design of the multi-input shift-accumulator is explored in Problem 24.

13.7.2 Distributed Arithmetic with Offset-Binary Coding

In this section, the offset-binary coding (OBC) [18] is introduced that can reduce the ROM size by a factor of 2 to 2^{N-1}.

Rewrite (13.21) as:

$$
\begin{aligned}
x_i &= \frac{1}{2}[x_i - (-x_i)] \\
&= \frac{1}{2}[-(x_{i,W-1} - \overline{x_{i,W-1}}) + \sum_{j=1}^{W-1}(x_{i,W-1-j} - \overline{x_{i,W-1-j}})2^{-j} - 2^{-(W-1)}],
\end{aligned}
$$

$$(13.25)$$

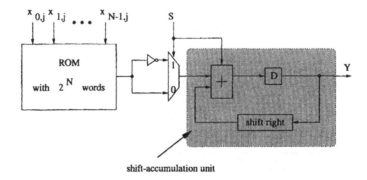

Fig. 13.36 Architecture of computing inner product of two length-N vectors using distributed arithmetic.

where

$$-x_i \;=\; -\overline{x_{i,W-1}} + \sum_{j=1}^{W-1} \overline{x_{i,W-1-j}}\, 2^{-j} + 2^{-(W-1)}.$$

Define

$$d_{i,j} = \begin{cases} x_{i,j} - \overline{x_{i,j}}, & \text{for } j \neq W-1 \\ -(x_{i,W-1} - \overline{x_{i,W-1}}), & \text{for } j = W-1 \end{cases} \tag{13.26}$$

and $d_{i,j} \in \{-1,+1\}$. Equation (13.25) can be rewritten as:

$$x_i = \frac{1}{2}\Big[\sum_{j=0}^{W-1} d_{i,W-1-j}\, 2^{-j} - 2^{-(W-1)}\Big]. \tag{13.27}$$

Using (13.27), (13.20) can be written as

$$Y \;=\; \sum_{i=0}^{N-1} \frac{1}{2} c_i \Big[\sum_{j=0}^{W-1} d_{i,W-1-j}\, 2^{-j} - 2^{-(W-1)}\Big] \tag{13.28}$$

$$=\; \sum_{j=0}^{W-1}\Big(\sum_{i=0}^{N-1} \frac{1}{2} c_i d_{i,W-1-j}\Big) 2^{-j} - \Big(\frac{1}{2}\sum_{i=0}^{N-1} c_i\Big) 2^{-(W-1)}.$$

Now define

$$D_j = \sum_{i=0}^{N-1} \frac{1}{2} c_i d_{i,j}, \quad \text{for } 0 \leq j \leq W-1 \tag{13.29}$$

and

$$D_{extra} = -\frac{1}{2}\sum_{i=0}^{N-1} c_i. \tag{13.30}$$

Therefore, we have

$$Y = \sum_{j=0}^{W-1} D_{W-1-j} 2^{-j} + D_{extra} 2^{-(W-1)}. \tag{13.31}$$

Equations (13.29)–(13.31) characterize the OBC scheme. Table 13.3 shows the content of the ROM.

Table 13.3 Content of the ROM with OBC Coding ($N=4$)

$x_{0,j}$	$x_{1,j}$	$x_{2,j}$	$x_{3,j}$	Content of the ROM
0	0	0	0	$-(c_0 + c_1 + c_2 + c_3)/2$
0	0	0	1	$-(c_0 + c_1 + c_2 - c_3)/2$
0	0	1	0	$-(c_0 + c_1 - c_2 + c_3)/2$
0	0	1	1	$-(c_0 + c_1 - c_2 - c_3)/2$
0	1	0	0	$-(c_0 - c_1 + c_2 + c_3)/2$
0	1	0	1	$-(c_0 - c_1 + c_2 - c_3)/2$
0	1	1	0	$-(c_0 - c_1 - c_2 + c_3)/2$
0	1	1	1	$-(c_0 - c_1 - c_2 - c_3)/2$
1	0	0	0	$(c_0 - c_1 - c_2 - c_3)/2$
1	0	0	1	$(c_0 - c_1 - c_2 + c_3)/2$
1	0	1	0	$(c_0 - c_1 + c_2 - c_3)/2$
1	0	1	1	$(c_0 - c_1 + c_2 + c_3)/2$
1	1	0	0	$(c_0 + c_1 - c_2 - c_3)/2$
1	1	0	1	$(c_0 + c_1 - c_2 + c_3)/2$
1	1	1	0	$(c_0 + c_1 + c_2 - c_3)/2$
1	1	1	1	$(c_0 + c_1 + c_2 + c_3)/2$

It is obvious that the D_j values are mirrored along the line between the 8-th and the 9-*th* rows in the ROM table. In other words, the term D_j has only 2^{N-1} possible values depending on the $x_{i,j}$ values. Therefore it is possible to reduce the ROM size by a factor of 2. Table 13.4 illustrates the new ROM table and Fig. 13.37 shows a typical architecture for the computation of an N-input inner product using distributed arithmetic with the OBC scheme. Again the computation starts from the lsb of x_i, i.e., $j = 0$. The XOR gates are used for address decoding, the MUX with the constant D_{extra} provides the initial value to the shift-accumulator and the MUX after the ROM is used to inverse the output of ROM when $j = W - 1$. Two control signals S_1 and S_2 are required, where S_1 is 1 when $j = W - 1$ and 0 otherwise, and S_2 is 1 when $j = 0$ and 0 otherwise.

Table 13.4 Content of the ROM (Reduced Size) with OBC Coding ($N=4$)

$x_{1,j}$	$x_{2,j}$	$x_{3,j}$	Content of the ROM
0	0	0	$-(c_0 + c_1 + c_2 + c_3)/2$
0	0	1	$-(c_0 + c_1 + c_2 - c_3)/2$
0	1	0	$-(c_0 + c_1 - c_2 + c_3)/2$
0	1	1	$-(c_0 + c_1 - c_2 - c_3)/2$
1	0	0	$-(c_0 - c_1 + c_2 + c_3)/2$
1	0	1	$-(c_0 - c_1 + c_2 - c_3)/2$
1	1	0	$-(c_0 - c_1 - c_2 + c_3)/2$
1	1	1	$-(c_0 - c_1 - c_2 - c_3)/2$

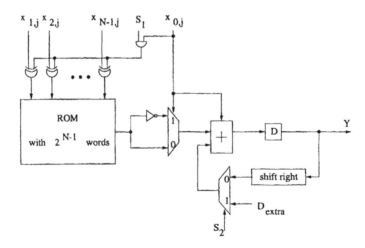

Fig. 13.37 Architecture of computing inner product of 2 length-N vectors using distributed arithmetic with OBC coding.

13.7.3 ROM Decomposition for Distributed Arithmetic

The ROM size of the conventional distributed arithmetic increases exponentially with N. Generally, ROM access time can be a bottleneck for speed of the whole system, especially when ROM size is large. Therefore, reducing the ROM size is very important and is of great practical concern. Due to the linearity of equation (13.24), one possible solution is to divide the N address bits of the ROM into N/K groups of K bits. Hence it is possible to decompose the ROM of size 2^N into N/K ROMs of size 2^K and add the outputs of these ROMs using a multiinput accumulator. Fig. 13.38 illustrates the architecture for computing an N-input inner product using conventional distributed arithmetic with ROM decomposition. The total size of storage is now reduced

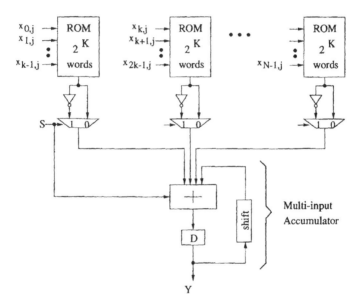

Fig. 13.38 Architecture for computing inner product of two length-N vectors using distributed arithmetic with ROM decomposition.

from 2^N to $(N/K)2^K$ which increases linearly with N. The ROM access time is also reduced along with the ROM size. This reduction of the storage size is balanced by a linear increase of the computation complexity of the accumulator. Carry-save arithmetic can be used to realize the multiinput accumulator to minimize the computation time. Note that ROM decomposition technique is applicable to OBC-coding-based distributed arithmetic as well.

13.8 CONCLUSIONS

This chapter has presented the design of bit-level arithmetic architectures. Design of bit-parallel multipliers, including carry-ripple array, carry-save array, Baugh-Wooley, and Booth-recoded multiplications has been introduced. The two efficient layout strategies, *interleaved floor-plan* and *bit-plane*, for digital filters have been discussed. Design of bit-serial multipliers using Horner's rule as well as using systolic mapping has been addressed. This chapter has also addressed the design methodologies for bit-level pipelined bit-serial FIR and IIR filters with constant coefficients. The CSD representation has been presented for the design of low-cost, high-speed constant multipliers. Latency reduction in serial and parallel computations using associativity and tree-height reduction has been discussed. Finally, the bit-level implementation schemes for vector-vector multiplication based on the distributed arithmetic approach has been addressed. Residue arithmetic [23], which is often used for implementation of FIR digital filters and transforms, is beyond the scope of this book.

Digit-serial architectures are also attractive for discrete wavelet transforms, where higher levels of wavelet can be implemented using smaller digit sizes [24]. For example, in a 3-level wavelet, digit-sizes $W/2$, $W/4$ and $W/8$ can be used for levels 1, 2, and 3, respectively. Higher levels require less computation rates and can be implemented using fewer hardware, assuming use of a single clock in the system. Traditionally, digit-serial multipliers are designed by folding bit-parallel multipliers, or unfolding bit-serial multipliers. Some resulting digit-serial architectures cannot be pipelined at the bit-level. A novel *cell replacement* transformation technique presented in [25] can be used to design low-power bit-level pipelined digit-serial multipliers from bit-serial multipliers.

13.9 PROBLEMS

1. (a) Verify that the circuit in Fig. 13.39 implements a binary full-adder.

   (b) The adder circuit in Fig. 13.39 uses 32 transistors. Derive an optimized architecture using CMOS-transmission gates with only 24 transistors (Hint: Try to share hardware of sum and carry parts).

   (c) What is the number of transistors in the critical path of an 8-bit carry-ripple adder?

2. Consider the addition of 2 two's complement 8-bit numbers X and Y in a ripple-carry manner as shown in Fig. 13.40.

   Derive a truth table and logic circuit for detecting overflow for this adder using the bits x_7, y_7, c_7, c_8, and s_7. (Hint: If $x_7 \neq y_7$, i.e., the sign bits

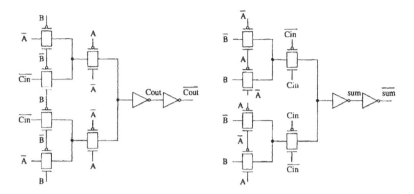

Fig. 13.39 Schematic of a complementary pass-transistor logic based CMOS full-adder.

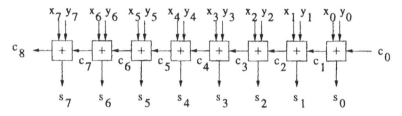

Fig. 13.40 Eight-bit ripple carry adder in Problem 2.

of X and Y are different, then there can never be overflow. If $x_7 = y_7$, then overflow occurs if $x_7 = y_7 \neq s_7$.)

3. Design bit-parallel architectures for computation of

$$y(n) = \sum_{i=0}^{5} x_i(n) \qquad (13.32)$$

using

(a) carry-save arithmetic and

(b) tree-height reduction technique,

using half and full adders and a VMA. Assume a wordlength of 8. Compute the latencies of these architectures without including the latency of the VMA.

4. This problem considers the derivation of the Baugh-Wooley multiplication algorithm shown in Fig. 13.8. Consider the 4×4-bit multiplication operation $X = A \times B$, where $A = a_3.a_2a_1a_0 = -a_3 + a_2 2^{-1} + a_1 2^{-2} + a_0 2^{-3}$, $B = b_3.b_2b_1b_0 = -b_3 + b_2 2^{-1} + b_1 2^{-2} + b_0 2^{-3}$.

Multiplying A and B is equivalent to perform

$$
\begin{aligned}
P &= (-a_3 + a_2 2^{-1} + a_1 2^{-2} + a_0 2^{-3})(-b_3 + b_2 2^{-1} + b_1 2^{-2} + b_0 2^{-3}) \\
&= (a_3 b_3 + (a_2 2^{-1} + a_1 2^{-2} + a_0 2^{-3})(b_2 2^{-1} + b_1 2^{-2} + b_0 2^{-3})) \\
&\quad -(a_3(b_2 2^{-1} + b_1 2^{-2} + b_0 2^{-3}) + (a_2 2^{-1} + a_1 2^{-2} + a_0 2^{-3})b_3).
\end{aligned}
\tag{13.33}
$$

(a) Prove that

$$
\begin{aligned}
&-(a_3(b_2 2^{-1} + b_1 2^{-2} + b_0 2^{-3}) + (a_2 2^{-1} + a_1 2^{-2} + a_0 2^{-3})b_3) \\
&= (\overline{a_3 b_2} + \overline{a_2 b_3})2^{-1} + (\overline{a_3 b_1} + \overline{a_1 b_3} + 1)2^{-2} + (\overline{a_3 b_0} + \overline{a_0 b_3})2^{-3},
\end{aligned}
\tag{13.34}
$$

where $\bar{a} = 1 - a$, for $a = 0$ or 1. Hint: The product of 2 numbers within the range $[-1, 1)$ should still be within this range. Hence, the nonzero bits at higher bit positions can be ignored.

(b) Using equations (13.33) and (13.34), and associativity property to rearrange all the terms involved in this multiplication, derive the Baugh-Wooley multiplication table shown in Fig. 13.8.

5. The Baugh-Wooley multiplication algorithm can also be implemented as follows:

$$
\begin{aligned}
P &= (-a_3 + a_2 2^{-1} + a_1 2^{-2} + a_0 2^{-3})(-b_3 + b_2 2^{-1} + b_1 2^{-2} + b_0 2^{-3}) \\
&= a_3 b_3 + (a_2 2^{-1} + a_1 2^{-2} + a_0 2^{-3})(b_2 2^{-1} + b_1 2^{-2} + b_0 2^{-3}) \\
&\quad + \overline{a_3} + (a_3 \overline{b_2} 2^{-1} + a_3 \overline{b_1} 2^{-2} + a_3 \overline{b_0} 2^{-3}) + a_3 2^{-3} \\
&\quad + \overline{b_3} + (\overline{a_2} b_3 2^{-1} + \overline{a_1} b_3 2^{-2} + \overline{a_0} b_3 2^{-3}) + b_3 2^{-3}
\end{aligned}
\tag{13.35}
$$

by rewriting (13.34) as

$$
\begin{aligned}
&-(a_3(b_2 2^{-1} + b_1 2^{-2} + b_0 2^{-3}) + (a_2 2^{-1} + a_1 2^{-2} + a_0 2^{-3})b_3) \\
&= a_3(-b_2 2^{-1} - b_1 2^{-2} - b_0 2^{-3}) + b_3(-a_2 2^{-1} - a_1 2^{-2} - a_0 2^{-3}).
\end{aligned}
\tag{13.36}
$$

Prove the Baugh-Wooley multiplication algorithm in (13.35) and derive the multiplication table for this algorithm. (Hint: Use the fact that $\sum_{i=1}^{3} -b_{3-i} 2^{-i} = \sum_{i=1}^{3}(1 - b_i)2^{-i} - 1 + 2^{-3}$.)

6. Consider the computation of

$$
x(n) + f x(n - 1) + g x(n - 2).
\tag{13.37}
$$

Using Baugh-Wooley multiplication algorithm and two's complement representation, draw the interleaved bit-parallel floor-plan architecture for this computation with

(a) bit-level pipelining, and

(b) 2-bit-level pipelining

for signals and coefficients of wordlength of 4.

7. Using the multiplication chart in Fig. 13.13, design a 2-bit-level pipelined bit-parallel architecture using modified bit-plane technique for the computation in Problem 6.

8. Show detailed schedules for the bit-serial multiplier in Fig. 13.19 and verify its correctness.

9. Show detailed schedules for the bit-serial Baugh-Wooley multiplier in Fig. 13.23 and verify the correctness of this architecture.

10. Find appropriate projection vector, scheduling vector, and processor space vector to design a bit-level pipelined version of Lyon's bit-serial carry-ripple multiplier from the DG in Fig. 13.3. This multiplier should be a pipelined version of the multiplier in Fig. 13.17. Complete the details of the design and show the switching instances of all multiplexers in the multiplier.

11. This problem is concerned with design of complete architecture for a bit-serial 5-level recoding-based modified Booth multiplier for a wordlength of 12 using Horner's rule expansion. Use the notation where the radix point is to the right of the msb (or sign bit) and bit number 11 is the msb and bit number 0 is the lsb.

(a) To obtain the recoded signal

$$y_i' = -2y_{2i+1} + y_{2i} + y_{2i-1}, \qquad (13.38)$$

we need to derive three control signals A_i, B_i, and C_i. $C_i = 1$ implies y_i' is negative, and $C_i = 0$ implies y_i' is nonnegative. $B_i = 1$ implies $|y_i'| = 2$ and $A_i = 1$ implies $|y_i'| = 1$. Draw the Karnaugh map for A_i, $B_{i,}$, and C_i and prove that

$$\begin{aligned} A_i &= y_{2i} \oplus y_{2i-1} \\ B_i &= (y_{2i+1} \oplus y_{2i})\overline{(y_{2i} \oplus y_{2i-1})} \\ C_i &= y_{2i+1}, \end{aligned} \qquad (13.39)$$

where the symbol $\oplus$ denotes exclusive OR, and the overbar indicates complementation. Using A_i, B_i and C_i, design the modified Booth recoding unit.

Table 13.5   Truth Table for Low-Power Booth Recoding Circuitry in Problem 12

y_{2j+1}	y_{2j}	y_{2j-1}	y_j'	neg	$x1$	$x2$	zp
0	0	0	0	0	0	1	1
0	0	1	1	0	1	0	*
0	1	0	1	0	1	0	*
0	1	1	2	0	0	1	0
1	0	0	-2	1	0	1	0
1	0	1	-1	1	1	0	*
1	1	0	-1	1	1	0	*
1	1	1	0	1	0	1	1

(b) Draw the complete modified Booth recoded bit-serial multiplier architecture and show all switching instances.

12. This problem considers design of a Booth recoding circuit for low power. The control circuitry for Booth recoding in Problem 11 contains only two XOR gates and one inverter. However, the generation of the control signals A_i, B_i, and C_i through different logic levels with different propagation delay time leads to an increase in the glitching activity in the partial product generation and accumulation circuit, hence leading to high power dissipation. Glitching and power consumption can be reduced by using a redundant recoding scheme, which balances the paths from each input to the outputs of the control circuitry [11].

Consider the multiplication $A \times Y$, and denote the recoded multiplier bits as y_j'. Four control signals are used in the new *race-free* Booth recoder, neg, $x1$, $x2$ and zp. $neg = 1$ implies y_j' is negative, and $neg = 0$ implies y_j' is nonnegative. $x1 = 1$ implies $|y_j'| = 1$; $x2 = \overline{x1}$. zp distinguishes $|y_j'| = 2$ from $|y_j'| = 0$. The new recoding scheme is summarized in the Table 13.5, where * denotes a *don't-care* condition. One bit-slice of the partial product generator obtained using this recoding scheme is shown in Fig. 13.41.

(a) Prove that the circuit in Fig. 13.41 generates the correct partial products for the Booth multiplication.

(b) Derive the Booth recoder (control) circuit such that the propagation delay of all paths from each input bit, including y_{2j+1}, y_{2j}, y_{2j-1}, a_i and a_{i-1}, to each bit of the partial product, Ay_j', are equal and are limited by one XOR/XNOR gate delay, one AND gate delay, and one NOR gate delay. The *don't care* conditions in zp signal can be used for logic minimization. Show those zp values that you use to substitute the *don't-care* conditions.

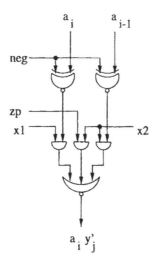

Fig. 13.41 One bit slice partial product generator for the *race-free* Booth multiplier in Problem 12.

13. Obtain a 2-unfolded carry-ripple digit-serial multiplier by unfolding the Lyon's multiplier in Fig. 13.17.

14. This problem is concerned with fixed-point bit-serial and digit-serial implementation of an all-pole second-order recursive filter

$$y(n) = -\frac{7}{8}y(n-1) + \frac{3}{4}y(n-2) + x(n).$$

Assume the signal wordlength to be 8 (i.e., the wordlengths for y and x are 8 bits). Assume the coefficient $-7/8$ is encoded as 1.001 and 3/4 is encoded as 0.11. In the multiplication with respect to coefficients, only multiplication with respect to nonzero bits is carried out.

(a) Draw the block diagram of the computation by exploiting associativity. The inner loop bound of your architecture should be limited by 1 multiply-add time.

(b) Design a functionally correct bit-level pipelined bit-serial architecture for the structure in part (a).

(c) The loop latency in part (b) imposes a constraint on the minimum wordlength for the signals y and x. What is the minimum feasible signal wordlength for the system in part (b)?

15. This problem considers bit-serial implementation of the 3rd-order fixed-coefficient IIR filter shown in Fig. 13.42. Assume the data wordlength to be 8, filter coefficient wordlength = 4, and filter coefficients $a = -1/4$,

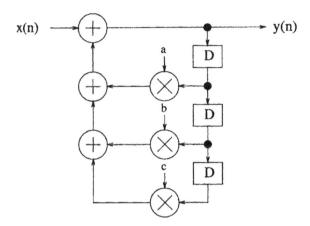

Fig. 13.42 IIR filter diagram for Problem 15.

$b = 1/8$, $c = -3/4$. Assume all numbers to be represented using two's complement representation.

(a) Obtain an equivalent structure by using associativity such that the inner loop bound is limited by 1 multiply-add time.

(b) Complete the bit-level pipelined bit-serial design of the structure in part (a). Treat minimization of delay elements in the design as a secondary objective.

16. This problem addresses a bit-level pipelined bit-serial implementation of the recursive computation

$$y(n) = \frac{3}{16}y(n-1) + \frac{5}{8}y(n-2) + \frac{1}{2}x(n)$$

using two's complement representation and a signal wordlength of 10. The bit-serial design must use Horner's rule to improve accuracy in the precision available. Associativity must be exploited so that the loop bound of the inner loop is limited by 1 multiply and 1 add time at the word level. Design the bit-serial architecture for a signal wordlength of 10. What is the minimum feasible wordlength for this computation?

17. Consider the bit-serial implementation of the computation

$$y(n) = 0.25y(n-1) + x(n) \tag{13.40}$$

shown in Fig. 13.43.

What wordlength has been used in the circuit? For this wordlength, complete the missing switching instances. Unfold this bit-serial structure by a factor of 3 to obtain a digit-serial implementation with digit size 3.

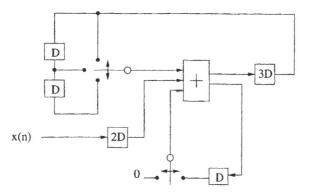

Fig. 13.43 Bit-serial implementation of the IIR filter in Problem 17.

18. This problem considers the design of a low-latency bit-serial multiplier by transforming the ripple-carry Lyon's multiplier using associativity and retiming.

   (a) Show that the architecture in Fig. 13.44(a) can be transformed to that in Fig. 13.44(b) using associativity and retiming. Compare the critical path and latencies of these 2 architectures.

   (b) Design a low-latency bit-serial multiplier by applying similar transformations as in part (a) to the Lyon's ripple-carry bit-serial multiplier or by recasting the Horner's rule multiplication equation into an appropriate form. Assume a wordlength of 12 for signal sample and the coefficient. Show all switching instances in your architecture.

   (c) Design a low latency constant bit-serial multiplier to compute $y(n) = ax(n)$, where $a = 0.01011100101$, by considering multiplication with respect to nonzero bits only using the architecture in part (b). Show all the switching instances in this architecture. Assume a signal wordlength of 12.

   (d) Based on the bit-serial multiplier derived in part (c), design a bit-serial implementation of the recursive computation $y(n) = ay(n-1) + x(n)$ for the same value of a in (c). Assume a signal wordlength of 12.

19. Obtain the CSD representation of the following two's complement numbers:

$$c_0 = 0.00010110, \quad c_1 = 0.01001100, \quad c_2 = 0.01100110,$$
$$c_3 = 0.00010110111.$$

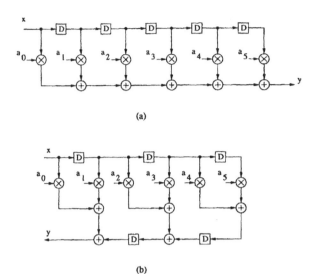

Fig. 13.44 Bit-serial multipliers in Problem 18.

20. Obtain the CSD representation of the following two's complement numbers:

$$c_0 = 1.11111111, \quad c_1 = 1.11110010, \quad c_2 = 0.01100110,$$
$$c_3 = 0.01001100111.$$

21. This problem considers a bit-serial implementation of the IIR filter

$$y(n) = a_1 y(n-1) + a_2 y(n-2) + x(n), \tag{13.41}$$

where $a_1 = 0.00011011100$ and $a_2 = 0.01001111110$.

(a) Represent the coefficients a_1 and a_2 in CSD representation.
(b) Using CSD representation and the data-flow graph in Fig. 13.27(b), obtain a bit-level pipelined bit-serial IIR filter architecture for a signal wordlength of 12. What is the minimum feasible wordlength of this architecture?
(c) Apply the Horner's rule and tree height reduction techniques to improve your design in part (b). What is the minimum feasible wordlength of this design?

22. Extend the OBC concept to implement a distributed arithmetic architecture using a ROM containing $2^N/4$ words.

23. Consider ROM decomposition with $N=16$, $K=4$. Calculate the reduction factor in ROM size. Realize the distributed arithmetic architecture using two-input accumulators and carry-save arithmetic.

24. This problem considers design of digit-serial distributed arithmetic architecture. Implement the computation

$$Y = \sum_{i=0}^{N-1} c_i x_i \qquad (13.42)$$

using a 3-bit digit-serial distributed arithmetic assuming a wordlength of 9. The bits $x_{i,3k+l}$ should be processed in the l-th ROM ($l = 0, 1, 2$) in k-th clock cycle ($k = 0, 1, 2$). Using 3 ROMs and a multi-input shift-accumulator, design the 3-bit digit-serial distributed arithmetic architecture. This architecture processes 3 consecutive input bits in a clock cycle and all input words are processed in 3 clock cycles. Assume the ROM contents to be represented using 16 bits. Design two forms of shift-accumulators using bit-parallel (i) carry-ripple and (ii) carry-save adders. The output of the shift-accumulator is represented using 16 bits. The critical path of the carry-ripple design should be $17t_{FA}$ and that of the carry-save design should be $3t_{FA}$, where t_{FA} is the propagation delay of a full adder. The carry-save design requires an additional carry-propagate adder at the end.

(a) Calculate the latencies of both designs in terms of t_{FA}.

(b) Which design is more suitable for high speed? Why?

(c) Which design is more suitable for low power? Why?

REFERENCES

1. L. B. Jackson, J. F. Kaiser, and H. S. McDonald, "An approach to implementation of digital filters," *IEEE Trans. on Audio Electroacoustics*, vol. 16, pp. 413–421, 1968.

2. P. B. Denyer and D. Renshaw, *VLSI Signal Processing: A Bit-Serial Approach*. Addison-Wesley, 1986.

3. R. Jain et al., "Custom design of a VLSI PCM-FDM transmultiplexor from system specification to circuit layout using a computer aided design system," *IEEE J. Solid State Circuits*, vol. 21, pp. 73–85, Feb. 1986.

4. K. K. Parhi, "A systematic approach for design of digit-serial processing architectures," *IEEE Trans. on Circuits and Systems*, vol. 38, no. 4, pp. 358–375, April 1991.

5. R. I. Hartley and K. K. Parhi, *Digit-Serial Computation*. Kluwer, 1995.

6. N. E. Weste and K. Eshraghian, *Principles of CMOS VLSI design: A Systems Perspective*. Addison-Wesley, 1993.

7. K. Hwang, *Computer Arithmetic: Principles, Architecture and Design*. Wiley, 1979.

8. I. Koren, *Computer Arithmetic Algorithms*. Prentice Hall, 1993.

9. C. R. Baugh and B. Wooley, "A two's complement parallel array multiplication algorithm," *IEEE Trans. on Computers*, vol. C-22, no. 12, pp. 1045–1047, Dec. 1973.

10. C. S. Wallace, "A suggestion for a fast multiplier," *IEEE Trans. on Computers*, vol. EC-13, pp. 14–17, Feb. 1964.

11. R. Fried, "Minimizing energy dissipation in high-speed multipliers," in *Proc. of ISLPED-97*, (Monterey, CA), pp. 214–219, Aug. 1997.

12. M. Hatamian and K. K. Parhi, "An 85-MHz fourth-order programmable IIR digital filter chip," *IEEE Journal of Solid State Circuits*, vol. 27, pp. 175–183, Feb. 1992.

13. T. G. Noll, "Semi-systolic maximum rate transversal filters with programmable coefficients," in *Proc. of 1986 International Conference on Systolic Arrays*, (Oxford, U.K.), pp. 5–13, July 1986.

14. R. F. Lyon, "Two's complement pipelined multipliers," *IEEE Trans. on Communications*, vol. 24, pp. 418–424, April 1976.

15. D. Ait-Boudaoud, M. K. Ibrahim, and B. R. Hayes-Gill, "Novel cell architecture for bit level systolic arrays multiplication," *IEE Proceedings-E*, vol. 138, Jan. 1991.

16. S. W. Reitwiesner, "Binary arithmetic," *Advances in Computers*, pp. 231–308, 1966.

17. M.-T. Sun, T.-C. Chen, and A.-M. Dottlieb, "VLSI implementation of a 16 × 16 discrete cosine transform chip," *IEEE Trans. on Circuits and Sytems*, vol. 36, no. 4, pp. 610–617, April 1989.

18. N. Demassieux and F. Jutand, "Orthogonal transforms," in *VLSI Implementations for Image Communications* (P. Pirsch, ed.), pp. 217–250, Elsevier, 1993.

19. A. Peled and B. Liu, "A new hardware realization of digital filters," *IEEE Trans. Acoustics, Speech, and Signal Processing*, vol. ASSP-22, no. 6, pp. 456–462, Dec. 1974.

20. C. S. Burrus, "Digital filter structures described by distributed arithmetic," *IEEE Trans. on Circuits and Systems*, Dec. 1977.

21. S. Uramoto et al, "A 100-MHz 2-D discrete cosine transform core processor," *IEEE Journal of Solid-State Circuits*, vol. 27, no. 4, pp. 492–499, April 1992.

22. Y. Katayama, I. Tamitani, A. Taniguchi, and Y. Ooi, "A single-chip MPEG1 audio/video decoder using macrocore and cell-based implementation," in *IEEE VLSI Signal Processing, VIII*, (Osaka, Japan), pp. 431–440, Oct. 1995.

23. F. J. Taylor, "Residue arithmetic: a tutorial with examples," *IEEE Trans. on Computers*, May 1984.

24. K. K. Parhi and T. Nishitani, "VLSI architectures for discrete wavelet transforms," *IEEE Trans. on VLSI Systems*, vol. 1, no. 2, pp. 191–202, June 1993.

25. Y.-N. Chang, J. H. Satyanarayana, and K. K. Parhi, "Design and implementation of low-power digit-serial multipliers," in *Proc. 1997 IEEE International Conference on Computer Design (ICCD)*, (Austin, TX), pp. 186–195, Oct. 1997.

14

Redundant Arithmetic

14.1 INTRODUCTION

In a conventional nonredundant radix-r number system, a digit can take on values $\{0, 1, \cdots, r-1\}$, and all the numbers can be represented in a unique way. A *radix-r redundant signed-digit* number system is based on a digit set $S \triangleq \{\overline{\beta}, \overline{\beta-1}, \cdots, \overline{1}, 0, 1, \cdots, \alpha\}$, where the notation $\overline{x}$ denotes $-x$, $1 \leq \beta, \alpha \leq r-1$, and the digit set S contains more than r values [1]. The last condition allows multiple representations for any number in signed-digit format, thus the name *redundant*. A symmetric signed-digit representation ($\alpha = \beta$) is generally used and considered in this chapter. For example, the digit set $\{\overline{1}, 0, 1\}$ is used for radix-2 ($r = 2$) redundant number system. In this case, the number 3 can be represented as 0011 or 010$\overline{1}$, etc. Signed-digit representations have been used in Chapter 13 in the context of CSD representation and Booth recoding; however, these representations are unique.

The attractiveness of the redundant signed-digit number systems lies in their "carry-free" addition property. This feature makes them very useful in digit-serial implementation of division and square root operations where the computations start from most significant digit (msd) first. Most significant digit (msd) first redundant arithmetic is also referred to as *on-line arithmetic*. On-line arithmetic is attractive for implementation of recursive digital filters where the carry-free property leads to low latency or high speed [2]. Note that two's complement arithmetic cannot be used for on-line arithmetic. Redundant arithmetic can also be used for least significant digit (lsd) first serial arithmetic. However, these may not be any more efficient than two's complement arithmetic.

Carry-save arithmetic also leads to a form of redundant number representation. The "carry-sum" digit in carry-save arithmetic can take values 0, 1, 2 as compared with -1, 0, 1 possible values in redundant representation for radix-2 representation. Because of the similarity between carry-save and redundant arithmetic, most redundant architectures can be adapted to carry-save case. This chapter, however, concentrates on redundant arithmetic.

This chapter starts with the basic concepts of redundant number representations and focuses on the design of arithmetic architectures in redundant number systems. Redundant number representations, including minimally and maximally redundant representations are presented in Section 14.2. Section 14.3 addresses radix-2 hybrid and signed-digit additions and subtractions. Minimally and maximally redundant radix-4 additions are discussed in Section 14.4. Design of radix-2 redundant multipliers is considered in Section 14.5. Finally, architectures for data format conversion between redundant representation and two's complement representation, in both lsd-first and msd-first modes, are described in Section 14.6.

14.2 REDUNDANT NUMBER REPRESENTATIONS

In a conventional two's complementation representation, all numbers are represented in a unique manner, thus they are nonredundant. As a consequence of nonredundancy, in a conventional addition, the carry can propagate all the way from the lsd to the msd [3]. In redundant representations, addition can be carried out in constant time independent of the wordlength W of the operands. Although the carry-ripple is limited to 2 or 3 positions to the left, redundant additions are referred to as carry-propagation-free, or simply carry-free [4],[5]. The carry-free property renders msd-first computation schemes or on-line arithmetic feasible [6] $-$[9].

A symmetric signed-digit representation uses the digit set $D_{<r.\alpha>} = \{\bar{\alpha}, \cdots, \bar{1}, 0, 1, \cdots, \alpha\}$, where r is the radix and α is the largest digit in the digit set. A number in this representation is written as:

$$X_{<r.\alpha>} \; = \; x_{W-1}.x_{W-2}\,x_{W-3} \cdots x_0 = \sum_{i=0}^{W-1} x_{W-1-i} r^i. \tag{14.1}$$

The sign of the number is given by the sign of the most significant nonzero digit.

If the number of digits in the digit set $D_{<r.\alpha>}$ is less than r, i.e., $\alpha < \frac{r-1}{2}$, the digit set is incomplete because some numbers cannot be represented. If the radix r is odd and the number of digits is equal to r, i.e., $\alpha = \frac{r-1}{2}$, the digit set is complete but not redundant, i.e., every number in the possible range is represented uniquely as it is the case for the conventional representation (Notice that for an even radix r, a signed-digit set cannot be complete and nonredundant). Finally, if the number of digits is greater than r, i.e., $\alpha \geq \lceil \frac{r}{2} \rceil$, the digit set is redundant. Moreover, if $\alpha = \lceil \frac{r}{2} \rceil$ the digit set is called *minimally redundant*, if $\alpha = r - 1$ it is called *maximally redundant*, and if $\alpha > r - 1$ it is called *over-redundant* [10],[11].

A measure of the redundancy of a signed-digit representation is the *redundancy factor*, ρ, defined as:

$$\rho = \frac{\alpha}{r - 1}. \tag{14.2}$$

Table 14.1 is a summary of the redundancy characteristics of the different signed-digit representations. Notice that the greater the redundancy factor the greater the redundancy of the representation. For example, if $\rho = \frac{1}{2}$ the digit set is complete but nonredundant (this is possible if r is odd), if $\frac{1}{2} \leq \rho < 1$ the digit set is minimally redundant, and if $\rho = 1$ the digit set is maximally redundant.

Table 14.1   Redundancy Characteristics of Signed-Digit Representations

Digit Set $D_{<r.\alpha>}$	α	Redundancy Factor ρ
Incomplete	$< \frac{r-1}{2}$	$< \frac{1}{2}$
Complete but nonredundant	$= \frac{r-1}{2}$	$= \frac{1}{2}$
Redundant	$\geq \lceil \frac{r}{2} \rceil$	$> \frac{1}{2}$
Minimally redundant	$= \lceil \frac{r}{2} \rceil$	$> \frac{1}{2}$ and < 1
Maximally redundant	$= r - 1$	$= 1$
Over-redundant	$> r - 1$	> 1

The radix-2 signed-digit representation $D_{<2.1>}$ is also referred to as signed-binary-digit (SBD), redundant-signed-digit (RSD), and borrow-save (BS) representations [4], [12]–[14].

The range of numbers that can be represented by a signed-digit representation is $\left[-\rho \left(r - r^{-W+1} \right), \rho \left(r - r^{-W+1} \right) \right]$. Notice that this range depends on both the wordlength W and the redundancy factor ρ.

14.3   CARRY-FREE RADIX-2 ADDITION AND SUBTRACTION

Redundant number representations limit the carry propagation to a few bit-positions, which is usually independent of the wordlength W. This carry-propagation-free feature enables fast addition [1]. The algorithm to carry out signed binary digit addition is not unique [5, 12],[15], and therefore its logic implementation can be diverse.

A radix-2 signed-digit number is coded using 2 unsigned binary numbers, 1 positive and 1 negative, as $X = X^+ - X^-$. Hence, each signed digit is represented using 2 bits as $x_i = x_i^+ - x_i^-$, where $x_i^+, x_i^- \in \{0, 1\}$ and $x_i \in \{\bar{1}, 0, 1\}$ [4],[13]. This section considers radix-2 hybrid and signed-digit additions and subtractions. In a hybrid operation, 1 input operand and the output operand are in redundant signed-digit representation, and the 2nd input operand is a conventional unsigned number. A signed-digit addition can be viewed as a concatenation of one hybrid addition and one hybrid subtraction.

14.3.1 Hybrid Radix-2 Addition

Consider the addition of a radix-2 signed-digit number $X_{<2.1>}$ and an unsigned conventional number Y

$$S_{<2.1>} = X_{<2.1>} + Y \tag{14.3}$$

where $X_{<r.\alpha>} = x_{W-1} . x_{W-2} x_{W-3} \cdots x_0, Y_{<b.\alpha>} = y_{W-1} . y_{W-2} y_{W-3} \cdots y_0$, and $x_i \in \{\bar{1}, 0, 1\}$ and $y_i \in \{0, 1\}$. This addition can be carried out in 2 steps.

The 1st step is carried out in parallel for all bit positions i ($0 \leq i \leq W - 1$). An intermediate sum $p_i = x_i + y_i$ is computed, which lies in the range $\{\bar{1}, 0, 1, 2\}$. This addition is expressed as

$$x_i + y_i = p_i = 2t_i + u_i, \tag{14.4}$$

where t_i is the *transfer digit* and has value either 0 or 1, and is denoted as t_i^+; u_i is the *interim sum* and has value either $\bar{1}$ or 0, and is denoted as $-u_i^-$. The least significant transfer digit t_{-1} is assigned the value zero, the same as the most significant interim sum digit u_W.

In the 2nd step, the sum digits s_i is formed by combining t_{i-1}^+ and u_i^- as 1 digit:

$$s_i = t_{i-1}^+ - u_i^- . \tag{14.5}$$

Table 14.2 summarizes the digit sets involved in hybrid radix-2 addition ($S_{<2.1>} = X_{<2.1>} + Y$). The last column of the table corresponds to the binary encoding of the digits.

Replacing the corresponding binary codes in Table 14.2 to (14.4), we get:

$$x_i^+ - x_i^- + y_i^+ = 2t_i^+ - u_i^- . \tag{14.6}$$

This arithmetic operation can be performed by a generalized type-1 full adder [16], known as plus-plus-minus adder (PPM) [4]. The sum digit can be formulated by simply combining the two wires t_{i-1}^+ and u_i^- as 1 digit, hence, $s_i = s_i^+ - s_i^- = t_{i-1}^+ - u_i^-$. Fig. 14.1 shows the structure of an 8-digit parallel hybrid radix-2 adder. Notice that the sum has 9 digits, i.e., 1 more digit than the addends.

Table 14.2   Digit Sets Involved in Hybrid Radix-2 Addition

Digit	Radix 2 Digit Set	Binary Code
x_i	$\{\bar{1}, 0, 1\}$	$x_i^+ - x_i^-$
y_i	$\{0, 1\}$	y_i^+
$p_i = x_i + y_i$	$\{\bar{1}, 0, 1, 2\}$	$\cdots$
u_i	$\{\bar{1}, 0\}$	$-u_i^-$
t_i	$\{0, 1\}$	t_i^+
$s_i = u_i + t_{i-1}$	$\{\bar{1}, 0, 1\}$	$s_i^+ - s_i^-$

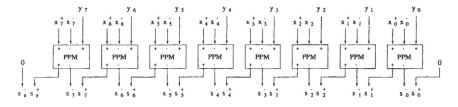

Fig. 14.1   Eight-digit hybrid radix-2 adder.

Hybrid redundant addition can also be carried out serially using one PPM adder. Digit-serial hybrid adders can be obtained by folding (see Chapter 6) the parallel adder in both lsd-first and msd-first modes. The lsd-first and msd-first digit-serial hybrid redundant adders are shown in Fig. 14.2(a) and (b), respectively. The lsd-first adder has zero latency and the msd-first adder has a latency of 1 clock cycle. For 8-digit addition the sum has 9 digits, hence, a zero digit needs to be inserted between 2 consecutive input operands and one addition takes 9 clock cycles. The inserted zero digit also generates the zero bits in the sum digits at lsd and msd positions.

14.3.2   Hybrid Radix-2 Subtraction

In hybrid subtraction, an unsigned conventional number Y is subtracted from a signed-digit radix-r number. The computation $S_{<2.1>} = X_{<2.1>} - Y$ can be carried out in a way similar to hybrid addition. The difference is that a negative transfer digit t_i is used here.

In the first step, an intermediate difference $p_i = x_i - y_i$ is computed digit-independently, which lies in the range $\{\bar{2}, \bar{1}, 0, 1\}$ and is expressed using the

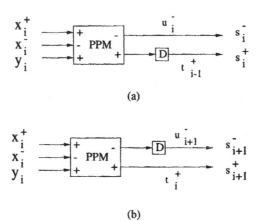

(a)

(b)

Fig. 14.2 Digit-serial hybrid radix-2 redundant adders. (a) Lsd-first adder; (b) msd-first adder.

following equation:

$$x_i - y_i = p_i = 2t_i + u_i, \tag{14.7}$$

where the transfer digit t_i has value either $\bar{1}$ or 0, and is denoted as $-t_i^-$, the interim difference u_i has value either 0 or 1, and is denoted as u_i^+. In the 2nd step, the sum digit s_i is formed by combining t_{i-1}^- and u_i^+ as 1 digit:

$$s_i = -t_{i-1}^- + u_i^+. \tag{14.8}$$

Table 14.3 lists the digit sets involved in hybrid radix-2 subtraction.

Table 14.3 Digit Sets Involved in Hybrid Radix-2 Subtraction

Digit	Radix 2 Digit Set	Binary Code
x_i	$\{\bar{1}, 0, 1\}$	$x_i^+ - x_i^-$
y_i	$\{0, 1\}$	y_i^-
$p_i = x_i - y_i$	$\{\bar{2}, \bar{1}, 0, 1\}$	$\ldots$
u_i	$\{0, 1\}$	u_i^+
t_i	$\{\bar{1}, 0\}$	$-t_i^-$
$s_i = u_i + t_{i-1}$	$\{\bar{1}, 0, 1\}$	$s_i^+ - s_i^-$

Replacing the corresponding binary codes from Table 14.3 in (14.7), we get:

$$x_i^+ - x_i^- - y_i^- = -2t_i^- + u_i^+. \tag{14.9}$$

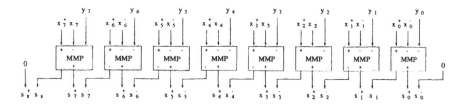

Fig. 14.3 Eight-digit hybrid radix-2 subtractor.

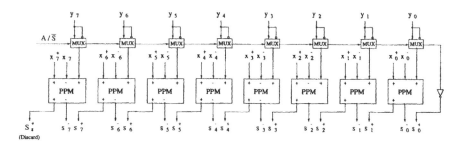

Fig. 14.4 Hybrid radix-2 adder/subtractor ($A/\overline{S} = 1$ for addition and $A/\overline{S} = 0$ for subtraction).

This arithmetic operation can be performed by a generalized type-2 full adder [16], known as minus-minus-plus adder (MMP) [4].

Furthermore, $s_i^+ = u_i^+$ and $s_i^- = t_{i-1}^-$. Therefore, step 2 of the hybrid radix-2 subtraction involves concatenation the 2 wires to form the sum digits. Fig. 14.3 shows the structure of an 8-digit parallel hybrid radix-2 subtractor.

14.3.3 Hybrid Radix-2 Addition/Subtraction

The hybrid adder (or subtractor) can add (or subtract) an unsigned number to (from) a signed-digit number. When 1 of the operands is in radix-r complement representation, i.e., two's complement representation for radix-2, hybrid subtraction can be carried out by hybrid addition where the two's complement of the subtrahend is added to the minuend and the carry-out from the most significant position is discarded. Hence, the same hardware can be used for both addition and subtraction. Fig. 14.4 shows the architecture of a hybrid radix-2 adder/subtractor.

Notice that each cell contains a two-to-one multiplexer to select either the number Y or its two's complement, depending on the operation.

14.3.4 Signed Binary Digit Addition/Subtraction

A signed-digit number is represented as $Y_{<r,\alpha>} = Y^+ - Y^-$, where Y^+ and Y^- are from the digit set $\{0, 1, \cdots, \alpha\}$. Therefore, a signed-digit number can be considered as the subtraction of 2 unsigned conventional numbers. Signed-digit addition can, therefore, be computed by sequentially performing hybrid addition and hybrid subtraction as follows:

$$\begin{aligned}
S_{<r,\alpha>} &= X_{<r,\alpha>} + Y_{<r,\alpha>} = X_{<r,\alpha>} + Y^+ - Y^-, \\
\Rightarrow \quad & S1_{<r,\alpha>} = X_{<r,\alpha>} + Y^+, \\
& S_{<r,\alpha>} = S1_{<r,\alpha>} - Y^-.
\end{aligned} \tag{14.10}$$

Fig. 14.5 illustrates such an approach for the case of radix-2. The figure also shows that the same hardware can be used to perform SBD addition as well as subtraction by simply including, in every position, a single two-by-two switching box [17], controlled by a suitable add/subtract control signal ($A/\overline{S}$). This is due to the fact that $-Y_{<2,1>} = Y^- - Y^+$, i.e., the sign of an SBD number can be easily changed by just exchanging the positive bit and the negative bit of the code of each signed-binary-digit. The critical path of the 2 adders in this design can be slow for some applications. A high-speed SBD addition circuit presented in [18] can be used in these cases.

Digit-serial SBD adders can be derived by folding (see Chapter 6) the digit-parallel adders in both lsd-first and msd-first modes, and their corresponding architectures are shown in Fig. 14.6. The lsd-first adder has zero latency and the msd-first adder has a latency of 2 clock cycles. For 8-digit addition the sum has 9 digits, hence, a zero digit needs to be inserted between 2 consecutive input operands and 1 addition takes 9 clock cycles.

It is clear that combined hybrid adder/subtractor is more efficient than the Signed-Binary-Digit adder/subtractor. The hardware cost of the hybrid radix-2 adder/subtractor is half of the SBD adder/subtractor.

14.4 HYBRID RADIX-4 ADDITION

In iterative or serial implementations of arithmetic operations, higher order radices can be employed to reduce the number of iteration cycles. Radix-4 is very appealing because it halves the number of iteration steps with regard to radix-2 and, in principle, is not much more complex to implement than radix-2.

This section considers the design of hybrid radix-4 addition. Designs of radix-4 architectures for subtraction or addition/subtraction are left as exercises to the reader. Radix-4 redundant signed-digit sets can be *maximally redundant* based on digit set $D_{<4.3>}$ or *minimally redundant* based on digit set $D_{<4.2>}$.

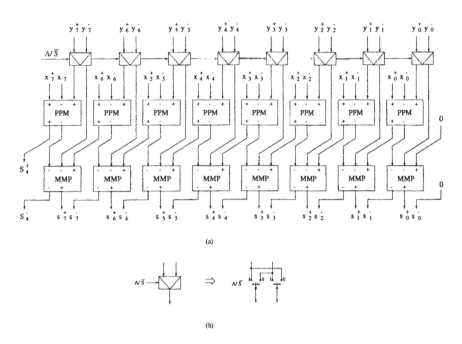

(a)

(b)

Fig. 14.5 (a) Signed binary digit adder/subtractor. (b) Definition of the switching box.

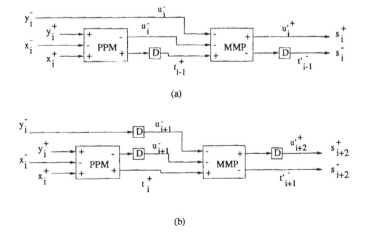

(a)

(b)

Fig. 14.6 Digit-serial SBD redundant adders. (a) Lsd-first adder; (b) msd-first adder.

14.4.1   Maximally Redundant Hybrid Radix-4 Addition

Hybrid radix-4 addition can be carried out in a way similar to the hybrid radix-2 addition. Table 14.4 summarizes the digit sets used in maximally redundant hybrid radix-4 addition (MRHY4A) $S_{<4.3>} = X_{<4.3>} + Y_4$. The last column of the table lists the binary codes assigned to the digits. Notice that the binary codes of the digits x_i and $s_i \in D_{<4.3>}$, and $y_i \in D_4$, correspond to the weighted addition of 2 consecutive radix-2 digits.

Table 14.4   Digit Sets Involved in Maximally Redundant Hybrid Radix-4 Addition

Digit	Radix 4 Digit Set	Binary Code
x_i	$\{\bar{3}, \bar{2}, \bar{1}, 0, 1, 2, 3\}$	$2x_i^{+2} - 2x_i^{-2} + x_i^+ - x_i^-$
y_i	$\{0, 1, 2, 3\}$	$2y_i^{+2} + y_i^+$
$p_i = x_i + y_i$	$\{\bar{3}, \bar{2}, \bar{1}, 0, 1, 2, 3, 4, 5, 6\}$	$\cdots$
u_i	$\{\bar{3}, \bar{2}, \bar{1}, 0, 1, 2\}$	$2u_i^{+2} - 2u_i^{-2} - u_i^-$
t_i	$\{0, 1\}$	t_i^+
$s_i = u_i + t_{i-1}$	$\{\bar{3}, \bar{2}, \bar{1}, 0, 1, 2, 3\}$	$2s_i^{+2} - 2s_i^{-2} + s_i^+ - s_i^-$

The arithmetic operation in step 1 of the hybrid addition computes

$$x_i + y_i = 4t_i + u_i. \tag{14.11}$$

Replacing the respective binary codes from Table 14.4 in (14.11), we get:

$$\left(2x_i^{+2} - 2x_i^{-2} + 2y_i^{+2}\right) + \left(x_i^+ - x_i^- + y_i^+\right) = 4t_i^+ + 2u_i^{+2} - 2u_i^{-2} - u_i^-. \tag{14.12}$$

A maximally redundant hybrid radix-4 adder cell (MRHY4A) is used for the foregoing computation. This cell contains 2 PPM adders that perform the 2 additions grouped inside the parentheses in parallel and reduce the number of bits from 6 to 4 with the weights indicated on the right-hand side of (14.12). Fig. 14.7 shows the structure of the MRHY4A cell. As can be seen, the MRHY4A cell is nothing more than 2 consecutive hybrid radix-2 adder cells.

Step 2 of the hybrid addition algorithm is defined by $s_i = u_i + t_{i-1}$. Replacing s_i, u_i and t_{i-1} by the corresponding binary codes (in Table 14.4) leads to $s_i^{+2} = u_i^{+2}$, $s_i^{-2} = u_i^{-2}$, $s_i^+ = t_{i-1}^+$, and $s_i^- = u_i^-$.

A hybrid radix-4 adder is shown in Fig. 14.8. From Fig. 14.8 and Fig. 14.1, it can be concluded that a W-digit MRHY4A has exactly the same structure as a $2W$-digit hybrid radix-2 adder.

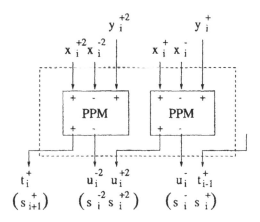

Fig. 14.7 Maximally redundant hybrid radix-4 adder cell (MRHY4A).

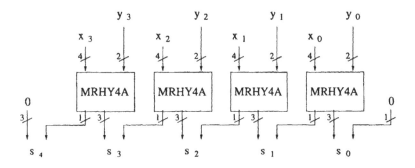

Fig. 14.8 Four-digit MRHY4A.

14.4.2 Minimally Redundant Hybrid Radix-4 Addition

Table 14.5 summarizes the digit sets used in a minimally redundant hybrid radix-4 addition (mrHY4A) $S_{<4.2>} = X_{<4.2>} + Y_4$. The last column of the table lists the binary codes assigned to the digits. Notice that the code of the digits x_i and $s_i \in D_{<4.2>}$ is represented by 3 bits, namely a negative bit of weight two and 2 positive bits of weight one.

The arithmetic operation in step 1 of the hybrid addition is described by (14.11).

Replacing the respective binary codes from Table 14.5 in (14.11), we get:

$$\left(-2x_i^{-2} + 2y_i^{+2}\right) + \left(x_i^+ + x_i^{++} + y_i^+\right) = 4t_i^+ - 2u_i^{-2} + u_i^+. \qquad (14.13)$$

Table 14.5   Digit Sets Involved in Minimally Redundant Hybrid Radix-4 Addition

Digit	Radix 4 Digit Set	Binary Code
x_i	$\{\bar{2}, \bar{1}, 0, 1, 2\}$	$-2x_i^{-2} + x_i^+ + x_i^{++}$
y_i	$\{0, 1, 2, 3\}$	$2y_i^{+2} + y_i^+$
$p_i = x_i + y_i$	$\{\bar{2}, \bar{1}, 0, 1, 2, 3, 4, 5\}$	$\cdots$
u_i	$\{\bar{2}, \bar{1}, 0, 1\}$	$-2u_i^{-2} + u_i^+$
t_i	$\{0, 1\}$	t_i^+
$s_i = u_i + t_i$	$\{\bar{2}, \bar{1}, 0, 1, 2\}$	$-2s_i^{-2} + s_i^+ + s_i^{++}$

Equation (14.13) leads to the mrHY4A cell shown in Fig. 14.9, where a full adder (FA) reduces the three bits of weight one (x_i^+, x_i^{++} and y_i^+) to two bits (u_i^+ and an intermediate carry c_i^{+2}), and then a PPM adder reduces the three bits of weight two (x_i^{-2}, y_i^{+2} and c_i^{+2}) to two new bits (t_i^+, u_i^{-2}). Notice this cell contains a local carry propagation.

In step 2 of the hybrid addition algorithm, the sum digits are generated using $s_i^{-2} = u_i^{-2}$, $s_i^+ = u_i^+$, $s_i^{++} = t_{i-1}^+$. Fig. 14.10 shows the structure of a 4-digit mrHY4A.

14.5   RADIX-2 HYBRID REDUNDANT MULTIPLICATION ARCHITECTURES

This section considers design of bit-serial radix-2 hybrid redundant number-based on-line multiplication. These redundant multipliers process the msd of the input data first and generate the msd of the result first. On-line arithmetic leads to low-latency architectures and is useful for operations such as division and square root which are inherently msd-first operations.

Consider multiplication of 2 numbers, $A = a_3.a_2a_1a_0$ and $B = b_3.b_2b_1b_0$, using the 2 multiplication dependence graphs (DGs) shown in Fig. 14.11 and Fig. 14.12. The basic processing element (the black solid circle in the DGs) carries out an add operation defined by the following equation :

$$a_i * b_j + carry_{in} + sum_{in} = 2 * carry_{out} + sum_{out} \tag{14.14}$$

where the dashed lines represent carry and the solid lines represent sum. The elliptic circles on the last row are dummy operations used only to group the bits together to form the product digits. In the DG of Fig. 14.11, the carry moves vertically down whereas it moves diagonally in the DG of Fig. 14.12

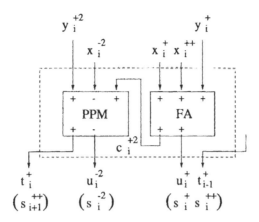

Fig. 14.9 Minimally Redundant HYbrid radix-4 Adder cell (*mrHY4A*).

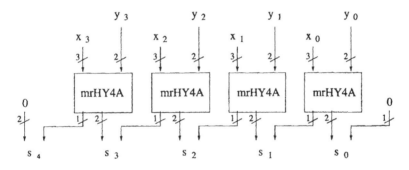

Fig. 14.10 Four-digit mrHY4A.

[19].

Using systolic design methodology (see Chapter 7), and the following projection vector, the processor space vector, and the scheduling vector

$$d = \begin{pmatrix} 1 \\ 0 \end{pmatrix}, \quad p^T = (\ 0 \quad 1\ ), \quad s^T = (\ 1 \quad 0\ ), \qquad (14.15)$$

we have the following edge mappings for the DG in Fig. 14.11:

e	$p^T e$	$s^T e$
a (1, 0)	0	1
b (0, 1)	1	0
carry (0, 1)	1	0
sum (1, 1)	1	1

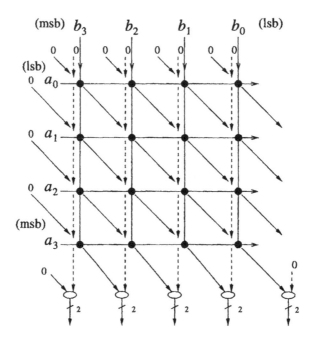

Fig. 14.11 Multiplication DG with vertical carry.

and the edge mappings for the DG in Fig. 14.12:

e	$p^T e$	$s^T e$
a (1, 0)	0	1
b (0, 1)	1	0
carry (1, 2)	2	1
sum (1, 1)	1	1
carry' (0, 1)	1	0

where "*carry'*" denotes the vertical carry edges in the last 2 rows.

The resulting bit-serial multipliers are shown in Fig. 14.13 and Fig. 14.14, respectively. They can be used to perform hybrid multiplication, as well as signed-digit multiplication, depending on the coding of the multiplicand and multiplier bits, and the definition of the single digit add operation in (14.14). In this section, hybrid radix-2 redundant multiplication is considered, where the multiplicand B is assumed to be a radix-2 redundant number, the multiplier A is assumed to be in two's complement representation. In this case, the sum and carry signals are restricted to the digit set $\{\bar{1}, 0\}$ or $\{0, 1\}$. Hence, each digit obtained by concatenating the sum bit and carry bit from the lower order position (in the last row in the DGs) is in the set of $\{\bar{1}, 0, 1\}$, and together they form the product in radix-2 redundant representation. Next, the detailed circuitry of the processing element (adder cell) is derived to obtain complete hybrid radix-2 multipliers.

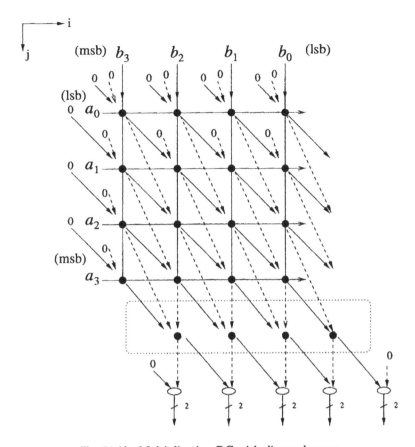

Fig. 14.12   Multiplication DG with diagonal carry.

Each digit $b_j = b_j^+ - b_j^-$ of a radix-2 redundant number B is recoded using a sign bit and a magnitude bit as follows:

b_j	$\bar{1}$	0	1
$\text{sign}(b_j)$	1	0	0
$|b_j|$	1	0	1

If the input bit b_j is positive, then the adder cell corresponding to coefficient $a_i, 0 \le i \le 2$ in Fig. 14.13 or Fig. 14.14 can be implemented as an full adder; the last adder cell, which involves the most significant sign bit of A with negative weight, carries out the following computation:

$$-a_3 * b_j + carry_{in} + sum_{in} = 2 * carry_{out} - sum_{out}, \qquad (14.16)$$

which can be implemented as a PPM adder consisting of an full adder and 2

$b_0 \, b_1 \, b_2 \, b_3$

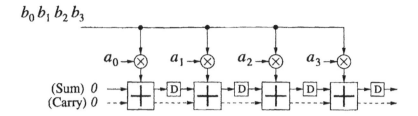

Fig. 14.13 Redundant multiplier architecture obtained from the DG of Fig. 14.11.

$b_0 \, b_1 \, b_2 \, b_3$

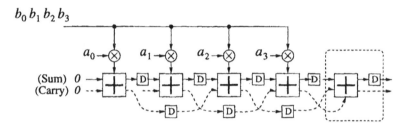

Fig. 14.14 Redundant architecture obtained from the DG of Fig. 14.12.

inverters. If the input digit b_j is negative, we have

$$-|b_j| * (-a_3 + a_2 2^{-1} + a_1 2^{-2} + a_0 2^{-3})$$
$$= \quad |b_j| * (-\bar{a}_3 + \bar{a}_2 2^{-1} + \bar{a}_1 2^{-2} + \bar{a}_0 2^{-3} + 2^{-3})$$
$$= \quad -|b_j|\bar{a}_3 + |b_j|\bar{a}_2 2^{-1} + |b_j|\bar{a}_1 2^{-2} + |b_j|\bar{a}_0 2^{-3} + |b_j| 2^{-3}. \quad (14.17)$$

Hence, the bits of A, $a_i, 0 \le i \le 3$, have to be inverted when the input b_j is negative. Combining these 2 cases, we have the following equation for the adder cells:

$$(a_i \oplus sign(b_j)) * |b_j| + carry_{in} + sum_{in}$$
$$= \quad 2 * carry_{out} + sum_{out}, \; for \; 0 \le i \le 2;$$
$$-(a_3 \oplus sign(b_j)) * |b_j| + carry_{in} + sum_{in}$$
$$= \quad 2 * carry_{out} - sum_{out}, \; for \; i = 3. \quad (14.18)$$

The detailed circuit diagrams of the 2 hybrid redundant multipliers are shown in Fig. 14.15 and Fig. 14.16. In these architectures, one guard digit 0 is required to isolate the successive processing of the input data words (and generate the 0 bit at the least significant digit position). Furthermore, as shown in Fig. 14.15 and Fig. 14.16, a *reset* signal is used to reset the latches when the next data word arrives at the input. Note that the guard digit can be eliminated at the expense of an increase in the control circuitry.

The hybrid multiplier shown in Fig. 14.16 has a critical path of 1 adder delay and has a fixed latency of 3 clock cycles, independent of the wordlength

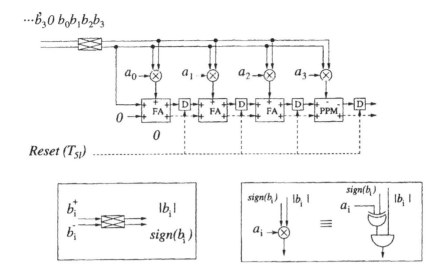

Fig. 14.15 Hybrid radix-2 redundant multiplier architecture obtained from the DG of Fig. 14.11.

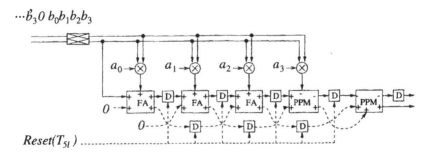

Fig. 14.16 Hybrid radix-2 redundant multiplier architecture obtained from the DG of Fig. 14.12.

W. It is the most efficient architecture in terms of critical path and computation latency. This multiplier also requires only 2 delay elements per stage. It may be noted that bit-level pipelined two's complement bit-serial multipliers require at least 3 delay elements per stage.

14.6 DATA FORMAT CONVERSION

In this section, conversion from nonredundant to redundant and vice-versa are presented for both radix-2 and radix-4 representations.

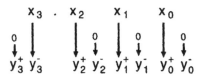

Fig. 14.17 Nonredundant to redundant radix-2 conversion for wordlength 4.

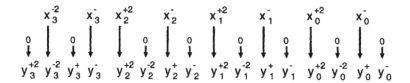

Fig. 14.18 Nonredundant to maximally redundant radix-4 conversion for wordlength 4.

14.6.1 Nonredundant to Redundant Conversion

This conversion process is relatively easy as the nonredundant input digit set is a subset of the redundant input digit set.

14.6.1.1 Radix-2 Representation Let the nonredundant number X be denoted by $X = x_3 . x_2\, x_1\, x_0$, and the corresponding redundant representation be denoted by $Y = y_3 . y_2\, y_1\, y_0$ where each digit y_i is encoded as $y_i^+ - y_i^-$ and each digit x_i represents a 1 or 0. Note that the bit x_3 has a weight -1 in two's complement number system. This conversion is shown in Fig. 14.17.

14.6.1.2 Radix-4 Representation Consider the conversion of a radix-4 complement number, X, to a maximally redundant number, Y. The digits of X, x_i, are encoded using 2 wires according to $x_i = 2x_i^{+2} + x_i^+$, and the digit y_i is encoded using $y_i = 2y_i^{+2} - 2y_i^{-2} + y_i^+ - y_i^-$. Equating the coefficients of the signal bits of similar weight, the converter in Fig. 14.18 is obtained for a wordlength of 4. Note that the sign digit x_3 can take values $-3, -2, -1$ or 0, and is encoded using $x_3 = -2x_3^{-2} - x_3^-$.

Next consider the conversion of a radix-4 complement number, X, to a radix-4 minimally redundant number, Y whose digits are encoded using $-2y_i^{-2} + y_i^+ + y_i^{++}$. This conversion is not as simple as conversion from nonredundant to maximally redundant case, because the digit for a radix-4 complement number belongs to the set $\{0, 1, 2, 3\}$ and that for a minimally redundant radix-4 representation belongs to the set $\{-2, -1, 0, 1, 2\}$. Therefore, a digit of value 3 has to be encoded using a transfer digit 1 (of value 4) and a corresponding digit -1. Similarly, the digit 2 is also reduced to a

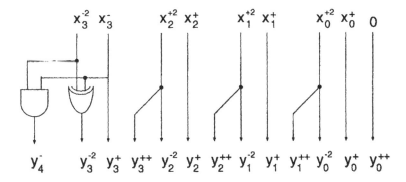

Fig. 14.19 Nonredundant to minimally redundant radix-4 conversion for wordlength 4.

transfer digit 1 and a corresponding digit -2. In general, if a radix-r number, x, is converted to $y_{< r.\alpha >}$, the digits in the range $[\alpha,\ r-1]$ are encoded using a transfer digit 1 and a corresponding digit $x_i - r$ where x_i is the i-th digit of x. This is equivalent to rewriting

$$2x_i^{+2} + x_i^+ \;=\; 4x_i^{+2} - 2x_i^{+2} + x_i^+ \qquad (14.19)$$
$$=\; y_{i+1}^{++} - 2y_i^{-2} + y_i^+.$$

The converter is described by the equations:

$$y_i^{-2} = x_i^{+2}, \quad y_i^+ = x_i^+, \quad y_{i+1}^{++} = x_i^{+2}. \qquad (14.20)$$

The converter for a wordlength of 4 is shown in Fig. 14.19. Note that a most significant value of -3 is not permitted for conversion without overflow.

14.7   REDUNDANT TO NONREDUNDANT CONVERTER

The problem of converting a redundant number to a nonredundant number is nontrivial and more interesting. For example, consider a radix-4 digit in maximally redundant format transmitted msd first, where the digits can take on values from the set $\{-3, -2, -1, 0, 1, 2, 3\}$. The problem is to transform this number into a parallel nonredundant number. It is important to note that in general it is not possible to know the value of any of the nonredundant digits until the least significant redundant digit becomes available. For example, consider the redundant number $1000\bar{1}$. In nonredundant radix-4 format this number is expressed as $(03333)_4$. However, changing the lsd from -1 to 1, it is immediately seen that the resulting number in nonredundant radix-4 format is $(10001)_4$, which means that changing the least significant digit from -1 to 1 causes all of the preceding (more significant) digits to be changed.

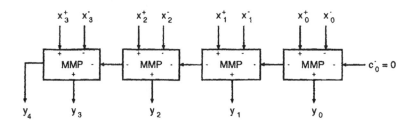

Fig. 14.20   Radix-2 redundant to nonredundant format converter operating in the lsd-first mode.

Therefore, if a redundant number is scanned msd-first and transformed to a nonredundant radix-4 format, it is impossible to output a single digit of the result until the lsd of the input has been processed.

14.7.1   LSD-First Conversion

The conversion process from redundant to nonredundant format in lsd-first mode can be carried out by considering x^+ and x^- as 2 independent unsigned numbers and subtracting x^- from x^+ as follows:

$$x_i^+ - x_i^- - c_i = -2c_{i+1} + s_i, \qquad (14.21)$$

where an MMP adder is used at each bit position.

A simple lsd-first redundant format to nonredundant format conversion circuit is shown in Fig. 14.20 for a wordlength of 4 bits. Note that the carry-out at any stage can be 0 or $\bar{1}$. Fig. 14.20 also illustrates the similarity between lsd-first redundant-to-binary conversion and binary addition.

14.7.2   MSD-First Conversion

The msd-first conversion is essential for on-line arithmetic where the digits are processed serially, 1 digit at a time, in an msd-first manner. The conversion described in this section assumes that the input digit is in radix-2 redundant format. This technique can be easily extended to any arbitrary radix input digits.

Since the converter is operated in msd-first mode, the carry-in signal at each digit is not known *a priori*. Therefore, the 2 possible output digits are computed assuming carry inputs -1 and 0, and the final output corresponding to carry input 0 is selected the output. Table 14.6 shows how the output is computed for a given input digit and two possible values of carry-in (note that the higher order bit in the box is the carry output).

the higher order bit in the box is the carry output).

Table 14.6 Conversion Mapping of a Radix-2 Redundant Number to a Nonredundant (Two's Complement) Number

Carry-In	$\bar{1}$	0	1
0	$\boxed{\bar{1}}\,1$	$\boxed{0}\,0$	$\boxed{0}\,1$
$\bar{1}$	$\boxed{\bar{1}}\,0$	$\boxed{\bar{1}}\,1$	$\boxed{0}\,0$

In this conversion, two partial results, X_i^0 and $X_i^{\bar{1}}$ (for $-1 \le i \le W-1$), are computed iteratively assuming the carry input equal to 0 and $\bar{1}$, respectively, with the initial value $X_{-1}^0 = 0$ and $X_{-1}^{\bar{1}} = 1$. The final result is X_{W-1}^0. During the conversion, at step i, X_i^0 and $X_i^{\bar{1}}$ are updated by selecting X_{i-1}^0 or $X_{i-1}^{\bar{1}}$ and by appending 0 or 1 based on the rule in Table 14.6. This updating procedure is summarized in Table 14.7, where *minus* and *plus* are used to select X_{i-1}^0 if *plus* $= 1$ or $X_{i-1}^{\bar{1}}$ if *minus* $= 1$. *Minus* is 1 if input digit is $\bar{1}$ and *plus* is 1 if input digit is 1. If the input digit is $\bar{1}$, the second column in Table 14.6 implies that the carry output is always equal to $\bar{1}$, no matter what the carry input is. Hence, *minus* is set to 1 and $X_{i-1}^{\bar{1}}$ is used for updating. The bits 1 and 0 are appended to $X_{i-1}^{\bar{1}}$ to form X_i^0 and $X_i^{\bar{1}}$, respectively, assuming possible carry inputs 0 and $\bar{1}$. If the input digit is 1, the 4th column in Table 14.6 implies that the carry output is always equal to 0. Hence, *plus* is set to 1 and X_{i-1}^0 is used for updating. Bits 1 and 0 are appended to X_{i-1}^0 to form X_i^0 and $X_i^{\bar{1}}$, respectively, for possible carry inputs 0 and $\bar{1}$. In the case when the input signal is 0, the 3rd column in Table 14.6 implies that X_i^0 and $X_i^{\bar{1}}$ can be obtained by appending a 0 and 1 to X_{i-1}^0 and $X_{i-1}^{\bar{1}}$, respectively.

Table 14.7 Computation of the Output Digit During the Conversion of a Radix-2 Redundant to a Nonredundant Number Operating in the MSD-First Mode

Input Digit	X_i^0	$X_i^{\bar{1}}$	*Minus*	*Plus*
$\bar{1}$	$X_{i-1}^{\bar{1}} + 1 \cdot 2^{-i}$	$X_{i-1}^{\bar{1}} + 0 \cdot 2^{-i}$	1	0
0	$X_{i-1}^0 + 0 \cdot 2^{-i}$	$X_{i-1}^{\bar{1}} + 1 \cdot 2^{-i}$	0	0
1	$X_{i-1}^0 + 1 \cdot 2^{-i}$	$X_{i-1}^0 + 0 \cdot 2^{-i}$	0	1

Example 14.7.1 *Using Table 14.7, the radix-2 number $1\bar{1}0\bar{1}$ can be converted to nonredundant representation as outlined in Table 14.8.* ∎

Table 14.8 Example Showing the Conversion of a Radix-2 Redundant Number to a Nonredundant Number

k	Input Digit	X_i^0	$X_i^{\bar{1}}$
-	-	0	$\bar{1}$
0	1	0 1	0 0
1	$\bar{1}$	0 0 1	0 0 0
2	0	0 0 1 0	0 0 0 1
3	$\bar{1}$	0 0 0 1 1	0 0 0 1 0
output $= X_3^0 = 0\ 0\ 0\ 1\ 1 = 3_{10}$			

From Example 14.7.1 and Table 14.8, it is clear that a W-digit radix-2 redundant number is converted to a $(W+1)$-digit two's complement number.

In order to design the converter, 2 basic cells, the $COPY$ cell and the $APPEND$ cell [20] are required. Depending on the values of the current input signed digit, the $APPEND$ cell generates the select signals *minus* and *plus*, and 2 output bits based on the input digit and both possible values of the carry-in signal. Depending on the values of the *minus* and *plus* select signals, the $COPY$ cell selects either X_{i-1}^0 or $X_{i-1}^{\bar{1}}$. The logic equation of the $COPY$ and the $APPEND$ cells can be derived from Table 14.7 as follows:

$$minus = \overline{x_i^+ x_i^-} \tag{14.22}$$
$$plus = x_i^+ \overline{x_i^-}$$
$$x_i^{\bar{1}} = \overline{x_i^+ \oplus x_i^-}$$
$$x_i^0 = x_i^+ \oplus x_i^-,$$

where $x_i^{\bar{1}}$ denotes the output bit (to be used to update $X_i^{\bar{1}}$) assuming a carry-in of $\bar{1}$, and x_i^0 denotes the output bit (to be used to update X_i^0) assuming a carry-in of 0. Based on these equations, the $COPY$ and the $APPEND$ cells are designed as shown in Fig. 14.21(a) and (b), respectively.

The DG of a radix-2 redundant to nonredundant converter for a wordlength of 4 digits operating in the msd-first mode is shown in Fig. 14.22 (in solid lines). This triangular DG in solid lines is extended to a parallelogram (with dummy cells in dashed lines) in order to obtain a digit-serial msd-first converter using systolic mapping (see Chapter 7). The dummy cells in dashed line are degenerated $COPY$ cells, which simply pass the inputs to the outputs on the next row. Using the projection vector, processor vector, and scheduling

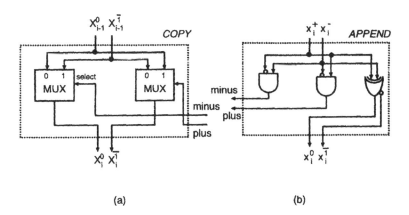

Fig. 14.21 (a) *COPY* cell (b) *APPEND* cell used in the conversion of a radix-2 redundant number to a nonredundant number.

vector

$$\mathbf{d} = \begin{pmatrix} 1 \\ 0 \end{pmatrix}, \quad \mathbf{p}^T = \begin{pmatrix} 0 & 1 \end{pmatrix}, \quad \mathbf{s}^T = \begin{pmatrix} 1 & 0 \end{pmatrix},$$

a serial msd-first converter can be derived. Its block diagram is shown in Fig. 14.23 and its detailed design is shown in Fig. 14.24. The reset signal in Fig. 14.24 is set to 1 at clock cycle $T = 5l$ (and 0 otherwise) such that the registers in the bottom row have the same contents as the top row, the bits of the two's complement number X_3^0. This ensures the bits of X_3^0 are output in the following cycles independent of subsequent *minus* and *plus* values.

14.8   CONCLUSIONS

This chapter has presented the basic concepts of redundant number systems and redundant arithmetic, which leads to carry-free addition property. Algorithms and architectures for hybrid radix-2 and radix-4 addition/subtraction, as well as signed-digit addition/subtraction have been developed. Two msd-first serial hybrid radix-2 redundant multipliers have been designed, which are also suitable for on-line computations. Finally, the design of data format converters including conversion from nonredundant to redundant in radix-2 and redundant to nonredundant in lsd-first and msd-first modes has been addressed. Fast redundant to nonredundant converters can be designed by using variations of known fast carry generation schemes such as carry-select and/or binary-tree configurations (see Appendix E). Interested readers may refer to [21] for a detailed description of the design of fast low-power redun-

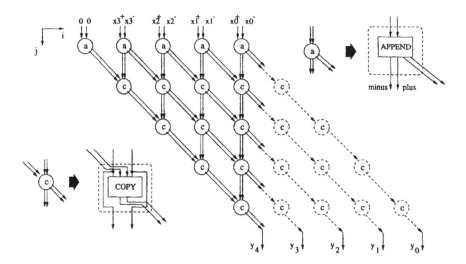

Fig. 14.22 Dependence graph for a radix-2 redundant to nonredundant converter for a wordlength of 4 digits operating in the msd-first mode.

dant to nonredundant converters, and their application to perform fast binary addition.

14.9 PROBLEMS

1. Consider the hybrid addition of a carry-save unsigned number X and an unsigned conventional number Y. Similar to the hybrid radix-2 redundant addition discussed in Section 14.3.1, the first step of this addition is computed as :

$$s_i = x_i + y_i = 2t_i + u_i \qquad (14.23)$$

   (a) Let $x_i = x_i^+ + x_i^{++}$ and $s_i = s_i^+ + s_i^{++}$. Design a parallel adder similar to the hybrid adder in Fig. 14.1 for a wordlength of 8. Specify appropriate encoding of t_i and u_i.

   (b) Design the corresponding msd-first and lsd-first serial architectures.

2. The adder in Fig. 14.5 computes $S_{<2,1>} = (X_{<2,1>} + Y^+) - Y^-$. Redesign another possible redundant adder architecture for the addition computation using $S_{<2,1>} = (X_{<2,1>} - Y^-) + Y^+$ in

   (a) digit-parallel,

   (b) lsd-first digit-serial, and

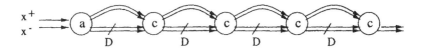

Fig. 14.23 Block diagram of msd-first redundant to nonredundant converter.

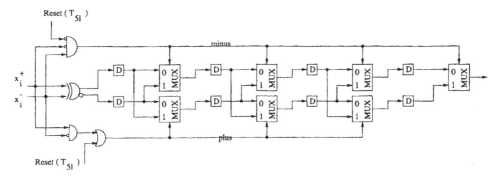

Fig. 14.24 Msd-first redundant to nonredundant converter.

(c) msd-first digit-serial

implementation styles.

3. Design the msd-first and lsd-first serial architectures for the addition of 2 carry-save numbers. Assume the carry-save digit x_i is assigned an arithmetic code of 2 bits x_i^+, x_i^{++} so that $x_i = x_i^+ + x_i^{++}$.

4. Design a radix-4 minimally redundant adder with critical path of 3 full adders assuming that a radix-4 digit x_i is encoded as $-2x_i^{-2} + x_i^+ + x_i^{++}$ using 3 wires. All input and output operands are in minimally redundant representation. Obtain the corresponding msd-first and lsd-first architectures using only 4 full adders and some delay elements. (Hint: For the 3rd-level adder, replace a single $-a$ by $-2a + a$.)

5. Design a radix-4 maximally redundant adder with critical path of 2 full adders assuming that a radix-4 digit x_i is represented as $2x_i^{+2} - 2x_i^{-2} + x_i^+ - x_i^-$ using 4 wires. Design the corresponding msd-first and lsd-first architectures using only 4 full adders and some delay elements.

6. Write a bit-level simulator and verify the functionality of the hybrid msd-first bit-serial radix-2 redundant multiplier shown in Fig. 14.14.

Simulate at least 10 multiplication operations. Assume the wordlength to be 4. Prove that one 0-bit must be input before the most significant bit of each word for proper functionality.

7. Design a radix-4 minimally redundant to nonredundant converter operating in the lsd-first mode for wordlength of 8 digits.

8. Design a radix-4 maximally redundant to nonredundant converter operating in the lsd-first mode for wordlength of 8 digits.

9. Design a msd-first radix-4 minimally redundant to nonredundant converter for wordlength of 8 digits.

10. Design a msd-first radix-4 maximally redundant to nonredundant converter for wordlength of 8 digits.

11. Faster and smaller radix-2 redundant to binary conversion circuits can be designed by rewriting $x = x^+ x^-$ as $x_r^+ x_r^-$ where a value 0 is represented as 00, and 1 and -1 are, respectively, represented as 10 and 01. In $(x_r^+ \ x_r^-)$ representation, 11 needs to be rewritten as 00 by a recoding circuitry. The $don't - care$ condition of 11 can then be exploited for design of simpler converters.

    (a) Show that a general $x^+ x^-$ representation can be rewritten using $x_r^+ x_r^-$ where

    $$x_r^+ = x^+ \overline{x^-}, \quad x_r^- = \overline{x^+} x^-$$

    and $(x_r^+ \ x_r^-)$ cannot be (11).

    (b) A fast lsd-first converter can be derived by using $(x_r^+ \ x_r^-)$ encoding and 2-input multiplexers only. Consider 1 MMP adder in Fig. 14.20 with this encoding shown in Fig. 14.25. Prove that the carry and sum outputs can be computed as

    $$c_{out}^- = c_{in}^- \ \overline{x_r^+} + \overline{c_{in}^-} \ x_r^-, \tag{14.24}$$

    $$s_{out}^+ = c_{in}^- \ \overline{x_r^+} \ \overline{x_r^-} + \overline{c_{in}^-} \ (x_r^+ + x_r^-). \tag{14.25}$$

    Implement the MMP adder using 2 multiplexers. You may use inverters and OR gates if necessary.

12. The sign of a redundant number is determined by the sign of the most significant nonzero digit. Consider a redundant representation where (11) digit has been rewritten as (00) as in Problem 11. (In this problem, x^+ and x^- are same as x_r^+ and x_r^- in Problem 11.) In this representation, x_i^- represents the sign of digit i, i.e., x_i^- is 1 if the digit i is -1 and x_i^- is 0 if the digit i is nonnegative. The sign of a redundant number can be detected by examining the most significant c_{out}^- bit of a redundant-to-binary converter with carry input 0. The s_{out}^+ need not be computed.

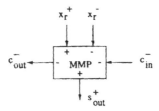

Fig. 14.25   The MMP adder for Problem 11.

(a) Design a sign detection circuit using only $(W - 1)$ multiplexers for a wordlength of W. The latency of this circuit is $(W - 1)t_{mux}$, where t_{mux} is the latency of a multiplexer.

(b) Design a fast sign detection circuit of latency $\log_2 W$ by using binary-tree and carry-look-ahead concepts. Assume W to be a power-of-2. Your design should require $2(W - 1) - \log_2 W$ multiplexers. Design the converter for $W = 16$. (Hint: Rewrite (14.24) as $c^-_{i+1} = c^-_i\, \overline{x^+_i} + \overline{c^-_i}\, x^-_i$ and iterate this equation once to determine the sign of a 2-digit number, twice to determine the sign of a 4-digit number, etc.)

13. This problem addresses the design of a digit-serial msd-first two's complement binary adder based on the msd-first redundant-to-binary converter in Fig. 14.24. Binary addition can be formulated in terms of a redundant-to-binary conversion by using the relation

$$X = A + B = A - (-B) = A - (\overline{B} + 1_{lsb}) = (A - \overline{B}) + (-1)_{lsb},$$

where $\overline{B}$ represents one's complement of B. $(A - \overline{B})$ can be interpreted as a redundant number where each digit $(a_i, \overline{b}_i)$ has a value $(a_i - \overline{b}_i)$. Thus, the msd-first addition can be designed by converting $(A - \overline{B})$ to a binary number and retaining the final result corresponding to input carry -1. Design the two's complement digit-serial msd-first adder for a wordlength of 8. The level of detail of your design should be similar to that of Fig. 14.24.

REFERENCES

1. A. Avizienis, "Signed digit number representation for fast parallel arithmetic," *IRE Trans. on Electronic Computers*, vol. EC-10, pp. 389–400, Sept. 1961.

2. S. C. Knowles, J. G. McWhirter, R. F. Woods, and J. V. McCanny, "Bit-level systolic architectures for high performance IIR filtering," *Journal of VLSI Signal Processing*, pp. 297–312, 1989.

3. D. S. Phatak and I. Koren, "Hybrid signed-digit number systems: a unified framework for redundant number representations with bounded carry propagation chains," *IEEE Trans. on Computers*, vol. 43, no. 8, pp. 880–891, Aug. 1994.

4. A. Guyot, Y. Herreros, and J. Muller, "JANUS, an on-line multiplier/divider for manipulating large numbers," in *Proc. of 9th Symposium on Computer Arithmetic*, pp. 106–111, 1989.

5. N. Takagi, H. Yassura, and S. Yajima, "High-speed VLSI multiplication algorithm with a redundant binary addition tree," *IEEE Trans. on Computers*, vol. C-34, no. 9, pp. 789–796, Sept. 1985.

6. J. Duprat, Y. Herreros, and J. Muller, "Some results about on-line computation of functions," in *Proc. of 9th Symposium on Computer Arithmetic*, pp. 112–118, 1989.

7. A. Skaf and A. Guyot, "VLSI design of on-line add/multiply algorithms," in *Proc. of ICCD'93*, (Cambridge, Massachusetts), pp. 264–267, Oct. 1993.

8. K. S. Trivedi and M. D. Ercegovac, "On-line algorithms for division and multiplication," *IEEE Trans. on Computers*, vol. C-26, no. 7, pp. 681–687, July 1977.

9. M. J. Irwin and R. M. Owens, "Design issues in digit serial signal processors," in *1989 IEEE International Symposium on Circuits and Systems*, (Portland, OR), pp. 441–444, 1989.

10. M. D. Ercegovac and T. Lang, *Division and Square Root.* Kluwer, 1994.

11. P. Montuschi and L. Ciminiera, "Over-redundant digit sets and the design of digit-by-digit division units," *IEEE Trans. on Computers*, vol. 43, no. 3, pp. 269–279, March 1994.

12. C. Y. Chow and J. E. Robertson, "Logical design of a redundant binary adder," in *Proc. of Symposium on Computer Arithmetic*, pp. 109–115, 1978.

13. H. R. Srinivas and K. K. Parhi, "High-speed VLSI arithmetic processor architectures using hybrid number representation," *Journal of VLSI Signal Processing*, vol. 4, pp. 177–198, April 1992.

14. A. Vandemeulebroecke, E. Vanzieleghem, T. Denayer, and P. Jespers, "A new carry-free division algorithm and its application to a single-chip 1024-b RSA processor," *IEEE Journal of Solid State Circuits*, vol. 25, no. 3, pp. 748–756, June 1990.

15. J. M. Muller, *Arithmétiques des Ordinateurs: Opérateurs et fonctions élémentaires.* Masson, 1989.

16. K. Hwang, *Computer Arithmetic: Principles, Architecture and Design.* Wiley, 1979.

17. K. Hwang and F. A. Briggs, *Computer Architecture and Parallel Processing.* McGraw-Hill, 1984.

18. H. Makino, Y. Nakase, H. Suzuki, H. Morinaka, H. Shinohara, and K. Mashiko, "A 8.8-ns 54 × 54 multiplier with high speed redundant binary architecture," *IEEE Journal of Solid State Circuits*, no. 6, pp. 773–783, June 1996.

19. G. Privat, "A novel class of serial-parallel redundant signed-digit multipliers," in *1990 IEEE International Symposium on Circuits and Systems*, (New Orleans, LA), pp. 2116–2119, May 1990.

20. L. Montalvo and A. Guyot, "Combinational digit-set converters for hybrid radix-4 arithmetic," in *Proc. of IEEE International Conference on Computer Design ICCD'94*, (Cambridge, MA), pp. 498–503, Oct. 1994.

21. K. K. Parhi, "Fast low-power VLSI binary addition," in *Proc. of 1997 IEEE Int. Conf. on Computer Design (ICCD)*, (Austin, Texas), pp. 676–684, Oct. 1997.

15

Numerical Strength Reduction

15.1 INTRODUCTION

Strength reduction at the algorithm level can be used to reduce the number of additions and multiplications (see Chapter 9). This chapter covers numerical transformation techniques for reducing strength of DSP computations. These transformations rely upon *subexpression elimination* (also referred to as *substructure sharing*) to restructure the computation in such a manner that the performance, in terms of speed, power and area, of the computation can be improved. Section 15.2 addresses the basic concepts of subexpression elimination. Section 15.3 describes how subexpression elimination can be applied to the multiple constant multiplication problem. Multiple constant multiplication is then extended to specific computations such as linear transformation and polynomial evaluation. Section 15.4 shows how subexpression elimination can be applied to digital filters. Section 15.5 discusses the application of additive number splitting to linear transformations including a detailed discussion of row-based and column-based splitting. This section also discusses multiplicative number splitting and shows how the technique can be applied to linear transforms to either reduce the power or the area of an implementation. Strength reduction reduces the total capacitance and, therefore, reduces power consumption.

15.2 SUBEXPRESSION ELIMINATION

Constant multiplications can be implemented efficiently by using dedicated shift-and-add multipliers. Subexpression elimination [1] is a numerical transformation of the constant multiplications that can lead to efficient hardware implementations in terms of area, power and speed. Subexpression elimination is applied to a set of constant multiplications with the same constant multiplicand. Subexpression elimination can only be performed on constant multiplications that operate on a common variable. Essentially, subexpression elimination is the process of examining the shift-and-add implementations of the constant multiplications and finding redundant operations. Once the redundancies are found, these operations can be performed once and shared among the constant multiplications.

Example 15.2.1 SubExpression Elimination
The operations $a \times x$ and $b \times x$ must be performed, where $a = 13$ and $b = 27$. In binary format, $a = 001101$ and $b = 011011$. Upon examination of a and b, the 1st and 4th bit positions from the right are found to be nonzero. The multiplications $a \times x$ and $b \times x$ can now be written in a slightly different yet equivalent form: $a \times x = 000100 \times x + 001001 \times x$ and $b \times x = 010010 \times x + 001001 \times x = (001001 \times x) << 1 + 001001 \times x$. As can be seen, the term $001001 \times x$ is used in the computation of both $a \times x$ and $b \times x$. Therefore, this term needs to be computed only once. If subexpression elimination were not used in this particular example, the implementation of a would require 2 shifts and 2 adds and the implementation of b would require 3 shifts and 3 adds. Using subexpression elimination, a and b can be implemented using a total of 3 shifts and 3 adds. Note that $b \times x = 2(a \times x) + x$. Hence, alternatively, the computation of $a \times x$ and $b \times x$ can be performed by computing $a \times x$ first, and then using it to compute $b \times x$, which also requires 3 shifts and 3 adds. ■

While this is a rather simple example, but it clearly demonstrates the basic principles used in the subexpression elimination transformation. Subexpression elimination can be realized in a variety of formats and can be applied to most designs that use constant multiplications. In the remainder of this chapter, some of the various forms of subexpression elimination are discussed.

15.3 MULTIPLE CONSTANT MULTIPLICATION

Subexpression elimination can be applied to a set of constant multipliers that multiply a common variable. The multiple constant multiplication (MCM) problem [1] determines how subexpression elimination can be applied to the set of constant multipliers so that the number of shifts and additions required for implementation is minimized. A general framework and algorithm for solving this problem has been presented in [1]. One of the attractive features

Table 15.1   Binary Representation of Constants from Example 15.3.1

Constant	Value	Unsigned
a	237	11101101
b	182	10110110
c	93	01011101

of this algorithm is its versatility and adaptability to various forms of the MCM problem. The algorithm uses an *iterative matching* process that consists of 5 basic steps.

Step 1: Express each constant in the set using a binary format (such as signed, unsigned, two's complement representation).

Step 2: Determine the number of bit-wise matches (nonzero bits) between all of the constants in the set.

Step 3: Choose the best match.

Step 4: Eliminate the redundancy from the best match. Return the remainders and the redundancy to the set of coefficients.

Step 5: Repeat Steps 2–4 until no improvement is achieved.

Although a few additional preprocessing steps can reduce the CPU run-time of the algorithm, these 5 steps represent the primary processing steps required to solve the MCM problem. Several applications of the MCM problem are considered in this section. The examples in this section assume an unsigned binary representation.

Example 15.3.1 Iterative Matching

We are required to implement the constant multipliers a, b, and c, where a = 237, b = 182, and c = 93. The unsigned binary representations of a, b, and c are shown in Table 15.1. Examining Table 15.1, we see that the number of matches between the 3 coefficients are as follows: a and b ⇒ 3 matches, a and c ⇒ 4 matches, b and c ⇒ 2 matches. The match between a and c is selected and this redundancy is removed and the remainders are placed back into the set of constants. Table 15.2 shows the set of constants after the 1st iteration. The constants are again examined to determine the number of bit-wise matches: b and Rem. (remainder) of a ⇒ 2 matches, b and Rem. of c ⇒ 1 match, b and Red. (redundancy) of a and c ⇒ 1 match. The best match is again chosen and the set of constants is updated. Matching in only 1 bit position between 2 constants does not reduce the number of shifts and adds required for implementation. The updated set of coefficients that result from the 2nd iteration of the matching algorithm are shown in Table 15.3. At this point, it should be clear that no more matching can be

Table 15.2   Updated Set of Constants, First Iteration, Example 15.3.1

Constant	Unsigned
Rem. of a	10100000
b	10110110
Rem. of c	00010000
Red. of a,c	01001101

Table 15.3   Updated Set of Constants, Second Iteration, Example 15.3.1

Constant	Unsigned
Rem. of a	00000000
Rem. of b	00010110
Rem. of c	00010000
Red. of a,c	01001101
Red. of Rem. a,b	10100000

performed. *The implementations of a, b and c that result from the iterative matching algorithm are as follows: a = [01001101+10100000], b = [00010110+ 10100000], c = [01001101 + 00010000]. The terms 01001101 and 10100000 represent the redundant subexpressions that were eliminated by the matching algorithm in iterations one and two, respectively. These terms need to be computed only once. They can then be shared among the constant multipliers. The implementation of these 3 constants requires only 9 shifts and 9 adds after subexpression elimination compared to the 14 shifts and 13 adds required for a standard implementation.* ■

As demonstrated by this example, the application of subexpression elimination to the MCM problems can significantly reduce the hardware required to implement constant multiplications. The hardware saving increases as both the wordlength of the constants and the number of constants grow.

While the iterative matching algorithm has been applied to multiple constant multiplications, this algorithm can also be extended for other applications such as linear transformations and polynomial evaluation.

15.3.1   Linear Transformations

Subexpression elimination can also be applied to linear transformations. When subexpression elimination is applied to constant multiplications, the constants are converted to a binary format and examined to determine the subexpressions that are common among the constants. The nonzero bits in the binary representation of a constant determine the number of partial products that need to be generated and summed in order to realize the constant multiplier. Consider the general form of the linear transformation: $y = T * x$, where T is a m by n matrix, y is a length-m vector, and x is a length-n vector (m may equal n). Writing this in an equivalent form, we have:

$$y_i = \sum_{j=1}^{n} t_{ij}x_j, \quad i = 1, ..., m. \tag{15.1}$$

When considering linear transformations, the subexpression elimination problem consists of 3 basic steps. The 1st step is to minimize the number of shifts and additions required to compute the products $t_{ij}x_j$. This is accomplished using the iterative matching algorithm described above.

Example 15.3.2 *Consider the following transformation matrix:*

$$T = \begin{bmatrix} 7 & 8 & 2 & 13 \\ 12 & 11 & 7 & 13 \\ 5 & 8 & 2 & 15 \\ 7 & 11 & 7 & 11 \end{bmatrix}. \tag{15.2}$$

The constants found in each column of the transformation matrix multiply a common variable. For example, x_1 is multiplied by the set of constants [7,12,5,7]. The iterative matching algorithm can be applied to the constants of each column to reduce the number of shifts and adds required to implement the constant multiplications. Table 15.4 shows the subexpressions required to realize the constant multiplications of each column assuming unsigned binary representation. For example, $7*x_1$ would be realized as $(0101)*x_1+(0010)*x_1$.

Table 15.4 Subexpressions Required for Each Column

Column 1	Column 2	Column 3	Column 4
0101	1000	0010	1001
0010	1011	0111	0100
1100			0010

The 2nd step involves the formation of the unique products using the subexpression found in the 1st step. These products will then be appropriately summed to form the y_i's. Looking at Table 15.4, the following list of products is obtained:

$$p_1 = 0101 * x_1, \quad p_2 = 0010 * x_1, \quad p_3 = 1100 * x_1,$$
$$p_4 = 1000 * x_2, \quad p_5 = 1011 * x_2, \quad p_6 = 0010 * x_3, \quad p_7 = 0111 * x_3,$$
$$p_8 = 1001 * x_4, \quad p_9 = 0100 * x_4, \quad p_{10} = 0010 * x_4.$$

Using these products, the y_i's can be formed:

$$\begin{aligned}
y_1 &= p_1 + p_2 + p_4 + p_6 + p_8 + p_9, \\
y_2 &= p_3 + p_5 + p_7 + p_8 + p_9, \\
y_3 &= p_1 + p_4 + p_6 + p_8 + p_9 + p_{10}, \\
y_4 &= p_1 + p_2 + p_5 + p_7 + p_8 + p_{10}.
\end{aligned}$$

$$(15.3)$$

The final step involves the sharing of additions, which is common among the y_i's. This step is very similar to the MCM problem discussed earlier in the chapter. Instead of sharing partial products, which are denoted by nonzero bit positions in the constant multipliers, we are sharing products formed after completing the first 2 steps of the process. We can represent the y_i's as a k-bit word $(1 \leq k \leq 10)$, where each of the k products formed after the 2nd step represents a particular bit position. Using this representation, we get:

$$\begin{aligned}
y_1 &= 1101010110, \quad y_2 = 0010101110, \\
y_3 &= 1001010111, \quad y_4 = 1100101101.
\end{aligned}$$

$$(15.4)$$

The iterative matching algorithm can now be applied to reduce the number of additions required to form y_1, y_2, y_3, and y_4. Applying the iterative matching algorithm, y_1, y_2, y_3, and y_4 are formed as follows:

$$\begin{aligned}
y_1 &= p_2 + (p_1 + p_4 + p_6 + p_8 + p_9), \\
y_2 &= p_3 + p_9 + (p_5 + p_7 + p_8), \\
y_3 &= p_{10} + (p_1 + p_4 + p_6 + p_8 + p_9), \\
y_4 &= p_1 + p_2 + p_{10} + (p_5 + p_7 + p_8).
\end{aligned}$$

$$(15.5)$$

The common expressions need to be computed only once. The iterative matching algorithm allows us to reduce the number of additions to form y_1, y_2, y_3 and y_4 from 19 to 13. The total number of additions required to form y_1, y_2, y_3, and y_4 including generation of the products p_1 through p_{10} has been reduced from 35 to 20. ■

As demonstrated by this example, the number of shift and addition operations required to implement a linear transformation with a constant coefficient transformation matrix can be significantly reduced through the use of subexpression elimination. This technique is very powerful as many of the transforms that are used in signal processing, including the discrete cosine transform (DCT) and the fast Fourier transform (FFT), are linear transforms.

15.3.2 Polynomial Evaluation

Subexpression elimination can be applied to polynomial evaluation to reduce the computational complexity. Suppose we are to evaluate the polynomial:

$$x^{13} + x^7 + x^4 + x^2 + x. \tag{15.6}$$

If the redundancies in this calculation are not considered, the evaluation of this polynomial would require 22 multiplications. However, if the exponents are examined, the number of multiplications required to evaluate this polynomial can be significantly reduced. Consider the unsigned binary representation of the exponents:

$$1 = 0001, \quad 2 = 0010, \quad 4 = 0100, \quad 7 = 0111, \quad 13 = 1101.$$

We can think of x^7 as $x^4 * x^2 * x^1$. By examing the binary representation of the exponents, we can find the common subexpressions that can be shared when evaluating the polynomial. For example, the exponents 7 and 13 share the subexpression 0101. If we apply subexpression elimination to the polynomial evaluation problem, the polynomial can be evaluated as follows:

$$x^8 * (x^4 * x) + x^2 * (x^4 * x) + x^4 + x^2 + x. \tag{15.7}$$

The terms x^2, x^4 and x^8 each require one multiplication:

$$x^2 = x * x, \quad x^4 = x^2 * x^2, \quad x^8 = x^4 * x^4.$$

Clearly, there is some redundancy being exploited when evaluating x^2, x^4, and x^8. However, this is not conceptually difficult and only involves the creation of the power-of-2 exponents of each bit position. For example, if the exponents of the polynomial were represented using 5-bit binary words, we would need to evaluate x^2, x^4, x^8, and x^{16} to have the proper "pieces" to build the polynomial exponents. Looking at (15.7), we see that (15.6) can be evaluated using only 6 multiplications compared to the 22 that are required if the evaluation of the polynomial is performed without exploiting any of the redundancies in the computation.

While it is clear that subexpression elimination can be applied to the evaluation of a single polynomial, we can also apply this technique to multiple polynomials evaluated over a single variable. Consider the following 3 polynomial equations:

$$
\begin{aligned}
w(x) &= 11x^5 + 3x^4 + 6x^3 + 5x \\
y(x) &= 13x^5 + 7x^4 + 11x^3 \\
z(x) &= 7x^5 + 15x^4 + 5x^2 + 7x.
\end{aligned}
$$

$$\tag{15.8}$$

Applying subexpression elimination to multiple polynomials is essentially a 2 step process. The 1st step involves reducing the number of multiplications required to generate the various powers of x. The 2nd step involves reducing the number of shifts and additions required to implement the multiplication of the power terms by the constant coefficients. The 1st step is similar to reducing the number of multiplications in the evaluation of a single polynomial. We examine the set of polynomials to determine which powers of x are required and then compute them using the fewest number of multiplications. Looking at (15.8), we see that we need to compute x^2, x^3, x^4, and x^5. Using the redundancies in the computation, these 4 powers of x can be calculated using 4 multiplications. Once the powers of x have been generated, the 2nd and final step is to reduce the number of shifts and additions needed for the constant coefficient multipliers. Subexpression elimination can be applied to the coefficients that multiply the same power of x. For example, 11 and 13 both multiply x^5 and share the subexpression 1001. After applying subexpression elimination to the constant coefficient multipliers, the constant coefficient multipliers can be implemented using 20 additions as opposed to 27 if no simplifications were made.

15.4   SUBEXPRESSION SHARING IN DIGITAL FILTERS

This section considers the implementation of FIR digital filters using common subexpressions. Both canonic signed digit (CSD) (see Section 13.6.1) and two's complement fixed-point representations with 1 integer bit are used in this section. Quantization of FIR digital filters using a specified number of signed power-of-two (SPT) terms is described in Appendix G.

Example 15.4.1 *This example considers an example of common subexpression elimination within a single multiplication*

$$y = 0.10\bar{1}00010\bar{1} * x \ .$$

This may be implemented as

$$y = (x >> 1) - (x >> 3) + (x >> 7) - (x >> 9),$$

where $>> i$ *denotes an arithmetic shift–right-by-i-bit operation, and is the same as the scaling operation* $\boxed{2^{-i}}$. *Alternatively, this multiplication can be implemented as*

$$x2 = x - x >> 2$$
$$y = (x2 >> 1) + (x2 >> 7)$$

which requires one less addition. ∎

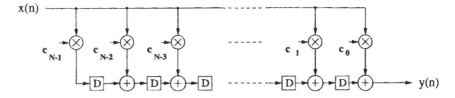

Fig. 15.1   General Transposed Direct-Form FIR Filter Structure.

As discussed in Section 15.3, subexpression elimination can be applied where several constants need to be multiplied to a common variable. These ideas can readily be applied to FIR filters to reduce the hardware complexity of the filter implementation. In order to realize the subexpression elimination transformation, the N-tap FIR filter

$$y(n) = c_0 x(n) + c_1 x(n-1) + \cdots + c_{N-1} x(n - N + 1) \qquad (15.9)$$

must be realized using a transposed direct-form structure (see Fig. 15.1). This FIR filter structure is often referred to as a data-broadcast filter structure (see Section 1.4.1). With this structure, one variable is multiplied to multiple constant coefficients. Subexpression elimination can then be applied to the data-broadcast FIR filters using a wide variety of techniques [2]–[4]. All of the methods are similar from the standpoint that the hardware implementation of the filter coefficients is examined to determine the hardware units that are common among the filter coefficients. These common hardware units can then be shared among the filter coefficients. The basic principles of subexpression elimination in digital filter design are demonstrated using several examples in this section.

To systematically obtain the subexpression sharing, a filter operation is represented by a table (matrix) $\{x_{ij}\}$, where the rows are indexed by delay i and the columns by shift j, i.e., the row i is the coefficient c_i for the term $x(n-i)$, and column 0 in row i is the most significant bit (msb) of c_i and column $W - 1$ in row i is the least significant bit (lsb) of c_i, where W is the wordlength. The row and column indexing starts at 0. The entries in the table are 0 or 1 if two's complement representation is used (except the sign bit), or they are from the digit set $\{0, 1 - 1\}$ if CSD representation is used. A nonzero entry (with absolute value 1) in row i, column j represents $x(n-i) >> j$. It is to be added or subtracted according to whether the entry is $+1$ or -1. In the following examples, $x1$ is used, instead of x, to denote the original multiplicand, and $x2$, $x3$, etc., are used to denote the intermediate subexpressions at step 2, 3, etc; $x1[-i]$ is used to represent $x(n-i)$, where the index $[-i]$ in general represents i sample delays.

Example 15.4.2 *Consider the constant coefficient (in CSD representation) FIR filter*

$$y(n) \; = \; 1.000\bar{1}00000 * x(n) + 0.\bar{1}0\bar{1}010010 * x(n-1)$$
$$+0.0001000\bar{1}0\bar{1} * x(n-2)$$

$$(15.10)$$

described by the following table:

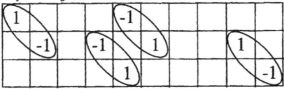

   This filter has 8 nonzero terms and would normally require 7 additions. However, we find that the subexpression $x1 + x1[-1] >> 1$ occurs 4 times in shifted and delayed forms by various amounts as circled in the table. Therefore, the filter may be written with 4 additions as

$$x2 \; = \; x1 - x1[-1] >> 1$$
$$y \; = \; x2 - (x2 >> 4) - (x2[-1] >> 3) + (x2[-1] >> 8) \; .$$

An alternative computation method is

$$x2 \; = \; x1 - (x1 >> 4) - (x1[-1] >> 3) + (x1[-1] >> 8)$$
$$y \; = \; x2 - (x2[-1] >> 1). \; \blacksquare$$

   This last example illustrates a novel feature, stated in the remark below.

Remark 15.4.1 *A subexpression of size m occurring n times is the same as a subexpression of size n occurring m times.*

An algorithm for subexpression matching is now illustrated using the following example.

Example 15.4.3 *Consider the 4-tap FIR filter*

$$y(n) \; = \; \bar{1}.01010000010 * x(n) + 0.\bar{1}000\bar{1}0\bar{1}0\bar{1}0\bar{1} * x(n-1)$$
$$+0.\bar{1}0010000010 * x(n-2) + 1.0000010\bar{1}000 * x(n-4),$$

$$(15.11)$$

where the coefficients are represented in CSD representation. The substructure matching procedure for this design is given as follows:

1. *Start with the table containing the coefficients of the FIR filter. An entry with absolute value of 1 in this table denote add or subtract of $x1$. Iden-*

tify the "best" subexpression of size 2. The best subexpression is chosen according to a benefit function in which the number of occurrences is an important factor.

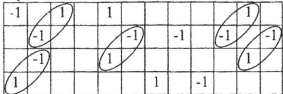

2. *Remove each occurrence of each subexpression and replace it by a value 2 or −2 in place of the 1st of the 2 terms making up the subexpression. By "first" it means 1st in row-major order on the table entries. In this table, an entry with absolute value 2 denotes add or subtract of x2, the 2nd level subexpression.*

-1		2		1				2	
					-2	-1			-2
		-2							
						1	-1		

3. *Record the definition of the subexpression. This may require a negative value for shift, but do not worry about that right now.*

$$x2 = x1 - x1[-1] >> (-1) .$$

4. *Continue by finding more subexpressions until done.*

-1		3						2	
					-3				-2
		-2							
						1	-1		

$$x3 = x2 + x1 >> 2 .$$

5. *Write out the complete definition of the filter.*

$$
\begin{aligned}
x2 &= x1 - x1[-1] >> (-1) \\
x3 &= x2 + x1 >> 2 \\
y &= -x1 + x3 >> 2 + x2 >> 10 - x3[-1] >> 5 - x2[-1] >> 11 \\
&\quad -x2[-2] >> 1 + x1[-3] >> 6 - x1[-3] >> 8 .
\end{aligned}
$$

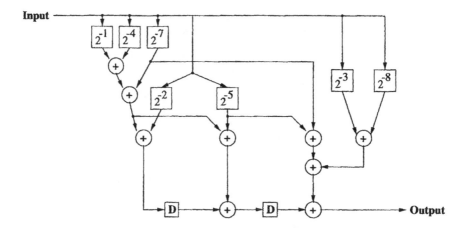

Fig. 15.2 Three-tap FIR filter with subexpression sharing in Example 15.4.4.

6. *If any subexpression definition involves negative shift, then modify the definition and subsequent uses of that variable to remove the negative shift as shown below.*

$$x2 = x1 >> 1 - x1[-1]$$
$$x3 = x2 + x1 >> 3$$
$$y = -x1 + x3 >> 1 + x2 >> 9 - x3[-1] >> 4 - x2[-1] >> 10$$
$$-x2[-2] + x1[-3] >> 6 - x1[-3] >> 8. \ \blacksquare$$

Note that in Example 15.4.3, the choice of which subexpressions to choose at each iteration is not only dependent on the number of times an expression occurs, but also on the expected reduction in the number of operators, which include adders and delay elements.

Example 15.4.4 *In this example, subexpression elimination is applied to a 3-tap filter with two's complement coefficients $c_2 = 0.11010010$, $c_1 = 0.10011010$ and $c_0 = 0.00101011$. Fig. 15.2 shows the 3-tap filter obtained with subexpression elimination. After subexpression sharing, the filter requires only 7 shifts and 9 additions compared to the 12 shifts and 11 additions required in the standard multiplierless implementation.*

Another subexpression sharing based structure is shown in Fig. 15.3, which requires 8 additions.

The structures in Fig. 15.2 and Fig. 15.3 can be implemented easily in bit-parallel style using carry-save addition. In bit-parallel designs, the shifters are realized by appropriate hard-wired interconnections. Accuracy in shifting can be improved by Horner's rule-based implementation (see Section 13.6.2.1). However, in bit-serial designs, the 2^{-1} shifters can only be implemented after proper synchronization has been achieved by inserting delay elements at

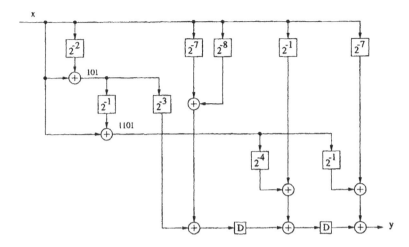

Fig. 15.3 Three-tap FIR filter with subexpression sharing in Example 15.4.4.

pipelining cutsets at appropriate locations. It may be noted that the bit-serial designs are often not very attractive because of the use of the large number of synchronizing delays. ∎

15.4.1 Using the Two Most Common Subexpressions in CSD Representations

Digital filters can be implemented with less hardware using a CSD representation. In CSD representation, the 2 most common subexpressions are $x - x >> 2$ and $x + x >> 2$, and statistically, this will always be so. Substantial gains in circuit area can be achieved very easily by finding the occurrences of only these 2 subexpressions. An expression $x - x >> 2$ corresponds to a sequence $10\bar{1}$ in one of the filter coefficients, and the expression $x + x >> 2$ corresponds to a sequence 101. It can be shown that asymptotically a W-bit CSD number can be broken down into $W/18 + O(1)$ pairs of type $10\bar{1}$, $W/18 + O(1)$ pairs of type 101, and $W/9 + O(1)$ isolated 1 or $\bar{1}$ bits [3]. Referring to pair $10\bar{1}$, a pair 101, or an otherwise isolated nonzero bit as a term, it can be shown that the asymptotic expected number of terms in a W-bit CSD number is $2(W + 1)/9$. This represents a 33% saving compared with the total number of nonzero bits, which is equal to $(3W + 1)/9$. Furthermore, taking advantage of these common subexpressions can be done without a major increase in routing cost. Fig. 15.4 shows a possible linear layout for an FIR filter designed using term sharing. The subexpression method used to transform this filter implementation relies upon the fact that all CSD coefficients can be "built" using 3 simple subexpressions: 101, $10\bar{1}$ and 1 [3]. These 3 subexpressions can be shifted and added to form the filter coefficients. In Fig. 15.4, the 2 terms $x + x >> 2$ and $x - x >> 2$ are precomputed. The 3

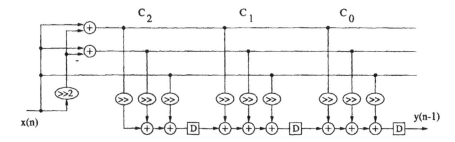

Fig. 15.4 An FIR filter using term sharing, where the 2 most common subexpressions in CSD numbers, 101 and 10$\bar{1}$, together with isolated 1 are shared among all filter coefficients.

terms, $x + x \gg 2$, $x - x \gg 2$ and x, are then fed along the row of cells. Each of the adders taps its inputs off the 3 buses. The right shift operator in the figure may represent multiple right shifts and additions, depending on the value of the corresponding coefficients. Although the 3 buses are shown above the data path, in reality, the best floor plan is to have them running right over the adder cells.

Example 15.4.5 *This example considers the design of a 3-tap FIR filter using the 2 most common subexpressions in CSD representation. The 12-bit coefficients of this filter are coded using a CSD binary format:*

$$c_2 = 0.\underline{101}0\underline{101}0\underline{10\bar{1}}, \quad c_1 = 0.100\underline{101}00\underline{10\bar{1}},$$
$$c_0 = 0.\underline{10\bar{1}0\bar{1}0}10000,$$

where the subexpressions 101 and 10$\bar{1}$ are underlined. Fig. 15.5(a) shows the filter implementation using the 2 most common subexpressions in CSD numbers. Notice that the 2 additions in the dotted square are the same, and these can be shared as shown in Fig. 15.5(b). As a result, the filter requires only 7 additions and 7 shifts compared to the 12 adds and 12 shifts required in the standard multiplierless implementation. ∎

The examples in this section have illustrated the effectiveness of substructure sharing when it comes to reducing the hardware cost of an FIR filter implementation. In FIR filters with a large number of taps, the possibility for substructure sharing is increased, which can lead to greater savings in hardware.

An alternative layout shown in Fig. 15.6 is possible, in which all the terms of each type are combined in a separate data path. Then the three partial results are summed to obtain the final output.

In this layout, best results will be achieved if the three data paths are to some extent balanced, i.e., these contain the same number of terms. One benefit of this may be layout convenience. Another important benefit relates

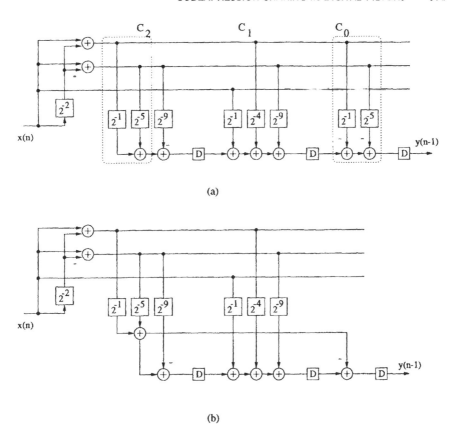

(a)

(b)

Fig. 15.5   Three-tap FIR filter example with CSD subexpression sharing.

to the clock rate. The maximum clock rate of the circuit is dependent on the maximum number of adders in one stage of the pipeline. In order to keep the number of adders in each stage at a minimum, it is desirable to keep the number of adders balanced in each of the 3 data paths. As remarked previously, however, the number of terms in the x data path is on the average twice as many as in the $x + x >> 2$ and $x - x >> 2$ paths. This inequality can be redressed by swapping x terms for $x + x >> 2$ and $x - x >> 2$ terms. This is done by departing from a strict adherence to CSD number representation. For instance, a bit sequence 1001 containing 2 isolated 1-bits and leading to terms $x + x >> 3$ can be rewritten as $101\bar{1}$. This gives rise to terms $(x + x >> 2) - x >> 3$. Thus, one of the x-terms has been replaced by an $x + x >> 2$ term. Similarly, a sequence 10001 can be written as $10\bar{1}00 + 00101$. In this way, 2 isolated 1-bits have been replaced by 2 pairs.

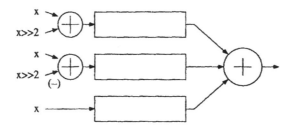

Fig. 15.6   Alternative layout for carry-save FIR filter.

15.5   ADDITIVE AND MULTIPLICATIVE NUMBER SPLITTING

Number splitting [2], which can be additive or multiplicative, is a numerical transformation that can be used to reduce the hardware complexity or power consumption of linear circuits. Additive number splitting is another form of subexpression elimination in multiple constant multiplication. Typically number splitting is performed on the infinite precision version of the constant coefficients before they are reduced to binary representation. This leads to strength reduction at a higher level. Additive number splitting can be either row based or column based.

Number splitting is an iterative technique used within the framework of an optimization algorithm. The optimization algorithm guides the number splitting algorithm through the use of a cost function. At each iteration, the number splitting that leads to the largest reduction in the cost function is chosen. The process is repeated until no further optimizations can be achieved through the use of number splitting. This section describes the basic principles of number splitting. The process of generating optimal solutions is not discussed (see [2],[5],[6]).

Before we examine how number splitting is performed, the notion of a linear circuit must be defined. The linear circuit is defined as

$$\mathbf{y} = \mathbf{Tx}$$

where

$$\mathbf{y} = \begin{bmatrix} y_0(n+1) \\ y_1(n+1) \\ \vdots \\ y_{N-1}(n+1) \end{bmatrix},$$

$$
\mathbf{T} = \begin{bmatrix} t_{0,0} & t_{0,1} & \cdots & t_{0,M-1} \\ t_{1,0} & t_{1,1} & \cdots & t_{1,M-1} \\ \vdots & \vdots & \ddots & \vdots \\ t_{N-1,0} & t_{N-1,1} & \cdots & t_{N-1,M-1} \end{bmatrix},
$$

$$
\mathbf{x} = \begin{bmatrix} y_0(n) \\ \vdots \\ y_{J-1}(n) \\ x_0(n) \\ \vdots \\ x_{K-1}(n) \end{bmatrix}.
$$

$$(15.12)$$

It should be noted that $M = J + K$. Notice that this definition of a linear circuit includes both recursive and nonrecursive circuits. In the case of a nonrecursive circuit, $y_0(n), \ldots, y_{J-1}(n)$ would be eliminated from $\mathbf{x}$ and $M = K$. Number splitting is used to transform the constant coefficients of the matrix $\mathbf{T}$ so that the area or power of the linear circuit is reduced. This corresponds to a transformation of the data-flow graph of the linear circuit. However, the functionality of the linear circuit remains unchanged.

15.5.1 Row-Based Additive Number Splitting

As the name implies, row-based number splitting is performed on the rows of the matrix $\mathbf{T}$. In order to perform row-based number splitting, a pivot element and a target element are first defined. Assuming that the number splitting is to be performed on the i-th row of $\mathbf{T}$, the pivot element of the i-th row is defined as $t_{i,p}$ and the target element is defined as $t_{i,q}$. The pivot element, $t_{i,p}$, is used to "split" the target element into 2 pieces, $t_{i,p}$ and δ ($t_{i,q} = t_{i,p} + \delta$), such that $\delta = t_{i,q} - t_{i,p}$. After performing row-based number splitting, the matrix $\mathbf{T}$ is transformed to a new matrix $\mathbf{T}'$

$$
\mathbf{T}' = \begin{bmatrix} t_{0,0} & \cdots & t_{0,p} & \cdots & t_{0,q} & \cdots & t_{0,M-1} \\ \vdots & \ddots & \vdots & \ddots & \vdots & \ddots & \vdots \\ t_{i,0} & \cdots & 0 & \cdots & \delta & \cdots & t_{i,M-1} \\ \vdots & \ddots & \vdots & \ddots & \vdots & \ddots & \vdots \\ t_{N-1,0} & \cdots & t_{N-1,p} & \cdots & t_{N-1,q} & \cdots & t_{N-1,M-1} \end{bmatrix}. \quad (15.13)
$$

In order to equate $\mathbf{T}'$ and $\mathbf{T}$, 2 additional matrices must be generated. The first matrix, $\mathbf{AG}$, contains rows that can be appropriately added to the rows of $\mathbf{T}'$ to produce $\mathbf{T}$. Initially, the $\mathbf{AG}$ matrix is empty. After each iteration of the row-based number splitting, the row that must be added to the i-th row of $\mathbf{T}'$ to produce the i-th row of $\mathbf{T}$ is appended to $\mathbf{AG}$. Clearly, after number splitting is performed on the i-th row of $\mathbf{T}$, the row $[0...0\ t_{i,p}\ 0...0\ t_{i,p}\ 0...0]$ must be added to the i-th row of $\mathbf{T}'$ to obtain the original matrix $\mathbf{T}$. After r iterations of row-based number splitting have been performed, $\mathbf{AG}$ will contain r rows, each having M entries.

The second matrix, $\mathbf{W}$, determines how the rows of $\mathbf{AG}$ should be added to the rows of $\mathbf{T}'$ to obtain the original matrix $\mathbf{T}$. $\mathbf{W}$ is initially set to an identity matrix of dimension $N \times N$. After each iteration of row-based number splitting, a column is appended to the right of $\mathbf{W}$. This columns contains N entries that are all set to zero except for the i-th entry, which is set to 1. Clearly, each column of $\mathbf{W}$ will contain only 1 nonzero entry This nonzero entry will always have a value of 1. Using this matrix along with $\mathbf{AG}$, we can equate $\mathbf{T}$ and $\mathbf{T}'$ as

$$\mathbf{T} = \mathbf{W} * \begin{bmatrix} \mathbf{T}' \\ \mathbf{AG} \end{bmatrix}. \tag{15.14}$$

In order to gain a better understanding of how row-based number splitting is performed, the technique is applied to the following linear circuit

$$\begin{bmatrix} y_0(n+1) \\ y_1(n+1) \\ y_2(n+1) \end{bmatrix} = \begin{bmatrix} .4 & .7 & .4 & .8 \\ .3 & .6 & .2 & .9 \\ .5 & .3 & .2 & .7 \end{bmatrix} \begin{bmatrix} y_0(n) \\ y_1(n) \\ y_2(n) \\ x_0(n) \end{bmatrix}. \tag{15.15}$$

Number splitting will be performed on the 1st row, using .4 (the 1st entry) as the pivot element and .4 (the 3rd entry) as the target element. The matrices $\mathbf{T}'$, $\mathbf{AG}$, and $\mathbf{W}$ that result are as follows

$$\mathbf{T}' = \begin{bmatrix} 0 & .7 & 0 & .8 \\ .3 & .6 & .2 & .9 \\ .5 & .3 & .2 & .7 \end{bmatrix},$$

$$\mathbf{AG} = \begin{bmatrix} .4 & 0 & .4 & 0 \end{bmatrix},$$

$$\mathbf{W} = \begin{bmatrix} 1 & 0 & 0 & 1 \\ 0 & 1 & 0 & 0 \\ 0 & 0 & 1 & 0 \end{bmatrix}. \tag{15.16}$$

Using these matrices, (15.14) becomes

$$\begin{bmatrix} .4 & .7 & .4 & .8 \\ .3 & .6 & .2 & .9 \\ .5 & .3 & .2 & .7 \end{bmatrix} = \begin{bmatrix} 1 & 0 & 0 & 1 \\ 0 & 1 & 0 & 0 \\ 0 & 0 & 1 & 0 \end{bmatrix} \begin{bmatrix} 0 & .7 & 0 & .8 \\ .3 & .6 & .2 & .9 \\ .5 & .3 & .2 & .7 \\ .4 & 0 & .4 & 0 \end{bmatrix}. \tag{15.17}$$

By performing the row-based number splitting, the method used to compute the output $y_0(n+1)$ has been changed to an equivalent form that requires less hardware. Originally, $y_0(n+1)$ is computed as $.4y_0(n) + .7y_1(n) + .4y_2(n) + .8x_0(n)$ requiring 4 multiplications and 3 additions. After the transformation, $y_0(n+1)$ is computed as $.4(y_0(n) + y_2(n)) + .7y_1(n) + .8x_0(n)$ requiring only 3 multiplications and 3 additions. Consider performing another iteration of the row-based number splitting on the 3rd row of $\mathbf{T}'$ using .2 as the pivot and .7 as the target:

$$\mathbf{T}' = \begin{bmatrix} 0 & .7 & 0 & .8 \\ .3 & .6 & .2 & .9 \\ .5 & .3 & 0 & .5 \end{bmatrix},$$

$$\mathbf{AG} = \begin{bmatrix} .4 & 0 & .4 & 0 \\ 0 & 0 & .2 & .2 \end{bmatrix},$$

$$\mathbf{W} = \begin{bmatrix} 1 & 0 & 0 & 1 & 0 \\ 0 & 1 & 0 & 0 & 1 \\ 0 & 0 & 1 & 0 & 0 \end{bmatrix},$$

$$\begin{bmatrix} .4 & .7 & .4 & .8 \\ .3 & .6 & .2 & .9 \\ .5 & .3 & .2 & .7 \end{bmatrix} = \begin{bmatrix} 1 & 0 & 0 & 1 & 0 \\ 0 & 1 & 0 & 0 & 1 \\ 0 & 0 & 1 & 0 & 0 \end{bmatrix} \begin{bmatrix} 0 & .7 & 0 & .8 \\ .3 & .6 & .2 & .9 \\ .5 & .3 & 0 & .5 \\ .4 & 0 & .4 & 0 \\ 0 & 0 & .2 & .2 \end{bmatrix}.$$

$$(15.18)$$

This iteration of the number splitting has modified the method for computing the output $y_2(n+1)$. In the original circuit, $y_2(n+1)$ is computed as $.5y_0(n) + .3y_1(n) + .2y_2(n) + .7x_0(n)$ requiring 4 multiplications and 3 additions. After number splitting is performed, $y_2(n+1)$ is computed as $.5y_0(n) + .3y_1(n) + .2(y_2(n) + x_0(n)) + .5 * x_0(n)$ requiring 4 multiplications and 4 additions. It appears that the transformation has actually caused the hardware complexity to grow. However, notice that originally the constant coefficient multiplier of $x_0(n)$ is .7. This has been replaced with a constant coefficient multiplier of .5. A multiplication by .5 can be implemented using a simple shift to the right. Therefore, the "expensive" multiplication by .7 has been replaced by an efficient multiplication by .5 at the cost of 1 addition. Number splitting has again reduced the hardware complexity of the linear circuit. The process of number splitting can be continued until it leads to no further reduction of the hardware complexity of the linear circuit.

15.5.2 Column-Based Additive Number Splitting

Column-based number splitting is essentially the same as row-based number splitting with the splitting being performed on a column of $\mathbf{T}$. Suppose that column-based number splitting is to be performed on the p-th column of

T. The i-th element of the p-th column, $t_{i,p}$, is referred to as the pivot element and the j-th element of the p-th column, $t_{j,p}$, is referred to as the target element. As before, the pivot element "splits" the target element into 2 pieces, $t_{i,p}$ and δ ($t_{j,p} = t_{i,p} + \delta$), such that $\delta = t_{j,p} - t_{i,p}$. The matrix **AG** is formed by appending rows of the form $[0...0 \; t_{i,p} \; 0...0]$ to **AG** after each iteration of column-based number splitting. This row, when added to the i-th and j-th rows of **T'**, produces the original transformation matrix **T**. Before number splitting is performed, **AG** is empty. As in row-based number splitting, the matrix **W** determines how the rows of **AG** should be added to **T'** to obtain the original transformation matrix **T**. **W** starts as an $N \times N$ identity matrix. After each iteration of number splitting, a column of the form $[0...0 \; 1 \; 0...0 \; 1 \; 0...0]$, with the 1's in the i-th and j-th entries, is appended to the right of **W**. The relationship that exists between **T'** and **T** is still given by (15.14).

Consider, once again, the linear circuit defined by (15.15)

$$\begin{bmatrix} y_0(n+1) \\ y_1(n+1) \\ y_2(n+1) \end{bmatrix} = \begin{bmatrix} .4 & .7 & .4 & .8 \\ .3 & .6 & .2 & .9 \\ .5 & .3 & .2 & .7 \end{bmatrix} \begin{bmatrix} y_0(n) \\ y_1(n) \\ y_2(n) \\ x_0(n) \end{bmatrix}. \qquad (15.19)$$

Column-based number splitting will be performed on the third column of **T** using the second entry, .2, as the pivot and the third entry, .2, as the target element. The matrices **T'**, **AG**, and **W** that result are as follows

$$\mathbf{T'} = \begin{bmatrix} .4 & .7 & .4 & .8 \\ .3 & .6 & 0 & .9 \\ .5 & .3 & 0 & .7 \end{bmatrix},$$

$$\mathbf{AG} = \begin{bmatrix} 0 & 0 & .2 & 0 \end{bmatrix},$$

$$\mathbf{W} = \begin{bmatrix} 1 & 0 & 0 & 0 \\ 0 & 1 & 0 & 1 \\ 0 & 0 & 1 & 1 \end{bmatrix}. \qquad (15.20)$$

Using these matrices, (15.14) becomes

$$\begin{bmatrix} .4 & .7 & .4 & .8 \\ .3 & .6 & .2 & .9 \\ .5 & .3 & .2 & .7 \end{bmatrix} = \begin{bmatrix} 1 & 0 & 0 & 0 \\ 0 & 1 & 0 & 1 \\ 0 & 0 & 1 & 1 \end{bmatrix} \begin{bmatrix} .4 & .7 & .4 & .8 \\ .3 & .6 & 0 & .9 \\ .5 & .3 & 0 & .7 \\ 0 & 0 & .2 & 0 \end{bmatrix}. \qquad (15.21)$$

By performing the column-based number splitting, the method used to compute the outputs $y_1(n+1)$ and $y_2(n+1)$ has been changed to an equivalent computation that requires less hardware. Originally, $y_1(n+1)$ is computed as $.3y_0(n) + .6y_1(n) + .2y_2(n) + .9x_0(n)$ and $y_2(n+1)$ is computed as

$.5y_0(n) + .3y_1(n) + .2y_2(n) + .7x_0(n)$ requiring 8 multiplications and 6 additions. After the transformation, the product term $.2y_2(n)$ is computed once and distributed to both of the outputs $y_1(n+1)$ and $y_2(n+1)$, saving a multiplication operation. The primary difference that exists between row-based and column-based number splitting is that row-based number splitting attempts to exploit redundancies in the computation of a single output while column-based number splitting attempts to exploit redundancies that occur in the computations of multiple outputs.

Number splitting is usually performed in conjunction with an optimization algorithm that uses a cost function to guide the number splitting. During each iteration of the number splitting, whether it be row based or column based, the pivot and target elements that will lead to the largest reduction in the cost function are chosen to perform the number splitting. Since the linear circuit is in reality a linear transformation, number splitting can be applied to linear transformations to reduce the computational complexity.

15.5.3   Multiplicative Number Splitting

Multiplicative number splitting [5],[6] is yet another numerical transformation that can be applied to a linear circuit (linear transform) to reduce the hardware complexity or the power consumption of the circuit. As in additive number splitting, multiplicative number splitting is an iterative technique that is guided by a cost function. The cost function, which is based upon the power or area of the circuit, determines the ideal splitting to be performed during each iteration of the multiplicative number splitting algorithm.

Referring back to (15.12), the linear transform in defined as

$$\mathbf{y} = \mathbf{Tx}. \tag{15.22}$$

Multiplicative number splitting operates on the matrix $\mathbf{T}$ in such a manner that the hardware complexity or power consumption of the linear circuit is reduced. Multiplicative number splitting is a relatively simple transformation that relies upon the following observation in linear algebra [5]:

The product $\mathbf{T_{i-1}T_i}$ remains unchanged if for some constant K

(1) the j-th row of $\mathbf{T_i}$ is transformed as

$$\text{Row}(j) = \text{Row}(j) - K*\text{Row}(k)$$

(2) the k-th column of $\mathbf{T_{i-1}}$ is transformed as

$$\text{Col}(k) = \text{Col}(k) + K*\text{Col}(j)$$

where j and k denote arbitrary valid row and column indices.

Using these observations, the multiplicative number splitting algorithm decomposes the original matrix $\mathbf{T}$ into a product of matrices, $\mathbf{T} = \mathbf{T_1 T_2 ... T_N}$. Consider applying multiplicative number splitting to the matrix

$$
\mathbf{T} =
\begin{bmatrix}
a_{1,1} & a_{1,2} & a_{1,3} \\
a_{2,1} & a_{2,2} & a_{2,3} \\
a_{3,1} & a_{3,2} & a_{3,3} \\
a_{4,1} & a_{4,2} & a_{4,3}
\end{bmatrix}.
\tag{15.23}
$$

The 1st step that must be performed is to write $\mathbf{T}$ as the product of an identity matrix and itself

$$
\mathbf{T} = \mathbf{T_1 T_2}
$$
$$
\begin{bmatrix}
1 & 0 & 0 & 0 \\
0 & 1 & 0 & 0 \\
0 & 0 & 1 & 0 \\
0 & 0 & 0 & 1
\end{bmatrix}
\begin{bmatrix}
a_{1,1} & a_{1,2} & a_{1,3} \\
a_{2,1} & a_{2,2} & a_{2,3} \\
a_{3,1} & a_{3,2} & a_{3,3} \\
a_{4,1} & a_{4,2} & a_{4,3}
\end{bmatrix}.
\tag{15.24}
$$

Now, using the observation above, $\mathbf{T_1}$ and $\mathbf{T_2}$ can be transformed without altering the functionality of the linear circuit. Consider multiplicative splitting with $K = 3$, $j = 1$, and $k = 2$

$$
\mathbf{T} = \mathbf{T_1 T_2}
$$
$$
\begin{bmatrix}
1 & 3 & 0 & 0 \\
0 & 1 & 0 & 0 \\
0 & 0 & 1 & 0 \\
0 & 0 & 0 & 1
\end{bmatrix}
\begin{bmatrix}
a_{1,1} - 3a_{2,1} & a_{1,2} - 3a_{2,2} & a_{1,3} - 3a_{2,3} \\
a_{2,1} & a_{2,2} & a_{2,3} \\
a_{3,1} & a_{3,2} & a_{3,3} \\
a_{4,1} & a_{4,2} & a_{4,3}
\end{bmatrix}.
$$
$$\tag{15.25}$$

Notice that $\mathbf{T_2}$ has been transformed using the 1st part of the observation: $\text{Row}(j) = \text{Row}(j) - K*\text{Row}(k)$. The matrix $\mathbf{T_1}$ has been transformed using the 2nd part of the observation: $\text{Col}(k) = \text{Col}(k) + K*\text{Col}(j)$. Consider transforming $\mathbf{T_1}$ and $\mathbf{T_2}$ a second time using multiplicative splitting with $K = 1$, $j = 2$, and $k = 3$

$$
\mathbf{T} = \mathbf{T_1 T_2}
$$
$$
\begin{bmatrix}
1 & 3 & 3 & 0 \\
0 & 1 & 1 & 0 \\
0 & 0 & 1 & 0 \\
0 & 0 & 0 & 1
\end{bmatrix}
\begin{bmatrix}
a_{1,1} - 3a_{2,1} & a_{1,2} - 3a_{2,2} & a_{1,3} - 3a_{2,3} \\
a_{2,1} - a_{3,1} & a_{2,2} - a_{3,2} & a_{2,3} - a_{3,3} \\
a_{3,1} & a_{3,2} & a_{3,3} \\
a_{4,1} & a_{4,2} & a_{4,3}
\end{bmatrix}.
$$
$$\tag{15.26}$$

At any time during the transformation process, another identity matrix can be added to either the left-hand side or the right-hand side of $\mathbf{T}$ in order to extend the possible number of transformations that can be performed.

Consider adding an identity matrix to the right-hand side of T

$$T = T_1 T_2 T_3 \qquad (15.27)$$

$$
\begin{bmatrix} 1 & 3 & 3 & 0 \\ 0 & 1 & 1 & 0 \\ 0 & 0 & 1 & 0 \\ 0 & 0 & 0 & 1 \end{bmatrix}
\begin{bmatrix} a_{1,1} - 3a_{2,1} & a_{1,2} - 3a_{2,2} & a_{1,3} - 3a_{2,3} \\ a_{2,1} - a_{3,1} & a_{2,2} - a_{3,2} & a_{2,3} - a_{3,3} \\ a_{3,1} & a_{3,2} & a_{3,3} \\ a_{4,1} & a_{4,2} & a_{4,3} \end{bmatrix}
\begin{bmatrix} 1 & 0 & 0 \\ 0 & 1 & 0 \\ 0 & 0 & 1 \end{bmatrix} .
$$

Multiplicative number splitting can now be performed to transform T_2 and T_3 in the same manner that T_1 and T_2 were transformed. Consider transforming T_2 and T_3 with $K = 1$, $j = 3$ and $k = 1$

$$T = T_1 T_2 T_3 \qquad (15.28)$$

$$
\begin{bmatrix} 1 & 3 & 3 & 0 \\ 0 & 1 & 1 & 0 \\ 0 & 0 & 1 & 0 \\ 0 & 0 & 0 & 1 \end{bmatrix}
\begin{bmatrix} a_{1,1} - 3a_{2,1} + a_{1,3} - 3a_{2,3} & a_{1,2} - 3a_{2,2} & a_{1,3} - 3a_{2,3} \\ a_{2,1} - a_{3,1} + a_{2,3} - a_{3,3} & a_{2,2} - a_{3,2} & a_{2,3} - a_{3,3} \\ a_{3,1} + a_{3,3} & a_{3,2} & a_{3,3} \\ a_{4,1} + a_{4,3} & a_{4,2} & a_{4,3} \end{bmatrix}
\begin{bmatrix} 1 & 0 & 0 \\ 0 & 1 & 0 \\ -1 & 0 & 1 \end{bmatrix} .
$$

The process of adding identity matrices and transforming the linear circuit through multiplicative number splitting can be repeated until no further gains can be made in terms of lowering the power consumption or hardware complexity of the circuit. Typically, the multiplicative splitting is guided by a greedy algorithm [6] that attempts all possible matrix transformations during each iteration of the splitting algorithm. The transformation leading to the largest reduction in power or hardware cost would be chosen. The splitting process would be continued until no further optimizations could be achieved.

The multiplicative number splitting algorithm is now illustrated using the linear transform

$$T = \begin{bmatrix} .4 & .7 & .4 \\ .6 & .8 & .2 \\ .1 & .3 & .2 \end{bmatrix} . \qquad (15.29)$$

T can be written in an equivalent form as the product of an identity matrix and itself

$$T = T_1 T_2$$

$$\begin{bmatrix} 1 & 0 & 0 \\ 0 & 1 & 0 \\ 0 & 0 & 1 \end{bmatrix} \begin{bmatrix} .4 & .7 & .4 \\ .6 & .8 & .2 \\ .1 & .3 & .2 \end{bmatrix}. \tag{15.30}$$

Now, transform T_1 and T_2 using multiplicative splitting with $K = 1, j = 2$, and $k = 3$

$$T = T_1 T_2$$

$$\begin{bmatrix} 1 & 0 & 0 \\ 0 & 1 & 1 \\ 0 & 0 & 1 \end{bmatrix} \begin{bmatrix} .4 & .7 & .4 \\ .5 & .5 & 0 \\ .1 & .3 & .2 \end{bmatrix}. \tag{15.31}$$

The 2nd row of T_2 has been transformed from 3 nontrivial multiplications to 2 trivial multiplications (a shift to the right by one position is all that is required to implemented a multiplication by .5). Consider transforming T_1 and T_2 a second time with $K = 2, j = 1$, and $k = 3$

$$T = T_1 T_2$$

$$\begin{bmatrix} 1 & 0 & 2 \\ 0 & 1 & 1 \\ 0 & 0 & 1 \end{bmatrix} \begin{bmatrix} .2 & .1 & 0 \\ .5 & .5 & 0 \\ .1 & .3 & .2 \end{bmatrix}. \tag{15.32}$$

The first row of T_2 has now been transformed from 3 nontrivial multiplications to 2 nontrivial multiplications. Now, consider adding an identity matrix to the right-hand side of T_2 in order that the columns of T_2 can be transformed

$$T = T_1 T_2 T_3$$

$$\begin{bmatrix} 1 & 0 & 2 \\ 0 & 1 & 1 \\ 0 & 0 & 1 \end{bmatrix} \begin{bmatrix} .2 & .1 & 0 \\ .5 & .5 & 0 \\ .1 & .3 & .2 \end{bmatrix} \begin{bmatrix} 1 & 0 & 0 \\ 0 & 1 & 0 \\ 0 & 0 & 1 \end{bmatrix}. \tag{15.33}$$

Using $K = -1, j = 2$, and $k = 1$, transform T_2 and T_3

$$T = T_1 T_2 T_3$$

$$\begin{bmatrix} 1 & 0 & 2 \\ 0 & 1 & 1 \\ 0 & 0 & 1 \end{bmatrix} \begin{bmatrix} .1 & .1 & 0 \\ 0 & .5 & 0 \\ -.2 & .3 & .2 \end{bmatrix} \begin{bmatrix} 1 & 0 & 0 \\ 1 & 1 & 0 \\ 0 & 0 & 1 \end{bmatrix}. \tag{15.34}$$

Now, consider applying 3 final transformations

$$T = T_1 T_2 T_3$$

$$\begin{bmatrix} -3 & 0 & 2 \\ -2 & 1 & 1 \\ -2 & 0 & 1 \end{bmatrix} \begin{bmatrix} .1 & .1 & 0 \\ 0 & .5 & 0 \\ 0 & .5 & .2 \end{bmatrix} \begin{bmatrix} 1 & 0 & 0 \\ 1 & 1 & 0 \\ 0 & 0 & 1 \end{bmatrix}, \tag{15.35}$$

$$\mathbf{T} = \mathbf{T_1 T_2 T_3}$$

$$\begin{bmatrix} -3 & 2 & 2 \\ -2 & 2 & 1 \\ -2 & 1 & 1 \end{bmatrix} \begin{bmatrix} .1 & .1 & 0 \\ 0 & .5 & 0 \\ 0 & 0 & .2 \end{bmatrix} \begin{bmatrix} 1 & 0 & 0 \\ 1 & 1 & 0 \\ 0 & 0 & 1 \end{bmatrix}, \tag{15.36}$$

$$\mathbf{T} = \mathbf{T_1 T_2 T_3}$$

$$\begin{bmatrix} -3 & 2 & 2 \\ -2 & 2 & 1 \\ -2 & 1 & 1 \end{bmatrix} \begin{bmatrix} 0 & .1 & 0 \\ -.5 & .5 & 0 \\ 0 & 0 & .2 \end{bmatrix} \begin{bmatrix} 1 & 0 & 0 \\ 2 & 1 & 0 \\ 0 & 0 & 1 \end{bmatrix}. \tag{15.37}$$

Clearly, the multiplicative splitting transformation has reduced the hardware complexity of the original transformation matrix $\mathbf{T}$. The original matrix required 9 nontrivial multiplications. Using multiplicative splitting, the 9 nontrivial multiplications have been reduced to 2 nontrivial multiplications at the expense of a few additions and shift operations.

15.6 CONCLUSIONS

Similar to the strength reduction at algorithm level, numerical strength reduction can reduce the hardware complexity significantly. This chapter has addressed various numerical strength reduction approaches based on subexpression elimination or substructure sharing. These approaches can be exploited to reduce the implementation complexity of fixed-coefficient digital filters such as FIR and IIR digital filters, multirate filters, and wavelet filters. It may be noted that subexpression elimination techniques are commonly used in compiler [7].

15.7 PROBLEMS

1. Assume that the multipliers a, b, c and d must multiply a common multiplicand x. Determine the number of shifts and additions required to implement $a \times x$, $b \times x$, $c \times x$ and $d \times x$ given the set of multiplier values (assume an unsigned binary representation):

   (a) $a = 54$, $b = 45$, $c = 43$, $d = 21$
   (b) $a = 93$, $b = 59$, $c = 55$, $d = 73$

2. Apply the MCM iterative matching algorithm to the multiplier set of Problem 1(a). For each iteration, find the number of bit-wise matches among all constant pairs in the set (see step 2). Determine the number of shifts and additions required after applying the algorithm. How many shifts and additions are saved?

3. Repeat Problem 2 for the multiplier set of Problem 1(b).

4. Apply subexpression elimination for computation $\mathbf{y} = \mathbf{Tx}$ using linear transformation matrix:

$$\mathbf{T} = \begin{bmatrix} 13 & 12 & 5 & 3 \\ 11 & 2 & 7 & 11 \\ 6 & 9 & 15 & 7 \\ 6 & 11 & 5 & 15 \end{bmatrix}$$

Assume an unsigned binary representation. Determine:

(a) the subexpressions required for each column;

(b) the unique product expressions;

(c) y_1, y_2, y_3, and y_4 in binary format where the bit positions represent the presence or absence of the product expressions. Apply the iterative matching algorithm to y_1, y_2, y_3, and y_4. Calculate the total number of shifts and adds required to realize $\mathbf{T}$ after subexpression elimination has been applied. How many shifts and additions have been saved compared to a realization of $\mathbf{T}$ that uses no sharing?

5. Repeat Problem 4 for the following linear transformation matrix (also used in (15.8)):

$$\mathbf{T} = \begin{bmatrix} 11 & 3 & 6 & 0 & 5 \\ 13 & 7 & 11 & 0 & 0 \\ 7 & 15 & 0 & 5 & 0 \end{bmatrix}.$$

Assume an unsigned binary representation.

6. Consider the YUV to RGB color format conversion

$$\begin{bmatrix} R \\ G \\ B \end{bmatrix} = \begin{bmatrix} 1 & 0 & 1.402 \\ 1 & -0.34414 & -0.71414 \\ 1 & 1.772 & 0 \end{bmatrix} \begin{bmatrix} Y \\ U - 128 \\ V - 128 \end{bmatrix},$$

which requires 4 multiplications and 6 additions for each pixel in the image. The efficiency of any color conversion algorithm depends on two criteria: implementation complexity and quality of the color converted image [8]. To reduce the implementation cost, this transformation matrix is approximated as:

$$\begin{bmatrix} 1 & 0 & 1.5 \\ 1 & -0.375 & -0.75 \\ 1 & 1.5 & 0 \end{bmatrix},$$

where each coefficient in unsigned form contains at most two 1's in their binary representation. Use unsigned representation for the coefficients and implement computations involving negative coefficients using subtraction. Design the color format converter using substructure sharing assuming a pixel wordlength of 8. Note that subtracting 128 from U and V can be handled simply by inverting the most significant bit of the value, which need not be counted as 1 subtract operation.

7. Repeat Problem 6 using the approximated transformation matrix

$$\begin{bmatrix} 1 & 0 & 1.375 \\ 1 & -0.34375 & -0.6875 \\ 1 & 1.75 & 0 \end{bmatrix},$$

where each coefficient contains at most three 1's in their binary representation.

8. Apply subexpression elimination to the following polynomials:

   (a) $x^{22} + x^{19} + x^{14} + x^7 + x$;

   (b) $x^{29} + x^{23} + x^{20} + x^{15} + x^9 + x$;

   (c) $x^{23} + x^{17} + x^8 + x^5 + x^4 + x$;

   Determine the number of multiplications required to evaluate the polynomials both before and after subexpression is applied?

9. Consider the implementation of the recursive computation

$$y(n) = \frac{37}{64}y(n-2) + \frac{5}{64}y(n-3) + \frac{1}{4}x(n). \qquad (15.38)$$

   Using two's complement fixed-point representation and substructure sharing, design a bit-serial implementation for wordlength of 8.

10. Design a bit-serial architecture for the 3-tap FIR filter based on the substructure sharing derived in Example 15.4.2. Assume a signal wordlength of 8.

11. This problem addresses bit-serial implementation of the FIR filter in Example 15.4.4. Assume a signal wordlength of 8. For each of the 2 designs in this example, insert proper pipelining cutsets to obtain feasible bit-level pipelined bit-serial architecture. Synchronizing delay elements need to be inserted at appropriate locations. Compare the number of delay elements required in these 2 architectures, including synchronization delays. Note that the synchronizing delays at cutset locations are bit-level delays, while the delays in the data-flow graph represent word-level delays. You do not need to implement the detailed bit-serial design.

12. Consider the implementation of the 5-tap FIR filter

$$y(n) = c_0 x(n) + c_1 x(n-1) + c_2 x(n-2) + c_1 x(n-3) + c_0 x(n-4), \quad (15.39)$$

where

$$c_0 = 0.00010110, \quad c_1 = 0.01001100, \quad c_2 = 0.01100110$$

in two's complementation representation. The output is computed as

$$y(n) = c_0(x(n) + x(n-4)) + c_1(x(n-1) + x(n-3)) + c_2 x(n-2).$$

(a) Represent the coefficients in CSD representation.

(b) Using CSD representation and substructure sharing, obtain a bit-serial implementation of the filter for a wordlength of 9. You do not need to complete a detailed design, i.e., switching instances need not be completed. In this part, assume substructure sharing is only permitted for each coefficient independently, i.e., no sharing among coefficients is permitted.

(c) Repeat part (b) by substructure sharing among coefficients.

(d) Evaluate the designs obtained in parts (b) and (c).

13. Design the bit-serial architecture for the computation

$$y(n) = \frac{83}{128}y(n-2) + \frac{37}{64}y(n-3) - \frac{83}{128}y(n-4) + x(n)$$

based on CSD representation and 2 most common subexpressions and substructure sharing. Assume a wordlength of 8 for signals and coefficients.

14. A length-15 linear phase FIR filter has the following coefficients given in two's complement binary representation:

$$c_0 = 0.00000010, \quad c_1 = 0.00001001, \quad c_2 = 1.11111111,$$
$$c_3 = 1.11110000, \quad c_4 = 1.11110010, \quad c_5 = 0.00010110,$$
$$c_6 = 0.01001100, \quad c_7 = 0.01100110, \quad c_8 = 0.01001100,$$
$$c_9 = 0.00010110, \quad c_{10} = 1.11110010, \quad c_{11} = 1.11110000,$$
$$c_{12} = 1.11111111, \quad c_{13} = 0.00001001, \quad c_{14} = 0.00000010$$

(a) Express all coefficients in CSD representation.

(b) The objective of this part is to implement this FIR filter using CSD coefficients and substructure sharing. Draw the filter implementation using adds, delays and shifts. Use the 2 most common CSD subexpression based substructure sharing to reduce the number of adds. The hardware complexity should be further reduced by exploiting the symmetry of the coefficients of the FIR filter. The implementation should use the smallest possible number of adds, delays, and shifts. Count the total number of adders, delay elements and shift operations used in your circuit.

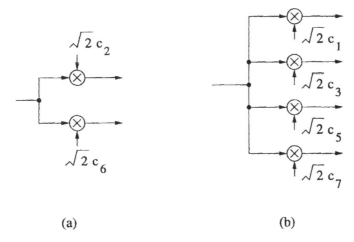

(a)   (b)

Fig. 15.7   DCT building blocks for Problem 16.

15. This problem addresses the implementation of a 7-tap equiripple linear-phase low-pass FIR filter designed using Parks-McClellan approach. The filter is designed for a passband edge of 0.2π and a stop-band edge of 0.25π using the remez command in MATLAB. The 12-bit filter coefficients are obtained as:

$$c_0 = c_6 = 0.0894 = 0.00010110111,$$
$$c_1 = c_5 = 0.3004 = 0.01001100111,$$
$$c_2 = c_4 = 0.1606 = 0.00101001000,$$
$$c_3 = 0.2544 = 0.01000001001.$$

$$(15.40)$$

This 7-tap filter can be implemented using 4 multiply operations due to the linear-phase property. Implement this filter using CSD representation of the coefficients and the 2 common subexpressions. Further subexpression sharing of the 2 common subexpressions based structure must also be exploited. Calculate the number of adders required in your implementation. How many adders would have been needed in the two's complement implementation without subexpression sharing?

16. Consider the design of a scaled 8-point DCT where all coefficients of the matrix are scaled by $\sqrt{2}$. The scaled DCT can be implemented using equations (9.53) and (9.54) with 20 multiplication operations (since $\sqrt{2}c_4 = 1$). This DCT can be implemented using the two building blocks shown in Fig. 15.7(a) and (b), where $c_i = \cos\frac{i\pi}{16}$.

(a) Represent $\sqrt{2}c_2$, $\sqrt{2}c_6$, $\sqrt{2}c_1$, $\sqrt{2}c_3$, $\sqrt{2}c_5$, $\sqrt{2}c_7$ in CSD number system with wordlength 14 that contains 12 fractional bits.

(b) Implement the structures in Fig. 15.7(a) and (b) using two common subexpressions, $x + x >> 2$ and $x - x >> 2$, with the goal of minimizing the number of adders.

(c) Calculate the total number of adders and scalers in the 8-point DCT implementation. You do not need to draw the complete DCT structure.

17. Using row-based additive number splitting, find a low complexity implementation of the transformation matrix in Problem 5.

18. Using row-based additive number splitting, find a low complexity implementation of

$$\begin{bmatrix} y_0(n) \\ y_1(n) \\ y_2(n) \end{bmatrix} = \begin{bmatrix} 0.875 & 0.5 & 0.90625 \\ -0.5 & 0.6875 & 1.1875 \\ 0.125 & 0.68625 & 0.625 \end{bmatrix} \begin{bmatrix} x_0(n) \\ x_1(n) \\ x_2(n) \end{bmatrix},$$

assuming all numbers to be represented in fixed-point two's complement representation.

19. Using column-based additive number splitting, find a low complexity implementation of

$$\begin{bmatrix} y_0(n) \\ y_1(n) \\ y_2(n) \end{bmatrix} = \begin{bmatrix} 0.8125 & 1.1875 & 0.875 \\ 0.25 & 0.4375 & 0.75 \\ 0.9375 & 0.1875 & 0.75 \end{bmatrix} \begin{bmatrix} x_0(n) \\ x_1(n) \\ x_2(n) \end{bmatrix},$$

assuming all numbers to be represented in fixed-point two's complement representation.

20. This problem considers low-complexity implementation of the transformation

$$\begin{bmatrix} y_0(n+1) \\ y_1(n+1) \\ y_2(n+1) \end{bmatrix} = \begin{bmatrix} 1.2 & 1 & -0.6 & 0.6 \\ 0.92 & -1.28 & 0.6 & -0.6 \\ 1 & -1.36 & 0.18 & 0 \end{bmatrix} \times \begin{bmatrix} y_0(n) \\ y_1(n) \\ y_2(n) \\ u(n) \end{bmatrix}$$

using row- and column-based multiplicative number splitting. Denote the original transformation matrix as $\mathbf{T}$, which requires 6 nontrivial multiplication operations. Find a 3×3 matrix $\mathbf{T}_1$ and a 4×4 matrix $\mathbf{T}_3$, such that $\mathbf{T} = \mathbf{T}_1 \mathbf{T}_2 \mathbf{T}_3$ and implementing this transformation matrix using $\mathbf{T}_1 \mathbf{T}_2 \mathbf{T}_3$ requires only 3 multiplications and some trivial shift operations.

Initially, $\mathbf{T}_1$ and $\mathbf{T}_3$ are indentity matrices and $\mathbf{T}_2$ equals $\mathbf{T}$. Use the following ordered column transformations on $\mathbf{T}_1$ and row transformations on $\mathbf{T}_3$ to obtain the resulting $\mathbf{T}_2$, which requires only 3 nontrivial multiplications:

- The 1st column of $\mathbf{T}_1$ is transformed as

$$Col(1) = Col(1) - 1 \times Col(2); \qquad (15.41)$$

- The 4th row of $\mathbf{T}_3$ is transformed as

$$Row(4) = Row(4) + 2 \times Row(1); \qquad (15.42)$$

- The 1st row of the updated matrix $\mathbf{T}_3$ is transformed as

$$Row(1) = Row(1) - 1 \times Row(2); \qquad (15.43)$$

- The 4th row of the updated matrix $\mathbf{T}_3$ is transformed as

$$Row(4) = Row(4) - 1 \times Row(3); \qquad (15.44)$$

- The 2nd row of the updated matrix $\mathbf{T}_3$ is transformed as

$$Row(2) = Row(2) - \frac{1}{2} \times Row(3). \qquad (15.45)$$

The resulting $\mathbf{T}_1$ and $\mathbf{T}_3$ matrices are as follows:

$$\mathbf{T}_1 = \begin{bmatrix} 1 & 0 & 0 \\ -1 & 1 & 0 \\ 0 & 0 & 1 \end{bmatrix}, \quad \mathbf{T}_3 = \begin{bmatrix} 1 & -1 & 0 & 0 \\ 0 & 1 & -0.5 & 0 \\ 0 & 0 & 1 & 0 \\ 2 & 0 & -1 & 1 \end{bmatrix}. \qquad (15.46)$$

Note that the product $\mathbf{T}_1\mathbf{T}_2\mathbf{T}_3$ is unchanged and equals to $\mathbf{T}$. A corresponding row operation on $\mathbf{T}_2$ is required whenever a column operation is performed on $\mathbf{T}_1$; a corresponding column operation on $\mathbf{T}_2$ is required whenever a row operation is performed on $\mathbf{T}_3$. Write down the necessary row/column operations on $\mathbf{T}_2$ corresponding to the above column/row linear transformations on $\mathbf{T}_1$ and $\mathbf{T}_3$, and explicitly show the $\mathbf{T}_2$ matrix at each step. Show that the final $\mathbf{T}_2$ matrix is obtained as

$$\mathbf{T}_2 = \begin{bmatrix} 0 & 1 & 0.5 & 0.6 \\ 0.28 & 0 & 0 & 0 \\ 1 & -0.36 & 0 & 0 \end{bmatrix}. \qquad (15.47)$$

REFERENCES

1. M. Potkonjak, M. B. Srivastava, and A. P. Chandrakasan, "Multiple constant multiplications: efficient and versatile framework and algorithms for exploring common subexpression elimination," *IEEE Trans. on Computer-Aided Design*

of Integrated Circuits and Systems, vol. 15, no. 2, pp. 151–165, Feb. 1996.

2. A. Chatterjee, R. K. Roy, and M. A. d'Abreu, "Greedy hardware optimization for linear digital circuits using number splitting and refactorization," *IEEE Trans. on VLSI Systems*, vol. 1, no. 4, pp. 423–431, Dec. 1993.

3. R. I. Hartley and K. K. Parhi, *Digit-Serial Computation.* Kluwer, 1995.

4. M. Potkonjak, M. B. Srivastava, and A. Chandrakasan, "Efficient substitution of multiple constant multiplications by shifts and additions using iterative pairwise matching," in *DAC-94, Proceedings of the 31st ACM/IEEE Design Automation Conference*, pp. 189–194, 1994.

5. A. Chatterjee and R. K. Roy, "An architectural transformation program for optimization of digital systems by multi-level decomposition," in *30th ACM/IEEE Design Automation Conference*, (Atlanta, GA), pp. 343–348, May 1993.

6. H. Nguyen, A. Chatterjee, and R. K Roy, "Activity measures for fast relative power estimation directed numerical transformation for low power DSP synthesis," *Journal of VLSI Signal Processing Systems*, vol. 18, no. 1, pp. 25–38, Jan. 1998.

7. A. Aho, R. Sethi, and J. D. Ullman, *Compilers: Principles, Techniques and Tools.* Addison-Wesley, 1986.

8. B. Gordon, N. Chaddha, and T. Meng, "A low-power multiplierless YUV to RGB converter based on human vision perception," in *Proc. of IEEE Workshop on VLSI Signal Processing*, (San Diego, CA), pp. 408–417, 1994.

16

Synchronous, Wave, and Asynchronous Pipelines

16.1 INTRODUCTION

The need for high performance and low cost digital systems for signal/image processing applications has resulted in a major thrust for high-speed VLSI design. Traditionally, high throughput is obtained by dividing the combinatorial logic into a number of stages separated by registers/latches controlled by a global clock. Various clocking styles can be used depending on the type of application; these include 2-phase, true single phase, etc. With the advent of technology, the number of transistors that can be integrated on a single chip has increased tremendously. Along with it the clock frequencies at which these chips can operate is also increasing at a rapid rate. Consequently, clock distribution and minimization of clock skew have become major bottlenecks in the design of synchronous systems. In fact, the clock skew may build up to dangerous proportions and cause malfunctioning of the circuit. Therefore, alternative techniques are being explored and most prominent among them are wave pipelining [1]–[6] and asynchronous pipelining [7]–[18].

Wave pipelining is a technique employed to decrease the effective number of pipeline stages in a digital system without increasing the number of physical registers in the pipeline. This is achieved by applying new data to the inputs of the combinational logic before the output (due to previous data inputs) is available, thus pipelining the combinational logic. The time of application of new data is determined by performing detailed system-level and circuit-level analysis. At the system level, the analysis should take into account the clock period, the intentional clock skew, and the global clock latency. At the circuit level, precise estimates of the maximum and minimum delays through combinational logic circuits are required.

Asynchronous pipelining is a technique where there is no global synchronization within the system; subsystems within the system are only synchronized locally by the communication protocols between them. Systems that involve some sort of request/acknowledge handshake protocol between the subsystems are often referred to as *self-timed* systems. Since most practical asynchronous systems are self-timed systems, these terms are often used synonymously in the literature. The results produced by subsystems in an asynchronous system can be consumed by other subsystems as soon as they are generated, without having to wait for a global clock change. As a result, asynchronous systems are limited by the average-case performance rather than the worst case (as in synchronous systems) of the subsystems. Moreover, a subsystem can be replaced by another subsystem with the same functionality but different performance with ease. However, in synchronous systems this task is not easy as the clock period may have to be recomputed. Finally, transitions in a particular subsystem are only produced when data is processed by it and therefore there is no dynamic power consumption when the subsystem is idle. This makes asynchronous systems attractive for low-power designs. However, the power consumption is increased by the handshaking circuits.

This chapter first presents a detailed discussion of synchronous pipelining and various clocking styles that can be used. Then, the issues of clock skew and clock distribution are addressed together with methods to minimize them. This discussion is followed by a broad overview of more recent techniques that have been proposed to overcome the problem of clock skew and clock distribution including wave pipelining and asynchronous pipelining. The organization of this chapter is as follows. Section 16.2 briefly describes synchronous pipelining and the various clocking styles that can be used. Section 16.3 addresses the problem of clock skew and clock distribution and presents some techniques that can be employed to minimize them. The theoretical background for wave pipelining is discussed in Section 16.4. The details about the levels of wave pipelining and their practical significance are presented in Section 16.5. In Section 16.6, an algorithm for wave pipelining of a given circuit using normal process complementary pass transistor logic (NPCPL) is presented. A brief introduction to asynchronous design style is given in Section 16.7. Here, various types of communication protocols including bundled data, dual-rail, 2-phase, and 4-phase are discussed. An introduction to signal transition graphs (STGs) for designing 4-phase handshake circuits is presented in Section 16.8. In Section 16.9, the application of STGs to design interconnection circuits is presented. Design examples of asynchronous circuits are presented in Section 16.10.

16.2 SYNCHRONOUS PIPELINING AND CLOCKING STYLES

Consider a typical synchronous nonpipelined system as shown in Fig. 16.1(a). Here, the system consists of a single combinatorial block surrounded by edge

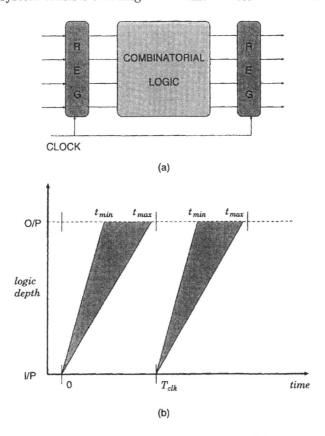

(a)

(b)

Fig. 16.1 (a) Synchronous nonpipelined system. (b) Data flow.

triggered registers. At the beginning of each clock cycle, data is initiated into the block from the input register. Due to the differences in circuit path lengths and other factors, the delay through the combinatorial block may vary. However, this delay is bounded between t_{min} and t_{max} as shown in Fig. 16.1(b). Here, the shaded regions depict the flow of data through the combinatorial block and the times at which particular parts of the logic are changing, while the unshaded regions depict the time at which the logic is stationary. Therefore, the output register is clocked in the unshaded region after the latest data has arrived at the output of the combinatorial block (allowing for register setup times). At the same time new input data is clocked into the logic at the input register. Therefore, the minimum clock period is bounded by the sum of the longest delay of the combinatorial logic and the

propagation, setup times of the register together with any unintentional clock
skew between input and output clocks.

The conventional method for decreasing the clock period of the system is
by *pipelining* the combinatorial block as shown in Fig. 16.2(a). Here, the
combinatorial block is divided into 2 parts and a register is inserted between

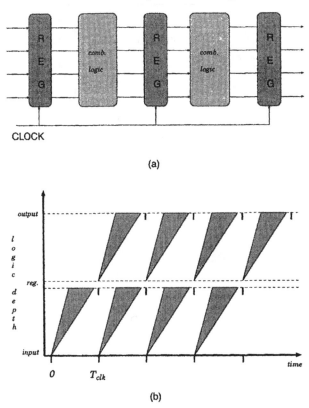

Fig. 16.2 (a) Synchronous pipelined system. (b) Data flow.

them. As a result, each computation takes 2 clock cycles to propagate through
the system, and a new computation is available at the output register every
clock period. The insertion of the register reduces the maximum delay of
the combinatorial block, and therefore the overall system clock period can be
reduced.

Various clocking styles that can be used to clock the registers in the synchronous pipelined system. The *2-phase clocking* was used in most of the
earlier designs of digital systems. The main idea behind this clocking style
is to use 2 nonoverlapping clocks ϕ_1 and ϕ_2 as shown in Fig. 16.3. Clock ϕ_1
is typically referred to as the *master* clock and ϕ_2 is referred to as the *slave*
clock. They both satisfy the important property that they are never high at
the same time. However, they can have a finite *underlap* time as shown in

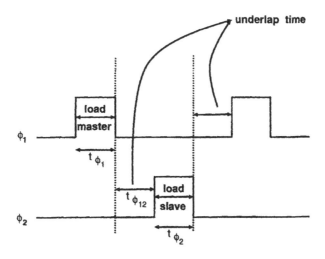

Fig. 16.3   Two-phase clocking strategy.

Fig. 16.3. A synchronous register can then be designed by cascading 2 latches in *master-slave* configuration as shown in Fig. 16.4, where the 1st latch is

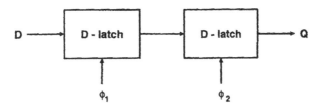

Fig. 16.4   A typical synchronous register.

clocked using ϕ_1, and the 2nd latch is clocked using ϕ_2. The nonoverlapping clock signals guarantee that the input signal D will not race through to the output Q. The nonoverlapping property of the clock signals can be expressed in a more formal way using the concept of *valid on phase* and *stable on phase*.

A signal X is said to be *valid on phase* ϕ_i ($[V\phi_i]$) if it is stable around the falling edge of ϕ_i as shown in Fig. 16.5(a). A signal Y is said to be *stable on phase* ϕ_i ($[S\phi_i]$) if it is stable for the entire duration when ϕ_i is high as shown in Fig. 16.5(b). It follows that a signal that is stable on phase ϕ_i will automatically be valid on phase ϕ_i since it is a stronger constraint. If a signal X is $[V\phi_i]$, then it can be wired to the D input of the D-type latch that is clocked on phase ϕ_i, because the $[V\phi_i]$ property guarantees that the setup/hold requirements will be met. It is intuitive to observe that if the input to a D-latch that is clocked using ϕ_1 is $[V\phi_1]$, then the output of the latch will automatically be $[S\phi_2]$. The concepts of $[V\phi_i]$ and $[S\phi_i]$ are very useful in the design of correct synchronous systems.

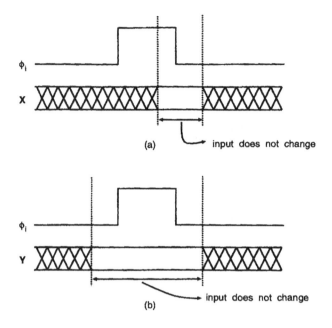

Fig. 16.5 (a) Valid on phase ϕ_i. (b) Stable on phase ϕ_i.

The D-latch shown in Fig. 16.4 can be implemented using static logic or dynamic logic. The architecture of a static latch is shown in Fig. 16.6 and consists of 8 transistors. There are 2 transmission gates numbered 1 and 2; one

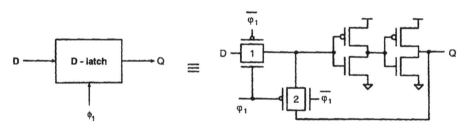

Fig. 16.6 Static D-latch.

clocked using ϕ_1 and the other using $\overline{\phi_1}$ (logic complement of ϕ_1). When ϕ_1 is high, the transmission gate numbered 1 is transparent and the input signal D passes through 2 inverters and becomes available at the output. When ϕ_1 is low, the transmission gate numbered 1 is opaque and the transmission gate numbered 2 becomes transparent. Therefore, the output signal Q is recirculated through the latch.

The architecture of a dynamic D-latch is shown in Fig. 16.7 and consists of 6 transistors for the generation of both Q and $\overline{Q}$. The main difference between this latch and the static latch is that the output is not fed back. A single

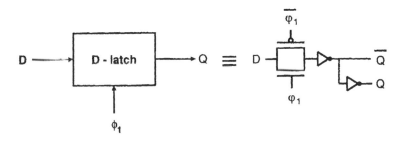

Fig. 16.7 Dynamic D-latch.

transmission gate clocked using ϕ_1 is present at the input end. When ϕ_1 is high, the transmission gate is transparent and the true and complement forms of the input are available at the output. When ϕ_1 is low, the transmission gate is opaque and the capacitor present at the output stores the last value of D. Although the dynamic latch uses fewer transistors than the static latch, the charge on the output capacitance stays only for a very short time. Therefore, the output might have to be refreshed periodically.

Although the idea behind 2-phase clocking sounds simple, the designer must ensure that the 2 phases ϕ_1 and ϕ_2 never overlap. This is sometimes not easy to achieve as the delays on the clock wires cannot be ignored for bigger designs. In addition the inverted clocks $\overline{\phi_1}$ and $\overline{\phi_2}$ should also never be low at the same time. Therefore, these clocks cannot be designed by a simple inversion of their corresponding true clocks. An efficient design for generating both the true and inverted clocks from 1 single external clock ϕ is shown in Fig. 16.8. This circuit ensures that ϕ_1 and ϕ_2 can never be high at the same

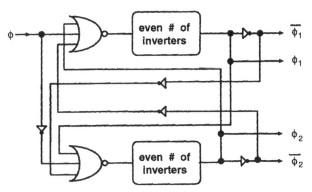

Fig. 16.8 Two-phase clock generator.

time, and that $\overline{\phi_1}$ and $\overline{\phi_2}$ can never be low at the same time. Initially let us assume that ϕ and ϕ_2 are one, and ϕ_1 is 0. When ϕ makes a transition from 1 to 0, the output of the bottom NOR gate becomes 0 and consequently ϕ_2 becomes 0. Now, the inputs to the top NOR gate are all 0 and therefore the output becomes 1. This in turn causes ϕ_1 to become 1 after a certain delay. Again when ϕ makes a transition from 0 to 1, the output of the top NOR gate becomes 0 causing ϕ_1 to become 0. This causes all the inputs of the bottom NOR gate to be 0. Consequently, ϕ_2 also becomes 1 after a certain inverter delay. Therefore, 2 nonoverlapping clocks are generated using 1 external clock.

With advancement in semiconductor technology, a large number of digital circuits are being integrated on a single chip. In addition, a significant portion of the chip area is also being used by registers. As a result, clock distribution using a 2-phase clocking scheme becomes difficult. Therefore, recently a novel clocking style known as *true single phase clocking* (tspc) has been developed [19]. The main feature of this clocking style is that there is just 1 clock ϕ (even $\bar{\phi}$ is not required). This results in a simpler clock distribution and potentially increased speeds. A tspc positive (negative) edge-triggered flip-flop is designed by cascading a tspc p-latch (n-latch) and a tspc n-latch (p-latch) as shown in Fig. 16.9.

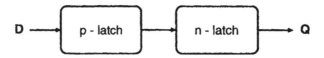

Fig. 16.9 Positive edge-triggered tspc flip-flop.

The architecture of a tpsc n-latch is shown in Fig. 16.10. It is clear from

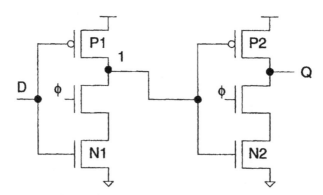

Fig. 16.10 Architecture of a tspc n-latch.

the figure that the latch consists of 6 transistors and only 1 single phase clock signal ϕ. The operation of the latch can be summarized in the following 2 steps:

1. $\phi = 1$: Both the NMOS clock transistors are ON. Therefore, the circuit behaves like 2 inverters in series and as a result the latch is transparent.

Consequently, any change in the input signal D is reflected at the output signal Q.

2. $\phi \to 0$: This step is analyzed using the following 2 cases:

   (a) Let us suppose that the input signal D had stabilized to 0 prior to this edge. Since ϕ is 0, both the clocked NMOS transistors are turned OFF and there is no path to GND. However, P1 is turned on as D is 0 and node 1 is pulled to Vdd. This in turn switches OFF P2 and the output signal Q remains at its previous value, i.e., 0. Now, let us assume that D changes to 1. This isolates node 1 (as P1 is turned OFF) and it retains its previous value of Vdd. Therefore, the output remains unchanged.

   (b) Let us suppose that the input signal D had stabilized to 1 prior to this edge. This meant that prior to this edge node 1 was discharged to GND and P2 was ON causing the output Q to be pulled up to Vdd. Now, since $\phi = 0$, node 1 remains isolated at 0 and Q remains at Vdd. If D changes to 0, P1 is turned ON and node 1 is pulled up to Vdd. This in turn causes P2 to be turned OFF and as before the output Q is isolated and retains its previous value of Vdd. It is clear from the analysis that $\phi = 1$ corresponds to the transparent phase and $\phi = 0$ corresponds to the opaque phase.

The architecture of the tspc p-latch is shown in Fig. 16.11 and consists of 6

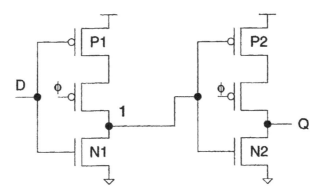

Fig. 16.11   Architecture of a tspc p-latch.

transistors and a single phase clock ϕ. As before, the functionality of the latch is analyzed in the following 2 steps:

1. Let us assume that $\phi = 0$. Consequently, the 2 PMOS clocked transistors are turned ON. The circuit then behaves like 2 inverters in series and the input signal D propagates to Q. Therefore, the latch is transparent during this phase.

2. Let us assume that $\phi = 1$. This can result in the following 2 cases:

   (a) Let us suppose that D had stabilized to 0 prior to this edge. As $\phi \to 1$, both the pull-up paths are turned OFF. Therefore, node 1 which has a value of Vdd is isolated and Q remains pulled to GND through N2. Now, if D changes to 1, N1 turns ON and node 1 is discharged to GND. Although this causes P2 to turn ON it is still in series with an OFF clocked transistor. Therefore, Q is isolated and retains its value of 0.

   (b) Let us suppose that D had stabilized to 1 prior to the clock edge. This means that prior to the clock edge node 1 would have been discharged to GND and Q would have been pulled up to Vdd. If D now goes to 0, node 1 becomes isolated and remains at GND and Q retains its value of Vdd. Therefore, it is clear that $\phi = 0$ corresponds to a transparent phase and $\phi = 1$ corresponds to an opaque phase.

The tspc register requires 12 transistors if the p-latch and the n-latch are cascaded together. However, an efficient implementation of the register that uses only 9 transistors (for the generation of $\overline{Q}$) exists and is shown in Fig. 16.12. The operation of this flip-flop is as follows. Let us assume initially

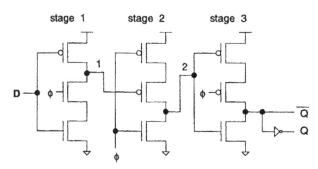

Fig. 16.12   Nine-transistor tspc negative edge-triggered flip-flop.

that $\phi = 1$. This implies that stage 1 is transparent and node 1 becomes equal to $\overline{D}$. At the same time node 2 of stage 2 is discharged to GND. In stage 3, $\overline{Q}$ is isolated and stores its previous value. Let us assume that ϕ goes to 0. The following 2 cases can arise depending on the value of D.

1. Let us assume that prior to ϕ becoming 0, D was 0. After ϕ becomes 0, node 1 stays at Vdd and node 2 stays at GND. In the 3rd stage the pull-up net is ON and $\overline{Q}$ is pulled up to Vdd.

2. Let us assume that prior to ϕ becoming 0, D was 1. This meant that node 1 and 2 would have been discharged to GND and $\overline{Q}$ would be isolated. Now, as soon as ϕ becomes 0, the pull-up net in stage 2 is

turned ON and node 2 is pulled up to Vdd. This in turn causes $\overline{Q}$ to be discharged to 0. Therefore, it is clear from the above discussion that the design functions as a *negative edge-triggered flip-flop.*

16.3 CLOCK SKEW AND CLOCK DISTRIBUTION IN BIT-LEVEL PIPELINED VLSI DESIGNS

The previous section presented various clocking styles that can be used for design of pipelined systems. Bit-level pipelined designs are used in high-speed or low-power applications and the problems of clock skew and clock distribution can be severe due to the large number of registers used. In large systems, the global clock is available to different registers at different times due to the propagation delay of the clock lines. The difference between the time of arrival of the global clock at different registers is referred to as *clock skew.* In this section, the clock skew problem is formulated and conditions resulting in clock skew are discussed. In addition, techniques are presented for clock distribution that can be used to minimize the clock skew.

16.3.1 Clock Skew

In synchronous systems, clock skew is a problem that grows with the speed and size of the system. As a result, in very high-speed bit-level pipelined systems this becomes a major bottleneck. Therefore, it is necessary to understand thoroughly the effects of clock skew before designing bit-level pipelined systems. In addition, the way the clock skew affects the operation of a system generally depends on the type of clocking style used and on the direction of data transfer with respect to the clock signal.

The issues of clock skew are analyzed with the help of Fig. 16.13 [20]. Here, the computational logic block (CLB) and the register R form 1 module of the

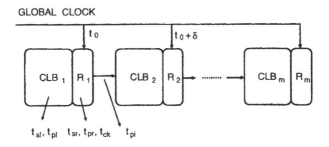

Fig. 16.13 A typical pipelined system for clock skew analysis.

synchronous system or 1 stage of the pipeline. Depending on the degree of pipelining each CLB can be a single logic gate, a full adder performing bit-level operations, or a multiplier performing word-level operations. Associated with each module, the following parameters are defined:

t_{sl}, t_{sr}: logic cell, register computation delay, or settling time.

t_{pl}, t_{pr}: logic cell, register propagation delay.

T_{clk}: register clock time.

t_{pi}: propagation delay time corresponding to the interconnection between adjacent pipeline stages.

The *propagation delay* is the time it takes before at least one of the outputs of the CLB starts a transition in response to a change at any one of its inputs. This delay is typically much shorter than the *settling time* of the CLB and plays an important role in the clock skew problem. The problem of clock skew is addressed for two different clocking styles, namely, edge-triggered single-phase and 2-phase clocking.

16.3.1.1 Edge-Triggered Single-Phase Clocking

Consider the data transfer between blocks CLB_1 and CLB_2 in Fig. 16.13. It is clear from the figure that at time $t = t_0$ the output of CLB_1 begins to be loaded into R_1, and at time $t = t_0 + \delta$ the output of CLB_2 begins to be loaded into R_2, where δ denotes the clock skew between the 2 registers. In addition, at time $t = t_0 + t_{pr} + t_{pi} + t_{pl}$, the response to the change in R_1 has propagated all the way up to the input of R_2. However, the loading time of R_2 is $t = t_0 + \delta$ and therefore the following condition must be satisfied.

$$t_0 + t_{pr} + t_{pi} + t_{pl} > t_0 + \delta. \tag{16.1}$$

Equivalently,

$$\delta < t_{pr} + t_{pi} + t_{pl}. \tag{16.2}$$

Therefore, the clock skew must be less than the sum of the propagation delay times of the register, interconnect, and the logic cell. In general, δ can be positive or negative depending on the direction of the clock with respect to the direction of the data flow. Since the propagation delays in (16.2) are always positive, this condition will always be satisfied if δ is negative. However, a negative δ has a significant effect on the clock period T_{clk} of the digital system. The clock period must be long enough to allow the computation to take place. It is easy to compute the computation time t_c of the CLBs as

$$t_c = t_{sr} + t_{pi} + t_{sl}. \tag{16.3}$$

Therefore, from Fig. 16.14(b) the constraint on the clock period for negative δ is expressed as

$$T_{clk} > t_c + |\delta| = t_{sr} + t_{pi} + t_{sl} + |\delta|. \tag{16.4}$$

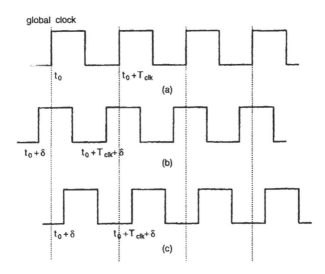

Fig. 16.14 (a) Clock as seen by register R_1. (b) Clock as seen by register R_2 for negative δ. (c) Clock as seen by register R_2 for positive δ.

Similarly, if δ is positive it is clear from Fig. 16.14(b) that the constraint on the clock period becomes

$$T_{clk} > t_c - \delta = t_{sr} + t_{pi} + t_{sl} - \delta. \tag{16.5}$$

Combining (16.4) and (16.5) one gets

$$T_{clk} > t_{sr} + t_{pi} + t_{sl} + |\delta|, \quad \delta \leq 0 \tag{16.6}$$
$$T_{clk} > t_{sr} + t_{pi} + t_{sl} - \delta, \quad \delta > 0.$$

This means that if the clock skew is negative, then condition (16.2) will always be satisfied and the propagation delays of the register, logic, and interconnection cannot cause disasters provided the system clock period is large enough. However, if the clock skew is positive, then condition (16.2) must be satisfied to prevent system failure. The throughput is slightly improved because the clock period can be shortened by δ. Another interesting observation is that for positive δ, if condition (16.2) is violated no matter how large the clock period is, the system will fail to perform correctly. Therefore, it is clear from the foregoing discussion that if the goal is to maximize the throughput then positive skew is better than negative skew. However, in a general synchronous system with feedback, the skew can be both positive and negative. In this case the worst possible skew must be considered.

The parameters defining the upper bound on the clock skew in (16.2) depend on the technology used, the speed of the CLBs, and the interconnection between the modules. For bit-level pipelined architectures, the interconnection propagation delay t_{pi} is typically small because data transfer takes place between modules that are close to each other on the chip. The propagation delay of the CLBs t_{pl} is also quite small as the largest computing module is typically a 1-bit full adder. If 1.25μ CMOS technology is used, typical values for $t_{pr} + t_{pi} + t_{pl}$ are found to be in the order of 1.2 nsec.

16.3.1.2 Two-Phase Clocking Consider the 2-phase clocking scheme shown in Fig. 16.3, where t_{ϕ_1} represents the phase-1 pulse width, t_{ϕ_2} represents the phase 2 pulse width, and $t_{\phi_{12}}$ represents the delay time between phase 1 and phase 2. The remaining parameters stay the same as that in the previous section except that t_{pr_1} and t_{sr_1} are used for the phase 1 latch, and t_{pr_2} and t_{sr_2} for the phase 2 latch. It is also assumed that the clock skew has the same pattern for both phase 1 and phase 2. At time $t = t_0$, the output of CLB_1 begins a transfer into the phase 1 latch of register R_1 and its effect is observed at the phase 1 input of R_2 at time

$$t = t_0 + t_{\phi_1} + t_{\phi_{12}} + t_{pr_2} + t_{pi} + t_{pl}. \tag{16.7}$$

For the digital system to operate correctly, this time should be greater than $t = t_0 + \delta + t_{\phi_1}$. Therefore, the condition for the clock skew becomes

$$\delta < t_{pr_2} + t_{pi} + t_{pl} + t_{\phi_{12}}. \tag{16.8}$$

Performing an analysis similar to that of the single-phase clocking, it is found that the clock period T_{clk} should satisfy the following conditions

$$T_{clk} > t_{\phi_1} + t_{\phi_{12}} + t_{sr_2} + t_{pi} + t_{sl} + |\delta|, \quad \delta \leq 0 \tag{16.9}$$
$$T_{clk} > t_{\phi_1} + t_{\phi_{12}} + t_{sr_2} + t_{pi} + t_{sl} - \delta, \quad \delta > 0.$$

In addition, one must also have $t_{\phi_1} > t_{sr_1}$ and $t_{\phi_2} > t_{sr_2}$. An interesting point in 2-phase clocking is that for positive δ, one can always increase $t_{\phi_{12}}$ to satisfy condition (16.8) at the cost of reducing the throughput. In other words, unlike the edge-triggered single-phase clocking scheme, in a 2-phase clocking approach, it is always possible to prevent failure of the digital system by slowing down the clock frequency. The parameter $t_{\phi_{12}}$ acts as a global parameter that can be used to control the clock skew.

The techniques just described can be followed for any other clocking scheme to understand the effect of clock skew on the operation of a bit-level pipelined digital system. These approaches have been used to design very high-speed digital integrated circuits including the $70 - MHz$ multiplier [21] and the $85 - MHz$ IIR digital filter [22].

16.3.2 Clock Distribution

The factors that determine the clock skew picture in a synchronous digital system are as follows:

- the resistance, inductance, and capacitance of the interconnection material used in the clock distribution network

- the shape of the clock distribution network

- fabrication process variation over the area of the chip or the wafer

- number of processing elements in the digital system and the load presented by each module to the clock distribution network

- rise and fall times and the frequency of the clock signal

- buffering schemes and clock buffers used.

In order to study these effects, a distributed RC model for the clock distribution network can be used. The most widely studied clock distribution network that minimizes skew is called as the H-tree network [23]−[25] shown in Fig. 16.15. Here, the architecture consists of an 8 × 8 array of cells iden-

GLOBAL CLOCK

Fig. 16.15 H-tree distribution network for an 8×8 array of cells.

tical in size. It is clear from the figure that since the cells are identical they present the same load and the paths from the clock source to all the cells are similar and as a result the clock skew is minimized. It was shown in [26] that for an N × N array of processing elements the clock pulse rise time and the clock skew associated with it are $O(N^3)$. Therefore, it appears that as

N increases, the clock skew would increase rapidly and become a stumbling block. However, this problem can be overcome by using a distributed buffering scheme as shown in Fig. 16.16 [23]. One of the disadvantages of introducing

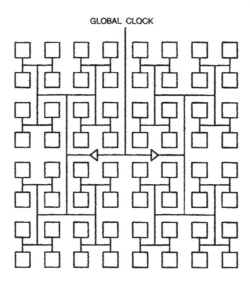

Fig. 16.16   H-tree distribution network with intermediate buffering.

buffers in the H-tree network is the area overhead. The other disadvantage is the increase in the sensitivity of the design to process variations. This is however offset by the improvement gained in speed. H-tree networks are most useful when all processing elements in the system are identical and the clock can be truly distributed in a binary fashion. An alternative to the H-tree network suitable for on-chip clock distribution is the network using a 2-level buffering scheme as shown in Fig. 16.17 [20]. Although, in theory, this network does not provide the minimum clock skew feature offered by an ideal H-tree network, it has been proved to be useful in practice, because the extent of clock skew minimization depends on the amount of clock skew tolerated by the system. This technique has been used to design bit-level pipelined multiply-accumulate systems [20].

16.4   WAVE PIPELINING

It is clear from the previous section that clocking styles play a very important role in the performance of digital systems. Conventional methods involve the identification of the *critical path* (the path with the longest delay) for the determination of the clock period. Therefore, the designer spends most of the time in trying to minimize this clock period. In digital systems, typically there exist many paths having delays that are much smaller than the critical

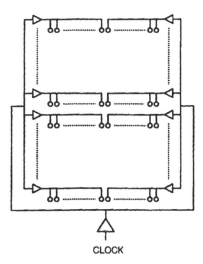

CLOCK

Fig. 16.17 Two-level distributed buffering scheme.

path. However, they are still clocked with the same clock period and as a result the logic gates along this path remain idle for a major portion of the clock period. This suggests that there is room for improvement in the clock speed where the noncritical paths remain idle. The concept of *wave pipelining* [4] is based on the fact that the clock speed can be increased if the idle time of the noncritical paths can be reduced.

It is intuitive to observe from Fig. 16.1(b) that the inputs to the output register are all stable for a significant portion of the clock period, suggesting that the combinatorial block is not operating at its maximum rate. One may then ask the question, is it possible to apply a new set of operands to the input of the combinatorial block before the results of the current operand appear at its output. The answer is yes, and in fact the clock period can be reduced as long as data from a particular clock cycle does not overwrite data from the previous clock cycle. This forms the basis of wave pipelining as shown by the logic depth-timing diagram in Fig. 16.18(b), where the clock period has been reduced as much as possible. The factor now limiting the clock period is the difference between the maximum (t_{max}) and minimum (t_{min}) data delays through the combinatorial block along with register setup/hold, propagation times, and unintentional clock skew.

The clock period (T_{clk}) in a wave-pipelined system is constrained by the difference between the maximum and the minimum combinational logic delay. Of course, nonideal effects like setup and hold times, clock skew at input and output registers should also be taken into account. These effects are best illustrated with the help of Fig. 16.19(b). Here t_{min} and t_{max} represent, respectively, the minimum and maximum combinational logic delays. The setup and hold times are denoted by t_{setup} and t_{hold}, and Δ_i and Δ_o represent

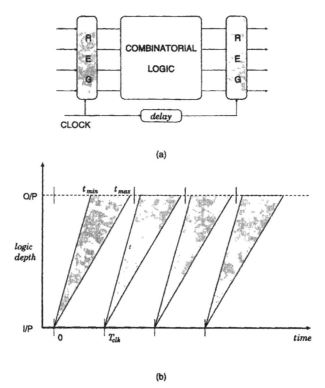

Fig. 16.18 (a) Wave-pipelined system and (b) data-flow.

the intentional delays added to the input and output registers. Moreover, Δt_e^i and Δt_l^i represent the earliest and latest possible clock skews, respectively, at the input register. The corresponding values at the output register are denoted by Δt_e^o and Δt_l^o.

In Fig. 16.19(b), the clock period should be such that the output data is latched *after* the latest data has arrived at the outputs and *before* the earliest data from the next clock period arrives. Let the output data be latched by the output register at some time t relative to the global clock. Then t corresponds to kT_{clk}, where k is called as the global clock latency [4]. Since the output register has a delay of Δ_o associated with it, the condition for t can be expressed mathematically as

$$t = kT_{clk} + \Delta_o. \tag{16.10}$$

Therefore, for correct clocking the output data must be sampled at time t at which the data is stable. This implies that the following constraint must be valid:

$$kT_{clk} + \Delta_o - \Delta t_e^o \geq \Delta_i + \Delta t_l^i + t_d + t_{max} + t_{setup}, \tag{16.11}$$

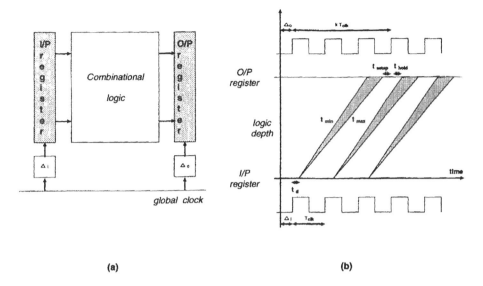

Fig. 16.19 (a) Wave-pipelined circuit with (b) corresponding timing diagram.

where t_d represents the delay time of the register. In addition to ensure that the earliest data is latched correctly, the following constraint must also be satisfied:

$$\Delta_i + T_{clk} + t_d + t_{min} - t_{hold} - \Delta t_e^i \geq kT_{clk} + \Delta_o + \Delta t_l^o. \quad (16.12)$$

Combining (16.11) and (16.12) and rearranging terms, one gets

$$T_{clk} + t_{min} - t_{hold} - \Delta t_e^i - \Delta t_l^o \geq kT_{clk} + \Delta - t_d \geq \qquad (16.13)$$
$$t_{max} + t_{setup} + \Delta t_l^i + \Delta t_e^o,$$

where

$$\Delta = \Delta_o - \Delta_i. \quad (16.14)$$

Equivalently,

$$T_{clk} \geq (t_{max} - t_{min}) + t_{setup} + t_{hold} + \Delta t_e^i + \Delta t_e^o + \Delta t_l^i + \Delta t_l^o. \quad (16.15)$$

It is clear from the foregoing expression that the clock rate is bounded by the difference of maximal and minimal delays between input and output registers. It is also evident that the unintentional clock skew and setup/hold times directly increase the possible clock period. In conventional pipelining, however, the clock period is bounded by just the maximal computational delay.

Example 16.4.1 *Let $t_{max} = 10$ nsec, $t_{min} = 8$ nsec. Then for conventional*

pipelining (ignoring setup/hold times) the minimum possible clock period is
$t_{max}=10$ *nsec. However, for wave pipelining the minimum possible clock pe-*
riod is $t_{max} - t_{min}=2$ *nsec. Therefore, the wave-pipelined system can be op-*
erated at least five times faster than the conventional pipelined system. ■

A condition similar to (16.15) can be derived for all the internal nodes
(ignoring the setup/hold requirements) in the system in accordance with

$$T_{clk} \geq \left\{ \max_{(i,j)\in C} (t_{max}(i)) - \min_{(i,j)\in C} (t_{min}(i)) \right\} \tag{16.16}$$

where C represents the set of all circuit connections in a combinational logic
block.

Example 16.4.2 *Consider the circuit shown in Fig. 16.20(a). Here,* $\mathcal{G}=\{3,4\}$
and $C=\{(1,4), (2,3), (3,4)\}$, *where* $\mathcal{G}$ *represents the set of all gate output*
nodes. Here, the terms inside the ovals represent the values of t_{min} *and* t_{max}.

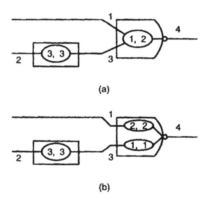

(a)

(b)

Fig. 16.20   Gate delay model circuit I (a) and II (b).

Therefore, (16.16) becomes

$$T_{clk} \geq max\{t_{max}(1), t_{max}(3)\} - min\{t_{min}(1), t_{min}(3)\}. \tag{16.17}$$

Upon simplification, one gets

$$T_{clk} \geq max\{0, 3\} - min\{0, 3\} = 3. \tag{16.18}$$

This means that in order to satisfy the internal node constraints, the minimum
clock period must be 3. *One can also see from Fig. 16.20(a) that the minimum*
delay among all paths from input to output is 1, *and the maximum delay is* 5.
Therefore, the output node constraint is

$$T_{clk} \geq \{5 - 1\} = 4. \tag{16.19}$$

From (16.18) and (16.19) it is clear that the output node constraint is stronger than the internal node constraint, and that the minimum clock period required for the system to operate correctly is $T_{clk} = 4$. ■

Example 16.4.3 *Consider the circuit shown in Fig. 16.20(b). Substituting the appropriate t_{min} and t_{max} values into (16.16), one gets*

$$T_{clk} \geq max\{0, 3\} - min\{0, 3\} = 3. \tag{16.20}$$

The output node constraint becomes

$$T_{clk} \geq \{4 - 2\} = 2. \tag{16.21}$$

In this example, the internal node constraint is stronger than the output node constraint, and the minimum clock period is $T_{clk} = 3$. ■

It is also clear from (16.15) that high throughput is achieved by minimizing the spread or the difference $t_{max} - t_{min}$. This means that the delays through all propagation paths have to be balanced, so that $t_{max} \approx t_{min}$. However, this is a formidable task in the case of large circuits for the following reasons:

- path variation due to logic depth in the architecture

- unequal rise/fall times

- delay variations in the basic building blocks

- temperature and process variations.

Many approaches have been proposed to counteract these factors, ranging from rough/fine tuning to inserting delay elements in the noncritical paths. A wave-pipelined architecture is said to be efficient if it satisfies the following properties:

- a logic that provides identical propagation delay and equal rise/fall times for all the input combinations

- a delay element perfectly emulating the delay of the combinational logic blocks

- an architecture having identical propagation paths in terms of the logic depth

- identical effect of temperature and process variations on all the propagation paths of the architecture.

16.5   CONSTRAINT SPACE DIAGRAM AND DEGREE OF WAVE PIPELINING

If the setup/hold times are ignored, the constraints expressed in (16.11) and (16.12) can be expressed as

$$kT_{clk} + \Delta \geq t_{max} \tag{16.22}$$

and

$$T_{clk} + t_{min} \geq kT_{clk} + \Delta. \tag{16.23}$$

The plot of these equations as a function of Δ and T_{clk} is referred to as the *timing constraint space diagram* and is shown in Fig. 16.21. The parameter k is referred to as the *degree of wave pipelining*. It is clear from the figure that for fixed values of k, distinct feasible regions of operation are available.

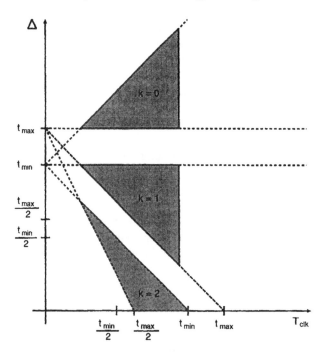

Fig. 16.21   Constraint space diagram.

Furthermore, as k is increased, the feasible region is reduced. Special values of k and Δ are interesting from a design point of view. In the following, these cases are analyzed and their effect on the clock period is also studied. The analysis is performed by using the simplified constraints of (16.22) and (16.23).

16.5.1 $\Delta \leq T_{clk}$

This constraint forces the designer to operate in the highest k region to achieve a low clock period. The simplified constraints of (16.22) and (16.23) can be expressed equivalently as

$$kT_{clk} + \Delta \geq t_{max} \tag{16.24}$$

and

$$t_{min} \geq (k-1)T_{clk} + \Delta. \tag{16.25}$$

The problem definition results in the additional constraint

$$T_{clk} \geq \Delta. \tag{16.26}$$

Finally, the internal node constraints result in the following constraint

$$T_{clk} \geq t_{internal}, \tag{16.27}$$

where $t_{internal}$ denotes the lower bound on the clock period due to the internal node constraints. Constraints (16.24) and (16.25) together imply

$$T_{clk} \geq t_{max} - t_{min}, \tag{16.28}$$

and constraints (16.24) and (16.26) together imply

$$T_{clk} \geq \frac{t_{max}}{k+1}. \tag{16.29}$$

Therefore, from (16.27), (16.28), and (16.29) the minimum clock period of the single stage system with $\Delta \leq T_{clk}$ is given by

$$T_{clk} = max\left(t_{internal}, \frac{t_{max}}{k+1}, t_{max} - t_{min}\right). \tag{16.30}$$

16.5.2 $\Delta \geq 0$

The delay Δ in an actual implementation of the wave-pipelined system is derived from the physical delay units at the input and output registers, i.e., $\Delta = \Delta_o - \Delta_i$. This can also be achieved by removing these physical delay units at the input and output registers and replacing them with a single delay Δ between the 2 registers. This type of system implicitly imposes an upper bound on the clock period as shown in the following.

The set of 4 constraints (16.24), (16.25), (16.26), and (16.27) become

$$kT_{clk} + \Delta \geq t_{max} \tag{16.31}$$

$$t_{min} \geq (k-1)T_{clk} + \Delta \tag{16.32}$$

$$\Delta \geq 0, \tag{16.33}$$

and

$$T_{clk} \geq t_{internal}. \tag{16.34}$$

As before, (16.31) and (16.32) can be combined to obtain the following constraint:

$$T_{clk} \geq t_{max} - t_{min}. \tag{16.35}$$

From (16.34) and (16.35), the effective constraint on the clock period is given by

$$T_{clk} = max\left(t_{internal}, t_{max} - t_{min}\right). \tag{16.36}$$

If an additional constraint of $\Delta = 0$ is added to the above system, then it can be easily shown that the constraint on the clock period reduces to

$$T_{clk} = max\left(t_{internal}, \frac{t_{max}}{k}\right). \tag{16.37}$$

Finally, the special case of $k = 1$, $\Delta = 0$ reduces to the case of a conventional pipelined system, and the clock period in this case is limited by t_{max}.

16.6   IMPLEMENTATION OF WAVE-PIPELINED SYSTEMS

The choice of an appropriate logic style is crucial in any wave-pipelined implementation because mismatches in propagation delays at the level of the basic building blocks may cause the architecture to fail. The use of CMOS technology is desirable as it offers increased packing density and reduced power dissipation. However, static CMOS is not an ideal choice for wave pipelining because its propagation delay is highly data dependent. For example, the rise/fall times of a 2-input NAND gate may vary as much as 50%, depending on whether both the input signals are 0 or only 1 of them is 0. Therefore, many logic styles have been proposed to design wave-pipelined architectures. This section addresses only one such style known as the NPCPL [2].

16.6.1   NPCPL

The normal process complementary pass transistor logic (NPCPL) attempts to exploit the advantages of NMOS-only pass transistor logic in a process that requires no threshold adjustment of the pass elements. It consists of

- true and complementary inputs
- two pass blocks generating true and complementary output variables
- level restoring inverters to restore the degraded voltage levels at the output of the pass block to full CMOS levels.

The logic threshold of the inverter used in the logic can be set in accordance with the equation

$$V_{TH} = \frac{\sqrt{K}(V_{dd} - |V_{Th_p}|) + V_{Th_n}}{1 + \sqrt{K}} \qquad (16.38)$$

where $K = k_p/k_n$, $k_p = k'_p(W/L)_p$, and $k_n = k'_n(W/L)_n$. The value thus obtained is taken as a starting point for further iterations. Fine tuning is done experimentally through SPICE simulations, and the W_p/W_n ratio is determined to achieve equal $0 \to 1$ and $1 \to 0$ transition delays and nominally equal rise/fall times. This procedure is highly process specific, and the design procedure may have to be repeated if the fabrication process is changed.

The most critical parameter in the NPCPL design is the logic threshold voltage (V_{TH}) of the level restoring inverter. An increase (decrease) in V_{TH} increases (decreases) the fall time and the transition delay of the NPCPL building block, thereby affecting the performance of the wave-pipelined circuit. The general structure of the NPCPL block is shown in Fig. 16.22, and can be configured to realize different Boolean functions by applying appropriate

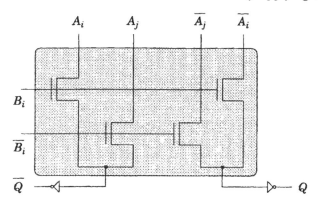

Fig. 16.22 Basic structure of the NPCPL block.

inputs. The salient feature of this block is that it can be used to realize all the major 2-input Boolean functions with identical propagation delays. By virtue of its symmetric structure, it provides identical logic depth and hence equal delay for all the logic gates. Moreover, it can also be used as a delay element, to mimic the delay of other 2-input logic gates. However, the NPCPL suffers from poor noise margin problems, when compared to static CMOS. This can be considered as a trade-off for obtaining identical logic depths.

16.6.2 Algorithm for Wave Pipelining a Given Circuit

NPCPL has the unique property that any circuit design can be conceived as a composition of NPCPL generic building blocks, which serve as universal logic elements. The delay through a circuit is determined by the number of basic building blocks in the longest path. A necessary and sufficient condition for wave pipelining is to ensure that all paths from input to output have equal delay. Therefore, it is necessary to balance delays on all paths in an NPCPL design before it can be exploited for wave pipelining. The concept of a CLB was introduced in [2] to design wave pipelined circuits. A CLB is an NPCPL building block with delay δ as shown in Fig. 16.23. Here, the output implements the Boolean function

$$out = f(in_1, in_2). \tag{16.39}$$

An *abstract CLB* is a CLB with zero delay in combination with a delay ele-

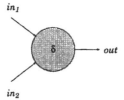

Fig. 16.23   Representation of a CLB.

ment D, either at the input or at the output of the CLB, such that $D = \delta$ as shown in Fig. 16.24. It follows that the delay elements can be transferred from input to output of a CLB and vice versa without any change in the functionality of the circuit; this is equivalent to retiming the CLB (see Chapter 4).

Consider an arbitrary circuit shown in Fig. 16.25 that has to be wave pipelined. Here, F_1, F_2, and F_3 represent, respectively, the 3 Boolean operations performed by the circuit. The 1st step in the algorithm is to recast the Boolean function to be implemented in terms of 2-input functions as shown in Fig. 16.26. The next step is to find the critical path in the circuit from input to output. This is achieved by finding the path with the maximum number of CLBs in series. For the example shown in Fig. 16.26, the length of the critical path is 5, consisting of f_1, f_2, f_3, f_4, and f_5. Next, the physical representation is translated into an abstract representation using zero delay CLBs as shown

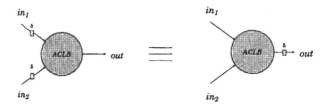

Fig. 16.24   Abstract representation of a CLB.

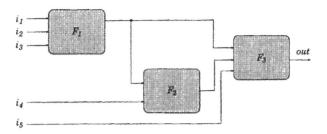

Fig. 16.25 An arbitrary circuit to be wave pipelined.

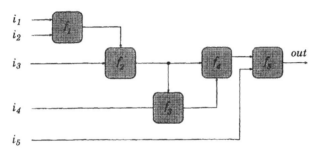

Fig. 16.26 Implementation in terms of 2-input functions.

in Fig. 16 27. Then, k delay elements, each of delay δ are introduced at the

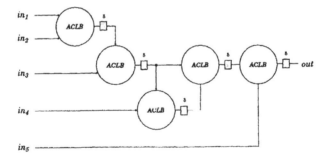

Fig. 16.27 Implementation in terms of abstract CLBs.

input of the system, where k is the length of the critical path. The circuit is then retimed such that each CLB is followed by at least 1 delay element and between any 2 delay elements there is either 0 or 1 CLB, and the resulting circuit is shown in Fig. 16.28. The final step in the algorithm is to combine the abstract CLB with the delay in front of it, and to transform it into a physical CLB as shown in Fig. 16.29. It is clear from the figure that every path from input to output has a delay equal to 5δ. This technique of delay balancing can be applied to any circuit in general, and a corresponding wave-pipelined realization can be obtained.

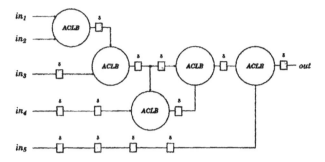

Fig. 16.28 Retimed version of the abstract representation.

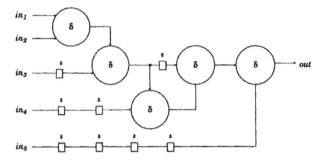

Fig. 16.29 Retimed version of the abstract representation.

The wave-pipelined implementation has some of the following attractive properties:

- The absence of pipeline latches leads to a decrease in area and a marginal decrease in power consumption.

- The absence of pipeline latches results in simpler clock distribution.

- It has higher throughput when compared to corresponding synchronous designs.

The disadvantages associated with the implementation are:

- Data dependent delay fluctuations cannot be fully eliminated, which degrades the performance from the ideal figure.

- The design requires accurate SPICE models for the transistors. Therefore, the basic building block may have to be resized when the design is ported a different fabrication process.

- Layout is critical for delay balancing and therefore an automatic layout generator is not recommended.

16.7 ASYNCHRONOUS PIPELINING

Most of the present-day systems are clock based or *synchronous*. These systems are built from subsystems, where each subsystem is a finite-state machine. The subsystems change from one state to another depending on a global *clock signal*, with flip-flops (registers) being used to store the different states. The state updates within the flip-flops are carried out on the rising (falling) edge of the clock signal. A typical synchronous system is shown in Fig. 16.30(a). Although this approach has made great strides in the design of digital systems, it is beginning to hit some fundamental limitations. A clock-based system can operate correctly only if all parts of the system see the clock at the same time, which can happen only if the delay on the clock wire is negligible. However, with advancement in technology, the systems tend to get bigger and bigger, and as a result the delay on the clock wires can no longer be ignored. The problem of *clock skew* is thus becoming a bottleneck for many system designers.

The second problem facing system designers is that of power. Logically speaking, this should correspond to the various gates in a system doing some useful work. However, in synchronous systems, this is not the case. Many gates switch unnecessarily just because they are connected to the clock, and not because they have to process new inputs. In fact, the biggest gate is the clock driver itself which must switch even if a small part of the system has something useful to do. As a result, synchronous systems tend to consume more power than necessary.

The design of clock-free or *asynchronous* systems has thus become attractive for digital system designers during the past few years. An asynchronous system is one in which there is no global synchronization within the system; subsystems within the system are only synchronized locally by the communication protocols between them. Systems that involve some sort of re-

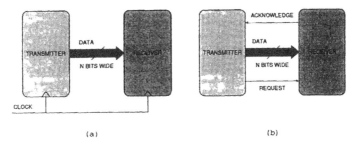

(a)   (b)

Fig. 16.30 Synchronous (a) and asynchronous (b) systems.

quest/acknowledge handshake protocol between the subsystems are often referred to as *self-timed* systems. Since most practical asynchronous systems are self-timed systems, these terms are often used synonymously in the literature. A typical asynchronous system is shown in Fig. 16.30(b).

In synchronous systems, avoiding clock skew becomes very costly in terms of power. However, in asynchronous systems, the absence of a global clock circumvents this problem. Moreover, transitions in a particular subsystem are only produced when data is passing through it and therefore there is no dynamic power consumption when the subsystem is idle. This makes them attractive for low-power designs.

The results produced by the subsystems in an asynchronous system can be consumed by other subsystems as soon as they are generated, without having to wait for a global clock change. As a result, asynchronous systems are limited by the average-case performance rather than the worst case (as in synchronous systems) of the subsystems. Moreover, a subsystem can be replaced by another subsystem with the same functionality but different performance with ease. However, in synchronous systems this is not an easy task as the clock period may have to recomputed.

The foregoing features make asynchronous design style very attractive for state of the art digital system design. Asynchronous systems come in many flavors, the most prominent among them being the bundled-data and dual-rail protocol. The communication protocol among these systems can also assume two forms, such as 2-phase and 4-phase.

16.7.1   Bundled-Data Versus Dual-Rail Protocol

The bundled-data protocol uses a single request (acknowledge) wire and a set of data wires (hence the name bundle) as shown in Fig. 16.31. The request wire is used to inform the receiver about the validity of the data on the data

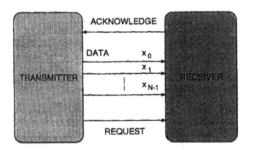

Fig. 16.31   Bundled-data protocol.

bundle. This inherently places a constraint on the request wire, known as the *bundling constraint*. According to this constraint, the request wire must be asserted only after the bundled data is valid at the receiver end. However, even though the request wire is asserted after the data becomes valid at the transmitter end, arbitrary wire delays mean that this condition may not hold at the receiver. Therefore, bundled data protocols are *not delay-insensitive*, where the term *delay* refers to arbitrary wire delays. The system designer should therefore ensure that the bundling constraint is met while designing bundled-data systems.

In contrast to bundled-data encoding, dual-rail encoding does not use a separate request wire, instead it is embedded within the data wires. Moreover, each data wire x_i (for i $\in$ [1, N]) is now represented by using 2 data wires $x_{i,0}$ and $x_{i,1}$ as shown in Fig. 16.32. A transition on the $x_{i,0}$ wire indicates

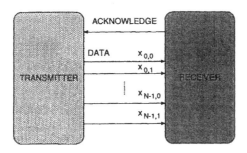

Fig. 16.32   Dual-rail protocol.

that a zero has been transmitted, while a transition on the $x_{i,1}$ wire indicates that a one has been transmitted. Since the request wire is embedded within the data wires, a transition on either $x_{i,0}$ or $x_{i,1}$ informs the receiver about the validity of the data. This makes dual-rail protocols *delay insensitive*, i.e., they will always produce functionally correct outputs independent of the wire delays.

The choice of either the bundled-data protocol or the dual-rail protocol depends on the nature of the data bundle. For example, if the data bundle is relatively large, bundled-data protocols may be more efficient since they require only 2 extra signals, a request and an acknowledge. Conversely, dual-rail protocols use 2 wires to represent each data-bit and therefore may result in greater area overheads. However, they are more robust because of their insensitivity to wire delays.

16.7.2   Two-Phase Versus Four-Phase Protocol

As seen in the preceding sections, the request wire is used to inform the receiver about the validity of the data. This can be achieved in two ways: either by a simple transition (low-to-high or high-to-low) on the request wire or by a transition from low-to-high only. The former is referred to as the 2-phase protocol, the latter as the 4-phase protocol.

The 2-phase protocol is illustrated in Fig. 16.33, and is summarized by the following steps:

1. Transmitter generates data.

2. Transmitter issues a request (denoted by a transition on the request

wire).

3. Receiver accepts data.

4. Receiver issues an acknowledge (denoted by a transition on the acknowledge wire).

5. Transmitter may disable data at will.

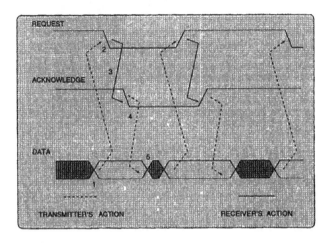

Fig. 16.33   Two-phase protocol.

Once the bundling constraint is satisfied, i.e., the foregoing steps are followed, the system becomes delay insensitive. Once designed, these systems can be placed in a library and reused to design arbitrary complex control structures.

The 4-phase protocol is similar to the 2-phase protocol, except for the fact that it is level sensitive, i.e., only a transition from low-to-high on the request wire will inform the receiver about the validity of the data. Therefore, the request wire has to go low before it can go high again, leading to an intermediate *return-to-zero* phase between two successive data values. The advantage of 4-phase protocol is that the logic processing elements can be much simpler and familiar logic gates can be used. Designs based on 2-phase protocol, however, require complex control circuits to process transitions.

16.8   SIGNAL TRANSITION GRAPHS

In this section, specification of asynchronous handshake circuits using signal transition graphs (STGs) [14] is discussed. Here, signal transitions instead of signal levels are used in the specification thereby reducing the complexity of the mapping. A typical STG is shown in Fig. 16.34, where a rising transition

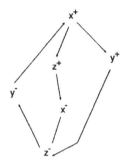

Fig. 16.34 A typical STG.

of a signal x is denoted by x^+, and a falling transition by x^-. Moreover, an arc in an STG represents a dependence relation. For example, the arc $z^- \to y^-$ means that z must go low before y can go low. Some of the terminologies associated with the STG are discussed next.

Liveness: An STG is said to be live if every transition can be enabled eventually.

For example, the STG shown in Fig. 16.35 is *not* live because once transition

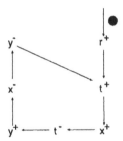

Fig. 16.35 STG that violates liveness.

r^+ has fired, it may never fire again.

Safety: An STG is said to be safe if no place or arc can ever contain more than one token.

For example, the STG shown in Fig. 16.36 is not safe, because after the firing sequence $s^+ \to r^- \to s^- \to r^+$, the arc from r^+ to y^+ has two tokens.

Persistence: An STG is said to be persistent if for all arcs $p^+(p^-) \to q^+$ in the STG, there must be other arcs that ensure that q^+ fires before $p^-(p^+)$.

The STG shown in Fig. 16.37 is not persistent because there is an arc $x^+ \to y^+$, and yet x^- can fire before y^+ fires.

Consistency: An STG is said to be consistent if the transitions of various signals strictly alternate between +'s and −'s (i.e., an already lowered signal cannot be lowered again and vice versa).

This condition is actually necessary for implementation purposes. The STG

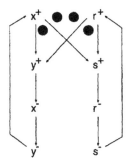

Fig. 16.36 An STG that violates safety.

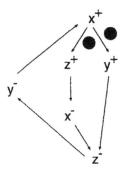

Fig. 16.37 An STG that violates persistence.

shown in Fig. 16.38 is not consistent because two consecutive x^+ can occur

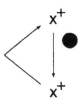

Fig. 16.38 An STG that violates consistency.

without an intervening x^-, and therefore it cannot be implemented.

Semimodularity: A signal transition is said to be semimodular if once the transition is enabled, only the firing of the transition can disable it. A circuit is semimodular if every single transition in the circuit is semimodular.

For example, if a^+ enables b^+, semimodularity requires that only after b has gone high a can go low. The STG shown in Fig. 16.34 is not semimodular, because the delay in the operation $x^+ \to y^+$ may be so long that another allowed sequence of transitions $x^+ \to z^+ \to x^-$ can take place before y can go high. This will cause y to lose its chance of going high, since the enabling condition x^+ does not hold anymore.

There exists an equivalence between hazard-free circuits and semimodular signal transition graphs under certain broad conditions. For the graph in Fig. 16.34, the equivalent semimodular graph is shown in Fig. 16.39. Here, a directed arc has been added from y^+ to x^- to prevent x from going low before

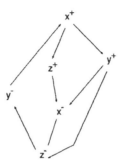

Fig. 16.39 Semimodular STG of the graph shown in Fig. 16.34.

y goes high. Other arcs such as the one directed from y^+ to z^+ also suffice to make the transition semimodular, but are too strong in that they prevent the possible simultaneous operation of y^+ and z^+.

In order to realize the STG shown in Fig. 16.39, the first step is to construct a state transition diagram as shown in Fig. 16.40. This diagram is constructed by starting from an initial state and then tracing through all possible transi-

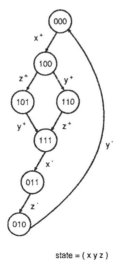

state $= (x\ y\ z)$

Fig. 16.40 State transition diagram for the STG shown in Fig. 16.39.

tions in the corresponding STG. The Karnaugh map is then constructed for the 3 outputs as shown in Figs. 16.41(a), (b), and (c). The resulting logic

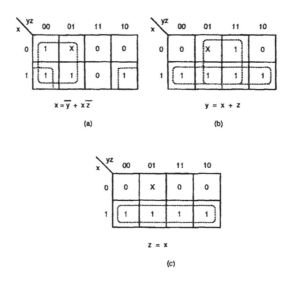

Fig. 16.41 Karnaugh maps for output signal (a) x (b) y (c) z.

equations can easily be implemented using simple gates. Note that the state 001 is not present; this leads to 'X' (don't-care) markings in the Karnaugh map. In the Karnaugh map for z, if the current state is 100, then z can be 0 or 1. Since z can change to 1, a 1 is placed in the Karnaugh map.

16.9 USE OF STG TO DESIGN INTERCONNECTION CIRCUITS

Consider a typical interconnection circuit shown in Fig. 16.42, where the 2 units A and B are connected in a pipeline. The handshake circuit enables the unit A to process the next data sample while the unit B processes the current data sample. Since unit B might take longer to finish or vice versa, an acknowledge signal is necessary to indicate when B has completed its task and is ready for the next data sample. The purpose of the handshake circuit is to ensure correct transmission of data samples and prevent any *run away* (overwriting of data) conditions.

There are two styles of interconnection circuits as shown in Fig. 16.43 [14], differing in their specifications relating the input and output signals. The specification for the STG in Fig. 16.43(a) is

$$*[R_{in}^+ \ \rightarrow \ R_{out}^+], \tag{16.40}$$

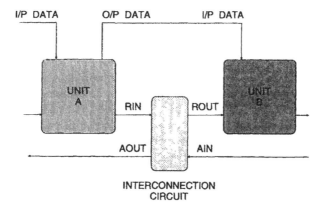

Fig. 16.42 An example of an interconnection circuit.

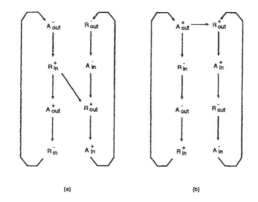

Fig. 16.43 Two different specifications of interconnect circuits.

and for that in Fig. 16.43(b) is

$$*[A_{out}^+ \to R_{out}^+]. \tag{16.41}$$

The first condition means that if the input sample is ready (R_{in}^+), then start computation (R_{out}^+). The requirement that the succeeding unit must be empty (A_{in}^-) before a new sample can be accepted is reflected in the 4-phase hand-shaking transition $A_{in}^- \to R_{out}^+$ as shown in Fig. 16.43(a).

The second condition tells unit A that its output data has been accepted (A_{out}^+) so that unit B can start computation (R_{out}^+) and R_{in} can be reset (R_{in}^-). As before, the need that the succeeding unit must be empty (A_{in}^-) before a new sample is accepted is reflected in the 4-phase handshaking transition $A_{in}^- \to R_{out}^+$ as shown in Fig. 16.43(b).

An STG has to satisfy the weakest semimodularity conditions to satisfy a hazard-free implementation. The algorithm that was proposed in [14] to derive the weakest semimodularity conditions in a live STG is discussed here. The first step in the algorithm involves the identification of the nonsemimodular transitions (those that enable multiple allowed sequences). Then, the weakest condition for semimodularity on a nonsemimodular transition is satisfied by adding arcs directed from the nonsemimodular transition to all the transitions whose inverse transitions enable this nonsemimodular transition. As new arcs are added, redundant arcs are deleted and the STG is updated. This process has to be repeated recursively until all transitions in the STG are semimodular. For example, consider the STG shown in Fig. 16.43(a), where the arc $R_{in}^+ \rightarrow R_{out}^+$ represents a nonsemimodular transition (because R_{in}^+ has multiple allowed sequences). According to the algorithm, an arc directed from $R_{out}^+ \rightarrow R_{in}^-$ should be added to the graph to make the transition from R_{in}^+ semimodular. However, R_{in} is an input signal, and a physical circuit cannot impose any constraints on any input signals; it can only impose constraints on the output signal, which in turn will influence the target input signal. Therefore, the 1st arc added to the graph is directed from $R_{out}^+ \rightarrow A_{out}^+$ as shown in Fig. 16.44(a), and the redundant arc from R_{in}^+ to A_{out}^+ is deleted. This in turn

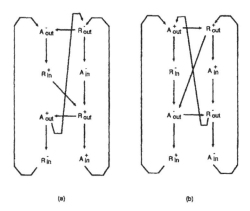

(a)   (b)

Fig. 16.44 Semimodular STGs (with the weakest conditions) for the graphs shown in Fig. 16.43.

results in a nonsemimodular transition R_{out}^+. Therefore, an arc directed from A_{out}^+ to R_{out}^- is added, resulting in A_{out}^+ becoming nonsemimodular. Finally, an arc directed from R_{out}^- to A_{out}^- is added, making the whole STG semimodular. A semimodular STG for the graph shown in Fig. 16.43(b) can be derived in a similar manner and the resulting STG is shown in Fig. 16.44(b). Finally, Karnaugh maps are constructed from the STGs as explained in the previous section and the corresponding realizations are shown in Figs. 16.45(a) and (b).

The implementations shown in Fig. 16.45 are not truly delay-insensitive because of the use of SR latches, since the mutual exclusion of the S and R inputs cannot be guaranteed through unbounded external gate delays. For

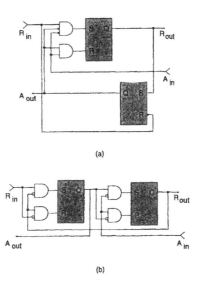

Fig. 16.45   Circuit diagrams for the handshake circuit derived from their corresponding STGs.

illustration, consider the SR latch in Fig. 16.45(b) that generates A_{out}. If the delay of the inverter gate at input R is greater than the additive delay of one AND gate plus one SR latch, both S and R inputs can become high at the same time, and lead to hazards. However, since this mismatch does not occur in practice, SR latches are still used extensively.

A purely delay-insensitive circuit can still be designed by the use of C-elements. A 2-input C-element implements the Boolean function $C = AB + BC' + AC'$, where A and B are the input signals, C' is the previous output signal, and C is the current output signal. The C-element has the property that the output signal will change to the input level only when both inputs are at the same level; otherwise the output stays at its previous value. It has also been proposed that delay-insensitive circuits use only C-elements. The actual implementation of the C-element is discussed in the next section. Since the SR latches derived from a semimodular circuit preclude any hazard conditions, the functionality of an SR latch is identical to that of a C-element with an inverter. Therefore, C-elements can be used to replace SR latches without any functionality difference. The resulting handshake circuits obtained by replacing the SR latches with C-elements are shown in Figs. 16.46(a) and (b), respectively.

The efficiency of hardware utilization of the 2 designs presented above can be derived from their corresponding STGs. In a live semimodular graph, once a request is accepted, each transition must be traversed only once before the next request can be accepted. The circuit delay in response to an external request is the longest delay of all the simple loops in the graph. The computa-

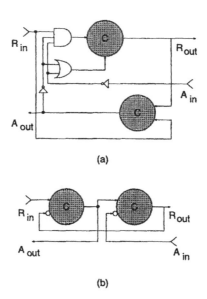

(a)

(b)

Fig. 16.46   Handshake circuits using C-elements.

tion latencies are much longer than the handshake transitions, and therefore the computation arcs in the STG have to be identified first. In the STG of Fig. 16.44(a), the loop of transitions $A_{out}^- \rightarrow R_{in}^+ \rightarrow R_{out}^+ \rightarrow A_{in}^+ \rightarrow R_{out}^-$ $\rightarrow A_{out}^-$ traverses 2 computation arcs $A_{out}^- \rightarrow R_{in}^+$ and $R_{out}^+ \rightarrow A_{in}^+$. If the latencies associated with the computation units are the same, then the handshake circuit specified by $*[R_{in}^+ \rightarrow R_{out}^+]$ will cause half of the computation units to be idle at any instant. Therefore this scheme of handshaking is commonly referred to as the *half handshake*. However in Fig. 16.44(b), there is no loop that contains both the computation arcs, and as a result the computation units are working at all times. This scheme of handshaking is therefore referred to as the *full handshake*.

The connection between computation units and interconnection blocks is dictated by the request-acknowledge signal pairs. Registers are usually considered as part of the interconnection blocks because they implement a pipeline stage in the signal processing sense. For example, in Fig. 16.46(b), the first C-element of the full handshake controls the acknowledge signal A_{out}, while the second C-element controls the request signal R_{out} to the next block. It follows that for any pipeline interconnection using a full-handshake circuit, A_{out} is the only signal that can be used for latching without corrupting either the input data or the output data. The completion detection circuitry used to detect register latching is shown in Fig. 16.47, where delay insensitivity has been ensured in the register latching operation. It is assumed that at the start of the operation, all signals have been initialized to logic zero. When the data is stable at the input of the register, a transition occurs on the request

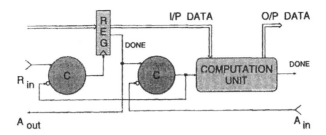

Fig. 16.47 Completion detection mechanism with the use of a register and full hand-shaking.

line R_{in}. This makes the output of the C-element go high and the data is latched. The register then informs the second C-element that data has been latched and is ready to be read by the computation unit. At the same time it also acknowledges the input end through the A_{out} signal. The input end is now free to proceed with its next computation. Meanwhile, since the A_{in} signal has been initialized to logic zero, the output of the second C-element is driven high. The computation is then carried out and once the output data is ready, the *Done* signal is set high.

16.10 IMPLEMENTATION OF COMPUTATIONAL UNITS

This section addresses the design techniques used to implement asynchronous computational units using either field-programmable gate arrays (FPGAs) or full custom VLSI.

16.10.1 Full Custom VLSI Implementation

It has been shown that 2 binary handshake signals, *request* and *acknowledge*, are necessary and sufficient to realize general asynchronous networks. For efficient hardware implementation, any combinational circuit can be combined into one computational block, provided that the request and acknowledge signals can be generated along the data path. The differential cascode voltage switch logic (DCVSL) has become popular among asynchronous circuit designers because it offers an elegant way to generate the completion signals. The general structure of a DCVSL block is shown in Fig. 16.48, where the *request* signal can be viewed as the *completion* signal from the previous block. When the *request* line is active low, the 2 output data lines will be pulled up by the PMOS transistors, and the *done* signal will be pulled down. When the *request* line goes high, indicating that the computation of the preceding stage has been completed and that the control/data signals are stable for evaluation, the two PMOS transistors will be turned off and the input lines will be

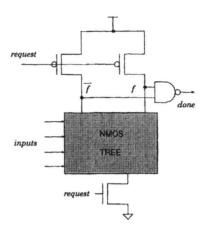

Fig. 16.48 Generic structure of a DCVSL block for asynchronous circuit design.

evaluated by the NMOS tree. The NMOS tree itself is designed such that only one of the output data lines $(f/\overline{f})$ will be pulled down by the NMOS tree, causing the *complete* signal to be set high by the NAND gate. The differential NMOS tree can be designed by using the existing logic minimization algorithms, and has been found to offer a performance advantage when compared with primitive NAND/NOR families. A simple example is considered next to illustrate the design of a DCVSL block.

Consider the implementation of a logic function f, described by the equation

$$f = AB + C(A + B). \tag{16.42}$$

The DCVSL implementation of this function requires the logic to be expressed in the *if-else* style as shown below.

$$
\begin{aligned}
&if \quad A = 1 \\
&\qquad if\ B = 1 \\
&\qquad\qquad\qquad f = 1; \overline{f} = 0 \\
&\qquad else \\
&\qquad\qquad\qquad if\ C = 1 \\
&\qquad\qquad\qquad\qquad\qquad f = 1; \overline{f} = 0 \\
&\qquad\qquad\qquad else \\
&\qquad\qquad\qquad\qquad f = 0; \overline{f} = 1 \\
&\qquad else \\
&\qquad\qquad\quad if\ B = 1 \\
&\qquad\qquad\qquad\quad if\ C = 1 \\
&\qquad\qquad\qquad\qquad\qquad f = 1; \overline{f} = 0 \\
&\qquad\qquad\qquad\quad else \\
&\qquad\qquad\qquad\qquad\quad f = 0; \overline{f} = 1 \\
&\qquad\qquad\ else \\
&\qquad\qquad\qquad f = 0; \overline{f} = 1
\end{aligned}
$$

This can then be translated into an implementation as shown in Fig. 16.49. Here, the *C*-block (starting with *if C* = *1*) is common to both the *if* and

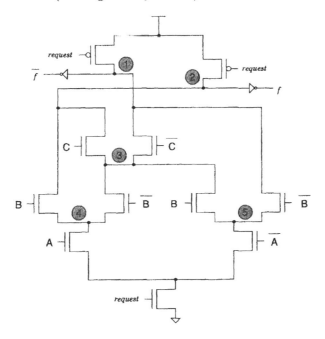

Fig. 16.49   A DCVSL implementation of the logic function $f = AB + C(A + B)$.

else blocks, and therefore has been shared between them. The problem of *charge sharing* may arise in the DCVSL design, and suitable precautions have to be taken to avoid them. For example, the capacitances at nodes 1 and 2 should be made large (achieved by the use of large precharge transistors), and explicit precharge transistors could be connected at nodes 3, 4, and 5 if necessary. Some typical examples of asynchronous circuits are discussed next.

16.10.1.1 Muller C-element   Consider the circuit of a Muller *C*-element as shown in Fig. 16.50, where *A* and *B* represent the input signals, and *C* represents the output signal. When *A* and *B* are both low, the 2 PMOS transistors P1 and P2 are turned ON and node 1 is pulled up to Vdd, which in turn makes the output go low. If either *A* or *B* is high, node 1 is isolated and therefore retains its previous value. When both *A* and *B* are high, the NMOS transistors N1 and N2 are turned ON and node 1 is pulled to ground, causing the output signal to go high.

16.10.1.2 An Asynchronous 2-Input Multiplexer   An asynchronous 2-input multiplexer is shown in Fig. 16.51, where *A* and *B* represent the 2 input signals, and *out* represents the output signal. When the *request* signal is active low, the 2 PMOS pull-up transistors are turned on, and *out*, $\overline{out}$ are set to logic

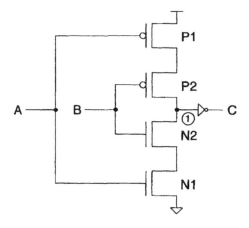

Fig. 16.50 Implementation of a Muller C-element.

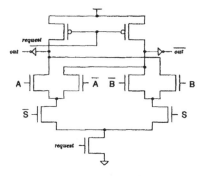

Fig. 16.51 Asynchronous 2-input multiplexer.

zero. When the *request* signal becomes active high, the PMOS transistors are turned off and depending on the value of the select signal S, either *out* or $\overline{out}$ is pulled to ground.

16.10.2 FPGA Implementation

This section considers FPGA implementations using the Actel FPGA. The chip is arranged much like a conventional channeled gate array with rows of logic cells interspersed with routing channels containing wire segments of various lengths. These segments are connected through a two-terminal electrically programmable device known as *antifuse*, which changes irreversibly from a high to a low resistance when programmed by applying an appropriate voltage across its terminals. Logic modules are connected to perform the desired function by programming selected antifuses and thus programming the chip to a desired function. Once programmed, an Actel FPGA cannot be reprogrammed for change of functionality. However, XILINX family FPGAs can be reprogrammed. In this section, the design of asynchronous circuits using Actel FPGAs will only be addressed.

16.10.2.1 C-elements A 2-input C-element, a gate first described by Muller, will force its output high when both inputs are high, and low when both inputs are low. If the inputs are in opposite states, the output retains its last value. The C-element can therefore be used like an AND function for transitions. A transition will occur at the output of a C-element only if transitions have occurred at both the inputs of the C-element, assuming that the inputs have been initialized to the same state.

Two different forms of the C-element are shown in Figs. 16.52(a) and (b) [8], the 1st one without a clear signal (CLR) and the 2nd one with a clear

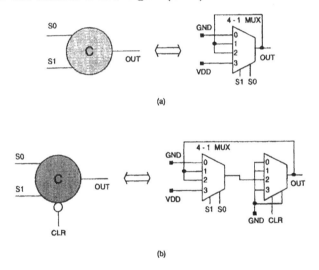

Fig. 16.52   Two types of C-elements.

signal. Both the circuits have been implemented with the use of a simple 4-1 multiplexer. It is clear from Fig. 16.52(a) that only when both inputs are in the same state will the output also attain the same state. In Fig. 16.52(b), two 4-1 multiplexers have been used to incorporate the active-low clear signal. When the clear signal is low the output of the 2nd multiplexer is cleared, and if it is high the output of the 1st multiplexer is transmitted straight through.

16.10.2.2 Transition Latch (Normally Opaque) A transition latch is a circuit that will capture and store data (D) in response to transition control signals. A new datum is captured on each transition on the control signal. Fig. 16.53(a) [8] shows the symbol for a *normally opaque* transition latch, while Fig. 16.53(b) shows its equivalent circuit diagram. Here, C and P represent, respectively, the *capture* and *pass* control signals, while D and Q represent,

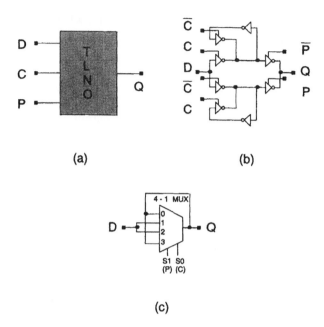

Fig. 16.53 (a) Symbol for a transition latch (normally opaque). (b) Equivalent circuit diagram. (c) Implementation using Actel FPGA.

respectively, the input and output data signals. This latch uses enabled inverters that form loops to capture data signals. After initialization, when the 2 control signals are at the same level, the latch is opaque from input to output, because a loop is formed at the top (if the control signals are initialized to logic 0) or at the bottom (if the control signals are initialized to logic 1). The first transition occurs on the C signal which breaks a loop and causes the latch to become transparent from input to output. When a transition occurs on the P line, the loop is formed again, only to be broken by another transition on the C line. The FPGA implementation using a 4-1 multiplexer is shown in Fig. 16.53(c), and its operation can be easily verified.

Variations of the foregoing latch are easily imagined. The latch could be transparent on initialization and later become opaque due to a transition on the control signal. This type of latch is called as a *normally transparent* latch, and the details can be found in [8].

16.10.2.3 Carry Completion Adder Module An important DSP operation is that of addition, and this section addresses the design of an adder module. The operation of addition could range anywhere from ripple-carry to carry-look-ahead to carry-save addition, but the challenge lies in identifying the worst-case data path and then developing a model that meets the bundling constraint. A simple way to treat the operation of addition in an asynchronous system is to treat it as a combinatorial function, and then build a general bundled module around that function. For example, in the case of ripple-carry addition, the bundling delay must model the case where the carry propagates from the lower order bit to the higher bit. The carry-completion adder (CCA) [7] shown in Fig. 16.54 employs carry-completion sensing, and has a 4-phase control interface and uses 2 internal carry signals: one for representing a carry to the next stage $(CIN/COUT)$, and one for don't-carry to the next stage $(DCIN/DCOUT)$. These signals are initialized to logic 0 at the start of

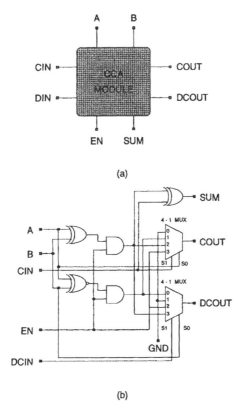

Fig. 16.54   (a) Symbol for a CCA. (b) FPGA implementation.

the addition operation. When the enable signal (EN) goes high, the adder starts computing the sum and the carry signals, and the subsequent assertion of either $COUT$ or $DOUT$ signals signifies the completion of the addition operation. The $DONE$ signal can then be easily generated as the OR of $COUT$ and $DOUT$ signals. A 2-phase to 4-phase protocol converter may be used if this adder is used in a 2-phase environment.

A 4-bit CCA is then designed by cascading the CCA modules as shown in Fig. 16.55, where the enable signals from each module are connected together to become the request line. The acknowledge signals from each module are

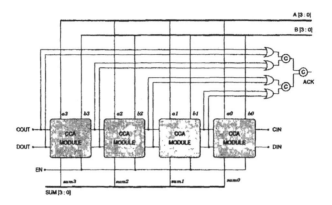

Fig. 16.55   A 4-bit CCA.

connected into a tree of C-elements to signal the condition that all the adder bits have produced their carry. A falling EN signal is used to initialize the adder for the next addition by pulling all the carry signals low. This in turn causes the Ack signal to fall, indicating that each bit has been reset and that the adder is ready to compute a new result.

16.10.2.4 First-In First-Out Buffer

A simple first-in first-out (FIFO) can be constructed by using transition latches and C-elements as shown by the diagram in Fig. 16.56. After initializing all the wires in the circuit to a low state,

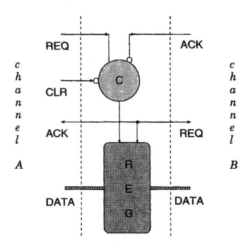

Fig. 16.56   One stage of a first-in first-out buffer.

the first action of the circuit is to accept data from channel A. To achieve this, the A channel places data on the data wires, and then makes a transition on the A channel request (REQ) wire. Since all the wires have been initialized low, the output of the C-element is forced high. This transition signals the register to latch the data present at its input. The register then acknowledges the A channel that the data has been latched, and also informs the B channel that the data is now available for reading. At this point the circuit connected to the A channel is free to send in more data by changing the values on the data wire and making another transition on the A channel request wire. The B channel may also accept the data currently held in the register by signaling with a transition on the B channel acknowledge wire (ACK) that it is no longer necessary to hold the data in the register. Only when both these events take place, i.e., there are transitions on both the inputs of the C-element, will the register be ready to accept more data from the A channel. A corresponding FPGA implementation is shown in Fig. 16.57, where the register has been designed using 8 normally transparent transition latches. The 1-word FIFO

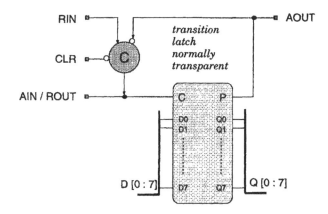

Fig. 16.57 An FPGA implementation of one word of an FIFO buffer.

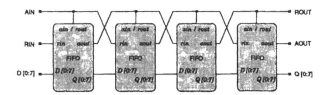

Fig. 16.58 An FPGA implementation of a 4-word 8-bit FIFO.

can be stacked together to make a deeper FIFO, similar to the one shown in Fig. 16.58. Here, 4 copies of the 1-word FIFO have been cascaded to form a 4-word 8-bit FIFO. The operation of this register is easily verified.

16.11 CONCLUSIONS

This chapter has presented a comprehensive discussion of various pipelining styles. First, a detailed discussion of synchronous pipelining and various clocking styles was presented. Then, the problems of clock skew and clock distribution were addressed and methods to overcome them were presented. Two recent techniques, namely, wave pipelining and asynchronous pipelining were addressed in the remainder of the chapter. Wave pipelining was used to increase the number of pipeline stages without the use of physical registers. This was achieved by performing accurate timing analysis of the design both at the circuit level and at the system level. The absence of registers results in a simpler clock distribution. Moreover, a significantly higher throughput is achieved when compared to synchronous systems. An algorithm was also presented to systematically design wave-pipelined circuits.

Asynchronous pipelining is an alternate pipelining style where the use of a global clock signal is totally eliminated and communication is carried out using handshake signals. The chapter has presented different types of asynchronous circuits classified based upon the handshake signals. The design of 4-phase handshake circuits using signal transition graphs was also presented. Many examples illustrating the design of asynchronous computational units were also presented.

16.12 PROBLEMS

1. Consider a typical sequential system shown in Fig. 16.59 which is de-

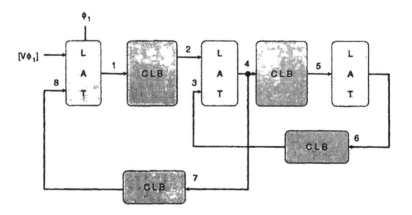

Fig. 16.59 A typical sequential system.

signed using CLBs and latches (LATs). Let us assume that the input signal to the leftmost latch is $[V\phi_1]$ and that the latch is clocked using

ϕ_1. Will this sequential circuit behave correctly? Explain. Also, what is the status of the signals at nodes 1–8, i.e., are they $[V\phi_1]$, $[V\phi_2]$, $[S\phi_1]$, or $[S\phi_2]$? Explain which latches are clocked using ϕ_1 and which are clocked using ϕ_2.

2. Consider the circuit shown in Fig. 16.60, where the input signal X is

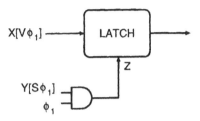

Fig. 16.60   Circuit for Problem 2.

$[V\phi_1]$ and the input signal Y is $[S\phi_1]$. The signal Z is used as the clock for the latch. Will this latch function correctly? If so, what is the main advantage of this circuit?

3. Draw the timing waveforms of ϕ, ϕ_1, and ϕ_2 for the circuit shown in Fig. 16.8 and verify the operation of the 2-phase clock generator.

4. Design a 9-transistor positive edge-triggered true single phase clocked flip-flop and explain its operation.

5. Let us assume that a bit-pipelined digital system is designed using a single-phase level sensitive clocking scheme with pulse width t_ϕ. Show that the clock skew δ for this clocking scheme is given by

$$\delta < t_{pr} + t_{pi} + t_{pl} - t_\phi. \tag{16.43}$$

Explain the behavior of the circuit for both positive and negative δ.

6. Draw an H-tree distribution network for a 4-bit × 4-bit array of regular cells with and without intermediate buffering.

7. Draw the equivalent wave-pipelined implementation of the circuit shown in Fig. 16.61 so that the every path has the same delay from input to output.

8. Draw the timing diagram of a 4-phase handshake communication system and explain the various steps involved.

9. Consider the STG shown in Fig. 16.62. Explain in each case if the STG is (a) live (b) safe (c) consistent (d) semimodular. If the STG is not semimodular, draw an equivalent semimodular representation of it.

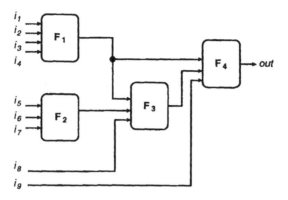

Fig. 16.61 Circuit for Problem 7.

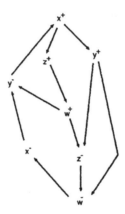

Fig. 16.62 Circuit for Problem 9.

10. Derive the circuit diagrams of the half-handshake and full-handshake circuits shown in Fig. 16.45(a) and (b), respectively by drawing Karnaugh maps for the corresponding STGs shown in Fig. 16.44(a) and (b). (Hint: see [14])

11. Draw the circuit diagram of a normally transparent asynchronous transition latch and explain its operation.

12. Design an asynchronous unsigned 4-bit × 4-bit multiplier using carry completion adders. Show clearly how the handshake signals are used.

13. Draw a DCVSL implementation for the logic function f described by the equation

$$f = AB + D(C + B) + \overline{AD}. \tag{16.44}$$

REFERENCES

1. D. Fan, T. Gray, W. Farlow, T. Hughes, W. Liu, and R. Cavin III, "A CMOS parallel adder using wave pipelining," in *Proc. Brown/MIT Conference Advanced Research in VLSI and Parallel Systems*, pp. 147–164, March 1992.

2. D. Ghosh and S. K. Nandy, "Design and Realization of high-performance wave-pipelined 8×8b multiplier in CMOS technology," *IEEE Trans. VLSI Systems*, vol. 3, no. 1, pp. 36–48, March 1995.

3. C. T. Gray, W. Liu, and R. Cavin III, "Timing constraints for wave-pipelined systems," *IEEE Trans. on Computer-Aided Design*, vol. 13, no. 8, pp. 987–1004, Aug. 1994.

4. C. T. Gray, W. Liu, and R. Cavin III, *Wave Pipelining: Thoery and CMOS Implementation*. Kluwer, 1994.

5. W.-H. Lien and P. Burleson, "Wave-domino logic: theory and applications," *IEEE Trans. Circuits and Systems, Part II—Analog and Digital Signal Processing*, vol. 42, no. 2, pp. 78–90, Feb. 1995.

6. V. Nguyen, W. Liu, C. T. Gray, and R. Cavin III, "A CMOS multiplier using wave-pipelining," in *Proc. Custom Integrated Circuits Conference*, pp. 147–164, May 1993.

7. E. Brunvand, "Using FPGAs to implement self-timed systems," *Journal of VLSI Signal Processing*, vol. 6, pp. 173–190, 1993.

8. E. Brunvand, "Designing self-timed systems using concurrent programs," *Journal of VLSI Signal Processing*, vol. 7, pp. 47–59, Feb. 1994.

9. P. Day and V. Woods, "Investigation into micropipeline latch design styles," *IEEE Trans. on VLSI Systems*, vol. 3, no. 2, pp. 264–272, June 1995.

10. M. E. Dean, D. L. Dill, and M. Horowitz, "Self-timed logic using current-sensing completion detection (CSCD)," *J. of VLSI Signal Processing*, vol. 7, pp. 7–16, 1994.

11. S. Hauck, "Asynchronous design methodologies: an overview," *Proc. IEEE*, vol. 83, no. 1, pp. 67–93, Jan. 1995.

12. G. M. Jacobs and R. W. Brodersen, "A fully asynchronous digital signal processor using self-timed circuits," *IEEE Journal of Solid-State Circuits*, vol. 25, no. 6, pp. 1526–2536, Dec. 1990.

13. A. J. Martin, "Compiling communicating processes into delay insensitive circuits," *Distributed Computing*, vol. 1, pp. 226–234, 1986.

14. T. H.-Y. Meng, R. W. Brodersen, and D. G. Messerschmitt, "Automatic synthesis of asynchronous circuits from high-level specifications," *IEEE Trans. on Computer-Aided Design*, vol. 8, no. 11, pp. 1185–1205, Nov. 1989.

15. P. Patra and D. S. Fussell, "Fully asynchronous, robust, high throughput arithmetic structures," in *Proc. 8th International Conference on VLSI Design*, pp. 141–145, Jan. 1995.

16. J. T. Udding, "A formal model for classifying delay-insensitive circuits and systems," *Distributed Computing*, vol. 1, pp. 197–204, 1986.

17. T. Williams, M. Horowitz, R. L. Alverson, and T. S. Yang, "A self-timed chip for division," in *Proc. of Stanford Conference on Advanced Research in VLSI*, pp. 75–95, March 1987.

18. T. E. Williams and M. A. Horowitz, "A zero-overhead self-timed 160-ns 54-b CMOS divider," *IEEE J. of Solid-State Circuits*, vol. 26, no. 11, pp. 1651–1661, Nov. 1991.

19. J. Yuan and C. Svensson, "High-speed CMOS circuit technique", *IEEE Journal of Solid-State Circuits*, vol. 24, no. 1, pp. 62–70, Feb. 1989.

20. M. Hatamian and G. L. Cash, "Parallel bit-level pipelined VLSI designs for high-speed signal processing," *Proc. IEEE*, vol. 75, no. 9, pp. 1192–1202, Sept. 1987.

21. M. Hatamian and G. L. Cash, "A 70-MHz 8-bit×8-bit parallel pipelined multiplier in 2.5-μ CMOS," *IEEE Journal of Solid-State Circuits*, vol. SC-21, no. 4, pp. 505–513, Aug. 1986.

22. M. Hatamian and K. K. Parhi, "An 85-MHz fourth-order programmable IIR digital filter chip," *IEEE Journal of Solid-State Circuits*, vol. 27, no. 2, pp. 175–183, Feb. 1992.

23. H. B. Bakoglu, J. T. Walker, and J. D. Meindl, "A symmetric clock-distribution tree and optimized high-speed interconnections for reduced clock skew in ulsi and wsi circuits," in *Proc. of IEEE International Conference on Computer Design*, (Rye Brook, NY), pp. 118–122, Oct. 1986.

24. A. L. Fisher and H. T. Kung, "Synchronizing large VLSI processor arrays," *IEEE Trans. on Computers*, vol. C-34, no. 8, pp. 734–740, Aug. 1985.

25. E. G. Friedman and S. Powell, "Design and analysis of a hierarchical clock distribution system for synchronous standard cell/macrocell VLSI," *IEEE Journal of Solid-State Circuits*, vol. SC-21, no. 2, pp. 240–246, April 1986.

26. S. Y. Kung and R. J. Gal-Ezer, "Synchronous versus asynchronous computation in very large scale integrated (VLSI) array processors," in *Proc. of SPIE Symposium*, vol. 341, pp. 53–65, 1982.

17

Low-Power Design

17.1 INTRODUCTION

Historically, *performance characteristics* of digital systems have been synchronous with circuit speed or processing power. For example, in the world of microprocessors, performance is often measured in terms of MFLOPS (millions of floating point operations per second) or MIPS (millions of instructions per second). The *cost* of the digital system is dependent on the implementation strategy being considered. For VLSI system design, there is a fair one-to-one correspondence between silicon area and cost. Consequently, increasing the implementation area tends to result in higher packaging costs as well as reduced fabrication yields with both effects leading to increased product cost. In addition, improvements in system performance generally come at the expense of silicon area. Therefore, historically, the task of VLSI designers has been to explore the AT (area-time) trade-offs and strike a reasonable balance between these often conflicting objectives.

Recently, it has been found that area and time are not sufficient metrics for evaluating the system performance. *Power consumption* is another very important metric. Until recently, power consumption was only a secondary concern in comparison to area and speed. However, this thinking has begun to change in recent years and power is being given comparable weight to area and speed considerations. Many factors contribute to this new trend. Perhaps the most visible factor has been the phenomenal growth of portable electronics. Personal digital assistants, laptop computers and cellular phones have enjoyed considerable success among consumers, and the market for these and other portable devices is on the rise. For these applications, the *average power* consumption has become the most critical design concern. For example, the power consumption of a portable multimedia terminal when implemented using off-the-shelf components not optimized for low-power operation is about 40 W. With advanced nickel-metal-hydride battery technologies yielding around 65 watt-hours/kilogram, this terminal would require an unacceptable 6 kilograms of batteries for 10 hours of operation [1]. Even with state-of-the-art battery technologies such as lithium ion, which yield about 100 watt-hours/kilogram, the multimedia terminal would require about 4 kilograms of battery cells for 10 hours of operation. Therefore, in the absence of low-power design techniques, current and future portable devices will suffer from either a very heavy battery pack or a very short battery life.

Even in the case of nonportable systems, reductions in power consumption play a very crucial role. For example, microprocessors optimized for performance dissipate typically about 40−80 W at 200−500 MHz clock rates. The speed of microprocessors is increasing at a steady pace and the clock speeds have reached 1 GHz already. At such high clock speeds, they would consume about 300 W of power, which is unacceptable as the cost associated with packaging and cooling such devices is huge. Therefore, unless the power consumption is dramatically reduced, the resulting heat will limit the packaging and the performance of VLSI systems.

In addition to cost, reliability is also a major issue in the design of digital systems. High-power systems often run hot and this tends to exacerbate failure mechanisms. It is found that the failure rate is doubled for every 10°C rise in operating room temperature. In addition, the maximum power dissipation is a critical factor as it determines the thermal and electrical limits of the system. Therefore, it is essential to have the peak power under control.

All of the foregoing factors have motivated the discussion in this chapter, which presents techniques for the design of low-power systems. The low-power design techniques are targeted towards digital CMOS circuits as they are widely used in industry for the design of portable systems to DSP architectures to microprocessors. The power consumption in digital CMOS circuits is expressed as

$$P = I_{standby}V_{dd} + I_{leakage}V_{dd} + I_{sc}V_{dd} + \alpha C_l V_{dd}^2 f_{clk} \qquad (17.1)$$

where
• the *standby current* $I_{standby}$ is the DC current drawn continuously from the power supply (V_{dd}) to ground,
• the *leakage current* $I_{leakage}$, is primarily determined by the fabrication technology, caused by (1) the reverse bias current in the parasitic diodes formed between source and drain diffusions and the bulk region in a MOS transistor, and (2) the subthreshold current that arises from the inversion that exists at the gate voltages below the threshold voltage,
• the *short-circuit current* I_{sc} is due to the DC path between the supply rails during output transitions,

• the last term refers to the capacitive power dissipation with α (referred to as the switching activity) being the average number of $0 \to 1$ output transitions, C_l the load capacitance at the output node, V_{dd} is the power supply voltage, and f_{clk} is the clock frequency. The product of the switching activity and the clock frequency is also referred to as the *transition density* [2].

The *standby current*, and hence standby power consumption, occurs when both the NMOS and the PMOS transistors are continuously on. This could happen, for example, in a pseudo-NMOS inverter, when the drain of an NMOS transistor is driving the gate of another NMOS transistor in a pass-transistor logic, or when the tristated input of a CMOS gate leaks away to a value between power supply and ground. The standby power is equal to the product of V_{dd} and the DC current drawn from the power supply to ground.

The diode *leakage current*, and hence leakage power, is proportional to the area of the source or drain diffusion and the leakage current density and is typically in the order of 1 *picoA* for a 1 *micron* technology. The subthreshold *leakage current* for long channel devices decreases exponentially with $V_{GS} - V_t$, where V_{GS} is the gate bias and V_t is the transistor threshold voltage, in accordance with

$$I_{st} = k e^{\frac{(V_{gs} - V_t)}{n V_T}} \left(1 - e^{\frac{V_{ds}}{V_T}} \right) \tag{17.2}$$

where k is a function of the technology parameters and V_T is the thermal voltage (KT/q). This is negligible at normal supply and threshold voltages but its effect can become pronounced at reduced power supply and device threshold voltages. Moreover, at short channel lengths, the subthreshold current becomes exponentially dependent on drain voltage instead of being dependent on V_{DS}, which is the difference between the drain and the source voltages.

The term *static power dissipation* refers to the sum of the standby and leakage power dissipations. Leakage currents in digital CMOS circuits can be reduced with the proper choice of device technology. Standby currents play an important role in design styles like pseudo-NMOS and NMOS pass transistor logic and in memory cores.

The *short-circuit power consumption* of a logic gate is proportional to the input rise time (t_r) and fall time (t_f), the load, and the transistor sizes of the gates. For example, for an inverter without load and assuming that $t_r = t_f = t_{rf}$, the short-circuit power consumption P_{sc} is expressed as [3]

$$P_{sc} = \frac{\beta}{12} (V_{dd} - 2V_t)^3 \frac{t_{rf}}{T_{clk}} \tag{17.3}$$

where T_{clk} is the period of the input waveform and β is the gain factor of the transistor and is dependent on both the process parameters and the device geometry, and is given by

$$\beta = \frac{\mu\epsilon}{t_{ox}}\left(\frac{W}{L}\right) \tag{17.4}$$

where μ is the effective surface mobility of the carriers in the channel, ϵ is the permittivity of the gate insulator, t_{ox} is the thickness of the gate insulator, W is the width of the channel, and L is the length of the channel. The gain factor β therefore consists of a process dependent factor $\mu\epsilon/t_{ox}$, and a geometry term (W/L) that depends on the actual layout dimensions of the device. The maximum short-circuit current flows when there is no load and it decreases as the load increases. Depending on the approximations used to model the currents and to estimate the input signal dependencies, different techniques have been derived for the evaluation of the short-circuit power. A useful expression was recently derived in [4] that shows the explicit dependence of the short circuit power dissipation on the design parameters. The idea is to adopt an alternative definition of the short-circuit power dissipation through an equivalent short-circuit capacitance C_{SC}. If the gate sizes are selected so that the input and output rise- and fall-times are about equal, the short-circuit power consumption will be less than 15% of the dynamic power consumption. However, if very high performance is desired and large gates are used to drive relatively small loads and if the input rise time is long, then the short-circuit power consumption cannot be ignored.

For well-designed CMOS circuits the capacitive power is the dominant source of power consumption. The term *dynamic power consumption* refers to the sum of the short-circuit and capacitive power dissipations. Using the concept of equivalent short-circuit capacitance described previously, the dynamic power dissipation can be calculated if C_{SC} is added to C_l.

The outline of this chapter is as follows. Section 17.2 gives some theoretical background on probability theory used in the remainder of the chapter. The effect of technology scaling on power consumption is discussed in Section 17.3. Here, it is shown that as the device sizes are reduced, the supply voltage also has to be reduced in order to maintain a constant power density. Moreover, the threshold voltage also has to be scaled along with supply voltage to maintain a constant circuit delay. A detailed analysis of the different factors that affect power consumption is presented in Section 17.4. Section 17.5 presents some recent techniques that have been developed for power reduction. Power estimation techniques for digital CMOS circuits are presented in Section 17.6.

17.2 THEORETICAL BACKGROUND

In this section some simple probabilistic measures that are useful in estimating power consumption of digital systems are defined. Let a signal $\hat{x}(t)$, $t \in (-\infty, +\infty)$, be a stochastic process [5], which makes transitions between logic

0 and logic 1 at random times. A logic signal $x(t)$ can then be thought of as a sample of the stochastic process $\hat{x}(t)$, i.e., $x(t)$ is one of an infinity of possible signals that make up the family $\hat{x}(t)$. In this chapter, it is also assumed that the input processes are *strict-sense stationary* [5], implying that its statistical properties are invariant to a shift in the time origin.

The digital CMOS circuits under consideration are assumed to be operating in a synchronous environment, i.e., they are being controlled by a global clock. Let T_{clk} denote the clock period, and T_{gd} denote the smallest gate delay in the circuit. To capture the glitches in the circuit, the clock period is assumed to be divided into S slots as shown in Fig. 17.1, where

$$S \triangleq \frac{T_{clk}}{T_{gd}}. \tag{17.5}$$

The duration of a time slot is determined by performing SPICE simulations

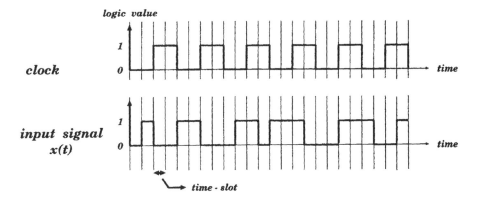

Fig. 17.1   Notion of a time slot.

with detailed device level parameters. Then, the probability of a signal x_i being 1 at a given time is defined as

$$p_{x_i}^1 = \lim_{N \to \infty} \frac{\displaystyle\sum_{n=1}^{N \times S} x_i(n)}{N \times S} \tag{17.6}$$

where N represents the total number of clock cycles, and $x_i(n)$ is the value of the input signal x_i between the time instances n and $n + 1$. Then, the probability that the signal x_i is 0 at a given time is defined as

$$p_{x_i}^0 = 1 - p_{x_i}^1. \tag{17.7}$$

Let us assume that the signal x_i makes a transition from 0 to 1. Then, the probability associated with this transition is defined as

$$p_{x_i}^{0 \to 1} = \lim_{N \to \infty} \frac{\sum_{n=1}^{N \times S} \overline{x_i(n)x_i(n+1)}}{N \times S}. \tag{17.8}$$

The other transition probabilities can be obtained in a similar manner. It is easy to verify that

$$p_{x_i}^{0 \to 1} + p_{x_i}^{1 \to 0} + p_{x_i}^{1 \to 1} + p_{x_i}^{0 \to 0} = 1, \tag{17.9}$$

and

$$p_{x_i}^{0 \to 0} + p_{x_i}^{1 \to 0} = p_{x_i}^{0} \tag{17.10}$$
$$p_{x_i}^{0 \to 1} + p_{x_i}^{1 \to 1} = p_{x_i}^{1}.$$

It should be noted that in the foregoing equations $p_{x_i}^{1 \to 0}$ and $p_{x_i}^{0 \to 1}$ are equal.

The conditional probabilities can be easily derived from the transition probabilities, where for example

$$p_{x_i}^{1/0} = \frac{p_{x_i}^{0 \to 1}}{p_{x_i}^{0 \to 1} + p_{x_i}^{0 \to 0}} \tag{17.11}$$

represents the probability that $x_i(n+1) = 1$ given that $x_i(n) = 0$.

The signal characteristics can be completely determined once the conditional or transition probabilities are known.

17.3 SCALING VERSUS POWER CONSUMPTION

Scaling is an important factor that affects power consumption. As technology is scaled, power supply voltage should also be scaled to maintain the same power density as shown in Fig. 17.2. It is clear from the figure that if the supply voltage is scaled by $1/k$ the power consumption is scaled by a factor $1/k^2$ although the power density remains constant. It is also clear that if supply voltage is not scaled then the power density increases in a cubic manner.

The reduction in supply voltage is also accompanied by an increase in circuit delay T_d in accordance with the 1st-order equation [6]

$$T_d = \frac{C_l \times V_{dd}}{\mu C_{ox} (W/L) (V_{dd} - V_t)^2}. \tag{17.12}$$

Fig. 17.3 shows a plot of delay with supply voltage for a threshold voltage of 0.7 V. It is clear from the figure that the delay for $V_{dd} = 1.5$ V is about 10 times the delay for $V_{dd} = 5$ V.

Parameters		Scaling effects	
		Scaled Vdd	Constant Vdd
Device size		$1/k$	$1/k$
Gate thickness	t_{ox}	$1/k$	$1/k$
Substrate doping		k	k^2
Supply voltage	V	$1/k$	1
Electric field	E	1	k
Current	I	$1/k$	k
Area	A	$1/k^2$	$1/k^2$
Capacitance	$C = \varepsilon A / t_{ox}$	$1/k$	$1/k$
Gate delay	VC/I	$1/k$	$1/k^2$
Power dissipation	VI	$1/k^2$	k
Power density	VI/A	1	k^3

Fig. 17.2 Effect of scaling on power consumption.

One approach to reducing the supply voltage without sacrificing speed is to modify the V_t of the devices. However, the limits on how much V_t can be reduced is set by adequate noise margins and subthreshold leakage currents. Typically, the optimum V_t is determined based on the gates of the CMOS devices and the control of the leakage currents. It is found that for 80–100 mV reduction in V_t (at room temperature), the subthreshold current is increased by an order of magnitude [1]. As a rule of thumb, the off current should remain at least two orders of magnitude smaller than the on current. This limits V_t to about 0.3 V for operation (at room temperature) of CMOS devices.

Fig. 17.4 shows a plot of delay versus V_t for different supply voltages. It is clear from the figure that the delay can change by as much as two times for a ΔV_t of 0.15 V when V_{dd} equals 1.1 V. Therefore, techniques that limit the V_t fluctuation to 0.05 V have been explored [7]. Another important characteristic observed from the figure is that in order to maintain a constant circuit delay, both supply voltage and the threshold voltage have to be scaled *simultaneously*. For example, from Fig. 17.4, it is observed that in order to have a normalized delay of 0.01 the following combinations of supply and threshold voltages have to be used: $V_{dd}=3$ V and $V_t=0.67$ V; $V_{dd}=1.5$ V and $V_t=0.33$

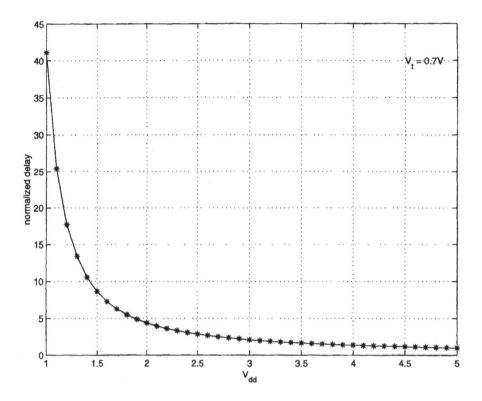

Fig. 17.3 Circuit delay as a function of supply voltage.

V; V_{dd}=1.1 V and V_t=0.11 V. It is clear from this discussion that reduction in supply voltage plays an important and tricky part in the reduction of power consumption.

17.4 POWER ANALYSIS

It is clear from Section 17.1 that essentially four factors determine the power dissipation in a digital CMOS circuit. However, reducing the clock frequency is generally not an option as all digital systems have certain minimum throughput requirements. The ramifications of scaling the supply voltage has already been discussed in the previous section. This section briefly analyzes the other two factors, namely switching activity and physical capacitance, describing their importance, as well as the interactions that make the design for low-power challenging.

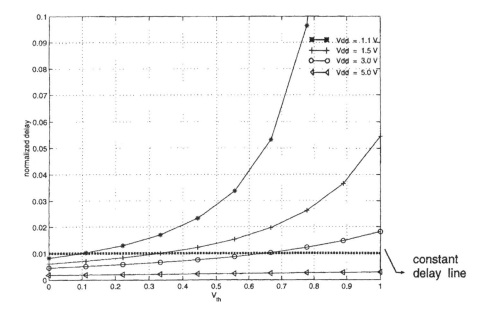

Fig. 17.4 Circuit delay as a function of supply voltage for varying threshold voltages.

17.4.1 Switching Activity

The switching activity of a circuit is the average number of $0 \to 1$ transitions that occur in 1 clock cycle at various output nodes in the circuit. It is difficult to estimate the switching activity for a general circuit because it is not only a function of the circuit inputs and the logic function the circuit implements but also a function of the temporal and spatial correlations among the circuit inputs. Furthermore, glitching or spurious transitions that occur at output nodes before they settle down also affect the switching activity.

The dependence of switching activity on the correlation among circuit inputs is illustrated with the help of a simple example. Consider an OR gate with two inputs x and y as shown in Fig. 17.5(a). If the inputs are independent and the signal probabilities are $1/2$ each, then the switching activity α is $3/16$ as the OR gate makes a $0 \to 1$ output transition in 3 out of 16 possible input transitions (see Fig. 17.5(b)). Now let us suppose that only patterns 00 and 11 can be applied to the OR gate and that both patterns are equally likely, then α is $1/4$ (see Fig. 17.5(c)). Alternatively, assume that every 0 applied to input x is immediately followed by a 1 while every 1 applied to input y is immediately followed by a 0, then α is $2/9$ (see Fig. 17.5(d)). Finally, assume that it is known that x changes exactly when y changes value, then α is $1/8$ (see Fig. 17.5(e)). Fig. 17.5(c) illustrates the case of *spatial* correlations between gate inputs, (d) illustrates the *temporal* correlations on gate inputs,

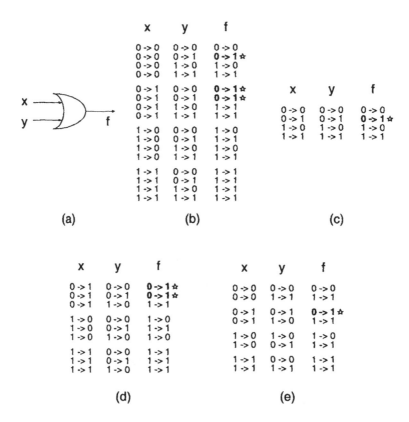

Fig. 17.5 Example illustrating the dependence of switching activity on correlation among circuit inputs.

and (e) instantiates the case of *spatiotemporal* correlations.

In the case of glitching at the output nodes, there may be an additional number of $0 \rightarrow 1$ transitions leading to increased switching activity. It is found that in the case of data-path intensive circuits like multipliers, the glitch power (or wasted power) could be as high as 40%. Therefore, while designing for low power, careful attention has to paid to all these factors. Although it is difficult to predict the exact glitching effects due to its complex dependence on the delays, an approximation is still possible. In this chapter, the notion of a time slot is employed to compute the switching activity in the presence of glitching.

Theorem 17.4.1 *Let us assume that the clock cycle is divided into S time slots numbered from 0 to $S-1$, where the duration of the time slot is equal to the smallest gate delay of all the cells in the library. Let us also assume that the inputs change only in the beginning of every clock cycle. Moreover, let the output of the circuit at the beginning of any time slot j in every clock cycle be defined as $f_j(Sn)$ where $j \in \{0, S-1\}$ and n is the time index. Then the* *switching activity at the output node f in the presence of glitching is computed as [8]*

$$\alpha_f = \sum_{j=0}^{S-1} \alpha_{f_{j,j+1}} = \sum_{j=0}^{S-1} p_{f_{j+1}} \left(1 - p_{f_j}\right) \left(1 - \rho_{f_{j,j+1}}\right) \qquad (17.13)$$

where p_{f_x} is the probability of the output f being 1 in time slot x, and

$$\rho_{f_{j,j+1}} = \frac{E\left[f_j(Sn)f_{j+1}(Sn)\right] - p_{f_j}p_{f_{j+1}}}{\sqrt{\left(p_{f_j} - p_{f_j}^2\right)\left(p_{f_{j+1}} - p_{f_{j+1}}^2\right)}}. \qquad (17.14)$$

In (17.14), the output of the circuit at time slot S is the same as the output of the circuit at time slot 0 in the next clock cycle.

Proof:
The switching activity of a node in the presence of glitching is expressed as (see Problem 4)

$$\alpha_f = p_f(1 - p_f)(1 - \rho_f) \qquad (17.15)$$

where p_f represents the probability of the output f being 1 and ρ_f is the autocorrelation coefficient of f. Since (17.15) is true for every clock cycle it must be true for every time slot. Therefore, (17.13) is a straightforward extension of (17.15).

The autocorrelation matrix for two successive time slots is computed as

$$\mathbf{R}_{f_{j,j+1}} = \begin{bmatrix} E\left[f_j(Sn)^2\right] & E\left[f_j(Sn)f_{j+1}(Sn)\right] \\ E\left[f_{j+1}(Sn)f_j(Sn)\right] & E\left[f_{j+1}(Sn)^2\right] \end{bmatrix} \qquad (17.16)$$

and the mean vector $\mu_{f_{j,j+1}}$ defined as

$$\mu_{f_{j,j+1}} = \begin{bmatrix} E\left[f_j(Sn)\right] \\ E\left[f_{j+1}(Sn)\right] \end{bmatrix}. \qquad (17.17)$$

The covariance matrix $\mathbf{C}_{f_{j,j+1}}$ is therefore computed as

$$\mathbf{C}_{f_{j,j+1}} = \mathbf{R}_{f_{j,j+1}} - \mu_{f_{j,j+1}} \cdot \mu_{f_{j,j+1}}^T \qquad (17.18)$$

Therefore, making use of (17.16) and (17.17), $\mathbf{C}_{f_{j,j+1}}$ is expressed as

$$\mathbf{C}_{f_{j,j+1}} = \begin{bmatrix} E\left[f_j(Sn)^2\right] - p_{f_j}^2 & E\left[f_j(Sn)f_{j+1}(Sn)\right] - p_{f_j}p_{f_{j+1}} \\ E\left[f_j(Sn)f_{j,j+1}(Sn)\right] - p_{f_j}p_{f_{j+1}} & E\left[f_{j+1}(Sn)^2\right] - p_{f_{j+1}}^2 \end{bmatrix}. \qquad (17.19)$$

Therefore, the correlation coefficient is computed as

$$\rho_{f_j, j+1} = \frac{E\left[f_j(Sn)f_{j+1}(Sn)\right] - p_{f_j}p_{f_{j+1}}}{\sqrt{\left(p_{f_j} - p_{f_j}^2\right)\left(p_{f_{j+1}} - p_{f_{j+1}}^2\right)}}. \blacksquare \qquad (17.20)$$

The theorem is best illustrated with the help of a simple example. Consider the circuit shown in Fig. 17.6 with 3 inputs. The numbers inside the

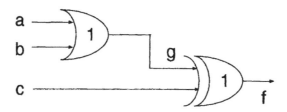

Fig. 17.6 An example circuit to illustrate computation of switching activity in the presence of glitching.

gates denote the delay in terms of the number of time slots for the gate to compute its output. The circuit is analyzed using uncorrelated inputs, inputs with temporal correlation, inputs with spatial correlation, and inputs with spatiotemporal correlation. The clock cycle is divided into 2 time slots for the switching activity analysis. Let the probability of the input signals a, b, c being 1 be p_a, p_b, and p_c, respectively.

A) Uncorrelated inputs: Based on the delay model, the final output is computed as

$$\begin{aligned}
f_2(2n) = f(2n+2) &= \{1 - c(2n)\}\, b(2n) + \qquad\qquad (17.21)\\
&\quad \{1 - c(2n)\}\, a(2n)\, \{1 - b(2n)\} + \\
&\quad c(2n)\, \{1 - a(2n)\}\, \{1 - b(2n)\}\,.
\end{aligned}$$

Here, the sum terms are expressed in such a way that they are disjoint with respect to each other. In a similar manner the intermediate output is expressed as

$$g(2n+1) = g(2n+2) = a(2n) + b(2n)\,\{1 - a(2n)\}\,. \qquad (17.22)$$

The output $f_1(2n)$ is computed as

$$\begin{aligned}
f_1(2n) = f(2n+1) &= g(2n) \oplus c(2n) \qquad\qquad\qquad (17.23)\\
&= \{1 - c(2n)\}\, a(2n-2) + \\
&\quad \{1 - c(2n)\}\, b(2n-2)\, \{1 - a(2n-2)\} + \\
&\quad c(2n)\, \{1 - a(2n-2)\}\, \{1 - b(2n-2)\}\,.
\end{aligned}$$

In deriving this expression, it is assumed that the inputs a, b, and c change only in the beginning of every clock cycle, i.e., in the beginning of time slots 0, 2, 4, etc. Making use of (17.21) $f_0(2n)$ is computed as

$$f_0(2n) = f(2n) = \{1 - c(2n-2)\}\, b(2n-2) + \tag{17.24}$$
$$\{1 - c(2n-2)\}\, a(2n-2) \{1 - b(2n-2)\} +$$
$$c(2n-2) \{1 - a(2n-2)\} \{1 - b(2n-2)\}.$$

Using the preceding equations, the expected values are computed as

$$E[f_0(2n)f_1(2n)] = (1-p_c)^2 p_a p_b + (1-p_c)^2 p_a(1-p_b) + \tag{17.25}$$
$$(1-p_c)^2 p_b(1-p_a) + p_c^2 (1-p_a)(1-p_b)$$
$$= \frac{1}{4}$$

$$E[f_1(2n)f_2(2n)] = (1-p_c)p_b p_a + (1-p_c)p_b^2(1-p_a) +$$
$$(1-p_c)p_a^2(1-p_b) + (1-p_c)(p_b - p_b^2)(p_a - p_a^2) +$$
$$p_c(1-p_a)^2(1-p_b)^2$$
$$= \frac{5}{16}.$$

In a similar manner, the probability values are computed as

$$p_{f_0} = p_{f_2} = (1-p_c)p_b + (1-p_c)p_a(1-p_b) + p_c(1-p_a)(1-p_b)$$
$$= \frac{1}{2}$$
$$p_{f_1} = (1-p_c)p_a + (1-p_c)p_b(1-p_a) + p_c(1-p_a)(1-p_b)$$
$$= \frac{1}{2}. \tag{17.26}$$

Making use of (17.14), the correlation coefficients are computed as

$$\rho_{f_{0,1}} = 0, \ \rho_{f_{1,2}} = \frac{1}{4} \tag{17.27}$$

and the switching activity factor is computed as

$$\alpha_f = \frac{1}{4} + \frac{3}{16} = \frac{7}{16}. \tag{17.28}$$

If a zero-delay model is assumed for the gates it is found that the switching activity factor is 1/4. Therefore, it is clear that the switching activity assuming glitching is about twice that without glitching.

B) Inputs with temporal correlation: Let us assume that the input a is correlated in time. That is, a 0 at input a is always followed by a 1. In a similar manner let us assume that a 1 at input b is always followed by a 0. This implies that $t_a = E[a(Sn)a(Sn-S)] = 1/3$ and $t_b = E[b(Sn)b(Sn-S)] = 0$.

Also $p_a = 2/3$ and $p_b = 1/3$.

Making use of the foregoing facts, one obtains

$$E\left[f_0(2n)f_1(2n)\right] \;=\; \frac{1}{4} \tag{17.29}$$

$$\begin{aligned}
E\left[f_1(2n)f_2(2n)\right] \;&=\; (1 - p_c)p_b p_a + (1 - p_c)t_b(1 - p_a) + \\
&\quad (1 - p_c)t_a(1 - p_b) + (1 - p_c)(p_a - t_a)(p_b - t_b) + \\
&\quad p_c(1 - 2p_a + t_a)(1 - 2p_b + t_b) \\
&=\; 5/18
\end{aligned}$$

$$p_{f_{0,1}} = p_{f_{1,2}} \;=\; \frac{1}{2}.$$

The correlation coefficients are then computed as

$$\rho_{f_{0,1}} = 0, \; \rho_{f_{1,2}} = \frac{1}{9}. \tag{17.30}$$

Finally, the switching activity is computed as

$$\alpha_f \;=\; \frac{1}{4} + \frac{2}{9} = \frac{17}{36}. \tag{17.31}$$

If a zero-delay model is assumed then the switching activity is found to be $1/4$. This example again illustrates in the case of temporal correlation among inputs, the switching activity considering glitching is about twice that without glitching.

C) Inputs with spatial correlation: Let us assume that the inputs a and b have spatial correlation. In particular, let us assume that the only possible values of ab are 00 or 11. This implies that $a(Sn) = b(Sn)$ and that $t_{ab} = E\left[a(Sn)b(Sn)\right] = 1/2$.

Proceeding in a similar manner as before, one obtains

$$\begin{aligned}
E\left[f_0(2n)f_1(2n)\right] \;&=\; (1 - p_c)^2 t_{ab} + (1 - p_c)^2(p_a - t_{ab}) + \tag{17.32} \\
&\quad (1 - p_c)^2(p_b - t_{ab}) + p_c^2(1 - p_a) \\
&=\; \frac{1}{4}
\end{aligned}$$

$$\begin{aligned}
E\left[f_1(2n)f_2(2n)\right] \;&=\; (1 - p_c)p_a^2 + p_c(1 - p_a)^2 \\
&=\; \frac{1}{4}.
\end{aligned}$$

The correlation coefficients are then computed as

$$\rho_{f_{0,1}} = 0, \; \rho_{f_{1,2}} = 0. \tag{17.33}$$

Therefore the switching activity factor is computed as

$$\alpha_f = \frac{1}{4} + \frac{1}{4} = \frac{1}{2}. \tag{17.34}$$

It should be noted that if a zero-delay model is used then the switching activity factor would be $1/4$. This example shows that even with spatially correlated inputs, the switching activity with glitching is more than that without glitching.

D) Inputs with spatiotemporal correlation: Let us assume that the inputs a and b have spatiotemporal correlation. An example of this kind of correlation is that a changes exactly when b changes. Consequently, the input $a(n)$ is expressed as

$$\begin{aligned}
a(Sn) =\ & a(Sn - S)b(Sn)b(Sn - S) + \tag{17.35} \\
& a(Sn - S)\{1 - b(Sn)\}\{1 - b(Sn - S)\} + \\
& \{1 - a(Sn - S)\}b(Sn)\{1 - b(Sn - S)\} + \\
& \{1 - a(Sn - S)\}\{1 - b(Sn)\}b(Sn - S).
\end{aligned}$$

The computation of the expected values requires the computation of the following quantities:

$$\begin{aligned}
t_1 =\ & E\left[a(Sn)b(Sn)\right] = E\left[a(Sn - S)b(Sn)b(Sn - S)\right] + \tag{17.36} \\
& E\left[1 - a(Sn - S)1 - b(Sn)b(Sn - S)\right] \\
=\ & \frac{p_b(1 - p_b - p_a)}{1 - 2p_b}. \tag{17.37}
\end{aligned}$$

Taking expected values of both sides of (17.35), one has

$$\begin{aligned}
p_a =\ & p_b t_1 + (1 - p_b)(p_a - t_1) + \tag{17.38} \\
& p_b(1 - p_b - p_a + t_1) + (1 - p_b)(p_b - t_1) \\
=\ & \frac{(1 - 2p_b)(p_b - 2t_1)}{2p_b} + \frac{1}{2}.
\end{aligned}$$

If $p_b = 1/2$, it is clear that $p_a = p_b = 1/2$. Therefore, when $p_b = 1/2$, t_1 reduces to $p_b/2 = 1/4$ for the circuit under consideration.

$$t_2 = E\left[a(Sn)b(Sn)b(Sn - S)\right] = p_b t_1 = \frac{1}{8} \tag{17.39}$$

$$t_3 = E\left[a(Sn)b(Sn - 1)\right] = p_b t_1 + (1 - p_b)(p_b - t_1) = \frac{1}{4}$$

$$t_4 = E\left[a(Sn)b(Sn - S)a(Sn - S)\right] = p_b t_1 = \frac{1}{8}$$

$$t_5 = E\left[a(Sn)b(Sn)a(Sn - S)b(Sn - S)\right] = p_b t_1 = \frac{1}{8}$$

$$t_6 = E[a(Sn)a(Sn-S)] = t_1(2p_b - 1) + p_a(1 - p_b) = \frac{1}{4}$$

$$t_7 = E[a(Sn)b(Sn)a(Sn-S)] = p_b t_1 = \frac{1}{8}.$$

Making use of (17.21), (17.23), and (17.24), one gets

$$
\begin{aligned}
E[f_0(2n)f_1(2n)] &= (1-p_c)^2 t_1 + (1-p_c)^2(p_a - t_1) + && (17.40) \\
&\quad (1-p_c)^2(p_b - t_1) + p_c^2(1 - p_a - p_b + t_1) \\
&= \frac{1}{4} \\
E[f_1(2n)f_2(2n)] &= (1-p_c)p_b p_a + (1-p_c)(p_b^2 - p_b t_1) + \\
&\quad (1-p_c)(t_6 - t_7) + (1-p_c)(t_3 - t_4 - t_2 + t_5) + \\
&\quad p_c(1 - 2p_a - 2p_b + 2t_1 + t_6 + t_3 - t_4 + p_a p_b + p_b^2 - \\
&\quad p_b t_1 - t_7 - t_2 + t_5) \\
&= \frac{3}{8}.
\end{aligned}
$$

The corresponding probabilities are easily computed as

$$
\begin{aligned}
E[f_0(2n)] &= E[f_1(2n)] = && (17.41) \\
&= p_b(1 - p_c) + (1 - p_c)(p_a - t_1) + p_c(1 - p_a - p_b + t_1) \\
&= \frac{1}{2}.
\end{aligned}
$$

Finally, the switching activity is computed as

$$\alpha_f = \frac{1}{4} + \frac{1}{8} = \frac{3}{8}. \tag{17.42}$$

If a zero-delay model is used for the gates, it is found by doing a similar analysis that the switching activity is 1/4. Therefore, we see that even with spatiotemporal correlation among inputs, the proposed approach can be applied to compute the switching activity in the presence of glitching.

Circuit style is also an important issue that affects power consumption. The analysis presented above assumed a static CMOS implementation style for all the logic gates. If a dynamic CMOS implementation style is assumed then the switching activity results are different. As an example let us consider the OR gate shown in Fig. 17.5 and let us assume that it is implemented using dynamic CMOS circuit style as shown in Fig. 17.7. If the inputs are uncorrelated, then the switching activity for the OR gate is nothing but the probability of the output being 1. This is because in dynamic logic the gate is always precharged before evaluation. Therefore, for this 2-input OR gate, α_f is 3/4. The reader may recall that the switching activity for the OR gate designed using static logic was 3/16. It is therefore observed that the switching activity for a circuit

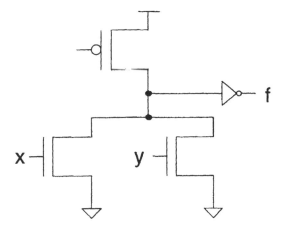

Fig. 17.7 An OR gate implemented using dynamic logic.

designed using dynamic logic is much more than that designed using static logic. Although the dynamic logic circuits have more switching activity, they have less glitching.

17.4.2 Physical Capacitance

Power consumption of a digital circuit is directly proportional to the physical capacitances seen by it at the output. However, estimation of capacitance at behavioral or logical levels of abstraction is imprecise because it requires estimation of the load capacitances that are not yet mapped to gates in a cell library. Therefore, analytical models have been developed for estimation of physical capacitance as a function of the circuit inputs, circuit fan-out, circuit complexity, and the technology information.

Interconnect capacitance also plays a very important role as devices shrink in size. Again, estimation of interconnect capacitance is a difficult problem even after technology mapping due to lack of detailed place and route information.

By intuition, reduction of physical capacitance is achieved by use of less area, shorter wires, and smaller devices. For example, area reduction can be achieved by using techniques like resource sharing, gate sizing, and logic minimization. Reduction of interconnect capacitance can be achieved by common subfunction extraction, register sharing, etc. Although smaller devices help in the reduction of physical capacitance, they have a negative effect on speed. Therefore, a suitable trade-off is desired.

17.5 POWER REDUCTION TECHNIQUES

Power optimization refers to the problem of reducing power consumption in a digital circuit at various abstractions of the design – from the software and algorithmic level down to the layout level. Traditional algorithmic transformations like pipelining and parallel processing can be used to reduce power consumption by operating the system with lower supply voltage (see Chapter 3). Power consumption can also be reduced by reducing capacitance by strength reduction transformation, either at the algorithmic level (see Chapter 9) or at the numerical level (see Chapter 15). In this section, some of the more recent techniques are briefly discussed.

17.5.1 Path Balancing

In order to reduce the glitching activity in a circuit, the delay of all true paths that converge at each gate must be roughly balanced, because *path balancing* leads to nearly simultaneous switching on the various gate inputs, and thus eliminates possible hazards at the output of the gate as shown in Fig. 17.8. This in turn reduces the average power dissipation in the circuit. Path bal-

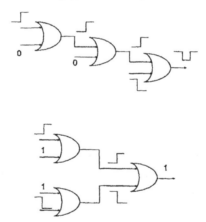

Fig. 17.8 Example illustrating the effect of path balancing.

ancing can be achieved before or after technology mapping. Before technology mapping it is achieved by logic decomposition or selective collapsing. After technology mapping it is achieved by delay insertion and pin reordering.

The idea behind selective collapsing is that by collapsing the fan-ins of a node, the arrival time at the output of that node can be changed. Logic decomposition leads to minimization of the level difference between inputs of the nodes that are driving high capacitive nodes. The delay insertion procedure tries to balance the delays of all paths in the circuit. The key issue in delay insertion is to use the minimum number of delay elements to achieve maximum reduction in spurious switching activity. Finally, pin assignments can be changed to balance path delays. This is possible because the delay characteristics of CMOS gates vary as a function of the input pin that is causing a transition at the output.

17.5.2 Transistor and Gate Sizing

It is well known that the power consumption is directly proportional to the size of the transistors; hence the bigger the size of the transistors, the greater the power consumption. Therefore, ideally to achieve the least power consumption, minimum-size transistors must be used throughout the design. However, this leads to extremely slow circuits. The *transistor sizing* problem reduces to that of finding a minimum power solution subject to meeting a given delay constraint.

A linear programming (LP) based approach is presented in [9] for generator-based gate sizing. This work is extended to handle setup and hold time constraints in [10]. This approach ignores short-circuit current and does not include the effect of input ramp time in the analysis. In [11], the LP-based approach is extended to handle short-circuit currents.

An approach for transistor sizing in a static CMOS layout to minimize short-circuit and capacitive power is presented in [12]. It is shown that power-optimal size for the transistors in a gate that is driving a given load can be larger than minimum size. Borah et al. also derive relationships for power-delay optimal sizes for these transistors and present a greedy algorithm for calculating the power optimal circuit. The algorithm presented by the authors starts out by doing an initial power-optimal transistor sizing on each gate. If the power-minimal layout satisfies the delay constraint, the process is terminated; or else, the power-delay sizing is applied until the delay constraints are satisfied. Using this approach the authors report about 15−20% reduction in total power dissipation.

A heuristic algorithm for library-based *gate sizing* for minimization of power subject to a given delay constraint is presented in [13]. Here, a minimum-size gate version is used to start with. Then, sizing is done along paths that have negative slacks so as to satisfy the delay constraints while increasing the switched capacitance of the circuit minimally. Alternatively, one can start with the fastest possible design and then size down gates along paths with positive slacks. In general, a dynamic programming approach can be applied to build power-delay trade-off curves and then perform gate selection in such a way that the delay constraints are met while minimizing the switched capacitance. In [14], a circuit that satisfies the timing constraint is used to begin with. Then, gates (not necessarily on the critical path) are sized to reduce power dissipation.

17.5.3   Transistor Reordering

It is well known that library gates have functionally equivalent pins, i.e., inputs can be permuted on those pins without changing the function of the gate output. However, these equivalent pins may have different pin loads and pin-dependent delays. Therefore, signal to pin assignment in a CMOS logic gate has a sizable effect on the propagation delay through the gate. If the parasitic power dissipation due to charging and discharging of source/drain to bulk diffusion capacitances inside a CMOS logic gate is ignored, then the high switching activity inputs should be matched with pins that have low input capacitance. This approach is not very effective for semicustom libraries since the difference in pin capacitances for logically equivalent pins is small. The parasitic power dissipation varies in turn as a function of the pin assignment of the input signals and switching activities [15]. Here, an optimization problem is solved to find the minimum power-pin assignment for a gate that accounts for the internal power dissipation. This approach is feasible as long as the number of functionally equivalent pins is not greater than 6.

Another approach is to assign the input signal with the largest probability of assuming a control value to the transistor near the output terminal of the gate [11]. The idea behind the approach is that this transistor will switch off more frequently, thus preventing the internal nodes from unnecessary charging and discharging. Another approach proposed in [16] states that the input that has the highest switching activity should be assigned to the input closest to the output terminal. The idea behind this approach is that assigning such a signal closest to the supply rails would lead to larger power dissipation. In [17] it is pointed out that if there is a conflict between the two rules, then the input with the highest ratio (probability of assuming controlling value over probability of making transitions) should be placed closest to the output terminal.

17.5.4   Retiming for Low Power

Retiming (see Chapter 4) was first proposed in [18] as a technique to improve the throughput by moving registers in a circuit while maintaining input-output functionality. The basic goal is to redistribute registers in the circuit to maximize throughput.

The use of retiming to minimize switching activity is proposed in [19] based on the observation that the register outputs have significantly fewer transitions than the register inputs. Consider the example shown in Fig. 17.9. The circuit shown in Fig. 17.9(a) has no glitching before the flip-flop, whereas the circuit shown in Fig. 17.9(b) has glitching before the flip-flop. As a result the switching activity at the input of the flip-flop in the latter case is higher. The effective switched capacitance in the 1st case is given by $\alpha_A C_f + \alpha_f C_B + \alpha_B C_C$ while that in the latter case is given by $\alpha_A C_B + \alpha'_B C_f + \alpha'_f C_C$. Depending

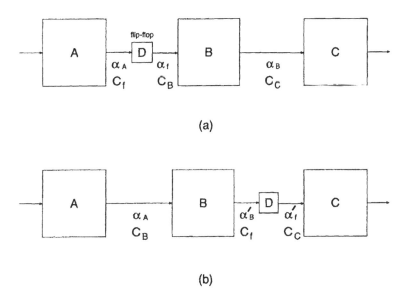

Fig. 17.9 Circuit illustrating the effect of retiming.

on the functionality implemented by the blocks A, B, and C, one of the implementations has lower switching activity. This method can be generalized to large circuits and heuristics can be applied to retime the circuit to obtain the minimum switching activity.

17.5.5 Voltage Scaling and Multiple Supply Voltages

Scaling of voltage levels will become an important issue in the design of future digital systems. The main driving force is the desire to produce complex, high performance systems on a chip and the exponential growth in the market for portable and wireless systems. It is projected that the various ASICs and memory will also switch to reduced supply voltages to meet stringent power constraints. One of the main problems in this approach is the availability of the complete chip set to make up systems at reduced supply voltages. This problem is overcome to some extent by mixing and matching different supply voltages on the chip.

In [20] two CMOS device and voltage scaling possibilities are described, one optimized for the highest speed and one trading off high performance for significantly lower power. The authors show that the low power scenario is similar to the electric field scaling theory. Improvements in speed and power-delay product can be obtained by the scaling of CMOS devices to submicron region, compared with high performance 0.6 micron devices at 5 V. The idea behind using multiple supply voltages is illustrated with the help of the following example.

Example 17.5.1 *Consider the system shown in Fig. 17.10 where all blocks are assumed to be identical. Let us assume that each block in the system has*

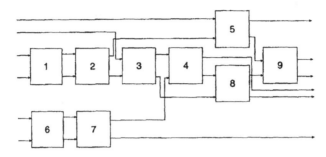

Fig. 17.10   Example to illustrate the use of multiple supply voltages.

a critical path of 1 time unit (u.t.) when the system is operated with a supply voltage of 3 V. The threshold voltage of the technology, V_{th}, is known to be 0.5 V. Assume a maximum of 3 supply voltages to be available. Also assume the minimum supply voltage to be 1.33 V. Use multiple supply voltages to obtain the least power consumption without altering the system latency of 6 u.t. Neglect loading effects.

   Solution: It is known that the delay t_d of a CMOS circuit is proportional to

$$t_d \propto \frac{V_{dd}}{(V_{dd} - V_{th})^2}. \tag{17.43}$$

Therefore, for supply and threshold voltages of 3V and 0.5V, respectively, the delay is found to be $t_d = 12/25$. Since the latency is 6 u.t., blocks 5, 6, and 7 can be operated much slower than 1 u.t. delay.

   In order to preserve the system latency of 6 u.t., it is observed that blocks 6 and 7 can be operated with a delay of $1.5t_d$ and block 5 with a delay of $3t_d$.

   For a delay of $1.5t_d$, the supply voltage can be reduced and the new supply voltage is obtained by solving

$$\frac{V_{dd}}{(V_{dd} - 0.5)^2} = \frac{18}{25}. \tag{17.44}$$

The new supply voltage for a delay of $1.5t_d$ is therefore $V_{dd} = 2.28$ V. In a similar manner the supply voltage for a delay of $3t_d$ is obtained by solving

$$\frac{V_{dd}}{(V_{dd} - 0.5)^2} = \frac{36}{25} \tag{17.45}$$

to obtain $V_{dd} = 1.53$ V.

   The system will now operate with 3 supply voltages; blocks 1, 2, 3, 4, and 8 with a supply voltage of 3 V, blocks 6 and 7 with a supply voltage of 2.28 V, and block 5 with a supply voltage of 1.53 V. Since the power is proportional to the square of the supply voltage, the initial power is computed as

$$Initial\ power\ \propto\ 9.(3)^2 = 81. \tag{17.46}$$

The final power is computed as

$$Final\ power\ \propto\ 6.(3)^2 + 2.(2.28)^2 + (1.53)^2 = 66.74. \tag{17.47}$$

Therefore, it is observed that by using multiple supply voltages a power reduction of about 18% is obtained without sacrificing the performance. ■

17.5.6 Dual/Multi-V_{th}

It is well known that the CMOS circuit propagation delay is approximately given by

$$T_d = \frac{C_l V_{dd}}{(V_{dd} - V_{th})^\alpha} \tag{17.48}$$

where α represents the velocity saturation effect and is typically 1.3 for submicron MOSFETs.

It is clear from the foregoing expression that there is a trade-off between power and delay. However, if V_{dd} and V_{th} are carefully chosen, better trade-offs can be found. Moreover, fluctuations in V_{dd} and V_{th} need to be reduced. In this way optimizing V_{dd} and V_{th} are essential for low-power high-performance design while they are treated as constants in conventional CMOS design. This leads to two important considerations: (1) degradation of worst-case speed due to V_{th} fluctuation at low V_{dd} [7],[21] and (2) increase in standby power dissipation at low V_{th} [22]–[24].

To solve these problems several schemes including the multi threshold-voltage CMOS (MTCMOS) scheme [23], a variable threshold-voltage CMOS (VTCMOS) scheme [25], and an elastic-V_{th} CMOS (EVTCMOS) scheme [26] have been proposed.

Typically in PCs, the power supply is turned off by a power management controller when a chip is inactive. The MTCMOS scheme employs 2 threshold voltages; a low V_{th} for fast circuit operation in logic circuits and a high V_{th} for cutting off the subthreshold leakage current in the standby mode. Since the parasitic capacitance is much smaller on a chip than on a board, power supply control can be performed much faster on a chip leading to efficient power management. The drawback of this approach is that it requires a large number of transistors for power supply control. Moreover, these area penalties become extreme below 0.9 V because the high V_{th} transistors become too slow in the active mode. An inverter operating under the MTCMOS scheme is shown in Fig. 17.11.

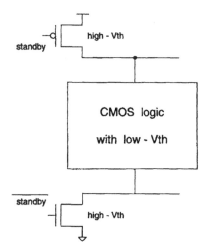

Fig. 17.11 Multithreshold CMOS inverter.

In VTCMOS, V_{th} can be dynamically varied through substrate bias V_{BB}. Typically, V_{BB} is controlled so as to compensate the threshold voltage fluctuations in the active mode, while in the standby mode deep V_{BB} is applied to increase the threshold voltage and thereby cut off the subthreshold leakage current. An inverter operating under the VTCMOS scheme is shown in Fig. 17.12.

EVTCMOS controls both the supply voltage and V_{BB} in such a way that when V_{dd} is lowered, V_{BB} becomes deeper. This in turn raises V_{th} and therefore reduces power dissipation in standby mode. In this approach the internal power supplies are provided by source-follower nMOS and pMOS transistors with controlled gate voltages.

The essential difference between the three schemes is that VTCMOS controls the substrate bias while the others control the power lines. Since a small current flows in the substrate when compared to the power lines, a smaller circuit can be used to control the substrate bias, which leads to negligible area and speed penalties in VTCMOS. Using a phase-locked loop and an SRAM in a VTCMOS array, the substrate noise influence has been shown to be negligible. A discrete cosine transform macro designed using the VTCMOS scheme [25] is found to consume one order of magnitude lower power than conventional CMOS design.

17.5.7 Clocking

In many synchronous applications, a significant amount of power is dissipated by the clock. Generally this is the only signal that switches all the time and it usually has to drive a very large clock tree. Moreover, in many cases the

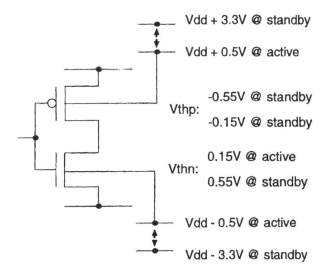

Fig. 17.12 Variable threshold CMOS inverter.

switching of the clock causes a lot of unnecessary switching activity. Consequently, more recent circuits are designed with controllable clocks. In other words, from the master clock other clocks are derived that can be slowed down or stopped completely with respect to the master clock under certain conditions. The circuit is therefore partitioned into small blocks that have their own derived clocks. The power savings achieved in this manner are very application dependent but can be significant.

In [27], power savings are achieved by stopping the clock fed into idle modules. Sections of the clock tree are turned on or off by gating the clock signals during the active or idle times of the clocked elements by associating every node in the clock tree with a binary string of 1s or 0s representing the active/idle status of the node in that time slot. The leaves of the clock tree are sinks and their activities are found from the high-level description of the system. The activity patterns of the internal nodes of the clock tree are computed by performing bitwise OR operations on the patterns of their children. Using this approach, significant power savings have been reported. An example of a true single phase clocked (tspc) latch is shown in Fig. 17.13 [28]. Here, the output can be forced to zero during the low phase of the clock using the transistor G. Without this device, it is not possible to generate rising edges for the gated clock on 2 consecutive rising edges of the system clock.

Another popular approach is to use a dual edge triggered flip-flop scheme as shown in Fig. 17.14. Here, the output is updated on both clock edges. As a result the effective data flow rate is twice the clock frequency. This extra speed can be traded with reduction in power supply voltage to achieve

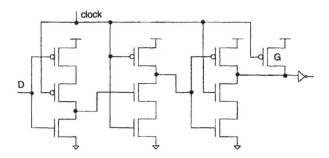

Fig. 17.13 Circuit illustrating the use of clock gating.

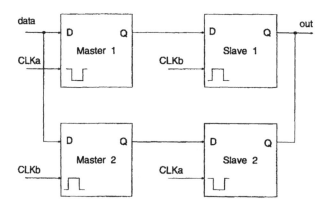

Fig. 17.14 Dual edge triggered flop-flop.

reduction in power consumption.

Asynchronous architectures use handshake signals to communicate between systems. As a result, they request operations only when they are needed. Although this approach offers what can be considered as optimal gated clocking, the handshaking control overhead has traditionally limited performance. However, for some applications such as a compact digital cassette error corrector chip, the performance requirements are easily met and the asynchronous approach yields savings up to a factor of five when compared with its synchronous counterpart [29].

17.5.8 Circuit Styles

Typically, a given logic function can be realized using many different logic styles such as static CMOS, dynamic CMOS, pass transistor, differential cascode voltage switch logic, etc. Among these, the pass transistor logic style is the most suitable for low-power design, because the pass transistor logic can be designed with many fewer transistors when compared with conventional static CMOS. As an example, the circuit of a static CMOS full adder requires 40 transistors, whereas a circuit designed using pass-transistor logic requires only 28 transistors. Researchers have therefore explored various pass transistor logic styles such as the complementary pass transistor logic (CPL) [30], swing-restored pass transistor logic (SRPL) [31], and differential cascade voltage switch with pass transistor gate (DCVSPG).

A CPL design uses only nMOS pass transistor circuits and therefore the high level drops by V_{th}. CMOS inverters are provided at the output stage to compensate for the dropped signal level as well as to increase the output drive capability. Although the output voltage is restored, the lowered high level increases the leakage current in the CMOS inverters. In order to avoid this, cross-coupled pMOS loads are added to recover the high level and enlarge the operation margin. Typically, small pMOS transistors are used to prevent degradation in switching speed. An example of a circuit designed using CPL style is shown in Fig. 17.15. The DCVS style is a slight variation of the CPL

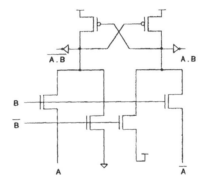

Fig. 17.15 Circuit realized using CPL design style.

style and uses nMOS pass transistor logic with cross-coupled pMOS loads as shown in Fig. 17.16.

An SRPL design uses nMOS pass transistor logic coupled with a CMOS latch. Since the CMOS latch flips in a push-pull manner, it exhibits greater operation margin, less static current, and faster speed compared to the cross-coupled CMOS loads. This approach is ideal for circuits with small load capacitance. Moreover, these circuits are more robust against process variations. An example of a circuit designed using SRPL style is shown in Fig. 17.17.

17.6 POWER ESTIMATION APPROACHES

Power estimation refers to the problem of estimating *average power dissipation* of digital circuits. Ideally the average power should include both the static and the dynamic power dissipations. However, for well-designed CMOS

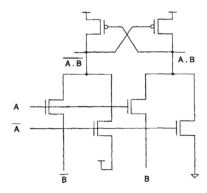

Fig. 17.16   Circuit realized using DCVS design style.

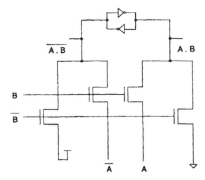

Fig. 17.17   Circuit realized using SRPL design style.

circuits, the capacitive power is dominant and therefore the average power generally refers to the capacitive power dissipation. This is much different from estimating the instantaneous or the worst-case power that is modeled as a voltage drop problem.

The design of low-power digital CMOS circuits cannot be achieved without accurate power prediction and optimization tools. Therefore, there is a critical need for CAD tools to estimate power dissipation during the design process to meet the power constraint without having to go through a costly redesign effort. The techniques for power estimation can be broadly classified into two categories: simulation based and nonsimulation based.

17.6.1   Simulation-Based Approaches

The main advantages of these techniques is that issues such as hazard generation, spatial/temporal correlation, etc. are automatically taken into account. The approaches under this category can be further classified into direct simulation and statistical simulation.

17.6.1.1 Direct Simulation The approaches in this category basically simulate a large set of random vectors using a circuit simulator like SPICE and then measure the average power dissipated. They are capable of handling various device models, different circuit design styles, tristate drivers, single and multiphase clocking methodologies, etc. The main disadvantage of these techniques is that they require large memory and have very long execution times. As a result they cannot be used for large, cell-based designs. Moreover, it is difficult to generate a compact vector set to calculate activity factors at various nodes.

Direct simulation can also be carried out using a transistor-level power simulator, which is based on an event-driven timing simulation algorithm. This uses simplified table-driven device models, circuit partitioning to increase the speed by 2–3 orders of magnitude over SPICE while maintaining the accuracy within 10% for a wide range of circuits. It also gives detailed information like instantaneous, average current, short-circuit power, capacitive power, etc.

Other techniques like Verilog-based gate-level simulation programs can be adapted to determine the power dissipation of digital circuits under user-specified input sequences. These techniques rely heavily on the accuracy of the macromodels built for the gates in the ASIC library as well as on the detailed gate-level timing analysis tools. The execution time is 3–4 orders of magnitude shorter than SPICE. Switch-level simulators like IRSIM [32] can be easily modified to report the switched capacitance (and thus dynamic power dissipation) during circuit simulations. This is much faster than the circuit-level simulation techniques but is not as versatile or accurate.

17.6.1.2 Statistical Simulation Techniques under this category are based on a *Monte Carlo simulation (MCS)* approach, which alleviates the pattern-dependence problem by a proper choice of input vectors. This approach consists of applying randomly generated input patterns at the circuit inputs and monitoring the power dissipation for T clock cycles using a simulator. Each such measurement gives a power sample that is regarded as a random variable. By applying the *central limit theorem*, it is found that as T approaches infinity, the sample density tends to a normal curve. Typically, a sample size of 30–50 ensures normal sample density for most combinatorial circuits. For a desired percentage error in the power estimate, ϵ, a given confidence level, ϑ, the sample mean, μ, and the sample standard deviation, σ, the number of required samples, N, is estimated as

$$N > \left(\frac{t_{\vartheta/2}\sigma}{\epsilon\mu}\right)^2 \tag{17.49}$$

where $t_{\vartheta/2}$ is defined so that the area to its right under the standard normal distribution curve is equal to $\vartheta/2$. In estimating the average power consumption of the digital circuit, the convergence time of the MCS approach is short when the error bound is loose or the confidence level is low. This method may converge prematurely to a wrong power estimate value if the sample density does not follow a normal distribution. Moreover, this approach cannot handle spatial correlations at the circuit inputs.

17.6.2 Non-Simulative Approaches

Nonsimulative approaches are based on library models, stochastic models, and information theoretic models. They can be broadly classified into those that work at the behavioral level and those that work at the logic level.

17.6.2.1 Behavioral Level Approaches Here, power estimates for functional units such as adders, multipliers, registers, and memories are directly obtained from the design library where each functional unit has been simulated using white noise data and the average switched capacitance per clock cycle has been calculated and stored in the library. The power model for a functional unit may be parametrized in terms of its input wordlength. For example, the power dissipation of an adder (or a multiplier) is linearly (or quadratically) dependent on its input wordlength. Although this approach is not accurate, it is useful in comparing different adder and multiplier architectures for their switching activity. The library can thus contain interface descriptions of each module, description of its parameters, its area, delay, and internal power dissipation (assuming white noise data inputs). The latter is determined by extracting a circuit or logic level model from an actual layout of the module by simulating it using a long stream of randomly generated input patterns. These characteristics are stored in the form of equations or tables. The power model thus generated and stored for each module in the library has to be modulated by the real input switching activities in order to provide power estimates that are sensitive to the input activities.

Word-level behavior of data input can be captured by its probability density function (pdf). In a similar manner, spatial correlation between data inputs can be captured by their joint pdf. This idea is to develop a probabilistic technique for behavioral level power estimation. The approach can be summarized in 4 steps: (1) building the joint pdf of the input variables of a data-flow graph (DFG) based on the given input vectors, (2) computing the joint pdf for some combination of internal arcs in the DFG, (3) calculating the switching activity at the inputs of each register in the DFG using the joint pdf of the inputs, (4) estimating power of each functional block using input statistics obtained in step 3. This method is robust but suffers from the worst-case complexity of the joint pdf computation and inaccuracies associated with the library characterization data.

An information theoretic approach is described in [33]−[35] where activity measures like entropy are used to derive fast and accurate power estimates at the algorithmic and structural behavioral levels. Entropy characterizes the uncertainty of a sequence of applied vectors and thus this measure is related to the switching activity. It is shown in [34] that under a temporal independence assumption the average switching activity of a bit is upper bounded by one half of its entropy. For control circuits and random logic, given the statistics of the input stream and having some information about the structure and functionality of the circuit, the output entropy bit is calculated as a function of the input entropy bit and a structure- and function-dependent information scaling factor. For DFGs, the output entropy is calculated using a compositional technique that has linear complexity in terms of its circuit size. A major advantage of this technique is that it is not simulative and is thus fast and provides accurate power estimates.

Most of the foregoing techniques are well suited for data paths. Behavioral level power estimates for the controller circuitry is outlined in [36],[37]. This technique provides a quick estimation of the power dissipation in a control circuit based on the knowledge of its target implementation style, i.e., dynamic, precharged pseudo-nMOS, etc.

17.6.2.2 Logic-Level Approaches From the discussion in Section 17.6.2.1, it is clear that most of the power in digital CMOS circuits is consumed during the charging/discharging of load capacitance. Therefore, in order to estimate the power consumption, one has to determine the switching activity α of various nodes in the digital circuit. If temporal independence among input signals is assumed, then the switching activity of a node with probability p_n is computed as

$$\alpha = p_n(1 - p_n). \tag{17.50}$$

If two successive values of a node are correlated in time, then the switching activity is computed using

$$\alpha = p_n(1 - p_n)(1 - \rho_n). \tag{17.51}$$

Computing the signal probabilities has therefore attracted a lot of attention from researchers in the past. In [38], some of the earliest work in computing the signal probabilities in a combinational network is presented. Here, variable names are assigned with each of the circuit inputs to represent the signal probabilities of these inputs. Then, for each internal circuit line, algebraic expressions involving these variables are computed. These expressions represent the signal probabilities for these lines. While the algorithm is simple and general, its worst-case complexity is exponential. An exact procedure based on ordered binary-decision diagrams (OBDDs) [39] can also be used to compute signal probabilities. This procedure is linear in the size of the corresponding function graph, however, may be exponential in the number of circuit inputs. Here, the signal probability of the output node is calculated by first building an OBDD corresponding to the global function of the node (i.e., function of the node in terms of the circuit inputs) and then performing a postorder traversal of the OBDD, which leads to a very efficient computational procedure for signal probability estimation. For example, if x_1, x_2, x_3 , and x_4 are the inputs of a 4-input XOR gate, then the probability of the output is computed using the OBDD shown in Fig. 17.18 and is expressed as

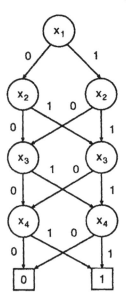

Fig. 17.18   Computing signal probabilities using OBDDs.

$$p_z = \overline{p_{x_1}}\,\overline{p_{x_2}}\,\overline{p_{x_3}}\,p_{x_4} + p_{x_1}p_{x_2}\,\overline{p_{x_3}}\,p_{x_4} + \overline{p_{x_1}}\,p_{x_2}p_{x_3}p_{x_4} + \quad (17.52)$$
$$p_{x_1}\,\overline{p_{x_2}}\,p_{x_3}p_{x_4} + \overline{p_{x_1}}\,\overline{p_{x_2}}\,p_{x_3}\,\overline{p_{x_4}} + p_{x_1}p_{x_2}p_{x_3}\,\overline{p_{x_4}} +$$
$$\overline{p_{x_1}}\,p_{x_2}\,\overline{p_{x_3}}\,\overline{p_{x_4}} + p_{x_1}\,\overline{p_{x_2}}\,\overline{p_{x_3}}\,\overline{p_{x_4}}.$$

where p_{x_i} represents the probabilities of the input signals.

All the foregoing techniques account for steady-state behavior of the circuit and thus ignore hazards and glitches and are therefore defined to be *zero-delay* model based techniques. Some previous work has been done in the area of estimation under a real delay model. In [40], the exact power estimation of a given combinational logic is carried out by creating a set of symbolic functions that represent Boolean conditions for all values that a node in a circuit can assume at different time instances under a pair of input vectors. The concept of a probability waveform is introduced in [41]. This waveform consists of an *event list,* which is nothing but a sequence of transition edges over time from the initial steady state to the final steady state where each event is annotated with a probability. The probability waveform of a node is a compact representation of the set of all possible logical waveforms at that node. In [2], an efficient algorithm based on Boolean difference equation is proposed to propagate the transition densities from circuit inputs throughout the circuit. The transition density $D(y)$ of each node in the circuit is calculated in accordance with

$$D(y) \;=\; \sum_{i=1}^{n} P\left(\frac{\partial y}{\partial x_i}\right) D(x_i) \tag{17.53}$$

where y is the output of a node and x_i's are the inputs of the node and the Boolean difference of the function y with respect to x_i gives all combinations for which y depends on x_i. Although this is quite effective it assumes that the x_i's are independent. This assumption is incorrect because x_i's tend to become correlated due to reconvergent fanout structures in the circuit. The problem is solved by describing y in terms of the circuit inputs, which are still assumed to be independent. Although the accuracy is improved in this case, the calculation of the Boolean difference terms becomes very expensive. A compromise between accuracy and efficiency can be reached by describing y in terms of some set of intermediate variables in the circuit.

17.6.2.3 Hierarchical approach

In this chapter, based on [42], we present a stochastic approach for power estimation of digital circuits and a tool based on this approach referred to as HEAT (hierarchical energy analysis tool). The salient feature of this approach is that it can be used to estimate the power of large digital circuits including multipliers, dividers, etc. in a short time. A typical approach to estimate power consumption of large digital circuits using stochastic methods would be to model them using state transition diagrams (STDs). However, this would be a formidable task as the number of states would increase exponentially with an increase in the number of nodes. Therefore, the digital circuits are decomposed into subcircuits, and the subcircuits are modeled using STDs. This greatly reduces the number of states in the STD, thereby reducing the computation time by orders of magnitude. For example, a typical Booth multiplier (designed using full adders, encoders, and multiplexers) is broken up into 3 subclasses, with the 1st subclass containing full adders, the 2nd subclass containing encoders, and the 3rd containing multiplexers. The circuit belonging to each subclass is then modeled with the help of an STD, facilitated through the development of analytic expressions for the state-update of each node in the STD. Then, the energy associated with each edge in the STD is computed using SPICE, and the total energy of the circuit belonging to a given subclass is computed by summing the energies of all the constituent edges in the STD. This procedure is repeated for all the subclasses, and the final energy of the digital circuit is computed by summing the energies of the constituent subclasses. An estimate of the average power is then obtained by finding the ratio of the total energy to the total time over which it was consumed.

Consider a typical digital circuit consisting of a regular array of cells as shown in Fig. 17.19. The array is treated as an interconnection of subcircuits arranged in rows and columns. The energy of the entire circuit is then com-

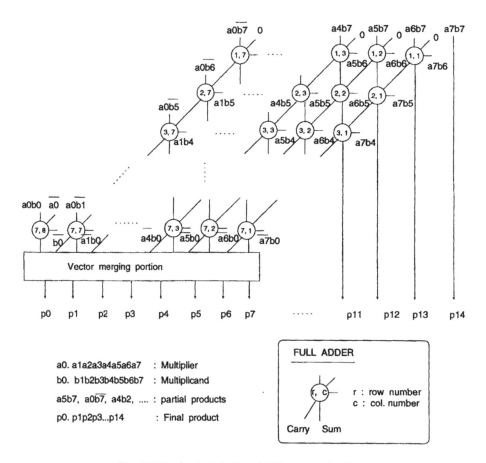

Fig. 17.19   An 8×8-b Baugh-Wooley multiplier.

puted by summing the energies of the individual subcircuits. The steps in the
proposed approach are summarized in the following algorithm.

Algorithm 17.6.1 *INPUT: # of rows, cols. in the circuit, type of subcircuits, parameters, i.e., signal, conditional probabilities of all input signals
OUTPUT: Estimated average power
est_power () {
total_energy = 0;
for r = 1 to rows
    for c = 1 to cols.
        model the sub_circuit(r,c) by using a STD;
        compute steady-state probabilities using MATLAB from the input
        signal parameters of sub_circuit(r,c), by treating the STD as an
        irreducible Markov chain;
        compute edge activities of the edges in the STDs using steady-state*

probabilities and MATLAB;
compute energy(r,c) associated with the edges of the STD using SPICE;
/* this step has to be executed only once */
total_energy = total_energy + energy(r,c);
compute the output signal parameters of sub_circuit(r,c);
  end;
end;
$$average\ power = \frac{total\ energy}{time\ over\ which\ the\ energy\ was\ spent}\ \} \blacksquare$$

State Transition Diagram Modeling

Here, a systematic approach is presented to model digital circuits using STDs. The modeling is done by deriving analytic expressions for the state-update of all nodes in the corresponding digital circuits.

A) Static CMOS NOR Gate

Consider a typical static CMOS NOR gate shown in Fig. 17.20, where x_1 and x_2, respectively, represent the 2 input signals and x_3 represents the output signal. It is clear from Fig. 17.20 that there are basically 2 nodes, $node_2$ and

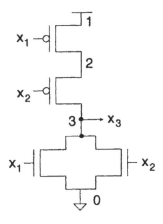

Fig. 17.20 A static CMOS NOR gate.

$node_3$, which have their values changing between 1 and 0. The presence of charging/discharging capacitances at these nodes enables us to develop the state update *arithmetic* equations for the nodes in accordance with

$$node_2(n + 1) = (1 - x_1(n)) + x_1(n) * x_2(n) * node_2(n) \qquad (17.54)$$

$$node_3(n + 1) = (1 - x_1(n)) * (1 - x_2(n)). \qquad (17.55)$$

The foregoing equations can be used to derive the STD for the NOR gate as shown in Fig 17.21, where for example, S_1 represents the state with node values $node_2 = node_3 = 0$, and the edge e_1 represents a transition (switching activity) from state S_1 to S_3.

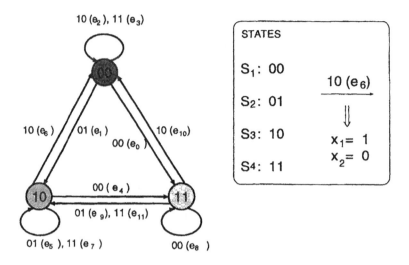

Fig. 17.21   State transition diagram for a static CMOS NOR gate.

B) Static CMOS NAND Gate

A static CMOS NAND gate is shown in Fig. 17.22, where as before x_1 and x_2 represent the 2 input signals and x_3 represents the output signal. The

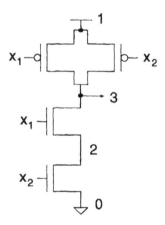

Fig. 17.22   A static CMOS NAND gate.

state update equations for the static CMOS NAND gate are expressed as

$$node_2(n+1) = (1 - x_2(n)) * (x_1(n) + (1 - x_1(n)) * node_2(n)) \quad (17.56)$$

$$node_3(n+1) = 1 - x_1(n) * x_2(n). \quad (17.57)$$

The equations (17.56) and (17.57) can be used to derive the STD for the

NAND gate as shown in Fig 17.23.

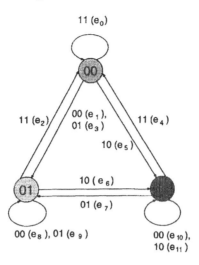

Fig. 17.23 State transition diagram for a static CMOS NAND gate.

C) A Static CMOS Full Adder

Consider the architecture of a static CMOS full adder as shown in Fig. 17.24. It is clear from the figure that the architecture is comprised of a carry gener-

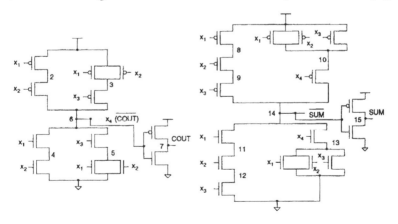

Fig. 17.24 Static CMOS full adder.

ation portion and a sum generation portion.

The state update equations can be determined in a similar manner for the carry and the sum portion of the full adder. Then, independent state transition diagrams are constructed for both the portions. For example, the state transition diagram for the carry portion of the full-adder is shown in Fig. 17.25. Here, for the sake of brevity only few edges have been shown. It

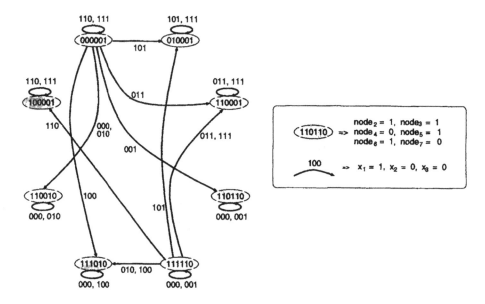

Fig. 17.25 State transition diagram for the carry portion of the static CMOS full adder.

is clear from Fig. 17.25 that the STD comprises of 8 states. Each state is associated with the 6 nodes present in the carry portion of the full-adder, and each edge is associated with the 3 inputs to the full-adder.

Computation of Steady-State Probabilities

An approach based on irreducible Markov chains is used to compute the steady-state probabilities of the various states in the STD. Consider the STD of the CMOS NOR gate shown in Fig. 17.21. Here, assuming that the input signals x_1 and x_2 are independent, the probabilities $p(e_j)$ associated with the various edges are computed in accordance with

$$p(e_j|e_j : x_m = q, x_n = r) = (q * p_{x_m}^1 + (1-q) * p_{x_m}^0) \tag{17.58}$$
$$\times (r * p_{x_n}^1 + (1-r) * p_{x_n}^0)$$

where $j \in \{0, 11\}$, $m, n \in \{1, 2\}$, and $q, r \in \{0, 1\}$. For example, the probability of edge e_1 in the STD is $p(e_1) = p_{x_1}^0 * p_{x_2}^1$. These edge probabilities are then used to compute the state transition matrix Π_{nor} in accordance with

$$\Pi_{nor} = \begin{bmatrix} p(e_2) + p(e_3) & p(e_1) & p(e_0) \\ p(e_6) & p(e_5) + p(e_7) & p(e_4) \\ p(e_{10}) & p(e_9) + p(e_{11}) & p(e_8) \end{bmatrix}. \tag{17.59}$$

Here, the $\Pi_{nor_{ij}}$-th element represents the transition probability from state S_i to state S_j, where $i, j \in \{1, 4\}$ and $i, j \neq 2$. Having modeled the transition diagram as an irreducible Markov chain, the steady-state probabilities are then computed by solving

$$P_S = P_S * \Pi_{nor} \tag{17.60}$$

where

$$P_S = \begin{bmatrix} P_{S_1} & P_{S_3} & P_{S_4} \end{bmatrix} \tag{17.61}$$

represents the steady-state probabilities of the different states. A simple approach to solve (17.60) is to first compute the eigenvalues associated with Π_{nor}^T. Then the normalized eigenvector corresponding to an eigenvalue of 1 would be the steady-state probability vector P_S. It may be noted that P_S is computed using MATLAB.

The steady-state probabilities computed by using the above Markov model are then used to compute the edge activities EA_j (for $j \in \{0, \#of\,edges - 1\}$). For example, the edge activity numbers for the NOR gate are computed using MATLAB in accordance with

$$EA_0 = P_{S_1} * N * S * P(00/10) + EA_3 * (P(00/11) - P(00/10)) \tag{17.62}$$

$$EA_1 = P_{S_1} * N * S * P(01/10) + EA_3 * (P(01/11) - P(00/10)) \tag{17.63}$$

$$\vdots$$

$$EA_7 = P_{S_3} * N * S * P(11/01) + (EA_{11} + EA_7) * (P(11/11) - P(11/01)) \tag{17.64}$$

$$\vdots$$

$$EA_{11} = P_{S_4} * N * S * P(11/00) \tag{17.65}$$

where, P(11/00) for example, represents the probability that $x_1(n + 1) = x_2(n + 1) = 1$ given that $x_1(n) = x_2(n) = 0$. The error in the edge activity numbers using the proposed approach was found to be less than 1.5%.

Energy Computation of Each Edge in the STD

This section presents an algorithm for the computation of energy associated each edge in the STD using SPICE. The first step in the algorithm is the identification of the initial state, and the sequence of inputs leading to that state. Two flag vectors, one for the state, and another for each edge in the STD are defined. The state flag vector is set whenever that state is first encountered. The edge flag vector on the other hand is set whenever the corresponding edge is traversed. The variable i stores the state number, while the variable k stores the number of the input sequence. For example in Fig. 17.21, i can vary from 1 to 4 (corresponding to states S_1 to S_4), and k can vary from 1 to 4 (corresponding to the sequence of inputs 00, 01, 10, 11). A matrix called edge_mat is formed, the rows of which store the sequence of inputs leading to the traversal of an edge in the STD. The steps in the algorithm are summarized below.

Algorithm 17.6.2 *INPUT: STD of the subcircuit; initial state (*init_state*), number of inputs to the subcircuit (*num_inputs*), initialized edge-matrix (*edge_mat*). OUTUT: energy of each edge in the STD.*
energy_edge() {
reset state flags and edge flags to zero;
i = init_state;k = 1;
while(all edge flags have not been set)
   m = new state;
   if(edge flag vector corresponding to input k not set)
      set edge flag vector;
      update edge_mat;
      if(flag corresponding to state m is not set)
         set flag corresponding to state m;
         update edge_mat;
         prev_state(i) = i;
         i = m;k = 0;
      else
         update edge_mat;
      end;
   end;
   k = k+1;
   if(k > 2^{num_inputs})
      k = 1;
      i = prev_state(i);
   end;
end; }
/* a matrix edge_mat with rows containing the sequence of inputs leading to the traversal of edges in the STD has been formed */
rows = number of rows in edge_mat;
cols. = number of columns in edge_mat;
for j = 1 to rows;
   run SPICE for input sequence edge_mat(j,cols-1);
   energy1 = resulting energy;
   run SPICE for input sequence edge_mat(j,cols.);
   energy2 = resulting energy;
   W_j *= energy2 - energy1;*
end;

                                            ■

Using this algorithm, the initial state for the NOR gate shown in Fig. 17.21 was found to be 11, and the edge_matrix was found to be

$$edge\_mat = \begin{bmatrix} 00 & 01 & 10 & 00 \\ 00 & 01 & 10 & 01 \\ 00 & 01 & 10 & 10 \\ 00 & 01 & 10 & 11 \\ 00 & 01 & 00 & \\ 00 & 01 & 01 & \\ 00 & 01 & 10 & \\ 00 & 01 & 11 & \\ 00 & 00 & & \\ 00 & 01 & & \\ 00 & 10 & & \\ 00 & 11 & & \end{bmatrix} \begin{matrix} \rightarrow e_0 \\ \rightarrow e_1 \\ \rightarrow e_2 \\ \rightarrow e_3 \\ \rightarrow e_4 \\ \rightarrow e_5 \\ \rightarrow e_6 \\ \rightarrow e_7 \\ \rightarrow e_8 \\ \rightarrow e_9 \\ \rightarrow e_{10} \\ \rightarrow e_{11} \end{matrix} \quad . \qquad (17.66)$$

The energy associated with the sub-circuit is then computed by taking a weighted sum of the energies associated with the various edges in the STD representing the sub-circuit, in accordance with

$$energy = \sum_{j=0}^{\# \; of \; edges \; - \; 1} W_j * EA_j. \qquad (17.67)$$

Computation of Output Signal Parameters

The final step in the hierarchical approach to power estimation is concerned with the computation of the signal parameters at the output of the subcircuits. This is best illustrated with the help of a simple example. Consider two NOR gates connected in cascade as shown in Fig. 17.26. Let $x_1(n)$ and $x_2(n)$

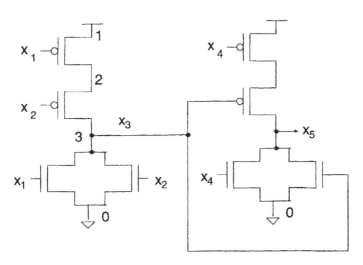

Fig. 17.26 Two NOR gates connected in cascade.

represent, respectively, the binary values of the input signals x_1 and x_2 at time instance n. Then, one can compute the value of the signal x_3 which will be the input to the 2nd NOR gate at time instance $(n + 1)$. Therefore, once $x_3(n)$ and $x_4(n)$ are well-defined for all time slots, the signal characteristics for the 2nd NOR gate can be computed. To compute the energy of the 2nd NOR gate using (17.67), we use the W_j values calculated previously for the 1st NOR gate and the new EA_j values obtained for the 2nd NOR gate. This enables the computation of the energy values in a very short time.

This method is easily generalized to multipliers (dividers) that are designed using type 0 or type 1 adders cascaded in a specific manner.

Loading and Routing Considerations

One of the disadvantages of the proposed approach is that it does not take into account the effect of loading and routing capacitances directly. In this section, we propose an approach that enables these effects to be taken into account.

Consider the CMOS digital circuit shown in Fig. 17.27, where an effective load/routing capacitance has been added. The proposed method involves

Fig. 17.27 Circuit with loading effects.

recomputation of the edge energies in the state transition diagram of the CMOS circuit with the load capacitance in place. The idea is to simulate the effect of loading when computing the edge energies. Therefore, we see that by a slight modification in the computation of the edge energies, the effect of loading can be taken into account.

One of the main advantages of this approach is that SPICE is used to characterize the effect of loading. Therefore, accurate device models can be used to incorporate the effect of loading. The approach involves adding a load/routing capacitance before estimating the edge energies using SPICE. This takes care of the loading effects.

Power Estimation of Sequential Circuits

In this section, the algorithm presented for combinational circuits is extended to handle sequential circuits as well. A sequential circuit has a combinational block and some storage elements like flip-flops, which can also be modeled using STDs.

Consider an edge-triggered D flip-flop as shown in Fig. 17.28. Here, D represents the input signal, Q represents the output signal, and $\phi_{1,2}$ represent the nonoverlapping 2-phase clock signals. It is clear from Fig. 17.28 that the

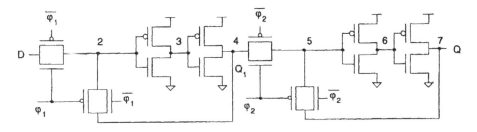

Fig. 17.28   An edge-triggered D flip-flop.

D flip-flop can be viewed as a cascade of 2 identical latches controlled by different clocks. Therefore, for power estimation it is sufficient to model a single latch with the help of an STD. The state update *arithmetic* equations for the 1st latch are

$$node_2(n+1) = D(n) * \phi_1(n) + (1 - \phi_1(n)) * node_4(n) \tag{17.68}$$

$$node_3(n+1) = 1 - node_2(n+1) \tag{17.69}$$

$$node_4(n+1) = node_2(n+1). \tag{17.70}$$

Using the foregoing equations, the STD for the latch is derived and is shown in Fig. 17.29. Here, the states represent the values of the nodes $node_2$, $node_3$,

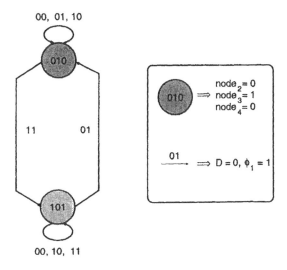

Fig. 17.29   State transition diagram for a latch.

and $node_4$ at some time instant. For example, S_1 represents the state with node values $node_2 = 0$, $node_3 = 1$, and $node_4 = 0$. The numbers associated with the edges represent the sequence D, phi_1. It is interesting to note that although there are 3 nodes in the latch, there are only 2 states. Intuitively, this means that the presence of a latch reduces the glitching activity. The STD for the 2nd latch can then be easily obtained by replacing phi_1 with phi_2, and D with Q_1.

Once the flip-flops have been modeled, the next step is to just simulate the entire sequential circuit without computing any energy values. This enables the computation of both the direct and feedback input signal values at all possible time slots, and the transition probabilities can then be determined by considering these values. As a result, the temporal correlation between the input signal values is taken into account. Then, the algorithm for power estimation of combinational circuits is used to estimate the power of sequential circuits as well.

17.7   CONCLUSIONS

This chapter has presented a comprehensive discussion on the design of low-power DSP systems. Different power optimization techniques such as path balancing, transistor sizing, transistor reordering, circuit styles, etc. are presented. These techniques can be used to achieve significant reduction in power consumption in digital systems. Finally, a tool for power estimation in digital systems is presented. This tool is fast due to its hierarchical nature and achieves accurate results. At algorithm level, power consumption can also be reduced by use of *approximate processing* where the filter length or the length of the DFT can be reduced dynamically for a marginal degradation of the system performance [43]. Furthermore, parameters such as wordlength can also be reduced by dynamic algorithm selection where the system SNR can be traded off for low power [44].

17.8   PROBLEMS

1. Assuming a 1-step Markov process, prove that for a signal x_i the probabilities $p_{x_i}^0$ and $p_{x_i}^1$ can be expressed in terms of the conditional probabilities as

$$p_{x_i}^0 = \frac{p_{x_i}^{0/1}}{p_{x_i}^{0/1} + p_{x_i}^{1/0}}, \quad p_{x_i}^1 = \frac{p_{x_i}^{1/0}}{p_{x_i}^{0/1} + p_{x_i}^{1/0}}. \tag{17.71}$$

2. Assuming a 1-step Markov process, prove that for a signal x_i the transition probabilities can be expressed in terms of the conditional probabilities as

$$p_{x_i}^{0 \to 0} = \frac{p_{x_i}^{0/1} \, p_{x_i}^{0/0}}{p_{x_i}^{0/1} + p_{x_i}^{1/0}}, \quad p_{x_i}^{0 \to 1} = \frac{p_{x_i}^{0/1} p_{x_i}^{1/0}}{p_{x_i}^{0/1} + p_{x_i}^{1/0}},$$

$$p_{x_i}^{1 \to 0} = \frac{p_{x_i}^{0/1} \, p_{x_i}^{1/0}}{p_{x_i}^{0/1} + p_{x_i}^{1/0}}, \quad p_{x_i}^{1 \to 1} = \frac{p_{x_i}^{1/0} p_{x_i}^{1/1}}{p_{x_i}^{0/1} + p_{x_i}^{1/0}}. \tag{17.72}$$

3. Assuming a 1-step Markov process, prove that for a signal x_i the conditional probabilities can be expressed in terms of the transition probabilities as

$$p_{x_i}^{0/0} = \frac{p_{x_i}^{0 \to 0}}{p_{x_i}^{0 \to 0} + p_{x_i}^{0 \to 1}}, \quad p_{x_i}^{1/0} = \frac{p_{x_i}^{0 \to 1}}{p_{x_i}^{0 \to 0} + p_{x_i}^{0 \to 1}},$$

$$p_{x_i}^{0/1} = \frac{p_{x_i}^{1 \to 0}}{p_{x_i}^{1 \to 0} + p_{x_i}^{1 \to 1}}, \quad p_{x_i}^{1/1} = \frac{p_{x_i}^{1 \to 1}}{p_{x_i}^{1 \to 0} + p_{x_i}^{1 \to 1}}. \tag{17.73}$$

4. Use the expressions for the transition and conditional probabilities for a 1-bit signal x_i derived in the previous 3 problems and the fact that its correlation coefficient is given by

$$\rho_{x_i} = \frac{E[x_i(n)x_i(n-1)] - p_{x_i}^2}{p_{x_i} - p_{x_i}^2} \tag{17.74}$$

to show that the switching activity for that signal can be computed as

$$\alpha_{x_i} = p_{x_i} (1 - p_{x_i}) (1 - \rho_{x_i}). \tag{17.75}$$

5. Consider a simple AND gate with 2 inputs x and y. Assume that the gate is implemented using static CMOS style. Compute the switching activity at the output of the gate assuming

   (a) uncorrelated inputs with uniform probability distribution.

   (b) temporal correlation in the inputs: let us assume that a 0 at x is always followed by a 1 and a 1 at y is always followed by a 0.

   (c) spatial correlation among inputs: let us assume that only the input combinations of 01 or 10 are allowed.

6. Repeat the previous problem assuming that the gate is implemented using n-type dynamic logic.

7. Consider the circuit shown in Fig. 17.30 and assume a zero-delay model. Here, a, b, and c are independent and change only in the beginning of every clock cycle. Also, let t_x denote $E[x(n)x(n-1)]$.

   (a) Let the successive values of a, b, and c be uncorrelated and let $p(a)$, $p(b)$, and $p(c)$ each be equal to 0.5. Derive $p(f)$ and t_f in terms of

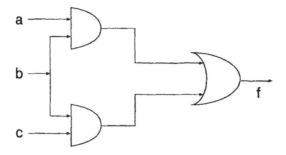

Fig. 17.30   Circuit of Problem 7.

$p(a)$, $p(b)$, and $p(c)$. Then, compute ρ_f and α_f.

(b) Let b and c be uncorrelated and let $p(b)$ and $p(c)$ each be 0.5. Let a be correlated such that $a = 0$ is always followed by $a = 1$, and $p(a) = 2/3$. Derive $p(f)$ in terms of $p(a)$, $p(b)$, $p(c)$, and t_a. Compute ρ_f and α_f.

(c) Let c be uncorrelated and let $p(c)$ be 0.5. Let a be correlated such that $a = 1$ is always followed by a $a = 0$ and let $p(a) = 1/3$. Let b be correlated such that a $b = 0$ is always followed by a $b = 1$, and $p(b) = 2/3$. Derive $p(f)$ and t_f in terms of $p(a)$, $p(b)$, $p(c)$, t_a, and t_b. Also, compute ρ_f and α_f.

8. Apply path balancing to equalize delays along all paths of the circuit shown in Fig. 17.10.

9. Consider the circuit shown in Fig. 17.31. Compute the switching activi-

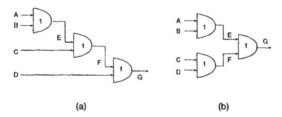

(a)   (b)

Fig. 17.31   Circuit to illustrate the effect of circuit topology on switching activity. (a) Chain structure. (b) Tree structure.

ties at nodes E, F, and G both with and without glitching. All the gates have 1 time slot delay. Let the total switching activity be computed as the sum of the switching activities at nodes E, F, and G. Which circuit has less switching activity? Explain. Assume that all the inputs are uncorrelated.

10. Repeat Example 17.5.1 assuming a latency of 10 u.t. Assume a maximum of 3 supply voltages with 1 supply voltage being 3 V. Also, assume a minimum supply voltage of 1.33 V. Find the minimum power solution.

11. Draw the state transition diagram for a static CMOS XOR gate. How many states and edges does it have ? How many states do not exist ?

12. Draw the STD for a tpsc n-latch. How does this compare with that of the tspc p-latch.

13. Derive equations for the edge activity numbers of the static CMOS NOR gate.

14. Consider the circuit shown in Fig. 17.32.

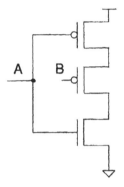

Fig. 17.32 Circuit of Problem 14.

(a) Draw the STD for this circuit.

(b) Let

$$X = \begin{bmatrix} 4/8 & 1/8 & 1/8 & 2/8 \\ 1/8 & 4/8 & 1/8 & 2/8 \\ 4/8 & 1/8 & 2/8 & 1/8 \\ 1/8 & 2/8 & 4/8 & 1/8 \end{bmatrix} \qquad (17.76)$$

represent the input conditional probability matrix. For example, the entry in the 3rd row and 4th column represents the probability $P(AB = 11/AB = 10)$. Using this matrix compute the input transition probability matrix where each entry represents $p(i \to j)$.

(c) Compute the steady-state probabilities of the states. Derive expressions for the edge activity numbers in terms of steady-state probabilities and the input conditional probabilities. Do not solve for these edge activity numbers. Assume the clock cycle to be denoted by N and the number of time slots in a clock cycle to be denoted by S.

(d) Compute the average power of the circuit assuming identical edge energies of 1 nJ for all edges and $N=1000$, $S = 66$, and $T_{clk} = 20$ nsec.

REFERENCES

1. M. Pedram, "Power minimization in IC design: principles and applications," *ACM Trans. on Design Automation of Electronic Systems*, vol. 1, no. 1, pp. 3–56, Jan. 1996.

2. F. N. Najm, "Transition density: a new measure of activity in digital circuits," *IEEE Trans. on Computer-Aided Design of Integrated Circuits and Systems*, vol. 12, no. 2, pp. 310–323, Feb. 1993.

3. N. H. E. Weste and K. Eshraghian, *Principles of CMOS VLSI Design: A Systems Perspective.* MA: Addison-Wesley, 1994.

4. S. Turgis, N. Azemard, and D. Auvergne, "Explicit evaluation of short circuit power dissipation for CMOS logic structures," in *Proc. IEEE International Symposium on Low Power Design*, pp. 129–134, April 1995.

5. A. Papoulis, *Probability, random variables, and stochastic processes.* McGraw-Hill, 2nd ed., 1984.

6. A. P. Chandrakasan, S. Sheng, and R. W. Brodersen, "Low-power CMOS digital design," *IEEE Journal of Solid State Circuits*, vol. 27, no. 4, pp. 473–483, April 1992.

7. T. Kobayashi and T. Sakurai, "Self-adjusting threshold-voltage scheme (SATS) for low-voltage high-speed operation," in *Proc. IEEE Custom Integrated Circuits Conference (CICC)*, pp. 271–274, May 1994.

8. J. H. Satyanarayana, *Design of Low-Power DSP Systems*, Ph.D. Thesis, University of Minnesota, 1998.

9. M. Berkelaar and J. Jess, "Gate sizing in MOS digital circuits with linear programming," in *Proc. ACM European Design Automation Conference (EDAC)*, pp. 217–221, 1990.

10. Y. Tamiya, Y. Matsunaga, and M. Fujita, "LP based cell selection with constraints of timing, area, and power consumption," in *Proc. IEEE International Conference on Computer Aided Design (ICCAD)*, pp. 4378–4381, 1994.

11. M. Pedram, "Power estimation and optimization at the logic level," *International Journal of High Speed Electronic Systems*, vol. 5, no. 2, pp. 179–202, June 1994.

12. M. Borah, R. M. Owens, and M. J. Irwin, "Transistor sizing for minimizing power consumption of CMOS circuits under delay constraint," in *Proc. of IEEE International Symposium on Low Power Design*, pp. 167–172, 1995.

13. C.-H. Tan and J. Allen, "Minimization of power in VLSI circuits using transistor sizing, input ordering and statistical power estimation," in *Proc. of IEEE International Workshop on Low-Power Design*, pp. 75–80, 1994.

14. H.-R. Lin and T.-T. Hwang, "Power reduction by gate sizing with path-oriented slack calculation," in *Proc. of 1st Asia-Pacific Design Automation Conference*, pp. 7–12, 1995.

15. C.-Y. Tsui, M. Pedram, and A. M. Despain, "Power efficient technology decomposition and mapping under an extended power consumption model," *IEEE Trans. on Computer Aided Design of Integrated Circuits and Systems*, vol. 13, no. 9, Sept. 1994.

16. S. C. Prasad and K. Roy, "Circuit optimization for minimization of power consumption under delay constraint," in *Proc. of IEEE International Workshop on Low-Power Design*, pp. 15–20, 1994.

17. W.-Z. Shen, J.-Y. Lin, and F.-W. Wang, "Transistor reordering rules for power reduction in CMOS gates," in *Proc. of 1st Asia-Pacific Design Automation Conference*, pp. 1–5, 1995.

18. C. E. Leiserson, F. M. Rose, and J. B. Saxe, "Optimizing synchronous circuitry by retiming," in *Proc. 3rd Caltech Conference on VLSI*, pp. 23–36, March 1983.

19. J. Monteiro, S. Devadas, and A. Ghosh, "Retiming sequential circuits for low power," in *Proc. IEEE International Conference on Computer Aided Design (ICCAD)*, pp. 398–402, Nov. 1993.

20. B. Davari, R. H. dennard, and G. G. Shahidi, "CMOS scaling for high performance and low power," *Proc. IEEE*, vol. 83, no. 4, pp. 408–425, April 1995.

21. S.-W. Sun and P. Y. Tsui, "Limitation of CMOS supply-voltage scaling by MOSFET threshold-voltage variation," *IEEE Journal of Solid-State Circuits*, vol. 30, no. 8, pp. 947–949, Aug. 1995.

22. T. Kuroda and T. Sakurai, "Threshold-voltage control schemes through substrate-bias for low-power high-speed CMOS LSI design," *Jour. of VLSI Signal Processing Systems*, vol. 13, no. 2/3, pp. 191–201, Aug./Sep. 1996.

23. S. Mutoh et al., "1-V power supply high-speed digital circuit technology with multithreshold-voltage CMOS," *IEEE Journal of Solid-State Circuits*, vol. 30, no. 8, pp. 847–854, Aug. 1995.

24. K. Seta et al., "50% active-power saving without speed degradation using standby power reduction (SPR) circuit," in *ISSCC Dig. Tech. Papers*, pp. 318–319, Feb. 1995.

25. T. Kuroda et al., "A 0.9V 150MHz 10mW $4mm^2$ 2-D discrete cosine transform core processor with variable-threshold voltage scheme," *IEEE Journal of Solid-State Circuits*, vol. 31, no. 11, pp. 1770–1779, Nov. 1996.

26. M. Mizuno et al., "Elasti-Vt CMOS circuits for multiple on-chip power control," in *ISSCC Dig. Tech. Papers*, pp. 300–301, Feb. 1996.

27. G. E. Tellez, A. Farrahi, and M. Sarrafzadeh, "Activity-driven clock design for low power circuits," in *Proc. of the IEEE International Conference on Computer Aided Design (ICCAD)*, pp. 62–65, 1995.

28. A. P. Chandrakasan and R. W. Brodersen, "Minimizing power consumption in digital CMOS circuits," *Proc. IEEE*, vol. 83, no. 4, pp. 498–523, April 1995.

29. C. H. Van Berkel et al., "A fully-asynchronous low-power error corrector for the digital compact cassette player," in *ISSCC Dig. Tech. Papers*, Feb. 1994.

30. K. Yano et al., "A 3.8-ns CMOS 16×16-b multiplier using complimentary pass transistor logic," *IEEE Journal of Solid-State Circuits*, vol. 25, no. 2, pp. 388–395, April 1990.

31. A. Parameswar, H. Hara, and T. Sakurai, "A high speed, low power, swing restored pass-transistor logic based multiply and accumulate circuit for multimedia applications," in *Proc. of Custom Integrated Circuits Conference (CICC)*, pp. 278–281, May 1994.

32. A. Salz and M. A. Horowitz, "IRSIM: an incremental MOS switch-level simulator," in *Proc. 26th IEEE/ACM Design Automation Conference (DAC)*, pp. 173–178, June 1989.

33. F. N. Najm, "Towards a high-level power estimation capability," in *Proc. IEEE International Symposium on Low Power Design*, pp. 87–92, April 1995.

34. D. Marculescu, R. Marculescu, and M. Pedram, "Information theoretic measures for energy consumption at register transfer level," in *Proc. IEEE International Symposium on Low Power Design*, pp. 81–86, April 1995.

35. N. R. Shanbhag, "A mathematical basis for power-reduction in digital VLSI systems", *IEEE Trans. on Circuits and Systems–II: Analog and Digital Signal Processing*, vol. 44, no. 11, pp. 935–951, Nov 1997.

36. P. E. Landman and J. Rabaey, "Activity-sensitive architectural power analysis for control path," in *Proc. IEEE International Symposium on Low Power Design*, pp. 93–98, April 1995.

37. S. Ramprasad, N. R. Shanbhag, and I. N. Hajj, "Analytical estimation of signal transition activity from word-level statistics", *IEEE Trans. on Computer-Aided Design of Integrated Circuits and Systems*, vol. 16, no. 7, pp. 718–733, July 1997.

38. K. P. Parker and E. J. McCluskey, "Probabilistic treatment of general combinatorial networks," *IEEE Trans. on Computers*, vol. C-24, pp. 668–670, June 1975.

39. R. Bryant, "Graph-based algorithms for Boolean function manipulation," *IEEE Trans. on Computers*, vol. C-35, pp. 677–691, Aug. 1986.

40. A. Ghosh, S. Devadas, K. Keutzer, and J. White, "Estimation of average switching activity in combinational and sequential circuits," in *Proc. 29th IEEE/ACM Design Automation Conference (DAC)*, pp. 253–259, June 1992.

41. R. Burch, F. Najm, P. Yang, and D. Hocevar, "Pattern independent current estimation for reliability analysis of CMOS circuits," in *Proc. 25th IEEE/ACM Design Automation Conference (DAC)*, pp. 294–299, June 1988.

42. J. H. Satyanarayana and K. K. Parhi, "HEAT: Hierarchical Energy Analysis Tool," in *Proc. IEEE/ACM Design Automation Conference (DAC)*, (Las Vegas, NV), pp. 9–14, June 1996.

43. S. H. Nawab, A. V. Oppenheim, A. P. Chandrakasan, J. M. Winograd, and J. T. Ludwig, "Approximate signal processing," *Journal of VLSI Signal Processing Systems for Signal, Image and Video Technology*, vol. 15, no. 1/2, Jan. 1997.

44. M. Goel, and N. R. Shanbhag, "Low-power reconfigurable signal processing via dynamic algorithm transformations (DAT)", in *Proc. of IEEE International Conference on Acoustics, Speech, and Signal Processing*, (Seattle, WA), May 1998.

18

Programmable Digital Signal Processors

18.1 INTRODUCTION

DSP has many applications including data/fax modems, digital audio broadcast, digital photography, digital video, multimedia computers, digital cellular phone, personal communication systems, etc. Traditionally, dedicated (application-specific) architectures have been used for high performance DSP applications. This trend continues today as more complex digital signal processing and image/video processing algorithms are implemented on single chips. Furthermore, at the same time, improvements in scaled VLSI technologies have also led to improvements of programmable microprocessors by orders of magnitude.

Digital representations of speech and audio and video signals (multimedia) can be handled in the same way as the text data are processed. However, their information rate is orders of magnitude higher than that of text data. As a result, conventional microprocessors cannot easily process these multimedia data in real time. This has led to the evolution of programmable digital signal processors (often denoted as PDSPs or DSP processors), which are specialized microcomputers designed for implementation of extensive arithmetic computation and DSP functions through downloadable or resident software. The PDSPs were first developed in 1980 for processing of speech signals in real time for communications applications such as voiceband data modem and low bit-rate speech codec [1], and have evolved through several generations. They distinguish themselves from general purpose microprocessors in low power, low cost, and high signal processing capabilities; they outperform application-specific architectures by offering high flexibility, low design cost, and reduced time-to-market. Current DSP processors are especially suitable for wireless applications and multimedia processing.

This chapter addresses the fundamental features of the PDSP architectures, and their evolution for the two ever-increasingly demanding applications, wireless communications and multimedia processing. Section 18.2 presents an overview of the evolution of PDSPs over the past 2 decades. Section 18.3 addresses the two most important features of DSP processor architectures, the data path containing fast multiply-accumulate unit(s) and the multiple-access memory architectures. The PDSP design trends in the area of wireless communications (*domain-specific* DSPs) and multimedia processing (*media* processors) are covered in Sections 18.4 and 18.5, respectively. Section 18.5 also discusses the multimedia extension in general purpose microprocessors.

18.2   EVOLUTION OF PROGRAMMABLE DIGITAL SIGNAL PROCESSORS

General purpose DSPs were first developed in the early 1980s for iterative and computation-intensive digital signal processing applications. These applications run mostly under tight real-time constraints and involve large numbers of memory accesses and repetitive executions of the same algorithm. To meet the performance requirements and to accommodate programmability at the same time, earlier DSP processors deviated from the general purpose microprocessors by introducing hardware multipliers for fast multiply-accumulate operation, and by using multiple-access memories. PDSPs do not provide all of the programmer friendly features typically available on general purpose processors. As a result, these achieve higher performance with low cost and low power consumption. The first generation DSPs were developed for high-throughput (millions of operations per second) audio signal processing. Their characteristics are compared with the microprocessor of the day (M68000) in Table 18.1 [2]. As can be seen, the DSP-1 exhibits a 50:1 performance advantage over M68000, for about the same cost and power [2].

DSP processors have experienced performance improvements, and price and power consumption reduction during the last 2 decades. Generally DSP processors exploit parallelism where one instruction can incorporate several operations in parallel. As a result, their MOPS (million operations per second) figures had been much higher than the microprocessors. This is, however, no longer true since the evolution of the latest generation of SIMD (single instruction multiple data) enhanced microprocessors (i.e., Intel MMX) which employ subword parallelism and obtain a significant performance advantage over the conventional microprocessors. Nevertheless, today's DSPs will remain dominant in the portable and wireless market due to their low power and low cost features.

Recently the introduction of efficient audio and video compression tech-

Table 18.1 Performance Characteristic Comparison of The First Generation DSP Processor and The Motorola 68000 Microprocessor

	DSP-1 (1980)	M68000 (1980)
Technology	5μ NMOS	3μ NMOS
Clock rate	5MHZ	8 MHZ
Bus width	20-bit data, 16-bit instruction	16-bit data, 16-bit instruction
Peak performance	5 M multiply-add/sec	100 K multiply-add/sec
Power	1.25 Watts	1.5 Watts

niques and their standardization has created a new category of devices: *media processors*. These processors are a special group of DSP processors equipped with audio, video, and graphics accelerators suitable for multimedia signal processing applications. These media processors exploit the parallelization potential in multimedia signal processing algorithms at both the instruction level (i.e., using very long instruction word (VLIW)) and the data level (i.e., SIMD), and are able to achieve peak performances of billions of operations per second with less than 100 MHz clock frequencies. These processors can operate either as stand-alone CPUs (central processing units) in applications such as video phone, or as multimedia accelerators in personal computers (PCs).

18.3 IMPORTANT FEATURES OF DSP PROCESSORS

DSP processors are designed to support repetitive, numerically intensive tasks [3]. To this end, most DSP processors not only have a powerful data path, but also have the ability to move large amounts of data to and from memory quickly. Moreover, DSP processors provide special instruction sets to exploit hardware efficiency.

The two most important features of DSP processor architectures, the data path containing fast multiply-accumulate unit(s) and the multiple-access memory architectures [4], are addressed in this section. The N-tap finite-impulse-response (FIR) filter:

$$y[n] = c_0 x[n] + c_1 x[n-1] + \cdots + c_{N-1} x[n-N+1] \qquad (18.1)$$

is used as a typical example in this section.

Pipelining (see Chapter 3) is often used to increase the performance of a processor. Almost all the processors on the market today use pipelining to some extent. However, in the process of improving performance, pipelining also makes programming difficult. In this section, two common programming techniques, referred to as *time-stationary* and *data-stationary* [5] coding, used for programming pipelined PDSPs, are discussed.

18.3.1 Data Path

Only fixed-point DSP processor data paths are addressed in this section. They typically incorporate a multiplier, accumulators, an ALU (arithmetic logic unit), one or more shifters, operand registers, and other specialized units such as saturation arithmetic unit.

18.3.1.1 Multiplier and Accumulator Multiplication is an essential operation in virtually all DSP algorithms. In many applications, half or more of the instructions executed by the processor involve multiplication. The presence of a hardware multiplier is central to the definition of a DSP processor.

In many DSP algorithms, multiplication is followed by accumulation. Therefore, in many DSP processors, the multiplier is integrated with an adder such that multiply-accumulate (MAC) operation can be carried out in one instruction cycle.

18.3.1.2 ALU DSP processor arithmetic logic units implement basic arithmetic and logical operations in a single instruction cycle. Common operations include add/subtract, increment, negate and logical AND, OR, NOT and XOR. In some processors, ALU is used to perform addition for MAC operations. In other processors, a separate adder is provided.

18.3.1.3 Shifter Multiplication and accumulation tend to result in growth in the bit width of the results. Hence scaling is an important operation in many fixed-point DSP applications. A shifter in the data path can be used to scale its input by a power of 2. A shifter is often found immediately following the multiplier and ALU. Some processors provide a shifter between the multiplier and ALU to allow scaling of the product. Both *limited-capability* shifter (which permits 1-bit shift at a time) and *barrel* shifter (which supports shifts by any number of bits in a single instruction cycle) are used.

18.3.1.4 Overflow and Saturation Most DSP algorithms involve accumulating a series. In this case, the magnitude of the sum may grow. Eventually, the magnitude of the sum may exceed the maximum or minimum value that can be represented by the accumulator register. This situation is referred to as *overflow*. When overflow occurs, an incorrect value is stored, which could be very different from the correct value. Overflow can be handled by either scaling down the result or by saturation arithmetic. Scaling can be effective, but it may not be able to maintain the adequate signal fidelity. Overflow is generally dealt with by using saturation arithmetic in DSP processors. In saturation arithmetic, a special circuit detects overflow and the largest posi-

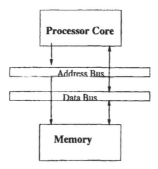

Fig. 18.1 Simple Von Neumann memory architecture, common among many kinds of non-DSP processors.

tive number or the smallest negative number is selected as the output in the case of overflow in the positive or negative direction, respectively. Fixed-point DSP processors generally provide special hardware for saturation arithmetic.

It is worth pointing out that the data paths in DSP processors are generally not used for memory addressing. Instead, a separate *address generation unit* is usually provided for address calculation.

18.3.2 Memory Architecture

The memory architecture, the organization of memory and its interconnection with the processor's data path, is as important as the data path itself to a high-performance DSP processor.

Consider the N-tap FIR filter in (18.1), where one filtering operation involves N multiply-accumulate operations. With the multiply-accumulate unit in the processor data path, a new output sample can be produced every N instruction cycles. However, to achieve this performance, the processor must be able to access the memory several times within one instruction clock cycle.

Traditionally, a processor contains a single bank of memory, which is accessed by the processor through a single set of address and data buses, as shown in Fig. 18.1. This is commonly referred to as a *Von Neumann architecture*. Both program instructions and data are stored in a single memory, and the processor can only access the memory once during each instruction cycle. This type of memory architecture is not suitable for DSP processors. Consider the FIR filter example. Although the processor's data path is capable of completing a MAC operation in one instruction cycle, more than 3 clock cycles are needed to perform the MAC operation in a processor with sequential memory access and one memory access per instruction cycle.

DSP processors make use of many variations of the Von Neumann architecture to improve memory access bandwidth. These processors use so called *Harvard architecture*, which refers to a memory structure where the processor

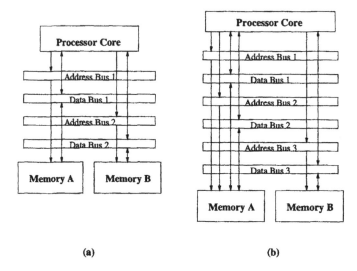

(a)   (b)

Fig. 18.2 (a) Basic Harvard architecture, where the processor can simultaneously access 2 memory banks using 2 independent sets of buses. (b) A Harvard architecture with a dual-ported data memory (A) and a single-ported program memory (B), where the processor can simultaneously perform 2 accesses to memory A and 1 access to memory B through 3 sets of buses.

is connected to 2 independent memory banks via 2 independent sets of buses, as shown in Fig. 18.2(a). In this architecture, one memory holds program instructions and the other holds data. It can also be extended to allow one memory bank to hold program and data, while the other memory bank holds data only. Nevertheless, at least 2 memory accesses can be made in each instruction cycle. It is also common for DSP processors to use 3 memory banks, 1 program bank and 2 data memory banks. In this case, it is possible for the processor to perform a 1-tap FIR filtering operation per instruction cycle. Besides using multiple, independent memory banks, a number of DSP processors use fast memories that support multiple, sequential accesses per instruction cycle over a single bus, or use multiported memories that allow multiple concurrent memory accesses over 2 or more independent sets of buses within 1 instruction cycle. The most common type of multiported memory is *dual-ported*, which provides two simultaneous accesses. The key disadvantage of multiported memories is that they are costly to implement in terms of chip area. Some DSP processors combine a modified Harvard architecture with the use of multiported memories, as shown in Fig. 18.2(b), which include a single-ported program memory with a dual-ported data memory and provides 1 program memory access and 2 data memory accesses per instruction cycle.

Parallel memory banks can increase memory bandwidth, but create a fundamental problem since the instructions must specify several memory accesses. For a reasonable address space, the number of bits required to specify each address is large enough that the width of the instruction word gets large. Hence a larger memory space is required to store the program, or more memory cycles are required to access each instruction (in the case of multiword instructions). To this end, *register-indirect* addressing (with pre- or post- increment or decrement) modes are used. Usually a set of address registers is provided for this purpose. As mentioned in last subsection, most DSP processors include one or more special address generation units (AGUs) dedicated for address calculation. An AGU can perform one or more complex address calculations per instruction cycle without using the processor's data path. This enables address calculations to take place in parallel with arithmetic operations on data.

Some DSP processors also provide special features designed to reduce the number of memory accesses required to perform certain kind of operations. These techniques include the use of program cache, modulo addressing mode, etc. The number of memory accesses can also be reduced by using algorithms (programs) that exploit more data locality.

With multiple functional units and multiple-access memory banks, DSP processors can issue specialized instructions that specify several simultaneous operations performed by different functional units in one instruction cycle, such as simultaneous operand fetches and execute operations. These specialized instruction sets are constructed to fully utilize the hardware resources. Furthermore, packing several operations into one special instruction can also reduce the program size.

18.3.3   Time-Stationary and Data-Stationary Coding in Pipelined DSP Processors

Pipelining is an implementation technique where a sequence of operations are broken into smaller pieces, which are executed in parallel. In processors, pipelining breaks instruction execution into several pipelining stages and allows multiple instructions to be overlapped in execution. Pipelining exploits parallelism among the instructions in a sequence of instruction stream, and yields a reduction in the average execution time per instruction.

Pipelining speeds up the computation, but makes programming complicated [6]. Usually, two assembly code formats, time-stationary and data-stationary, are used for programming of pipelined DSP processors.

18.3.3.1 Time-Stationary Coding   In time-stationary coding, programmers have more explicit control over the pipeline stages. An instruction explicitly specifies several operations, such as simultaneous operand fetch and execute operations, to be performed in parallel by different functional units. For example, the following instruction specifies 2 memory fetches and 1 multiply-accumulate (MAC) operation in parallel.

$$\text{MAC X0, Y0, A \quad X:(R0)+, X0 \quad Y:(R4)-, Y0}$$

In this case, the multiplier and accumulator are integrated together such that the MAC operations can be carried in 1 cycle. The operands of the MAC operation are the contents of the X0 and Y0 registers, which were loaded from memory in a *previous* instruction; the MAC operation computes the product of X0 and Y0, and adds it to the A register. Meanwhile, the other two parts specify operand fetches for the *next* instruction.

Another good example of time-stationary coded multiply-accumulate instruction looks like:

$$\text{a0 = a0+p \quad p = x*y \quad x = *r0++ \quad y = *r1++}$$

The product of register p from previous multiplication is added to $a0$; at the same time a new product is formed using the contents of the x and y registers; meanwhile, the x and y registers are loaded with new values from memory using the address registers r0 and r1, and the values in r0 and r1 are incremented and these point to their corresponding next memory locations. Note that in this example, the multiplier and accumulator in the processor are independent of each other, and 1 MAC operation takes 2 instruction cycles.

18.3.3.2 Data-Stationary Coding In data-stationary coding, a single instruction specifies all the operations performed on a set of operands from memory, but does not indicate the exact time when these operations are executed. Consider the following example:

$$\text{a1 = a1 \quad + \quad (*r5++ \quad = \quad *r4++) \quad * \quad *r3++}$$

which specifies the following operations: the values in the memory locations pointed by registers $r3$ and $r4$ are fetched and multiplied, the value that was pointed to by register $r4$ is written back to the memory location pointed to by register $r5$, and the result of multiplication is accumulated in register $a1$. Note that the data-stationary approach uses operands that refer to memory directly. Instead of multiplying two registers, the instruction multiplies the contents of 2 memory locations. The values of these locations are fetched and brought to the multiplier, but the programmer need not specify this directly, as in the time-stationary case.

The time-stationary and data-stationary approaches each have their advantages and disadvantages. In time-stationary coding, the programmers carry out part of the scheduling tasks, while in data-stationary coding, the programmers specify the operations to be performed and leave the scheduling tasks to the compiler. In general, the data-stationary model is easier to read out, but is not as flexible as the time-stationary approach.

Table 18.2   Evolution of DSP Processors

Year	Generation	Feature	Example
1982	1st	Basic Harvard 1 data bus, 1 program bus 1 multiply - ALU unit	TMS32010, NEC 7720
1986	2nd	"Modified" Harvard 1 data/program bus, 1 data bus	TMS320C25, AT&T DSP16A
1990	3rd	Extra addressing modes Extra functions	TMS320C5x, AT&T DSP161x
1994	4th	2 data buses, 1 program bus separate MAC, ALU	TMS320C540
1995	5th	2 data buses, 1 program bus 2 MACs, 1 ALU	Lode

18.4 DSP PROCESSORS FOR MOBILE AND WIRELESS COMMUNICATIONS

DSP processors achieve high throughput by exploiting parallelism with specialized data paths at moderate clock frequencies. Different generations of DSPs have emerged using variations of the basic Harvard architecture, as summarized in Table 18.2 [7]. The main difference between the generations evolve around the bus structure and memory bandwidth such that the multiply-accumulate operation can be executed in 1 cycle or less.

Although VLIW and SIMD approaches (see next section for details) can be used to further improve the processor performance, they are expensive in terms of area and power, which makes them unsuitable for mobile and wireless communications, where low area and low power consumption are critical factors. Instead, a *domain-specific* concept is used keeping in mind the targeted application of the processor. The Lode DSP [7] listed in Table 18.2 as 5th generation DSP is a domain-specific processor designed with wireless communication and speech processing in mind. Its data path contains 2 MAC units and 1 AMU (Arithmetic Manipulation Unit), which can operate in parallel. In general, this would lead to a 3 fold increase in the memory bandwidth. In this domain-specific DSP, input combinations to the 3 functional units are restricted. The input combinations and the bus structure have been selected such that typical DSP operations and especially operations for wireless communications and speech processing are optimally supported. The instruction set also reflects the choice for a domain-specific DSP. Instructions, such as *Square Distance And Accumulate* for vector quantization, *Add-Compare-Select* for Viterbi algorithm, and *Galois field operations* for forward error-control coding, are provided.

18.5 PROCESSORS FOR MULTIMEDIA SIGNAL PROCESSING

Multimedia signal processing involves processing of digital information in various representations. It covers a broad range of applications including audio and speech processing, image and video processing, two-dimensional (2D) and three-dimensional (3D) graphics, etc. Multimedia signal processing applications generally have very high data rate and demand real-time processing capabilities. Their important characteristics, from an algorithmic perspective, can be summarized as [8]:

- Frequent use of small integer operands;

- Highly regular computation-intensive operations;

- Intensive input/output (I/O) or memory access, data reusability, and data locality;

- Complex control operations in less computationally intensive tasks.

Conventional microprocessors and DSP processors do not support these characteristics of multimedia signal processing. Therefore, special architectural approaches are used to achieve the required high processing power with efficient utilization of hardware resources. To this end, one special class of *media processors* has been created to handle multimedia applications with high quality in real time. They can be used as stand-alone CPUs or as multimedia accelerators in PCs. Meanwhile, general purpose microprocessors have been extended using new instructions and resources by *multimedia extensions* to improve the performance of media processing programs.

Several general approaches to accelerate multimedia signal processing are introduced in this section. Then, special strategies used in media processors and multimedia extensions of general purpose microprocessors are discussed.

18.5.1 Enhancements for Multimedia Signal Processing

Two general enhancements can be identified in adapting programmable DSPs for multimedia applications. One is to exploit instruction- or data-level parallelism in order to achieve a significant increase in computational power; the other approach is to introduce specialized instructions and integrate dedicated hardware modules. Within this broad framework, many approaches are possible as outlined in this section.

18.5.1.1 Multiprocessing Multiprocessing can be exploited in the form of SIMD or MIMD (multiple instruction multiple data) [6]. In a SIMD machine, the same instruction is executed by multiple processors on different data streams. Each processor has its own data memory, but there is only one instruction memory and control processor, which fetches and dispatches

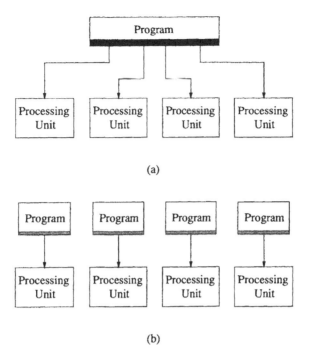

Fig. 18.3 (a) Simplified SIMD architecture; (b) MIMD architecture.

instructions. A simplified SIMD architecture is shown in Fig. 18.3(a). In a MIMD machine, each processor fetches its own instructions and operates on its own data. These processors either utilize centralized shared-memory architecture, or each has its own memory and they communicate with each other through crossbar networks. A simplified MIMD architecture is shown in Fig. 18.3(b). SIMD processors can exploit data parallelism, but are not as flexible as MIMD processors. They are suitable for algorithms with high data parallelism and little data-dependent control flow. MIMD processors are more flexible; they can either function as single-user machines focusing on high performance for one particular application, or as multiprogrammed machines running many tasks simultaneously. However, they are much more complicated and expensive due to replication of control hardware, high instruction memory bandwidth requirement and synchronization of data paths. Besides pure SIMD and MIMD approaches, a combination of both SIMD and MIMD approaches is also possible where these hybrid architectures aim at exploiting the advantages of both SIMD and MIMD architectures.

18.5.1.2 Subword Parallelism: Data-Level Parallelism Data in image processing, video processing, and graphics rendering computations generally can be represented using less than 16-bit. For example, 8-bit precision is sufficient for pixels in ordinary image processing and 12-bit data can be used in medical

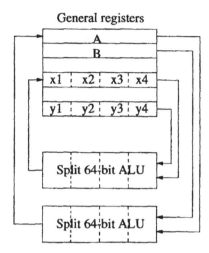

Fig. 18.4 Example of subword parallelism, where the same ALU operations can be performed on the four 16-bit subwords in parallel, or on one 64-bit word.

imaging. However, the length of a processing unit in a general processor, the wordlength, is usually 32-bit or 64-bit. These low-precision data in multimedia programs do not exploit full utilization of processors' computation power. To this end, subword parallelism is introduced.

In subword parallelism, a standard computation or storage unit, a word, is partitioned into smaller units called *subwords*. For example, a 64-bit word can be partitioned into four 16-bit subwords. The same operation can be performed on the subwords simultaneously in parallel, which provides a form of SIMD parallel processing. Subwords can be of different sizes, 8-bit, 16-bit, or 32-bit, depending on the range of targeted applications. In practice, subwords are nonoverlapping and completely fill the word.

Unlike a normal SIMD approach where multiprocessors are used, in subword parallelism, the functional units of 1 wordlength are split into smaller subword-long units. For example, a 64-bit integer two's complement adder can be partitioned into four 16-bit subword integer adders, by conditionally blocking the carries at the three 16-bit boundaries for subword additions. Such a split adder allows four 16-bit additions, as well as a single 64-bit add, to be performed in 1 instruction cycle. Usually partitionable ALUs are used. Fig. 18.4 illustrates the subword parallelism concept in a processor with 2 partitionable ALUs. Notice that the packed word also increases the effective memory bandwidth, since 4 subwords can be accessed as 1 word from and to memory.

With subword parallelism and their corresponding special instruction sets, many computation-intensive tasks (loops) can be efficiently coded and executed. For example, consider the following matrix-vector multiplication, where all elements are 16-bit long.

$$\begin{bmatrix} A0 \\ A1 \end{bmatrix} = \begin{bmatrix} M00 & M01 & M02 & M03 \\ M10 & M11 & M12 & M13 \end{bmatrix} \times \begin{bmatrix} V0 \\ V1 \\ V2 \\ V3 \end{bmatrix}$$

In a processor of 64-bit wordlength and partitionable functional units, this matrix-vector multiplication can be computed as shown in Fig. 18.5.

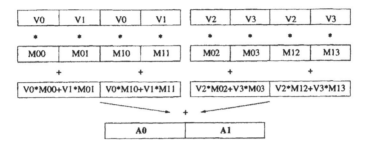

Fig. 18.5 Flow graph of matrix-vector multiplication as an example of subword parallelism.

Subword parallelism provides a small-scale SIMD parallelism in a word-oriented processor with very low cost [9]. The partitionable functional units have very little hardware overhead, and the packed data type reduces memory access requirements. This scheme is applicable not only for special-purpose multimedia processing, but also for other applications with low-precision data and high data-parallelism.

18.5.1.3 LIW (Long Instruction Word)/VLIW (Very Long Instruction Word): Instruction-Level Parallelism   (V)LIW architectures belong to the family of *multiple-issue* processors [6]. The goal of multiple-issue processors is to allow multiple instructions to be issued in a clock cycle, such that the CPI (cycle per instruction) can be reduced to less than one. The (V)LIW architectures exploit available instruction level parallelism by specifying multiple LIW or VLIW operations within a single instruction word. This requires multiple functional units in order to enable simultaneous execution of all operations contained in the instruction word. (V)LIW processors can be viewed as small-scale MIMD processors with centralized memory architectures and multiple functional units. VLIW architectures use a much wider instruction divided into fixed-length fields, which fully specify simple, atomic, and completely independent operations. Fig. 18.6 illustrates a typical VLIW architecture.

The VLIW operations rely on the compiler to perform *static scheduling* in contrast to *superscalar* architectures (another type of multiple-issue processors) which determine instructions to be concurrently executed dynamically.

VLIW Instruction

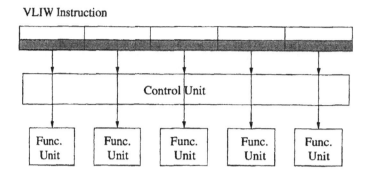

Fig. 18.6 A typical VLIW architecture.

This results in a simplified architecture for the VLIW processors as scheduling tasks are taken care of at software level. On the other hand, a very sophisticated compiler is needed to ensure efficient utilization of hardware resources. Thus, VLIW architectures shift complexity from hardware to software. The efficiency of VLIW architectures strongly depends on the degree of exploitable instruction level parallelism inherent in a particular algorithm. Video compression algorithms have typically short inner loops and loop-unrolling can be applied to increase the efficiency of static scheduling performed by the compiler.

In addition to above parallel processing techniques, special instruction sets and coprocessors are also often used for multimedia signal processing applications.

18.5.1.4 Special Instruction Sets A conventional and widely used adaptation approach is to introduce specialized hardware and instruction sets for frequently recurring operations with relatively higher complexity, such as multiply-accumulate with saturation. Specialized instructions significantly reduce instruction count and result in faster program execution. This approach, employed by DSP processors over the last two decades, is recently being used by some general purpose microprocessors to accelerate multimedia signal processing programs.

18.5.1.5 Coprocessors Coprocessor architectures combine both parallelization and adaptation. A coprocessor architecture typically comprises a processor core (usually RISC (reduced instruction set computer) type) coupled with several modules adapted to specific tasks. One possibility is to combine a standard RISC core suited for the execution of irregular data-dependent algorithms with specialized modules suited for regular, computation-intensive program parts. Another approach is to add highly specialized units to an otherwise powerful general purpose processor core in order to perform a specific subtask. Coprocessors result in higher efficiency for specific algorithms

Table 18.3 Announced Media DSP Processors

Processors	TI C8x	Chromatic Mpact	Philips Tri-Media	TI C6x
Architecture	4 × 64b DSPs +31b RISC +cross-bar	VLIW/SIMD 4 ALUs +ME engine +792b bus	VLIW +25 Exe. Units +Video/Audio +VLD units	VLIW 8 instr./clk 2 MACs/clk
Technology	–	0.5μ	–	0.25μ
# Trans.	4M	1.5M	–	–
Chip Size(mm^2)	340	100	–	196
Clock (MHz)	40	62	100	200
Perk Rate	1.2 GOPs/sec	2 GOPs/sec	4 GOPs/sec	1.6 GOPs/sec
Power(watts)	8	–	–	–
Memory	DRAM 400 MB/s	RAMBUS 500 MB/s	SDRAM 400 MB/s	SDRAM 400 MB/s
Programming	Compiler +assembler	in-house	VLIW compiler	VLIW compiler

as function-specific optimizations are possible and the control circuitry can be simplified.

18.5.2 Media Processors

Current media processors not only support SIMD-like subword parallelism to exploit data parallelism, but also adopt efficient VLIW architectures to exploit instruction parallelism. They are able to achieve peak performance of more than 1 gigaoperations per second (GOPs/sec), with a clock rate of around 100 MHz. The performance characteristics of several typical media processors are shown in Table 18.3.

18.5.2.1 Texas Instruments C8x The TI TMS320C8x [10] is a fully programmable MIMD processor and integrates RISC, floating-point, multiple high-performance fixed-point DSPs, on-chip memory controller, and static RAM technology on a single chip. Fig. 18.7 illustrates the TI TMS320C8x processor architecture. The 32-bit RISC master processor targets efficient execution of high-level languages; it controls on-chip parallel processing, supports communications with other devices (such as a host PC if C8x is used in a PC-based environment), and executes most high-level processing such as control protocols and floating-point-intensive algorithms. The four advanced DSP processors combine efficient multiply-accumulate processing with enhanced ability for image processing using splittable ALU and bit-stream manipulations. They are responsible for computationally intensive integer processing and are designed to efficiently support a wide range of DSP algorithms, including frequency domain transformations (such as discrete-cosine transform),

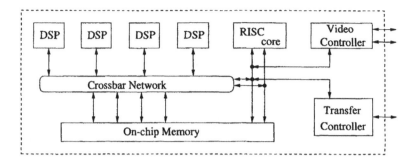

Fig. 18.7 The TI TMS320C8x media processor architecture.

correlation, filtering, and bit-stream manipulations. These processors execute their own instruction streams and communicate with each other using the shared-memory architecture. With the MIMD architecture, SIMD-like sub-word instructions and 40 MHz clock frequency, the TI C8x processor can achieve a peak performance of 1.3 GOPs/sec. The TI TMS320C8x digital signal processors support desktop videoconferencing, videophones, 3D virtual reality, real-time MPEG-1 decompression, high-quality audio processing, and document image processing.

18.5.2.2 Chromatic MPact Mpact media processor [11],[12] is designed to accelerate multimedia functions for PCs and requires a host processor for operation. It comprises the processor controller, the data path, and SRAM (static RAM), as shown in Fig. 18.8. The processor data path, as shown in Fig. 18.9, contains five ALU units that can operate concurrently. The Mpact instruction set has VLIW-style control over the data path and also supports packed data types (subword instructions). The SRAM has 4 read and 4 write ports to support the high data bandwidth required for the VLIW instruction set architecture (ISA). Operated at 62 MHz frequency, the Mpact processor has a peak performance close to 2 GOPs/sec. Mpact supports real-time MPEG-1 encoding and MPEG-1 and MPEG-2 decoding, 2D and 3D graphics, high-quality audio processing, fax/modem, and video conferencing.

18.5.2.3 Philips Trimedia Philips Trimedia processor [13] has a multimedia repertoire similar to Chromatics' Mpact. It can be used as a stand-alone CPU or an accelerator in a PC. Trimedia processor combines a powerful VLIW CPU with 4 autonomous direct memory access (DMA) units, and also contains a variable-length decoder (VLD) coprocessor and an image coprocessor (ICP), as shown in Fig. 18.10. The VLIW DSP core has 27 execution units turned to match the computing requirements of actual multimedia code (see Fig. 18.11). Its instruction set also supports subword parallelism. The 2 coprocessors are used to offload simple but high-bandwidth tasks from the processor core. With

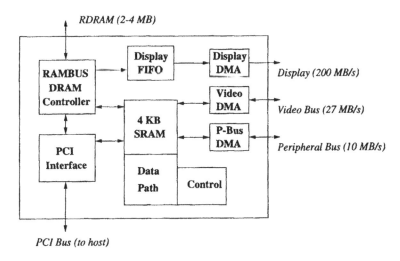

Fig. 18.8 Chromatic Mpact media processor architecture.

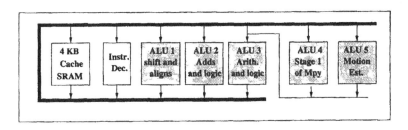

Fig. 18.9 Chromatic Mpact media processor data path architecture.

100 MHz clock frequency, the Trimedia processor has a peak performance of 3.8 GOPs/sec.

18.5.2.4 TI C6x TI C6x processors [14] use a new *VeliciTI* architecture, which is an advanced VLIW architecture that provides simple and cost-effective access to the power of on-chip parallelism. Fig. 18.12 shows the block diagram of the novel *VeliciTI* VLIW architecture. The key feature of TI C6x is that they are developed based on *processor-compiler* codesign techniques. As a result, their complier, on average, achieves 84% efficiency of an assembly language programmer. Note that for ordinary DSP processors, compilers achieve only about 20 − 50% of the efficiency of assembly language programmers [15]. TI's C6x generation enables real-time applications for cable modems, central office switches, digital imaging, advanced multifunction wireless personal digital assistants (PDAs), digital subscriber loop (xDSL) systems, etc. Readers may refer to [15] and [14] for detailed explanations of the novel *VeliciTI* architecture.

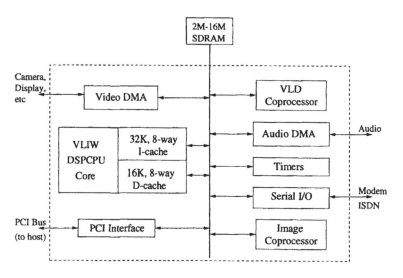

Fig. 18.10 Philips Trimedia (TM) processor architecture. TM combines a powerful VLIW CPU with 4 autonomous DMA units.

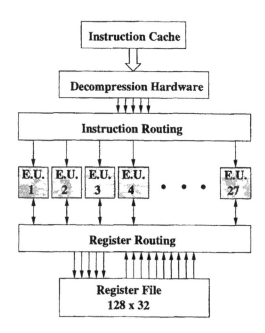

Fig. 18.11 Philips Trimedia data path architecture.

VLIW Instruction

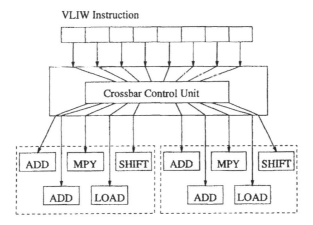

Fig. 18.12 The TI TMS320C6x *VelociTI* advanced VLIW architecture.

18.5.3 General Purpose Microprocessors with Multimedia Extensions

An increasing trend in general purpose microprocessor design is the incorporation of DSP-like functions to better handle multimedia signal processing tasks. Generally, the multimedia extensions in general purpose processors, i.e., MAX (multimedia acceleration extensions) in HP PA-RISC workstations [16] and MMX (multimedia extensions) in Intel ix86 processors [17], etc., implement the concept of subword parallelism, which accelerate all data-parallel computations with low-precision data, including media processing. The processor architectures are modified and special instructions are added in such a way that these not only accelerate multimedia programs, but also are fully compatible to their previous instruction set architectures.

As it is relatively easy to split ALU operations into subword level, both MAX and MMX support parallel subword ALU operations such as *Parallel Add* and *Parallel Subtract* with saturation arithmetic. However, multiplication is one area that makes the greatest differences among different multimedia instruction-set extensions. The problems with multiplications are: an integer multiplication takes about three to fours times the area of an integer adder, it takes about three times the latency, and it generates a result that is longer than each operand. To reduce the area, current MMX implementations implement only one 16-bit integer multiplier, which is reused iteratively to perform subword multiplications in *Parallel Subword Multiply* instruction. MAX does not have any 16-bit multiply hardware. It use a 2-pronged strategy for supporting multiplication [9]. Those media computations that require extensive, full-function multiplications with precision greater than 16-bit are implemented using the existing PA-RISC floating-point functional units, i.e., multiplications in this case are carried out using existing floating-point multiply-accumulate units. Those computations with frequent multiplications by constants with precision less than 16 bits are implemented on existing integer adders with preshifters using the *Parallel Shift Left/Right and Add* instructions.

18.6   CONCLUSIONS

This chapter has introduced the features of ordinary DSP processors, with focus on data path and memory architectures. Special requirements for low-power DSP processors in mobile and wireless communications were discussed. General parallelization and adaptation techniques for multimedia processing were addressed. Media processors and multimedia extensions of general purpose microprocessors were discussed.

Mobile and wireless communications and multimedia processing will continue to be the driving force of both DSP processors and microprocessors. The typical requirements for DSP processors include [2]:

- **flexibility** - the applications and their standards keep changing faster than their system counterparts.

- **high throughput** - on the order of hundreds to thousands of MOPS.

- **low power and low cost** - the need for desktop and portable solutions with silicon costing under $40.

For mobile and wireless communication applications, the flexibility and low power and cost are extremely important. One example of promising applications in this area is software radio. When all functions, from baseband modulation and channel processing to voice codec, become available in software supported by programmable hardware, we can travel all over the world with our own wireless terminal. Adaptation to local standards and specifications in different countries can be realized by the replacement of software. For multimedia processing applications, the flexibility and high throughput are extremely important. One example of future applications in this area is digital TV with easily programmable media processor, which will be able to support a broad range of standards and deliver movie-quality picture and sound.

REFERENCES

1. T. Nishitani, "Trend and perspective on domain specific programmable chips," in *Proc. of IEEE Workshop on Signal Processing Systems (SiPS-97)*, pp. 1–8, 1997.

2. B. Ackland, "Programmable multimedia signal processors," in *Circuits and Systems in the Information Age* (Y.-F. Huang and C.-H. Wei, eds.), pp. 23–30, IEEE Press, 1997.

3. P. Lapsley, J. Pier, A. Shoham, and E. Lee, *DSP Processor Fundamentals: Architectures and Features.* Elsvier, 1993.

4. E. A. Lee, "Programmable DSP architectures: part I," *IEEE ASSP Magazine*, pp. 4–19, Oct. 1988.

5. E. A. Lee, "Programmable DSP architectures: part II," *IEEE ASSP Magazine*, pp. 4–14, Jan. 1989.

6. J. Hennessy and D. Patterson, *Computer Architecture A Quantitative Approach*, 2nd ed., Morgan Kaufmann Publishers, 1996.

7. I. Verbauwhede and M. Touriguian, "A low power DSP engine for wireless communications," *Journal of VLSI Signal Processing Systems*, vol. 18, no. 2, Feb. 1998.

8. P. Pirsh, H. Stolberg, Y. Chen, and S. Kung, "Implementation of media processors," in *IEEE Signal Processing Magazine*, July 1997.

9. R. Lee, "Multimedia extensions for general-purpose processors," in *Proc. of IEEE Workshop on Signal Processing Systems (SiPS-97)*, pp. 9–23, 1997.

10. *Digit Signal Processing Selection Guide.* Texas Instruments, 1996.

11. D. Epstein, "Chromatic raises the multimedia bar," *Microprocessor Report*, pp. 23–27, Oct. 1995.

12. P. Kalapathy, "Hardware-software interactions on Mpact," *IEEE Micro*, vol. 17, pp. 20–26, 1997.

13. B. Case, "First trimedia chip boards PCI bus," *Microprocessor Report*, pp. 22–25, Nov. 1995.

14. *TMS320C6x– The Future of DSP Solutions Just Arrived.* Texas Instruments, 1997.

15. R. Simar Jr., "Dsp architectures, algorithms, and code-generation: fission or fusion?," in *Proc. of IEEE Workshop on Signal Processing Systems (SiPS-97)*, pp. 50–59, 1997.

16. R. B. Lee, "Subword parallelism with MAX-2," *IEEE Micro*, vol. 16, no. 4, pp. 51–59, Aug. 1996.

17. A. Peleg and U. Weiser, "MMX technology extension to the Intel architecture," *IEEE Micro*, vol. 16, no. 4, pp. 42–50, Aug. 1996.

Appendix A: Shortest Path Algorithms

A.1 INTRODUCTION

In this appendix, the Bellman-Ford algorithm and the Floyd-Warshall algorithm shortest path algorithms are described. These algorithms can be used to solve several problems in VLSI signal processing such as computing the iteration bound of recursive DFGs (see Chapter 2), retiming (see Chapter 4), and retiming for folding (see Chapter 6).

The level of detail included here is intended to be enough so that the reader can use these algorithms to solve the problems mentioned above. The theory behind these algorithms has been omitted; however, for the interested reader, there is a reference that discusses the theory behind these algorithms (e.g., [1], [2]).

The concepts of shortest paths and negative cycles are demonstrated using the DFG in Figure A.1. The length of a path is the sum of the weights on the edges of the path. The path $2 \rightarrow 3 \rightarrow 4$ has length $1 + 2 = 3$. There are 2 paths from node 2 to node 4, namely the path $2 \rightarrow 4$ with length 1 and the path $2 \rightarrow 3 \rightarrow 4$ with length 3. The shortest path from node 2 to node 4 is $\min\{1, 3\} = 1$. A negative cycle in a directed graph is a directed cycle such that the sum of the lengths on the edges of the cycle is negative. Figure A.1

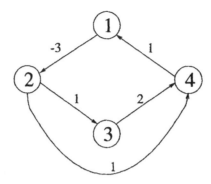

Fig. A.1   A graph containing 1 negative cycle.

contains the 2 cycles $2 \to 4 \to 1 \to 2$ and $2 \to 3 \to 4 \to 1 \to 2$. The cycle $2 \to 4 \to 1 \to 2$ is a negative cycle because the sum of the edge weights is $1 + 1 + (-3) = -1$. The other cycle, $2 \to 3 \to 4 \to 1 \to 2$, is not a negative cycle because the sum of the edge weights is $1 + 2 + 1 + (-3) = 1$. With this in mind, each of the 2 shortest path algorithms works as follows. If there are no negative cycles in the graph, the algorithm returns TRUE and provides some information about the lengths of the shortest path between the nodes (the amount of information varies between the two algorithms, as we will see in the following sections). If there exists at least 1 negative cycle in the graph, the algorithm returns FALSE. To summarize, each of the algorithms searches for a negative cycle and provides shortest path information if no negative cycle exists.

The following assumptions and notation are used. We assume that no parallel edges exist in the graph, i.e., for 2 nodes U and V, there is at most 1 edge from U to V ($U \overset{e}{\to} V$) and at most 1 edge from V to U ($V \overset{e}{\to} U$). Let

$$w(U \overset{e}{\to} V) = \begin{cases} \text{the length of the edge } U \overset{e}{\to} V, & \text{if } U \overset{e}{\to} V \text{ exists} \\ \infty, & \text{otherwise} \end{cases},$$

where the length of the edge is simply a number associated with the edge. Let n be the number of nodes in the graph, and assume that the n nodes are numbered $1, 2, \ldots, n$. The shortest path from the node U to the node V is denoted as S_{UV}.

A.2   THE BELLMAN-FORD ALGORITHM

The Bellman-Ford algorithm is a single-point shortest path algorithm. If no negative cycles exist in the graph, it finds the shortest path from an arbitrarily chosen node U (called the origin) to each node in the graph. For a graph with n nodes, the algorithm constructs $n - 1$ vectors $\mathbf{r}^{(k)}$, $k = 1, 2, \ldots, n - 1$, which

1. $r^{(1)}(U) = 0$
2.   For $k = 1$ to n
3.   If $k \neq U$
4. $r^{(1)}(k) = w(U \xrightarrow{e} k)$
5.   For $k = 1$ to $n - 2$
6.   For $V = 1$ to n
7. $r^{(k+1)}(V) = r^{(k)}(V)$
8.   For $W = 1$ to n
9.   If $r^{(k+1)}(V) > r^{(k)}(W) + w(W \xrightarrow{e} V)$
10. $r^{(k+1)}(V) = r^{(k)}(W) + w(W \xrightarrow{e} V)$
11.   For $V = 1$ to n
12.   For $W = 1$ to n
13.   If $r^{(n-1)}(V) > r^{(n-1)}(W) + w(W \xrightarrow{e} V)$
14.   return FALSE and exit
15.   return TRUE and exit

Fig. A.2   The Bellman-Ford algorithm.

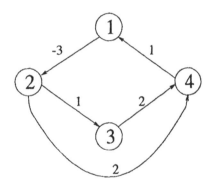

Fig. A.3   A graph containing no negative cycles.

are each of size $n \times 1$, as described in Figure A.2. Note that $\mathbf{r}^{(k)}(U)$ represents the U-th entry in the column vector $\mathbf{r}^{(k)}$.

If TRUE is returned, then $r^{(n-1)}(V)$ is S_{UV}, which is the shortest path from the node U to the node V. If FALSE is returned, then the graph contains at least one negative cycle.

Example A.2.1 *In this example, the Bellman-Ford algorithm in Figure A.2 is used to find the shortest path from the node $U = 2$ to the nodes in the graph in Figure A.3. The values of $r^{(k)}(V)$ for $k = 1, 2, 3$ and $V = 1, 2, 3, 4$ are shown in Table A.1. The Bellman-Ford algorithm returns TRUE in this example, so the value of $r^{(3)}(V)$ is the shortest path from node 2 to node V for $V = 1, 2, 3, 4$.* ∎

Table A.1   Values of $r^{(k)}(V)$ for $k = 1, 2, 3$ and $V = 1, 2, 3, 4$ from Example A.2.1

$r^{(k)}(V)$	$k = 1$	$k = 2$	$k = 3$
$V = 1$	∞	3	3
$V = 2$	0	0	0
$V = 3$	1	1	1
$V = 4$	2	2	2

Table A.2   Values of $r^{(k)}(V)$ for $k = 1, 2, 3$ and $V = 1, 2, 3, 4$ from Example A.2.2

$r^{(k)}(V)$	$k = 1$	$k = 2$	$k = 3$
$V = 1$	∞	2	2
$V = 2$	0	0	-1
$V = 3$	1	1	1
$V = 4$	1	1	1

Example A.2.2 *In this example, the Bellman-Ford algorithm is used to find the shortest path from the origin $U = 2$ to the nodes in the graph in Figure A.1. The values of $r^{(k)}(V)$ for $k = 1, 2, 3$ and $V = 1, 2, 3, 4$ are shown in Table A.2. In this example, the Bellman-Ford algorithm returns FALSE because $r^{(3)}(3) > r^{(3)}(2) + w(2 \overset{e}{\to} 3)$, so a negative cycle is detected. This negative cycle can be seen in Figure A.1, where the cycle $2 \to 4 \to 1 \to 2$ has length $1 + 1 - 3 = -1$.*
■

A.3   THE FLOYD-WARSHALL ALGORITHM

The Floyd-Warshall algorithm is an all-points shortest path algorithm. If no negative cycles exist in the graph, the algorithm finds the shortest path between all possible pairs of nodes in the graph. The algorithm constructs $n + 1$ matrices $\mathbf{R}^{(k)}$, $k = 1, 2, \ldots, n + 1$, which are each of size $n \times n$, as described in Figure A.4.

If TRUE is returned, then $r^{(n+1)}(U, V)$ is S_{UV}, which is the shortest path from the node U to the node V. If FALSE is returned, then the graph contains a negative cycle.

Example A.3.1 *In this example, the Floyd-Warshall algorithm in Figure A.4 is used to solve the all-pairs shortest path problem for the graph in Figure A.3. The values of $r^{(k)}(U, V)$ for $U, V \in \{1, 2, 3, 4\}$ and $k = 1, 2, 3, 4, 5$ are given in Table A.3, where $r^{(k)}(U, V)$ is the element U, V in the matrix $\mathbf{R}^{(k)}$. The*

1.   For $V = 1$ to n
2.   For $U = 1$ to n
3. $r^{(1)}(U, V) = w(U \xrightarrow{e} V)$
4.   For $k = 1$ to n
5.   For $V = 1$ to n
6.   For $U = 1$ to n
7. $r^{(k+1)}(U, V) = r^{(k)}(U, V)$
8.   If $r^{(k+1)}(U, V) > r^{(k)}(U, k) + r^{(k)}(k, V)$
9. $r^{(k+1)}(U, V) = r^{(k)}(U, k) + r^{(k)}(k, V)$
10.   For $k = 1$ to n
11.   For $U = 1$ to n
12.   If $r^{(k)}(U, U) < 0$
13.   return *FALSE* and exit
14.   return *TRUE* and exit

Fig. A.4   The Floyd-Warshall algorithm.

Floyd-Warshall algorithm returns TRUE because all of the diagonal elements in the matrices $\mathbf{R}^{(k)}$, $k = 1, 2, 3, 4$, are nonnegative, so $r^{(5)}(U, V)$ is the shortest path from the node U to the node V. ∎

Example A.3.2 *In this example, the Floyd-Warshall algorithm is used to solve the all-pairs shortest path problem for the graph in Figure A.1. The values of $r^{(k)}(U, V)$ for $U, V \in \{1, 2, 3, 4\}$ and $k = 1, 2, 3, 4, 5$ are given in Table A.4, where $r^{(k)}(U, V)$ is the element U, V in the matrix $\mathbf{R}^{(k)}$. The Floyd-Warshall algorithm returns FALSE because some of the diagonal elements in the matrices $\mathbf{R}^{(k)}$, $k = 3, 4$ and 5, are negative. Therefore, the graph contains a negative cycle.* ∎

A.4   COMPUTATIONAL COMPLEXITIES

The Bellman-Ford algorithm detects negative cycles and solves the *single-source* shortest path problem if no negative cycles exist in $\mathcal{O}(n^3)$ time, while the Floyd-Warshall algorithm detects negative cycles and solves the *all-pairs* shortest path problem if no negative cycles exist in $\mathcal{O}(n^3)$ time. The Bellman-Ford algorithm requires $\mathcal{O}(n^4)$ time to solve the all-pairs shortest path problem since it needs to be run once for each of the n nodes. The Floyd-Warshall algorithm is preferred for applications that require all-pairs shortest path solution, and the Bellman-Ford algorithm and Floyd-Warshall algorithm can be used interchangeably for applications that require a single-source shortest path solution.

Modifications to the Bellman-Ford algorithm and early exit conditions for both algorithms can be utilized to improve computational efficiency. The

Table A.3   Values of $r^{(k)}(U, V)$ for Example A.3.1

$\mathbf{R}^{(1)}$

$$\begin{bmatrix} \infty & -3 & \infty & \infty \\ \infty & \infty & 1 & 2 \\ \infty & \infty & \infty & 2 \\ 1 & \infty & \infty & \infty \end{bmatrix}$$

$\mathbf{R}^{(2)}$

$$\begin{bmatrix} \infty & -3 & \infty & \infty \\ \infty & \infty & 1 & 2 \\ \infty & \infty & \infty & 2 \\ 1 & -2 & \infty & \infty \end{bmatrix}$$

$\mathbf{R}^{(3)}$

$$\begin{bmatrix} \infty & -3 & -2 & -1 \\ \infty & \infty & 1 & 2 \\ \infty & \infty & \infty & 2 \\ 1 & -2 & -1 & 0 \end{bmatrix}$$

$\mathbf{R}^{(4)}$

$$\begin{bmatrix} \infty & -3 & -2 & -1 \\ \infty & \infty & 1 & 2 \\ \infty & \infty & \infty & 2 \\ 1 & -2 & -1 & 0 \end{bmatrix}$$

$\mathbf{R}^{(5)}$

$$\begin{bmatrix} 0 & -3 & -2 & -1 \\ 3 & 0 & 1 & 2 \\ 3 & 0 & 1 & 2 \\ 1 & -2 & -1 & 0 \end{bmatrix}$$

Table A.4   Values of $r^{(k)}(U, V)$ for Example A.3.2

$\mathbf{R}^{(1)}$

$$\begin{bmatrix} \infty & -3 & \infty & \infty \\ \infty & \infty & 1 & 1 \\ \infty & \infty & \infty & 2 \\ 1 & \infty & \infty & \infty \end{bmatrix}$$

$\mathbf{R}^{(2)}$

$$\begin{bmatrix} \infty & -3 & \infty & \infty \\ \infty & \infty & 1 & 1 \\ \infty & \infty & \infty & 2 \\ 1 & -2 & \infty & \infty \end{bmatrix}$$

$\mathbf{R}^{(3)}$

$$\begin{bmatrix} \infty & -3 & -2 & -2 \\ \infty & \infty & 1 & 1 \\ \infty & \infty & \infty & 2 \\ 1 & -2 & -1 & -1 \end{bmatrix}$$

$\mathbf{R}^{(4)}$

$$\begin{bmatrix} \infty & -3 & -2 & -2 \\ \infty & \infty & 1 & 1 \\ \infty & \infty & \infty & 2 \\ 1 & -2 & -1 & -1 \end{bmatrix}$$

$\mathbf{R}^{(5)}$

$$\begin{bmatrix} -1 & -4 & -3 & -3 \\ 2 & -1 & 0 & 0 \\ 3 & 0 & 1 & 1 \\ 0 & -3 & -2 & -2 \end{bmatrix}$$

interested reader can find these details in [1].

REFERENCES

1. E. L. Lawler, *Combinatorial Optimization: Networks and Matriods.* Rinehart and Winston, 1976.

2. T. H. Cormen, C. E. Leiserson and R. C. Rivest, *Introduction to Algorithms,* MIT Press, 1990.

Appendix B: Scheduling and Allocation Techniques

B.1 INTRODUCTION

Scheduling and allocation are two important tasks in hardware or software synthesis of DSP systems [1],[2]. They are both interrelated and dependent on each other and are among the most difficult problems of high-level synthesis. *Scheduling* involves assigning every node of the DFG to *control time steps*. Control time steps (or simply, time steps) are the fundamental sequencing units in synchronous systems and correspond to clock cycles. *Resource allocation* is the process of assigning operations to hardware with the goal of minimizing the amount of hardware required to implement the desired behavior. The hardware resources consist primarily of functional units, memory elements, multiplexers, and communication data paths.

DSP synthesis systems take a set of inputs, including a behavioral description of the algorithm, a set of resources and a set of constraints and goals, and generate a register-transfer level (RTL) architecture. The set of constraints and goals define the desired performance and characteristics of the final architecture. The most common constraints are area and performance constraints. Area constrained problems provide the designer with a set of resources (or more specifically a set of functional units), and the goal is to

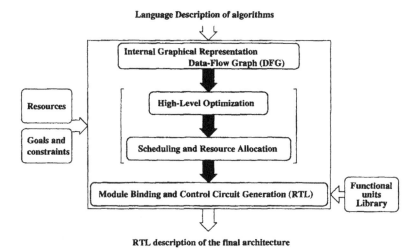

Fig. B.1   The high-level DSP synthesis system.

implement the application using those resources such that it has the highest performance. This is known as *resource-constrained synthesis*. The performance constrained problem is known as *time-constrained synthesis*, where the designer is given a desired sample rate or iteration period and the goal is to minimize the total area of the final architecture. Other goals during the synthesis problem include minimizing the number of memory elements, reducing the power consumption, minimizing the number of busses, incorporating reliability and testability into the design, etc.

The design flow in a high-level DSP synthesis system is illustrated in Fig. B.1. The first step in high-level synthesis is to convert the behavioral description into a graph-based internal representation in the form of a *control and data-flow graph* (CDFG) or DFG. The intermediate tasks in high-level synthesis include high-level optimizations, scheduling and resource allocation, module binding, and control circuit generation. The final architecture produced by high-level synthesis is typically at the RTL and can be represented by a netlist that consists of a network of functional units, registers, multiplexers, and busses. Low-level optimization tools can be used to map the generated RTL description into a physical design. Many high-level synthesis systems have been designed and a great deal of progress has been made in finding good techniques for optimizing and exploring design tradeoffs [3] −[15]. In addition, the trend towards more automation at higher levels of the design process is expected to continue.

In this appendix, we consider both the CDFG and the DFG to be the same. This is valid for DSP systems that do not contain control-dominated operations such as conditional operations and nested loops.

High-level synthesis is believed to be NP-hard because many of the subtasks of synthesis, such as scheduling and allocation, are known to be NP-complete [16], which means the number of steps required to find an optimal solution is believed to grow exponentially as the problem size grows linearly. Because many of the subtasks are interdependent and cannot be isolated, the overall synthesis task is also NP-hard.

This appendix addresses various time-constrained scheduling and allocation techniques, including iterative/constructive scheduling (Section B.2), transformational scheduling (Section B.3), and integer linear programming (ILP) (Section B.4).

B.2 ITERATIVE/CONSTRUCTIVE SCHEDULING ALGORITHMS

An iterative/constructive algorithm generates a schedule by adding the nodes of the DFG to the schedule one node at a time until all nodes have been scheduled. They differ from one another by the methods employed to choose the nodes that will be scheduled and where they will be scheduled. Two of the more simple methods are "As Soon as Possible" and "As Late as Possible" scheduling. These scheduling algorithms are illustrated using the example of an iterative formulation of a 2nd-order differential equation solver.

Consider the 2nd-order differential equation and its corresponding C program formulation:

$$y'' + 3xy' + 3y = 0 \qquad u = y' = \frac{dy}{dx}$$

$$\frac{du}{dx} = y'' = \frac{d^2y}{dx^2} = -3xy' - 3y = -3xu - 3y$$

```
while (x < a) {
    xl  =  x  +  dx;
    ul  =  u  -  (3 * x * u * dx)  -  (3 * y * dx);
    yl  =  y  +  u * dx;
    x   =  xl; y  =  yl; u  =  ul;
}
```

whose DFG is shown in Fig. B.2. In this DFG, the multiplication and addition operations are assumed to be executed in one time step. Many synthesis systems construct and use a more simplified version of the DFG by removing all edges with weights greater than zero. This leaves a DFG that only contains the precedence constraints for one iteration or the *intra-iteration precedence constraints* and is known as the *precedence graph*. Fig. B.2(b) shows the precedence graph for the DFG of Fig. B.2(a). Note that the precedence graph is always guaranteed to be acyclic.

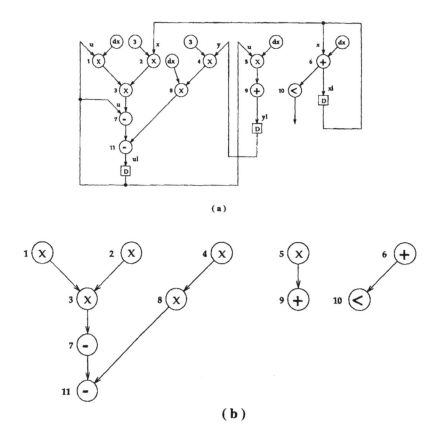

(a)

(b)

Fig. B.2 (a) The DFG of the 2nd-order differential equation formulation. (b) The precedence graph as generated from the DFG.

B.2.1   As Soon As Possible Scheduling Algorithm

"As soon as possible" (ASAP) scheduling is one of the earliest and simplest scheduling algorithms [3]. With this approach, the node selection technique and the method used to place the node into a schedule use local criteria. ASAP scheduling assumes that there are unlimited resources. Nodes are first topologically sorted; i.e., if a node n_j is constrained to follow the node n_i by a precedence constraint, then n_j will topologically follow n_i. From this sorted list, nodes are taken one at a time and placed in the earliest available time step, depending upon its precedence constraints. The ASAP algorithm is shown in Fig. B.3. Fig. B.4 shows the ASAP schedule for the DFG of Fig. B.2, assuming unlimited resources.

Input: DFG $G = (N, E)$.
Output: ASAP Schedule.
1. $TS_0 = 1$; /* Set initial time step */
2.   While   (Unscheduled nodes exist) {
　　2.1   Select a node n_j whose predecessors have already
　　　　been scheduled;
　　2.2   Schedule node n_j to time step $TS_j = \max\{TS_i + (C_i)\}$
　　　　$\forall\ n_i \rightarrow n_j$;
　　}

Fig. B.3   The ASAP scheduling algorithm.

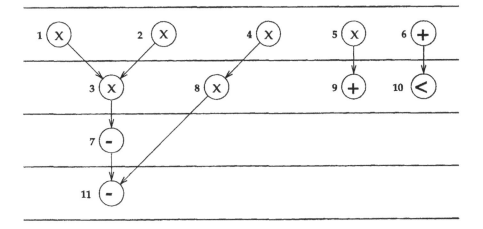

Fig. B.4   The ASAP schedule for the 2nd-order differential equation.

B.2.2   As Late As Possible Scheduling Algorithm

"As late as possible" (ALAP) scheduling is similar to the ASAP scheduling algorithm. ASAP and ALAP scheduling approaches differ in the way nodes are placed in the schedule. As the name indicates, ALAP scheduling algorithm builds the schedule from the bottom up and the nodes are topologically sorted in reverse order. Therefore, this algorithm must have an inherent knowledge of the iteration period in order to build the schedule from the bottom up. The desired iteration period must be long enough to allow the algorithm to schedule all of the nodes in the DFG or it will fail. The ALAP scheduling is shown in Fig. B.5. Fig. B.6 shows the ALAP schedule for the DFG of Fig. B.2.

Although both ASAP and ALAP algorithms do not produce very good results, they are still used extensively to determine *scheduling ranges* for more

Input: DFG $G = (N, E)$, $IterationPeriod = T$.
Output: ALAP Schedule.
1. $TS_0 = T$; /* Set initial time step */
2.   While   (Unscheduled nodes exist) {
            2.1   Select a node n_i whose successors have already
                    been scheduled;
            2.2   Schedule node n_i to time step $TS_i = \min\{TS_j - (C_i)\}$
                    $\forall \; n_i \rightarrow n_j$;
        }

Fig. B.5   The ALAP scheduling algorithm.

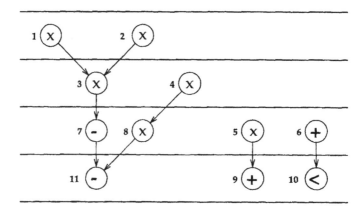

Fig. B.6   The ALAP schedule for the 2nd-order differential equation.

sophisticated techniques as shown later in this appendix. Generally the ASAP schedule defines the minimum values for the start times of the nodes and the ALAP schedule provides the maximum values. The difference between the two values provides the scheduling range for each node in the DFG. ASAP schedules are also used to generate initial schedules, which are then modified by other more efficient scheduling techniques.

B.2.3   List-Scheduling Algorithms

The main problem with ASAP and ALAP scheduling algorithms is that no priority is given to the nodes on the critical path. As a result, less critical nodes may be scheduled ahead of the critical nodes. This is generally not a problem when there is an unlimited number of functional units; however, when the resources are limited (i.e., in a resource-constrained problem), the less critical nodes may block the critical nodes and thus produce inferior schedules

---

Input: DFG $G = (N, E)$, $R = (FU)$.
Output: Final Schedule.
1. $TS_0 = 1$; /* Set initial time step */
2.   While   (Unscheduled nodes exist) {
      2.1   Locate all nodes whose predecessors have already been scheduled and place into list L;
      2.2   Sort nodes in L by decreasing criticalness;
      2.3   While   (L is not empty) {
          2.3.1   Select the first node n_j from L.
          2.3.2   Determine time step $TS_j = \max \{ TS_i + (C_i) \}$
                $\forall \ n_i \rightarrow n_j$;
          2.3.3   If   (FUs at TS_j are not full)
                Schedule node n_j to time step TS_j
            else
                Remove node from L.
        }
   }

Fig. B.7   A simple list-scheduling algorithm that prioritizes nodes by decreasing criticalness.

To overcome this problem, *list scheduling techniques* were developed to utilize more global node selection criteria [6].

In list-scheduling algorithms, all nodes that are ready to be scheduled are sorted into a list by some priority function and nodes are taken from this list and scheduled until the number of functional units are exhausted. Then any remaining nodes and newly ready nodes are sorted into a new list. This iteration continues until all nodes are scheduled. The drawback of list scheduling is that these algorithms require some prior knowledge of the number of resources and, therefore, can only be applied to the resource-constrained problem. Fig. B.7 provides a simple list-scheduling algorithm that prioritizes nodes that are ready to be scheduled by decreasing criticalness. Criticalness is determined by the scheduling range; the smaller the range, the more critical the node. In Fig. B.7, R represents the set of resources and the restricted resources are the functional units (FU).

B.3   TRANSFORMATIONAL SCHEDULING ALGORITHMS

A transformational scheduling algorithm begins with an initial schedule that is either maximally serial or maximally parallel. Transformations are then applied to the initial and intermediate schedules to obtain other schedules

```
Input:    DFG  G = (N, E), Iteration Period = T.
Output:   Final FDS Schedule.
1.   While   (Unscheduled nodes exist) {
        1.1   Compute the time frames for each node;
        1.2   Build the distribution graph;
        1.3   Compute the self-forces;
        1.4   Compute the predecessor and successor forces;
        1.5   Schedule the node into the time step that
              minimizes the total force;
     }
```

Fig. B.8 The force-directed scheduling algorithm.

until a final solution is produced. The fundamental transformations move the nodes that are in serial (parallel) to locations in the schedule where they are more in parallel (serial). These types of approaches differ from one another by the type of transformations they employ. These scheduling algorithms generally provide better results than the iterative/constructive algorithms.

B.3.1 Force Directed Scheduling Algorithm

A good example of transformational scheduling is *force-directed scheduling* (FDS) developed in the HAL system where its node selection criteria and its node scheduling technique utilize more global information [5]. HAL calculates a *force* that is exerted between an operation and a particular time step. This force is proportional to the number of operations that can be scheduled to the same functional unit at a particular time step. The scheduling process then minimizes the overall force which tends to balance the concurrency of the nodes in the DFG. Fig. B.8 shows the basic force-directed scheduling algorithm.

As can be seen from Fig. B.8, the first step of the basic FDS approach involves the determination of the *time frames* (scheduling ranges) for each node from the ASAP and ALAP schedules. These time frames represent the probability of the node being assigned to a particular time step and therefore, the areas of the time frames are equal to 1 for every node. If a node can be scheduled within the range of time steps $[S_i, L_i]$ (where $S_i \leq L_i$), then the probability of this node being scheduled to each time step in this interval is $\frac{1}{L_i - S_i + 1}$. Fig. B.9(a) shows the time frames of the DFG of Fig. B.2 and the associated probabilities. Next a *distribution graph* (DG) is created for each functional unit type by summing all of the probabilities for each time step (See Fig. B.9). These graphs are a graphical representation of the concurrency of similar operations within the DFG.

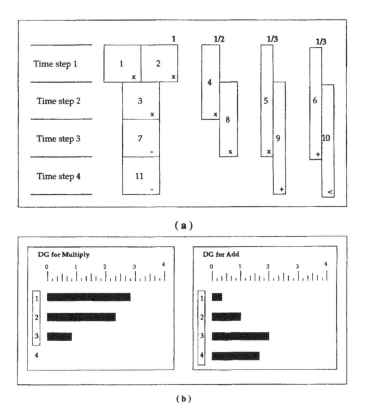

(a)

(b)

Fig. B.9 (a) The initial time frame for the 2nd-order differential equation which shows the probabilities of each node being scheduled to a specific time frame (note that each node's area is equal to the other node's areas). (b) The DGs for the 2nd-order differential equation.

From the DG we can calculate the forces applied when a node is scheduled to a certain time step. Two types of forces are determined for each node in the DFG: a *self force* and *predecessor/successor forces*. Self force reflects the effect on the overall concurrency by attempting to schedule a node to the time step. It is positive if the assignment causes an increase in concurrency and negative for a decrease. For each possible assignment of a node, n_j, to a time step, TS_j, within the node's time frame $(S_j \leq TS_j \leq L_j)$, a self force is calculated as:

$$Self\_Force(j) = \sum_{i=S_j}^{L_j} [DG(i) * x(i)]$$

where $DG(i)$ is the distribution value at time step i, and $x(i)$ is the change in the probability associated with time step i. The predecessor and successor forces are the self forces of predecessor and/or successor nodes that will be affected by the assignment of a node to a time step. The total force exerted on a node becomes the summation of the self, the predecessor, and the successor forces. The node with the lowest total force is then assigned to the time step. After a node has been assigned to a time step, the whole process is repeated for the remaining nodes of the DFG until all nodes have been assigned to a time step.

As an example, consider the scheduling of node 4 in Fig. B.9, using force-directed scheduling. We can see that node 4 can be scheduled into time step 1 or time step 2. Therefore we must calculate the self forces for both cases.

$$
\begin{aligned}
Self\_Force_4(1) &= Force_4(1) + Force_4(2) \\
&= (DG_M(1) * x_4(1)) + (DG_M(2) * x_4(2)) \\
&= (2.833 * (1 - 0.5)) + (2.333 * (0 - 0.5)) \\
&= (2.833 * (+0.5)) + (2.333 * (-0.5)) \\
&= +0.25
\end{aligned}
$$

$$
\begin{aligned}
Self\_Force_4(2) &= Force_4(1) + Force_4(2) \\
&= (DG_M(1) * x_4(1)) + (DG_M(2) * x_4(2)) \\
&= (2.833 * (-0.5)) + (2.333 * (+0.5)) \\
&= -0.25
\end{aligned}
$$

If node 4 is scheduled into time step 1, it does not affect the time frame for its successor, node 8; therefore, the total force caused by scheduling node 4 to time step 1 will be $Force_4(1) = +0.25$. However, if node 4 is scheduled into time step 2, it will cause its successor node to be scheduled into time step 3. In this case the successor force must also be calculated and included into the total force.

$$
\begin{aligned}
Succ\_Force_4(2) &= Self\_Force_8(2) + Self\_Force_8(3) \\
&= (DG_M(2) * x_8(2)) + (DG_M(3) * x_8(3)) \\
&= (2.333 * (0 - 0.5)) + (0.833 * (1 - 0.5)) \\
&= (2.333 * (-0.5)) + (0.833 * (+0.5)) \\
&= -0.75
\end{aligned}
$$

$$
\begin{aligned}
Force_4(2) &= Self\_Force_4(2) + Succ\_Force_4(2) \\
&= -0.25 - 0.75 = -1.00
\end{aligned}
$$

After calculating the total force for node 4 for each time step within the time frame, the assignment that has the lowest force is chosen and node 4

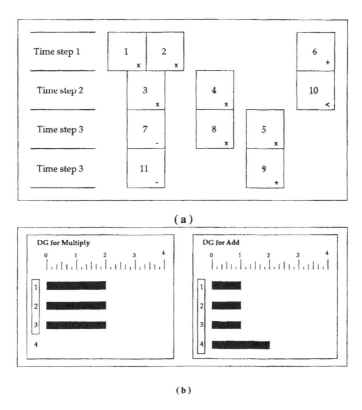

(a)

(b)

Fig. B.10 (a) The final time frame and schedule for the 2nd-order differential equation. (b) The final DGs for the 2nd-order differential equation.

is scheduled to time step 2. We can repeat the process by determining the new time frames and building a new distribution graph and then scheduling another node. Fig. B.10 shows the final time frames and DGs that represent the final schedule.

Because the total forces must be recalculated for every remaining node every time a node is scheduled into a time step, the run times for this approach can become large. To reduce the execution time of the scheduling task, transformational heuristics can be utilized that produce similar results faster. It may be noted the scheduling algorithms discussed up to this point are *critical path* schedulers; i.e., these can only generate schedules for iteration periods equal to or larger than the critical path. They only exploit concurrency within a single iteration and only utilize the intra-iteration precedence constraints.

As another example, Fig. B.11(a) shows a simple 2nd-order IIR filter or biquad filter that realizes the following function:

$$y(n) = x(n) + b_0 x(n-1) + b_1 x(n-2) - a_0 y(n-1) - a_1 y(n-2).$$

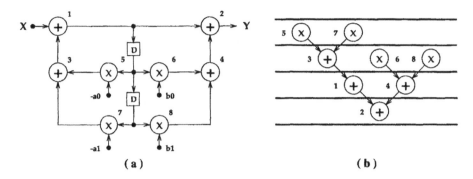

Fig. B.11 (a) The DFG of a simple biquad filter. (b) A schedule generated by a critical path scheduler that has a lower bound iteration period of 4 u.t.

If we assume the addition and multiply operations require computation times of 1 u.t. then this filter has a critical path of CP = 4 u.t. Fig. B.11(b) shows one schedule that might be generated by a critical path scheduler. Note that the iteration period is 4 u.t. and that it requires 2 multipliers and 2 adders. To generate better schedules one could apply high-level transformations to optimize the DFG, such as pipelining and retiming, to reduce the critical path as a preprocessing step. If the DFG of Fig. B.11(a) is pipelined and retimed, the critical path can be reduced to 3 u.t. and the number of allocated functional units can also be reduced. Some recent techniques eliminate this preprocessing step by incorporating these high-level transformations within the scheduling process. Two examples include the iterative loop based scheduling algorithm [9]–[12] and the use of integer linear programming models [13]–[15].

B.3.2   Iterative Loop Based Scheduling Algorithm

An example synthesis system based on iterative loops is the minnesota architecture synthesis or the MARS system [11],[12]. MARS uses a loop-based heuristic scheduling technique which also implicitly pipelines and retimes the DFG as it builds the schedule. Loop-based scheduling algorithms are developed from the fact that feedback or recursive loops are the most restrictive sections within a DFG. Loops, which are commonly found in DSP applications, are created by feedback edges; therefore, the next iteration cannot be initiated until the current iteration has been completed. These feedback edges must contain one or more delays to ensure the DFG is valid and these edges represent *inter-iteration precedence constraints*. During the scheduling process MARS exploits both the intra- and inter-iteration precedence constraints to implicitly pipeline and retime the DFG for better results. The basic MARS iterative loop based scheduling algorithm is shown in Fig. B.12.

In a loop-based approach, the first step is to locate all of the loops and sort them by decreasing *loop bounds*. The loop bound is the lower bound on

Input: DFG $G = (N, E)$, *Iteration Period* $= T$.
Output: Final Schedule.
1.   Locate all loops within the DFG;
2.   Sort loops by decreasing criticalness;
3.   Locate subset of loops that cover all nodes located in the loops;
4.   Allocate lower bound functional units;
5.   Build the initial schedule ;
6.   Locate all resource conflicts;
7.   While   (Resource conflicts exist in the schedule) {
    7.1   For $(TS = 1; TS \leq T; TS + +;)$ {
        7.1.1   If   (a resource conflict exists at TS)
            Resolve conflict by rescheduling or
            allocating additional functional units;
        7.1.2   Update resource conflicts;
        }
    }
8.   Locate all feed-forward paths;
9.   Sort paths by decreasing criticalness;
10.   Locate subset of paths that cover all nodes in the paths;
11.   Allocate remain functional units;
12.   Build the initial schedule;
13.   Locate all resource conflicts;
14.   While   (Resource conflicts exist in the schedule) {
    14.1   For $(TS = 1; TS \leq T; TS + +;)$ {
        14.1.1   If   (a resource conflict exists at TS)
            Resolve conflict by rescheduling or
            allocating additional functional units;
        14.1.2   Update resource conflicts;
        }
    }

Fig. B.12 The MARS iterative loop based scheduling algorithm.

the time required to execute one iteration of a loop and can be calculated for each loop by:

$$T_{lb_l} = \frac{t_l}{w_l}$$

where t_l is the total computation time and w_l is the number of delays within the loop l. From the set of all loops, a subset of loops that contain all of the recursive (loop) nodes is identified and used by MARS to schedule the recursive nodes. The nonrecursive nodes are not considered with the recursive nodes because they belong to feed-forward paths that can be easily pipelined when necessary, while recursive nodes belong to loops and cannot be easily pipelined.

The next step is to create a schedule matrix where columns represent loops and rows represent time steps. Starting with the loop with the largest loop bound, every unscheduled node of each loop is entered into the schedule matrix such that the intra-iteration precedence constraints are satisfied by assuming that an unlimited number of resources are available. This constitutes the initial schedule and transformations are iteratively applied to generate the final schedule. Before initiating any transformations, MARS calculates the lower bound on the number of functional units required by the DFG:

$$M_{t_k} = \left\lceil \frac{N_{t_k} * T_{t_k}}{P_{t_k} * T} \right\rceil$$

where M_{t_k} is the lower bound on the number of t_k type functional units, N_{t_k} is the number of nodes computed by t_k type functional units, T_{t_k} is the computation time, P_{t_k} is the number of pipelined stages, and T is the desired iteration period. This lower bound assumes that no intra-iteration precedence constraints exist in the DFG. MARS then allocates these functional units to be used during the scheduling process. At this point, MARS begins to iteratively search the initial schedule for resource conflicts (time steps where more nodes are scheduled than allocated functional units) and attempts to resolve the conflicts by rescheduling nodes to different time steps. In choosing and rescheduling a node, MARS exploits the inter-iteration precedence constraints to obtain more efficient schedules. By resolving the most area expensive processor conflicts first, MARS utilizes the inter-iteration precedence constraints on the more costly functional units in order to minimize the need to allocate any additional expensive resources. If resource conflicts cannot be resolved by rescheduling the conflicting nodes, MARS allocates another functional unit.

Continuing with the 2nd-order differential equation example, MARS locates three loops and all are required for scheduling recursive nodes. Next MARS determines the lower bounds on the number of multipliers and ALUs to be:

$$Multipliers: \quad M_{mult} = \left\lceil \tfrac{6*1}{1*4} \right\rceil = 2.$$
$$ALUs: \quad M_{alu} = \left\lceil \tfrac{5*1}{1*4} \right\rceil = 2.$$

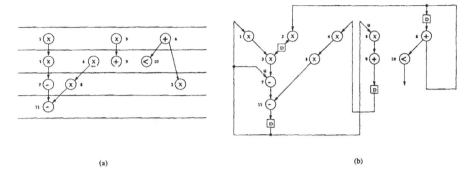

(a)   (b)

Fig. B.13   (a) The final schedule for the 2nd-order differential equation as generated by MARS. (b) The retimed and pipelined DFG of the 2nd-order differential equation that is derived from the final schedule.

After allocating this set of functional units MARS generates the final schedule as shown in Fig. B.13(a). Fig. B.13(b) shows the retimed and pipelined DFG as derived from the final schedule.

To demonstrate the usefulness of implicit transformations, consider the biquad filter of Fig. B.11 once again. First MARS locates 2 loops in the DFG and both loops are required to schedule the recursive nodes. Next MARS determines the lower bounds on the number of multipliers and adders to be:

$$Multipliers: \quad M_{mult} = \left\lceil \tfrac{4*1}{1*4} \right\rceil = 1.$$
$$Adders: \quad M_{add} = \left\lceil \tfrac{4*1}{1*4} \right\rceil = 1.$$

After allocating one multiplier and one adder, MARS is able to generate the final optimal schedule for the biquad filter as shown in Fig. B.14(b). Fig. B.14(a) shows the retimed and pipelined DFG as derived from the final schedule. Note that with an iteration period of 4 u.t., this schedule is optimal and that the number of processors is also reduced. Here we only require 1 multiplier and 1 adder as compared to 2 multipliers and 2 adders for critical path schedulers. Critical path schedulers would require a pipelining preprocessing step to achieve the same result.

B.3.3   Other Heuristic Scheduling Algorithms

Several other heuristic scheduling algorithms have been proposed and several new approaches are being developed. Some have been derived from software design techniques [7]. Others are based upon general iterative methods such as simulated annealing. Another transformation-based technique iteratively applies the retiming transformation on existing schedules to obtain more efficient ones [17]. Genetic algorithms have also been applied to the scheduling problems. For more optimal results, heuristic techniques must utilize the full

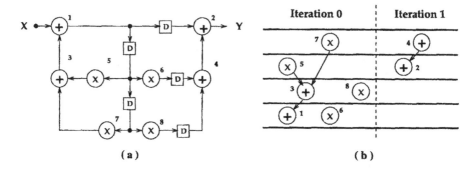

Fig. B.14 (a) The pipelined DFG of the simple biquad filter that is derived from the final schedule. (b) The optimal schedule generated by MARS that utilizes implicit pipelining.

scheduling range [18] of the nodes in a DFG to exploit both the intra- and inter-iteration precedence constraints as was done in the MARS system and in [18]. The main point to be made is that because high-level synthesis is a difficult problem, many different heuristic approaches can be utilized to obtain good results in less time. Most approaches produce similar results in comparable run times; however, heuristic techniques cannot guarantee optimal solutions.

B.4   INTEGER LINEAR PROGRAMMING MODELS

Integer linear programming (ILP) models provide a formal method to describe and solve the scheduling problems in an optimal manner. The models primarily differ in the manner they are described and their objective functions. Although ILP models provide a formal method to address the scheduling problem, they have been used sparingly until recently, because they require longer execution times and when constraints are relaxed, the run times increase exponentially. New models have been developed to reduce the execution time [13]–[15]. ILP models are attractive because they can produce optimal solutions and can be easily modified to accommodate additional constraints.

A general description of ILP modeling for high-level synthesis consists of an objective function to be minimized (or maximized) and a set of constraints to be satisfied. Most approaches also utilize scheduling ranges to reduce the design space and run times. When constructing an ILP model, integer variables are used to describe the objective function and the constraints. The primary variables are binary decision variables, $x_{i,j}$, which represent whether node i can be scheduled into time step j. Other important variables are M_{t_k}, which represent the number of t_k type functional units that will be allocated. Costs associated with each t_k type functional unit are represented by constants: c_{t_k}. Using these variables and constants, the scheduling problem can be formulated as minimizing the total cost of all of the functional units:

$$\sum_{k=1}^{m} (c_{t_k} * M_{t_k})$$

where m represents the number of different types of functional units that can be used to build the final architecture. This objective function is also subjected to the design constraints. The first constraint states that no schedule will have a time step that contains more operations than M_{t_k} functional units (no resource conflicts):

$$\sum_{o_i \in FU_{t_k}} x_{i,j} - M_{t_k} \leq 0, \quad for \ 1 \leq j \leq T, \quad 1 \leq k \leq m.$$

where T represents the desired iteration period of the final architecture. The variable o_i is a node in the DFG that is an operation capable of being processed by a t_k type functional unit, FU_{t_k} represents the functional unit types able to compute the o_i operation, and $x_{i,j}$ represents the binary decision variable associated with o_i ($x_{i,j} = 1$ if o_i is scheduled into step j, otherwise $x_{i,j} = 0$).

The next constraint states that o_i can only be scheduled within the scheduling range bounded by S_i and L_i ($S_i \leq j \leq L_i$ as determined by the ASAP and ALAP schedules) and can only appear once in the schedule.

$$\sum_{j=S_i}^{L_i} x_{i,j} = 1, \quad for \ 1 \leq i \leq n.$$

The last constraint ensures that the intra-iteration precedence constraints are maintained.

$$\sum_{j=S_i}^{L_i} (j * x_{i,j}) - \sum_{j=S_i}^{L_i} (j * x_{k,j}) \leq -1, \quad \forall \ o_i \rightarrow o_k.$$

If we apply this simple model to the 2nd-order differential equation example of Fig. B.2 we obtain the following sets of inequalities that can be solved by hand (for small problems) or by an ILP solver program (such as GAMS [19]):

$$Assume \quad c_{mult} = 5 \ u.t. \quad and \quad c_{alu} = 1 \ u.t.$$

$$Minimize \ (5 * M_{mult} + 1 * M_{alu})$$

Subject to no resource conflicts:

$$Multiplier: \quad x_{1,1} + x_{2,1} + x_{4,1} + x_{5,1} - M_{mult} \leq 0$$
$$x_{3,2} + x_{4,2} + x_{8,2} + x_{5,2} - M_{mult} \leq 0$$
$$x_{8,3} + x_{5,3} - M_{mult} \leq 0.$$

$$ALU: \quad x_{6,1} - M_{alu} \leq 0$$
$$x_{9,2} + x_{6,2} + x_{10,2} - M_{alu} \leq 0$$
$$x_{7,3} + x_{9,3} + x_{6,3} + x_{10,3} - M_{alu} \leq 0$$
$$x_{11,4} + x_{9,4} + x_{10,4} - M_{alu} \leq 0.$$

The nodes of the DFG can only appear once in the schedule. This is described by the constraints:

$$x_{1,1} = 1, \quad x_{2,1} = 1, \quad x_{3,2} = 1, \quad x_{7,3} = 1, \quad x_{11,4} = 1$$
$$x_{4,1} + x_{4,2} = 1, \quad x_{8,2} + x_{8,3} = 1$$
$$x_{5,1} + x_{5,2} + x_{5,3} = 1, \quad x_{9,2} + x_{9,3} + x_{9,4} = 1$$
$$x_{6,1} + x_{6,2} + x_{6,3} = 1, \quad x_{10,2} + x_{10,3} + x_{10,4} = 1.$$

The intra-iteration precedence constraints of the DFG lead to:

$$x_{4,1} + 2x_{4,2} - 2x_{8,2} - 3x_{8,3} \leq -1$$
$$x_{5,1} + 2x_{5,2} + 3x_{5,3} - 2x_{9,2} - 3x_{9,3} - 4x_{9,4} \leq -1$$
$$x_{6,1} + 2x_{6,2} + 3x_{6,3} - 2x_{10,2} - 3x_{10,3} - 4x_{10,4} \leq -1.$$

The solution to this set of inequalities generates a similar schedule as shown in Fig. B.10 and is shown below:

$$x_{1,1} = 1, \quad x_{2,1} = 1, \quad x_{3,2} = 1, \quad x_{4,2} = 1,$$
$$x_{5,3} = 1, \quad x_{6,1} = 1, \quad x_{7,3} = 1, \quad x_{8,3} = 1,$$
$$x_{9,4} = 1, \quad x_{10,2} = 1, \quad x_{11,4} = 1.$$

The power behind ILP models lies in the ease to redefine the problem and to add additional constraints. Other models are also robust enough to generate schedules for both homogeneous and heterogeneous environments [15]. We define a heterogeneous environment as a system where the data format of every processor may not be the same. For example, some processors may be bit-parallel while others may be bit-serial, and still others may be digit-serial where the digit sizes may also vary. The objective function for these models is to minimize the overall area, which includes the automatic allocation of data-format converters as well as functional units and the minimization of registers.

REFERENCES

1. M. C. McFarland, A. C. Parker, and R. Camposano, "The high-level synthesis of digital systems," *Proc. IEEE*, vol. 78, no. 2, pp. 301–318, Feb. 1990.

2. R. Camposano and W. Wolf, eds., *High Level VLSI Synthesis*. Kluwer, 1991.

3. T. C. Hu, "Parallel sequencing and assembly line problems," *Operations Research*, no. 9, pp. 841–848, 1961.

4. N. Park and A. C. Parker, "Sehwa: a software package for synthesis of pipelines from behavioral specifications," *IEEE Trans. on Computer-Aided Design*, vol. 7, no. 3, pp. 356–370, March 1988.

5. P. G. Paulin and J. P. Knight, "Force-directed scheduling for the behavioral synthesis of asic's," *IEEE Trans. on Computer-Aided Design*, vol. 8, no. 6, pp. 661–679, June 1989.

6. H. De Man, J. Rabaey, P. Six, and L. J. Claesen, "Cathedral-II: A silicon compiler for digital signal processing," *IEEE Design and Test*, vol. 3, no. 6, pp. 13–25, Dec. 1986.

7. G. Goossens, J. Rabaey, J. Vandewalle, and H. De Man, "An efficient microcode compiler for application specific DSP processors," *IEEE Trans. on Computer-Aided Design*, vol. 9, no. 9, pp. 925–937, Sept. 1990.

8. J. Rabaey et al., "Fast prototyping of datapath-intensive architectures," *IEEE Design and Test*, vol. 8, no. 3, pp. 40–51, June 1991.

9. P. R. Gelabert and T. P. Barnwell III, "Optimal automatic periodic multiprocessor scheduler for fully specified flow graphs," *IEEE Trans. on Computer-Aided Design*, pp. 858–888, Feb. 1993.

10. T. F. Lee et al., "A transformation-based method for loop folding," *IEEE Trans. on Computer-Aided Design*, no. 4, pp. 439–450, April 1994.

11. C.-Y. Wang and K. K. Parhi, "Resource-constrained loop list scheduler for DSP algorithms," *Journal of VLSI Signal Processing*, vol. 11, Oct. 1995.

12. C.-Y. Wang and K. K. Parhi, "High-level synthesis using concurrent transformations, scheduling, and allocation," *IEEE Trans. on Computer-Aided Design*, vol. 14, no. 3, March 1995.

13. C. H. Gebotys and M. Elmasry, "Global optimization approach for architecture synthesis," *IEEE Trans. on Computer-Aided Design*, vol. 12, pp. 1266–1278, Sept. 1993.

14. C.-T. Hwang, J.-H. Lee, and Y.-C. Hsu, "A formal approach to the scheduling problem in high-level synthesis," *IEEE Trans. on Computer-Aided Design*, vol. 10, no. 4, pp. 464–475, April 1991.

15. K. Ito, L. E. Lucke, and K. K. Parhi, "ILP based cost-optimal DSP synthesis with module selection and data format conversion," *IEEE Trans. on VLSI Systems*, vol. 6, no. 4, Dec. 1998.

16. M. R. Garey and D. S. Johnson, *Computers and Intractability*. Freeman and Co., 1979.

17. L.-F. Chao, A. LaPaugh, and E. Sha, "Rotation scheduling: a loop pipelining algorithm," *IEEE Trans. on Computer-Aided Design*, no. 3, pp. 229–239, March 1997.

18. S. M. Heemstra de Groot, S. Gerez, and O. Herrmann, "Range-chart-guided iterative data-flow-graph scheduling," *IEEE Trans. on Circuits and Systems-I: Fundamental Theory and Application*, vol. 39, no. 5, pp. 351–364, May 1992.

19. A. Brooke, D. Kendrick, and A. Meeraus, *GAMS: A User's Guide, Release 2.25*. The Scientific Press, 1992.

Appendix C: Euclidean GCD Algorithm

C.1 INTRODUCTION

There are two versions of Euclidean greatest common divisor (GCD) algorithms, one for integers, the other for polynomials. Both of them are presented in this appendix.

C.2 EUCLIDEAN GCD ALGORITHM FOR INTEGERS

Theorem C.2.1 (Division Algorithm) *For every pair of integers c and d with d nonzero, there is a unique pair of integers Q (the quotient) and r (the remainder) such that $c = dQ + r$, where $0 \leq |r| < |d|$.*

Using the division algorithm, the GCD of 2 integers can be found.

Example C.2.1 *$GCD(993,186)$ can be found as follows:*

$$993 = 5 \times 186 + 63 \qquad \text{(C.1)}$$
$$186 = 2 \times 63 + 60$$

$$63 = 1 \times 60 + 3$$
$$60 = 20 \times 3 + 0.$$

Since GCD(993,186) divides 993 and 186, it must divide the 1st remainder 63. Because it divides 186 and 63, it must divide the 2nd remainder 60. Because it divides 63 and 60, it divides 3. On the other hand, 3 divides 60, and hence 63, and hence 186 and 993. Therefore, GCD(993,186)=3. ∎

Following is the Euclidean GCD algorithm for integers.

Theorem C.2.2 (Euclidean GCD Algorithm) *Given 2 positive integers s and r, their greatest common divisor can be computed by iteratively applying the division algorithm. Suppose $r < s$, then the algorithm is continued iteratively as shown below:*

$$
\begin{aligned}
s &= Q_1 r + r_1, & \text{(C.2)} \\
r &= Q_2 r_1 + r_2, \\
r_1 &= Q_3 r_2 + r_3, \\
&\cdots \\
r_{n-2} &= Q_n r_{n-1} + r_n, \\
r_{n-1} &= Q_{n+1} r_n,
\end{aligned}
$$

and the process stops whenever the remainder is zero. The last nonzero number, r_n is the greatest common divisor.

Corollary C.2.1 *For any positive integer s and r, there exist integers a and b such that*

$$GCD(s,r) = as + br. \qquad \text{(C.3)}$$

The integers a and b can be obtained by computing the equation (C.3) backward, rewriting $r_i = r_{i-2} - Q_i r_{i-1}$ and using back substitution as follows:

$$
\begin{aligned}
GCD(s,r) &= r_n & \text{(C.4)} \\
&= r_{n-2} - Q_n r_{n-1} \\
&= r_{n-2} - Q_n(r_{n-3} - Q_{n-1} r_{n-2}) \\
&= (Q_n Q_{n-1} + 1)r_{n-2} + (-Q_n)r_{n-3} \\
&= \cdots
\end{aligned}
$$

until it is expressed in terms of integers s and r, as in (C.3).

Example C.2.2 *Express GCD(993,186) in terms of 993 and 186.*

$$
\begin{aligned}
GCD(993, 186) &= 3 & \text{(C.5)} \\
&= 63 - 1 \times 60
\end{aligned}
$$

$$\begin{aligned}
&= & 63 - 1 \times (186 - 2 \times 63) \\
&= & 3 \times 63 - 1 \times 186 \\
&= & 3 \times (993 - 5 \times 186) - 1 \times 186 \\
&= & 3 \times 993 - 16 \times 186.
\end{aligned}$$

Hence we conclude that for $a = 3$ and $b = -16$, GCD(993,186) can be expressed using equation (C.3) as

$$GCD(993, 186) = 3 = a \times 993 + b \times 186. \quad \blacksquare \tag{C.6}$$

This completes the computation of GCD of 2 integers. The computation of GCD of 2 polynomials is addressed next.

C.3 EUCLIDEAN GCD ALGORITHM FOR POLYNOMIALS

Theorem C.3.1 (Division Algorithm for Polynomials) *For 2 polynomials $c(x)$ and $d(x)$ with $d(x)$ not equal to zero, there is a unique pair of polynomials $Q(x)$ (the quotient polynomial) and $r(x)$ (the remainder polynomial) such that*

$$c(x) = Q(x)d(x) + r(x) \tag{C.7}$$

and deg $r(x) <$ deg $d(x)$.

Theorem C.3.2 (Euclidean GCD Algorithm for Polynomials) *Given the polynomials $s(x)$ and $r(x)$ over certain field, their greatest common divisor can be computed by applying iteratively the division algorithm. Suppose deg $s(x) \geq$ deg $r(x) \geq 0$, then this computation is carried out iteratively as:*

$$\begin{aligned}
s(x) &= & Q_1(x)r(x) + r_1(x), \tag{C.8} \\
r(x) &= & Q_2(x)r_1(x) + r_2(x), \\
r_1(x) &= & Q_3(x)r_2(x) + r_3(x), \\
& \cdots & \\
r_{n-2}(x) &= & Q_n(x)r_{n-1}(x) + r_n(x), \\
r_{n-1}(x) &= & Q_{n+1}(x)r_n(x)
\end{aligned}$$

and the process stops when a remainder of zero is obtained. Then

$$GCD(s(x), r(x)) = \alpha r_n(x), \tag{C.9}$$

where α is a scalar.

Corollary C.3.1 *For any polynomials $s(x)$ and $r(x)$, there exist polynomials $a(x)$ and $b(x)$ such that*

$$GCD(s(x), r(x)) = a(x)s(x) + b(x)r(x). \tag{C.10}$$

The procedure to find the polynomials $a(x)$ and $b(x)$ is the same as that for the integers.

Example C.3.1 *Find $GCD(s(x), r(x))$, given $s(x) = x^3 - x^2 + x - 1$ and $r(x) = x^2 - 2x + 1$. Express $GCD(s(x), r(x))$ in terms of $s(x)$ and $r(x)$ as in (C.10).*

From Euclidean algorithm, we have

$$\begin{aligned} s(x) &= (x+1)r(x) + (2x - 2), \tag{C.11}\\ r(x) &= (\frac{1}{2}x - \frac{1}{2})(2x - 2). \end{aligned}$$

Therefore, $GCD(s(x), r(x)) = 2(x - 1)$. By using back substitution to (C.12), we get

$$GCD(s(x), r(x)) = s(x) - (x + 1)r(x) \tag{C.12}$$

with $a(x) = 1$ and $b(x) = -(x + 1)$. ∎

Appendix D:
Orthonormality of Schur Polynomials

D.1   ORTHOGONALITY OF SCHUR POLYNOMIALS

From (12.21),
$$\langle \Phi_N(z), \Phi_i(z) \rangle = 0, \quad \text{for } 0 \le i \le N-1, \tag{D.1}$$
since the coefficient of z^N of each $\Phi_i(z)$, for $0 \le i \le N-1$ is zero.

Next, using (12.4), (12.26), (12.27), (12.21), (12.22) and (12.37), the inner product $\langle \Phi_{N-1}(z), \Phi_{N-2}(z) \rangle$ can be calculated as

$$
\begin{aligned}
&\langle \Phi_{N-1}(z), \Phi_{N-2}(z) \rangle \\
&= \langle \frac{z^{-1}\{\Phi_N(z) - k_N \Phi_N^*(z)\}}{\sqrt{1 - k_N^2}}, \frac{z^{-1}\{\Phi_{N-1}(z) - k_{N-1}\Phi_{N-1}^*(z)\}}{\sqrt{1 - k_{N-1}^2}} \rangle, \\
&= \langle \frac{\Phi_N(z) - k_N \Phi_N^*(z)}{\sqrt{1 - k_N^2}}, \frac{\Phi_{N-1}(z) - k_{N-1}\Phi_{N-1}^*(z)}{\sqrt{1 - k_{N-1}^2}} \rangle, \\
&= \frac{-k_N}{\sqrt{(1 - k_N^2)(1 - k_{N-1}^2)}} \langle \Phi_N^*(z), \Phi_{N-1}(z) - k_{N-1}\Phi_{N-1}^*(z) \rangle,
\end{aligned}
$$

$$= \frac{-k_N}{\sqrt{(1-k_N^2)(1-k_{N-1}^2)}} \frac{1}{\phi_N} \{\Phi_{N-1}(0) - k_{N-1}\Phi_{N-1}^*(0)\},$$

$$= 0.$$

This approach can be extended to the inner product

$$\langle \Phi_i(z), \Phi_j(z) \rangle, \quad \text{for } 0 \le j < i < N. \tag{D.2}$$

Notice that any $\Phi_i(z)$ can be expressed as a function of $\Phi_N(z)$ and $\Phi_N^*(z)$ as shown in Example D.1.1 where the notation $f(a, b, c, d, \cdots)$ denotes the dependence of the function on parameters a, b, c, d and does not represent a specific function.

Example D.1.1

$$\begin{aligned}
\Phi_{N-1}(z) &= z^{-1}f(\Phi_N(z), \Phi_N^*(z)). \\
\Phi_{N-1}^*(z) &= z^{N-1}\Phi_{N-1}(z^{-1}), \\
&= f(\Phi_N(z), \Phi_N^*(z)). \\
\Phi_{N-2}(z) &= z^{-1}f(\Phi_{N-1}(z), \Phi_{N-1}^*(z)), \\
&= z^{-1}f(\Phi_N(z), \Phi_N^*(z), z^{-1}\Phi_N(z), z^{-1}\Phi_N^*(z)). \\
\Phi_{N-2}^*(z) &= z^{N-2}\Phi_{N-2}(z^{-1}), \\
&= f(\Phi_N(z), \Phi_N^*(z), z^{-1}\Phi_N(z), z^{-1}\Phi_N^*(z)). \quad \blacksquare
\end{aligned}$$

From the foregoing example, it is obvious that $\Phi_i(z)$, for $0 \le i < N$ can be expressed as

$$\Phi_i(z) = z^{-1}f(\Phi_N(z), \Phi_N^*(z), \cdots, z^{-(N-i-1)}\Phi_N(z), z^{-(N-i-1)}\Phi_N^*(z)). \tag{D.3}$$

Also, $\Phi_j(z)$ can be expressed as

$$\Phi_j(z) = \frac{z^{-1}\{\Phi_{j+1}(z) - k_{j+1}\Phi_{j+1}^*(z)\}}{\sqrt{1-k_{j+1}^2}}. \tag{D.4}$$

Then, using (D.3-D.4), the inner product in (D.2) becomes

$$\langle \Phi_i(z), \Phi_j(z) \rangle = \langle P(z), \frac{\Phi_{j+1}(z) - k_{j+1}\Phi_{j+1}^*(z)}{\sqrt{1-k_{j+1}^2}} \rangle, \tag{D.5}$$

where

$$P(z) = f(\Phi_N(z), \Phi_N^*(z), \cdots, z^{-(N-i-1)}\Phi_N(z), z^{-(N-i-1)}\Phi_N^*(z)). \tag{D.6}$$

Let's first consider the inner product by $z^{-m}\Phi_N(z)$ in $P(z)$ as

$$\langle z^{-m}\Phi_N(z), \frac{\Phi_{j+1}(z) - k_{j+1}\Phi^*_{j+1}(z)}{\sqrt{1 - k^2_{j+1}}} \rangle$$

$$= \langle \Phi_N(z), \frac{z^m\Phi_{j+1}(z) - k_{j+1}z^m\Phi^*_{j+1}(z)}{\sqrt{1 - k^2_{j+1}}} \rangle. \tag{D.7}$$

By (12.21), the above inner product becomes zero when the order of $z^m\Phi_{j+1}(z)$, i.e., $m + j + 1$ is less than N. Notice that, from (D.6), the maximum value of m is $N - i - 1$. Therefore, the maximum value of $m + j + 1$ is $N - (i - j)$, which is less than N from the condition on i and j in (D.2). Therefore, the terms, $z^{-m}\Phi_N(z)$, for $m = 0$ to $N - i - 1$ in $P(z)$ can be removed from $P(z)$ without affecting the inner product.

Next, consider the inner product by $z^{-m}\Phi^*_N(z)$ in $P(z)$ as

$$\langle z^{-m}\Phi^*_N(z), \frac{\Phi_{j+1}(z) - k_{j+1}\Phi^*_{j+1}(z)}{\sqrt{1 - k^2_{j+1}}} \rangle$$

$$= \langle \Phi^*_N(z), \frac{z^m\Phi_{j+1}(z) - k_{j+1}z^m\Phi^*_{j+1}(z)}{\sqrt{1 - k^2_{j+1}}} \rangle. \tag{D.8}$$

When $m = 0$, the above inner product becomes zero since

$$\frac{\Phi_{j+1}(0) - k_{j+1}\Phi^*_{j+1}(0)}{\sqrt{1 - k^2_{j+1}}} = 0. \tag{D.9}$$

When $m > 0$, the inner product in (D.8) is obviously zero since the constants of $z^m\Phi_{j+1}(z)$ and $z^m\Phi^*_{j+1}(z)$ are zeros.

From the above discussions we conclude that

$$\langle \Phi_i(z), \Phi_j(z) \rangle = 0, \quad \text{for } 0 \le j, \ i \le N, \tag{D.10}$$

which means that the Schur polynomials $\{\Phi_N(z), \Phi_{N-1}, \cdots, \Phi_0(z)\}$ are orthogonal to each other.

D.2   ORTHONORMALITY OF SCHUR POLYNOMIALS

In the previous section, we proved the orthogonality of the Schur polynomials using the inner product formulation. Therefore, to prove the orthonormality of Schur polynomials, we only need to show

$$\langle \Phi_i(z), \Phi_i(z) \rangle = 1, \quad \text{for } 0 \leq i \leq N. \tag{D.11}$$

For convenience, an i-th order Schur polynomial is expressed as

$$\Phi_i(z) = \sum_{m=0}^{i} \phi_m^{(i)} z^m. \tag{D.12}$$

Using this notation, (12.37) can be rewritten as

$$k_i = \frac{\phi_0^{(i)}}{\phi_i^{(i)}}. \tag{D.13}$$

Then, from (12.4) and (D.13), the coefficient of z^{N-1} of $\Phi_{N-1}(z)$ is

$$
\begin{aligned}
\phi_{N-1}^{(N-1)} &= \frac{\phi_N^{(N)} - k_N \phi_0^{(N)}}{\sqrt{1 - k_N^2}}, \\
&= \frac{\phi_N^{(N)}(1 - k_N^2)}{\sqrt{1 - k_N^2}}, \\
&= \phi_N^{(N)} \sqrt{1 - k_N^2}.
\end{aligned}
\tag{D.14}
$$

By the same way, the coefficient of z^i of $\Phi_i(z)$ can be expressed as

$$\phi_i^{(i)} = \phi_{i+1}^{(i+1)} \sqrt{1 - k_{i+1}^2}. \tag{D.15}$$

By repeated application of (D.15),

$$\phi_i^{(i)} = \phi_N^{(N)} \sqrt{1 - k_N^2} \sqrt{1 - k_{N-1}^2} \cdots \sqrt{1 - k_{i+1}^2}. \tag{D.16}$$

To evaluate the inner product in (D.11), $\Phi_i(z)$ can be expressed using (D.3) and (D.6) as

$$\langle \Phi_i(z), \Phi_i(z) \rangle = \langle P(z), z\Phi_i(z) \rangle, \tag{D.17}$$

The reverse Schur polynomials in $P(z)$ do not have any effect on the above inner product since the constant of $z\Phi_i(z)$ is zero. The only term in $P(z)$ that produces a nonzero result is $z^{-(N-i-1)}\Phi_N(z)$ since

$$\langle z^{-(N-i-1)}\Phi_N(z), z\Phi_i(z) \rangle = \langle \Phi_N(z), z^{N-i}\Phi_i(z) \rangle, \tag{D.18}$$

where the degree of $z^{N-i}\Phi_i(z)$ is N.

By repeated application of (12.4), the coefficient of $z^{-(N-i-1)}\Phi_N(z)$ in

$P(z)$ can be shown to be $1/\sqrt{(1-k_N^2)(1-k_{N-1}^2)\cdots(1-k_{i+1}^2)}$. Therefore,

$$\langle \Phi_i(z), \Phi_i(z) \rangle = \frac{1}{\sqrt{(1-k_N^2)(1-k_{N-1}^2)\cdots(1-k_{i+1}^2)}} \langle \Phi_N(z), z^{N-i}\Phi_i(z) \rangle,$$

$$= \frac{1}{\sqrt{(1-k_N^2)(1-k_{N-1}^2)\cdots(1-k_{i+1}^2)}} \frac{\phi_i^{(i)}}{\phi_N^{(N)}}. \tag{D.19}$$

From (D.16), it is obvious that the above inner product reduces to 1, which means that the Schur polynomials are orthonormal.

Using the orthonormality of the Schur polynomials, we can prove the following:

$$\langle \Phi_i^*(z), \Phi_i^*(z) \rangle = \frac{1}{2\pi j} \oint_C \frac{\Phi_i^*(z)\Phi_i^*(z^{-1})}{\Phi_N(z)\Phi_N(z^{-1})z} dz,$$

$$= \frac{1}{2\pi j} \oint_C \frac{\{z^i\Phi_i(z^{-1})\}\{z^{-i}\Phi_i(z)\}}{\Phi_N(z)\Phi_N(z^{-1})z} dz,$$

$$= \frac{1}{2\pi j} \oint_C \frac{\Phi_i(z)\Phi_i(z^{-1})}{\Phi_N(z)\Phi_N(z^{-1})z} dz,$$

$$= \langle \Phi_i(z), \Phi_i(z) \rangle,$$

$$= 1. \tag{D.20}$$

Also,

$$\langle \Phi_{i-1}(z), \Phi_{i-1}(z) \rangle = \langle \frac{z^{-1}\{\Phi_i(z) - k_i\Phi_i^*(z)\}}{\sqrt{1-k_i^2}}, \frac{z^{-1}\{\Phi_i(z) - k_i\Phi_i^*(z)\}}{\sqrt{1-k_i^2}} \rangle,$$

$$= \frac{1}{1-k_i^2}\{1 - 2k_i\langle \Phi_i(z), \Phi_i^*(z) \rangle + k_i^2\}. \tag{D.21}$$

From the orthonormality of the Schur polynomials, (D.21) should be 1. Therefore, we conclude

$$\langle \Phi_i(z), \Phi_i^*(z) \rangle = k_i. \tag{D.22}$$

Appendix E: Fast Binary Adders and Multipliers

E.1 INTRODUCTION

This appendix addresses implementation of fast binary adders and multipliers. In Section E.2, fast adders are designed based on Manchester, carry-select, and carry-look-ahead techniques. These adders differ from those in other textbooks in the sense that these are implemented using multiplexers only. Section E.3 addresses design of fast multipliers based on Wallace tree and Dadda multipliers.

E.2 MULTIPLEXER-BASED FAST BINARY ADDERS

This section considers implementation of Manchester, carry-select, and carry-look-ahead based fast binary adders using multiplexers only.

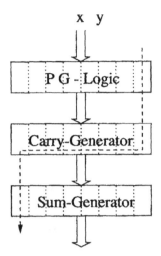

Fig. E.1 Block diagram of a Manchester adder.

E.2.1 Multiplexer-Based Manchester Adder

In a binary addition, a carry c_i can be either generated at stage i or propagated from the preceding stage. A carry is generated at stage i if x_i and y_i are both 1, and a carry is propagated from stage i-1 to stage i+1 if only one of the operands (x_i, y_i) is 1 but not both [1]. Let g_i and p_i denote the carry generation and the propagation at stage i. These can be computed as:

$$g_i = x_i \cdot y_i, \tag{E.1}$$
$$p_i = x_i \oplus y_i, \tag{E.2}$$

where $\oplus$ denotes XOR operation. The carry c_{i+1} and the sum s_i at each stage are computed by:

$$c_{i+1} = g_i + p_i \cdot c_i. \tag{E.3}$$
$$s_i = p_i \oplus c_i. \tag{E.4}$$

Hence, an adder based on this principle consists of 3 sequential stages:

- PG-logic: compute all pairs of (g_i, p_i) based on (E.1) and (E.2) in parallel;

- Carry-generator: computes all carries c_{i+1} based on (E.3);

- Sum-generator: computes all sum bits s_i based on (E.4);

as shown in Fig. E.1. The critical path computation time of this adder (shown by the dashed line in Fig. E.1) is equal to $t_{pg} + (W-1)t_{carry} + t_{sum}$, where t_{pg},

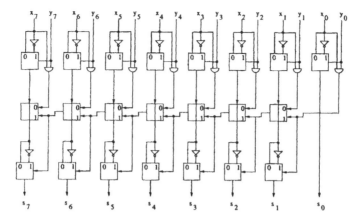

Fig. E.2 8-bit multiplexer-based Manchester adder.

t_{carry}, and t_{sum} denote the computation delay of 1-bit slice PG-logic, carry-generator and sum-generator, respectively. The computation delay of the carry chain, $(W-1)t_{carry}$, limits the speed of the adder. To this end, Manchester adders are designed to expedite the carry generation. This subsection addresses multiplexer-based Manchester adder, where the carry-generator is implemented using multiplexers only.

It can be observed from (E.1) and (E.2) that g_i and p_i can never both be simultaneously 1. Applying this constraint, (E.3) can be rewritten as

$$c_{i+1} = \overline{p_i} \cdot g_i + p_i \cdot c_i, \qquad (E.5)$$

which can be implemented using a multiplexer only [2]. Fig. E.2 shows an 8-bit multiplexer-based Manchester adder. The critical path of this adder equals $9t_{mux}$, where t_{mux} denotes the computation delay of 1 multiplexer.

Although the computation delay of binary addition has been reduced from Wt_{FA} (t_{FA} denotes 1 full-adder delay) to $(W+1)t_{mux}$ by using the multiplexer-based Manchester adder, it is still proportional to the wordlength W.

E.2.2 Fast Binary Addition

Fast binary adders can be designed based on carry-select or carry-look-ahead (also referred to as binary-look-ahead or tree-based) adders.

E.2.2.1 Carry-Select Approach In a carry-select adder, the word is divided into multiple blocks (not necessarily of same length). For each block, duplicate sum and carry bits are generated assuming carry-input to the block can be 1 and 0. The appropriate sum bits are selected as soon as the carry generated from the less significant block is known [3]. Fig. E.3 illustrates an

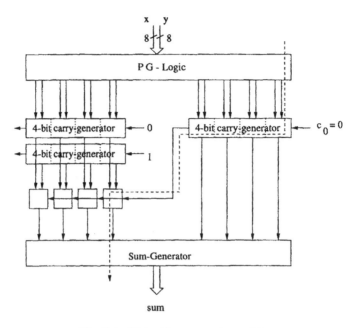

Fig. E.3   Eight-bit carry-select adder.

8-bit multiplexer based carry-select adder where the carry-generator contains 2 blocks of size $L = 4$ each. The critical path or latency of this adder (shown in dashed line in Fig. E.3) equals $6t_{mux}$. The reader can verify that this design requires a total of 29 multiplexers and 8 AND gates.

E.2.2.2 Tree-Based Approach   Multiplexer-based fast carry generators can also be designed by exploiting a tree-based binary-look-ahead or carry-look-ahead concept [4].

Define a logic operator o between consecutive (p, g) pairs as follows:

$$(g, p) \ o \ (g', p') = (g + p \cdot g', \ p \cdot p'). \tag{E.6}$$

Note that g and p cannot be 1 at the same time, neither can g' and p'. Hence, the o operator can be rewritten as

$$(g, p) \ o \ (g', p') = (\bar{p} \cdot g + p \cdot g', \ p \cdot p') \tag{E.7}$$

and can be implemented using 1 multiplexer and 1 AND gate. Let Γ_i, Π_i be defined as:

$$(\Gamma_i, \Pi_i) = \begin{cases} (g_0, p_0) & if \ i = 0, \\ (g_i, p_i) o(\Gamma_{i-1}, \Pi_{i-1}) & if \ 0 < i \leq W - 1. \end{cases} \tag{E.8}$$

Hence, we have

$$(\Gamma_i, \Pi_i) = (g_i, p_i) \, o \, (g_{i-1}, p_{i-1}) \, o \cdots o \, (g_0, p_0) \, . \qquad \text{(E.9)}$$

It can be proved that $\Gamma_i = c_{i+1}$ and $\Pi_i = p_i \cdot p_{i-1} \cdots p_0$. It can also be shown that the o operator is *associative*. Therefore, the computation in (E.9) for 8-bit carry generation can be carried out in a binary-tree manner as follows:

1. The following computations are carried out in parallel in the first step:

   - $(\Gamma_0, \Pi_0) = (g_0, p_0)$ and $c_1 = \Gamma_0$.
   - $(g_1, p_1) o (\Gamma_0, \Pi_0) = (\Gamma_1, \Pi_1)$ and $c_2 = \Gamma_1$.
   - $(g_3, p_3) o (g_2, p_2)$.
   - $(g_5, p_5) o (g_4, p_4)$.
   - $(g_7, p_7) o (g_6, p_6)$.

2. The 2nd step computes

   - $[(g_3, p_3) o (g_2, p_2)] o (\Gamma_1, \Pi_1) = (\Gamma_3, \Pi_3)$ and $c_4 = \Gamma_3$.
   - $[(g_7, p_7) o (g_6, p_6)] o [(g_5, p_5) o (g_4, p_4)]$.
   - $(g_2, p_2) o (\Gamma_1, \Pi_1) = (\Gamma_2, \Pi_2)$ and $c_3 = \Gamma_2$.

3. The 3rd step computes

   - $([(g_7, p_7) o (g_6, p_6)] o [(g_5, p_5) o (g_4, p_4)]) o (\Gamma_3, \Pi_3) = (\Gamma_7, \Pi_7)$ and $c_8 = \Gamma_7$.
   - $[(g_5, p_5) o (g_4, p_4)] o (\Gamma_3, \Pi_3) = (\Gamma_5, \Pi_5)$ and $c_6 = \Gamma_5$.
   - $(g_4, p_4) o (\Gamma_3, \Pi_3) = (\Gamma_4, \Pi_4)$ and $c_5 = \Gamma_4$.

4. Finally, Γ_6 and Π_6 can be computed as

   - $(g_6, p_6) o (\Gamma_5, \Pi_5) = (\Gamma_6, \Pi_6)$ and $c_7 = \Gamma_6$.

This 8-bit tree-based carry-generator is shown in Fig. E.4, where the o operations are highlighted in shaded regions. This adder requires a total of 27 multiplexers and 19 AND gates, and has a latency of $6t_{mux}$. The latency of a carry-generator is reduced from proportional to $W t_{mux}$ to proportional to $(\log_2) W t_{mux}$ in a binary-look-ahead or tree-based adder.

Carry-select and binary-look-ahead concepts can be combined to design fast, low-area and low-power binary adders. Readers may refer to [2] for further reading on this topic.

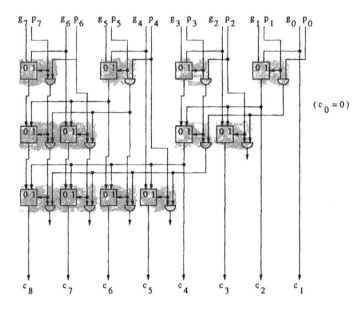

$(c_0 = 0)$

Fig. E.4 Eight-bit multiplexer-based tree binary-look-ahead carry generation.

E.3 WALLACE TREE AND DADDA MULTIPLIER

The principle of Wallace tree multiplication [5] is shown in Fig. E.5(a). It is clear from the figure that there are 16 partial products (shown as black dots) that have to be summed. The 1st step in the addition process involves grouping the partial products into sets of 3. For example, if there are p rows of partial products, $3 * (\lfloor p/3 \rfloor)$ rows are grouped and the remaining $p \bmod 3$ rows are passed to the next stage. Therefore, in Fig. E.5 3 rows of partial products are grouped together in stage 1. These 3 rows are summed using full adders if there are 3 dots in 1 column and using half adders if there are 2 dots in 1 column. The resulting sum and carry signals from the half and full adders are passed on to the next stage. It turns out that this stage has exactly 3 rows of partial products to be summed. The resulting sum and carry signals are passed on to the 3rd stage. Since there are only 2 rows of partial products to be summed, this stage can be implemented using a fast carry-propagate adder. The implementation of the 4 × 4-bit Wallace tree multiplier is shown in Fig. E.5(b). The architecture requires only 5 full adders and 3 half adders to sum the 16 partial products.

The principle of Wallace tree multiplication can easily be extended to longer wordlengths. Fig. E.6 shows the operation of a 8 × 8-bit multiplier, where the partial products are added in 5 stages. As before, stage 5 involves the use of fast carry-propagate adder.

The Wallace tree operation was generalized in [6], where it was shown that

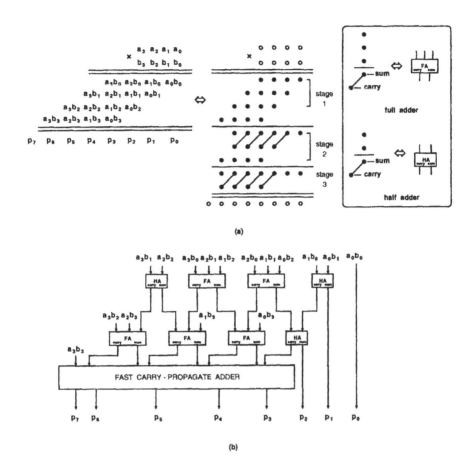

Fig. E.5 (a) Operation of the Wallace tree multiplier. (b) Architecture of a 4 × 4 Wallace tree multiplier. The operands are assumed to be unsigned numbers.

the height of the matrix at each stage could be reduced by at most a factor of 1.5. The generalized multipliers are referred to as Dadda multipliers. It was also shown that at each stage only the minimum amount of reduction should be done in order to reduce the current height of the partial product matrix to that of the next stage. Therefore, if the height of the partial product matrix is p at stage n, then the maximum height of the partial product matrix at stage $n + 1$ should be $\lceil \frac{2p}{3} \rceil$. As an example, if the height of the matrix is initially 8, then the height of the matrix at subsequent stages should be 6, 4, 3, 2, respectively. The operation of an 8 × 8-bit Dadda multiplier is illustrated in Fig. E.7. This architecture consists of 5 stages and a final vector merging portion. A comparison between the 8 × 8-bit Dadda and Wallace tree multipliers reveals that while the Wallace tree multiplier uses 38 full

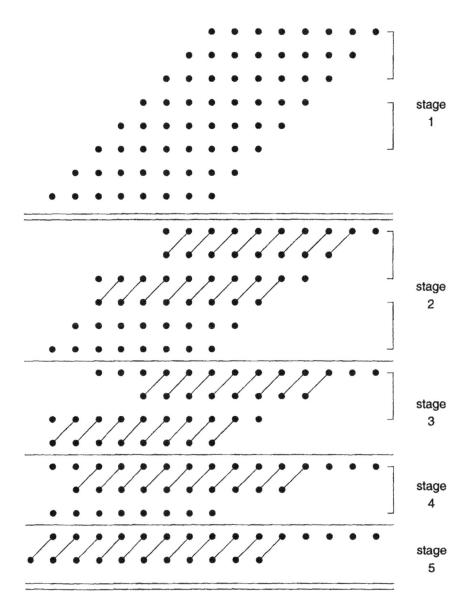

Fig. E.6 Operation of a 8×8-bit Wallace tree multiplier.

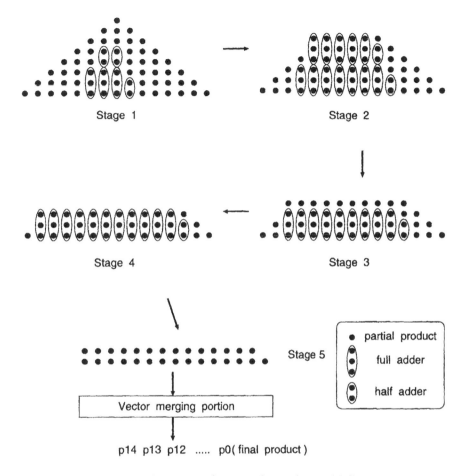

Fig. E.7 Operation of a 8 × 8-bit Dadda multiplier.

adders and 15 half adders, the Dadda multiplier uses only 35 full adders and 7 half adders. The Wallace tree multiplier, however, requires a carry-propagate adder that is only 10 bits wide, while the Dadda multiplier requires an adder that is 14 bits wide. The other disadvantage of the Dadda multiplier is that it is less regular than the Wallace tree multiplier, making it more difficult to layout in VLSI design.

REFERENCES

1. A. R. Omondi, *Computer Arithmetic Systems: Algorithms, Architecture, and Implementations.* Prentice Hall International, 1994.

2. K. K. Parhi, "Fast low-power VLSI binary addition," in *Proc. of 1997 IEEE In-*

ternational Conference on Computer Design (ICCD), (Austin, Texas), pp. 676–684, Oct. 1997.

3. S. Waser and M. J. Flynn, *Introduction to Arithmetic for Digital Systems Designers*. CBS College Publishing, 1982.

4. R. P. Brent and H. T. Kung, "A regular layout for parallel adders," *IEEE Trans. on Computers*, vol. C-31, no. 3, pp. 260–264, March 1982.

5. C. S. Wallace, "A suggestion for a fast multiplier," *IEEE Trans. on Computers*, vol. EC-13, pp. 14–17, Feb. 1964.

6. L. Dadda, "Some schemes for parallel multipliers," *Alta Frequenza*, vol. 34, pp. 349–356, 1965.

Appendix F: Scheduling in Bit-Serial Systems

F.1 INTRODUCTION

A special case of high-level synthesis is the synthesis of bit-serial architectures. In bit-serial systems, no allocation is performed, i.e., each algorithm operation is mapped to a unique bit-serial functional unit. In bit-serial architectures, a complete word is not computed in a single clock but is computed over a series of clock cycles. Therefore the task of scheduling bit-serial architectures is important to ensure the inputs and outputs are synchronized correctly. This appendix presents an algorithm for optimal resource-constrained scheduling of bit-serial architectures. In this algorithm, it is assumed that a one-to-one mapping of operations to hardware functional units exist and that there is no need for functional unit allocation. The goal of the bit-serial scheduling algorithm is to assign the operations to time steps while minimizing the number of required synchronizing registers.

A bit-serial architecture is often represented by the timing model shown in Fig. F.1 and is used in the bit-serial scheduling algorithm. This model represents the necessary *relative timing* of the inputs and outputs of a bit-serial operator. In Fig. F.1, a functional unit (or operator) i scheduled to begin computations at time step T_i expects to see the first bit of input x_1 at

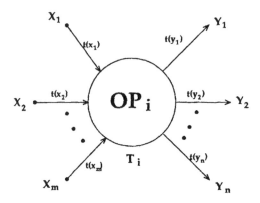

Fig. F.1   The timing model of a general bit-serial operator.

time $T_i + t(x_1)$, input x_2 at time $T_i + t(x_2)$, ..., and input x_m at time $T_i + t(x_m)$. Operator i produces the first bit of output y_1 at time $T_i + t(y_1)$, output y_2 at time $T_i + t(y_2)$, ..., and output y_n at time $T_i + t(y_n)$. As an example of this model, consider the bit-serial architecture shown in Fig. F.2. From this figure, one can see that functional unit M is scheduled at time step 0 and A is scheduled at time step 4. The inputs $y(n-1)$ and $x(n)$ arrive together at relative time 0. M can consume the first bit of input $y(n-1)$ immediately and then generate the first output bit 4 time steps later. Because A must wait for the output of M before beginning its computation as shown by its scheduled time, input $x(n)$ must be delayed by 4 time steps to properly synchronize the input data. Therefore in this example, the bit-serial scheduling algorithm must insert 4 delays onto the $x(n)$ input to properly synchronize the incoming data as shown in the figure.

F.2   OUTLINE OF THE SCHEDULING ALGORITHM

The bit-serial scheduling algorithm consists of assigning a "schedule time" to every operator in a bit-serial architecture. This time represents the time when the operation will nominally take place. Informally, each operator must be scheduled at a time after all of its inputs become available (i.e., they have been generated by a previous operator). The scheduling problem can be formulated as a linear programming problem and because all scheduled time of the operators must be integers, the scheduling algorithm must find the optimal integer solution to this problem.

Consider a pair of operators joined by an edge as shown in Fig. F.3. One of the outputs produced by the operator OP_i is the operand $OPND_x$. This operand in turn is the input to the operator OP_j (and possibly to others). The scheduled times of operators OP_i and OP_j are denoted by T_i and T_j

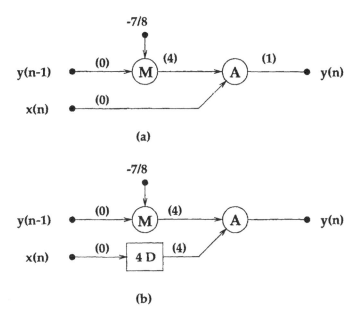

(a)

(b)

Fig. F.2 Example of the bit-serial scheduling problem. (a) DFG prior to scheduling. (b) DFG after scheduling showing allocated synchronization registers.

respectively. The timing specifications of the relevant output and input ports of OP_i and OP_j are denoted by t_i and t_j, respectively.

Since OP_i is scheduled at time T_i, the output $OPND_x$ will become available at time $T_i + t_i$ as shown. Further, this same operand will be required as an input to the operator OP_j at time $T_j + t_j$. By the requirement that the operand cannot be used by operator OP_j before it is produced by operator OP_i, the following inequality can be derived:

$$T_j + t_j \geq T_i + t_i,$$

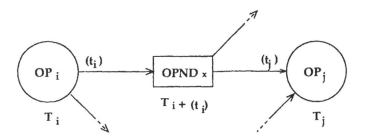

Fig. F.3 A pair of operators showing the timing information.

or otherwise stated,

$$T_j - T_i \geq t_i - t_j. \tag{F.1}$$

Such an inequality holds for each pair of operands joined by an edge in the DFG. In these inequalities, T_i and T_j are the unknowns, whereas the value $t_i - t_j$ is a known constant.

In order to correctly handle the primary or system input and output operands of the circuit, the scheduling algorithm utilizes special input and output psuedo-operators. An input operator is an operator with no inputs and a single output acting as the source of an input operand to the circuit. Conversely, an output operator has a single input attached to an output of the circuit.

A solution to the set of inequalities can be determined by using common techniques for solving linear programming problems such as the shortest path problem as seen in Section A.2 and Section A.3. Alternatively a software package that solves integer linear programming problems such as GAMS [1] can be used. Once a solution is found to this set of inequalities, the circuit may be correctly synchronized by inserting a delay equal to $T_j - T_i - (t_i - t_j)$ clock cycles between operators OP_i and OP_j [2].

F.3   MINIMUM COST SOLUTION

In general, the bit-serial scheduling problem will have many solutions that satisfy the set of inequalities for a given architecture and hence there are many ways to synchronize the circuit. The goal of optimal bit-serial scheduling is to generate a solution that provides the minimal cost, where cost is defined to be the total number of shift-register delays required to properly synchronize the circuit. If a linear cost function can be defined, the minimum cost problem can be easily formulated as a linear programming problem.

Minimizing the total number of synchronization delays required for each edge between functional units of a circuit is not sufficient. Note that there exists the possibility of multiple fanout from any functional unit. Therefore, the delays from a multiple fanout output should be allocated sequentially and not in parallel. Consider a simple case where an output of some operator OP_O is used as an input to several other operators as shown in Fig. F.4. In this figure, the output of OP_O is used as an input to 3 other operators, OP_A, OP_B, and OP_C. As shown in this example, delays of 10, 12, and 25 clock cycles need to be applied to the operand before it is input to the three operators. The total number of delays is equal to $10 + 12 + 25 = 47$. Fig. F.5 shows an alternative arrangement of the delays, where the delays are arranged sequentially. The total number of delays in this alternative solution is equal to 25, which is the length of the longest delay. This leads to an observation:

Observation F.3.1 *The total number of delays that need to be allocated to*

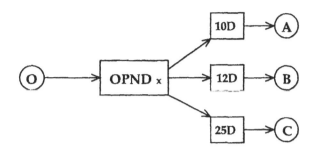

Fig. F.4 Operator O with a fanout of three and no delay sharing.

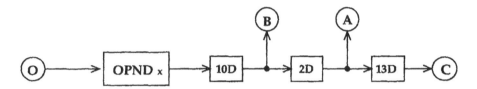

Fig. F.5 Operator O with a fanout of three and sharing delays.

any node in the circuit is equal to the maximum delay that must be allocated.

Let D_x represent the maximum delay that must be allocated to an operand $OPND_x$ of width w_x. A total cost function to be minimized can now be derived:

$$Cost = \sum_x D_x\, w_x \qquad (F.2)$$

where the sum is over each operand node in the circuit.

For each node as shown in Fig F.3, there exists a constraint as described in (F.1) and is repeated here:

$$T_j - T_i \geq t_i - t_j . \qquad (F.3)$$

The maximum delay on operand $OPND_x$ from OP_i to OP_j is less than the maximum delay, D_x. This is described by the constraint:

$$T_j - T_i - (t_i - t_j) \leq D_x . \qquad (F.4)$$

These two constraints, (F.1) and (F.4), along with the cost function (F.2) that will be minimized, describe a linear programming problem capable of providing the minimum cost schedule for the bit-serial architecture.

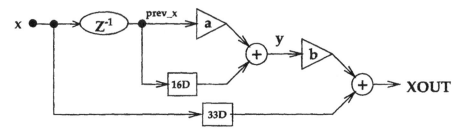

Fig. F.6 Scheduling of circuit with a z^{-1} operator.

F.4   SCHEDULING OF EDGES WITH DELAYS

The bit-serial scheduling algorithm described to this point will generate optimal solutions for DFGs that consist of delay-free edges. Many DSP algorithms are inherently recursive and contain delay elements. Purely feed-forward circuits are not also guaranteed to contain all delay-free edges either. Therefore the bit-serial scheduling algorithm must be able to handle edges that contain delays.

Consider the simple circuit described by the following equations:

$$
\begin{aligned}
prev_x &:= x[-1]; \\
y &:= prev_x * a + prev_x; \\
xout &:= b * y + x;
\end{aligned}
$$

Where a and b are constants, and it is assumed that $W = 16$, a constant multiplication is assumed to have a latency of 16 u.t., and an addition is assumed to have a latency of 1 u.t. The data-flow diagram for this circuit is shown in Fig. F.6 along with scheduling delays. The triangular symbols represent constant multiplications. If the z^{-1} operator is removed, one can see that the two delays of 16 and 33 cycles may be amalgamated, but this is not possible with the z^{-1} operator in the DFG, since the two branches are applied to apparently different signals, x and $x[-1]$. It is possible to find more complicated examples in which the scheduling of hardware operators will be affected in a nonoptimal way by the presence of the z^{-1} operators during the scheduling.

A preferable method is to incorporate the word delays right into the linear programming equations. This is done by slightly modifying equations (F.2)–(F.4) to take into account the presence of z^{-1} operators. Specifically, Fig. F.7 shows a general situation in which the output of some operator OP_i undergoes a z^{-n} transformation before being used as input to the operator OP_j. The equations describing the scheduling constraints, corresponding to (F.1) and (F.4) are

$$T_j - T_i \geq t_i - t_j - nW \tag{F.5}$$

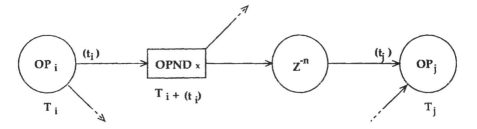

Fig. F.7   General node to be scheduled including z^{-1} operators.

$$T_j - T_i - (t_i - t_j) + nW \le D_x \tag{F.6}$$

where W is the number of clock cycles in a word or wordlength. In this case, as before, $T_j - T_i - (t_i - t_j) + nW$ is the delay applied to the connection shown in the diagram, and D_x is the maximum delay applied to this variable. Constraints (F.5) and (F.6) may be put in a form that can be solved as a linear-programming problem using integer scheduling programming techniques.

REFERENCES

1. A. Brooke, D. Kendrick, and A. Meeraus, *GAMS: A User's Guide, Release 2.25.* The Scientific Press, 1992.

2. R. I. Hartley and J. R. Jasica, "Behavioral to structural translation in a bit-serial silicon compiler," *IEEE Trans. on Computer-Aided Design*, vol. 7, no. 8, pp. 877–886, Aug. 1988.

Appendix G: Coefficient Quantization in FIR Filters

G.1 INTRODUCTION

In order to implement a digital filter in hardware, the ideal filter coefficients must first be quantized using a power-of-two representation of a given wordlength, K (not including the sign-bit to the left of the decimal). Traditionally, the quantization process consists of a direct binary conversion of the coefficients in conjunction with a truncation or rounding scheme. This quantization method is straightforward and time-efficient. However, the quantized filter coefficients contain large number of nonzero bits. In this appendix, the NUS (National University of Singapore) quantization algorithm is presented for multiplierless implementation of FIR digital filters using signed power-of-two terms [1]. All filter coefficients are assumed to be in the range $[-1, 1)$.

G.2 NUS QUANTIZATION ALGORITHM

In [1],[2] it is shown that if the filter coefficients are first scaled before the quantization process is performed, the resulting filter will have much better frequency-space characteristics. By using the appropriate scale factor, the filter coefficients collectively "settle" into the optimal power-of-two quantization space. The NUS algorithm employs a scalable quantization process and produces excellent results in terms of the frequency space-characteristics of the quantized filters.

To begin the process, the ideal filter is normalized so that the largest coefficient has an absolute value of 1 and the quantized filter is initialized with zeros. The normalized ideal filter is then multiplied by a variable scale factor (VSF). The VSF steps through the range of numbers from .4375 to 1.13 with a step size of $2^{-(K+1)}$. Signed power-of-two (SPT) terms are then allocated to the quantized filter coefficient that represents the largest absolute difference between the scaled ideal filter and the quantized filter. The NUS algorithm iteratively allocates SPT terms until the desired number of SPT terms has been allocated or until the absolute differences between all of the scaled ideal coefficients and the quantized coefficients are less than 2^{-K}. Once the allocation of terms has stopped, the Normalized Peak Ripple (NPR) is calculated. The process is then repeated for a new scale factor. The quantized filter leading to the minimum NPR is chosen. The NUS algorithm is described by the following pseudocode.

NUS Quantization Algorithm

Normalize the set of filter coefficients so that the magnitude of the largest coefficient is 1;
For VSF = Lower Scale:Step Size:Upper Scale,
{

      Scale normalized filter coefficients with VSF;
      Quantize the scaled coefficients using SPT term allocation scheme
          in NUS algorithm;
      Calculate NPR of the quantized filter;

}
Choose the quantized coefficients that leads to the minimum NPR;

When the quantized filter is implemented, a post-processing scale factor (PPSF) is used to properly rescale the magnitude of the resulting data stream. The value of the PPSF is determined as follows:

$$PPSF = \frac{Max[Abs(Ideal\ Filter\ Coeffs.)]}{VSF}. \tag{G.1}$$

Essentially, the PPSF reverses the normalization and scaling introduced in the quantization process. While the scaling process changes the magnitude of the filter response, it should be noted that it does not change the functionality of the filter.

The INUS algorithm [2] slightly modifies the term allocation process by using some searching techniques. The NPR of the quantized filters is slightly improved, but at the expense of computation time.

In order to understand more clearly the need for scaling in the process of coefficient quantization, three quantization examples are given. In the first and third examples, it should be noted that the scaling process has been carried out for only one scale factor. In the second example, no scaling is used which causes the quantized filter to be very poor representative of the ideal filter. The benefits of the scaling process should be clear from these examples.

Example G.2.1 *Quantization with Scaling*

- *The wordlength, K, equals 2.*

- *Ideal Filter (IF) = [.26 .131], Initial Quantized Filter (QF) = [0 0].*

- *Normalize the Ideal Filter, IF = [1 .5038].*

- *Scale with a variable scale factor of 1/2, IF = [.5 .2519].*

- *Begin quantization.*

- *Iteration One, QF = [.5 0].*

- *Iteration Two, QF = [.5 .25].*

- *Difference between IF and QF is less than 1/4, stop SPT allocation.*

- *Implement filter as QF = [.5 .25] and PPSF = .26/.5.* ■

Example G.2.2 *Quantization without Scaling*

- *The wordlength, K, equals 2.*

- *Ideal Filter (IF) = [.26 .131], Initial Quantized Filter (QF) = [0 0].*

- *Begin quantization.*

- *Iteration One, QF = [.25 0].*

- *Difference between IF and QF is less than 1/4, stop SPT allocation.*

- *Implement filter as QF = [.25 0].* ■

Example G.2.3 *Quantization with Scaling*

- *The wordlength, K, equals 7.*

- *Ideal Filter (IF) = [.26 .131 .087 .011], Initial Quantized Filter (QF) = [0 0 0 0].*

- *Normalize the Ideal Filter, IF = [1 .5038 .3346 .0423].*

- *Scale with a variable scale factor of 1/2, IF = [.5 .2519 .1673 .0212].*

- *Iteration One, QF = [.5 0 0 0].*

- *Iteration Two, QF = [.5 .25 0 0].*

- *Iteration Three, QF = [.5 .25 .125 0].*

- *Iteration Four, QF = [.5 .25 .1563 0].*

- *Iteration Five, QF = [.5 .25 .1563 .0156].*

- *Difference between IF and QF is less than 1/64, stop SPT allocation.*
  ■

The reader is referred to [3], [4] for efficient quantization of parallel FIR filters using SPT terms.

REFERENCES

1. D. Li, J. Song and Y. C. Lim, "A polynomial-time algorithm for designing digital filters with power-of-two coefficients," in *Proc. of IEEE International Symposium on Circuits and Systems*, (Chicago, IL), pp. 84–87, May 1993.

2. C. L. Chen, K. Y. Khoo and A. N. Willson, Jr, "An improved polynomial-time algorithm for designing digital filters with power-of-two coefficients," in *Proc. of IEEE International Symposium on Circuits and Systems*, (Seattle, WA), pp. 223–226, May 1995.

3. D. A. Parker and K. K. Parhi, "Low-area/power parallel fir digital filter implementations," *Journal of VLSI Signal Processing*, no. 1/2, pp. 75–92, Sept. 1997.

4. J.-G. Chung, Y.-B. Kim, H.-G. Jeong, K. K. Parhi, and Z. Wang, "Efficient parallel FIR filter implementations using frequency spectrum characteristics," in *IEEE International Symposium on Circuits and Systems*, (Monterey, CA), vol. 5, pp. 354–358, June 1998.

Index

Printed and bound by CPI Group (UK) Ltd, Croydon, CR0 4YY

27/10/2024

14580262-0001